THE EVOLUTION
OF MANAGEMENT
THOUGHT

A Volume in the Wiley Series
in Management and Administration

THE EVOLUTION OF MANAGEMENT THOUGHT

Second Edition

DANIEL A. WREN

The University of Oklahoma

JOHN WILEY AND SONS

New York • Chichester • Brisbane • Toronto

Library of Congress Cataloging in Publication Data

Wren, Daniel A
The evolution of management thought.

(Wiley series in management & administration)
Bibliography: p.
Includes index.
1. Management—History.   I. Title.

HD30.5.W73 1979   658'.009   78-10959
ISBN 0-471-04695-7

Printed in the United States of America

10 9 8 7 6 5 4 3

To Leon and Maude, my links with the past;
to Karen, my link with the present;
and to Jonathan, Laura, and Lynda, my links with the future.

ABOUT THE AUTHOR

DANIEL A. WREN, Ph.D., University of
Illinois, is Professor of Management and Curator
of the Harry Bass Business History Collection
at the University of Oklahoma. He has served as
President of the Southern Management
Association and Chairman of the Management
History Division of the Academy of
Management. Previously he taught at the Florida
State University, and is the author, with Dan
Voich, Jr., of *Principles of Management—Process
and Behavior,* published by The Ronald Press
Company, now a division of Wiley.

PREFACE

There has been more research and teaching in management history in the past ten years than in any preceding period. The reasons for this increasing interest are manifold: (1) more and more of the younger scholars are finding management history as challenging and rewarding as any other field of research and teaching; (2) a growing group of "veteran" observers of management have become interested in recording their experiences and recollections for posterity; (3) a professional interest group, the Management History Division, has been formed within the Academy of Management as a forum for collegial exchanges; and (4) there is a growing recognition that a discipline which aspires to be a "profession" must include its intellectual heritage as part of the educational process.

The purpose of this new edition is to refine and extend the earlier materials pertaining to the evolution of management thought. Users of the first edition will find the same basic chronological framework in the present edition. The changes are primarily to refine the telling of history, to incorporate recent research findings, and to bring developments up to the present. Materials have been added on figures such as Pierre DuPont and Harry Hopf; more is included in personnel and labor history; the changing expectations regarding business and society receive a greater emphasis; and developments in the modern era are brought up to date. My continuing hope is that students will find in these pages the reward of knowing the past as a prologue to the future.

I tried to make the book an unfolding story about the lives and the times of those who are our intellectual predecessors. These individuals have left us a heritage that we often take for granted, frequently do not acknowledge, and sometimes reject because we do not think yesterday's solutions have any practical value for tomorrow's problems. But these men and women were very much as we are: they were attempting to cope with the manifold problems of administering mass assemblages of human and physical resources; they were trying to develop philosophies and theories about human behavior and motivation; they were agents for change; and they were struggling with the age-old problem of allocating scarce resources to meet the goals and desires of organizations and people. Our problems today are basically the same, only the proposed solutions have changed as we have learned more, as we have sharpened our diagnostic tools, and as cultural values have changed.

This book traces the evolution of management thought from its earliest, informal days to the present by examining the backgrounds, ideas, and influence of the major contributors. In doing this, it outlines and depicts the significant eras in the development of management thought and analyzes the various trends and movements throughout this development. In addition, it illustrates the impact of environmental forces on the development of ideas. Management is an open-ended activity in that what is done and thought is affected by the prevailing economic, social, and political values and institutions.

Throughout, the organization is chronological, in order to demonstrate the evolutionary nature of management theory and practice and to show how assumptions about people and organizations change with shifting economic, social, and political values and institutions. Finally—in keeping with the concept that management theory is a product of past historical forces—the concluding chapter summarizes the functions of the manager and discusses the history of management as a prologue to the future.

I am most grateful to those who helped me in my own evolution of thinking. Professor Robert G. Cook of the University of Missouri gave me an excellent introduction to management history. At the University of Illinois, Professors Joseph Litterer, Dwight Flanders, Harvey Huegy, and M. J. Mandeville encouraged me to approach problems from an interdisciplinary and environmental point of view. Professors John Mee and Richard Whiting willingly shared materials and ideas; Kenneth Trombley helped on some of the finer points of the life of Morris L. Cooke; Fritz Roethlisberger clarified some origins of human relations ideas; Ernestine Gilbreth Carey reviewed what I had written of the Gilbreths; Ralph C. Davis gave generously in writing of his own evolving ideas; and William B. Wolf was of invaluable assistance on the life and work of Chester Barnard.

My colleagues in the Management History Division of the Academy of Management contributed in many ways, and I applaud their quest to improve our understanding of management history. My students continue to provide feedback, which challenges my own thinking and helps me to refine the materials. I especially thank Hilda Cooney who typed much of the manuscript and ran the office so I could complete my task. I am also grateful to readers of the first edition, since it is their encouragement that led to this revision. Now, let us unroll the past so that we can be prepared for the future.

Daniel A. Wren
Norman, Oklahoma, 1979

CONTENTS

PART FOUR

THE MODERN ERA   437

I | EARLY MANAGEMENT THOUGHT

Part I will cover a wide span of time and trace developments in management thought up to the scientific management era in America. After a brief introduction to the role of management in organizations, we will examine examples of very early management thought and then demonstrate how changes in the economic, social, and political environment were setting the stage for the Industrial Revolution. This revolution created certain management problems in the embryonic factory system and led to a need for the formal study of management. The genesis of modern management thought will be found in the work of early pioneers in management thought who sought to solve the problems created by the factory system. We will conclude part I by tracing this genesis of management thought to America and examine our early experiences with the factory, some early management writers, and the cultural environment of America before the scientific management era.

1

A Prologue to the Past

The activity of management is ancient, but formal study of the discipline of management is relatively new. Management is essential to organized endeavors, and for a broad working definition let us view management as an activity which performs certain functions in order to obtain the effective acquisition, allocation, and utilization of human efforts and physical resources in order to accomplish some goal. Management "thought," then, is the existing body of knowledge about the activity of management, its functions, purpose, and scope.

The purpose of this study is to trace the significant periods in the evolution of management thought from its earliest informal days to the present. The study of management, like the study of people and their cultures, is an unfolding story of changing ideas about the nature of work, the nature of human beings, and the functioning of organizations. The methodology of this study of management will be analytic, synthetic, and interdisciplinary. It will be analytic in examining people who made significant contributions, their backgrounds, their ideas, and their influence. It will be synthetic in examining trends, movements, and environmental forces that furnish a conceptual framework for understanding individuals and their approaches to the solution of management problems. It will be interdisciplinary in the sense that it includes—but moves beyond—traditional management writings to draw upon economic history, sociology, psychology, social history, political science, and cultural anthropology in order to place management thought in a cultural historical perspective. The author's objective is to place management thought in the context of its cultural environment and thereby to understand not only *what* management thought was and is, but also to explain *why* it developed as it did.

Management history as a separate area of study is generally neglected in most schools of business administration. A smattering of history is taught at various levels but the area generally lacks depth, direction, and unity. Henry Wadsworth Longfellow said "let the dead past bury its dead," but there is much to be said for resurrection. We live and study in an age which is represented by a diversity of approaches to management. Students are presented with quantitative, behavioral, functional, and other approaches in the various courses they take. While such a variety of intellectual inputs may be stimulating, it typically leaves students with a fragmented picture of management and assumes that they have the ability to integrate these various ideas for themselves.

In many cases, this burden is far too great. A study of evolving management thought can provide the origins of ideas and approaches, trace their development, provide some perspective in terms of the cultural environment, and thus provide a conceptual framework which will enhance the process of integration. A study of the past contributes to a more logical, coherent picture of the present. Without a knowledge of history, individuals have only their own limited experiences as a basis for thought and action. History should therefore equip perceptive people with additional alternatives and answers to build into their decision-making models. Intellectual flexibility and a mental set for the inevitability of change can be facilitated through the study of the past. Present pedagogy can be improved, knowledge expanded, and insights gained by examining the lives and labors of management's intellectual progenitors. Theory, a legitimate goal in any discipline, is based upon the warp and woof of individuals' ideas in the fabric of management. By tracing the origin and development of modern management concepts, we can better understand the analytical and conceptual tools of our trade. In understanding the growth and development of large-scale enterprise, the dynamics of technology, the ebb and flow of cultural values, and the changing assumptions about the nature and nurture of people, we can better equip young men and women with the skills and attitudes they need to prepare themselves for future positions of responsibility. The study of management history not only furnishes insights into our own culture but also reveals notions of how management skills and knowledge might be applied to other organizations and to other cultures.

Today is not like yesterday, nor will tomorrow be like today; yet today is a synergism of all our yesterdays, and tomorrow will be the same. There are many lessons in history for management scholars; the important one is the study of the past as prologue.

A Cultural Framework

How have our concepts of managing organizations evolved throughout history? To understand this evolution, this dynamic process of change and growth, we need to establish a cultural framework of analysis for the evolution of management thought. Management is not a closed-end activity since managers operate organizations and make decisions within a given set of cultural values and institutions. Thus management has "open-system" characteristics in that managers affect their environment and in turn are affected by it.

Culture is our total community heritage of nonbiological, humanly transmitted traits and includes the economic, social, and political forms of behavior associated with mankind. Generally, we speak of a specific culture within geographic or physically contiguous boundaries, such as that of the United States, or Mexico, or that of Germany. However, there are "levels" of culture, such as the "Western" culture and "Eastern" cultures of the world. Or there may be subcultures within one culture, such as a "middle-class" culture, that of the "hippies," or of other groups sharing a common set of cultural forms of behavior. Here the term "culture" will apply to a set of people having in common an economic, social, and political system. Culture is the broadest possible concept for study, and here the study of management will be confined to more specific economic, social, and political ideas which influence the job of managing an organization. Human behavior is a product of past and present cultural forces and the discipline of management is also a product of the economic, social, and political forces of the past and present. Cultures are generally taken for granted, much like the goldfish who takes the water in his fishtank as a natural state of affairs. Modern individuals examine present organizations, read contemporary authors, and yet they have little appreciation of the background of our technology, political bodies, or arrangements for the allocation of resources. Management thought did not develop in a cultural vacuum; managers have always found their jobs affected by the existing culture.

To study modern management, the past must be examined to see how our communal heritage was established. The elements of our culture were described above as economic, social, and political. In practice, these elements are closely interrelated and interact to form our total culture; they are separated here and throughout the following pages only for ease of presentation. Here our attention shall be confined to the portions of our culture which apply most directly to management, omitting other cultural phenomena such as art forms, music, and so on.

The Economic Facet

The *economic* facet of culture is the relationship of people to resources. Resources may be man-made or natural; the term denotes as well both tangible objects and intangible efforts which have the capability of being utilized to achieve some stated end. Physical resources include land, buildings, raw materials, semifinished products, tools, and equipment or other tangible objects used by people and organizations. Human thought and effort are also resources because they design, assemble, shape, and perform other activities which result in the production of some product or service.

Every society has the economic problem of a scarcity of resources and a multiplicity of economic ends. The mobilization of these scarce resources to produce and distribute products, services, and satisfactions has taken a variety of forms throughout history. Heilbroner has characterized these methods of allocating resources as by tradition, by command, and by the market.[1] The *traditional* method operates on past societal precepts; technology is essentially static, occupations are passed down from one generation to the next, agriculture predominates over industry, and the social and economic systems remain essentially closed to change. The *command* method is the imposition of the will of some central person or agency upon the rest of the economy about how resources will be allocated and utilized. The economic commander-in-chief may be the monarch, the fascist dictator, or the collectivist central planning agency. What is to be produced, what prices and wages will be, and how economic goods and services are to be distributed are decisions to be made by some central source. The *market* method, which Heilbroner has noted as a relatively recent phenomenon, relies upon an impersonal network of forces and decisions to allocate resources. Prices, wages, and interest rates are set by a bargaining process between those who have the product or service and those who want it; all resources flow to their best reward and no central agency nor prior precepts need to intervene.

In actual practice, modern societies display a mixture of the elements of tradition, command, and the market. Much of our total cultural heritage has been influenced by tradition and command as the predominant economic philosophies. However, we will see later that the market philosophy created the need for the formal, systematic development of a body of management thought. In brief, the state of technology and the source of decisions about the societal allocation of resources have a large bearing upon how managers go about their job. A tradition-directed economy would circumscribe the role of the manager with prior precepts; the command orientation would make the manager an executor of central decisions; but the market system opens the way to the innovative utilization of resources to meet a multiplicity of ends.

The Social Facet

The *social* facet refers to the relationship of people to other people in a given culture. Mankind does not live alone but finds advantages in forming groups for mutual survival or for the furtherance of personal goals. In forming groups, the initial input is a variety of people of differing needs, abilities, and values. Out of this heterogeneity, some homogeneity must evolve or the group will not survive. Thus all participants form a "contract" which en-

[1]Robert L. Heilbroner, *The Making of Economic Society*, Englewood Cliffs, N.J.: Prentice-Hall, 1962, pp. 10–16.

compasses some common rules and agreements about how to be-
have to preserve the group.[2] The unwritten but nevertheless binding contract defines assumptions about the behavior of others and
expectations about the reciprocal treatment of the individual. It includes some agreement about how best to combine and coordinate efforts to accomplish a given task, be it the making of an economic product or achieving the satisfactions of social fellowship.

Values, or cultural standards of conduct defining the pro-
priety of a given type of behavior, are another part of social interactions. Thus ethics in interpersonal relations is an age-old problem. Economic transactions, deeply imbedded in social trust, are
an integral part of a societal contract. Values shift from one time
period to another and from one culture to another. Managerial efforts are affected by the relationships between individuals and the
group, and by the social values prevailing in the culture.

The Political Facet

The *political* part of culture is the relation of the individual to the
state and includes the legal and political arrangements for the establishment of social order and for the protection of life and property. The absence of state and order is anarchy; unless there is
some provision for protection of rational beings from irrational
ones, the result is total economic, social, and political chaos.
Where order begins, anarchy ends. Political institutions to bring
order and stability take a variety of forms, ranging from representative government to a monarchy or dictatorship. Political assumptions about the nature of mankind range from one end of the
continuum, self-governing people, to the other extreme position,
direction from one person or a ruling body at the top which im-
poses its will on others based on the assumption that people cannot, or will not, govern themselves. Provisions for property, contracts, and justice are also key concepts in the political aspect of
cultures. In a democracy, people typically have the right of private
property, the freedom to enter or not to enter into contracts, and
an appeal system for justice. Under a dictatorship or monarchy,
the right to hold and use private property is severely restricted,

[2] Pitirim A. Sorokin, *Society, Culture, and Personality*, New York: Cooper Square
Publishers, 1962, pp. 371–373.

the right to contract is limited, and the system of justice depends upon the whims of those in power. The cultural role of management is affected by the form of government, by the power to hold or not hold property, by the ability to engage in contracts for the production and distribution of goods, and by the appeal mechanism available to redress grievances.

Interacting to form any culture, the economic, social, and political facets are useful tools of analysis for examining the evolution of management thought. Managers are affected by their cultural environment, and the ways in which they allocate and utilize resources have evolved within the changing views about economic, social, and political institutions and values.

People, Management, and Organizations

From this introduction to the cultural environment of management, let us turn more specifically to the basic elements of our study. Even before people began to record their activities, they encountered the necessities of managing their efforts in cooperative endeavors. As an overview, Figure 1-1 begins with the state of nature and traces the quest for need satisfaction through organizations. Management, an activity essential to organized endeavors, facilitates the operation of organizations in order to satisfy the needs of people.

The Human Being

The human being is the fundamental unit of analysis in the study of mankind, the study of organizations, and the study of management. Humans have always faced a relatively hostile environment characterized by scarce food supplies, inadequate shelters, and in general a scarcity of other resources with which to satisfy their manifold needs. Humans are not biologically stronger than many of the other species which exist or have existed on earth. To explain their survival one must look beyond their physical powers for other characteristics which can explain the proliferation of the human race to the point where people today can control and manipulate their environment, within certain natural physical boundaries which themselves are constantly being challenged as we seek outer space and expand our technology.

The solution to the question of why humans have survived is found in their ability to reason, their ability to cope with the problems of reality. In the long evolutionary process, it was not always the most *physically* fit who survived, for they were still inferior to the behemoths and the carnivorous animals, but it was the most *mentally* fit who are our ancestors. Paleoanthropologists tell us that the first true human, *Homo erectus*, appeared some

THE CULTURAL ENVIRONMENT

```
┌─────────────────────────────────┐
│ The state of nature:            │
│   general scarcity of resources │
│   and hostility in nature       │
└─────────────────────────────────┘
            │ Gives
            │ rise to
            ▼
┌──────────────────────┐   To satisfy      ┌──────────────────────┐
│ Economic, social,    │   needs,          │ Economic, social,    │
│ and political        │─── people form ──▶│ and political        │
│ needs of people      │                   │ organizations        │
└──────────────────────┘                   └──────────────────────┘
            ▲                                          │
            │ The management of                        │ Organized
            │ organizations                            │ efforts
            │ facilitates                              │ require
            │ satisfaction of                          │
            │ people's needs                           ▼
            │           ┌───────────────────────────────┐
            │           │ Management—the                │
            │           │   activity which per-         │
            │           │   forms certain functions     │
            │           │   in order to obtain the      │
            └───────────│   effective acquisition,      │◀─
                        │   allocation, and utili-      │
                        │   zation of human efforts     │
                        │   and physical resources      │
                        │   in order to accomplish      │
                        │   some goal                   │
                        └───────────────────────────────┘
```

Fig. 1-1.   People, management, and organizations.

500,000 years ago. Evidence uncovered at Olduvai Gorge by Louis and Mary Leakey suggests that *Homo erectus* became a capable tool and weapon maker, mastered the use of fire, had a low level of conceptual thought, had powers of speech, and engaged in activities which required a marked degree of planning and co-operation. His brain was at the evolutionary mid-point in cranial capacity between the chimpanzee and modern man; other evidence shows a steady evolution in brain size toward the present and strongly suggests that the human mind has been the species' main means of survival. These were the people who fashioned equalizing clubs and spears for defense, who formed implements for tilling the soil, and who developed organizational means which gave humans a differential advantage over their natural enemies.

Humans are not only *Homo sapiens* but also *Homo faber*, the maker, the doer. They are active, not passive, creative, not idle, and ever-changing in their quest to better themselves and their species. Their most basic needs are economic ones, those necessary to physical survival in a harsh world in which food, drink, shelter and other fundamental needs of life must be obtained. With cultural advancement, these economic needs become more complex but they still form a base of human existence. Beyond these basic needs, which are essential to existence itself, are social needs. These needs for affiliation most probably arose out of physiological drives in the sex act and the selection of a mate. The family became the most elementary unit of human group relationships, an organization which provided both satisfactions as well as new duties. Survival of the family became a goal and humans found that they could better protect and enhance their welfare by forming groups or tribes for mutual advantage in food-gathering, defense, and family care activities.

Early humans found that the knowledge and skills of one generation must be transmitted to the next if the species was to survive. Such were the elementary beginnings of education and the transmission of knowledge. In forming groups and living with their fellow humans to minister to both economic and social needs, they found need of rules and means to insure the viability of the organization. They formed elementary political units which had agreed-upon codes about economic, social, political, and often religious behavior. It was out of these economic, social, and political needs that organized human activity began. People found advantages in participating and cooperating with others to achieve their own goals.

Organizations and Management

As humans have evolved, so have organizations. People found that they could magnify their own abilities by working with others and thereby better satisfy their own needs. The inputs of various skills and abilities into the group led to the recognition that some were better at some tasks than others. Group tasks were *differentiated*, that is, there was a division of labor to take advantage of these varying skills. Once labor was divided, some agreement had to be reached about how to structure and interrelate these various work assignments in order to accomplish group objectives. Quite logically, the group also *stratified* tasks and developed a hierarchy of authority or power. Perhaps the assignment of work to others was made by the strongest, the eldest, or the most articulate of the group who became the earliest leader. In any case, the group had to achieve some unity of agreement about what was to be done, how, and who would be responsible for accomplishment.

This most elementary appearance of the first organization reflected essentially the same common elements of organizations throughout history. First, there had to be a goal, a purpose, an objective, or something to be accomplished. Perhaps it was the annual berry-picking, the hunt, the sowing of a crop, or the defense of the group from marauding nomads. Second, people had to be attracted to the purpose or the common will in order to participate. They had to perceive that it was in their best interest to work toward the group goal. The first bonds of organization were in people's attraction to the group as a means of satisfying their own needs. Third, the organizational members needed something with which to work or fight. These were the resources or means to the end and comprised the people themselves, the weapons, the tilling implements, or whatever. Fourth, there was a need for a structuring of the various activities of the participants in order that their actions would interact and be interrelated in achieving the common goal. If each proceeded without timing and coordination of effort, the result would be chaos. Finally, the group discovered that results could be better achieved if someone had the assigned task of keeping the whole group on its course toward the goal. Someone had to resolve differences of opinion, decide on strategy and timing, and maintain the structure of activities and relationships toward the objective. This emergence of an activity of *managing* apart from the activities of *doing* was to become an essential aspect of all types of cooperative endeavors. Management as an activity has always existed in order to make people's desires manifest through organized effort. Management facilitates the efforts of people in organized groups and arises when people seek to cooperate to achieve goals.

People have always participated in organizations and organizations have always existed to serve the ends of people. These ends are manifold and are reflected in organizational arrangements for the satisfaction of economic needs and wants, for the provision for individual and social desires, for the transmission of knowledge from one generation to the next, and for the protection of life and property from internal and external threats. As people's conceptual ability has been refined through evolution, they have also refined their understanding of the art of arranging physical and human resources for guidance toward purposeful ends. We call this art *management,* and its evolution is the focal point of our study.

Summary

Our ideas about people, management, and organizations have evolved within the context of various cultural values and institutions throughout history. The development of a body of knowledge about how to manage has also evolved within a framework of the economic, social, and political facets of various cultures. Management thought is both a process in and a product of its cultural environment. Having these open-system characteristics, management thought must be examined within this cultural framework. In nature, people have economic, social, and political needs which they seek to satisfy through organized efforts. Management is an essential activity which arises as individuals seek to satisfy their needs through group action, and it facilitates the accomplishment of goals for the individual and the group. Various organizations such as the family, the tribe, the state, and the church have appeared throughout history as means to people's ends. People create organizations to enlarge upon their own specialized talents, to protect themselves, to enrich their lives, and to satisfy a variety of other needs. To reach these ends, organizations are formed of people who have a common purpose and who are attracted to the group in order to satisfy their needs. These organizations must be managed and our study will focus upon how our ideas about management have evolved over time.

2

Management Before Industrialization

Historically, industrialization is a relatively recent phenomenon. Mankind existed for eons before the great advances were made in power, transportation, communications, and technology which came to be known as the Industrial Revolution. Before industrialization, organizations were primarily the household, the tribe, the church, the military, and the state. Some people did engage in small-scale economic undertakings, but not on a scale to compare with what would emerge as a result of the Industrial Revolution. Nevertheless, there was still a need for management in the conduct of military campaigns, in household affairs, in the administration of government, and in the operation of the church. It is in these organizations that we see the earliest notions of management. In examining preindustrial management, two themes consistently appear: (1) the relatively parochial view of the management function; and (2) the low esteem of commerce held by the prevailing cultures. This chapter will examine these first attempts at management in early civilizations and will discuss the changing cultural values which would lead to the Industrial Revolution.

Management in Early Civilizations

The Near East

As group affiliations evolved from the family to the nation, the question of organizational authority became a problem. In the family authority rested in the patriarch or the matriarch, but in the nation there was often a conflict between chiefs and priests, the former claiming secular power, the latter, heavenly dominion. From this struggle, this division of authority, came the idea of the priest-ruler or divine king. A king was not a king until the priests ordained him, a tradition that long endured.

One such divine king was the Babylonian, Hammurabi (2123–2081 B.C.), who received his right to rule and his famous code from the sun god.[1] Babylon, near modern Baghdad, rested in what was once called the ancient cradle of civilization between the Tigris and the Euphrates rivers. For his state, Hammurabi issued a unique code of 282 laws which governed business dealings, personal behavior, interpersonal relations, wages, punishments, and a host of other societal matters. One law was the first historical mention of accounting and dealt with the handling of receipts. Another might appeal to modern consumer advocates:

> *If a builder builds a house for a man and does not make its construction firm, and the house which he has built collapses, and causes the death of the owner of the house, that builder shall be put to death.*

In ancient Mesopotamia, lying just north and west of Babylon, the temples developed an early concept of a "corporation," or a group of temples under a common body of management. Flourishing as early as 3000 B.C., temple management operated under a dual control system: one high priest was responsible for ceremonial and religious activities, while an administrative high priest coordinated the secular activities of the organization. Records were kept on clay tablets, plans made, labor divided, and work supervised by a hierarchy of officials.[2] From these early civilizations, we can observe some ancient practices of management.

The Far East

The ancient Chinese civilization has opened its doors occasionally

---

[1] Robert F. Harper (ed.), *The Code of Hammurabi: King of Babylon*, Chicago: University of Chicago Press, 1904.

[2] Richard L. A. Sterba, "The Organization and Management of the Temple Corporations in Ancient Mesopotamia," *Academy of Management Review*, Vol. 1, No. 3 (July, 1976), pp. 16–26.

to let Westerners peek in. The oldest known military treatise is the product of the Chinese general Sun Tzu (ca. sixth century B.C.). He wrote of marshaling the army into subdivisions, of gradations of rank among the officers, and of using gongs, flags, and signal fires for communications. He advocated lengthy deliberations and sound plans before going into battle: "Thus do many calculations [plans] lead to victory, and few calculations to defeat." It is possible that General Sun Tzu held a staff officer's position: "The General that hearkens to my counsel and acts upon it, will conquer. . . . The General that hearkens not to my counsel nor acts upon it, will suffer defeat."[3] It appears that the problems of line and staff relationships are at least 2,500 years old.

Confucius (551 or 552–479 B.C.) left his mark on the ages through his moral teachings and only incidentally through his advocacy of a merit system. In Confucius' time, the highest respectable goal was service in the government: merchants ranked only slightly above convicts in social esteem. The competition for governmental posts was severe and Confucius advocated that offices should go to men of proven merit and ability. It was during the Han dynasty (206 B.C.–A.D. 220) that merit exams started, based on Confucian advice. Merit as a basis for selection would in turn lead to merit rating (performance appraisal) for promotions. Although the record is spotty, the Sung dynasty started a merit rating system around A.D. 962. Research indicates that the Chinese had problems with bureauracy, much as we moderns experience. Selection of officials on the basis of classical scholarship qualities did not always bring the best administrators to office. Much corruption and manipulation by officials and lesser functionaries were common, leading to numerous attempts to reform the system.[4]

The Chinese bureaucracy was fully developed into a hierarchy of officials perhaps as early as 1000 B.C., long before Confucius. Indeed, the Confucian philosophy was in contradiction to the "legalists" of that time. The legalists sought to use rewards and punishments through a system of laws to insure performance,

---

[3] Lionel Giles (ed. and trans.), *Sun Tzu on the Art of War*, London: Luzac and Co., 1910, p. 5.

[4] Richard L. A. Sterba, "Clandestine Management in the Imperial Chinese Bureaucracy," *Academy of Management Review*, Vol. 3, No. 1 (January, 1978), pp. 69–78.

while Confucius advocated cultivating and improving the moral nature of people to secure cooperation.[5] How ancient this struggle between the formalists and the humanists, the system and the individual! There is also evidence that the Chinese were familiar with the division of labor and the departmental form of organization as early as A.D. 1. An inscription on a rice bowl indicates it was made in a government workshop in which there was a high degree of specialization of labor among the various artisans. The workshop was divided into three departments: accounting, security, and production.[6] Such artifacts enable us to understand the age-old practice of management.

Chanakya Kautilya (ca. 332–298 B.C.) was a noted and feared minister to Chandragupta Maurya, the greatest statesman of Hindu India. Kautilya's *Arthasastra* founded Indian public administration and contained advice on how to establish and maintain economic, social, and political order. Kautilya wrote on the qualifications of administrators ("of high ancestry . . . blessed with wisdom . . . eloquent . . . intelligent, enthusiastic . . . sociable") and how to select personnel through interviews and checking references. He wrote of the use of staff advisers ("never listen to just one or two"), established departments with directors, and prepared detailed job descriptions for various offices.[7] Although his work was public administration, it reinforces the idea of how ancient many of our management concepts are.

Egypt

The Egyptians developed extensive irrigation projects as an adjunct to the annual inundation by the Nile, and their engineering feats of the pyramids and canals were marvels superior to anything the Greeks and Romans later developed. Mining and most engineering projects were state monopolies and required the de-

[5] Chan K. Hahn and Warren C. Waterhouse, "Confucian Theories of Man and Organization," *Academy of Management Journal,* Vol. 15, No. 3 (September, 1972), p. 358.

[6] Rodger D. Collons, "Factory Production—1 A.D.," *Academy of Management Journal,* Vol. 14, No. 2 (June, 1971), pp. 270–273.

[7] T. N. Ramaswamy (ed.), *Essentials of Indian Statecraft: Kautilya's Arthasastra,* London: Asia Publishing House, 1962.

velopment of an extensive bureaucracy to administer state affairs. The labor supply consisted of both freemen and slaves. Strong cultural traditions bound freemen to occupations, and chains took care of other labor problems.

There is evidence that the Egyptians were aware of limits to the number of people one manager could supervise. In the earliest dynasties, it was the custom to kill and bury workers and servants with the departed pharaoh. With more civilization came the progressive idea of burying carvings or of making engravings to *represent* or symbolize the presence of servants rather than killing them. Whether this was due to a moral advancement or to a scarcity of labor cannot be determined historically. The interesting thing learned from the excavated engravings of servants (*ushabtis* or "answerers") was that there was a ratio of about 10 servants to each supervisor. Excavations also revealed distinctive dress for managers and workers. The supervisors wore kilts or robes while the *ushabtis* were dressed so as to represent their trade or occupation.[8] The "rule of ten" in the span of management was an Egyptian practice which influenced the Hebrews, as we shall see shortly.

One of the most ancient terms used to describe a "professional" managerial role is that of vizier. The record that this office existed goes back to at least 1750 B.C., although it is probably more ancient than that. One of the best known viziers was the Hebrew Joseph, who had been sold into bondage by his brothers. Because of Joseph's ability to forecast, the pharaoh made him his vizier. This was delegation, leaving spiritual matters in the hands of the pharaoh and temporal matters in the hands of Joseph. The office of vizier thus was an ancient office of director, organizer, coordinator, and decision maker. Beneath the vizier, an elaborate bureaucracy was developed to measure the rise of the river upon which every part of the economy depended, to forecast the grain crop and revenues, to allocate these revenues to the various governmental units, and to supervise all industry and trade. Here were some rather sophisticated (for the times) methods of managing through forecasting, planning work, dividing the work among the various people and departments, and establishing a "profes-

[8]W. M. Flinders Petrie, *Social Life in Ancient Egypt,* London: Constable & Co. Ltd., 1924, pp. 21–22.

sional" full-time administrator to coordinate and control the state enterprise.

The Hebrews

The Old Testament is a story of the leadership of a people in quest of a land. The great leaders of the Hebrew people combined spiritual and secular powers; examples include Abraham (ca. 1900 B.C.), Joseph (ca. 1750 B.C.), Moses (ca. 1300 B.C.), and David (ca. 1000 B.C.). Even after the great kings had passed away, tribal leadership became the task of judges who led by virtue of their possession of spiritual power or what has come down to us as "charisma." The Book of Judges tells how 12 judges, in successive reigns amounting to 410 years, held sway over Israel.

It is very likely, however, that it was the Egyptians who provided the seeds for the managerial concepts we see reported in the Bible. Joseph was sold into slavery, rose to be the vizier, and gained valuable administrative experience. Moses, while in captivity in Egypt, observed the Egyptian "rule of ten." The Bible tells us that it was upon the advice of his father-in-law Jethro (thus making Jethro the first known management consultant) that Moses:

> . . . chose able men from all over Israel and made them judges over the people–thousands, hundreds, fifties, and tens. They were constantly available to administer justice. They brought the hard cases to Moses but judged the smaller matters themselves. (Living Bible, Exod. 18:25–26.)

Thus Moses was able to employ an "exception principle" in managing as well as to establish a more orderly organizational structure for tribal management.

Greece

Will Durant captured the essence of the rise and fall of many civilizations with his "a nation is born stoic, and dies epicurean."[9] In the stoic phase of the cycle, adversity breeds cohesion and deprivation fosters initiative. Self-control, thrift, hard work, and an

[9]Will Durant, *The Story of Civilization, Part I: Our Oriental Heritage*, New York: Simon and Schuster, 1935, p. 259.

orderly life bring prosperity. As affluence reigns, self-control becomes self-indulgence, thrift becomes a vice, industry and perseverance yield to opportunism, and social order breaks down. Epicureans take no thought for the morrow and decline begins; the fall comes not from without, but from internal decay. The cycle was true for Greece and for Rome. America was founded by stoics, the Puritans; does the past foretell the future?

The institutions, art, language, drama, and literature of Greece form a significant part of our own culture. However, Greek economic philosophy was antibusiness, and trade and commerce were considered beneath the dignity of the Grecian ideal. Work, being ignoble to the aristocratic or philosophical Greek, was to be carried out by slaves and less than respectable citizens. Manual workers and merchants were excluded from citizenship in the Greek democracy because of the low esteem of manual and trade occupations. Government administration was based solely on election and participation by all citizens and the prevailing philosophy discouraged "professional" experts as administrators.

Socrates observed that managerial skills were transferable between public and private affairs. In this early recognition of the universality of management, Socrates noted that "the conduct of private affairs differs from that of public concerns only in magnitude"; both involved the management of men and if one could not manage his private affairs he certainly could not manage the public business. However, the Athenians may have followed the Socratic notion of universality too far. Military and municipal leaders were regularly rotated, creating chaos in governmental affairs and becoming a terrible burden when Athens was threatened by the better organized, more professional armies of Philip of Macedonia, Alexander the Great, and the government of Sparta.

In his *Politics*, Aristotle noted that "He who has never learned to obey cannot be a good commander."[10] In his discussion of household management (*oeconomia*) he, like Socrates, spoke of the similarity between the art of managing a state and managing a household. Both involved the management of property and of slaves and freemen with the only difference being the magnitude of the total operation. In his *Metaphysics*, Aristotle developed the

[10] Aristotle, *Politics* (trans. by Benjamin Jowett), Chicago: Great Books of the Western World, Vol. 9, Encyclopaedia Britannica, Inc., 1952, p. 474

thesis that reality is knowable through the senses and through reason. By rejecting mysticism, Aristotle became the father of the scientific method and established the intellectual foundation for the Renaissance and the age of reason. Eventually this spirit of scientific inquiry would form a basis for scientific management.

It was another Grecian, Xenophon, who wrote the first known description of the advantages of the division of labor (ca. 370 B.C.):

> . . . There are places [workshops] even where one man earns a living by only stitching shoes, another cutting them out, another by sewing the uppers together, while there is another who performs none of these operations but only assembles the parts. It follows . . . that he who devotes himself to a very highly specialized line of work is bound to do it in the best possible manner. [11]

Greece fell before the Romans, a hardy stock of people from the banks of the Tiber. It destroyed itself first by depleting its forests and natural resources, by internal moral decay, by political disorder, and by decimating its leaders through revolts and counterrevolts. Stoicism, like its later Christian counterparts Calvinism and Puritanism, produced the strongest characters of that time. Despite the antitrade philosophy, the age of Greece illustrates the first seeds of democracy, the advent of decentralized participatory government, the first attempts to establish individual liberty, the beginnings of the scientific method for problem solving, and an early, though sketchy, insight into the notion that managing different undertakings requires essentially the same managerial skills.

Rome

Rome was born stoic and conquered the decaying Hellenic civilization. The Romans developed a quasi-factory system to manufacture armaments for the legions, for the pottery makers who produced for a world market, and later for textiles which were sold for export. The famous Roman road system was built to speed the distribution of goods, as well as to speed the movement of troops to dissident colonies. The Romans inherited the Greek

---

[11]Cited by Friedrick Klemm, *A History of Western Technology*, New York: Charles Scribner's Sons, 1959, p. 28.

disdain for trade and left business activities in the hands of Greek and Oriental freedmen. A growing external trade required commercial standardization and the state developed a guaranteed system of measures, weights, and coins. The first resemblance of a corporate organization appeared in the form of joint-stock companies which sold stocks to the public in order to carry out government contracts to supply the war effort. There was a highly specialized labor force which, with few exceptions, worked in small shops as independent craftsmen selling for the market rather than for individual customers. Free workers formed guilds (*collegia*) but these were for social aims and mutual benefits, such as to defray the cost of funerals, rather than for establishing wages, hours, or conditions of employment. The state regulated all aspects of Roman economic life: it levied tariffs on trade, laid fines upon monopolists, regulated the guilds, and used its revenues to fight a multitide of wars. Large-scale organizations could not exist since the government prohibited joint-stock companies for any purpose other than the execution of government contracts.

The Romans also had a genius for order, and the military autocracy ran the empire with an iron hand. Behind this authoritarian organizational structure lay two fundamental concepts— discipline and functionalism. The latter provided for a specific division of work among the various military and governmental agencies and the former provided a rigid framework and hierarchy of authority to insure that the functions were carried out. The contributions of Rome to our heritage lay chiefly in law and government which were manifestations of this concern for order. Roman law became a model for later civilizations and the Roman separation of legislative and executive powers provided a model system of checks and balances for later constitutional governments.

The Catholic Church

The Roman Catholic church could be considered a legacy of Rome in an indirect manner. Gibbon held that Christianity was the chief cause of Rome's fall because it destroyed the old faiths of Rome which had given character to the Roman people and stability to the Roman state. Christianity was more probably the effect rather than the cause of Rome's downfall and it brought consolation to poverty, hope to slavery, and the promise of a better afterlife. Christianity became a legacy for mankind, guiding the morality of Western culture to the present.

The Catholic church itself posed some interesting organizational problems. As the faith spread, novel sects grew and the first blush of a youthful theology threatened to become an adolescence of diversity. Early congregations operated independently, each defining its own doctrine and conditions for membership. Bishops became heads of various local churches and the roles of presbyters and deacons began to emerge as assistants for the bishop. By the third century A.D., an ordered hierarchy was more apparent with the addition of subdeacons and acolytes, who performed personal and secretarial duties, and exorcists and readers who performed liturgical duties. All of these ranks were enumerated by Bishop Cornelius in a message to Fabius of Antioch (A.D. 251). At the Council of Arles (A.D. 314) some bishops were made "more equal" than others, giving rise to a chief bishop, the bishop of Rome. Matthew (16:18–19) is the only gospel which provides this base of authority in Rome, i.e., Peter's church. At the Council of Nicaea (A.D. 325), the bishop of Rome was named to the office of pope. The outcome was centralized doctrine and authority in Rome and the papacy. However, the conflict between centralized and decentralized authority has reappeared throughout history, not only in the Catholic church but in other organizations. In modern organizational terms, the Catholic church leaders perceived a need to "institutionalize" the organization: that is, the need to specify policies, procedures, doctrine, and authority. The problem is a recurring one even today: the need for unanimity of purpose, yet discretion for local problems and conditions.

Feudalism and the Middle Ages

Renaissance writers coined the phrase "Middle Ages" to refer to what occurred from the decline of Rome to the Renaissance period. Slavery became uneconomical in the late Roman period: the upkeep of slaves was costly and they showed no particular enthusiasm for their work. The abolition of slavery came not with moral progress but with economic change. Development of free men as tenant farmers proved to be more economical for the landholder, for they were less expensive to keep and avoidance of starvation yielded a crude but effective incentive system. The growth of large estates and the political disorder following the fall of Rome led to economic, social, and political chaos, ripe for the emergence of the feudal system. Feudalism as a cultural system prevailed from about A.D. 600 to about A.D. 1500. At the base of the feudal system was the serf who was free, yet tied more than the slave before him to his master. The serf tilled a plot of land owned by the manorial lord, much like modern share croppers, and was given military protection in exchange for a portion of the products of his labors. The feudal system tied man to the land, fixed rigid class distinctions, established an age of landed aristocracy that was to endure to the Industrial Revolution, forced education to a standstill, made poverty and ignorance the hallmark of the masses, and completely stifled human progress until the age of reformation. It is no wonder that some historians prefer to call this period the "Dark Ages."

The Catholic church dominated medieval life and provided the hope of an afterlife as the only consolation for this one. The church also became the largest landholder in Europe and employed serfs; as Durant said, "feudalism feudalized the Church."[12] With the church as superstate, the admonitions of doctrine against lending for interest, against desiring anything from this world other than subsistence, and against materialistic trade and profits, continued the opinion of business as an evil necessity. The complete domination of life by the church led men to think not of this world, but of the other; not of gain, but of salvation. The self-interest of trade diverted men's thoughts from God to gain, from obedience to initiative, and from humility to activity. The seeds of doubt and despair were sown and only a great cultural revolution could pave the way for an industrial society.

The Revival of Commerce

Feudalism gave birth to the Crusades and, in turn, died as a result of them. Two centuries of religious fervor had left Jerusalem in the

---

[12] Will Durant, *The Story of Civilization, Part IV: The Age of Faith,* New York: Simon and Schuster, 1950, p. 564.

hands of the Moslems and Europe was seething with the potential for change. The Crusades also stimulated commerce by opening new trade routes and exposing parochial, feudal Europe to the wealth of the East. The Crusades weakened Christian belief. Embarking on their journeys with invincible religious conviction, the Crusaders returned with the realization that the Middle Eastern culture was superior in manners, morals, trade, industry, and warfare. The results of this cultural confrontation led to a more secular life in Europe through weakening religious bonds. Interest arose in exploration and a new spirit of trade and commerce arose to fill the land of feudalism. New markets, new ideas, the rise of towns, the first seeds of a new middle class, freer circulation of money and credit instruments, and the resurgence of political order created the soil for the Renaissance and the Reformation.

Old cities were revitalized by trade, and new cities arose as trade centers. Industrial growth followed the securing of trade routes and textiles became a leading facet of economic growth. The first method of industrial organization was the *domestic* system of production. Under the domestic or "putting out" system, a merchant procured the raw materials, farmed them out to individual workers or families who, using their own equipment, would complete the product in their home and then deliver it to the employer for a wage. Indeed, the domestic system of production lingers even today in the weaving of tweed cloth in Ireland and Scotland. The faults of the domestic system lay in the simple tools and technology, with little incentive to improve them, and in the inefficiencies of small-scale production with a limited division of labor. As the volume of trade grew, the domestic system proved inefficient and the need for more capital, the benefits to be gained from specializing labor, and the economies of scale of a centralized workplace led to the factory system.

Growing trade also required a rationalization of the methods of keeping accounts. Although Genoese, Florentine, and Venetian bankers were using the essentials of double entry bookkeeping as early as 1340, it was the task of a Franciscan monk, Luca Pacioli, to first describe it in print in 1494 in his *Summa de Arithmetica, geometrica, proportioni, et proportionalita*. Pacioli's system was the first information system for management; it told the entrepreneur his cash and inventory position and enabled a check on his cash flow.

It did not tell him his costs and it was not until the twentieth century that any advancements were made upon Pacioli's system.

As trade expanded, ethics also became a more pressing matter of concern among merchants. The first known study of business ethics in the Western world was the work of Friar Johannes Nider.[13] Nider opposed the prevailing church doctrine against the charging of interest and the profit motive. He made a distinction between "just" and "unjust" contracts and argued that contracts for gain or profit should be spiritually acceptable as well as temporally legal. Ethical practices in business is thus an ancient concern which has long been woven in our social fabric.

Feudalism was dead, interred by the expansion of trade, the growth of urbanization, the creation of a merchant class, and the development of strong central governments. But the age of industrialization had not yet arrived. New wine was fermenting, straining the old societal containers. What was needed now was a new spirit, a new sanction for human efforts.

The Cultural Rebirth

The new wine that was straining the cultural containers was a trinity of forces which would eventually lead to the Industrial Revolution and a new culture for mankind. These forces established the cultural foundations of a new industrial age which brought people from subservience to new-found freedoms in economic arrangements for the allocation of resources, in social relations, and in political institutions. The rediscovery of the ancient classics and renewed interest in reason and science epitomized the Renaissance and broke the ancient hold of theology on people through the Protestant Reformation and the subsequent Protestant ethic. The liberty ethic established new concepts in relations between people and the state through constitutional government. Another facet, the market ethic, brought forth the notion of a market-directed economy. These three "ethics," or standards for cultural conduct, interacted in practice to change cultural values toward people, toward work, and toward profits. The outcome of this cultural

---

[13] Johannes Nider, *De Contractibus Mercatorum*, Cologne: Ulrich Zell, 1468; translated by Charles H. Reeves and edited by Ronald B. Shuman as *On The Contracts of Merchants*, Norman, Okla.: The University of Oklahoma Press, 1966.

rebirth was the creation of a new environment which would lead
to the need for the formal study of management.

The Protestant Ethic

The loosening of religious bonds by the Crusades and the spread
of general prosperity through the revival of commerce was bound
sooner or later to lead to a revolt against the church. It began in
Germany with Martin Luther and shook the world. By no stretch
of the imagination could Martin Luther be considered as pro-
capitalism. He agreed with the church in condemning interest,
considered commerce a "nasty business," and spoke out vehe-
mently against the Fuggers, the leading commercial family in Germany. John Calvin was inspired by the reformation attempts of
Luther and, like Luther, he followed the Augustinian creed of pre-
destination and brought to the Reformation a somber view of the
smallness and weakness of man. He viewed as ideal a combination of church and state which led to his theocracy of Geneva
and clearly repudiated the philosophy of the Renaissance. His
concept of the "elect," those predestined to be saved, gave a new
spirit to his followers. Since all was predetermined, each should
believe that he was of the elect and, based on this divine election,
each would have the courage to face the tribulations of any harsh
world. Did the stern Protestantism of Luther and Calvin provide
the religious sanctions for capitalism? Certainly their ideas did not
espouse the cause of capitalism, but (as often happens when disciples are given free rein) did their ideas create a new man for a
new age?

Max Weber would answer in the affirmative by stating the
case for Protestantism having created the spirit of capitalism.[14]
Weber began his search for an explanation of the capitalistic spirit
by noting the overwhelming number of Protestants as business
leaders and entrepreneurs, and as the more skilled laborers and
the more highly technically and commercially trained personnel.
In Weber's view, Luther developed the idea of a "calling" in the
sense of a task set by God, a life task. This was a new idea

[14] Max Weber, *The Protestant Ethic and the Spirit of Capitalism* (trans. by Talcott Parsons),
New York: Charles Scribner's Sons, 1958. Originally published in Germany (1905)
and revised in 1920 to include answers to various critics.

brought about during the Reformation which became a central dogma of Protestant denominations. It discarded Catholic notions of subsistence living and monastic asceticism by urging the individual to fulfill the obligations imposed upon him in this world, i.e., in his "calling" (German, *Beruf*). It placed worldly affairs as the highest form of moral activity for the individual and gave the performance of earthly duties a religious significance and sanction. Every person's occupation was a calling and all were legitimate in the sight of God. Weber did not say that Luther intended capitalism to follow from his concept of the calling; on the contrary, it was later connotations which led to refinement of this idea into a success-oriented spirit of capitalism. The calling did place a new interpretation on the purpose of life; instead of waiting in his station for the Judgment Day, the worker should pursue whatever occupation he had chosen, not for the purpose of material gain beyond needs, but because it was divine will. The result of this Protestant dogma was a worldly asceticism which asked people to renounce earthly sensuality to labor in this world for the glorification of God. Each person must consider himself as one of the "elect" and if he did not his lack of confidence was interpreted as a lack of faith. To attain self-confidence, each individual must engage in intense worldly activity for it and it alone dispelled religious doubts and gave certainty of grace. In practice, this came to mean that God helps those who help themselves.

The Catholic layman, in contrast, fulfilled his required religious duties conscientiously. Beyond that minimum his good works need not form a rationalized system of life. He could use his good works to atone for particular sins, to better his chances for salvation, or as a sort of insurance premium for his later years. To make a sharper distinction, Weber described the demands of Calvinism:

> *The God of Calvinism demanded of his believers not single good works, but a life of good works combined into a unified system. There was no place for the very human Catholic cycle of sin, repentance, atonement, release, followed by renewed sin. Nor was there any balance of merit for a life as a whole which could be adjusted by temporal punishments or the Churches' [sic] means of grace.* [15]

[15] Ibid., p. 117.

The Calvinist was therefore required to live a *life* of good works, not an inconsistent series of wrongs balanced by repentant rights. Weber saw this as a keystone in developing a spirit of effort and gain; people were no longer able to give free rein to irrational impulses but were required by dogma to exercise self-control over their every action. They proved their faith by worldly activity, acting with zeal and self-discipline.

This new Protestant asceticism, which Weber also characterized as Puritanism, did not condone the pursuit of wealth for its own sake, for wealth would lead to pleasure and to all the temptations of the flesh. Instead activity became the goal of the good life. Numerous corollaries developed in practice: (1) that the waste of time was the deadliest of sins since every hour wasted was negating the opportunity to labor for the glory of God; (2) willingness to work: "he who will not work shall not eat"; (3) that the division and specialization of labor was a result of divine will since it led to the development of a higher degree of skill, to improvement in the quality and quantity of production, and hence served the good of all; and (4) that consumption beyond basic needs was wasteful and therefore sinful: "Waste not, want not."[16] According to Weber, each of these ideas had a significant impact on the motivations of people, leading to a spirit of enterprise.

Intense activity moved people from a contemplative life to one of continuous physical and mental labor. Willingness to work placed the motivational burden on individuals and their self-directed, self-controlled lives gave them an internal gyroscope.[17] The specialization of labor placed each person in his calling, required him to do his best, and the nonspecialized worker demonstrated a lack of grace. The Protestant ethic postulated that God desired profitability, that this was a sign of grace, and to waste anything and reduce profits, or to forgo what might be a profitable venture, worked against God's will. By not seeking luxury, people created a surplus or profit from their labors. The created wealth could not be consumed beyond a person's basic needs and

[16] Ibid., p. 157–173.

[17] Cf., David Riesman, Nathan Glazer, and Reuel Denney, *The Lonely Crowd*, Garden City, N.Y.: Doubleday and Co., 1950, pp. 29–32. Riesman and his associates characterized the product of the Protestant ethic as "inner-directed man."

thus the surplus was to be reinvested in other ventures or the improvement of present ones.

Protestantism resulted in specific guidelines for the creation of a capitalistic spirit. According to Weber, people had a duty to work, a duty to use their wealth wisely, and a duty to live self-denying lives. An unequal distribution of goods in the world was divine providence at work since each person had unequal talents and therefore reaped unequal rewards. Wealth was no assurance of heaven and the poor need not worry as long as they performed their calling properly. For Weber, the spirit of capitalism was created by the Protestant ethic, which equated spiritual worth and temporal success. With no room for self-indulgence and with the tenets of self-control and self-direction, a new age of individualism had been born.

A Criticism of the Weberian Thesis

Every thesis generates its antithesis and Weber's Protestant ethic is no exception. R. H. Tawney reversed Weber's thesis and argued that capitalism was the cause and justification of Protestantism, not the effect.[18] Tawney noted that Catholic cities were chief commercial centers, Catholics were leading bankers, and that the "capitalistic spirit" was present in many places far in advance of the sixteenth- and seventeenth-century influences that Weber discussed. According to Tawney:

> Is it not a little artificial to suggest that capitalist enterprise had to wait, as Weber appears to imply, till religious changes had produced a capitalist spirit? Would it not be equally plausible, and equally one-sided, to argue that the religious changes were themselves merely the result of economic movements?[19]

In Tawney's view, the rise of capitalism was action and reaction, molding and in turn being molded by other significant cultural forces. The Renaissance brought a new focus on reason, on discovery, on exploration, and on science; all were challenges to the monolithic authority of the church. The Renaissance contributed the humanist's views that made life on earth more important and brought the promise of a new social order in which there would

[18] R. H. Tawney, *Religion and the Rise of Capitalism*, London: John Murray, 1926.

[19] R. H. Tawney, "Foreword" to Max Weber's *The Protestant Ethic*, p. 8.

be mobility for people; it signaled the mastery of people over their environment rather than the reverse case of the Middle Ages.[20] Growing economic life posed new problems for church doctrine and merchants and tradesmen engaged in profit-making activities regardless of dogma. Perhaps, then, the Reformation was an attempt to create materialistic loopholes for the emerging merchant class.

With two sets of assumptions two different conclusions are reached: one, Weber's notion that the church changed and then the spirit of capitalism abounded; or two, Tawney's view that economic motivation was steam pushing on the lid of church authority until the safety valve of a change in dogma (i.e., the Reformation and its later proliferation into various sects) could sanction economic efforts.

Modern Support for Weber

Despite the criticisms of Weber's thesis there is modern evidence that Protestants hold different values toward work. In his *Achieving Society*, McClelland began a search for the psychological factors which were generally important for economic development.[21] The factor he isolated was the "need for achievement" or the shorthand version, "*n* achievement." McClelland's study was both historical and cross-cultural and his findings support Weber's thesis. First, McClelland found that high *n* achievement was essential to engaging in entrepreneurial activities; second, that high *n* achievement in a society was significantly correlated to rapid economic development; and third, that certain ethnic, religious, and minority groups showed marked differences in *n* achievement. He found that Protestants produced children with higher *n* achievement than Catholics, and Jews produced children with higher *n* achievement than either one. McClelland concluded that "individualistic" religions, for example the Protestant ones, tended to be associated with a high need for achievement, while "authoritarian" ones, such as traditional Catholicism, tended to have a

---

[20]Tawney, *Religion and the Rise of Capitalism*, pp. 61–63.

[21] David C. McClelland, *The Achieving Society*, New York: Van Nostrand Rinehold Co., 1961. See also John W. Atkinson, *A Theory of Achievement Motivation*, New York: D. Van Nostrand Co., 1966.

lower need for achievement. He did concede, however, that at the present there are wide variations and subcultures among various modern Catholic communities.

What was involved in the need for achievement was not so much the need to reach certain goals, such as wealth, status, respect, etc., as to enjoy the satisfactions of success. Wealth was a way of keeping score, not the goal. The entrepreneurial personality was characterized by special attitudes toward risk-taking, willingness to expend energy, willingness to innovate, and a readiness to make decisions and accept responsibility. Historically the concern for achievement appeared in a culture some fifty or so years before a rapid rate of economic growth and prosperity. McClelland found this to be true in ancient Greece (before its golden age), in Spain in the Middle Ages (before the age of exploration), and in England during two different periods. The first period was from 1500–1625 when Protestantism and Puritanism were growing in strength in England concurrently with a rising need for achievement. The second period came in the eighteenth century just prior to the Industrial Revolution. The reasoning that McClelland used to support Weber was basically thus: (1) the Protestant Reformation emphasized self-reliance rather than reliance on others in all facets of life; (2) Protestant parents changed child-rearing practices to teach self-reliance and independence; (3) it has been empirically demonstrated by McClelland and his associates that these practices lead to a higher need for achievement in sons; and (4) a higher need for achievement leads to spurts of economic activity such as that which Weber characterized as the spirit of capitalism.[22] Therefore, McClelland was able to draw a relationship empirically between the influence of Protestantism and Weber's "spirit of modern capitalism."

Lenski has summarized the criticisms of Weber, evaluated them, and presented the evidence both for and against Weber. On balance, he found evidence more in favor of Weber than against him. Lenski examined vertical mobility and concomitant characteristics of aspirations, ambition, and attitudes toward work in an attempt to define the relationship between religious affiliation and the ability of people to move upward in the job world. The

[22]McClelland, pp. 47–53.

findings resulted in a ranking of: first (most mobile), Jews; second, Protestants; and third (least mobile), Catholics. Lenski's explanation resided in the differences among the above three groups with respect to "achievement" motivation and their attitudes toward work. Jews and Protestants showed a positive attitude toward work and derived satisfactions from work. Catholics held neutral attitudes toward work and indicated that it was done for some other purpose than the satisfaction that came from work itself. In Lenski's view:

> Catholics continued to regard work primarily as a necessary evil; a consequence of Adam's fall and a penalty for sin. By contrast, Protestants come to view it as an opportunity for serving God, or, in the Deist version, for building character. [23]

The implications of McClelland's and Lenski's findings can be far-reaching for modern man. Not only did they find empirical support for Weber, but their work suggests that achievement values can be taught and instilled in various societies. In underdeveloped nations and in America's ghettos, inculcation of achievement values would provide means for self-help programs to speed the progress of or the adjustment to industrialization. [24]

The Liberty Ethic

Given the postulates of a need for achievement and the sanctions of individual rewards for worldly efforts, the political system must be conducive to individual liberty. The divine right of kings, the aristocracy of the manor lord, the exercise of secular authority by the church, and serfdom as a birthright were not favorable conditions for developing an industrialized society. In the Age of Enlightenment, new political philosophers began to stimulate the thoughts of people with such new ideas as equality, justice, the rights of citizens, a rule of reason, and notions of a republic governed by the consent of the governed. These were radical ideas in those times, ideas that threatened the existing order with a pro-

---

[23] Gerhard Lenski, *The Religious Factor: A Sociological Study of Religious Impact on Politics, Economics, and Family Life,* Garden City, N.Y.: Doubleday and Co., 1961, p. 83.

[24] For examples of how this might be done, see David C. McClelland and David G. Winter, *Motivating Economic Achievement,* New York: Free Press, 1969.

found revolution in the views of the relationship between citizen and state.

Before this facet of the cultural rebirth, political theory called for the domination of the many by the few and found its best proponents in Machiavelli and Thomas Hobbes. Nicolo Machiavelli, an out-of-office administrator and diplomat in the city-state of Florence, wrote *The Prince* in 1513.[25] He was an experienced observer of the intrigues of state and papacy and set forth a "how to do it" book for a rule or any aspiring ruler. *The Prince,* dedicated to Lorenzo di Piero de Medici, was an exposition on how to rule, not how to be good or wise, but how to rule successfully. Machiavelli's basic assumption about the nature of people was indicative of his rationale for the type of leadership he advocated:

Whoever desires to found a state and give it laws, must start with the assumption that all men are bad and ever ready to display their vicious nature, whenever they may find occasion for it.[26]

To cope with these brutes, the ruler was justified in pursuing any leadership style that suited his purpose. He should be concerned with having a good reputation, but not with being virtuous; should he have to choose between being feared and being loved, he would find it better to be feared; and above all, he must be like a lion and a fox, employing force and deceit. For Machiavelli, it was the end and not the means which was important; if the ruler succeeded, he would win approval and his villainies would be forgotten. "Machiavellian" has come to connote the unscrupulous, crafty, and cunning in policy. For that time, and perhaps for this one, Machiavelli has personified the command philosophy of governing people.[27]

Thomas Hobbes' *Leviathan* (1651) was a later argument for a strong central leadership.[28] He began his analysis with mankind in a state of nature, without civil government, and proceeded to the conclusion that some greater power, the *Leviathan,* must exist

[25] Nicolo Machiavelli, *The Prince* (trans. by Luigi Ricci), New York: New American Library, 1952.

[26] Nicolo Machiavelli, *Discourses on Livy,* trans. by Alan H. Gilbert, reprinted in *Machiavelli: The Chief Works and Others,* Durham, N.C.: Duke University Press, Vol. 1, 1956, p. 203

[27] An interesting analysis of Machiavellian practices in modern corporate life may be found in Antony Jay, *Management and Machiavelli,* New York: Holt, Rinehart, and Winston, 1967.

to bring order from chaos. This person or body became sovereign; since it was given all rights by the governed, its powers could not be revoked, and it became an absolute sovereign. It made no difference to Hobbes whether the sovereign be civil or ecclesiastical, as long as the central power regulated all overt conduct and expression, both civil and religious. The sovereign ruled all, and the individual was subordinate to the system.

In the history of human liberty, John Locke's essay *Concerning Civil Government* (1690) must stand as a great contribution to political theory and as an effective instigator of political action. It served to state the principles of the English "bloodless revolution" of 1688 which brought about substantial fundamental changes in the British constitution. It also set the stage for the American Revolution of 1776 by inspiring the authors of the Declaration of Independence and furnished inspiration to Jean Jacques Rousseau's *Social Contract* and the ensuing French Revolution. Perhaps no other one man has had such a profound effect on political theory and action. Locke attacked the divine right of kings, whose proponents traced this right to Adam's God-given right to rule his children, and set forth some new concepts of authority:

> . . . *who shall be judge whether the prince or legislative body act contrary to their trust? . . . To this I reply, the people shall be judge. . . .*[29]

This notion found more explicit support in the Declaration of Independence:

> *We hold these truths to be self-evident, that all men are created equal; that they are endowed by their creator with certain inalienable rights; that among these are life, liberty, and the pursuit of happiness. That to secure these rights, governments are instituted among men deriving their just powers from the consent of the governed.*

Locke's work is so broad that it is possible only to sample his

---

[28] Thomas Hobbes, *Leviathan, or the Matter, Form and Power of a Commonwealth Ecclesiastical and Civil*, Chicago: Great Books of the Western World, Vol. 23, Encyclopaedia Brittanica, 1952. Originally published as *Leviathan, or the Matter, Forme, and Power of a Common-Wealth Ecclesiasticall and Civill*, London: printed for Andrew Ckooke, at the Green Dragon in St. Paul's Churchyard, 1651.

[29] John Locke, *Second Essay Concerning Civil Government*, Chicago: Great Books of the Western World, Vol. 35, Encyclopaedia Britannica, 1952, p. 81. Originally published in 1690.

main contributions: first, that people were governed by a natural law of reason and not by the arbitrary rules of tradition or the whims of a central authoritarian figure. Second, that civil society was built upon private property. The law of nature and reason commanded one not to harm another's possessions and individuals entered into a civil society in order to preserve more perfectly their liberty and property, which were then protected by both natural law and civil law. Since people had a natural right to property, the state could not take it away, but must rather protect their rights to it.

Locke was a Puritan in the England of Cromwell. His writing must have affected that of Adam Smith and most certainly established the basis for Rousseau's writings. In the emergence of the philosophical Age of Enlightenment, he put forth a new civil order: one, a law based on reason, not arbitrary dictates; two, a government deriving its powers from the governed; three, liberty to pursue individual goals as a natural right; and four, private property and its use in the pursuit of happiness as a natural and legally protected right. These four ideas interwove in practice to form a solid political foundation for industrial growth. It provided a sanction for *laissez-faire* economics, sanctioned the pursuit of individual rewards, guaranteed the rights of property, gave protection to contracts, and provided for a system of justice among people.

The Market Ethic

Economic thinking was basically sterile during the Middle Ages since localized, subsistence-level economies needed no economic theory to explain their workings. Early people perceived the main factors of production as land and labor, and even the latter did not pose much of a problem. Capital as an input factor was scorned and its return damned. Any idea that management was a resource input to the organization was completely lacking in early economic thought.

In the sixteenth and seventeenth centuries, the reemergence of strong national entities began to reshape economic thought. As new lands were discovered through explorations, new trade routes and new products created an international market. This revolution in trade resulted in the economic philosophy of mercantilism and injected the government into a central role of financing and protecting trade in order to build strong national economies. This economic chauvinism meant that the state intervened in all economic affairs, engaged in state economic planning, and regulated private economic activity to a large degree.[30] Mercantilism eventually fell of its own weight. Much of its planning went awry because it tried to keep alive uneconomic enterprises, curbed private initiative, built elaborate bureaucratic, red-tape controls, and fostered wars and trade rivalries and destroyed the very markets it was trying to create.[31] The mercantilists were a philosophical contradiction to the emerging eighteenth-century "Age of Enlightenment." The mercantilists thought only of the state while the philosophy of the enlightenment championed individual rights and viewed all human institutions in terms of the contribution they could make to the happiness of each individual.[32]

In the eighteenth century, the physiocratic school of economic thought emerged to challenge mercantilism. Francois Quesnay, its founder, maintained that wealth did not lie in gold and silver but sprang from agricultural production. He advocated *laissez-faire* capitalism, meaning that the government should "let alone" the mechanisms of the market; for him, economics had a natural order and harmony and government intervention interfered with the natural course of events. Adam Smith (1723–1790), a Scottish political economist, was not a physiocrat *per se* but was influenced by their view of a natural harmony in economics. In his *Wealth of Nations,* Smith established the "classical" school and became the father of liberal economics.[33] Smith thought that the tariff policies of mercantilism were destructive and, rather than protecting industry, these policies penalized efficiency by a state fiat and consequently misallocated the nation's resources. Smith

[30] John Fred Bell, *A History of Economic Thought,* 2d ed., New York: Ronald Press, 1967, p. 53.

[31] Shepard B. Clough, *The Economic Development of Western Civilization,* New York: McGraw-Hill Book Co., 1959, Chapter 11.

[32] John Bowditch and Clement Ramsland (ed.), *Voices of the Industrial Revolution,* Ann Arbor: University of Michigan Press, 1961, pp. iv–v.

[33] Adam Smith, *An Inquiry Into the Nature and Causes of the Wealth of Nations,* Chicago: Great Books of the Western World, Vol. 39, Encyclopaedia Britannica, 1952. Originally published in 1776.

proposed that only the market and competition be the regulator of economic activity. The "invisible hand" of the market would insure that resources flowed to their best consumption and their most efficient reward, and the economic self-interest of each person and nation, acting in a fully competitive market, would bring about the greatest prosperity of all.

For Adam Smith, the specialization-of-labor concept was a pillar of this market mechanism. He cited the example of the pinmakers who, when each performed a limited operation, could produce 48,000 pins a day, whereas one unspecialized worker could do no more than twenty pins per day. He admitted that this was a trifling example but he found the same principles of division of labor operating successfully in many industries:

> *This great increase of the quantity of work which, in consequence of the division of labour, the same number of people are capable of performing, is owing to three different circumstances; first, to the increase of dexterity in every particular workman; secondly, to the saving of the time which is commonly lost in passing from one species of work to another; and lastly, to the invention of a great number of machines which facilitate and abridge labour, and enable one man to do the work of many.*[34]

While Smith saw the benefits of specialized labor, he also foresaw its dysfunctional consequences:

> *The man whose whole life is spent in performing a few simple operations . . . naturally loses, therefore, the habit of [mental] exertion, and generally becomes stupid and ignorant as it is possible for a human creature to become . . . . His dexterity at his own particular trade seems . . . to be acquired at the expense of his intellectual, social, and martial virtues.*[35]

Smith argued that it was the province of government, through public education, to overcome the debilitating effects of the division of labor. In his view, the manager, in order to gain productivity, must rely upon the division of labor. The division-of-labor concept benefited all of society and provided an economic

---

[34] Ibid., p. 4. Smith also enunciated the first marketing principle when he noted that the division of labor was limited by the extent of the market, i.e., there would be no economic rationale in having 18 men producing 48,000 pins per day if the market could absorb only 20,000 per day. Ibid., Chapter 3.

[35] Ibid., p. 340.

rationale for the factory system. When markets were limited, a household or domestic production arrangement could meet market needs. As the population grew and as new trade territories became feasible, a greater division of labor was possible and the factory system as a productive device began to gain momentum.

When his writing appeared in the early stages of the Industrial Revolution, Smith found a large number of vocal supporters and fertile soil for his liberal economics. He was in tune with the philosophy of the Enlightenment and the newly emerging group of entrepreneurs who wished to sweep away the restrictions of mercantilism and the controlling power of the landed aristocracy. England found in the market ethic an economic sanction for private initiative rather than mercantilism, competition rather than protection, innovation rather than economic stagnancy, and self-interest rather than state interest as the motivating force. The market ethic was another element in this trinity of forces which created the cultural environment for the flowering of the industrial system.

Summary

Early management thought was dominated by cultural values which were antibusiness, antiachievement, and largely anti-human. Industrialization could not emerge when people were bound to their stations in life, when monarchs ruled by central dictates, and when people were urged to take no thought of individual fulfillment in this world but to wait for a better one. Before the Industrial Revolution, economies and societies were essentially static, and political values involved unilateral decision making by some central authority. While some early ideas of management appeared, they were largely localized. Organizations could be run on the divine right of the king, on the appeal of dogma to the faithful, and on the rigorous discipline of the military. There was little or no need to develop a formal body of management thought under these nonindustrialized circumstances.

Three forces were interacting and combining to provide for a new age of industrialization. Characterized as "ethics," or standards governing human conduct, they illustrate how economic, social, and political attitudes were changing during the cultural rebirth. The "ethics" discussed were in reality a struggle between the old traditional and the newly emerging society. The Protestant ethic was a challenge to the central authority of the church and a response to the needs of people for achievement in this world; the liberty ethic reflected the ancient struggle between monolithic and representative forms of government and sought to protect individual rights; and the market ethic was a gauntlet flung before the landed aristocracy who preferred mercantilism. The struggle represented here is an old one: the state versus the individual, human rights and due process versus whimsical autocracy, and centralization versus decentralization. The struggle goes on.

This cultural rebirth would establish the preconditions for industrialization and subsequently the need for a rational, formalized, systematic body of knowledge about how to manage. The emergence and refinement of the market economy required managers to become more creative and to be better informed about how best to administer an organization. Faced with a competitive, changing environment, the manager had to develop a body of knowledge about how best to utilize resources. People began thinking of individual gain and had to be accommodated in some rational administrative framework. The emergence of modern management had to be based on *rational* ways of making decisions; no longer could the organization be operated on the whims of a few. This change did not come suddenly but evolved over a long period of time as the culture changed. How these changes came about and how they affected the evolution of management thought is the subject of this book. It is an intriguing story.

3

The Industrial Revolution: Problems and Perspective

The Industrial Revolution heralded a new age for civilization. The cultural rebirth had created new social, economic, and political conditions which were ripe for advances in science and technology. Subsequent improvements in technology made possible large combinations of physical and human resources and ushered in the factory system to replace the domestic system of production. This chapter will examine the salient characteristics of the Industrial Revolution and the managerial problems it created, and attempt to achieve some perspective on the consequences of this cultural revolution.

The Industrial Revolution in England

Industrial progress is always closely tied to advancements in science and technology. In the fifteenth century, Johann Gutenberg (1400–1468) developed the first metallic movable type for a printing press and opened the door to an information revolution which has yet to cease. While medieval scientists attempted to deduce physical laws from the writings of Plato, Aristotle, St. Augustine, and the Bible, a new age of scientific inquiry began in the sixteenth and seventeenth centuries as church bonds loosened. This Age of Reason, this revolution in scientific thought, was the product of such individuals as Francis Bacon, Nicholas Copernicus, Galileo Galilei, William Gilbert, William Harvey, Isaac Newton, and others. This scientific revolution emphasized the spirit of observation and inquiry and established the foundation for the technological revolution which was to follow.

A shift in land-use policy in England was also a contributing factor to industrial development in an indirect way. Starting as early as the thirteenth century, the feudal land owners began to enclose lands which had formerly been for communal use. Proceeding irregularly, this "enclosure" movement reached twin peaks in the sixteenth and late eighteenth centuries, the latter coming just before the Industrial Revolution. The enclosures were made possible by improved agricultural practices such as row (rather than broadcast) planting, crop rotation, and iron hoes drawn by horses. By enclosing over one-half of the common lands, small farm units were consolidated into larger, more profitable ones. Further, fewer farmers were required, releasing them for employment in the emerging factory system. Without the agricultural revolution, the industrial one would not have been possible.

Even since mankind began to improve methods of tilling the soil, of making weapons, or of weaving cloth, there have been advancements in technology or the art of making and using tools and equipment. Technology has been evolving and advancing for thousands of years but a "revolution" came in late eighteenth-century England that marked the beginning of a more rapid advance in technology than ever before. The essence of this revolution was the substitution of machine power for human power and it brought about marked changes in everyday life. Phyllis Deane, in pinpointing the emergence of the Industrial Revolution, illustrated the difference between preindustrialized societies and industrialized ones. Preindustrial societies are characterized by low per capita income, economic stagnation, dependence on agriculture, a low degree of specialization of labor, and very little geographical integration of markets. Industrial societies are characterized by rising or high per capita income, economic growth, low dependence on agriculture, a high degree of specialization of labor, and a widespread geographical integration of markets.[1] Using these factors as indicators, Deane concluded that the shift in

[1] Phyllis Deane, *The First Industrial Revolution*, London: Cambridge University Press, 1965, pp. 5–19.

England from a preindustrial to an industrial nation became most evident in 1750 and accelerated thereafter.

The Age of Machines

The physical elements of the Industrial Revolution were coal, iron, transportation, machinery, power, and factories; the human elements were the entrepreneurs with a zeal for innovation and profits and a largely agrarian and handicraft labor force. Iron and coal are the sinews of industry and England had ample quantities of both. Early blast furnaces used water-driven power to fan the coke. In 1760, an enterprising John Smeaton replaced the water-driven bellows in his furnaces with one partially driven by steam and increased his iron production from 12 to 40 tons per furnace per day. Iron declined in price with added productivity and new uses were found; in 1763, the first known railway, the first iron bridge in 1779, and the first iron ship in 1787.[2] Birmingham, close to large coal and iron deposits, became the leading city in the English iron industry. Transport was costly and difficult and the construction of canals greatly reduced the cost of commercial traffic in Britain so that cities sprang up along the waterways.

The growing market for textiles proved a boon to further innovations. Increasing imports of cotton and a larger world market made mechanical improvements imperative. John Kay began the mechanization of weaving by his "flying shuttle" in 1733; in 1765, James Hargreaves changed the position of the spinning wheel from vertical to horizontal, stacked the wheels on top of one another, and wove eight threads at once by turning them all with one pulley and belt. He called his gadget the "spinning jenny" (Jenny was Mrs. Hargreaves) and added more wheels and power until he was weaving 80 threads at once. In 1769, Richard Arkwright developed a "water frame" that stretched the cotton fibers into a tighter, harder yarn. His factories grew with this innovation until by 1776 he employed 5,000 workers, including many children who could operate the very simple machinery.

---

[2] A. P. Usher, *An Introduction to the Industrial History of England,* Boston: Houghton-Mifflin Co., 1920, p. 323. Another excellent history of technological advancement is R. Whatley Cooke Taylor, *Introduction to a History of the Factory System,* London: Richard Bentley & Sons, 1886.

Despite these mechanical improvements, the heart of the Industrial Revolution was really the steam engine. The steam engine was not new; Hero of Alexandria (ca. A.D. 200) developed one for the sake of amusement. Others had built models but had mechanical problems. Thomas Newcomen developed a steam-propelled engine to pump water out of coal mines which were flooding as deeper and deeper shafts went down. It was the task of James Watt, who was trained as a maker of scientific instruments, to perfect the earlier work of others. Watt developed his first workable steam engine in 1765 but finances and moving from the prototype to an industrial installation took 12 years. During this time he formed a partnership with Matthew Boulton, a leading English ironmaker, to make steam engines. In 1776, Watt's first engine was sold to John Wilkinson for use in his iron works. Not knowing what price to charge, an agreement was made that the steam engine would be "rated" at the equivalent of how many horses could do the same amount of work; hence the derivation of "horsepower" for mechanical engines. In 1781, Watt made his greatest breakthrough in technology with the development of an engine with a rotary, rather than an up-and-down, movement. This made the machine more adaptable to factory uses and the applications became more numerous as Watt's new engine turned mills for grinding grain (replacing water wheel power), drove textile machines, and blew bellows for iron works. In 1788, Watt patented a "fly-ball governor" which adjusted the flow of steam to promote the uniform speed of the engine. This first cybernetic control device operated on a centrifugal principle; as the engine sped up, arms on a rotating shaft raised and the steam intake vents closed, reducing power intake; as the engine slowed, the arms dropped, allowing more power.

The historian Arnold Toynbee has noted that two men, Adam Smith and James Watt, were the most responsible for destroying the old England, building a new one, and launching the world toward industrialization. Smith brought about the revolution in economic thought; Watt, the revolution in the use of steam power.[3] Harnessed to the wheels of a hundred industries, the steam engine provided more efficient and cheaper power; power for ships, trains and factories, revolutionizing English commerce and industry. Steam power lowered production costs, lowered prices, and expanded markets. A spirit of innovation led to inventions, inventions led to factories, and factories led to a need for direction and organization. The expanded market called for more workers, more machines, and a larger production scale on a regular basis. Capital was needed to finance these larger undertakings and the men who could command the capital began to bring together workers and machines under one common authority. Labor was divided, each worker specializing in some task; parts of products had to become interchangeable such that the division of labor would lead to a common final result. Out of the division of labor would come the need for the direction and coordination of efforts. The "factory system" as a method of production was born, the age of machines began, and the infant capitalism toddled forth to create an abundance such as the world had never seen.

Management: The Fourth Factor of Production

Before the Industrial Revolution, economic theory focused on basically two factors of production, land and labor, and recognized capital as an input factor only as church bonds loosened. The physiocrats recognized a "farmer-entrepreneur" but held that manufacturing and commerce were "sterile" and unable to produce a surplus. Adam Smith recognized the entrepreneur as a factor but treated his return or the surplus he created as a return to capital. Jean Baptiste Say (1767–1832), a French economist, was the first to explicitly recognize a fourth factor of production. Say noted that some "adventurers" (entrepreneurs) owned the undertaking but more frequently than not they owned only a share, having borrowed from others or having formed a partnership. The "adventurer" thus became a manager for others and assumed an additional risk in combining the factors of land, labor, and capital:

> . . . at one time he must employ a great number of hands; at another, buy or order the raw material, collect labourers, find consumers, and give at all times a rigid attention to order and economy; in a word, he must possess the art of superintendence and

[3] Arnold Toynbee, *The Industrial Revolution*, Boston: Beacon Press, 1956, p. 89; originally published in 1884.

administration. . . . There is always a degree of risk attending such undertakings . . . [and] the adventurer may . . . sink his fortune, and in some measure his character . . .[4]

For assuming the added risk in combining the traditional three factors of production, the "adventurer" received a separate reward for administration in addition to a return of his own invested capital.

Some authors make a further distinction between an entrepreneur and a manager; Fritz Redlich, for example, said the entrepreneur made "strategic" decisions, those pertaining to broader competitive policies of the total firm; while the manager made "tactical" decisions concerning the use of resources within the broad policy framework.[5] Joseph Schumpeter saw the entrepreneur as an innovator-manager who was the prime mover in bringing about economic change by introducing new products, new methods of production, new markets, new sources of raw material supplies, or a new organization of industry.[6] Professor Collins and his associates viewed the entrepreneur as an organization builder and innovator and distinguished between those who "build" (the innovating entrepreneur) and those who administer the organization after it has been built ("the bureaucratic entrepreneur").[7]

The early entrepreneur was the fourth factor of production in the sense that he was an "innovator" as well as a manager. As his organization grew, the entrepreneur found that he alone could not direct and control all activities and he began to delegate some of them to a level of submanagers. These submanagers were the first non-owning, salaried managers who had the responsibility of

[4] Jean Baptiste Say, *A Treatise on Political Economy*, New York: Augustus M. Kelley, 1964, pp. 330–331; originally published in 1803.

[5] Fritz Redlich, *The Entrepreneur*, Cambridge, Mass.: Harvard University Press, 1957, pp. 50–51.

[6] Joseph A. Schumpeter, *The Theory of Economic Development*, Cambridge, Mass.: Harvard University Press, 1963, p. 66 passim.

[7] Orvis F. Collins, David G. Moore, and Dareb B. Unwalla, *The Enterprising Man*, East Lansing, Mich.: Bureau of Business Economic Research, 1964, pp. 19–20. The whole subject of entrepreneurship has been dealt with at length under the sponsorship of the Harvard Center for Entrepreneurial Studies, in the journal *Explorations in Entrepreneurial History* (two series), and in a collection by Hugh G. J. Aitken (ed.), *Explorations in Enterprise*, Cambridge, Mass.: Harvard University Press, 1965.

making decisions within a broader framework of policies established by the entrepreneur. It was in the process of delegation that
many problems were to arise as the entrepreneur expanded his organization and took on an increasing number of lower-level
managers.

Management Problems
in the Early Factory

The emerging factory system posed different management problems than ever encountered before. The church could organize
and manage its properties because of dogma and the devotion of
the faithful; the military could control large numbers of men
through a rigid hierarchy of discipline and authority; and governmental bureaucracies could operate without having to meet competition or show a profit. The managers in the new factory system
could not resort to any of these devices to insure the proper utilization of resources.

The Industrial Revolution spawned a number of industries
and the early 1800s were characterized by the growth of these
firms in an ever increasing competitive environment. For the firm,
the pressure for size came from the need for economies of scale to
compete more effectively. Some advocated resisting the pressures
for size; for example, a report of the Committee on Woollen Manufacturers of 1806 stated that the development of large factories
would not lead to many advantages for the entrepreneur. By continuing the domestic system, the entrepreneur could save much
capital investment and would not need to "submit to the constant
trouble and solicitude of watching over a numerous body of workmen."[8] Competition still demanded growth but the retarding factor was the lack of a pool of trained managers who could cope
with large-scale factory problems. Hence the size of the early firm
was often limited by the number of people the entrepreneur himself could effectively supervise. The result was a dual line of ad-

[8]Sidney Pollard, *The Genesis of Modern Management: A Study of the Industrial Revolution in Great Britain,* Cambridge, Mass.: Harvard University Press, 1965, p. 11.
Pollard's research into the early factory is quite extensive and is the most thorough
of all works pertaining to early managerial problems created by the factory
system.

vance for the factory system: on the one hand, technology and capital made a larger scale of production possible and forces of competition made a larger size imperative; on the other hand, the enlargement of operations created a myriad of managerial problems.

The Search for Managerial Talent

The shortage of managerial talent posed all sorts of problems for the early entrepreneurs. Judging from early literature, the salaried manager, i.e., those in the layer of management below entrepreneur, were usually illiterate workmen promoted from the worker ranks because they evidenced a greater degree of technical skills or had the ability (often the physical strength) to keep discipline. Typically they were paid only a little more than the other workers and more often than not were attracted to the managerial position because it gave them the power to hire wives and children to work in the factory. Untrained in the intricacies of managing, the manager was left on his own to develop his own leadership style. Problems were met and solved on an *ad hoc* basis, and only a few managers could learn from the experiences of others in solving factory problems or handling people. The general view of leadership was that success or failure to produce results depended upon the "character" of the leader, upon his personal traits and idiosyncrasies, and not upon any generalized concepts of leadership.

Other sources of management talent provided little enlightenment. Entrepreneurs used relatives in managerial positions frequently, presumably based on the assumption that they were more trustworthy or would act to preserve their potential inheritance. This device also served as a training ground to secure ownership and control in the family for the next generation. Another source of talent was the "counting-house"; entrepreneurs recruited likely looking bank clerks and tellers, thinking they probably had both business and financial acumen. For developing managers, the entrepreneurs relied on osmosis and experience on the job to furnish these recruits with the necessary knowledge.

The matriculation of England from an agrarian to an industrial society meant that there was no "managerial class" or in modern terms, no "professional" managers. First, there was no common body of knowledge about how to manage. The training of managers supplemented experience on the job with teaching the fledgling manager the techniques of production, the sources and characteristics of materials, the operations of machine processes, trade practices, and the legal obligations of the firm. This training was oriented toward a specific industry, cotton, woolen, mining, or whatever, and did not lend itself readily to generalization. The manager, trained in one industry, found himself bound to that industry since he would need to relearn his skills if he moved to another. Second, there was no common code of management behavior, no universal set of expectations about how a manager should act. Codes were developed for specific industries and gave advice about the manager's responsibility for safety, for the security of the plant and equipment, design standards for engineering, and for procedures to follow in safeguarding the owner's interests.

James Montgomery of Glasgow (Scotland) prepared what were most probably the first "management" texts.[9] Montgomery's managerial advice was largely technical in nature; he advised how to discern quality and quantity of work, how to adjust and repair machinery, how to keep costs down, and how to "avoid unnecessary severity" in disciplining subordinates. He noted that a manager must be "just and impartial—firm and decisive—always on the alert to prevent rather than check faults after they have taken place. . . ."[10] This latter comment on controlling was very perceptive and indicated an early understanding that the control function is essentially looking forward rather than backward. However, Montgomery's advice was for the cotton industry and, like most other early writers, he did not seek to develop any generalized principles of management.

Montgomery was so highly regarded as a manager that he

---

[9] James Montgomery, *The Carding and Spinning Masters' Assistant; or the Theory and Practice of Cotton Spinning,* Glasgow: J. Niven, Jr., 1832; and James Montgomery, *The Cotton Spinner's Manual,* Glasgow: J. Niven, Jr., 1835. Montgomery's contributions are discussed and portions of the 1832 work are reproduced in James P. Baughman (ed.), "James Montgomery on Factory Management, 1832," *Business History Review,* Vol. 42, No. 2 (Summer, 1968), pp. 219–226.

[10] Baughman, quoting Montgomery, p. 226.

was brought to America in 1836 to become superintendent of the York Mills, Saco, Maine. This gave Montgomery the opportunity to do what was probably the first comparative study of management through the analysis of different economies. He found that the United States had higher costs of production, paid higher wages (including wages for women), but had lower costs of materials. The British firms had lower costs, paid lower wages, but paid more for raw materials. The relative competitive efficiency resided in England, in Montgomery's opinion, because the English firms were better managed.[11] Montgomery's study was of cotton mills only, but it gives some idea of the differing states of managerial knowledge in America and Britain in 1840.

Early managerial salaries left much to be desired. The first-line supervisors, or "overlookers," were paid little more than the workers. Often the white-collar salaried managers were paid on the basis of their social class rather than on the extent of their responsibility. By 1800, however, Pollard noted that the shortage of talent had forced payment based on the job and not the person.[12] By 1830, the salaries of nonowner managers had risen rapidly and compressed the differential between their pay and that of the owner managers. In England, but not in France or Italy, the status of the entrepreneur was rising, inducing many young men to seek their fortunes in commerce, or at least to become a junior partner in a large firm. The second- and third-generation offspring of the founder-entrepreneur changed their style to give more status to the salaried manager. They tended to delegate more and depended more upon the salaried manager. Perhaps their affluence, built by the success of their forefathers, made them less desirous of becoming personally involved in daily activities; or perhaps the firms had grown to such a size and the fund of managerial talent had reached a point where they could find more reliable subordinates than their predecessors. In the early factory, the problems of finding and developing managerial talent were acute. There were no business schools for recruiting, no systematic programs for developing people into managers, and managerial skill was judged a localized, idiosyncratic matter.

[11] James Montgomery, *The Cotton Manufacture of the United States of America Contrasted and Compared with that of Great Britain,* London: John N. Van, 1840, p. 138.

[12] Pollard, p. 139.

The Labor Problem

The managerial problem was acute but the problems with labor made even the strongest "bull-of-the-woods" supervisor blanch. The factory had to attract laborers from rural to urban life; and peasants, with their traditional family ties and heritage, their long links with the past and their community, had to absorb a whole new culture in their shift to the factory.

Broadly conceived, the labor problem had three aspects: recruitment, training, and motivation. In itself, the recruitment problem was multi-faceted. The existing labor force consisted of unskilled agrarian workers who had a definite aversion to factory life and work. This aversion was largely due to the necessity of abiding by the rules and rigorous discipline that factory work required; although certainly much of it also came from the distaste for the noise, dirt, and apparent squalor in many of the factories themselves. The shift from a small workshop, from the farm, or from a family-operated operation, was a drastic one for the workers. They had to pull up roots from a long-familiar milieu and go to the brawling, bustling city for employment. They were required to accept a new culture and not exactly an inviting one at that. As Sombart has noted, people who were nonaccumulative, nonacquisitive, and accustomed to working for a subsistence income had to be made obedient to a cash stimulus for the prospect of maximization of income; further they had to be stimulated within the bounds of a predictable, controllable manner set by management.[13]

Andrew Ure and others complained that factory work was uncongenial to the typical workers who were accustomed to the domestic or agrarian life and did not look kindly upon the monotony of factory jobs, the year-round regularization of hours, and the constant demands of attention to their work. Workers tended to be restless, shiftless, and deviant. The firm of Roebuck and Garrett, for example, moved their factory from Birmingham (England) to Scotland because they found the Scots to be more reliable

---

[13] Werner Sombart, *The Jew and Modern Capitalism* (trans. by M. Epstein), London: T. Fisher Unwin, 1913, pp. 809, 829–831.

and obedient.[14] A contemporary observer described early textile weavers as fiercely independent and generally insubordinate. For the most part, they were Puritans and were as opposed to factory regimen and the managerial hierarchy of authority as they were to the Church of England.[15] It was with workers such as these that the early factory managers had to work.

The Shortage of Skilled Labor

The other facet of the recruitment problem resided in the extreme shortage of skilled labor. The paradox of early nineteenth-century England was a large amount of unemployment existing simultaneously with employers begging for help. It was structural unemployment partially in that the former agrarian workers did not possess factory skills but largely it was due to the refusal of workers to accept factory life. Some skilled labor did exist in small, scattered guilds and workshops; however, these craftsmen preferred this arrangement to the routine of factory work. Employers had to offer all sorts of inducements to these workers and had to make major concessions to keep them on the job. The loss of strategic or key craftsmen could shut down the whole factory. James Watt had pressing problems with finding men who could cut and fit the valves and cylinders to the proper tolerances; indeed, many of his early failures were of execution, not design. Arkwright kept his skilled people working extra hours because they were so scarce. Many iron mills kept their furnaces going even in slack times in order to keep from losing their labor force. These practices cast doubt on Marx's claim of the "reserve army of the unemployed"; the unemployment problem was a technological one and also one of personal inclination. If workers had the skills, or if they were willing to work in the factory to learn these skills, they need not have been unemployed. It was necessity, not malice, that led early entrepreneurs to employ domestic servants, women, children, parish paupers, displaced farmers, and anyone else they could obtain. Employers used every possible medium to advertise for

[14]Pollard, p. 161.

[15]Richard Guest, *A Compendious History of the Cotton Manufacture*, Manchester: Joseph Pratt, 1823, pp. 40–43.

workers and one authority reported that children and paupers were employed only after other sources of labor were absorbed.[16]

Training

The second major problem was that of training. Once the personnel were recruited, they had to be taught the new skills of an industrial life. Literacy was uncommon and basic educational skills were lacking; drawings, instruction sheets, and procedures for machine operation demanded some ability to read, figure, and to respond with predictable results. Training was conducted largely by oral instruction, demonstration, and trial and error. The new employee learned from someone else, usually a coworker, how to operate a machine or process a piece of material. Standardized methods were unheard of and each worker blithely followed the precepts of someone else who knew little more than he. The shortage of skilled workers, such as machinists, millwrights, and instrument makers, was of course a serious problem. Even more serious, however, were the *new* skills required by the factory since no previous jobs had exactly the same skills as the new ones. To transfer the worker's existing skills to new ones met both problems of learning as well as resistance to the new methods. The traditional prejudices against anything new added to management's discomfort. Finally, workers were not accustomed to abiding by the accuracy and tolerances demanded by the technique of interchangeable parts upon which many factories were based. Even the relatively crude measuring tools required instruction for use. The craftsmen, accustomed to individualizing their work, resisted the standardization of parts, methods, and tools required by the interchangeable-parts method of production.

The haphazard acquisition of knowledge from coworkers or inept supervisors, the lack of standard methods of work, and worker resistance to new methods posed serious problems for efficient factory operation. Employers resorted to developing their own schools to teach elementary arithmetic and geometry and other skills needed in the factory and not available in the populace. With this knowledge of the early factory it is easier to explain

---

[16]Stanley D. Chapman, *The Early Factory Masters: The Transition to the Factory System in the Midlands Textile Industry*, New York: Augustus M. Kelley, 1967, p. 168.

a number of managerial practices which modern writers often use to criticize early factory pioneers. Jobs were de-skilled, i.e., specialized and divided into minute tasks, because of the ease of teaching them to the worker. The goal was not only efficiency but also to solve the practical problems of finding and training personnel. Job enrichment would have been totally impractical for the early factory worker. The establishment of centralized, even autocratic, leadership was in large part probably necessitated by the need to get predictable results from an unwilling work force. Participation by the worker in decision making would have been impractical; of course even benevolent autocracy, though practiced by some, would have been an improvement. Not fully accustomed to democracy in their daily life and with memories of the authority of the feudal lord, the workers probably saw little change in their relations with their new superiors. The workers, lacking skills and motivation, would have frustrated a twentieth-century manager who espoused participative or democratic leadership. Viewed in its cultural perspective, the early factory probably demanded task-oriented leadership to cope with the vagaries of the existing labor force.

Discipline and Motivation

The third problem, and by no means the least one, was that of discipline and motivation. Accustomed to the craft traditions of independence and the agrarian mores of self-sufficiency, workers had to develop "habits of industry" such as punctuality, regular attendance, the acceptance of a new regime of supervision, and the mechanical pacing of work effort. Instead of supervision by the traditional aspects of craftsmanship and hallowed master-servant relationship, the factory substituted a different discipline. It demanded regularity rather than spurts of work, accuracy and standardization rather than individuality in design and methods, and the use of equipment and material of others, not pride in one's own tools of production. Apparently the new habits did not come easily: worker attendance was irregular, "feast days" which were common traditions in the domestic system caused large-scale absenteeism for factory operators, and workers tended to work in spurts by laboring long hours, collecting their money, and then disappearing for countless days of dissipation. To combat the feast-days problem, some early employers resorted to using the traditional holidays for company-sponsored outings and feasts to build company loyalty, to break the monotony of the work year, and to cement personal relations. For example, Arkwright held a feast for 500 employees at his Cromford mill in 1776 and Matthew Boulton hosted 700 at his Soho plant. Punctuality, or "time-thrift" in the early employer's terms, posed all sorts of problems. Employers levied fines for tardiness and often resorted to locking the plant gates and workshop doors at starting time.

Machine smashing, although it was sporadic, was another disciplinary problem. However, much of this behavior antedated the perfection of the steam engine and the growth of large factories. In 1753, John Kay's flying shuttle and other inventions were smashed and his home destroyed by workers protesting the introduction of this labor-saving machinery. James Hargreaves suffered a similar fate at his Blackburn mill in 1768. Operators of the old hand spinners were convinced that the new "jenny" would put them out of work so they raided Hargreave's house and smashed his machines. The machine-breaking era peaked in 1811–1812, although it appears that the workers' motives were changing from their previous fear of unemployment due to technological advancement. The changing times brought a label for the machine smashers, the "Luddites," which originated because a youth in Ludlam had smashed his knitting frame when his father had been too harsh with him. The Luddite movement never had any unified purpose, nor a single leader. Scattered groups did their smashing under the guise of "Ned Ludd," who was their "general." The name Luddite was first used in 1811, when a rash of machine breaking occurred, primarily in the hosiery knitting trade around Nottingham. However, these protests appeared to be based on different grounds than technological advancement. Wages were falling, unemployment rampant, and food prices were rising due to the government's policy on food imports. Machine smashing was a convenient way to protest dissatisfaction, although it was other latent forces, not technology, that caused the problem.[17]

[17]Malcolm I. Thomis, *The Luddites: Machine Breaking in Regency England*, Hamden, Conn.: Archer Books, 1970.

Disciplinary efforts against the Luddites were rather draconian. One Luddite, a fellow by the name of Mellor, assassinated a mill owner, and he and his followers were duly hanged in York (1812). Public fears of further violence led to more hangings of Luddites (Nottinghamshire, Lancaster, and Chester), and the movement soon died for lack of leadership.

Efforts to motivate people fell into three categories and, upon close inspection, appear to have changed only in application, not theory, up to the present day. The offering of positive inducements ("the carrot"), negative sanctions ("the stick"), and efforts to build a new "factory ethos" became the methods for bringing deviant workers into the fold. For the carrot, early employers developed two devices, subcontracting and payment by results. Subcontracting will be examined in greater depth later, but in essence it involved the employer contracting with an overseer for certain bits of work. This transferred responsibility for keeping the workers going to the overseer who had an incentive to accomplish a specified amount of output with the least possible costs. Individual piecework, or payment by results, appeared at an early point in the factory system. By 1833, 47.5 percent of the cotton mill workers were on a piece-rate incentive.[18] The firm of Boulton and Watt introduced piece-rate payments in 1778. Performance standards were based on the average times for the jobs which was taken from historical records; however, there was no scientific study of the jobs themselves and the time that workers *should* have taken for task completion.

Establishment of the concept of payment by results represented a major psychological break with tradition. The old attitude that the worker must be kept at the subsistence level and that the best worker was the hungriest one was replaced by an early concept of "economic man." This notion held that monetary incentives brought out the best in people and that they would work harder to get more. Economic man was born, to survive for many years. The piece-rate system engendered, even in these early years, the same animosities which are seen today. Employers resorted to the "speed-up," to rate-cutting, the quality of work often deteriorated, and employer-employee friction often arose over the standards and the computation of payment. These problems

[18] Pollard, p. 190.

should not be surprising, however: there is no evidence of any attempts to study job design nor of any efforts to systematically determine performance standards, even in such progressive firms as Boulton and Watt.

The "stick," negative sanctions, became a practice for which the early industrial system is frequently criticized. Corporal punishment, especially of children, was used, though authors disagree on its frequency and severity. The subcontracting system may have contributed to many of these abuses since the owner relinquished control and often left disciplinary policy in the hands of unlettered overseers who took their job of getting out production a little too seriously. Graduated fines were more common methods of discipline: one plant fined workers 30 cents for being absent Monday morning, and 70 cents for singing, swearing, or being drunk.[19] Since wages often amounted to two or three dollars a week, this was a fairly large portion of the worker's pay. Disciplinary policies probably varied widely between factories and fluctuated according to the relative scarcity or abundance of workers. Skilled workers, who were in short supply, were probably not dealt with too severely and labor shortages in general also must have diminished the employer's ability to be too harsh. It must be remembered that the prevailing attitude toward children, even in respectable homes, was that they should be seen and not heard, and that to "spare the rod" was to "spoil the child." In the context of the period, employers treated children as they were accustomed to being treated at home,[20] although that does not condone what did happen.

The third method of motivation was general in conception and oriented toward creating a new factory ethos. The goal was to use religious morals and values to create the proper attitudes toward work. The encouragement of moral education, even on company time and in early company towns, reading of the "good book," regular church attendance, and exhortations to avoid the deadly sins of laziness, sloth, and avarice were methods of inculcating in the working population the right habits of industry. A coalition of employers and ministers exhorted the populace to guard against the moral depravities which were not only sinful,

[19] Ibid., p. 187.
[20] Chapman, p. 203.

but led to a lackadaisical, dissipated work force. The Quaker Lead Company, for example, punished workers for "tippling [drinking], fighting, and night rambling."[21] Doubtless this moral suasion emanated from more than a concern for the soul of the worker. Pollard presented a succinct statement of these attempts to create a new ethos:

> *The drive to raise the level of respectability and morality among the working classes was not undertaken for their own sake, but primarily . . . as an aspect of building up a new factory discipline.*[22]

Management Functions in the Early Factory

In addition to the difficulties of staffing the factory with a reluctant labor force, the task of acquiring competent submanagers, and the avoidance of the Luddites, early managers faced planning, organizing, and controlling problems similar to those of the modern manager. Workmen's "combinations" were forbidden by law and early employers resorted to a "black-list" and the firing of anyone who conspired to form a union. Although employers could agree on what to do with threats from labor, they did not attempt to share their knowledge about how to manage other aspects of their operations.

In planning operations, the early factory required more farsightedness than the domestic system. As the factory system developed, the new industrialist became more rational, more pragmatically interested in laying a foundation for long-term growth rather than short-term speculative gains. Early mines required long-range planning to develop the veins and early factories required costly equipment. As capital was "sunk," businessmen had to be more rational and more aware of the long-term implications of their decisions. Examples of planning in industry are few and those which do exist are largely technically oriented rather than comprehensive in company scope and application. Robert Owen and Richard Arkwright led the way in preplanning factory layout. Their "requirements," or principles, emphasized

[21]Pollard, p. 193.
[22]Ibid., p. 197.

the orderliness of the work flow and factory cleanliness. Factory technology demanded the planning of power sources and connections, the arrangement of machinery and space for a smooth flow-through of work, and the reduction of confusion through bins and well-placed stores of materials.[23] The firm of Boulton and Watt also stressed factory layout and developed detailed systems for controlling stocks of materials and parts. They engaged in rudimentary work study for production planning, for work flow, and for assembly methods at their Soho factory (the engine works).[24] The use of standardized, interchangeable parts made planning necessary, both in design and execution of the assembly. James Watt, Jr., saw at an early stage that standard parts would lessen the tasks of controlling work and that detailed planning and proper initial execution would insure that the final product would meet specifications. Standard parts also eased repairs for the customer and reduced both the company's and customer's inventory of spare parts, thus simplifying the stock control system.

In organizing, managers were limited to a large extent by the caliber of the subordinate managers. Early departmentation, or the grouping of activities, was often based on the number of partners or relatives. With a gesture toward egalitarianism, each became department heads with one or two salaried managers below them supervising the workers. Some companies did develop what would be called a typical line structure with a single director above other managers in an orderly organizational box format.

There is evidence in the textile industry that technology played an important role in how activities and relationships were structured in the emerging factory system.[25] In the beginning, most workshops followed a "batch" processing technology; that is, there were relatively short runs of manufacturing a quantity of

[23] Jennifer Tann, *The Development of the Factory System*, London: Commarket Press, 1970.

[24] Erich Roll, *An Early Experiment in Industrial Organization: Being a History of the Firm of Boulton and Watt, 1775–1805*, London: Longmans, Green and Co., 1930. The development of relatively advanced managerial techniques at Boulton and Watt is credited to the sons of the firm's famous founders, Matthew Robinson Boulton and James Watt, Jr. Roll, p. xv.

[25] Stanley D. Chapman, "The Textile Factory Before Arkwright: A Typology of Factory Development," *Business History Review*, Vol. 48, No. 4 (Winter, 1974), pp. 468–473.

like products at the same time, followed by another batch of slightly different products, and so on. This description seems to characterize the textile industry until the early 1800s.

As new applications of steam power were made, another technology emerged as being more efficient. The new strategy was to arrange the power-driven machines in a line sequence to flow toward completion of the product. This "flow" technology resembled more the mass production assembly line with an output of large quantities of standardized products, made at a lower per unit cost, and intended for a mass market. With this increase in production quantity, it became more economical to specialize labor even further, with each person adding his efforts to the flow of work. It was not a moving assembly line as we know it today, but the product was moved from one stage of production to another by carts, workers, chutes, etc. Departments were established for the various operations necessary to the product flow. With more departments came the need for another level of management to coordinate the work as it flowed from one stage to another. The consequence was scalar organizational growth, creating a taller hierarchy of management and more elaborate procedures and systems so efforts could be integrated. It appears that early textile firms discovered long ago what modern contingency theorists espouse: that is, that technology affects the organizational structure. Early "batch" production methods allowed more informality; however, the application of steam-driven power led to a new factory technology, flow manufacturing, and required more formality in organizational design.

In controlling performance, entrepreneurs faced numerous problems. Needing to delegate authority to cope with larger-sized enterprises since they could no longer personally oversee all operations, they found the shortage of trained and trusted submanagers posed problems of accountability. Adam Smith observed that it was a rare salaried manager who would exercise the same vigilance over other people's money as he would over his own. Accounting knowledge had not advanced since Pacioli and its use as an aid to managers was an almost unheard-of phenomenon. Books were kept to account for earnings, wages, material, and sales, but there is no evidence that managers knew how to use the accounting function as an aid to decision making. The accounting information they had was in gross form, undigested and erratic. Charles Babbage did suggest a descriptive cost accounting system but it was not until the twentieth century that accounting and management thought developed to the point where costs and information became a focal point of study. This lag in knowledge is really not surprising since the prevailing view was that it was the personality of the manager that meant success or failure, not accounts nor procedures.

Pollard cited numerous examples of business failures occurring when the "principals," or owners, left the management of firms up to a salaried staff of managers. These managers were often dishonest, absconding, and alcoholic, and their mismanagement led many early entrepreneurs to establish a "contracting out" system in an effort to insure control. The entrepreneurs set a contract price for the finished work and let the contractor managers pay their own workers, procure their own materials, and assume all factory risk.[26] Working to keep costs down to insure a profit as the margin between their contract price and their costs, the subcontractors had an important incentive which was lacking under the direct factory work system. Contracting out provided control for the entrepreneur and motivation for the contractor without necessitating direct supervision by the principal. Of course there were disadvantages in practice; the contractor often stressed short-run return to the detriment of worker safety and this practice often led to a deterioration in the condition of mines or in the maintenance of equipment. The drive to produce more or speed up the worker gave rise to abuses and some very crude managerial techniques which often led to dissatisfaction and riots. Yet many early managers kept this system rather than try to supervise a large-scale operation directly.

Through trial-and-error experience, early entrepreneurs attempted to cope with the problems of managing a factory and a work force. The emphasis on technical rather than managerial problems was probably due to the crude state of the technological art and the pressure to keep abreast of competition and to make the new gadgets work. Management was deemed a localized matter, not subject to generalization, and success was thought to de-

[26] Pollard, pp. 19–23.

pend upon the personal qualities of the managers, not upon their grasp of broader principles of management. Management was a personal art, not a discipline; pragmatic, not theoretical; and parochial, not universal.

There were some individuals who were attempting to fill this void in management knowledge; their efforts will be the subject of chapter 4. But first, let us try to gain some perspective on the cultural impact of the Industrial Revolution.

Cultural Consequences of the Industrial Revolution

The revolution was not only technological but cultural. The new machines, the new factories, and the new cities shook people's tradition-based roots and demanded participation in a new era. In the hearts of many there is an idealization of the agrarian life before industrialization. Critics have charged that capitalism, together with its offspring—the market and factory systems—robbed people of a golden age of equality and freedom. More specifically, the criticisms have been that people were enslaved to the owners of capital, that they became little more than a commodity in the marketplace of life, that capitalists exploited child and female labor, and that industrialization created poverty, urbanization, pollution, and a host of other societal ills. Let us examine some of these criticisms and attempt to gain a perspective on the cultural consequences of this new age of industrialization and capitalism.

The Condition of the Worker

Economics earned its sobriquet, "the dismal science," during the early nineteenth century. Thomas Malthus set out to disprove the optimism of Adam Smith and liberal economics with his famous "population" argument. Malthus postulated that population increases in geometric proportion while the food supply at best increases only arithmetically. The population is limited by the means of subsistence and the masses tend to reproduce beyond these means, preventing any improvement in their condition. Government relief of the poor only encourages a population increase, food prices go up, and the poor are no better off. The only answer for Malthus (he was not very optimistic about the outcome) was to restrict the supply of labor and to encourage self-restraint in the reproduction of the masses.[27] His was a hopeless view of people as no more than commodities in the market place of life who were basically powerless to overcome their disadvantage. David Ricardo did not appear much more optimistic; his "iron law of wages" said that in the long run real wages would always tend to stabilize at some minimum level which would provide the worker with just enough means to subsist.[28] The "Utopian socialists," such as Robert Owen, saw people as powerless in their environment and wanted to replace the individualism of the market with a communal life. The Utopians did not write of the necessity of revolt but felt they could achieve change through their writings and by example. An opposite view was developed by Karl Marx and Friedrich Engels, who advocated the need for force as the midwife of history. Because people were powerless, in their view, and because they were being kept at the subsistence level by the exploitation of the factory masters, workers must combine to break their chains. While the writings of Marx and Engels are more political essays that economic analyses, they did reflect the economist's dismal view of the world at that time.

Were people powerless and exploited to the poverty level by capitalism? The subsistence level for the masses was not new; they had spent the previous thousand or more years in essentially the same status but as agrarian peasants tied to a feudal landlord. The Industrial Revolution did not create poverty; it inherited it. The rise of capitalism was creating the means for releasing people from drudgery through labor-saving machines, making people more productive and better paid for less exertion of effort.[29] Further, it is difficult to agree with Marx and Engels that the workers were exploited by the factory owners for basically two reasons: first, the severe shortage of labor which would have diminished the managers' power to do as they liked with their labor; and sec-

---

[27] John Fred Bell, *A History of Economic Thought*, 2d ed., New York: Ronald Press Co., 1967, pp. 180–186.

[28] Ibid., p. 221.

[29] Friedrich A. Hayek, "History and Politics," in F. A. Hayek (ed.), *Capitalism and the Historians*, Chicago: University of Chicago Press, 1954, pp. 15–16.

ond, the fact that workers' real wages were steadily rising from 1790 to 1830 and the workers' lot was improving "well above the level of mere subsistence."[30] For those who were willing to enter the factory and learn its new skills, the new machines and methods made them more productive and raised wages; in turn, added industrial efficiency reduced the prices of goods and raised real wages. The increasing use of incentive payment plans held out a promise of economic betterment for people; no longer tied to remitting a tithe to the feudal lord, workers could, through effort, enhance their own well-being. It is also likely that wages were rising to reduce the onus of factory work and to overcome the short supply of labor. Were people powerless? Were they a commodity exploited by the new entrepreneur? Their lack of power appears to have been more of a reluctance to accept the new discipline of the factory; as for the commodity charge, no employers of the time would have agreed that they could buy and sell labor as they pleased.

Child and Female Labor

Child and female labor were not inventions of the Industrial Revolution. The domestic system required the participation of all and feudalism was built upon the family as the basic economic unit. One authority noted that child labor was at its worst in the domestic system long *before* the factory system.[31] Up to 75 percent of the labor force in many factories depended upon child and female labor. However, it is doubtful that employers made any profit on child labor, whose upkeep usually cost more than it produced.[32] Employers would have preferred a mature, stable, adult work force but these individuals were scarce and hard to attract. Concern in Britain over child labor practices led to two famous parliamentary investigations; the first in 1819 at the behest of Robert Owen, and chaired by Sir Robert Peel, himself an extensive employer of children in his factories; and that of the Sadler Committee of 1832. Extensive and detailed evidence was given be-

[30] T. S. Ashton, "The Standard of Life of the Workers in England: 1790–1830," in Hayek, p. 158.

[31] R. Whatley Cooke Taylor, p. 402.

[32] Stanley D. Chapman, *The Early Factory Masters*, p. 171.

fore these committees.[33] Children often began work at age five and occasionally spent a 14-hour day at the factory. This practice was widespread, being found in the cotton, wool, flax, and silk mills, and existing legislation concerning child labor provided no enforcement mechanism. In their testimony, witnesses described the hours (long), wages (low), working conditions (often extremely poor), and the methods of discipline (often harsh). One witness testified that children often fell asleep at work and were kept awake by an overseer who grasped the child by his legs and dipped him head first in a barrel of water.

Female labor, attracted to the factory for the wages to build a dowry, for the opportunity of finding a husband, or driven to the factory to supplement the family income, fared little better in some cases. Mantoux depicted the early entrepreneur as

> . . . *tyrannical, hard, sometimes cruel, their passions and greeds were those of upstarts. They had the reputation of being heavy drinkers and of having little regard for the honour of their female employees. They were proud of their newly acquired wealth and lived in great style with footmen, carriages and gorgeous town and country houses.*[34]

Mantoux is guilty of overgeneralization; ample examples can be given, such as Josiah Wedgewood, Matthew Boulton, James Watt, John Wilkinson, Robert Owen, and a host of others for whom there is no evidence that they played loose and fancy free with their female employees.[35] Only one specific case was cited in parliamentary testimony and the tenor of the critics' position was that of the "temptations and opportunities" presented by the presence of both males and females in the same workshop.[36] Evidently if the workers had been segregated by sex, no testimony would have appeared at all. There was great concern that unemployed girls would be forced by circumstances to prostitution; but a Doc-

---

[33] For some excerpts, see E. Royston Pike, *'Hard Times': Human Documents of the Industrial Revolution,* New York: Praeger Publishers, 1966, especially pp. 100–218.

[34] Paul J. Mantoux, *The Industrial Revolution in the Eighteenth Century,* trans. by Marjorie Vernon, New York: MacMillan Co., 1928, p. 397.

[35] See W. O. Henderson, *J. C. Fischer and His Diary of Industrial England 1814–1851,* New York: Augustus M. Kelley, 1966, p. 57. Undoubtedly some of these individuals existed, as they do in all ages, but Fischer maintained that they were not representative of the era.

[36] Pike, p. 285, with the lurid title of "Seduction in the Mill."

tor Hawkins presented evidence for Manchester that of the 50 prostitutes who had been apprehended in the past four years (1829–1833), only 8 came from the factories, while 29 came from the ranks of former household servants.[37]

Evidence concerning child and female labor is contradictory; most testimony hints of the moral degradation of factory life but the hard statistics are lacking. It appears that emotional and religious overtones were given more credence, isolated instances were ballooned, and no rigorous empirical investigation was undertaken to compare the past with the prevailing state of affairs. One cannot condone child labor whether it be of the domestic system or of the factory system. Employers of the times were driven to employment of children by the low level of technology and the great demand for unskilled labor. What the critics overlooked was the fact that capitalism was slowly but surely allowing the release of children from the work force. As better machines were developed to perform the simple jobs, it became uneconomical to employ children. It was an economic force—broadening capitalism, not legislative fiat nor a moral rebirth—that freed the child from the looms.[38] As for legislation and governmental bodies, it was the Poor Law Authorities, a government office, which sent the paupers into the factories! The paupers were poor or deserted children legally in the care of the state; to relieve the state of the burdens of maintenance, they were sent to whomever would accept their care and feeding.

To understand the critics of the factory system, one must consider that the Victorian value system was operating. The "Victorian" period began *before* Queen Victoria ascended the throne in 1837.[39] Victorian values of a profound social conscience and a formal adherence to strict standards of personal and social morality began forming around 1800. Economic and social conditions had been worse *before* the Industrial Revolution, but the Victorian value sets of people like Charles Dickens established the rationale for criticizing the emerging factory system.

---

[37] Ibid., p. 297.

[38] W. H. Hutt, "The Factory System of the Early Nineteenth Century," in Hayek, p. 184.

[39] John W. Osbourne, *The Silent Revolution: The Industrial Revolution in England as a Source of Cultural Change*, New York: Charles Scribner's Sons, 1970, pp. ix–xi.

There is evidence that the factory system led to a general rise in the standard of living (something lacking in the previous thousand years), to falling urban death rates and decreasing infant mortality. These factors led to a population explosion in England: its inhabitants increased from 6 million in 1750 to 9 million in 1800 and to 12 million in 1820. Further, infant mortality before the age of five fell from 74.5 percent in 1730–1749 to 31.8 percent in 1810–1829. Since there were no significant medical advances apparent during the period, one can only conclude that people were better able to feed, clothe, and care for themselves.[40] Heilbroner has pointed out that factory life, even with urban poverty, represented an improvement over life in an agrarian and domestic system.[41] Poverty was not new, it had just been collected in one place, the city, and made more easily visible to the legislators, intellectuals, and others. Isolated and scattered, agrarian poverty did not shock the sensibilities, but next door and down the street, it became a problem. Heilbroner further answered the critics of the Industrial Revolution in saying that the criticism was based on political and not economic unrest. England of that period was characterized by a surging interest in rights and justice and in political reform; the populace had "a critical temper of mind before which *any* economic system would have suffered censure."[42] This criticism was directed at the entrepreneur, not because he was to blame, but because he was a convenient symbol of change.

One cannot tax capitalism with the unsavory conditions and practices of the Industrial Revolution. The factory system inherited child and female labor, poverty, and long working hours from the past, it did not create them; the new age of industrial capitalism was creating through the factory a method for people to gain leverage for a better life.

---

[40] Margaret C. Buer, *Health, Wealth and Population in the Early Days of the Industrial Revolution, 1760–1815*, London: George Routledge & Sons, 1926, p. 30. Cited by Robert Hessen, "The Effects of the Industrial Revolution on Women and Children," in Ayn Rand, *Capitalism: The Unknown Ideal*, New York: American Library, 1966, p. 104.

[41] Robert L. Heilbroner, *The Making of Economic Society*, Englewood Cliffs, N.J.: Prentice-Hall, 1962, p. 85.

[42] Ibid., p. 86.

Summary

The Industrial Revolution created a new cultural environment and a revised set of problems for management. People's needs were becoming more complex as they sought to adjust to life in the city and to the new rigor of the factory. Organizations were being re-shaped by the demands for heavy infusions of capital, by the division of labor, and by the need for economical, predictable performance. Organizations needed to innovate and compete in a market economy and this created pressures for growth and the economies to be obtained from large-scale production and distribution. Economic theory recognized that the entrepreneur-manager performed a distinct role in combining the traditional three factors of production in the ever growing factory system. With size came the need for managers, the need for a capable, disciplined, trained, motivated work force, and the need for rationalizing the planning, organizing, and controlling of operations in the early enterprise. The problems were present and the next chapter will examine some early management pioneers who proposed solutions for coping with the growing factory system.

4

Management Pioneers in the Factory System

A prevailing theme so far has been the relationship of management thought to its cultural environment. The factory system posed new problems for owners, managers, and for society at large. This chapter will focus on four individuals who pioneered in proposing solutions to the manifold pressures of coping with the earliest large-scale industrial organizations. History leaves a notoriously scanty scent. Records and memorabilia are lost or destroyed, notable ideas may never be committed to writing, and judgments must be made on perhaps a small part of what actually occurred. Of the early management pioneers, history has provided us with the best records for four men: Robert Owen, Charles Babbage, Andrew Ure, and Charles Dupin.

Robert Owen: The Search for a New Harmony

Robert Owen (1771–1858) was a paradox in the turbulent era of the Industrial Revolution.[1] A successful entrepreneur himself, he attempted to halt the surge of industrialism and the evils he saw in it as he called for a new moral order based on a social reorganization. He had a vision of a new industrial society which was to be a combination of agricultural and industrial commune and

[1]This description of Owen's life and work is based on his autobiography: Robert Owen, *The Life of Robert Owen,* London: Effingham Wilson, 1857; reissued by Augustus M. Kelley, 1967 (Volumes I and IA).

harkened back to the lost days of more primitive people. Philosophically, he viewed people as powerless, held in the grips of revolutionary forces of the new age of machinery which destroyed moral purpose and social solidarity. His struggle was a long and frustrating one and he appears in history as a King Canute ordering the waves of progress to recede.

Early Managerial Experiences

A self-made man imbued with the self-confidence which typified the early entrepreneurs, Owen, at the age of 18, founded his first factory in Manchester during an age of war prosperity when many were getting rich. There was a great impetus in cotton trade and the new water frame, the weaving machines of Arkwright and Crompton, and the power sources of Watt made large factories feasible. Owen teamed with a mechanic named Ernest Jones, Jones taking the technical responsibility and Owen the management; and Owen described his introduction to managing:

> *I looked very wisely at the men in their different departments, although I really knew nothing. But by intensely observing everything, I maintained order and regularity throughout the establishment, which proceeded under the circumstances far better than I had anticipated.* [2]

Jones proved a burden to the firm, and Owen set out on his own after buying up Jones's share. His firm became profitable but he decided to become a salaried manager and sold his equipment to a Mr. Drinkwater and became employed by him. Still with a modicum of experience, he applied himself to the new position:

> *I looked grave, inspected everything very minutely . . . I was in with the first [workers] in the morning, and I locked up the premises at night. I continued this silent inspection and superintendence day by day for six weeks, saying merely yes or no to the questions . . . I did not give one direct order about anything. But at the end of that time I felt myself so much master of my position as to be ready to give directions in every department.* [3]

Owen, left on his own by Mr. Drinkwater, made a success of the mill. He rearranged the equipment, bettered the conditions of

[2] Ibid., p. 31–32.
[3] Ibid., p. 39.

the workers, and achieved a great deal of influence over his subordinates. He later attributed his success with the workers to his "habits of exactness" and to his knowledge of human nature. He left Drinkwater in 1794 or 1795 to establish a new partnership, the New Lanark (Scotland) venture. At New Lanark, he encountered the ubiquitous problem of scarcity of labor and noted: "It was most difficult to induce any sober, well-doing family to leave their home to go into cotton mills as then conducted."[4] Perhaps this difficulty in attracting labor influenced his personnel policies; he began forming his visions of a new society. At New Lanark, he employed between 400 and 500 parish apprentices, the pauper children furnished by the Poor Law authorities to whomever would take them. The children worked 13 hours per day including an hour and a quarter off for meals. Owen continued to employ children but tried to improve their living and working conditions even though he could not persuade his partners to accept all of his reforms. His reform efforts aimed to reshape the whole village of New Lanark, including the streets, houses, sanitation, and the educational system.

At New Lanark, Owen encountered the same disciplinary problems as other manufacturers. Similar to the attempts of others to create a new factory ethos, he tried to use moral suasion rather than corporal punishment. He developed one particularly unique device, the "silent monitor," to aid discipline. Under this system, Owen awarded four types of marks to each superintendent and each of them in turn rated his subordinates. These marks were translated into color codes of black, blue, yellow, and white in ascending order of merit. A block of wood was mounted on each machine and the four sides painted according to the code. At the end of each day, the marks were recorded, translated, and the appropriate color side of the block turned to face the aisle. Anyone passing, and knowing the code, could immediately assess the workers' last day's effort. This wooden albatross worked to motivate laggards to overcome their deficiency and supposedly to induce the white block "good guys" to maintain theirs. It was most certainly a precursor of modern management's public posting of sales and production data to instill departmental pride or to encourage competition.

[4] Ibid., p. 79.

The Call for Reform

Pre-dating Mayo, Roethlisberger, Likert, and others who have urged concern for the human resource asset of the firm, Owen set forth his rationale for a new philosophy:

> . . . *you will find that from the commencement of my management I viewed the population [the labor force] . . . as a system composed of many parts, and which it was my duty and interest so to combine, as that every hand, as well as every spring, lever, and wheel, should effectually cooperate to produce the greatest pecuniary gain to the proprietors. . . . Experience has also shown you the difference of the results between a mechanism which is neat, clean, well-arranged, and always in a high state of repair; and that which is allowed to be dirty, in disorder, without the means of preventing unnecessary friction, and which therefore becomes, and works, much out of repair. . . . If, then, due care as to the state of your inanimate machines can produce such beneficial results, what may not be expected if you devote equal attention to your vital machines [the human resource], which are far more wonderfully constructed?*[5]

Owen chided his fellow manufacturers for not understanding the human element. He charged that they would spend thousands on the best machines, yet buy the cheapest labor. They would spend time improving machines, specializing labor, and cutting costs, yet make no investment in the human resource. He appealed to their pecuniary instincts, claiming that money spent on improving labor "would return you, not five, ten, or fifteen per cent for your capital so expended, but often fifty, and in many cases a hundred per cent."[6] He claimed a 50 percent return at New Lanark, and said it would shortly reach 100 percent. He claimed that it was more profitable to show such concern for people and that it also served to relieve the "accumulation of human misery." Owen's venture at New Lanark was profitable but there is at least one doubter about whether or not this was due to his personnel policies. One biographer noted that profits in the cotton spinning industry at that time were so large, averaging 20 percent or more on capital invested, that *any* personnel policy could have been profit-

[5] Ibid., Appendix B. p. 260.
[6] Ibid., p. 261.

able. "In fact the margin of profit was so wide that we need scarcely look for any other explanation of Owen's success as a manufacturer."[7] Whatever the reasons for his own success, Owen deplored the commercialism of life. He declared an intellectual war on capitalism and also attacked the church because it condoned the evils of the new industrial age. These views branded him as a radical and made it more difficult for him to persuade others of the need for reform. Owen felt that the crucial error of all established religions was the preaching of the doctrine of human responsibility. He held that man was the creature of his environment, relatively incapable of escaping it without a moral rearmament through education. Contrary to the church view that good character was promoted by the promise of rewards and punishment, especially in the hereafter, Owen felt that character developed solely if the material and moral environment of men was proper. To these ends, he became more active politically about 1813 and proposed a factory bill to prohibit all employment under age 10 and to limit hours to 10½ per day with no night work for children. His proposal was too radical for other manufacturers and politicians of that time. After many political intrigues, the bill became law in 1819 but instead of applying to all factories, it applied only to cotton mills and set the age limit at 9 and not 10. With no provision for inspection to insure compliance, the law was toothless.

A biographer suggests that, frustrated in his attempts to reform society, Owen became slightly "mad" in 1817.[8] Failing to change Britain, he sought the openness of America and established the first cooperative community based on his principles at New Harmony (Indiana) in 1824. That venture too was doomed to fail within three years and Owen found himself both financially and emotionally broken. Owen had thought that what he had learned and applied in his cotton mills could be applied to the whole society but he was unable to persuade others that his new moral order was realistic and not Utopian. As a reformer, Owen devised laws for relief of the poor and proposed solutions to un-

---

[7] Frank Podmore, *Robert Owen*, New York: Appleton-Century-Crofts, 1924, p. 642.

[8] G. D. H. Cole, *The Life of Robert Owen*, 3rd ed., Hamden, Conn.: Archon Books, 1966, p. 197.

employment problems. He proposed "Villages of Cooperation" (like New Harmony) which would have a communal sharing of surplus and be based on agriculture. He fought against the Malthusian doctrine of overpopulation, saying that, if all shared, none would hunger. He deplored the evils of the division of labor; in his ideal system, each man would do a number of different jobs, switching easily from one to another. For him, it was the evils of the wage system and capitalism that caused life at a subsistence level. In 1834, Owen led the British Trade Union movement which was a working-class movement based on the idea of collective action to control the means of production. He failed. Nevertheless, Robert Owen, a Utopian Socialist, sowed the first seeds of concern for the human element in industry.

Charles Babbage: The Irascible Genius

To call Charles Babbage (1792–1871) an irascible genius is to pay him the greatest compliment, for he fitted both qualities and emerged as a significant figure in management thought long before Frederick W. Taylor. Largely technique oriented like his contemporaries, Babbage's application of technological aids to human effort has earned him a place in history as the patron saint of operations research and management science. He theorized and applied a scientific approach to management long before the scientific management era in America. Born in Devonshire as the son of a wealthy banker, he used his inheritance in a life-long quest "into the causes of all those little things and events which astonish the childish mind."[9] He remarked that his first question after receiving a new toy was invariably "Mamma, what is inside of it?" and he also invariably broke open the toy if the answer did not appear satisfactory. The value of his work was recognized by few of his contemporaries, and he was generally considered a crackpot by his neighbors. His personal traits were not endearing to those who disturbed his cogitations. In retaliation against the ubiqui-

[9]Charles Babbage (autobiography), *Passages From the Life of a Philosopher*, London: Longman & Green, 1864, reprinted in Philip and Emily Morrison (eds.), *Charles Babbage and His Calculating Engines*, New York: Dover Publications, 1961, p. 9.

tous English street organ grinders, he blew bugles and created a commotion outside his house to scare them away. One contemporary, perhaps a neighbor, wrote: "He spoke as if he hated mankind in general, Englishmen in particular, and the English Government and organ grinders most of all."[10]

The First Computer

Babbage's scientific output was phenomenal.[11] He demonstrated the world's first practical mechanical calculator, his "difference engine," in 1822. Ninety-one years later its basic principles were being employed in Burroughs' accounting machines. Babbage had governmental support in his work on the difference engine but his irascibility cost him the support of government bureaucrats for his "analytical engine," a versatile computer that would follow instructions automatically.[12] In concept, Babbage's computer had all the basic elements of a more modern version. It had a store or memory device, a mill or arithmetic unit, a punch card input system, an external memory storage, and conditional transfer.[13]

Babbage's computer never became a commercial reality nor did he develop a punch-card machine. However, Herman Hollerith, inventor of the earliest practical punched card tabulating machine, perhaps had read Babbage's work or even more certainly

[10]No author, "The Cranky Grandfather of the Computer," *Fortune*, March, 1964, p. 112–113. The life and peccadilloes of Babbage are pieced together from this source; from Morrison and Morrison, op. cit.; and from an excellent biography by Maboth Moseley, *Irascible Genius: A Life of Charles Babbage, Inventor*, London: Hutchinson & Co. Publishers, 1964.

[11]Babbage was recognized as a genius by his contemporaries and the prevailing theory of the day was that there had to be physiological differences in the human brain which would explain variations in human intelligence. Accordingly, Babbage willed his brain to the Royal College of Surgeons (England) who, after a post-mortem examination, found nothing extraordinary in Babbage's brain mass or structure. Babbage's brain is still preserved by the Museum of the Royal College of Surgeons. Maboth Moseley, p. 257.

[12]Babbage conceived the analytical engine in 1833 and worked on it intermittently throughout the remainder of his lifetime. Jeremy Bernstein, *The Analytical Engine*, New York: Random House, 1963, p. 36.

[13]"Conditional transfer" in computer terminology is the "if" statement: i.e., instructions to the computer that "if such and such occurs, follow this path; if not, proceed in the normal sequence of control."

knew of the Jacquard loom which was developed in 1801 by Joseph-Marie Jacquard. The Jacquard loom, still in use in the textile industry, used "pattern" or punch-cards in which a hole signaled the loom to lift a thread and a blank corresponded to a depressed thread, thus guiding the machine weave. In short, the Jacquard loom anticipated by 100 or so years the zero/one, on/off, yes/no, binary system of the modern digital computer. Babbage probably borrowed the Jacquard concept but demonstrated foresight in his use of punch-cards for the storage of information as well as the guidance of machine operations. For more than a century Babbage's computer concepts lay dormant, awaiting the development of electronic technology. In 1939, Howard Aiken, then a graduate student in physics and now professor emeritus at Harvard, began to work on a large-scale computer. With the help of International Business Machines, he completed it in 1944. He was well along in his work when he discovered the work of Babbage and found that the irascible genius had been there before him by more than a hundred years.

One of the few bright spots in Babbage's life was his friendship with Augusta Ada, Countess of Lovelace and daughter of the poet Lord Byron. The countess was attractive, had a gift for mathematics and engineering, and was one of the few who really understood Babbage's work. She wrote treatises on his work, expressed his ideas better than he could, and actually wrote programs for the computer. Together with Babbage, she developed a sure-fire system for betting on the horses; unfortunately, the fillies did not fit the system and the countess had to pawn her jewels. Undaunted by the countess's loss of the family jewels, though the Count of Lovelace was upset, Babbage continued his work and developed gaming programs for his computer which were a forerunner of modern business gaming techniques. He limited his research to developing a computer program to play tick-tack-toe and chess but he saw that the machine (he called it an "automaton") could be programmed to make the best possible combinations of positions and moves, including anticipation as far as three moves in advance. Development of this automaton to play chess and tick-tack-toe certainly must have brought him to the fringe of probability theory in programming for player positions and decision alternatives.

Analyzing Industrial Operations

Inevitably, Babbage's inquisitive mind and wide interests led him to write of management. Babbage was more of a starter of projects than a finisher, as his computer work demonstrates. He frequently lost interest in his projects once his initial curiosity was satisfied, an unfortunate characteristic of many men of his genius. His most successful book was *On the Economy of Machinery and Manufactures* in 1832.[14] Babbage became interested in manufacturing and management as a result of his problems of supervising construction of his own "engine" and visited a wide variety of English factories. He described in great detail the tools and machines, discussed the "economical principles of manufacturing" and, in the true spirit of inquiry for an operations research man, analyzed operations, the kinds of skills involved, the expense of each process, and suggested directions for improving the then current practices.

Babbage, like Adam Smith, was fascinated by the principle of division of labor and felt that all advanced civilizations had achieved their positions through this process. For Babbage, the division of labor brought more efficiency because:

1. Of the time required for learning . . . *the greater the number of distinct processes, the longer will be the time which the apprentice must employ in acquiring it. . . . If, however, instead of learning all the different processes for making a needle, for instance, his attention be confined to one operation, the portion of time consumed unprofitably . . . will be small, and all the rest of it will be beneficial to his master . . .*

2. Of waste of materials in learning. *A certain quantity of material will . . . be consumed unprofitably, or spoiled by every person who learns an art . . . if each man commit this waste in acquiring successively every process, the quantity of waste will be much greater than if each person confine his attention to one process . . .*

3. *Another advantage resulting from the division of labor is,* the saving of that portion of time which is always lost in changing from one occupation to another. . . . *Long habit also pro-*

---

[14]Charles Babbage, *On the Economy of Machinery and Manufactures*, London: Charles Knight, 1832; reprinted by Augustus M. Kelley (New York), 1963.

duces in the muscles exercised a capacity for enduring fatigue to a much greater degree than they could support under other circumstances . . .

4. Change of tools. *The employment of different tools in the successive processes is another cause of the loss of time in changing from one operation to another . . . in many processes of the arts the tools are of great delicacy, requiring accurate adjustment every time they are used; and in many cases the time employed in adjusting bears a large proportion to that employed in using the tool . . .*

5. Skill acquired by frequent repetition of the same processes. *The constant repetition of the same process necessarily produces in the workman a degree of excellence and rapidity in his particular department, which is never possessed by a person who is obliged to execute many different processes . . .*

6. The division of labor suggests the contrivance of tools and machinery to execute its processes. *When each process, by which any article is produced, is the sole occupation of one individual, his whole attention being devoted to a very limited and simple operation, improvements in the form of his tools, or in the mode of using them, are much more likely to occur to his mind, than if it were distracted by a greater variety of circumstances. Such an improvement in the tool is generally the first step towards a machine.* [15]

Babbage also saw that the division of labor could be applied to mental as well as manual operations. He cited as an example G. F. Prony, Director of the École des Ponts et Chaussées (School of Bridges and Roads), who successfully divided his workers into skilled, semiskilled, and unskilled categories for the purpose of preparing an elaborate set of mathematical tables. By this method, Prony could conserve his high-powered mathematicians by giving them the more complex tasks and shifting to those who could only add and subtract the more menial, but necessary, chores.

As a management scientist, Babbage was interested in machinery, tools, the efficient use of power, developing "counting machines" to check quantity of work, and economy in the use of

[15] Ibid., pp. 170–174.

raw materials; these he called the "mechanical principles" of manufacturing. He developed a "method of observing manufactories"
which was closely akin to a scientific, systematic approach to the
study of operations. The observer must prepare a list of questions
about the materials used, normal waste, expenses, tools, prices,
the final market, workers, their wages, skill required, length of
work cycle, and so on.[16] In essence it was the same procedure as
that an operations analyst or a consultant would use in his approach to an assignment. Babbage also discussed the advantage of
large factories where capital investment made for more efficiency
and the proper location of these factories with respect to sources of
raw materials. On the human side, he recalled the Luddite movement and pleaded with the workers to recognize that the factory
system worked to their betterment:

> It is of great importance that the more intelligent amongst the
> class of workmen should examine the correctness of these views;
> because . . . the whole class may . . . be led by designing persons
> to pursue a course, which . . . is in reality at variance with their
> own best interests.[17]

His attempts to show the mutuality of interests between the
worker and the factory owner were somewhat similar to what
Taylor said 75 years later:

> . . . the prosperity and success of the master manufacturer is es-
> sential to the welfare of the workman . . . whilst it is perfectly
> true that workmen, as a class, derive advantage from the pros-
> perity of their employers, I do not think that each individual par-
> takes of that advantage exactly in proportion to the extent to
> which he contributes to it . . . it would be of great importance, if
> . . . the mode of payment could be so arranged, that every person
> employed should derive advantage from the success of the whole;
> and that the profits of each individual should advance, as the fac-
> tory itself produced profit, without the necessity of making any
> change in wages.[18]

---

[16]Babbage's list begins on p. 115 and continues through p. 117. It should be noted
that Babbage's discussion of "expenses" has the appearance of an early form of
cost accounting. However, it differed from modern cost accounting in that it described costs rather than providing for an analysis of what costs ought to be as under a standard cost system.

[17]Ibid., p. 230.

[18]Ibid., pp. 250–251.

Babbage's profit-sharing scheme had two facets: one, that a portion of wages would depend on factory profits; and two, that the worker "should derive more advantage from applying any improvement he might discover," i.e., a bonus for suggestions. Workers would receive a fixed salary based on the nature of their task plus a share in the profits, and the suggestion system would use a committee to determine the proper bonus for production savings. Babbage saw a number of advantages in his proposal: (1) each worker would have a direct interest in the firm's prosperity; (2) each would be stimulated to prevent waste and mismanagement; (3) every department would be improved; and (4) only workmen of high skill and character would be admitted since "it would be the common interest of all to admit only the most respectable and skillful." In effect, the work group, operating under a profit-sharing plan, would act to screen out undesirables who would reduce their share. Finally, Babbage saw his scheme as removing the necessity for "combinations" of workmen since their interests would be the same as the employers. With this mutuality of interests between worker and manager, neither would oppress the other and all would prosper.

Beyond his significant scientific contributions, Charles Babbage made significant advancements in understanding the problems of the emerging factory system. His analytic, scientific approach to the study of manufacturing, his recognition of the need for new incentives to enlist the cooperation of the worker, and his search for new harmonies between manager and worker place him as a man of vision in management. His contributions were not recognized until much later, however, and then by Frank B. Gilbreth, one of the pioneers in scientific management.[19]

Andrew Ure: Pioneering in Management Education

It was the task of Andrew Ure (1778–1857) to provide academic training for fledgling managers in the early factory system. Ure studied at Edinburgh and Glasgow Universities, receiving his

---

[19] John H. Hoaglund, *Charles Babbage: His Life and Works in the Historical Evolution of Management Concepts,* Columbus, Ohio: unpublished Ph.D. dissertation, The Ohio State University, 1954, pp. 333–339.

M.D. from the latter school in 1801. In 1804, Ure became professor of chemistry and natural philosophy at Anderson's College in Glasgow, where he was to remain until 1839. Dr. Anderson, the founder of the college, had lectured on science and through his will founded an institution to educate the working man on science. Educational pressures for technically trained white-collar workers and managers soon shifted the composition of Dr. Ure's classes from the working man to clerks, warehousemen, small tradesmen, and shopkeepers; it was from these classes that managers for the ever growing factory system were to be recruited. Ure knew the French engineer and management writer Charles Dupin and when Dupin visited Great Britain in 1816–1818, Ure escorted him around the Glasgow factories. Dupin commented that many of the managers of these factories were Ure's own students. This fact was acknowledged by Ure who said that his students were "spread over the [United] Kingdom as proprietors and managers of factories."[20] Dupin's work was influenced by Ure and in turn, it will be suggested below that Dupin influenced Henri Fayol.

Principles of Manufacturing

Ure, deeply concerned with industrial education, set out to prepare for publication a systematic account of the principles and processes of manufacturing. The essential principle of the factory system was the substitution of "mechanical science for hand skill . . . [and to provide] for the graduation of labor among artisans."[21] Although Ure devoted a large portion of his book to the technical problems of manufacturing in the silk, cotton, woolen, and flax industries, he eventually dealt with the problems of managing. Obviously promanagement in his analysis, Ure sought an "automatic plan" to prevent individual intractable workers from stopping work as they pleased and thereby throwing the whole factory into disorder. According to Ure, workers must recognize the benefits of mechanization and not resist its introduction. To establish this

---

[20]Andrew Ure, *The Philosophy of Manufactures: or an Exposition of the Scientific, Moral and Commercial Economy of the Factory System of Great Britain*, London: Charles Knight, 1835; reprinted by Augustus M. Kelley, (New York), 1967, p. viii.

[21]Ibid., p. 20.

automatic plan, management must "arrange and connect" manufactures to achieve a harmony of the whole. In every establishment there were "three principles of action, or three organic systems; the mechanical, the moral and the commercial."[22] While these formed no clear-cut notions of organizing work, Ure did seek to place them in the harmony of a "self-governing agency." "Mechanical" referred to the techniques and processes of production; "moral" to the condition of personnel; and "commercial" to sustaining the organization through selling and financing.

The mechanical part of manufactures was treated extensively by the scientist Ure; the moral aspect brought out the pro-management side of the educator. The factory system of Ure's day was under attack from a number of sources and Ure set out to defend industrial practices. He argued that factory operatives were better treated "as to personal comforts" than artisans or other workers in nonindustrial establishments. They ate better, enjoyed more leisurely labor because of the machines provided by the factory owner, and were better paid. Instead of appreciating this largesse, they engaged in strikes, sabotaged equipment, and caused capital losses for their employers, thus working against their own continued employment. Rebutting the investigations into child labor, Ure noted that most of the witnesses had never visited the factories; he also engaged in some character assassination, charging that one witness was an atheist, one a tavern keeper, and one an assaulter of women. For positive evidence, Ure noted that children lived in well-kept cottages, received both practical and religious education, were better fed, and enjoyed better health than otherwise available in the general community. Children employed in agriculture were paid half the factory wages and kept in sloth and ignorance. Citing medical investigations sponsored by the Factory Commission, Ure concluded that the incidence of disease, the dietary habits, and the general state of health of all factory workers were better than in the general population.

To illustrate worker nonappreciation of employers' concern for their health, Ure cited an instance in which large ventilating fans had been installed in one factory to reduce the foulness of the

[22] Ibid., p. 55.

air. Instead of thanking the employer, the workers complained that the fresh air had increased their appetites and therefore they were entitled to a corresponding wage increase! The factory owner reached a compromise with his workers by running the fan only half the day, thereafter hearing no more complaints about either the foul air or appetites. In terms of the evidence presented in chapter 3, Ure was probably more right than wrong concerning the condition of labor. He was a defender of the factory system, seeing more benefits accruing to society than there were disadvantages. His instruction in management was largely technically oriented and he exhorted workers not to resist but to accept the advance of mechanization. In Ure's work, there are very few generalizations about management, and his concern for the management of certain industries, e.g. textiles, reflects the parochial views of other early writers such as Montgomery.

Charles Dupin: Industrial Education in France

A second individual who pioneered in industrial education was the French engineer, Baron Charles Dupin (1784–1873). As noted above, Dupin had visited Great Britain (1816–1818) and observed the results Andrew Ure was obtaining in preparing individuals for factory management. In 1819, Dupin was named professor of mathematics and economics at the Conservatory of Arts and Professions (Paris).[23] He must have immediately initiated his own curricula, for in 1831 he wrote: "For 12 years I have had the honor of teaching geometry and mechanics applied to the arts, in favor of the industrial class . . . on the most important questions to the well-being, education, and morality of the workers, to the progress of national industry, to the development of all means of prosperity that work can produce for the splendor and happiness of our country."[24]

One of Dupin's colleagues at the conservatory was Jean Baptiste Say, a professor of political economy. Say, the reader will recall, was the person who brought Adam Smith's ideas to France

[23]*La Grande Encyclopédie*, Volume 15, p. 81.

[24]Charles Dupin, *Discours sur le Sort des Ouvriers*, Paris: Bachelier Librairie, 1831, p. 1. Translated, the title is *Discourse on the Condition of the Workers*.

and added to them by identifying management as a fourth factor of production. It is possible that both Say and Ure influenced Dupin's view of management. Dupin's contribution occurs in the influence he had on the course of industrial education and, though there is no direct historical support, perhaps on the later work of Henri Fayol. Fayol is generally credited with being the first to distinguish between technical and managerial skills and the possibility and necessity of teaching management. Yet examine this passage from Dupin, eight or so decades earlier:

> *It is to the director of workshops and factories that it is suitable to make, by means of geometry and applied mechanics,* a special study *of all the ways to economize the efforts of workers. . . . For a man to be a director of others, manual work has only a secondary importance; it is his intellectual ability* (force intellectuelle) *that must put him in the top position, and it is in instruction such as that of the Conservatory of the Arts and Professions, that he must develop it.*[25]

The "special study" would be the classes Dupin and Ure were teaching and Dupin clearly distinguished this type of program from manual or technical instruction. Fayol, himself educated as an engineer in France, could possibly have read Dupin and gleaned his own notions of teaching management.

John H. Hoaglund reported that by 1826 Dupin's materials on management had been presented in 98 French cities to 5,000 or more workers and supervisors.[26] Since his *Discours* was not published until 1831, the number of people he influenced must be greatly expanded. Dupin also demonstrated a rudimentary grasp of the concept of time study and the need to balance workloads after labor was divided:

> *When [the] division of work is put into operation the most scrupulous attention must be exercised to calculate the duration of each type of operation, in order to proportion the work to the particular number of workers that are assigned to it.*[27]

[25] Ibid., pp. 12–13. Emphasis added.

[26] John H. Hoaglund, "Management Before Frederick Taylor," *Proceedings of the Academy of Management*, December, 1955, pp. 15–24; reprinted in Paul M. Dauten, Jr., (ed.) *Current Issues and Emerging Concepts in Management*, Boston: Houghton Mifflin Co., 1962, p. 28.

[27] Charles Dupin, *Géométrie et Mécanique des Arts et Métiers et des Beaux Arts*, Paris: Bachelier III, 1926. Cited and translated by John H. Hoaglund, ibid., p. 30.

He wrote of the need for clear, concise instructions to workers, of the need for producing the desired level of work with the least expenditure of worker energy, and of the necessity of studying each type of industry in order to find and publish the best results of industrial practice.

The *Discours* was not so much an examination of management as it was an exhortation to remove industrial strife. Dupin recognized worker "uneasiness" over the introduction of mechanization into French industry, discussed the work of James Watt, and encouraged workers and managers to recognize the benefits of mechanization to themselves and to society. Regarding the dangers of technological displacement, he noted that before Watt's engine (1780), British industry employed fewer than 1 million men; by 1830, over 3 million were employed in industry and combined with machinery equivalent to the power of 7 million men. For Dupin this was ample proof that mechanization created jobs rather than destroyed them. Evidently the French had their own Luddites and Dupin indicated that such resistance to mechanization was futile; the solution called for was widespread industrial training to permit the agrarian and unskilled worker to share in the prosperity of industrialization: "He who perfects the machines tends to give them the advantage over the worker; he who perfects the worker, gives him the same fighting chance, and makes the machine serve his well-being, instead of having to suffer from their competition. Let us concern ourselves with man involved with the difficulties of the work and of the industry."[28] These were insights not only applicable to early nineteenth-century France but also to a world of the twentieth and the twenty-first centuries.

The Pioneers: A Final Note

The four pioneers discussed above were formulating the seeds of a management discipline. But, at their best, these were sparse and rudimentary. What prevented the formalization of a body of management thought during this early stage rather than some three-quarters of a century later? Why did Taylor get the credit for being

[28] Dupin, *Discours*, p. 9.

the father of scientific management and not Charles Babbage? In perspective, the reasons are manifold: first, the stress of early writings was on the techniques and not managing *per se*. In an age of expanding technology, it was difficult for early writers to separate the managerial function from the technical and commercial aspects of running a firm. Management was more concerned with finance, production processes, selling, and acquiring labor, all of which were indeed critical at the time, rather than with developing principles or generalizations about management. An analogy might be that of young children learning to walk: the motor urge is so great and consumes so much of their energy and attention that their development of speech is retarded. As the skill of walking is perfected, speech develops. The early entrepreneurs were just learning to walk in the new factory system; the technical and human problems consumed so much of their time that they had little left over for being articulate in stating generalizations about management. Second, the period was dominated by the technical genius, the inventor-pioneer, and the owner-founder. Success or failure was more likely to be attributed to their individual characteristics rather than to any generalized ideas about what skills managers would need. Each industry and its problems were considered unique and hence the principles derived by one entrepreneur were not considered applicable to different situations. Finally, the state of the art of disseminating knowledge must be considered. Few were literate, books were expensive, and schools were either classically oriented toward developing scholars or technique-oriented toward the artisan. Scholars read the books of other scholars; it is not likely that Babbage, Dupin, and Ure were widely read by the practicing manager. The classes of Ure and Dupin undoubtedly reached into some factories but this was probably only a minor fraction of the total management market.

Summary

In England, and France to a lesser extent, can be found the genesis of modern management thought. Robert Owen appealed to the heart as well as to the pocketbook in his search for a New Harmony between the human factor and the age of machines. Charles Babbage appealed to the mind, became the grandfather of scientific management, and applied a scientific approach to management before Taylor. Andrew Ure taught his experiences and observations and developed managers for the new factories. Dupin learned from Ure, started management classes in France, and perhaps influenced Henri Fayol. With the genesis of management thought in England, the exodus of our story will be the study of management in America before Taylor.

5

Early American Management

The nineteenth century in America was an age of dynamic growth and expansion of the factory system. A colony of mighty England 24 years before the beginning of this age and torn by half a decade of internecine strife in mid-century, America was to become the world's leading political and industrial force by the close of the century. Pre–Civil War America may be characterized as the emergence of the industrial system and post–Civil War America as an age of changing cultural values as industry grew toward maturity. This chapter will explore the emergence and growth of American industry, the work of some early management pioneers, and the changing cultural environment as a prelude to the emergence of the scientific management era.

Antebellum Industry and Management

America was a colony for almost as many years as it has been a nation. For its settlers the lure of America was manifold: social betterment, economic opportunity, religious freedom, and political separation. No element explains the whole, for the nation that was to emerge was a conglomerate of parts that defy a separate identification and explanation. The newcomers to these alien and often hostile shores were aristocrats as well as felons, and tramps and tarts as well as budding tycoons. Efforts to develop colonial manufactures were frowned upon by England for they posed the possibility of dangerous competition for England's early factories. After the Revolution, America sought independence both politically and economically. The War of 1812 severed America economically from England and spurred the growth of indigenous manufacturing operations. Conditions for industry were ripe; America was a land rich in natural resources, a growing labor supply, and a political system which encouraged the creation of wealth as a way of life. Many merchant capitalists had made their fortunes in trade; and these funds, aided by the dictums of thrift of early Puritanism, made increasing amounts of capital available for manufacturing. Technological advancements were rapid and the Americans became known for their inventiveness as well as their Yankee ingenuity.

The Industrial Revolution in America had three facets: power, transportation, and communication. The foundations of steam power had been built in England but soon took on a powerful upward surge in America. A craze of canal building in the 1820s and an ever expanding rail network opened new markets for producers. As the market expanded, mass production based on interchangeability of parts and division of labor became more feasible. The lowered costs of transportation and the new markets helped break down regional monopolies and barriers, stimulating entrepreneurs to explore and develop new production techniques.

Early Industrial Development

England sought to prevent industrial development by prohibiting the sale of manufacturing equipment and the emigration of skilled labor to America. Samuel Slater, a textile engineer for Richard Arkwright, disguised himself as a "farmer" on his emigration papers, memorized detailed blueprints of the textile equipment, and reconstructed the necessary equipment upon his arrival in America. Together with Moses Brown, a Quaker merchant of means, he launched America's first textile factory in 1790 with a 72-spindle mill at Pawtucket, Rhode Island. On a visit to England, Francis Cabot Lowell had also observed textile manufacturing; he copied the designs of mechanical weaving equipment, brought them surreptitiously to America, and established the Boston Manufacturing Company at Waltham, Massachusetts. Other factories and other entrepreneurs followed until the New England textile industry grew to rival that of England.

In textiles and other industries, labor posed a problem as it had in England. The labor force was largely unskilled, since England attempted to prevent skilled workers from leaving the country.[1] To attract labor, early textile manufacturers developed two distinct labor relations policies: the "Rhode Island system," begun by Slater at Pawtucket and later at Fall River (Massachusetts); and the "Waltham system" of Lowell and his associates. The Rhode Island system was patterned after English practices of employing the whole family if possible and it therefore resulted in more child labor. In contrast, the Waltham system was designed to attract female labor to the factory by establishing company "boarding houses." Workers in the textile factories were mainly "Yankee" girls and they were brought to the factories from the neighboring farms by agents touring the countryside and emphasizing the moral and educational advantages of factory work.[2] The girls had to be in at 10:00 P.M. and their moral conduct was carefully watched by a housemother.

Even that vocal critic of the English factory system, Charles Dickens, praised the Lowell and Waltham factories for their treatment of labor. He reported that the factory girls were clean, healthy, and of sound moral deportment. He felt the English could learn a great deal by the American example.[3] However, it appears that the Waltham plan was less successful in keeping a labor force since Ware estimated that the girls working in New England cotton mills stayed on the average one year.[4] Growing immigration, however, provided a steady source of replacements for the eastern factories. The western frontier was a safety valve which presented opportunities for workers who found the wilderness more attractive than the factories. Consequently, the American factory did not demonstrate in the same depth the evils as did the English

[1] Theodore Marburg, "Aspects of Labor Administration in the Early Nineteenth Century," *Business History Review*, Vol. XV, No. 1 (February, 1941), pp. 1–10.

[2] Thomas C. Cochran and William Miller, *The Age of Enterprise*, New York: Harper and Row, 1961, p. 19.

[3] Charles Dickens, *American Notes for General Circulation*, London: Chapman and Hall, 1842, Vol. I, pp. 156, 163–164. Corroborating evidence for Dickens's observations may be found in William Scoresby, *American Factories and Their Female Operatives*, Boston: W. D. Ticknor Co., 1845.

[4] Norman Ware, *The Industrial Worker: 1840–1860*, Glouchester, Mass.: Peter Smith Co., 1959, p. 149.

factory. Employers were paying high wages to attract and hold their labor, child labor was not as prevalent (perhaps since there were no "Poor Law Authorities" to encourage it), and abuses were less frequent and less severe.[5] The American worker was less resistant to the introduction of machinery and the Luddites found few followers, except in Pittsburgh, where some hand loom weavers rioted and destroyed their machines. Guilds were less entrenched and the American employer found innovation more acceptable to the worker.

Textiles represented America's entry into the industrial age but railroads and the steel industry were not far behind. The iron rail, flanged wheel, and the puffing locomotive began to develop around 1830. Opposed initially by the canal supporters who were fearful of its competition, the rail industry by 1850 had brought a new dimension to American life. It all started with Colonel John Stevens of Hoboken, New Jersey, who obtained from the New Jersey legislature America's first railroad charter in 1815.[6] Deemed "eccentric," he could not obtain financial backing until 1830 when he built the 23-mile-long Camden and Amboy Railroad. Stevens made numerous other technical contributions and earned the title "father of American engineering." He also endowed the Stevens Institute of Technology (Hoboken, N.J.), which was to become the alma mater of Frederick W. Taylor and Henry L. Gantt, pioneers in scientific management. After the Camden and Amboy, other lines such as the Chesapeake and Ohio and the Baltimore and Ohio were built and expanded until by 1850 there were 9,000 miles of track reaching all the way into Ohio.[7] The new age of rails was sweeping away local trade barriers, opening up new markets, and revolutionizing trade and communications.

Steel is the sinew of any industrial economy. Iron, because of

[5] Ross M. Robertson, *History of the American Economy*, New York: Harcourt, Brace, Jovanovich, 1955, p. 184. Based on his own research, Ware agreed with Robertson that there were fewer evils in the American factory system.

[6] An interesting account of John Stevens's various activities, including his anticipation by three years of Fulton's steamboat, may be found in Dorothy Gregg, "John Stevens: General Entrepreneur," in William Miller (ed.), *Men in Business*, New York: Harper and Row, 1957, pp. 120–152.

[7] John F. Stover, *American Railroads*, Chicago: University of Chicago Press, 1961, p. 29.

its impurities, caused many problems for early machine designers and factory owners. The race to improve iron production proceeded, as is often the history of invention, on separate concurrent paths in England and America. William Kelly of Kentucky began his experiments in 1847 and perfected a system of refining iron by subjecting it to a blast of hot air in a specially built furnace. Unfortunately, Kelly did not apply for a patent until 1857, two years after Sir Henry Bessemer had obtained his patent in England. The Bessemer process, based on the same idea, was quite an improvement over the very slow process of "puddling" iron, or the removal of carbon and other impurities by passing heated gases over the molten iron. Until 1908 and the perfection of the "open hearth" method of making steel, the Bessemer process formed the basis for the world's steel industry. The Americans made the most of their ingenuity in production; in 1868 the United States produced 8,500 tons of steel, Britain 110,000; in 1879, the countries' outputs were nearly equal; but by 1902, America produced 9,138,000 tons and England 1,826,000. American industry was showing its mettle.

The Railroads: Pioneering in American Management

The railroads were truly America's first "big business." The textile industry, though growing and dominating the Northeast, never developed into companies of the size and scope of the railroads. The management of textile firms was largely tied to England's early managerial methods, and perhaps the New England entrepreneurs read Montgomery, Ure, or Babbage for advice on managing cotton manufactures. The railroads, however, posed completely new problems; developing slowly in England concurrently with advances in America, there was no body of literature nor an extant fund of practical experience. The railroads were the first American business which grew to such a size and complexity that means had to be developed of coping with massive financial requirements, of developing integrated systems of trackage and station agents, of spreading large fixed costs, and of handling a labor force dispersed over a wide geographical area.[8] These factors required managers to develop ways of managing America's first industry of larger than local scope. Railroad pioneers had to develop the first organizational structures of any size and substance and likewise developed the nation's earliest professional managers. Unlike textile and other plants, railroad operations were dispersed and could not be controlled by frequent personal inspection of the hundreds of stations and thousands of miles of track, thus making communications a significant problem. The investments in track and rolling stock were immense and required extensive long-range planning to prevent large fixed capital outlays from being placed in the wrong market area. Passenger safety and the prevention of damage or loss in transit of cargo were critical to successful operations. Scheduling of service required planning and coordination, and standing rules and policies had to be developed to guide the decisions of lower organizational elements.[9] With these immense problems of allocating and utilizing resources, it is no wonder that railroad managers were forced into developing a management system.

Daniel McCallum: System and Organization

Daniel Craig McCallum (1815–1878) was born in Scotland but came to America in 1822.[10] He received some elementary schooling in Rochester, New York, but decided not to follow his father's

---

[8]Evidence of the scope of railroad problems may be made by comparing America's largest industry of the 1850s, the Pepperell Manufacturing Company (textiles), with some of the rail companies. Pepperell had expenses in excess of $300,000 in only one year during the 1850s; the New York and Erie spent $2,861,875 and the Pennsylvania spent $2,149,918 in 1855. Pepperell employed an average of 800 workers, the Erie 4,000, and by the 1880s, the Pennsylvania employed close to 50,000. (Alfred D. Chandler, Jr. (ed.), *The Railroads: The Nation's First Big Business, Sources and Readings*, New York: Harcourt, Brace, Jovanovich, 1965, p. 97.)

[9]Ibid., pp. 9–10. Another excellent source on railroad history is Leland H. Jenks, "Early History of a Railway Organization," *Business History Review*, Vol. 35 (Summer, 1961), pp. 153–179.

[10]Personal data on McCallum are from W. Jerome Arnold, "Big Business Takes the Management Track," *Business Week*, April 30, 1966, pp. 104–106; and Dumas Malone (ed.), *Dictionary of American Biography*, New York: Charles Scribners' Sons, Vol. VI, p. 565.

occupation as a tailor. He left home and school, and apprenticed himself as a carpenter. He became an accomplished carpenter and architect and designed and built numerous buildings. He left this occupation to join the New York and Erie Railroad Company in 1848. He showed a talent for administration as well as engineering and became superintendent of the Susquehanna Division, where he developed an early set of procedures to govern that segment's operations. Faced with growing problems of rail integration and a high accident rate, the Erie management made McCallum general superintendent of the Erie line in May 1854. In June of 1854, the workers struck for 10 days; not for shorter hours nor more pay, but in defiance of McCallum's institution of his system.

To McCallum, good management was based on good discipline, specific and detailed job descriptions, frequent and accurate reporting of performance, pay and promotion based on merit, a clearly defined hierarchy of authority of superiors over subordinates, and the enforcement of personal responsibility and accountability throughout the organization. He stated his principles of management as:

1. *A proper division of responsibilities.*

2. *Sufficient power conferred to enable the same to be fully carried out, that such responsibilities may be real in their character.*

3. *The means of knowing whether such responsibilities are faithfully executed.*

4. *Great promptness in the report of all derelictions of duty, that evils may at once be corrected.*

5. *Such information, to be obtained through a system of daily reports and checks that will not embarrass principal officers, nor lessen their influence with their subordinates.*

6. *The adoption of a system, as a whole, which will not only enable the General Superintendent to detect errors immediately, but will also point out the delinquent.* [11]

McCallum developed a high degree of organizational specificity to carry out these principles. First, he separated and identified each grade of worker as to task and required each worker to

[11] Daniel C. McCallum, "Superintendents' Report," March 25, 1856, in *Annual Report of the New York and Erie Railroad Company for 1855*, Chandler, p. 102.

wear a prescribed uniform with the insignia of his grade. Second, he developed comprehensive rules to limit the ability of individuals to do their tasks as they pleased. Rule No. 6, for example, required the engineers to stop their engines and personally see that the yard switches were properly set. The engineers saw this as an encroachment of their esteemed position; McCallum perceived it as a control device for safety.

Finally, McCallum developed a formal organizational chart (which his advocate Henry Varnum Poor had lithographed and put on sale to the general public for a price of $1.00). The chart took the form of a tree and depicted the lines of authority and responsibility, the division of labor among operating units, and the communication lines for reporting and control. The roots of the tree represented the board of directors and the president; the branches were the five operating divisions plus the staff service departments of engine repairs, car, bridge, telegraph, painting, treasurer's, and secretary's offices; the leaves were the various local freight and ticket forwarding offices, subordinate supervisors, crews, foremen, and so on to the lowest element. Adherence to the formal lines of authority was to be absolute:

> *The enforcement of a rigid system of discipline . . . is indispensable to success. All subordinates should be accountable to, and* be directed by their immediate superiors only; *as obedience cannot be enforced where the foreman in immediate charge is interfered with by a superior officer giving orders directly to his subordinates.* [12]

McCallum saw no exceptions to this unity of command principle; to do otherwise would break down his control system, which was based on personal accountability.

McCallum also developed information management to probably the highest state of the art for the times. He used the telegraph to make operations safer as well as to facilitate administration by requiring hourly reports to show the position of every train in the system, daily reports on passengers and cargo, and monthly reports to give management "statistical accounts" for planning, rate making, and control. He designed a clever cross-check control system by requiring both freight and passenger con-

---

[12]McCallum, *Annual Report,* in Chandler, p. 104.

ductors to report on train movements, loadings, damaged freight, etc.; by comparing the reports, he could readily see discrepancies and any dishonesty.

McCallum's system was successful from management's point of view, but trouble was brewing over Rule No. 6. The engineers had never forgiven McCallum, and 29 engineers had been dismissed for breaking Rule No. 6 and for avoiding various other safety rules he had devised. A six-month strike ensued, and McCallum was unable to replace the striking engineers. He resigned, along with the company president, in 1857. However, McCallum had earned the highest praise of Henry Varnum Poor, the eminent editor of the *American Railroad Journal* and spokesman for the industry. Poor later had some doubts about the system but thought that it was a step in the right direction.

McCallum's managerial days were not over, however. While on the Erie, he had invented and patented (1851) an inflexible arched truss bridge. In 1857 he established the McCallum Bridge Company and built bridges throughout the country, earning an income of $75,000 per year. In 1862 he was asked by Secretary of War Stanton to manage the nation's railways with the power to seize and operate any railroad necessary to the Union's war effort. By the end of the war he was a major general and his major feat was supplying Sherman's 200-day Atlanta campaign.[13]

After the war, McCallum served as a consultant for the Atlantic and Great Western Railroad and the Union Pacific. Failing health prompted an early retirement to Brooklyn, where he did not get into the bridge business, but wrote poetry. His best-known poem was *The Water-Mill* which concluded:

> *Possessions, Power, and blooming health,*
> *   must all be lost at last,*
> *The mill will never grind with water*
> *   that is past.*

McCallum's approach to management was not lost, despite his setbacks at the Erie. Henry Poor publicized his work widely

---

[13] An extensive account of McCallum's managerial feats in running the Northern railroads during the Civil War may be found throughout Thomas Weber, *The Northern Railroads in the Civil War*, New York: Columbia University Press, 1952.

and numerous others followed McCallum's style in systematizing America's first big business. Albert Fink developed a cost accounting system which used information flows, classification of costs, and statistical control devices which became a model for modern corporate control.[14] Charles E. Perkins, president of the Chicago, Burlington, and Quincy Railroad, made refinements in McCallum's organization by pointing out the limits to how much work a manager could supervise and the necessity to push authority and responsibility downward in the organization, and proposed a means of resolving conflicts between lower elements by moving them to a higher common level of authority.[15]

The most faithful adoption of McCallum's system came on the Pennsylvania Railroad. J. Edgar Thomson and Thomas A. Scott applied McCallum's ideas for geographical departmentation, formal lines of authority and responsibility, communications, line and staff duties, measuring performance, and cost accounting. It was the Pennsy tree that bore the fruit of systematic management, not the Erie. On the Pennsy was a young manager who learned McCallum's system from Thomson and Scott; his name was Andrew Carnegie and he will enter our story again shortly.

Henry V. Poor: A Broader View of Management

Henry Varnum Poor (1812–1905), through his editor's position on the *American Railroad Journal,* essayed to become the conscience of America's first large business. Whereas McCallum spoke of internal operating problems, Poor looked for broader principles of railroad operations including financing, regulation, and the role of the railroad in American life. Poor was well educated and came from a more select background than McCallum; his biographer tells us that Poor was thoroughly imbued with the romance and optimism of nineteenth-century America.[16] As editor of the *Jour-*

[14] Albert Fink, "Classification of Operating Expenses," in *Annual Report of the Louisville and Nashville Railroad Company* (1874), Chandler, pp. 108–117.

[15] From the personal papers of Charles E. Perkins, written in 1855, ibid., pp. 118–125.

[16] Alfred D. Chandler, Jr., *Henry Varnum Poor: Business Editor, Analyst, and Reformer,* Cambridge, Mass.: Harvard University Press, 1956. An interesting sidelight is that Professor Chandler is the great-grandson of Henry Varnum Poor.

nal in the pre–Civil War years, Poor made it the leading business periodical of the day and a reliable source of information for the railroad investor as well as the manager. His editorials discussed railroad developments, problems, and needed reforms in operating practices, and presented detailed financial and operating data. After the war, his *Manual of Railroads in the United States* continued his efforts to further the dissemination of financial and operating information. His life was marked throughout by the critical age of railroads coming from infancy to maturity and by their amazing impact on opening the West and tying America together with a web of steel.

In its early years, the Erie was one of Poor's favorite targets, for it was poorly managed and financed. The advent of McCallum's reforms soon made Poor the biggest booster of the Erie as an example of proper management. Poor saw a need for managerial reform through development of a group of professional managers rather than speculators and promoters to build the nation's transportation system. Poor looked for a science or "system" of management and from McCallum's work Poor gleaned three fundamental principles: organization, communication, and information.[17] Organization was basic to all management; there must be a careful division of labor from the president down to the common laborer, each with specific duties and responsibilities. Every person would be directly accountable to his immediate superior; Poor repeatedly used the terms "responsibility" and "accountability" in his editorials. Second, communication was devising a method of reporting throughout the organization to give top management a continuous and accurate accounting on operations. Finally, information was "recorded communication"; Poor saw the need for a set of operating reports to be compiled for costs, revenues, and rate making. This third principle was an early appearance of a "data bank" concept in management literature in the sense that management would build up a fund of data on operations to analyze the present system and to provide a base for changes to improve service. One can readily see the influence of McCallum on Poor's writing and can trace the

[17] Ibid., pp. 146–147. Chandler's work is based on Poor's editorials in the *Journal* and will be cited here without referring to specific dates and issues of that *Journal*. In the case of Poor's three principles, for example, Poor was influenced by McCallum and not vice versa. Ibid., p. 147.

development of the third principle through Albert Fink's efforts to install statistical control systems in the corporate structure.

Just as McCallum's work was becoming widely known, in large part due to Poor's editorials, Poor began having his doubts about whether organization, communication, and information were adequate principles to encompass the task of management. Poor visited England in 1858 to view its railway system and upon his return he wrote concerning "the grave difficulties of adapting human capabilities and current business practices and institutions to the severe requirements demanded by the efficient operation of such large administrative units."[18] Both in England and on the Erie Poor saw worker resistance developing to the discipline required by systematic management. The tighter control required to bring order from chaos, the limiting of individual discretion in the performance of tasks, and the rigid hierarchical specifications of a formal organization, were all leading to worker protests against the tyranny of the system. This protest was not new in the annals of management history, nor has the issue ever been fully resolved to this day. Poor, however, thought these protests were too extreme and defended the need for systematization: "We can see no other way in which such a vast machine can be safely and successfully conducted,"[19] i.e., except through order, system, and discipline.

Accordingly, Poor began to look for some broader principles to overcome the dangers of "regarding man as a mere machine, out of which all the qualities necessary to be a good servant can be enforced by the mere payment of wages. But duties cannot always be prescribed and the most valuable are often voluntary ones."[20] Close prescription of duties and the bureaucratization of management reduced incentives and inevitably would lead the railroads, in Poor's view, to the problems inherent in the rigid managerial structures along the patterns of the military and the government. Poor's solution was a leadership which would overcome dullness and routine by infusing the organization with an *esprit de corps*. Top management should become "the soul of the enterprise, reaching and infusing life, intelligence and obedience into every

[18] Ibid., p. 155.
[19] Ibid.
[20] Ibid.

portion of it. This soul must not be a fragmentary or disjointed one—giving one direction to the head, another to the hands, and another to the feet. Wherever there is lack of unity there will be a lack of energy—of intelligence—of life—of accountability and subordination."[21]

In anticipating Fayol's unity-of-direction principle by 60 years, he regarded the problems of top management as those of assuming and of getting subordinates to assume a total systems view of the organization. Leaders must not only know all aspects of railroad operation and administration but also needed to be able to handle people, to know the total system, and to prevent interdepartmental conflicts which destroyed unity of purpose. The breakdown in leadership came from two sources: one, selection on some basis other than ability or training and, two, the lack of an information system to pinpoint weak managers. Poor's pleas for professional managers to manage well the property of others were not too dissimilar to the problems Adam Smith had pointed out nearly a century before.

As spokesman for the industry, Poor lashed out against the promoters and speculators who manipulated and "watered" stock for short-run gains at the expense of the total industry. He reflected the *laissez-faire* spirit by calling for unrestricted competition. Rates should not be regulated by government and the only legislation necessary was that to protect "honest rational men" from the dishonest promoters. He insisted that the rapid development of the American railroad system was "proof that reliance on the self-interest of individuals operating under conditions of unrestricted competition resulted in the greatest good for the greatest number."[22] Through publicity to inform stockholders and the public, through professionalization of management, and through protection of the rational from the irrational, the railroads could achieve their proper role in the economy.

Henry Varnum Poor was truly a remarkable man who came to grips with the broader problems of management and its environment. He stated issues which face management today and will be there tomorrow. His position that the role of government was to protect, not to control, illustrates an ever recurring problem of

[21] Ibid., p. 157.
[22] Ibid., p. 260.

management vis-à-vis government. His search for order out of chaos without destroying individual incentive and dignity is yet a current problem too. Long before Frederick Taylor he called for a system; long before Elton Mayo he called for a recognition of the human factor; and long before Chris Argyris he called for leadership to remove the rigidities of formal organization. He was one of our most outstanding early contributors to management thought.

Systematic Management: A Final Note

It was Daniel McCallum who pioneered systematic management and now we need to trace one more thread of his influence. When one thinks of Andrew Carnegie (1835–1919), the portrait is of an entrepreneur who built an empire in steel and left a fortune in millions. But where did Carnegie learn his management skills? Carnegie, an immigrant like so many other entrepreneurs of this age, early learned the trade of a telegrapher. Thomas A. Scott, superintendent of the Western Division of the Pennsylvania Railroad, hired Carnegie as his personal telegrapher for dispatching trains over the mountainous divisional lines. Carnegie learned fast, and made his mark one day when he untangled a traffic tie-up after a derailment. Scott was absent at the time, and Carnegie sent out orders, using Scott's initials. He was rewarded for this usurpation of authority and his initiative led to a change in the organization by providing for a delegation of dispatching authority (formerly, only the superintendent had the authority).

Carnegie learned of railroad management from Scott and J. Edgar Thomson, who, as the reader will recall, had applied McCallum's ideas to the Pennsy. It was McCallum's system of organization, reporting, accounting, and control that Carnegie learned on the Pennsy. At age 24, Carnegie moved up to become superintendent of the Pennsy's Western Division, which at the time was the largest division of the nation's largest railroad. Under Carnegie's supervision, divisional traffic quadrupled, track mileage doubled, and it had the lowest ton-mile costs of any railroad in America. He was offered the post of general superintendent (1865), but declined as he wanted to become an entrepreneur rather than a salaried manager. The rest of Carnegie's development can be found in many sources: it was his early years and the influence of McCallum's management system that provides the link for our story. It was on the Pennsy that Carnegie learned how to measure performance, to control costs, and to assign authority and responsibility: it was in the steel industry that he applied these lessons.[23]

Big Business and its Changing Environment

The years of internecine strife from 1861 to 1865 were a tragic pause in the nation's move toward world industrial leadership. The Civil War was as much an economic struggle between agrarian and industrial societies as it was a political and social one. The South, predominantly agricultural, was dealt a harsh blow, leaving the industrialized North in control. In the years that followed would occur a concatenation of events that would help the American business system mature.

The Economic Environment: The Accumulation of Resources

No nation can undergo a transformation of society as America did in the nineteenth century without substantial repercussions. An examination of America's response to industrialism is necessary in order to understand the forces that would shape the twentieth century. American economic conditions encouraged a rapid growth in corporate size, and mass markets and mass production had ushered in an era of intense competition. Aggressive entrepreneurs responded by overbuilding capacity which further intensified price competition. To protect themselves from this sharp competition, businesses sought to combine through pools, trusts, mergers, and holding companies to insulate themselves from the market.

Corporations possessed enormous potential for growth and,

[23] Numerous parallels between McCallum and Carnegie may be found in Harold C. Livesay, *Andrew Carnegie and the Rise of Big Business*, Boston: Little, Brown, and Company, 1975.

as industrialization proceeded, they grew in size, scope, resources, and power. Alfred Chandler has developed an interesting thesis about the historical growth of large corporations and their subsequent organizational forms. By tracing the history of various firms, he delineated four phases in the history of the large American enterprise: one, "the initial expansion and accumulation of resources"; two, "the rationalization of the use of resources"; three, "the expansion into new markets and lines to help assure the continuing full use of resources"; and finally "the development of a new structure to make possible continuing effective mobilization of resources to meet both changing short-term market demands and long-term market trends."[24] Hence the cycle runs to accumulate resources, rationalize resource utilization, expand resources, and rerationalize resource utilization; presumably *ad infinitum*. For different companies, the cycle starts and ends at different times, depending upon the state of technology and the firm's ability to react to and capitalize on market opportunities. During the latter part of the nineteenth century, many major industries were forming and would fit into Chandler's phase I or "resource accumulation stage."

Chandler further noted two facets of industrial growth and their time periods: (1) *horizontal* growth from 1879 to 1893; and (2) *vertical* growth from 1898 to 1904. Horizontal growth occurred when producers in similar fields combined through mergers, pools and/or trusts in order to gain economies of scale in manufacturing. Examples would be firms in oil, beef, sugar, tobacco, rubber, distillers, and so on. These mergers into larger units enabled the firm or firms to *control* their market, gain financial leverage, and cut costs of production. Viewed as monopolistic by some, the producers saw this as necessitated by the chaos of cutthroat competition. The vertical growth period (1898–1904) occurred when firms moved "backward" or "forward" in terms of the production process. Moving "backward" meant the acquisition of raw material sources or suppliers; moving "forward" meant establishing marketing outlets for one's own products. For example, a petro-

---

[24] Alfred D. Chandler, Jr., *Strategy and Structure: Chapters in the History of the Industrial Enterprise*, Cambridge, Mass.: MIT Press, 1962, p. 385. See also: Alfred D. Chandler, Jr., *The Visible Hand: The Managerial Revolution in American Business*, Cambridge, Mass.: Harvard University Press, 1977.

leum refining company would move backward to explore, acquire oil leases, drill, and build pipelines to its refinery; it would move forward to acquire wholesale agents and perhaps its own retail stations.

As these forces of industrial concentration worked, there emerged new titles for companies such as the "Americans," the "Nationals," and even the "Internationals." Examples of each would be the American Locomotive Company, the National Can Company, and International Harvester. By 1905, 40 percent of American manufacturing was controlled by some 300 companies with a capital investment of $7 billion. It was during this era that big business became Big Business. The stage was set for phase two and scientific management, but we will deal with that later.

The farmers, like the businessmen, also undertook collective action to protect themselves from economic adversity. The Granger movement, in a large part, aimed at state supervision of railroad rates and was intended to give the farmer greater control over his environment. Farmer cooperative ventures also constituted a persistent effort of the farm movement to protect itself. Joining the farmer and the businessman, labor also attempted to organize for concerted effort.

In essence, the new age threatened everyone with the unknowns of change. Worker, farmer, and businessman alike organized for collective action. Producers joined to control the conditions under which they sold their products; distributors combined to wield influence over marketing and transportation; and laborers formed trade unions to bargain with management. This organizational revolution revealed the degree to which industrialism had shifted the context of economic decisions from personal relationships among individuals to a struggle for power among well-organized groups.

The Social Environment: Barons or Benefactors?

Virtuous conduct seldom makes news. Historians and journalists are awed by the extraordinary and more frequently than not overstress it to the detriment of those quiet, sturdy, responsible people

who, unheralded, are the true productive builders. Matthew Josephson developed the idea of "robber barons" to such a point
that the public is quick to equate any business leader with this
type of value system.[25] Josephson noted that honesty toward customers, respectability, and conservatism in business practices, all
those characteristics of the early American entrepreneur, were beginning to depart in the 1840s. The new breed of businessmen left
home early to seek their fortune; for the most part they came from
the aggressive Yankee stock of New England, had grown up in
relative poverty, were immigrants or the sons of immigrants, were
acquisition motivated, and were puritanical and pious men who
took their Calvinistic origins seriously.[26] There were exceptions—
some were contradictions in character such as Daniel Drew who
spent his evenings, often drunk, in a cheap hotel room reading
the Bible and chewing tobacco. They all saw the potential of
growth in the burgeoning economy and vowed to take advantage
of it. It would be impossible to chronicle all of their activities but
some thumbnail sketches will reveal why Josephson felt that some
entrepreneurs were behaving in socially irresponsible ways.

Commodore Cornelius Vanderbilt gained control of the New
York and Harlem line by bribery of the New York state legislature
and by stock manipulation. He later built the New York Central
system, watered the stock, increased his fortune, and once remarked: "What do I care about the law? Hain't I got the power?"[27]
Daniel Drew has the dubious honor of being the first to engage in
the practice which came to be called "watering stock." He had
purchased a herd of cattle with an enlistment bonus he had received from his Civil War Army days. In transporting the herd to
market, he fed them salt to make them thirsty, then offered them
all the water they could drink and sold at a very large profit some
temporarily overweight cattle. Together with Jay Gould and Jim
Fisk, Drew turned to railroading and soon gave the Erie line its
reputation for mismanagement in the days following Daniel
McCallum. The Western railroaders were especially malignant; led
by Collis P. Huntington and aided by Leland Stanford, Sr., they

[25] Matthew Josephson, *The Robber Barons*, New York: Harcourt, Brace, Jovanovich, 1934.

[26] Ibid., pp. 30–32.

[27] Ibid., p. 72.

purchased the favors of legislators who could grant them free government land, give franchises, and pass enabling legislation. One year Huntington paid $200,000 to get a bill through Congress; he later complained that Congress was costing up to a half a million dollars a session and moaned, "I am afraid this damnation Congress will kill us."[28]

Not all of the "barons" were railroad men. John D. Rockefeller combined audacity and cunning in building his South Improvement Company and the Standard Oil colossus. By conspiring with the railroads, he was able to extract rebates on his freight and to receive rebates on the oil that his rivals shipped.[29] Andrew Carnegie at one point owned or controlled two-thirds of the nation's young steel industry. The Homestead strike earned Carnegie a poor press when he met union efforts with a force of Pinkerton detectives (hired to protect the plant) who were brutally stoned and beaten by the striking workers; state troops moved in and secured the plant for a wholly nonunion crew. In the process 14 were killed and 163 wounded. These men represented, at least for Josephson, the most unsavory practices in American entrepreneurship.

What motivated the "robber barons"? For some social historians, it was the publication of Charles Darwin's book in 1859, *On the Origin of Species by Means of Natural Selection, or the Preservation of Favored Races in the Struggle for Life.* This set forth his theories concerning evolution and natural selection through the struggle for existence. Social scientists seized Darwin's theories in an attempt to apply them to human society and the result was "social Darwinism."[30] Since the most striking phrases of Darwinism were "struggle for existence" and "survival of the fittest," it was suggested that nature would provide that the "most fit" in a competitive situation would win. In the struggle for existence in a competitive society, money was the measure of success; this explained the huge fortunes millionaires acquired in a competitive system. Being the most fit, their huge fortunes were the legitimate

[28] Ibid., p. 357.

[29] Ibid., pp. 115–119. See also Ida Tarbell, *History of Standard Oil,* New York: Harper and Row, 1905.

[30] Richard Hofstadter, *Social Darwinism in American Thought,* Boston: Beacon Press, 1945, p. 4.

wages of efficiency. Thus, through unrestricted competition, the fittest would survive and move up the social ladder of success and the unfit would occupy the lower class structures and would eventually be eliminated through evolution. Ruthless business rivalry and unprincipled politics were to be justified by the survival philosophy.

Are these allegations true? One historian has suggested that "Darwinism may have done no more for the business community than to furnish a new terminology for old ideas."[31] He claimed that businessmen were pragmatic doers who worked out the rules as they met them; they read or heard little of Darwin or Adam Smith and cared little for abstract social and economic theories. Another agrees: "It is not true that this commitment [to competition] was grounded on Darwinian premises."[32] Few knew enough of Darwin "to turn biology to the uses of self-justification." What can be concluded about the effect of social Darwinism on the thought and practices of the businessman? The peak of social Darwinism in America saw businessmen and others trying to avoid competition through cooperative efforts of pools, Granges, and unions instead of allowing the laws of nature to run their course. Businessmen, being of a practical bent, have never been noted for their interest in the social theories of the intellectuals; here again social Darwinism falls short. Another strike against the proponents is the known pious nature of the entrepreneurs, at least on Sunday, and the thought of Darwinian concepts appealing to them is doubtful. Social Darwinism may have provided a rationalization for some practices, but the conclusion that it was the dominant philosophy is tenuous.

What was the relationship between business and society in terms of nineteenth-century values? Were the "barons" without conscience, or did they provide some benefactions to society? The philanthropy of business people is as ancient as business itself, including patrons of arts and letters, providers of funds for com-

---

[31]Edward C. Kirkland, *Dream and Thought in the Business Community, 1860–1900*, Ithaca, N.Y.: Cornell University Press, 1956, p. 14. Another who shares this pragmatic view is Peter d. A. Jones (ed.), *The Robber Barons Revisited*, Boston: D. C. Heath and Company, 1968, pp. v–xi.

[32]Raymond J. Wilson (ed.), *Darwinism and the American Intellectual: A Book of Readings*, Homewood, Ill.: Dorsey Press, 1967, p. 93.

munity projects, church givers, and endowers of educational institutions. No one would question the right of successful persons to give away some or all of their fortunes; after all, it was their money to do with as they pleased. But what of this new phenomenon, the corporation? Could it have a conscience? Could its managers and directors give away a portion of its profits to non-business-related endeavors? Or were the managers to work only in the interest of the owners, the stockholders? The legal question of corporate philanthropy was clouded because of a precedent set in an 1883 British case, *Hutton v. West Cork Railway Corporation.* In this case, the court ruled that the corporation existed only as a profit-making enterprise whose purpose was the equitable distribution of its earnings to its owners, the stockholders. Given this precedent, corporate officers would be hesitant to dole out money to other claimants in fear of stockholder lawsuits.

While corporate philanthropy might be questioned, it would be unlikely that the hand of individual charity would be nipped. Individual philanthropy would be the vehicle for expressing the social conscience of the nineteenth-century entrepreneur. Only a few of the great philanthropist-businessmen can be mentioned. Ezra Cornell pioneered in telegraphy, made a fortune out of the Western Union Company, and provided the money to found a college (Ithaca, N.Y.) which would naturally be named for him; William Colgate helped people get closer to godliness with his manufacture of soap and he and his heirs gave so much to a college that it changed its name to his; Moses Brown, Samuel Slater's partner, founded Rhode Island College in Providence (1770), which became Brown University in 1804; Johns Hopkins, founder of the Baltimore and Ohio Railroad, also founded the famous university in Baltimore which bears his name; and Cornelius Vanderbilt (the Commodore) made a large bequest in 1873 which converted a small Methodist Seminary in Nashville, Tennessee, into a well-known university which would receive its name from him.

There were more: Joseph Wharton, whose $100,000 grant enabled the nation's first school of business at the University of Pennsylvania; Edward Tuck, who honored his father with a gift of $300,000 to Dartmouth College to start the Amos Tuck School of Administration and Finance (1899); Leland Stanford, who honored his son with a university (1891); John Stevens, who provided for an institute of technology (1870); and James B. Duke, who established the trust fund to create Trinity College (later renamed for the Duke family). Good fortune did not smile on all colleges who hoped for a philanthropist. Daniel Drew gave a $250,000 promissory note to endow a Methodist Theological Seminary in Madison, New Jersey. The seminary started its work, but Daniel Drew went bankrupt and was never able to deliver the promised money.[33] The seminary was named Drew University anyway.

Other philanthropists are better known: Rockefeller endowed the University of Chicago in 1896, gave millions through a general education fund to educate southern Negroes, and by the time of his death in 1937 had given away half a billion dollars as well as providing for the future of the foundation which bears the family name. Carnegie had given away $350 million by his death in 1919 and left this world as he entered it, penniless. His libraries, universities, and foundation are enduring monuments to his expressed "stewardship of wealth" philosophy. Despite such generosity, both Carnegie and Rockefeller were denounced by the Congressional Committee on Industrial Relations in 1915 as "menaces" to society.[34] Their efforts were seen as intrusions into the province of government and reflected the fear that business charity had the potential of increasing the control of the business community over society.

Times have changed: income and inheritance taxes make it difficult to accumulate as much wealth as the entrepreneurs of the nineteenth century, the legal question of corporate philanthropy has been clarified (as we shall see later), and public expectations about the role of business in society have changed. But we are the recipients today of the benefactions of the nineteenth-century builders of America.

The Political Environment: From Adam Smith to the Twentieth Century

Two documents of 1776 tolled the death of mercantilism: the

[33]Josephson, p. 20.

[34]Cited by Clarence C. Walton, *Corporate Social Responsibilities*, Belmont, Calif.: Wadsworth Publishing Company, 1967, pp. 41–42.

American Declaration of Independence, and Adam Smith's *The Wealth of Nations*. America's economic heritage was largely mercantile, but the pressures for an escape from the policies of England were strong. Coincident with the Declaration of Independence in America, Smith's book appeared in England. It was a declaration of *economic* independence.

In the years between 1776 and 1787 the ideas of Adam Smith were widely read and discussed by American business and political leaders. Smith's writings fit into the philosophical concept of the new nation held by those who protested the strong role of government in economic matters. Smith's *laissez-faire* inclinations were acceptable to the framers of the Constitution. Article I, Section 8, gave Congress the power to impose and collect taxes, borrow money, coin money, fix standards of weights and measures, punish counterfeiters, issue patents, and to "regulate commerce with foreign nations and among the several states." Except for those powers, government was evidently to maintain a relatively hands-off approach to economic affairs and to act primarily to maintain uniformity and order among the states. The American experience with the mercantilistic restrictions and duties had led to a desire to limit the role of government in economic matters. This policy would persist until almost the close of the nineteenth century.

This "hands-off" policy extended to organized labor as well as business. An American legacy from England was the view that combinations of workers were "conspiracies" in restraint of trade and therefore illegal. Local craft guilds made some headway in America but often ran into court-ordered injunctions when they sought to strike. In a landmark case in 1842 (*Commonwealth v. Hunt*), the Supreme Court of Massachusetts held that a combination of workers was not illegal *per se*. If the object of the combination was criminal, then it could be prohibited. The court held that seeking a closed shop (workers must be union members) and striking were not illegal goals, and worker alliances for those purposes were proper. Although the decision applied only to Massachusetts, it discouraged attempts in other states to prosecute worker organizations on conspiracy grounds.

The organization of labor by unions made little progress among industrial workers, although craft workers in the building trades and railroad brotherhoods were relatively strong. Despite the *Commonwealth v. Hunt* decision, a relatively hostile public opinion retarded unionization. For the industrial workers (that is, noncraft workers such as those in the building trades), two abortive attempts were made to organize. They were labor's countervailing responses to the growth of business. The National Labor Union, headed by William H. Sylvis, sought to supplant the wage system with cooperative production in which the workers would pool their resources, supply their own labor, and manage the factories. The Noble Order of the Knights of Labor, organized in 1867, sought an eight-hour day, the establishment of a bureau of labor statistics, protection of child labor, a graduated income tax, government ownership of railroads and telegraph lines, the abolition of national banks, and a system of cooperation to take the place of wages. Neither of these organizations was to survive.

Labor violence in the 1880s and 1890s fueled public fears of unions. The Molly Maguires terrorized the populace with murders and other atrocities in the Pennsylvania coal fields. The Haymarket Affair (1886), in which the Knights of Labor tried to enforce a general strike in Chicago, led to several deaths. The Homestead strike (1892) and the Pullman strike (1894) were other examples of violence brought about by confrontations between labor and management. Public fear of "radicals" and "anarchists," who were often equated with legitimate union organizers, kept the union movement at a relative standstill. One success was the American Federation of Labor, organized in 1886 as a federation of craft unions that concentrated on the pursuit of immediate economic gains for the worker on the job rather than on distant political reforms. Under Samuel Gompers' leadership, the union membership increased from fewer than 200,000 in 1886 to more than 2,865,000 at the time of Gompers' death in 1924.[35] Industrial workers, however, had to await other times and a changing public opinion to legitimize their attempts at organization.

There were few effective efforts at national regulation of business as government held true to a narrowly construed commerce clause. The first attempts to reform business practices came very logically with the railroads. In 1869 Massachusetts passed the first

[35] Philip A. Taft, *The A.F.L. In The Time of Gompers,* New York: Harper and Row, 1957, Chapter 3.

statutes regulating railroads, the Granger laws of the seventies brought regulation to others, and the Interstate Commerce Act of 1887, which proved generally ineffective in practice, became the first national regulation. Beyond the railroads, the Sherman Antitrust Act of 1890 sought to check corporate trusts and monopoly practices "in restraint of trade." Poorly defined and narrowly construed, it was generally ineffectual. To illustrate further the "hands-off" policy, even taxpayers benefited. The first peacetime federal income tax was imposed by the Wilson-Gorman Tax Act of 1894. It levied a 2 percent personal tax on all incomes above $4,000 and a 2 percent tax on all corporate net income. In 1895, the Supreme Court declared the act unconstitutional. Taxpayers could rest easy for a few more years. In brief, the nineteenth-century political environment remained relatively *laissez-faire*, true to the precepts of Adam Smith; the twentieth century would bring a host of changes in this philosophy.

Summary of Part I

Part I of this study has been an examination of management thought prior to the scientific management era in America and may be visually conceptualized as Figure 5-1. People, a fundamental focus of our study, have manifold needs and wants which they seek to satisfy through organized endeavors. In organizations, management is an activity which performs certain functions in order to obtain the effective acquisition, allocation, and utilization of human efforts and physical resources in order to meet the organization's objectives and to yield positive benefits to organizational members. The cultural environment, characterized as having economic, social, and political facets, shapes values and forms institutional arrangements which have a large bearing upon people, upon organizations, and upon management as an activity.

Early civilizations reflected some early attempts to relate individuals to organizations but generally placed a low value on economic activity and held a parochial view of the management function. The cultural rebirth brought a new view of people, of economic activity, of social values, of political arrangements, and established the preconditions for the Industrial Revolution. This technological and cultural revolution created the factory system to

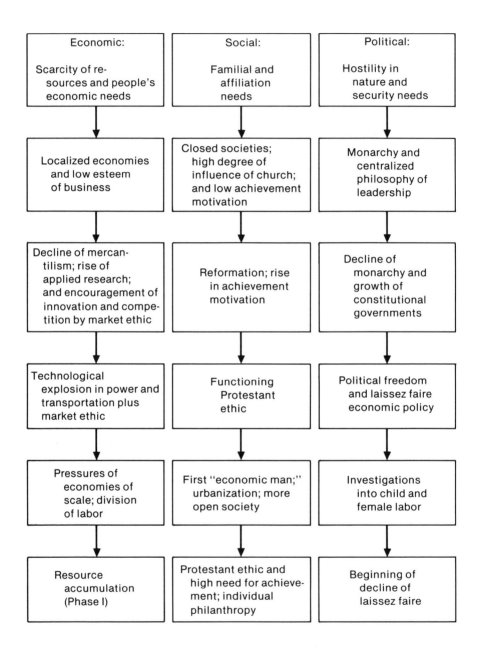

Fig. 5-1.   Synopsis of early management thought and the cultural environment.

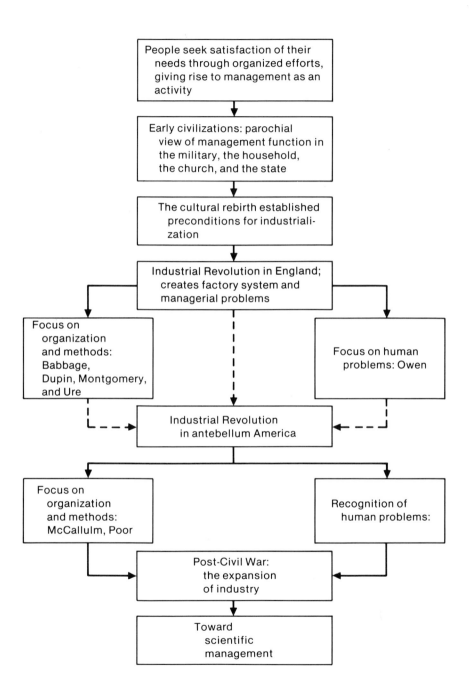

replace the domestic system and posed managerial problems on a scale never encountered before. Broadly viewed, these problems may be grouped in three categories: (1) the organizational and methods problems of melding technology, materials, organizational functions, and productive processes in an efficient manner; (2) the human problems of acquiring, developing, stimulating, and controlling human behavior toward preconceived ends; and (3) the managerial problem of fusing both of the above facets in order to accomplish objectives.

Throughout our study of management thought, we will see that various writers will shift their relative emphasis on the importance of the organization and methods facet vis-à-vis the human facet. This does not mean that these two facets are mutually exclusive but that it is a matter of relative focus and this to a large degree will be influenced by the cultural environment. For example, Charles Babbage was concerned with the human problems of the factory but his primary concern was with the analysis of production techniques. Robert Owen, on the other hand, was more concerned with the impact of industrialization on people. Likewise, Henry Varnum Poor was more concerned with the systematization of the railroads but recognized the interaction of the organization and methods facet with the human facet.

Figure 5-1 illustrates in summary form management thought before scientific management. It shows the interaction of the cultural environment with early ideas about management activity, depicts the relative emphases of management pioneers, and provides the basis for the beginnings of the scientific management era in America.

THE SCIENTIFIC MANAGEMENT ERA

Part II will begin with the work of Frederick W. Taylor and will examine management thought in Europe and America up to the early 1930s. Taylor provided the major thrust for an era which will be characterized as a search for efficiency and systematization in management thought. Around Taylor there were others, such as Carl Barth, H. L. Gantt, Frank and Lillian Gilbreth, Morris Cooke, and Harrington Emerson, who were spreading the gospel of efficiency in America. Though the work of Taylor and his followers dominated this era, there were also some early behavioral contributions and these will be examined as a prelude to the emergence of human relations in industry. Next, we will examine the work of Henri Fayol and Max Weber, who wrote during the scientific management era, but whose discovery for the development of management thought came much later. We will conclude part II by examining the critics of Taylorism and by presenting a conceptual viewpoint of the economic, social, and political conditions which comprised the cultural environment of scientific management.

6

The Advent of Scientific Management

The last decades of the nineteenth century resulted in unprecedented accumulations of resources in American industry. With resources accumulated and technology developing, the major impediment to added industrial productivity was in the crude forms of developing, organizing, controlling, and administering this mass of resource efforts. At no place in the firm was this more crucial than in the production shop itself. Labor was highly specialized, standardized methods and procedures were in short supply, and there was little emphasis on coordinating, integrating, and systematizing work.[1]

Another pressing problem was what referred to in the literature of the late 1800s as "the labor question." The productivity of labor was deemed low and the concern was how labor could be brought up to its potential. One author advocated better machines as labor-saving devices, another sought profit-sharing schemes, while others felt that better procedures, methods, and "systems" were the answer.[2] Frederick W. Taylor, a young manager-engineer

---

[1] Two excellent analyses of these industrial problems preceding Taylorism may be found in Joseph A. Litterer, "Systematic Management: The Search for Order and Integration," *Business History Review*, Vol. 35 (Winter, 1961), pp. 461–476; and Joseph A. Litterer, "Systematic Management: Design for Organizational Recoupling in American Manufacturing Firms," *Business History Review*, Vol. 37 (Winter, 1963), pp. 369–391.

[2] J. Schoenhof, *The Economy of High Wages*, New York: G. P. Putnam's Sons, 1892; Mary W. Calkins, *Sharing the Profits*, Boston: Ginn and Co., 1888; Oberlin Smith, "Systems in Machine Shops," *American Machinist*, Vol. 8 (October 31, 1885); and John Tregoing, *A Treatise on Factory Management*, Lynn, Mass.: Thomas P. Nichols, 1891.

at this time, was aware of these proposed solutions because of his membership in the American Society of Mechanical Engineers. Taylor knew from his experience the problems of the factory and he was to propose another solution to "the labor question." What was so revolutionary in Taylor's solution was that the answer resided only partially in labor and mostly in the poor state of existing management practices. But we are getting ahead of our story.

Frederick Winslow Taylor: The Early Years

Frederick Winslow Taylor (1856–1915) was born in Germantown, Pennsylvania, as the son of a fairly prosperous lawyer of Quaker stock and a mother who traced her Puritan ancestry to a Plymouth, Massachusetts, ancestor who arrived in 1629.[3] This Quaker-Puritan stock and training gave Taylor an unusual preparation for his life's work: an intense spirit of inquiry for the truth, an urge to observe and verify facts, and a Puritan zeal to eradicate the evils of waste and slothfulness. Taylor's early education was liberally sprinkled with the classics, the study of French and German, and occasional trips to Europe. As a young man, he was "enamored of scientific investigation, research, and experiment . . . [with] a passion for improving and reforming things on the basis of fact, and early was filled with a divine discontent with anything short of the *one best way*."[4] He put to careful study and analysis the game of croquet, found the best method with the least fatigue of taking a cross-country walk, and devised other ingenious devices which were early evidence of the intensely meticulous nature which became his hallmark in later work.

His parents intended that he follow his father's profession of law and duly enrolled him at Phillips Exeter to prepare for Harvard. The competition was stiff and Taylor's zeal and restless energy led to late nights and long hours, eventually impairing his

[3]The life of Taylor is presented in complete detail in Frank Barkley Copley, *Frederick W. Taylor: Father of Scientific Management* (2 vol.), New York: Harper and Row, 1923. A more recent work on Taylor uses a "psycho-historical" approach to examine his life and conflicts: see Sudhir Kakar, *Frederick Taylor: A Study in Personality and Innovation*, Cambridge, Mass.: MIT Press, 1970.

[4]Copley, vol. I, pp. 55–56.

eyesight. Though he passed the Harvard exams with honors, his poor health and eyesight forced him to turn away from law school and into an apprenticeship as a pattern-maker and machinist with the Enterprise Hydraulic Works of Philadelphia.[5] He started his four-year apprenticeship at no wage (since his father was a "man of means") and was making the grand sum of $3 a week when he finished his apprenticeship in 1878. Living an ascetic life which would have pleased Ben Franklin (he neither smoked nor drank stimulants such as alcohol, coffee or tea), his apprentice years were grueling; he attributed his success to "character," which to Taylor was "the ability to control yourself, body and mind . . . the ability above all to do things which are disagreeable."[6] His early concern with self-control, with character, and with doing even the tiresome and dull things because they developed a person, were manifestations of a later concern for discipline and adherence to the "one best way."

At Enterprise, Taylor developed an empathy for the workers' point of view; he could swear with the best of them and admired their sense of pride in workmanship.[7] However, he saw about him what he called the "bad industrial conditions," which consisted of worker soldiering on the job, the poor quality of management, and the lack of harmony between workers and managers.

Taylor at Midvale

Taylor moved to Midvale Steel (Philadelphia) in 1878 as a common laborer. The economic consequences of the financial panic of 1873 still lingered and jobs were scarce. The steel industry had developed slowly and was reaching its apex in the 1880s with the introduction of better machine tools and power. Midvale, under the presidency of William Sellers, was one of the leading steel firms of

[5] Ibid., pp. 77–79. Professor Kakar suggests that Taylor's change of plans was not due to failing eyesight but due to his rejection of his father's choosing his profession for him. Thus Taylor was passing through an adolescent "identity crisis" and in this manner sought to establish his own independence and personality. Kakar, pp. 26–27.

[6] Copley, p. 84.

[7] Copley, pp. 88–93 and p. 4. Kakar's analysis holds that Taylor's swearing and identification with the workers served as an outlet for his "aggressive impulses" against his family whose life style he was repudiating. Kakar, pp. 36–37.

the era. At Midvale, Taylor would rise from common laborer to clerk, to machinist, to gang boss of the machinists, to foreman of the machine shop, to master mechanic in charge of repairs and maintenance throughout the plant, and to chief engineer—all in six years; a meteoric rise for this intense young man. The twelve years at Midvale (1878–1890) were years of experimentation which provided the basis for his system of shop management and for his experiments with metals. Realizing his lack of scientific education, he enrolled in a home study course from Stevens Institute of Technology of Hoboken, New Jersey. He never attended classes except to take examinations and graduated with a degree in mechanical engineering in 1883. In total, it was two and a half years of study, all while pursuing his full-time duties at Midvale.

Taylor had no training in management and relied solely upon his own investigations as to what should be done. His frontal attack on shop problems led to an early confrontation with the workers. When Taylor became gang boss, the company had established a piecework incentive system which Taylor knew to be ineffective from his own working days. Midvale management felt that the workers would control their own behavior and would be properly motivated once given the piece-rate incentive. Taylor knew otherwise; he knew their output was only a third of what was possible and he set about to correct the situation as soon as he received the authority. To see a worker operating at less than full capability was morally shocking to the Quaker-Puritan Taylor. To do less than your best was bad for the character and probably this was a greater sin to Taylor than any mere unused capacity of machines or workers.

The restriction of output at Midvale was classified by Taylor in "natural soldiering" and "systematic soldiering." Natural soldiering proceeded from "the natural instinct and tendency of men to take it easy"; while the systematic form came from the workers' "more intricate second thought and reasoning caused by their relations with other men."[8] Natural soldiering could be overcome by a manager able to inspire or force workers to come up to the mark. Systematic soldiering posed a different problem and man-

[8]Frederick W. Taylor, *Shop Management*, New York: Harper and Row, 1903, p. 30. Reissued as part of Frederick Winslow Taylor, *Scientific Management*, New York: Harper and Row, 1947. Pagination is the same in both editions.

agers for years had been attempting to cope with the tendency to conform to group output standards. Why do workers soldier? Taylor answered as follows: first, they believed that to work faster would throw large numbers of workers out of work; second, the defective management systems then in use forced workers to work slowly to protect their own interests; and third, because of the adherence to rule-of-thumb work methods handed down from generation to generation.[9] Taylor placed the blame on management, not on the workers, for he thought that it was management's job to design the jobs properly and to offer the proper incentives to overcome their soldiering.

In no small part, systematic soldiering arose out of a "lump of labor" theory that postulated a limited amount of work in the world and that to do more today left less to be done tomorrow; i.e., you could work yourself or your fellow employees out of a job if you worked too fast. A daily or hourly wage system encouraged soldiering because pay was based on attendance and position, not effort. To work harder brought no reward and actually encouraged the lazy worker. Piece-rate systems, old long before Taylor, sought to encourage individual incentive and initiative by paying workers on the basis of their output. Such systems had been generally failures before Taylor; standards were often poorly set, employers cut the rates when workers earned too much, and workers hid their shortcut methods and improvements from management to protect themselves. With ample experience of cuts when they exceeded a certain amount of income, workers developed a consensus about how much each should produce and earn, not only to protect themselves but undoubtedly also to avoid the ridicule of the less capable. The workers perceived that management envisioned some maximum sum of pay and any earnings beyond that would lead to rate cuts. Taylor did not blame the workers; in fact he sympathized with them, because he felt that it was the wage *system*, not the workers, that was at fault.

Taylor's initial experiences as a machine shop foreman resulted in a bitter encounter with the workers. He told them that

---

[9] Frederick W. Taylor, *The Principles of Scientific Management*, New York: Harper and Row, 1911, pp. 15–16. Reissued as part of Frederick Winslow Taylor, *Scientific Management*, New York: Harper and Row, 1947. Pagination is the same in both editions.

he knew they could do more and that he was going to see that they did. Taylor started by showing them how to use the lathes to get more output with very little more effort by using his methods. He failed in retraining those machinists because they refused to follow his instructions; he then turned to training common laborers who, after learning the method, joined the group and resisted increased production. Taylor admitted "I was up against a stone wall. I did not blame these laborers in my heart; my sympathy was with them all the time . . .;"[10] but he had a job to do and the obstreperous workers only challenged the young Taylor. He turned to more drastic means by cutting the rate to make the men work harder to earn the same pay. The men retaliated by breaking and jamming the machines; Taylor countered by a system of fines (the proceeds going to a worker benefit fund) for equipment damage. Eventually Taylor not only won the battle with the machinists but learned a valuable lesson as well. Never again would he use the system of fines, and he later established strict rules against rate cutting. More importantly, the young Taylor realized that a new industrial scheme was essential to prevent such bitter labor-management encounters. It was at this time that Taylor began his search for a science of work.

The Search for Science in Management

Though sympathetic with the effort to soldier, Taylor thought that he could overcome it by a careful investigation of work which would then be used in setting rates. Once the workers saw that the rate was properly set, they would know that it was based on facts and not whims and that this would reduce their motivation to soldier. The problem was in defining a full and fair day's standard for each task. Taylor set out to determine scientifically what the workers ought to be able to do with their equipment and materials, and this became the true beginning of scientific management, i.e., the use of a scientific fact-finding method to determine empirically instead of traditionally the right ways to perform

---

[10] Copley (I), p. 162. Kakar notes that this battle with the machinists reflected his own internal conflicts and anxieties, that is, a struggle to control them while trying to control his own rebellious strivings. Kakar, pp. 61–62.

tasks. Initially, Taylor probably never envisioned that any theory would ensue nor that this step was the beginning of further applications to many jobs and industries. He did it because he felt that this would be a way to overcome the worker antagonism and resistance he encountered earlier. He had the worker's interests in mind when he thought that management should have the responsibility for determining standards, planning work, and devising incentive schemes; he abhorred the previous methods of setting a rate based on past performance, leaving it up to the worker to motivate himself to meet that rate, and cutting the rate if the worker earned too much.

Time study became the foundation of the Taylor system and some questioned Taylor's claim to originality. Charles Babbage had demonstrated the use of a watch in recording the labor operations and times necessary in the manufacture of pins. Copley said that Taylor probably had never heard of Babbage when Taylor began his time studies in the early 1880s.[11] In 1912, a subcommittee of the American Society of Mechanical Engineers issued a report on time study which made no mention of Taylor's work but referenced Adam Smith and Charles Babbage. Taylor contributed to a discussion of this report in an effort to clarify his concept of time study and to answer the doubters of his originality.

> *Time study was begun in the machine shop of the Midvale Steel Company in 1881. . . . It is true that the form of Tables 1 and 2 [the Babbage contribution to the A.S.M.E. report] is similar to that of the blanks recording time study, but here the resemblance ceases. Each line in Table 2, for instance, gives statistics regarding the average of the entire work of an operative who works day in and day out, in running a machine engaged in the manufacture of pins. This table involves no study whatever of the movements of the man, nor of the time in which the movements should have been made. Mere Statistics as to the time which a man takes to do a given piece of work do not constitute "time study": "time*

[11]Copley, p. 221. For support of Copley, see Lyndall Urwick and E. F. L. Brech, *The Making of Scientific Management*, vol. I, London: Management Publications Trust, 1943, p. 37; for the opposite view, i.e., that Taylor must have known of Babbage, see John Hoaglund, "Management Before Frederick Taylor," reprinted in Paul M. Dauten, Jr. (ed.), *Current Issues and Emerging Concepts in Management*, Boston: Houghton Mifflin Co., 1962, pp. 23–25.

study," as its name implies, involves a careful study of the time in which work ought *to be done . . . [rather than] the time in which the work actually was done.*[12]

Taylor's distinction supported his claim to originality since he was using time study for analytical rather than descriptive purposes; that is, future versus past uses of data. Taylor's time study formed the basis for his scientific approach to the job and had two phases: "analytical" and "constructive." In analysis, each job was broken into as many simple elementary movements as possible, useless movements were discarded, the quickest and best methods for each elementary movement were selected by observing the most skilled workman at each, and the movement was timed and recorded. To the recorded time, a percentage was added to cover unavoidable delays and interruptions, another percentage to cover "the newness" of workmen to a job, and yet another percentage for rest periods. It was in the determination and addition of these percentages that most critics said Taylor's method was not "scientific" since these were based on the experience and intuition of the time study observer. The constructive phase involved building a file of elementary movements and times to be used wherever possible on other jobs or classes of work; further, this phase led to consideration of improvements in tools, machines, materials, methods, and the ultimate standardization of all elements surrounding and accompanying the job.[13]

Whereas Babbage was content with gross times of actual performance, Taylor's method broke the job into component parts, tested them, and reconstructed the job as it *should* be done. Taylor thought that such scientific study of the job would form a "proof" to the worker to overcome resistance. In a later defense before his critics, Taylor denied that he sought exactness: "All we hope to do through time study is to get a vastly closer approximation as to time than we ever had before."[14]

The Quest for New Incentives

Since management relied heavily on engineers for advice in the

[12]Copley, pp. 225–226.
[13]Taylor, *Shop Management*, pp. 149–176.
[14]Copley (I), pp. 234–235.

factory, it is not coincidental that associations of engineers were the first to examine and write about managerial problems. The American Society of Mechanical Engineers was founded in 1880 and became the first proponents of the search for systematic, scientific management. An important point for the group came in 1886 with a paper by Henry R. Towne, President of the Yale and Towne Manufacturing Company, on "The Engineer as Economist."[15] Towne stressed that the engineer must look beyond the mere *mechanical* efficiency criteria of an economic (i.e., costs and revenues) nature. Engineers employed by industry must broaden their intellectual interests to learn to think and act as economists who were concerned with broader questions of total resource utilization. Since there were no management schools nor management associations, Towne suggested that the A.S.M.E. become a clearing house for information on managerial practices. Towne's ideas affected the thinking and life of Taylor, who had joined the A.S.M.E. in 1886. They had less impact on future papers for the A.S.M.E., as only four other papers were presented on management up to 1895. One was another Towne paper on "gain sharing" in which he contended that profit sharing was not an appropriate solution to the problem of greater worker productivity. In profit sharing, savings from worker efforts in one department could be offset by a lack of diligence in others. Instead, Towne proposed to determine costs and productivity for each work unit or department and to return to them the "gains" according to their own performance. Towne's plan guaranteed a wage rate to each employee, plus a 50–50 split of the "gain" in the worker's department.[16] Another significant paper was Frederick A. Halsey's "The Premium Plan of Paying for Labor," in which he attacked the evils of both profit sharing and individual piece-work systems.[17] He saw a lack of motivation in profit sharing and abuses in the piece-rate system. Halsey proposed that incentives be based on past production records, plus a guaranteed minimum wage, plus a premium for doing more work. The premium would amount to about one-third more than the daily or hourly rate and leave two-thirds

[15] *Transactions*, A.S.M.E., Vol. 7 (1886), pp. 428–432.

[16] Henry R. Towne, "Gain Sharing," *Transactions*, A.S.M.E., Vol. 10, (1889).

[17] *Transactions*, A.S.M.E., Vol. 12 (1891), pp. 755–764.

of the added value to accrue to the employer, who would be therefore less inclined to cut the rate.

Enter Frederick Taylor at this point. Taylor's first formal statement of his new system was "A Piece-Rate System" in which he attacked both the Towne and the Halsey plans.[18] The weakness in both, in Taylor's view, was that they sought to induce the worker to produce more by sharing the gain from their extra efforts with management. Taylor proposed a new system consisting of three parts: one, observation and analysis through time study to set the "rate" or standard; two, a "differential rate" system of piece-work; and three, "paying men and not positions." In Taylor's opinion, profit sharing failed because: (1) it discouraged personal ambition because all shared in profits regardless of their contribution; and (2) the "remoteness of the reward." Taylor's second criticism of profit sharing was an early insight into the psychological principle of temporal contiguity, i.e., the timing of the reinforcement with regard to the behavior, and reflected Taylor's view that a share of the profits at the end of the year gave no incentive for maximum daily performance.

In this paper, Taylor had clearly put the onus on management to take charge, to accept its responsibilities, and to move away from the old system of leaving the work up to the worker. A rate setting department planned the work and divided it into its various elements and set a rate or standard for each element. Based on thorough study, this rate moved job performance from guesswork and tradition to a more rational basis. The principle of the differential rate worked two ways: it forced those who did not meet the standard to receive a very low rate of pay, and greatly rewarded those who did attain the standard.[19] The incentive became that of following the proper methods and making the standard in order to be rewarded. The notion of paying workers and not positions was designed partially to overcome soldiering but mainly to individualize the worker by paying for his efforts and

---

[18] Frederick W. Taylor, "A Piece-Rate System," *Transactions*, A.S.M.E., Vol. 16 (1895), pp. 856–883.

[19] The "high" rate was set such that the average employee who met the standard earned 125 percent of the base standard pay: the "low" rate, for those who failed to meet the standard, was set at 80 percent. C. W. Lytle, *Wage Incentive Methods*, New York: Ronald Press Co., 1942, pp. 179–180.

not for his class of work. Taylor's paper of 1895 on the piece-rate system outlined his view on unions, an opinion he never changed, and one which would bring him a barrage of criticism:

> *The writer is far from taking the view held by many manufacturers that labor unions are an almost unmitigated detriment to those who join them, as well as to employers and the general public. The labor unions . . . have rendered a great service not only to their members, but to the world, in shortening the hours of labor and in modifying the hardships and improving the conditions of wage workers. . . . When employers herd their men together in classes, pay all of each class the same wages . . . the only remedy for the men lies in combination; and frequently the only possible answer to encroachment on the part of their employers is a strike. . . .*
>
> *This state of affairs is far from satisfactory and the writer believes the system of regulating wages and conditions of employment of whole classes of men by conference and agreement between the leaders, unions and manufacturers to be vastly inferior . . . to the plan of stimulating each workman's ambition by paying him according to his individual worth, and without limiting him to the rate of work or pay of the average of his class.*[20]

Taylor had no personal vendetta against unions per se (a view often misconstrued), but saw no necessity for them under his system of incentive management. Unions, to maintain their group solidarity, must insist on a "common rule" and a standardization of wages and conditions for all. Individualized treatment is a threat to the group. For Taylor, this view prevented each worker from fulfilling his personal desires because he was to be treated as one of the masses. People should be inspired to better themselves à la the Protestant ethic, not lumped into one class and treated like everyone else.

This early paper on incentives and the proper relation between worker and manager anticipated his philosophy of mutual interest between those parties. Countering a "more-less" assumption that if the workers got more, the employer naturally got less, Taylor saw a mutuality of interests rather than natural conflict be-

---

[20]Taylor, "A Piece-Rate System," pp. 859–860; also in *Shop Management*, pp. 185–186.

tween labor and management. This was his statement of the "paradox of high wages and low costs" which, on the surface, appear to be diametrically opposed concepts. Instead of the employers' practice of buying the cheapest labor and paying the lowest wages possible and the worker's desire to gain all he could get for the least he could give, Taylor advocated paying the first-class worker a high wage, thereby inducing him to produce more under standard, efficient conditions with no greater expenditure of effort than formerly. The result was more productivity, hence lower per unit labor costs to the employer and higher wages to the worker, thus satisfying both parties to the transaction. To summarize his system of payments, Taylor said the aim of each establishment should be:

(a)   *That each workman should be given as far as possible the highest grade of work for which his ability and physique fit him.*

(b)   *That each workman should be called upon to turn out the maximum amount of work which a first-rate man of his class can do and thrive.*

(c)   *That each workman, when he works at the best pace of a first-class man, should be paid from 30 percent to 100 percent according to the nature of the work which he does, beyond the average of his class.*[21]

The First-Class Man

This new notion of a "first-class man" formed a basis for the scientific selection of workmen and caused Taylor much grief in trying to explain it to others. In testimony before a special Congressional committee, Taylor defined his first-class man:

I believe the only man who does not come under "first-class" as I have defined it, is the man who can work and will not work. I have tried to make it clear that for each type of workman some job can be found at which he is first class, with the exception of those men who are perfectly well able to do the job but won't do it.[22]

[21] *Shop Management*, pp. 28–29.

[22] *Hearings before Special Committee of the House of Representatives to Investigate The Taylor and other Systems of Shop Management under Authority of House Resolution 90*, Washington D.C.: U.S. Government Printing Office, 1912, p. 1451.

Under these terms "non-first-class" workers would be either those who were physically and/or mentally unsuited for the work assigned, (in which case they should be retrained or transferred to another job for which they were suited), or any workers who were unwilling to give their best. In setting rates for each job, Taylor set the standard at the pace a first-class man "can keep up for a long term of years without injury to his health. It is a pace under which men become happier and thrive."[23] The first-class pace was not based on spurts of activity nor on strain but on the normal pace that a worker could sustain. Basically, Taylor was laying the foundations for sound personnel management, i.e., the match of workers' abilities to the job.

It was management's task to find the work for which employees were best suited, to assist them in becoming first-class workers, and to provide them with an incentive to give their best. Taylor's views on the first-class man were closely intertwined with his personal philosophy of "the will to get there" or that success drive which was the basis of his own life. It was his observation that the major difference between individuals was not in brains, but in *will*, the drive to achieve.[24] The first-class man was a person with ambition who was suited to his work, not some "superhuman," as the term came to connote to many people.

The Task Management System

At Midvale Taylor was laying the foundations of what he preferred to call task management. An essential ingredient was time study and the development of a science of work; a second ingredient was the selection of workers who could meet those standards when motivated by the differential piece rate. But the system was yet incomplete and Taylor began to build further. Taylor defined management as "knowing exactly what you want men to do, and then seeing that they do it in the best and cheapest way." Taylor added that no concise definition could fully describe the art of management but that "the relations between employers and men form without question the most important part of this art."[25]

[23] *Shop Management*, p. 25.
[24] Copley (I), p. 183.
[25] *Shop Management*, p. 21.

He saw unevenness in the quality of management in the shop and challenged the assumption that if you hired the right person the methods would take care of themselves. Management had the explicit responsibility to design the work system so that the greatest productivity was possible rather than relying upon the offering of incentives to induce people to produce more.

Recognizing that his work system depended upon careful advance planning, he developed the concept of "task management," a term he preferred over its later designation as "scientific management." Task management consisted of two parts: (1) each worker each day was given a definite task with detailed written instructions and an exact time allowance for each element of the work; and (2) the worker who performed the task in the time allotted would receive extraordinarily high wages while ordinary wages would go to those who took more time than allotted. The task was based upon detailed time study, and methods, tools, and materials were standardized. Once the tasks were defined and assigned to first-class individuals, the total work system had to be organized. An immediate problem of organization was the pressure that task management placed on the manager to minutely plan the work and guide it toward completion. To cope with this increasing complexity in managing, Taylor developed a unique form of supervision called "functional foremen." Taylor specified nine qualities that made up a "well-rounded" foreman:

Brains;
Education;
Special or technical knowledge; manual dexterity or strength;
Tact;
Energy;
Grit;
Honesty;
Judgment or common sense; and
Good health. [26]

Taylor thought that to find a man with three of these traits was not too difficult; with five or six, more difficult, but with seven or eight almost impossible. This led him to abandon the military type of line organization of a single boss and to develop

[26] Ibid., p. 96.

his functional foreman concept, for he hypothesized that not all foremen's duties required all these traits.[27] By specializing the foreman's job, physical and mental demands on the incumbent would be accordingly reduced. Initially, Taylor employed assistants to prepare instruction cards and perform other detailed tasks for Taylor as foreman. As his system evolved, he gave more and more responsibility to these men by further segregating the functions and delegating them. The result was a new organizational technique of functionalism rather than the previously typical hierarchical "military" arrangement. The typical manager of that day was not much of a planner; layout largely dictated planning; no one had developed task planning to the degree that Taylor had. Taylor's new style began with a distinction between the planning of work and its performance, a notable advance for the times. The "foremen," a rather misleading term because each was little more than a specialized clerk, were given final responsibility over some aspect of the work, thus negating the military hierarchy of one boss for the workers.

Taylor divided the responsibility into two major areas, performance duties and planning duties. In the performance segment of supervisory responsibilities, the "gang boss" had charge of all work up to the time that the piece was placed in the machine; the "speed boss" began his work when the material was in the machine and he determined the tools, the cut, and machine speed; the "inspector" was responsible for quality of work; and the "repair boss" was in charge of care and maintenance of the machinery. In the planning department, the "order of work route clerk" determined the flow of the work and the exact order of work by each class of men and machines; the "instruction card clerk" furnished written information on tools, materials, the piece rate and premium, and other operating instructions; the "time and cost clerk" sent the time ticket for recording times taken and costs in-

---

[27]Whiting has found that Taylor's concept of the functional foremen was also used as early as 1884 by John Richards, owner and manager of the San Francisco Tool Company. Richards, apparently also having difficulty in finding well-rounded foremen, created five separate functional areas in the shop with one man in charge of each. Richard J. Whiting, "John Richards—California Pioneer of Management Thought," *California Management Review*, Vol. 6, No. 2 (Winter, 1963), p. 37.

curred and insured the return of this data; the "shop disciplinarian" kept a record of each man's "virtues and defects,"
served as a "peacemaker," and performed the employment function of selecting and discharging employees.

The functional foreman concept (Figure 6-1) was an expediency; it provided a shop with supervision in a relatively short
time versus the long-range search for and development of well-
rounded managers. Taylor saw no conflict in his system with the
unity-of-command idea of the military. To him, *knowledge* must
prevail; orders were given to workers on the basis of the specialized knowledge of the clerk or boss and not on the basis of the authority inherent in the position. Hence there was no conflict since
each man had only one boss on any one particular aspect of his
job, such as speed of machine, repairs, etc. With his general objectives of harmony and mutuality of interests between workers
and management, Taylor foresaw that the spirit of cooperation
would obviate any inherent conflicts under the functional arrangement. Training of bosses would be easier since each had to learn
only limited duties. Evidently Taylor was encountering a problem
seen frequently in the earlier factories, the shortage of management talent.

Taylor had little difficulty in selling his functional principle to

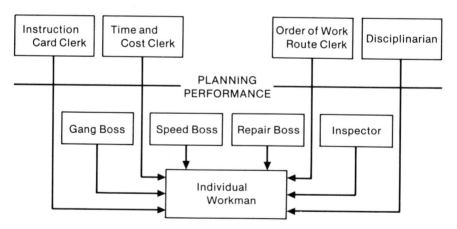

**Fig. 6-1.   Taylor's functional foremen. (Adapted from Frank B.
and Lillian M. Gilbreth, *Applied Motion Study*, New York: Sturgis
and Walton Co., 1917.)**

the workers; the bosses, however, resisted the system because it contracted their authority and range of activities.[28] Taylor did not specify that *one person* had to be in charge of each function; in smaller units, one person might perform all of the planning tasks or some other grouping of duties. Taylor's purpose was to focus specialized management knowledge on the work. As his concept has evolved to the present, this is now done by *functional authority* over a task, not over the worker, and without circumventing the supervisor. Taylor's functional foreman concept never became widespread in practice and its failures did not arise from confusion of workers or a violation of unity of command but from the recognition that it failed to develop well-rounded managers who could cope with a variety of shop problems through the use of staff assistants. In essence, functionalization was an attempt at decentralization, intending to strip authority from the general manager to place it in the hands of specialized lower-level managers.

This early attempt at decentralization of authority was designed to bring about a shift in the duties of the general manager. As a corollary to this redefinition, Taylor developed a special role for the general works manager. This person was to avoid the minutiae of shop management, leaving that to specialists, and concern himself only with "exceptions." The "exception principle" was one of Taylor's more important contributions:

> *Under it the manager should receive only condensed, summarized, and* invariably *comparative reports, covering . . . all of the exceptions to past averages or to the standards . . . both the especially good and especially bad exceptions . . . leaving him free to consider broader lines of policy and to study the character and fitness of the important men under him.*[29]

For Taylor all authority was based on knowledge, not position, and the exception principle enabled a check on who was and who was not meeting his delegated responsibility.

Onward and Upward

The years at Midvale had been full ones; his fulltime duties and

---

[28]Copley (I), p. 292.

[29]*Shop Management*, p. 126. Copyright 1947, Harper and Row; by permission.

meteoric rise on his job, teaming up with Clark to win the U.S. Amateur doubles tennis championship in 1881, the M.E. degree from Stevens Institute in 1883, marriage in 1884, scientific studies of the art of cutting metals and machine belting, and the essentials of task management all yielded a busy 12 years for Taylor. In 1890 he left Midvale to become general manager of the Manufacturing Investment Company, a converter of wood products into paper fiber. Perceiving a need for a new profession of a consulting engineer for management, he left his job at Manufacturing Investment Company and set up his own practice, which lasted from 1893 to 1901.

One of Taylor's early clients was the Steel Motor Company (Johnstown, Pa.), a division of the Johnson Company. To prepare himself for his consulting work, Taylor had paid William D. Basley, a public accountant who had many years of experience in railroad accounting, to tutor him. It was from Basley that Taylor learned of the accounting and reporting methods pioneered by McCallum and Fink, who were discussed earlier. For the Steel Motor Company, Taylor developed a system of cost accounts for material purchases, inventories, and issuance of stores. Taylor also devised a "routing" or assembly chart showing how all of the parts were brought together to form the electrical motor.[30] The men who hired Taylor were Tom L. Johnson, the firm's founder; A. J. Moxham, who would later become an executive with the DuPont Company; and Coleman DuPont. When Pierre DuPont wanted a cost accounting system for the DuPont Powder Company, it was Moxham who brought Taylor's system to that organization.[31]

Another of Taylor's clients was the Simond's Rolling Machine Company, where he conducted his experiments in the manufacture of bicycle ball bearings. In the finishing room, 120 women inspected the final product for flaws, a most tedious job for 10½

[30] Michael Massouh, "Technological and Managerial Innovation: The Johnson Company, 1883–1889," *Business History Review*, Vol. 50, No. 1 (Spring, 1976), pp. 66–67.

[31] H. Thomas Johnson, "Management Accounting in an Early Integrated Industrial: E. I. Dupont De Nemours Powder Company, 1903–1912," *Business History Review*, Vol. 49, No. 2 (Summer, 1975), p. 194.

hours per day. Over a period of time, Taylor began to improve the selection of the women, shortened the work day gradually to 8½ hours, introduced morning and afternoon rest periods, and put them on piece work. The interaction of the variables in the situation were complex and it would be impossible to fix causes and results. However, the outcome was that 35 women did the work of 120, accuracy improved by two-thirds, productivity increased from 5 million to 17 million bearings per month, wages were averaging 80 to 100 percent more than formerly, and "each girl was made to feel that she was the object of especial care and interest on the part of management."[32]

Taylor at Bethlehem

The Bethlehem Steel Company maintained its main plant in Lehigh, Pennsylvania, a community largely composed of Pennsylvania Dutch. It was to this environment that Taylor as a consultant brought his methods in 1893, developed with Maunsel White a self-hardening steel for machine tools, and continued to build his philosophy of task management. Taylor came to Bethlehem largely at the instigation of the entrepreneur Joseph Wharton, founder of the first school of business, who owned one-quarter of Bethlehem's stock. Bethlehem's management was in poor shape, since promotions were made and positions held because of influence rather than ability. Taylor's early attempts to install his methods met immediate resistance from management, although he early earned the nickname of "Speedy" Taylor from the workers. For assistance, Taylor called in loyal lieutenants such as Dwight V. Merrick, who became in later years a leading authority on time study, and Henry L. Gantt, who had worked with him at Midvale. Taylor never felt that Gantt fully grasped the underlying philosophy of his system; however, he respected Gantt's abilities and knew that he at least understood how to implement Taylor's methods. Pur-

---

[32] Taylor, *Principles*, pp. 95–96. This comment leads to the possible conclusion that Taylor, not Mayo, discovered what came to be known as the "Hawthorne effect," i.e., that concern for and attention to the worker by the experimenter led to a substantial increase in productivity.

suing his metal-cutting experiments jointly with installing his management system at Bethlehem, Taylor also called in Carl Barth, a mathematical genius, to help him with his research. Taylor's relations with Barth, as with Gantt, were often less than genial. Taylor hired Gantt and Barth not because of compatibility, but because they had the skills he needed. The outcome was mutual respect but not always mutual agreement. While Barth was developing a slide rule to solve the complex equations involved in handling the multitude of variables in cutting metals, Taylor was proceeding to systematize the utilization of yard labor at the mill.

The yard gang, consisting of 400 to 600 men, depending upon the season, was engaged in unloading raw materials of ore, limestone, sand, etc. from incoming rail cars as well as loading finished products on rail cars for shipment. The workers were all paid basically the same wage of $1.15 per day and the foremen were workers promoted from the ranks. Taylor was challenged when informed that these men were "slow and phlegmatic, and that nothing would induce them to work fast."[33] Taylor attacked the pig iron handling by a gang of 75 men first. It was a simple job in which the worker picked up a "pig" of iron weighing 92 pounds, walked up an inclined plank, and placed the pig in the car for shipment. Taylor felt that here was a good chance to show that his methods could be applied to even the simplest task. At Midvale, he had set out to discover some "law of fatigue" which would determine how much rest a worker needed when performing arduous manual tasks; he failed at Midvale, but tried with the help of Barth to find the law at Bethlehem. Barth was doubtful and amused at Taylor's ideas, but he went along, perhaps to escape the intense wrath of Taylor. Using his slide rule, Barth found that the pig iron handler could work under a heavy load only 42 percent of the day and that 58 percent of the day must be spent "free of load" or not actually toting pigs. Before Taylor undertook to apply his system, the handlers were loading on the cars an average of twelve and a half long tons of pig iron per man per day. After analyzing his data, Taylor concluded that a man *should* be able to load 47 to 48 long tons per day with no greater fatigue due to the

---

[33]*Shop Management,* p. 47.

rest pauses.[34] He contrived an incentive piece rate which would enable the worker to earn about 60 percent more, or $1.85 per day, if he met the standard of 47½ tons per day.

To institute his new method, Taylor had to select his first-class man. He chose a physically fit Dutchman who placed a high value on a dollar. "A penny looks about the size of a cart-wheel to him," was the comment of one worker. Taylor chose to call the man "Schmidt" (his real name was Henry Knolle and he stood 5 feet 7 inches and weighed 135 pounds). Taylor challenged "Schmidt" to be a "high priced man" (i.e., earn $1.85 per day) and admonished him to follow the prescribed methods.[35] Schmidt took the offer and succeeded at the task. As Schmidt continued to earn his high pay, the resistance of the other workers began to fade like the tan from a winter vacation. They gradually came around to Taylor asking to be shown the new method to earn the $1.85 per day. Only about one man in four proved to be a first-class man and Taylor pruned the yard gang accordingly; to those who protested the displacement of the remainder, Taylor indicated they were shifted to other company jobs for which they were better suited and then went on to earn higher wages.

Taylor had his critics for his handling of Schmidt. A young Socialist named Upton Sinclair wrote the editor of *The American Magazine* to protest "that he [Taylor] gave about a 61% increase in wages, and got a 362% increase in work."[36] Sinclair protested that

[34]*Principles,* pp. 60–61. Taylor furnished proof for the mathematically skeptical. Forty-seven and one-half long tons (one long ton = 2,240 pounds) at 92 pounds per pig = 1156 pigs per day. Forty-two percent of the day "under load" = 252 working minutes ÷ 1156 pigs = 0.22 minutes per pig. The pigs were moved an average distance of 36 feet. Therefore, 36 feet in 0.22 minutes (13.2 seconds) means that while *under load* the worker was traveling at a rate of 1.84 m.p.h. (normal walking pace is about 4 m.p.h.).

[35]*Principles,* pp. 44–47. There is a wide variance between earlier reports of this episode and later versions. In *Shop Management* (1903), the incident is scantily mentioned; in *Principles* (1911) it receives a detailed treatment. Wrege and Perroni believe that the conversation reported in *Principles* is entirely fictional. They do note, however, that Taylor must not be responsible for the "fiction" since notes were added to the original manuscript in the handwriting of someone other than Taylor. Charles D. Wrege and Amadeo G. Perroni, "Taylor's Pig-Tale: A Historical Analysis of Frederick W. Taylor's Pig-Iron Experiments," *Academy of Management Journal,* Vol. 17, No. 1 (March, 1974), pp. 6–26.

[36]February 24, 1911, cited by Copley (II), pp. 50–51.

this was exploitation and that the solution was for the workers to "take possession of the instrument and means of production" in order to get full value for their effort. In his response to Sinclair, Taylor put forth his philosophy of scientific management, saying that Sinclair's sympathies were inappropriately focused and that he overlooked the larger benefits of the system. Schmidt earned more with no greater effort because he had been taught *how.* The *method* enabled greater productivity and it was not exploitation or speeding up the worker but improvement in the *method* which freed the worker from wasteful efforts. Hence Schmidt's added earnings were for working no harder. Taylor's defense was a larger societal view that *all* benefited, the worker by receiving higher wages with no greater expenditure of effort, management by having greater profits, and the consumer by paying lower prices for products. The worker earned more because someone else taught him how and established the proper procedures. The primary concern for Taylor was the total benefits derived for all people, worker, employer, and consumer.[37] Taylor did not feel that he had done Schmidt an injustice, and the eagerness of other workers to become "high priced men" seemed to bear this out.[38]

Taylor also encountered opposition from management and from the citizens of the city of Bethlehem. The owners saw that the work force could be cut to about one-fourth its previous level if Taylor had his way. As Taylor told it:

> They [the owners] did not wish me, as they said, to depopulate South Bethlehem. They owned all the houses in South Bethlehem and the company stores, and when they saw we were cutting the labor force down to about one fourth, they did not want it . . . I said: You are going to have it . . . You employed me with the distinct understanding that is what I was going to do . . . [they responded] Well, we did not think you could do it.[39]

Taylor continued to clash with Bethlehem management and it was

[37]The complete response is quite lengthy and may be found in Copley (II), pp. 51–55; and also in *Principles*, pp. 136–140.

[38]Rumors in 1911 that Schmidt died as a result of working for Taylor were completely refuted; a physician testified that, at age 44, Schmidt was still in good physical condition and working 10 to 12 hours per day. Copley (II), p. 55.

[39]Copley (II), p. 46.

only the strong influence of Joseph Wharton that kept him in his position as long as he stayed.

Another part of Taylor's work at Bethlehem earned him the further animosity of management. Taylor introduced a cost accounting system and referred to it as "in general the modern railroad system of accounting adapted and modified to suit the manufacturing business."[40] This was the accounting system in which Taylor had been tutored and which he had installed at the Steel Motor Company earlier in his career. Taylor's system called for a rigorous classification of costs and the reporting procedures clearly reflected his exception principle. His thinking had an impact on the accounting profession by stimulating interest in costs. Taylor abhorred the futility of *post-mortem* accounting which gave the manager annual, semiannual, or monthly reports, considering these as being too late for managerial action. He moved the cost accounting function to his planning department and thereby generated his cost reports coincident with daily operations reports. Costs then became an integral part of daily planning and control, not a subject for analysis after a long period of time had passed. The system was effective, in fact so effective that management tried to throw the system out. Apparently Bethlehem management did not like such an accurate appraisal of their performance.

Taylor eventually lost the struggle with Bethlehem's management and left the company in 1901 despite entreaties from Wharton. In that same year, Bethlehem was sold to Charles M. Schwab, a Carnegie protégé, who ordered the Taylor system abandoned. As production fell afterward, some lower-level supervisors returned to Taylor's ideas, deceived Schwab by saying their practices were not based on Taylorism, and succeeded in restoring productivity.[41]

Taylor: The Peripatetic Philosopher

In 1901, Taylor moved his wife and three newly adopted children

[40] Ibid., p. 364.

[41] Copley (II), pp. 159–163. Based on a letter from Taylor to General William Crozier.

from Bethlehem to face a new world. Financially assured by his patents and his savings from past earnings, Taylor turned to the task of articulating his system in print and lectures.[42] A man of action and clearly uncomfortable at the demands of a desk and pen, he began the preparation of *Shop Management*, which appeared in 1903. About him Taylor witnessed various adoptions of his system; among the more notable was the work of James Mapes Dodge at the Link-Belt Company and that of Wilfred Lewis at the Tabor Company, a manufacturer of molding machines. Other conversions to the Taylor system were occurring steadily and must have brought some pride to the post-Bethlehem Taylor. During these years Taylor was not connected with any particular firm. In his spare time, he landscaped and renovated Boxly (near Philadelphia) as the new family home, developed new mixtures for soils for better golf greens, thoroughly investigated the best grasses for them, and set out to design some new concepts in golf clubs. He developed a putter with a "Y" shaft, experimented with lengths and thicknesses of shafts, and spent a great deal of time in practice on the links, or more euphemistically "experimentation."[42]

In 1906, Taylor became president of the prestigious American Society of Mechanical Engineers. His fame was spreading and those who were to spread the Taylor gospel were gathering. Henri Le Chatelier, Horace K. Hathaway, Morris L. Cooke, Sanford E. Thompson, Frank Gilbreth, and others were joining the earlier apostles, Gantt and Barth. Asked to teach a course at Harvard in the area which was to become the Graduate School of Business Administration (1908), Taylor refused, saying that his system could be learned only in the shop. Professor Edwin Gay, soon to be dean of the school, told Taylor that the course on scientific management would be taught with or without him, period. Taylor succumbed, though he was never entirely happy about teaching his system in a classroom. Taylor was not antibusiness education but felt that experience was the only way to learn his own particular system.

[42] Kakar concludes that this step in Taylor's life was a reaction to his perceived failure at Bethlehem Steel and was a typical reaction in terms of a person's life cycle. That is, a striving to overcome the depression of failure, a turning from "work to good works," and an attempt to prove his self-worth. Kakar, pp. 162–166.

Although he detested travel, he began to travel widely and lectured to a variety of groups. His lectures on "Success" at the University of Illinois in 1909 capsulized his views on business education:

> *I have selected some ten or fifteen instances . . . illustrating the all important fact that the ordinary qualities of common sense, character, grit, endurance, etc., count far more in attaining success than book learning or intellectual attainments.*[43]

Taylor's Harvard lectures began in 1909 and were given each winter through 1914. An interesting, though not polished speaker nor writer, he illustrated his material with anecdotes, punctuated them with curse words from his early mill worker days, and must have appeared as quite dramatic within the staid ivy-covered walls. For all his lectures, Taylor never accepted a penny of reimbursement, not even for traveling expenses. Likewise, he refused payment for the years of consulting he did in the Navy shipyards at Brooklyn and in the Army's Ordnance Department.

The Eastern Rate Case

Taylor also found his system getting some extraordinary free publicity. The Boston lawyer Louis D. Brandeis was becoming noted in the early twentieth century as "the people's lawyer." In 1910, when the Eastern railroads asked the Interstate Commerce Commission for an increase in freight rates, Brandeis took up the cause of the shippers and brought about an unusual series of hearings which thrust Taylor's task management into the public eye. At a loss for a name to apply to the Taylor system, Brandeis, Gilbreth, Gantt, and several other engineers met at Gantt's New York apartment to discuss the matter. Brandeis noted that Taylor frequently used the phrase "scientific" in his work: the others agreed with Brandeis and "scientific management" was the outcome. Brandeis's argument before the Interstate Commerce Commission was based on the inefficiency of railroad management and his proposition was that no rate increase would be necessary if the railroads applied scientific management. Proof of his case was a parade of witnesses who testified to the efficiencies to be gained; James M.

[43] Copley (II), p. 294.

Dodge, H. K. Hathaway, Henry R. Towne, and Harrington Emerson were some of the proponents of adopting more efficient management methods based on the Taylor principles. Taylor accepted the Brandeis-coined phrase "scientific management," but with reluctance, fearing that it sounded too "academic." The phrase caught on with the press, however, and Taylor gained a place in the public spotlight. The hearings, with the decision going against the railroads, concluded that it was too early to judge the merits of the new management system; nevertheless, the publicity furnished an impetus to Taylor's ideas that had both desirable and undesirable characteristics. Harrington Emerson's testimony that the railroads could save a million dollars a day by applying scientific management had great appeal to cost-conscious manufacturers and to the public. On the other hand, organized labor, especially the entrenched railway brotherhoods, were rising up to protest the introduction of these methods. For management to admit to using scientific management was to invite labor trouble.

Watertown and the Congressional Investigation

The railroad hearings brought publicity but had some unusual repercussions. As noted above, Taylor was serving to bring his system to improve the efficiency of governmental units, especially the Brooklyn Navy Yards and the Army Ordnance Department. Taylor had failed in bringing more efficiency to the Navy Yards and received a few verbal bruises from the naval bureaucracy as his reward. At the head of the Army Ordnance Department was General William Crozier, who had read Taylor's work and saw its applicability to Army arsenals. Crozier chose as test plants the arsenals at Watertown, Massachusetts, and Rock Island, Illinois. The time studies and other procedures were going smoothly at Watertown but trouble was brewing elsewhere. At Rock Island, a representative of the International Association of Machinists appeared to agitate the workers against time studies. The national union offices took up the fight against Taylorism in all government offices and sought to resist its introduction in other enterprises. As early as 1911, organized labor began to wage an all-out war on Taylorism. At this time, public interest in scientific management was at its height due to the hearings on railroad rates.

Taylor wrote to Crozier to install the system at Watertown carefully, step by step, despite the resistance at Rock Island, including sounding out the sentiments of the workers in each department before the beginning the time study. Dwight Merrick was doing the study and attempted to begin an analysis of the molders at Watertown. One of the molders refused, citing "the organization" (the union) as the reason for his refusal; he was fired, and in August of 1911 the first strike under Taylorism occurred at the Watertown Arsenal. Taylor attributed the whole problem to a mistake in tactics; the sentiments of the molders had not been examined nor had they been briefed on the purposes of the time study. Taylor did not blame the union but thought the cause was a premature attempt to make the study without following his recommended technique of consulting the workers first.[44] However, the agitation continued, and it was represented to Congress that the Watertown strike was due to unsatisfactory treatment of labor due to the introduction of the Taylor system. As a consequence, the House appointed a special committee to investigate. It consisted of three men, William B. Wilson, a former official of the United Mine Workers, then chairman of the House Labor Committee, and later secretary of labor under President Wilson; William C. Redfield, a manufacturer who later became secretary of commerce under Wilson; and John Q. Tilson, the only Republican member, as an umpire.

The hearings began in October, 1911, and ended in February, 1912. Taylor spent twelve hours scattered over four days in the witness chair. As Copley stated, "terrorism was in the air" as the unions set out to harass Taylor. From the testimony one can see the hostility and sharpness in the questions and answers. For example, this clash ensued over "the first-class man" with the Honorable Mr. Wilson, the labor man, presiding. (Previous to this tes-

[44]Milton J. Nadworny, *Scientific Management and the Unions: 1900–1923*, Cambridge, Mass.: Harvard University Press, 1955, p. 80, agrees that the workers were not objecting to the time studies and the production bonus but to the *method* of introducing the system.

timony, there were some questions and discussion on the effect of scientific management on worker displacement.).

The Chairman. Is it not true that a man who is not a good workman and who may not be responsible for the fact that he is not a good workman, has to live as well as the man who is a good workman?

Mr. Taylor. Not as well as the other workman; otherwise, that would imply that all those in the world were entitled to live equally well whether they worked or whether they were idle, and that certainly is not the case. Not as well.

The Chairman. Under scientific management, then, you propose that because a man is not in the first class as a workman that there is no place in the world for him—if he is not in the first class in some particular line that this must be destroyed and removed?

Mr. Taylor. Mr. Chairman, would it not be well for me to describe what I mean by a "first-class" workman. I have written a good deal about "first-class" workmen in my books, and I find there is quite a general misapprehension as to the use of that term "first-class."

The Chairman. Before you come to a definition of what you consider a first-class workman I would like to have your concept of how you are going to take care, under your scientific management, of a man who is not a first-class workman in some particular line?

Mr. Taylor. I cannot answer that question until I define what I mean by "first-class." You and I may have a totally different idea as to the meaning of these words, and therefore I suggest that you allow me to state what I mean.

The Chairman. The very fact that you specify "first-class" would indicate that in your mind you would have some other class than "first-class."

Mr. Taylor. If you will allow me to define it I think I can make it clear.

The Chairman. You said a "first-class" workman can be taken care of under normal conditions. That is what you have already said. Now, the other class that is in your mind, other than "first-class," how does your system propose to take care of them?

Mr. Taylor. Mr. Chairman, I cannot answer that question. I cannot answer any question relating to "first-class" workmen until you know my definition of that term, because I have used these words technically *throughout my paper, and I am not willing to answer a question you put about "first-class" workmen with the assumption that my answer applies to all I have said in my book.*

The Chairman. *You yourself injected the term "first-class" by saying that you did not know of a condition in normal times when a "first-class" workman could not find employment.*

Mr. Taylor. *I do not think I used that term "first-class."*

Mr. Redfield. *Mr. Chairman, the witness has now four times, I think, said that until he is allowed to define what he means by 'first-class" no answer can be given, because he means one thing by the words "first-class" and he thinks that you mean another thing.*

The Chairman. *My question has nothing whatever to do with the definition of the words "first-class." It has to do with the other class than "first-class" not with "first-class." A definition of first-class will in no manner contribute to a proper reply to my question, because I am not asking about "first-class," but the other than "first-class" workmen.*

Mr. Taylor. *I cannot describe the others until I have described what I mean by "first-class."*

Mr. Redfield. *As I was saying when I was interrupted, the witness had stated that he cannot answer the question for the reason that the language that the chairman uses, namely, the words "first-class" do not mean the same thing in the Chairman's mind that they mean in the witness's mind, and he asks the privilege of defining what they do mean, so that the language shall be mutually intelligible. Now, it seems to me, and I think it is good law and entirely proper, that the witness ought to be permitted to define his meaning and then if, after his definition is made, there is any misunderstanding, we can proceed.*[45]

Then the chairman, Mr. Redfield, and Mr. Tilson engaged in spirited discussion of whether or not Taylor should be allowed to define his terms; Redfield and Tilson prevailed and Taylor proceeded to his ideas of a first-class man and concluded:

. . . among every class of workmen we have some balky workmen—I do not mean men who are unable to work, but men who, physically well able to work, are simply lazy, and who through no amount of teaching and instructing and through no amount of kindly treatment,

[45]*Hearings,* pp. 1452–1453.

can be brought into the "first-class." That is the man whom I call "sec-ond-class." They have the physical possibility of being "first-class," but they obstinately refuse to do so.

Now, Mr. Chairman, I am ready to answer your question, having clearly in mind that I have these two types of "second-class" men in view; the one which is physically able to do the work, but who refused to do it—and the other who is not physically or mentally fitted to do that particular job. These are the two types of "second-class" men.

The Chairman.   *Then, how does scientific management propose to take care of men who are not "first-class" men in any particular line of work?*

Mr. Taylor.   *I give it up.*

The Chairman.   *Scientific management has no place for such men?*

Mr. Taylor.   *Scientific management has no use for a bird that can sing and won't sing.*

The Chairman.   *I am not speaking about birds at all.*

Mr. Taylor.   *No man who can work and won't work has any place under scientific management.*

The Chairman.   *It is not a question of a man "who can work and won't work" it is a question of a man who is not a "first-class" man in any one particular line, according to your own definition.*

Mr. Taylor.   *I do not know of any such line of work. For each man some line can be found in which he is first-class.*[46]

In another instance, Taylor was being questioned by Mr. John R. O'Leary (third vice president of the International Molder's Unions of North America) on the fines he had levied on workers at Midvale Steel:

Mr. O'Leary.   *Did I understand you to say that you had the permis-sion and cooperation of the men in putting in that system?*

Mr. Taylor.   *Yes . . . they ran it, invested the funds, took care of the sick; they furnished the doctor and nurse . . .*

Mr. O'Leary.   *What did they charge the men who were injured, for the Doctor?*

Mr. Taylor.   *Not a cent. The services were all free.*

Mr. O'Leary.   *Are you aware that there have been many suits insti-*

[46]Ibid., pp. 1455–1456

tuted against the Midvale Steel Co. to recover those fines, and that they were recovered?

Mr. Taylor.   No; I am not aware of it.

Mr. O'Leary.   Are you aware that men are fined a dollar for going to the urinal?

Mr. Taylor.   I have not the slightest idea that is true. Who ever said that told an untruth. Nothing of that kind was done while I was there.[47]

No support for O'Leary's charges ever appeared in any other testimony.

As Ida M. Tarbell, the muckraker of the Standard Oil days, declared:

> One of the most sportsmanlike exhibits the country ever saw was Mr. Taylor's willingness to subject himself to the heckling and the badgering of labor leaders, congressmen, and investigators of all degrees of misunderstanding, suspicion and ill will. To a man of his temperament and highly trained intellect, who had given a quarter of a century of the hardest kind of toil to develop useful truths, the kind of questioning to which he was sometimes subjected must have been maddening.[48]

From Miss Tarbell, this was quite a compliment. Baited, insulted, and made to appear a beast, Taylor staggered from the stand at the close of his testimony. Taylor's pride was sorely wounded, his life work reviled before a congressional committee. There was no victory for anyone in the final report of the committee. Phrased in good political double talk, the report said that it was too early "to determine with accuracy their [Taylor's and other scientific management systems] effect on the health and pay of employees and their effect on wages and labor cost."[49] The committee found no evidence to support abuses of workers nor any need for remedial legislation. It did refer to possible abuses, perhaps as a bone for opponents, but presented no evidence that they had occurred.

---

[47] *Ibid.*, pp. 745–746.

[48] *New Ideals in Business*, p. 315, cited by Copley (II), p. 347.

[49] *Hearings*, p. 1930.

Despite the recommendation that no legislation was needed, prolabor forces began introducing riders to appropriation bills specifying that no part of the Taylor system could be used under operating funds granted by that bill. In considering appropriation bills for the Army and Navy in 1914–1915, a heated debate occurred in the Senate. Among the anti-Taylor, prorider advocates was Henry Cabot Lodge, descendant of the early Massachusetts textile tycoons, who spoke of ending "the days of slavery" brought about by men such as Taylor who thought it "profitable to work the slaves to the last possible point and let them die."[50] Such demagoguery clearly indicated his ignorance of what Taylor was attempting. The rider failed in the Senate, but was restored in conference between the two Houses. After that, Congress after Congress continued to attach such riders to Army, Navy, and Post Office appropriation bills.[51] Taylorism and the attempt to bring efficiency to government agencies was clearly crippled.

The Mental Revolution

In the first decade of the twentieth century, great national concern was voiced by President Theodore Roosevelt and others over the depletion of America's resources. This national impetus exceeded a mere concern for natural resources to a much larger need for what the president called "national efficiency." Taylor, who had for almost three decades fought against the misuse of both physical and human resources, found himself as a result of the railroad hearings the man of the hour. Taylor wrote to meet that need for national efficiency in his *Principles of Scientific Management*, where he stated his objectives as:

First. *To point out, through a series of simple illustrations, the great loss which the whole country is suffering through inefficiency in almost all of our daily acts.*

[50] Copley (II), p. 351. Mary Barnett Gilson, an early employment counselor and later lecturer at the University of Chicago, called Senator Lodge an "exhibitionist" who tilted at windmills. M. B. Gilson, *What's Past is Prologue*, New York: Harper and Row, 1940, p. 55.

[51] Such antiscientific management legislation persisted until 1949 when time study and incentive bonus restrictions were removed from the statutes through the efforts of Senator Taft (Ohio) and Senator Flanders (Vermont). Nadworny, p. 103.

Second. *To try to convince the reader that the remedy for this inefficiency lies in systematic management, rather than in searching for some unusual or extraordinary man.*

Third. *To prove that the best management is a true science, resting upon clearly defined laws, rules, and principles, as a foundation. And further to show that the fundamental principles of scientific management are applicable to all kinds of human activities, from our simplest individual acts to the work of our great corporations, which call for the most elaborate cooperation.*[52]

"The principal object of management," said Taylor, "should be to secure the maximum prosperity for the employer, coupled with the maximum prosperity for each employee."[53] Taylor deplored short-run shortcuts which gave one side advantage over another; his mutuality of interests emphasized a long-term growth of both parties to insure prosperity for each. In *Principles*, Taylor was becoming a philosopher, looking beyond mere shop-level efficiency to show how scientific management, when applied to the lowest level, could then be generalized to bring about prosperity on the national or even international level. Taylor recognized that the "efficiency experts" were giving scientific management a black eye. He warned that "the mechanism of management must not be mistaken for its essence, or underlying philosophy."[54] This philosophy was based on a mutuality of interests and had four basic principles:

First. *The development of a true science.*

Second. *The scientific selection of the workman.*

Third. *His scientific education and development.*

Fourth. *Intimate friendly cooperation between the management and the men.*[55]

But neither these principles, nor any single part of Taylor's system, could be isolated as a major factor:

It is no single element, but rather this whole combination, that constitutes scientific management, which may be summarized:

[52]Taylor, *Principles*, p. 7. Copyright 1947, Harper and Row; by permission. This third point is a statement of the universality of scientific management but it does not necessarily hint at the same level of universality of management that will be seen later in the work of Henri Fayol.

[53]Ibid., p. 9.

[54]Ibid., p. 128.

[55]Ibid., p. 130. Copyright 1947, Harper and Row; by permission.

Science, not rule of thumb.

Harmony, not discord.

Cooperation, not individualism.

Maximum output, in place of restricted output.

The development of each man to his greatest efficiency and prosperity.[56]

A good many "efficiency experts" suddenly appeared in 1911 promising great cost reductions and improvements to those employers who would hire their services. Taylor deplored these experts, fearing, and properly so, that they promised quick panaceas without grasping the fundamental attitudes that had to be changed and the necessity of gaining acceptance and the step-by-step study, restudy, and installation of his methods. Taylor made a marked distinction between true scientific management and the efficiency craze; the difference was in a "mental revolution" on the part of the employer and the employee, something which came about from mutual respect over a period of time and not from the adoption of the mechanics of the system. At the hearings, Taylor tried to clarify first what scientific management was *not*, and then what it was:

Scientific management is not any efficiency device, not a device of any kind for securing efficiency; nor is it any bunch or group of efficiency devices. It is not a new system of figuring costs; it is not a new scheme of paying men; it is not a piecework system; it is not a bonus system; it is not a premium system; it is no scheme for paying men; it is not holding a stop watch on a man and writing things down about him; it is not time study; it is not motion study nor an analysis of the movements of men; it is not the printing and ruling and unloading of a ton or two of blanks on a set of men and saying, "Here's your system; go use it." It is not divided foremanship or functional foremanship; it is not any of the devices which the average man calls to mind when scientific management is spoken of. The average man thinks of one or more of these things when he hears the words "scientific management" mentioned, but scientific management is not any of these devices. I am not sneering at cost-keeping systems, at time study, at functional foremanship, nor at any new and improved scheme of pay-

---

[56]Ibid., p. 140. Copyright 1947, Harper and Row; by permission.

*ing men, nor at any efficiency devices, if they are really devices
that make for efficiency. I believe in them; but what I am emphasizing is that these devices in whole or in part are not scientific
management, they are useful adjuncts to scientific management,
so are they also useful adjuncts of other systems of management.*

*Now, in its essence, scientific management involves a complete
mental revolution on the part of the workingman engaged in any
particular establishment or industry—a complete mental revolution on the part of these men as to their duties toward their work,
toward their fellow men, and toward their employers. And it involves the equally complete mental revolution on the part of those
on the management's side—the foreman, the superintendent, the
owner of the business, the board of directors—a complete mental
revolution on their part as to their duties toward their fellow
workers in the management, toward their workmen, and toward
all of their daily problems. And without this complete mental revolution on both sides scientific management does not exist.*

*That is the essence of scientific management, this great mental
revolution.*[57]

What was the result of this mental revolution?

*The great revolution that takes place in the mental attitude of
the two parties under scientific management is that both sides take
their eyes off of the division of the surplus as the all-important
matter, and together turn their attention toward increasing the
size of the surplus until this surplus becomes so large that it is unnecessary to quarrel over how it shall be divided. They come to
see that when they stop pulling against one another, and instead
both turn and push shoulder to shoulder in the same direction, the
size of the surplus created by their joint efforts is truly as-
tounding. They both realize that when they substitute friendly cooperation and mutual helpfulness for antagonism and strife they
are together able to make this surplus so enormously greater than
it was in the past that there is ample room for a large increase in
wages for the workmen and an equally great increase in profits
for the manufacturer. This, gentlemen, is the beginning of the
great mental revolution which constitutes the first step toward
scientific management.*[58]

[57]*Hearings*, p. 1387.
[58] Ibid., pp. 1388–1389.

Taylor knew that his prime antagonists were the leaders of labor, not the laborers themselves, and was convinced of a conspiracy among union leaders to oppose his system. He made repeated offers to Samuel Gompers, president of the American Federation of Labor, to come and see plants using scientific management and to get the facts for himself; Mr. Gompers refused.[59] The same was true of John Mitchell of the mine workers. Taylor stuck with his early ideas that unions were fine in theory but lacked in practice any semblance of openness to improve the economic system. In Taylor's view, union philosophy and that of scientific management were directly antagonistic in that unions built and encouraged antagonisms setting the worker apart from management, while scientific management encouraged a mutuality of interests. To Gompers, "more, more, more" meant labor's gains came from the employer's pocket; for Taylor "more" came to both through improved productivity.

Taylor and the Human Factor

In answer to charges of the coldness and impersonality of scientific management and in rebuttal to omission of the human factor from his management equation, Taylor spoke on systems and men:

> No system can do away with the need of real men. Both system and good men are needed, and after introducing the best system, success will be in proportion to the ability, consistency, and respected authority of the management.[60]

On human relations:

> No system of management, however good, should be applied in a wooden way. The proper personal relations should always be maintained between the employers and men; and even the prej-

[59]Copley (II), pp. 403–404. In his testimony before the committee, Gompers categorically denied the existence of soldiering and labor resistance. *Hearings*, p. 27. Gompers' biographer, Philip Taft, has suggested that Gompers *himself* was not unalterably opposed to scientific management. According to Taft, Gompers yielded to the influence of the "socialist" president of the International Association of Machinists, William H. Johnston, because the Machinists were the largest and most powerful affiliate in the AFL. Philip Taft, *The A. F. of L. in the Time of Gompers*, New York: Harper and Row, 1957, pp. 299–300.

[60]*Shop Management*, p. 148.

udices of the workmen should be considered in dealing with them.

The employer who goes through his works with kid gloves on, and is never known to dirty his hands or clothes, and who either talks to his men in a condescending or patronizing way, or else not at all, has no chance whatever of ascertaining their real thoughts or feelings.

Above all is it desirable that men should be talked to on their own level by those who are over them. Each man should be encouraged to discuss any trouble which he may have, either in the works or outside, with those over him. Men would far rather even be blamed by their bosses, especially if the 'tearing out' has a touch of human nature and feeling in it, than to be passed by day after day without a word, and with no more notice than if they were part of the machinery.

The opportunity which each man should have of airing his mind freely, and having it out with his employers, is a safety-valve; and if the superintendents are reasonable men, and listen to and treat with respect what their men have to say, there is absolutely no reason for labor unions and strikes.

It is not the large charities (however generous they may be) that are needed or appreciated by workmen so much as small acts of personal kindness and sympathy, which establish a bond of friendly feeling between them and their employers.

The moral effect of this system on the men is marked. The feeling that substantial justice is being done them renders them on the whole much more manly, straightforward, and truthful. They work more cheerfully, and are more obliging to one another and their employers. They are not soured, as under the old system, by brooding over the injustice done them; and their spare minutes are not spent to the same extent in criticising their employers.[61]

On resistance to change:

Through generations of bitter experiences working men as a class have learned to look upon all change as antagonistic to their best interests. They do not ask the object of the change, but oppose it simply as change. The first changes, therefore, should be such as to allay the suspicions of the men and convince them by actual contact that the reforms are after all rather harmless and are only such as will ultimately be of benefit to all concerned.

[61] Ibid., pp. 184–185. Copyright 1947, Harper and Row; by permission.

> *Such improvements then as directly affect the workmen least should be started first. At the same time it must be remembered that the whole operation is of necessity so slow that the new system should be started at as many points as possible and constantly pushed as hard as possible.* [62]

Taylor stated that it took from two to five years to install his system fully. Scientific management was not an overnight panacea and required diligence and understanding when installations were attempted. Three weeks before his death, he spoke to the Cleveland Advertising Club:

> *Scientific management at every step has been an evolution, not a theory. In all cases the practice has preceded the theory . . . all the men that I know of who are connected with scientific management are ready to abandon any scheme, any theory, in favor of anything else that can be found which is better. There is nothing in scientific management that is fixed.* [63]

If there was a "one best way," Taylor in the twilight years knew from experience that it came after much experimentation and perhaps even then was not rigid but subject to further examination.

Worried by the declining health of his wife, bedeviled by the antagonism of organized labor, and frustrated by the efficiency experts who borrowed the techniques and forgot the philosophy, Taylor's last days were nigh. In a drafty drawing room of a rail car while returning from one of his speaking trips, he caught pneumonia. He died in the hospital one day after his fifty-ninth birthday. In a grave on a hill with a view of the steel smokestacks of Philadelphia, his epitaph reads "Frederick W. Taylor, Father of Scientific Management."

Summary

Frederick W. Taylor, the father of scientific management, and his associates represent the first age of synthesis in management thought. Management has been characterized as a process of fusing the physical resource or the technical facet of organizations with the human resource facet in order to achieve organizational

---

[62] Ibid., p. 137. Copyright 1947, Harper and Row; by permission.
[63] Copley (II), p. 348.

objectives. Prior to Taylor, no other person had developed to the same degree a systematic approach to management's problems and coupled it with a philosophical framework.

On the technique side, Taylor's scientific approach sought to analyze existing practices, study them for standardization and improvement, and rationalize resource utilization. On the human side, Taylor sought the highest degree of individual development and reward through fatigue reduction, scientific selection, matching men's abilities to jobs, and through incentive schemes. He did not neglect the human element, as is so often suggested, but stressed the individual and not the group side of people. Taylor's synthesis came through his call for a "mental revolution" which sought to fuse the interests of labor and management into a mutually rewarding whole.

7

Spreading the Gospel of Efficiency

Space and time rarely allow the full measure of a man and his work. This is true of Frederick W. Taylor and also applies to those who worked with and followed Taylor in propagating the scientific management movement. Taylor became the rallying point and this chapter will focus on six individuals who were prominent in the embryonic days of scientific management: Carl G. Barth, Henry L. Gantt, Frank and Lillian Gilbreth, Harrington Emerson, and Morris L. Cooke. These were the individuals who were in the vanguard in spreading the gospel of efficiency.

The Most Orthodox: Carl Barth

Of all the disciples in the vanguard of the scientific management movement, Carl Georg Lange Barth (1860–1939) was the most orthodox. Barth was recruited from his position as a mathematics teacher by Taylor at the suggestion of Wilfred Lewis for purposes of handling the complex mathematical problems in Taylor's metal-cutting experiments. Born in Norway, Barth was a stern man whose rimless glasses and close-cropped beard gave him a Teutonic professorial look. He was even more demanding than Taylor on standards and waste, to such an extent that Taylor pleaded with Barth to display more "tact." Barth joined Taylor at Bethlehem and his first assignment was to help Henry L. Gantt with the feed and speed problems which had plagued Taylor since Midvale. Barth's solution was "a combination of a crude or embryonic logarithmic slide rule and a set of tables" of formulae which allowed the instantaneous solution of any machine feed and speed problem. The operator, knowing the power of the machine and the cutting tool being used, could determine the proper rate at which the material to be processed could be fed into the machine and the proper speed of the lathe. Taylor credited Barth's "mathematical genius" for solving the variables and complexities of metal cutting.

When Taylor left Bethlehem at the urging of top management, Carl Barth went with him and assisted in the first installations of scientific management at the Tabor Manufacturing Company, the Link Belt Company, Fairbanks Scale, Yale and Towne, and later at the Watertown Arsenal. He also assisted George Babcock in installing scientific management in the Franklin Motor Car Company (1908–1912) and thus was a pioneer in the rationalization of that infant industry. Barth lectured on scientific management at Harvard (1911–16 and 1919–22) and was "exceedingly proud of being accused of being Mr. Taylor's most orthodox disciple."[1] He resisted any tampering with Taylor's precepts and later maintained that only those who had worked directly with Taylor, such as himself, were the "direct disciples" who fully understood the task management system.[2] Carl Barth's contribution to management thought was confined to his faithful execution of Taylor's precepts; his slide rule was unique and helpful but was confined to a narrow aspect of the whole philosophy of scientific management. It was the work of others that would lead to more unique derivations in the gospel of efficiency.

The Most Unorthodox:
H. L. Gantt

Henry Laurence Gantt (1861–1919) was born into a prosperous Maryland farm family and, when the Civil War left the family destitute, Gantt learned at an early age the demands of hard work, frugal living, and the self-discipline required to make one's way

[1] Carl G. Barth, "Discussion," *Transactions of the A.S.M.E.*, Vol. XXXIV (1912), p. 1204.

[2] Carl G. Barth, "Discussion," *Bulletin of the Taylor Society*, (September, 1920), p. 149.

in the world.[3] Graduating with distinction from Johns Hopkins in 1880, he became a teacher of natural science and mechanics at his old prep school, McDonagh (1880–1883). He returned to college at the Stevens Institute of Technology, gained his degree as a mechanical engineer in 1884, became a draftsman for an engineering firm, returned to his teaching post at McDonagh during 1886–1887, and then joined the Midvale Steel Company in 1887 as an assistant in the Engineering Department. It was here that the then 26-year-old Gantt met and began to work with a man who would have a significant influence on his future career, F. W. Taylor. Taylor and Gantt were an unusual team; they had mutual interests in their quest for science in management and developed a deep mutual admiration for each other's work. Gantt, however, was more cautious than Taylor in approaching problems, a sign interpreted by Taylor as pussyfooting. Gantt was also prone to severe headaches and to outbursts of irritation throughout his entire life. However, he grasped the essence of Taylor's work and, though they clashed at times, became a prime disciple of Taylor. Working closely with Taylor at Midvale, following him to the Simond's Rolling Machine Company to become superintendent, and joining him again at Bethlehem Steel, Gantt's early years and work were closely related to Taylor's. After 1901, however, he became a consulting industrial engineer on his own and, although he espoused the views of scientific management, his later years saw the development of a different Gantt. During his lifetime he published over 150 titles, including three major books, made numerous presentations before the A.S.M.E. (becoming vice-president of that group in 1914), patented more than a dozen inventions, lectured at Stevens, Columbia, Harvard, and Yale, and became one of the first successful management consultants.[4]

The Task and Bonus System

Gantt's ideas were largely influenced by Taylor, and the same el-

[3] Biographical data on Gantt is from L. P. Alford, *Henry L. Gantt: Leader in Industry*, prepared originally as a memorial volume for the A.S.M.E. and later published by Harper and Row (New York), 1934.

[4] A complete bibliography of Gantt's work may be found in Alford. Much of Gantt's work is reprinted in a subject heading format by Alex W. Rathe, *Gantt on Management*, New York: American Management Association, 1961.

ements appear in his early writings. The stress on the mutuality of interests between labor and management, the scientific selection of workmen, the incentive rate to stimulate performance, detailed instructions on work, and all of the other familiar concepts are reflected in Gantt's work. Gantt also sought the efficient utilization of labor through scientific investigation and "harmonious cooperation" between labor and management. In his words:

> ... the only healthy industrial condition is that in which the employer has the best men obtainable for his work, and the workman feels that his labor is being sold at the highest market price.[5]

On this road to high wages and low costs, Gantt saw some different possibilities for incentive systems. His view on unions paralleled that of Taylor but he was more persuasive and philosophical in stating the issue:

> If the amount of wealth in the world were fixed, the struggle for the possession of that wealth would necessarily cause antagonism; but, inasmuch as the amount of wealth is not fixed, but constantly increasing, the fact that one man has become wealthy does not necessarily mean that someone else has become poorer, but may mean quite the reverse, especially if the first is a producer of wealth. . . . As long . . . as one party—no matter which—tries to get all it can of the new wealth, regardless of the rights of the other, conflicts will continue.[6]

The "more, more, more" of organized labor hence became an antagonistic force unless it cooperated in producing more for the benefit of the other party to the transaction, management, and vice versa. Gantt was not convinced that the differential piece rate of Taylor was adequate to the task of bringing this desired cooperation to the operative workers. Instead, Gantt devised his "task work with a bonus" system which paid the worker a bonus of 50 cents per day if he did all of his work assigned for any particular day. Gantt later discovered that this plan offered little incentive beyond meeting the standard. To overcome this defect, he modified the plan to pay the workers for the time allowed plus a percentage of that time if they completed the job in the allowed

---

[5]H. L. Gantt, *Work, Wages, and Profits*, 2d ed., New York: Engineering Magazine Company, 1916, p. 33.

[6]Ibid., p. 55.

time or less. Hence, a worker could receive four hours pay for doing a three-hour job in three hours or less.[7]

Further, the foreman was to be given a bonus for each worker who made the standard plus an extra bonus if *all* the workers made it. Thus, if 9 of 10 workers made the standard, the foreman would receive 10 cents per worker or $.90; if all ten made the standard, he received 15 cents per worker or $1.50. To Gantt, this extra bonus for the foreman was for "bringing the inferior workmen up to the standard [and] made him devote his energies to those men who most needed them."[8] This is the first recorded attempt to make it in the financial interest of the *foreman* to teach the worker the right way. From his own schoolmaster experience, Gantt learned the importance of teaching and he felt that the bonus system would shift the foreman from a "driver" to a teacher and helper of his subordinates. In this shift from concern for production to concern for the worker through instruction and subsequently improved production, Gantt's work stands as an early landmark in early human behavioral thought. In Gantt's works: "Whatever we do must be in accord with human nature. We cannot drive people; we must direct their development."[9] Like Taylor, Gantt encountered more resistance from the foremen than from the workers. The main managerial obstacle was their reluctance to define and give tasks precisely and to exert the higher caliber of work which management must do to make the system succeed. As under the Taylor system, Gantt's plan called for the scientific investigation of the task, analysis and study of movements and times, standardization of conditions, and winning worker cooperation. Gantt's addition was the more direct involvement of management through a direct financial interest.

The "Habits of Industry"

In teaching the worker, Gantt felt the foreman should do more than increase the worker's skill and knowledge and added an in-

---

[7] Ibid., p. 165. For a detailed explanation and the computations necessary to Gantt's task and bonus plan, see C. W. Lytle, *Wage Incentive Methods*, New York: Ronald Press Co., 1942, pp. 185–200.

[8] *Work, Wages and Profits*, p. 115.

[9] Ibid., p. 124.

gredient to industrial education called the "habits of industry." These habits would be those of industriousness and cooperation which would facilitate the acquisition of all other knowledge. This too called for a break with the past and Taylor's influence is seen once more:

> the general policy of the past has been to drive; but the era of force must give way to that of knowledge, and the policy of the future will be to teach and lead, to the advantage of all concerned. [10]

The habits that must be taught the worker were those of "doing promptly and to the best of his ability the work set before him."[11] Stress must be placed on the pride that comes from quality as well as quantity of work. Gantt cited an example of a group of women who, working under the task and bonus system, formed a society of bonus producers with group admission available only to those who consistently earned the premium. To Gantt, this was the proper condition for all workers since he was also concerned with worker morale. However, this could come about only after management had created the proper atmosphere of cooperation and confidence with the employees. The results of his inculcation of "habits" were higher wages, increased skill, and greater pleasure and pride for the worker, coupled with lower costs and greater productivity for the employer. Beyond these tangible manifestations of efficiency, the harmonious cooperation between labor and management created that intangible élan or morale so vital to successful cooperative endeavors.

Graphic Aids to Management

As a former schoolmaster, Gantt was oriented toward the dramatization of data through graphic means. One of his early subjects for graphing was the "fixing of habits of industry" through horizontal bars illustrating the progress of workers toward meeting the task standard. For each worker, a daily record was kept of whether he made the standard and received a bonus, recorded in black, or did not, recorded in red. The graph served to aid both management and the worker since progress as well as reasons for

[10] Ibid., p. 148.
[11] Ibid., p. 154.

not making the bonus were recorded, enabling management to pinpoint deficiencies and feeding back progress data to the worker. In converting shops or departments from day work to task work, the progress of the shop could be seen by everyone as the chart contained progressively more and more solid black lines. As this method of charting succeeded in getting better performance, Gantt expanded his visual aids to include a chart on the daily production balance, cost control, quantity of work per machine, quantity of work per man in comparison with the original estimates, the expense of idle machinery, and others. However, his major breakthrough in charting came when he was serving as a dollar-a-year consultant to the Department of the Army during World War I.

The conversion of American industry to wartime production did not come quickly and smoothly. America had the productive capacity, but the integration and coordination of private industrial efforts with the governmental agencies were haphazard. Plants were scattered all over the nation, shipments were late, warehouses crowded or disorganized, and the Ordnance Department and the Navy were utilizing their resources poorly. Gantt had had some contact with governmental work before the war. In 1911, with Charles Day and Harrington Emerson, he was commissioned to study the organization and management of Navy shipyards. Their efforts went for naught when the secretary of the navy announced that he would never allow scientific management in the shipyards. The reader will recall that this was the period of the Congressional hearings and the general ill-will against the efficiency movement. Gantt had also served as a consultant to General William Crozier at the Frankford Arsenal just prior to the war. Crozier, influenced by Gantt's graphic displays, developed a series of "progress and performance" charts to aid in managing the Ordnance Arsenals. However, Crozier was removed from his position in 1917 and his successors allowed the system to lapse. When Gantt gave up his lucrative consulting work to aid the war effort, he puzzled over the problem of keeping track of the vast work of the various departments. Scheduling was especially crucial and management lacked the necessary information to control and coordinate private contractors' efforts with those of the gov-

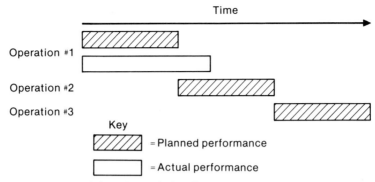

Fig. 7-1.   A simplification of the Gantt chart concept.

ernment agencies. Gantt spent three months trying to unravel the mess before the thought came to him that:

> *We have all been wrong in scheduling on a basis of quantities; the essential element in the situation is time, and this should be the basis in laying out any program.* [12]

Gantt's solution was a bar chart for planning and controlling work. Although numerous variations were developed, the essence of the Gantt chart concept was to show how work was routed and scheduled through various operations to its completion (Figure 7-1). For example, a manager could see from the data in Figure 7-1 that this particular project or product was behind schedule. Corrective action would then be taken to get the project back on schedule or to notify the customer of a late shipment or an expected completion date.

Gantt's graphic aids to management planning and controlling were revolutionary for this period in management thought. In a ready graphic form, management could see how plans were progressing and take whatever action necessary to keep projects on time or within budget authorizations. Gantt never patented the concept, nor profited from it, but his achievement did earn him the Distinguished Service Medal from the government. A member of Gantt's consulting firm, Wallace Clark, popularized the idea of the Gantt chart in a book that was translated into eight languages, formed the basis for the Russian central planners to control their

[12] Alford, p. 207.

"five-year plans," and provided the whole world with a graphic means of planning and controlling work.[13] All subsequent production control boards and charts drew their inspiration from Gantt's original work; the modern variation became Program Evaluation and Review Technique (PERT), which was a computerized, more intricate scheme but nevertheless founded upon the principles of planning and controlling times and costs. In Washington, the war effort took a measurable turn as the result of Gantt's contributions. Materials flowed more smoothly, boat-building blossomed, and America's productive might was brought to its greatest outpouring of goods. Surely these must have been some consolation for the man whose efforts to systematize governmental operations had been spurned so few years before.

Gantt: The Later Years

After the death of Taylor, Gantt began developing some very different ideas regarding the role of the industrial engineer and the business firm as an institution. In 1916, he deplored the failure of American industrial leadership which, in his opinion, was caused by the rise of leaders to power based on their influence and not their merit. Gantt's new leadership would be based on fact, not opinion, and on ability, not favoritism. The industrial engineer would be the new leader, not the financier nor the labor leader, because only the engineer could cope with the American problem of production as the creation of wealth. The engineers would be an educated elite to lead America, not with a concern for profits, but by stressing productive efficiency. Gantt's own notions regarding these changes were partially due to his reading of Thorstein Veblen but mostly attributable to Charles Ferguson.[14] In 1916, Gantt formed an organization called the "New Machine" whose membership comprised engineers and other sympathetic

---

[13] Wallace Clark, *The Gantt Chart: A Working Tool of Management*, New York: Ronald Press Co., 1922. For further information on Wallace Clark, see Harold Smiddy, "Wallace Clark's Contribution to International Management," *Advanced Management*, Vol. 23 (March, 1958), pp. 17–26.

[14] Alford, p. 264.

reformers who sought to acquire political as well as economic power. Charles Ferguson, Gantt's inspiration, was a minister who had served as an idea man for Colonel Edward M. House, President Wilson's adviser. Ferguson was a "joyous mystic" who preached a "religion of democracy" which would summon forth "an aristocracy of the capable to put down the rule of the mob and destroy privilege."[15] Gantt's New Machine operated on the premise that the engineer would form this "aristocracy of the capable." In a letter to President Wilson, the leaders of the New Machine called on the president to transfer the "control of the huge and delicate apparatus [i.e., industry] into the hands of those who understand its operation," to set up employment bureaus for better placement of men, and for "public service banks" to extend credit on the basis of ability and personality rather than property.[16]

Once the New Machine was rolling, Gantt lost his concern for mere factory matters and sought broader areas for reform. He attacked the profit system itself and on this point he appears to have been largely influenced by the swirl of world events. In 1917, the czar was overthrown and collectivism came by violent bloodshed in Russia. America herself had a "great red scare" in 1919 and anarchists were seen lurking everywhere. The Socialist Eugene Debs was something of a folk hero, there had been Communist uprisings in Bavaria and Hungary, the "Wobblies" (the International Workers of the World) were provoking labor unrest, and most Americans were firmly convinced that the Bolsheviks were about to overturn society. In the preface to his last book, written in 1919, Gantt said:

> The attempt which extreme radicals all over the world are making to get control of both the political and business systems on the theory that they would make the industrial and business system serve the community, is a real danger so long as our present system does not accomplish that end . . . in order to resume our advance toward the development of an unconquerable democratic civilization, we must purge our economic system of all autocratic practices of whatever kind, and return to the democratic principle

[15] Samuel Haber, *Efficiency and Uplift,* Chicago: University of Chicago Press, 1964, p. 45.

[16] Alford, pp. 269–277.

of rendering service, which was the basis of its wonderful growth. [17]

Gantt said that businessmen had emphasized profits, sought monopolies, and had forgotten to give "service" to the community. He said the businessman "has forgotten that his business system had its foundation in service, and as far as the community is concerned has no reason for existence except the service it can render." [18] Gantt's answer was that America could be saved without revolution by forming "public service corporations." These corporations would be financed by public money and profits would be returned to the community. Gantt did not specify any industries, nor the extent of such a plan, but he felt that this plan would insure that both labor and management would get their deserved shares and the "push and pull" wastes of competition would be eliminated. As he saw the situation: ". . . *the business system must accept its social responsibility and devote itself primarily to service, or the community will ultimately make the attempt to take it over in order to operate it in its own interest.*" [19] This position posed a paradox, for in an interview shortly before his death, he said:

> I am in favor of an organization similar to a cartel system. If in every industry we had a committee consisting of representatives of producers, distributors, and consumers, such a committee could fix prices with due regard to supply and demand . . .[20]

And further:

> . . . the engineer, who is a man of few opinions and many facts and many deeds, should be accorded the economic leadership which is his proper place in our economic system.[21]

Unfortunately, Gantt's ideas in his later years are vague and contradictory. On the one hand he called for service and social responsibility; on the other, a socialistic device of public service corporations. He wanted labor and management to receive rewards according to "services rendered," yet he would want a committee to fix prices of products. He would replace autocracy with democ-

[17] H. L. Gantt, *Organizing for Work*, New York: Harcourt, Brace, Jovanovich, 1919, pp. iv–v.

[18] Ibid., p. 5.

[19] Ibid., p. 15.

[20] *New York Sunday World*, October 12, 1919, cited by Alford, p. 298.

[21] Ibid., p. 296.

racy yet felt that a managerial elite, composed primarily of engineers, would be the most capable in running the system. In November 1919, Gantt was stricken with a "digestive disturbance" and died at the age of 58. After Gantt's death, the New Machine dissolved. Henry Laurence Gantt, the most unorthodox of Taylor's followers, had come to the ultimate conclusion that the mental revolution must be in the hands of the engineer and that the mutuality of interests was to be found in cartels and public service corporations.

Partners for Life: The Gilbreths

Frank Bunker Gilbreth (1868–1924) and Lillian Moller Gilbreth (1878–1972) formed a husband-and-wife team that brought not only color but significance to the early management movement. Frank was the son of a Maine hardware merchant and he learned early the virtues of frugality and thrift characteristic of New England puritanism.[22] When he was three, his father died and the family moved to Boston where he was educated at Andover and the Rice Grammar School. He prepped for the Massachusetts Institute of Technology, passed the qualifying exams, but decided instead to become an apprentice bricklayer at the tender age of 17. He rose to become chief superintendent of the Whidden Company and then launched his own career as an independent contractor in 1895 where his work formed the basis for his first investigations and publications. Though working independently of Taylor, Gilbreth's early work closely paralleled what Taylor was doing. In his later years, he formed his own management consulting company and became closely associated with the scientific management movement.

It was to the good fortune of modern management that Frank married Lillian Moller, for they formed a complementary team whose combined intellectual interests and assets brought a new

[22] Biographical information on the Gilbreths is from Edna Yost, *Frank and Lillian Gilbreth: Partners for Life*, New Brunswick, N.J.: Rutgers University Press, 1949. Popularized versions of their lives may be found in *Cheaper by the Dozen*, by Frank B. Gilbreth, Jr. and Ernestine Gilbreth Carey, New York: Thomas Y. Crowell Co., 1948; and (same authors) *Belles on Their Toes*, New York: Thomas Y. Crowell Co., 1950.

dimension to the inchoate field of management. Lillian was the daughter of a German-born sugar refiner and spent her early years in Oakland, California. Her family was relatively prosperous and she was schooled early in the responsibilities of home and children. Lillian was an exceptionally bright student, receiving her bachelor's and master's degrees in English from the University of California. She interrupted her work on her doctor's degree for a trip east; on that trip she met Frank, and their marriage in 1904 brought together two people who lived a most significant partnership, reminiscent of the Curies. After the marriage, Lillian decided to change her academic interests to psychology, for she thought that this field would best complement the work her husband was doing. Combining marriage and the ever-growing family (there were eventually 12 children) with her assistance to Frank's work, Lillian continued to do her research on her doctor's thesis and finally submitted it in 1912. The greatest blow came when the University of California informed her that the thesis was acceptable but that she would have to return to campus for a year of residency before the degree could be granted. Lillian had been led to believe that this requirement would be waived in her case but the university officials were steadfast. Frank was furious and began shopping around for a publisher. The *Industrial Engineering Magazine* published the thesis in serial form (May 1912–May 1913) and it was eventually published in book form by the firm of Sturgis and Walton with the proviso that the author be listed as "L. M. Gilbreth" with no mention that the author was a woman.[23] The thesis-turned-book, *The Psychology of Management*, stands in the literature as one of the earliest contributions to understanding the human factor in industry. Eventually the California authorities agreed that she could spend her "residency" in any college which gave an advanced degree in industrial psychology or management. These were scarce at that time but Frank discovered that Brown University was planning to offer a Ph.D. degree in "Applied Management"; after the proper preparation and waiting Lillian received her Ph.D. in 1915. This was not the culmination but

[23] Yost, p. 213. Lillian, like many women of that period, faced discrimination at every turn. Though she had earned a Phi Beta Kappa key at California, her name was omitted from the list of recipients. The "key" was later granted by the university.

the beginning of many years of hard work. Frank's work became more famous and Lillian's work on fatigue and psychology was a valuable supplement.

But that fruitful partnership was to end June 14, 1924, when Frank dropped dead of a heart attack. What does a woman with a Ph.D. do at age 46 when her husband has just died, she has a household full of children ranging in ages from two to nineteen, and she has felt the rebuffs of being a woman in a "man's world"? The situation demanded courage, and the "First Lady of Management" was never found wanting in that characteristic. She went to Europe and presented the paper that Frank was to have presented at the International Management Conference in Prague; she continued the motion study seminars for managers; she relied upon friends such as Wallace Clark to provide entrees for consulting jobs; she lectured; and she became a professor of management at Purdue University (1935–1948). When she wrote Frank's biography she said, "The Quest goes on."[24] She was to continue what she and Frank had started and the following pages are but a summary of their "quest."

Systematizing the Construction Industry

Though Frank Gilbreth was a contemporary of the founders of the scientific management movement, his own early work was done apart from any knowledge of what was happening at Midvale Steel. One of the first things he noted as a bricklayer's apprentice was the diversity in methods and speeds used by the workers. One set of motions was used for working fast, another for the slow pace, and yet another for teaching others how to lay bricks. Though bricklaying was one of man's oldest occupations, Gilbreth set out to develop in writing the best ways of laying bricks, handling materials, rigging scaffolding, training apprentices and in general improving methods while lowering costs and yet paying

[24] Lillian Moller Gilbreth, *The Quest of the One Best Way: A Sketch of the Life of Frank Bunker Gilbreth*, Easton, Pa.: Hive Publishing Company, 1973, p. 64. This reprint of a rare book is but one of the many contributions Yisrael Avishai and the Hive Publishing Company have made to the preservation of materials pertaining to the history of management.

higher wages. The essence of the system of work he was developing as a superintendent, as a contractor, and later as a consultant was published as the *Field System*, the *Concrete System*, and the *Bricklaying System*.[25]

The *Field System* was an accounting system without a set of books. It was designed to aid the construction contractor by showing costs, costs related to estimates, and the total cost of the job each Saturday up to the previous Thursday. No bookkeepers were needed since the original memorandum or receipt was filed and there was no general ledger. Gilbreth developed other facets of the field system and included detailed instructions for its use, even including a rule about no smoking on the job and the admonition that whistle blasts at starting and quitting time should not be over 4 seconds long. He established a suggestion system, including a $10 first prize each month for the best idea on how to improve work, give better service to customers, or secure additional construction jobs. Included in the field system were provisions for photographing working conditions at the time of any accident for use in lawsuits or other claims. Another part of the system was a "white list" card. This was an early appraisal form for workers which the foreman filled out on both desirables and undesirables. In an intermittent, transient trade such as construction, the Gilbreth "white list" became a valuable source of information for employers. Though his advice was quite detailed and applicable to construction, it was indicative of Gilbreth's desire to rationalize the workplace and is reminiscent of what the whole scientific management movement was attempting.

The *Concrete System* contained detailed advice to concrete contractors. Gilbreth wrote here too of directing the workers, including the necessity of "athletic contests" between work groups to give them a spirit of competition in completing the job. The total job was divided into equal groups of workers who competed to finish a wall or build concrete pillars. The *Bricklaying System* was also technical but brought forth a new facet of study to the young Gilbreth. The original concern was with the training of young apprentices and Gilbreth saw the wastes of hand-me-down instruction from experienced workers. He proposed the remedial step of

[25] Portions of these are reprinted in William R. Spriegel and Clark E. Meyers (eds.), *The Writing of the Gilbreths*, Homewood, Ill.: Richard D. Irwin, 1953, pp. 3–65.

finding the best way of laying bricks through motion study, followed by instruction and insisting that the emphasis be placed on *learning* the right way before maximum output was expected of the young worker. This early work was but a prelude to his later in-depth analysis of motions and fatigue.

One characteristic of Gilbreth's lifelong quest was that he asked the workers to help improve methods and achieve motion economy for *their own sake* as well as for management's. He not only taught the workers how to handle bricks but *why* that way was best. He thought pride was an essential part of learning a trade and that this came only if you knew your trade well. He stressed economy of effort, not speed, and sought to show how to improve productivity with no greater physical exertion. The result of his extensive analysis of bricklaying showed that motions could be reduced from 18½ to 4 and that workers could increase their output from 1,000 to 2,700 bricks laid per day with no greater effort. Like Taylor, Gilbreth found that the conditions of work greatly affected output; accordingly, he developed different types of scaffolding to suit the job, precise instructions on mortar consistency and trowel usage, and a "packet system" for proper conveyance and placement of bricks for the worker. Being a trained bricklayer himself undoubtedly helped Gilbreth win worker cooperation; however, he demonstrated early the need for worker involvement in making improvements, including incentives to do so, an emphasis on training, and finally the need to systematize without speeding up the worker.

Extending Motion and Fatigue Study

In 1907, after he had developed the rudiments of his construction systems, Gilbreth met Frederick Taylor. They had a great deal in common and Gilbreth soon developed into one of Taylor's most fervent advocates.[26] Their work interests were essentially parallel

[26]Nadworny has presented evidence that Gilbreth admired Taylor but not vice versa. Taylor and his followers distrusted Gilbreth because his consulting and micromotion analysis conflicted with Taylor's time study. Only after Taylor's death was there a *rapprochement* between micromotion study and time study. See Milton J. Nadworny, "Frederick Taylor and Frank Gilbreth—Competition in Scientific Management," *Business History Review*, Vol. 31, No. 1 (Spring, 1957), pp. 23–34.

although they differed in terminology: Taylor called his work "time study" and Gilbreth called his "motion study." In practice they were measuring the same thing, with similar objectives of eliminating motions to reduce fatigue and improve productivity. Gilbreth maintained that the stop watch was not an essential ingredient to his system and his bricklaying studies were of motions only. After Gilbreth came into contact with Taylor and began to refine his own system, he developed more and more intricate uses of the time dimensions of work. In one of the many amusing anecdotes about the Gilbreths in *Cheaper by the Dozen*, the children wrote that Frank was always the "efficiency expert" at home and on the job. He buttoned his vest from the bottom up, instead of top down, because the former took only three seconds and the latter took seven. He used two shaving brushes to lather his face and found that he could reduce shaving time by 17 seconds. He tried shaving with two razors, found that he could reduce the total shaving time by 44 seconds, but abandoned this scheme because it took two minutes per bandage applied to the cuts. His children suggest that it was the two lost minutes that bothered him and not the cuts. [27]

At Providence, Rhode Island, while Lillian was working on her doctorate, Gilbreth turned his attention away from construction and extended motion study to the general field of manufacturing. Fatigue became a major focus of attention and he received help from Mrs. Gilbreth in studying its causes and effects. The prevailing theory of the period was that fatigue was caused by a toxin generated by physical exertion and released in the blood. Every motion caused fatigue; hence any elimination of motions reduced fatigue. Gilbreth's analysis proceeded to isolating worker variables such as anatomy, habits, mode of living, etc., and variables in worker surroundings such as clothes, colors of walls, lighting, heating, tools, etc. He finally isolated 15 worker variables, 14 variables in the surroundings, and 13 "variables of motion" such as acceleration, length, path, etc. As he developed his study, he found it difficult for the human eye to follow motions and the study of gross movements was inadequate for the preciseness he needed.

[27] Gilbreth and Carey, *Cheaper By The Dozen*, p. 3.

He developed two techniques to overcome this deficiency: one, a list of micromotions of the most elementary motions; and two, the use of motion picture cameras and lights. Gross analysis of movements, such as "reach for tool," told Gilbreth little about the elements of that move. Accordingly, he developed a list of 17 basic motions, each called a *therblig* (*Gilbreth* spelled backward with the "th" transposed) such as "search," "select," "transport loaded," "position," "hold," etc.[28] These fundamental motions could not be further subdivided and gave Gilbreth a more precise way of analyzing the exact elements of any worker movement.

The second technique used the then infant technology of the motion picture camera. Gilbreth placed a large-faced clock, calibrated in fractions of minutes, in the camera's field of vision of the worker being studied. The pictures enabled Gilbreth to time the smallest motion of the worker. This was the beginning of what Gilbreth called "micromotion" study.

He also developed the "cyclegraphic" technique of attaching a small electric light bulb to the hand, finger, or arm of the worker which allowed photographs to show a path of light through space as the worker moved. His "chronocyclegraph" used a flashing bulb which showed acceleration and deceleration of movements by appearing in the film as a series of pear-shaped dots. Gilbreth found these laborious, meticulous methods necessary to improve methods, demonstrate correct motions, and to train new operators.[29]

One should not confuse the techniques with what the Gilbreths were trying to build. Their search for efficiency and economy included flow charts of both products and work, a three-position plan of promotion, and the impact of motion study on

[28] In 1851, Charles Babbage published his *Laws of Mechanical Notation* which contained methods for studying machine movements. According to Mrs. Gilbreth, Frank was an admirer of Babbage's work and Hoaglund suggests that Gilbreth applied to human movements the same ideas and symbols that Babbage used for machine movements. John H. Hoaglund, "Management Before Frederick Taylor," reprinted in Paul M. Dauten, Jr. (ed.), *Current Issues and Emerging Concepts in Management*, Boston: Houghton Mifflin Co., 1962, p. 27.

[29] The preceding material is a summary of more detailed descriptions found in F. B. Gilbreth, *Motion Study*, New York: Van Nostrand Reinhold Co., 1911; F. B. and L. M. Gilbreth, *Fatigue Study*, New York: Sturgis and Walton Co., 1916; and F. B. and L. M. Gilbreth, *Applied Motion Study*, New York: Sturgis and Walton Co., 1917.

the worker. All of their techniques were focused on eliminating waste in industry. The promotion plan was designed to prepare workers for advancement and as a morale and incentive booster. Each worker was considered to hold three positions in the organization: first, the position he last occupied and in which he was now serving as a teacher to his successor; second, his present position; and third, as one preparing for the next highest position. The system required charting promotion paths and records for appraising performance, and kept the worker from getting lodged in blind alley jobs. The psychology of motion study was to impress upon the worker the benefits of reducing fatigue and improving pay through motion study. According to the Gilbreths, monotony came not from performing the job the same way each time, but from the "lack of interest" of management in the worker. Motion and fatigue study displayed management's interest and facilitated the elimination of monotony.

Support for the Scientific Management Movement

During 1911, a number of A.S.M.E. members were finding it difficult to get papers on management recognized by that organization. A rump faction, led by Frank Gilbreth, formed a separate organization, first called the Society to Promote the Science of Management, then after Taylor's death, the Taylor Society.[30] Gilbreth was a vocal supporter of Taylor's in the Eastern rate hearings and participated in coining the term "scientific management." Like Taylor, he preferred the term "Taylor system" but his *Primer of Scientific Management* was designed to answer questions about this "new" phenomenon made famous by the rate hearings and the Congressional investigation. In the foreword, Louis Brandeis said:

> . . . the Primer will prove of greatest value in helping to remove from the minds of workingmen misapprehensions which have led

[30]In 1936, the Taylor Society and the Society of Industrial Engineers merged to form the Society for Advancement of Management.

some well-meaning labor leaders to oppose a movement from which labor has most to gain.[31]

Gilbreth proceeded in the *Primer* to pose common questions about scientific management and to provide answers in very basic terminology about the philosophy and practice of scientific management. No new information was provided but the expository device of questions and answers reflected an excellent approach to win over adherents to the cause. The following are merely examples:

Q. Does it [scientific management] not make machines out of men?

A. *. . . Is a good boxer, or fencer, or golf player a machine? He certainly approaches closely the 100% mark of perfection from the standpoint of the experts in motion study. It is not nearly so important to decide whether or not he is a machine as to decide whether or not it is desirable to have a man trained as near perfection as possible. . . .*[32]

Q. Does not the monotony of the highly specialized subdivision of work cause the men to become insane?

A. *. . . No, he will not become insane, for if his brain is of such an order that his work does not stimulate it to its highest degree, then he will be promoted, for under Scientific Management each man is specially trained to occupy that place that is the highest that he is capable . . .*[33]

Q. Does not the "speed boss" speed up the men to a point that is injurious to their health?

A. *"Speed boss," like "task," is an unfortunate name . . . the speed boss does not tell the men how fast they shall make their motions . . . [but he does] tell the men at what speeds their machines shall run.*[34]

[31] F. B. Gilbreth, *Primer of Scientific Management*, New York: Van Nostrand Reinhold Co., 1912, p. vii.

[32] Ibid., pp. 49–50.

[33] Ibid., pp. 53–54.

[34] Ibid., p. 65.

Q. If Scientific Management is a good thing for the workers, why do the labor leaders all oppose it?

A. *They do not all oppose it. Some oppose it for the simple reason that they do not understand it; the others have visions that Scientific Management is something that will reduce the value of their jobs,—and all are afraid, because of the bad treatment that workmen as a whole have had in the past, that Scientific Management is simply a new 'confidence game,' presented in a more attractive manner than ever before . . . they simply cannot imagine Dr. Taylor or any other practical man working for their interests unless there is a "comeback" somewhere . . .*[35]

Like Taylor, Gilbreth reaped the wrath of labor as he became more closely aligned with the scientific management movement. He had never encountered any strikes under his methods until 1910. Unlike Taylor, who thought that standards were the sole prerogative of management, Gilbreth had enlisted the cooperation of organized labor on the jobs. The continued ill-will of labor and the necessity to get to a campus for Lillian's work resulted in his leaving the contracting business and becoming an efficiency engineer in his own consulting company in 1914.

The Psychology of Management

Dr. Lillian Moller Gilbreth played an important role in her husband's work and earned as well a substantial reputation on her own.[36] Her doctor's thesis applied the findings of psychology to the workplace. She was not the originator of industrial psychology, since Hugo Munsterberg had opened up that field earlier, but she brought a human element into scientific management through her training, insight, and understanding.

She began by defining the psychology of management as "the effect of the mind that is directing work upon that work

[35] Ibid., pp. 87–88.

[36] For instance, Dr. Gilbreth made significant contributions to the field of home economics by applying the principles and techniques of scientific management to the home. See Lillian M. Gilbreth, *The Home-Maker and Her Job,* New York: Appleton-Century-Crofts, 1927; and *Management in the Home: Happier Living Through Saving Time and Energy,* New York: Dodd, Mead and Co., 1955.

which is directed, and the effect of this undirected and directed work upon the mind of the worker."[37] Heretofore, management had been considered an area in which no one could hope to succeed unless he had the inherited "knack"; with scientific management, it became possible to found management on laws and to study it in the classroom. Successful management "lies on the *man*, not on the work," and scientific management provided a means to make the most of people's efforts. Dr. Gilbreth characterized three historical styles of management: (1) traditional; (2) transitory; and (3) scientific. Traditional management was the "driver" or "Marquis of Queensbury" style that followed the unitary line of command and was typified by centralized authority. The Marquis of Queensbury term was adapted from prizefighting because she felt that it typified the physical and mental contest waged between worker and manager "according to the rules of the game." "Transitory" management referred to all forms in the interim stage between the traditional and the installation of scientific management. "Scientific," with synonyms of "measured functional," "ultimate," or the "Taylor plan of management," described the goal toward which all firms should be striving.

Dr. Gilbreth compared and contrasted these three styles of management according to how they affected individuality, functionalization, measurement, analysis and synthesis, standardization, records and programs, teaching, incentives, and welfare. On individuality, she noted that psychologists up to that time had been largely concerned with the "psychology of the crowd." Comparatively little work had been done on the psychology of the individual. Under traditional management, individuality was stifled by the power of the central figure; under scientific management, it became a fundamental principle in selection, incentives, and in overall consideration of worker "welfare," i.e., "general well-being, mental, physical, moral and financial."[38] The object of scientific management was to develop each person to the fullest po-

---

[37] L. M. Gilbreth, *The Psychology of Management: The Function of the Mind in Determining, Teaching and Installing Methods of Least Waste*, New York: Sturgis and Walton Co., 1914; reissued in 1921 by the Macmillan Co., p. 1.

[38] Ibid., p. 30.

tential by strengthening personal traits, special abilities, and skills. The focus was upon how management could develop the individual for their mutual benefit, not upon the worker's use and exploitation as under the Marquis of Queensbury type.

Functionalization promoted worker welfare by improving skills through specialization, enabling greater pride in output and higher wages; measurement insured that individuals received the product of their labors; standardization improved morale and prevented the worker from becoming a machine; and teaching overcame fear and instilled pride and confidence in the worker. Traditional management relied solely on rewards and punishment while scientific management attempted to enlist worker cooperation. The rewards under scientific management differed because they were predetermined (insuring against fear of rate cutting), were prompt (rather than delayed under profit sharing), and "personal" (in the sense that workers were rewarded for their efforts and not by their class of work). Under scientific management, the worker gained "mental poise and security" rather than the anxiety created by traditional management. Concerning welfare, scientific management promoted regular work, encouraged good personal habits, and fostered the physical, mental, moral, and financial development of the worker.

Dr. Gilbreth was pioneering in the psychology of management; she did not have the benefit of a half-century of empirical evidence and statistical sophistication that has been the evolution of the field of psychology. The state of the art in psychology was embryonic also: Wilhelm Wundt was fathering experimental psychology; Hugo Munsterberg was opening the vistas of industrial psychology; Ebbinghaus was experimenting with the memorization of nonsense syllables; and William James was developing his theories of emotions and habit formation. Dr. Gilbreth's work was more management than psychology; nevertheless, it illustrated concern for the worker and attempted to show how scientific management would foster and not stifle the individual worker. It is not easy to be on the foremost fringes of a new idea. But someone must be there or all frontiers vanish. The Gilbreths were in the vanguard and the field of management is indebted to them.

Efficiency Through Organization: Harrington Emerson

Harrington Emerson (1853–1931) was a Presbyterian minister's son who believed in the Protestant virtues of thrift and the economical use of resources. Educated at the Royal Bavarian Polytechnik in Munich, he was symbolic of the new breed of "efficiency engineers" who were bringing new methods of time and cost savings to the burgeoning American industry. Emerson began as a troubleshooter for the general manager of the Burlington Railroad and went on from there to become a consultant to the Santa Fe Railroad, which was on the verge of a serious work stoppage. In three years (1904–1907), Emerson was able to restore harmonious labor relations, reduce costs 25 percent, and yield the company $1.5 million in annual savings.[39] At this point in his career, Emerson perceived the need for applications of his efficiency concepts in areas other than the railroads. His work was largely independent of the Taylor movement although he had been corresponding with Taylor from 1903 onward. *The Engineering Magazine* was one of the earliest forums for the new management movement, and in 1908 and 1909 it published a series of articles by Emerson which were later issued as a single volume to become the basis of his system.[40]

Waste and inefficiency were the evils that Emerson saw pervading the entire American industrial system. His experience had shown that railroad repair shops averaged 50 percent efficiency and that preventable labor and material wastes were costing the railroad industry $300 million annually (hence his well-publicized testimony of $1 million a day savings).[41] Inefficiency was not con-

[39] Biographical data and the early work of Harrington Emerson is from "High Priest of Efficiency," *Milestones of Management*, vol. 1, editors of *Business Week*, 1964, pp. 8–9.

[40] Harrington Emerson, *Efficiency as a Basis for Operations and Wages*, New York: Engineering Magazine, 1911 (copyright 1909 by John R. Dunlap).

[41] One authority calls Emerson's testimony "pure hokum" and presents data to show that $50 million a year savings would have been the maximum possible rather than $300 million. Albro Martin, *Enterprise Denied: Origins of the Decline of American Railroads, 1897–1917*, New York: Columbia University Press, 1971, p. 222.

fined to the railroads but could be found in manufacturing, agriculture, and education. National productivity was not a function of the abundance or of the lack of natural resources among different countries but the cause of prosperity was "ambition, the desire for success and wealth."[42] America had the wealth of resources and the stimulus of individual ambition for gain, which had led to the rise of the United States as a world industrial power, yet she was losing her advantage due to inefficiency and wasted resource efforts. To Emerson, one of the greatest problems was the lack of *organization*. Only through proper organization could machines, materials, and human efforts be directed to improve efficiency and reduce waste.

Line and Staff Organization

Taylor's functional foreman ideas did not appeal to Emerson. He agreed with Taylor that the specialized knowledge of staff personnel was necessary but differed in how to bring this about. Influenced by his European education, Emerson admired the organizational efforts of General Von Moltke, who had developed the general staff concept and made the Prussian army the tremendously efficient machine it was in the mid-nineteenth century.[43] The theory of the general staff concept was that each subject vital to military efforts was studied to perfection by a separate staff specialist and that the combined wisdom of these specialists emanated from a supreme general staff to advise the commander.

Standing alone and unaided, the line organization had serious deficiencies. Emerson sought to apply these staff principles to industrial practice to bring about "complete parallelism between line and staff, so that every member of the line can at any time have the benefit of staff knowledge and staff assistance."[44] Each firm was to have a "chief of staff" and four major subgroupings of staff head under him: one for "men" to "plan, direct, and advise"

[42]Emerson, *Efficiency as a Basis for Operations and Wages*, p. 37. Cf. McClelland's thesis in chapter 2.

[43]Ibid., pp. 64–66. Karl von Clausewitz noted the use of the general staff concept in the Prussian Army as early as 1793. Karl von Clausewitz, *On War*, New York: Random House, 1943, p. 489; originally published in 1832.

[44]Emerson, *Efficiency as a Basis for Operations and Wages*, p. 69.

on everything pertaining to the well-being of employees; a second to advise on "structures, machines, tools, and other equipment"; a third for "materials" to include their purchase, custody, issue, and handling; and the fourth for "methods and conditions" to include standards, records, and accounting. Staff advice was available to all organizational levels and focused on planning: "It is the business of staff, not to accomplish work, but to set up standards and ideals, so that the line may work more efficiently."[45] The distinction between Emerson and Taylor is thus apparent: instead of making one person responsible for and with authority over each particular shop function, Emerson leaves supervision and authority to the line which operates on the basis of planning and *advice* by the staff. This shift maintained the advantages of specialized knowledge without the disadvantages of splitting the chain of command.

Principles of Efficiency

Emerson made other contributions in the areas of cost accounting, the use of Hollerith punch card tabulating machines in accounting records, and in setting standards for judging worker and shop efficiency. In cost accounting, for example, Emerson made a clear distinction between historical cost accounting (descriptive) and "the new cost accounting" which estimated what costs *should be* before the work started.[46] His work indicates that he was a pioneer in standard cost accounting because of this distinction. He also devised an incentive system which paid the worker a 20 percent bonus for 100 percent efficiency (the standard time); above the 100 percent efficiency level the worker received in addition his wages for the time he saved plus the 20 percent bonus. For example, at 100 percent efficiency, the bonus for 20 cents per $1.00 of wages; at 120 percent efficiency, 40 cents per $1.00 of wages; and 140 percent, 60 cents.[47]

[45] Ibid., p. 112.

[46] Ibid., p. 102. For other developments in cost accounting, see Michael Chatfield, *A History of Accounting Thought*, Hinsdale, Ill.: The Dryden Press, 1974, chap. 12.

[47] Emerson, *Efficiency as a Basis for Operations and Wages*, pp. 193–196. A table for computing bonus at all levels is found on p. 195. At 120 percent, for example, 40 cents = 20 cents for bonus and 20 cents for working 20 percent more efficiently.

Emerson's efficiency work was somewhat overshadowed by the Taylor system and in part this was due to the railroad rate hearings. Emerson was one of the witnesses and his studies of railroad efficiency were used by Louis Brandeis to show that the railroads did not need a rate increase if they applied the methods of the newly named "scientific management." Subsequent to the hearings, Emerson published his *Twelve Principles of Efficiency*, which became another landmark in the history of management thought. A chapter was devoted to each of the twelve principles; broadly conceived, the first five concerned relations with people and the remainder concerned methods, institutions, and systems. The "principles" were not isolated ones but interdependent and coordinated to form a structure for building a management system. In the preface, Emerson stated his basic premise:

> *It is not labor, not capital, not land, that has created modern wealth or is creating it today. It is* ideas *that create wealth, and what is wanted is more ideas—more uncovering of natural reservoirs, and less labor and capital and land per unit of production.*[48]

Ideas were the dominant force that must be focused on eliminating waste and creating a more efficient industrial system. Principles were the instruments to reach this goal and the basis of all principles was the line-staff form of organization because Emerson felt that "the industrial hookworm disease is defective organization."[49] The first principle was "clearly defined ideals." This principle made explicit the need for agreement among all organizational participants as to ideals and to pull in a "straight line." He did not use the term "objectives" as modern authors do, but "ideals" meant essentially the same thing. He hoped to reduce intraorganizational conflict, vagueness, uncertainty, and the aimlessness which arose when people did not understand and/or share a common purpose. Second, "common sense"; this principle exhorted managers to take a larger view of problems and their relationships and to seek special knowledge and advice wherever it could be found. Third, "competent counsel" was related to the second principle in that it pertained to building a competent staff force. "Discipline" became the fourth and provided for obedience

---

[48] Harrington Emerson. *The Twelve Principles of Efficiency*, New York: Engineering Magazine, 1913, p. x.

[49] Ibid., p. 29.

and adherence to organizational rules. It was a foundation for the other eleven principles and made the organization a system rather than anarchy. The fifth and final principle pertaining to people was the "fair deal." The fair deal depended upon the ability of the manager to establish a system of justice and fairness in all dealings with the worker. It was not a patronizing or altruistic relationship but one of mutual advantage.

The seven principles pertaining to methods were more mechanistic and largely self-explanatory: "reliable, immediate, accurate, and permanent records" (information and accounting systems); "despatching" [sic] (planning and routing of work); "standards and schedules" (methods and time for tasks); "standardized conditions"; "standardized operations"; "written standard practice instructions"; and "efficiency reward" (the incentive plan). Each principle was liberally sprinkled with examples of Emerson's consulting experience and formed a thorough, though often redundant, statement of his system.

Harrington Emerson achieved renown in his own time and his consulting firm endures today. He testified before the House committee on Taylorism and other efficiency systems, served as one of the experts on the Hoover Committee, which published *Elimination of Waste in Industry*, helped found the Efficiency Society (1912), and through his associates tried to bring more ethical practices to the field of management consulting by forming the Association of Consulting Management Engineers (1933). Harrington Emerson was a pioneer in spreading the gospel of efficiency.

The Gospel in Nonindustrial Organizations: Morris Cooke

While Taylor, Barth, the Gilbreths, Gantt, and Emerson were searching for efficiency in industrial enterprises, Morris Llewellyn Cooke (1872–1960) was extending the gospel of efficiency to educational and municipal organizations. After receiving a B.S. in mechanical engineering from Lehigh University (1895), Cooke went to work in industry and was soon applying a "questioning method" to the wastes of industry long before he met or heard of

F. W. Taylor.[50] As Taylor began to publish and be known more widely, Cooke became an avid reader and defender of what Taylor was espousing. He eventually met Taylor and evidently impressed him, since Taylor asked Cooke to become a member of a committee studying the administrative effectiveness of the A.S.M.E. Taylor personally financed the study and paid Cooke's salary; during the year-and-a-half study their friendship grew and Cooke became one of the "insiders" in the scientific management movement. Distrustful of the so-called new breed of "efficiency engineers," Taylor designated only four men as his disciples: Barth, Gantt, H. K. Hathaway, and Cooke. Once, on one of his assignments, Cooke saw a sign over the workers' entrance to a factory reading "Hands Entrance"; he asked the owner "where do the heads and hearts enter?"—the sign was promptly removed.[51] Perhaps he was being flippant, but he made his point—scientific management called for more than "hands."

In 1909, the president of the Carnegie Foundation for the Advancement of Teaching wrote Taylor asking for help in "an economic study" of administration in educational organizations. Taylor sent Cooke and the resulting study was a bombshell in the academic world.[52] Although only physics departments were studied since it was believed that they were representative of the existing level of teaching and research, Cooke included nothing in his final report that he did not feel applied to other departments as well. The report was quite lengthy and detailed and Cooke attempted something that few had been, or are today, eager to do, i.e. measure the cost of input efforts and the resulting output in teaching and research.

His findings were quite upsetting: inbreeding (hiring your own graduates) was widespread; management practices in education were even worse than the acknowledged poor state of industrial practice; committee management was a curse; departments enjoyed excessive autonomy which worked against sound univer-

[50]An excellent biography of Cooke is by Kenneth E. Trombley, *The Life and Times of a Happy Liberal: Morris Llewellyn Cooke*, New York: Harper and Row, 1954.

[51]Ibid., p. 10.

[52]M. L. Cooke, *Academic and Industrial Efficiency*, New York: Carnegie Foundation for the Advancement of Teaching, Bulletin No. 5, 1910.

sity coordination; professional pay should be based on merit and not longevity; and life tenure for professors should be scrapped and unfit teachers retired. Cooke recommended a "student hour" (one hour in class or laboratory per single student) as a standard to gauge the efficiency of professional effort. Professors should spend more time in teaching and research, leaving administration to specialists and not to committees. Assistants should be used more widely, allowing the higher-priced talent to take more complex jobs. Salary increases should be based on merit or efficiency and the costs of teaching and research should be more closely controlled by the central administration.

Initial reactions to the report were predictable: the president of the Massachusetts Institute of Technology said it read "as if the author received his training in a soap factory."[53] Nevertheless, some changes did come about and, though there are still inefficiencies and abuses, educational administration has made some progress, except perhaps, in the realm of committees.

The educational study had marked Cooke as an iconoclast, and there is no evidence that he was dismayed by the criticism he received. Following in Taylor's path, he knew the inevitability of resistance. In 1911, a newly elected reform mayor of Philadelphia asked Taylor to help out with municipal administration. Once more, Taylor sent Cooke into the breach. Cooke had been itching for reform ever since, as a poll watcher for the reform party, he had been bullied by a machine politician. In the new administration, Cooke became the director of public works and brought scientific management to the governance of Philadelphia. In four years he saved the city over $1 million in garbage collection costs, achieved a $1¼ million reduction in utility rates, fired 1,000 workers who were inefficient, established pension and benefit funds, opened channels of communication for workers and managers, and moved municipal administration from smoke-filled rooms into the sunshine. His book *Our Cities Awake* put forth his case for better-managed municipalities through application of the principles of scientific management.[54] He successfully established a "functional management" organization patterned after Taylor's

---

[53] Trombley, p. 11.

[54] M. L. Cooke, *Our Cities Awake*, New York: Doubleday and Co., 1918.

ideas, revamped budgeting procedures, hired numerous "experts" to replace political favorites, espoused management of the city by a professional "city manager," and sought to replace committees by individuals who had responsibility and authority. He called for "cooperation" by offering an early idea of participation in management decision making:

> Here then is a work [job] in which we can all have a hand, a work which will always be ineffectually done if it is confined to well-educated and highly trained men at the top . . . administrative leadership will in the future more and more consist in getting the largest possible number "into the play" in having the great body of employees increasingly critical in their judgments about both their own work and the work which is going on around them.[55]

Cooke saw that it was not the system, but the *confidence* of the people in the system that made scientific management effective.

After his work in Philadelphia and the pleas for municipal reform, Cooke opened his own consulting firm in 1916. Like the other pioneers, he contributed his knowledge to the War Department during World War I. Always concerned with gaining the cooperation of labor, he became increasingly interested in the growing national labor movement. He became a close friend of and adviser to Samuel Gompers, president of the American Federation of Labor. Cooke saw his task as that of bringing the labor and management factions together in a time when they were becoming more antagonistic. His advice was that labor was just as responsible for production as management; increased production improved the lot of both and it would form an effective barrier against both unemployment and low wages.[56] This thesis was repeated in Cooke's last book, coauthored with Philip Murray.[57] During the administration of Franklin D. Roosevelt, Cooke held numerous positions, chief among them administrator of the Rural Electrification Administration and of the New York State Power Authority. He also served as a trouble-shooter for President Harry

---

[55] Ibid., p. 98.

[56] Trombley, pp. 90–91.

[57] M. L. Cooke and Philip Murray, *Organized Labor and Production*, New York: Harper and Row, 1940. Murray was president of the Congress of Industrial Organizations (CIO) and the United Steel Workers of America.

S. Truman; and when Cooke was asked by his biographer to list his lifetime accomplishments, he replied: "Rural electrification, inexpensive electricity in our homes, progress in labor-management relations, conservation of our land and water and scientific management in industry."[58] To scientific management Morris Cooke had brought new ideas to develop harmonious cooperation between labor and management. He wanted more participation by workers, but most of all he sought to enlist the aid of the leaders of organized labor. If scientific management was to make any headway in the twentieth century, it required a man like Cooke to open the new vistas in nonindustrial organizations and to gain the support of the American labor movement.

Summary

The adolescence of a movement is analogous to life's teen-age years in growth, rebellion, and the search for the mellowing of adulthood. From Taylor's notion of science in management at Midvale and Bethlehem to the maturity of the movement in the 1920s, scientific management had its adolescence of diversity in the individuals examined in this chapter. Carl Barth was the true believer who became a faithful executioner of Taylor's orthodoxy. Henry Gantt began under Taylor's guidance, contributed significantly, and then strayed from the flock in his later years. The Gilbreths added refinement to Taylor's time study, enlarged the study of fatigue, and emphasized the psychology of scientific management. Harrington Emerson polished Taylor's notions of efficiency, rejected his functional foremen and wage-incentive schemes, and brought national recognition to the movement at the Eastern rate hearings. Morris Cooke, nurtured by Taylor, brought the system to academic and municipal undertakings and sought a *rapprochement* between scientific management and organized labor. The gospel of efficiency had its doctrine, but cracks were beginning to appear in the edifice as changing times brought new emphases.

---

[58]Trombley, p. 249.

8

Scientific Management in Europe and America

While Taylor and his associates furnished the impetus for scientific management, there were a number of individuals who were bringing the movement to its maturity along a number of dimensions. First, there was the immediate acceptance and applicability of scientific management in Europe, especially as an aid to management in World War I. Second, there was emerging recognition of the need to formalize the study of management in college curricula as well as in educating the industrial leader. Finally, there were numerous installations of scientific management in industry and a general spreading of its influence on other disciplines. This chapter will examine scientific management along these dimensions as well as discuss a number of other individuals who were adding to, amending, and otherwise bringing the notion of science in management to its maturity.

Scientific Management Goes Abroad

Whereas the Industrial Revolution began in Europe and spread to America, the "scientific management revolution" began in America and spread abroad. As early as 1907, Taylor's time study methods were being introduced in France, and World War I brought Europe's immediate attention to the possibilities of using scientific management to improve productivity.

Taylorism and Fayolism

The Frenchman Henri Fayol published his *Administration Industrielle et Générale* in 1916. Fayol's work, though recognized in Europe, remained in the intellectual shadow of Taylorism during the early part of the twentieth century. This was due to two primary forces: (1) the immediate applicability of Tayloristic efficiency devices to the French war effort; (2) the translation and popularization of Taylor's work by Henri Le Chatelier and Charles de Freminville. Georges Clemenceau, France's minister of war, ordered all plants engaged in the war effort to study and apply Taylor's methods of systematic management. Despite America's intense interest in management, Henri Fayol was unknown until other times and other cultural conditions could bring his ideas to the fore. To Le Chatelier fell the task of propagating Taylorism in French-speaking Europe. He translated *The Principles of Scientific Management*, became a close friend of Taylor, and was a leading exponent of his views in Europe. Le Chatelier added little to management thought himself; his contributions consisted in the elucidation of Taylor's philosophy, principles, and methods, and this did much to demonstrate the validity of scientific management in Europe.[1] Charles de Freminville was of lesser renown than Le Chatelier but likewise contributed to pioneering the management movement in France. As president of the Comité de l'Organisation Française, which served as the focal point for all activities devoted to the advancement of management in France, he helped fuse (for France) the two pioneering lives of Fayol and Taylor.[2]

The International Scientific Management Movement

The seeds having been sown, scientific management was soon to find other proponents who sought to bring its ideas and techniques under an ever-widening circle of influence. Edward Albert Filene (1860–1937) had pioneered in applying scientific methods

---

[1] Lyndall Urwick and E. F. L. Brech, *The Making of Scientific Management; Thirteen Pioneers*, vol. 1, London: Sir Isaac Pitman and Sons, 1951, pp. 93–103.

[2] Ibid., pp. 105–110.

to retail distribution in his family's Boston store. He had employed Frank Gilbreth as a consultant on employee training and evaluation and had attempted through other devices to bring science as well as human concern to retailing. In 1927, Filene was instrumental in forming the International Management Institute, located at Geneva, Switzerland, as an organization dedicated to spreading information about management abroad. The institute's first director was Lt. Col. Lyndall Urwick, who will be discussed in more detail later, and the office began functioning as a clearing house for international management. Unfortunately, the effort was short-lived. With the rise of Adolf Hitler to power, financial backers withdrew the organization's source of support and the institute closed in 1933.[3]

The international management movement received mixed acceptance and underwent various transformations in various countries. In England, Taylorism was not well received. Taylor had engendered some bitterness with British manufacturers over patent rights to high-speed steel and organized labor posed opposition so formidable that it made scientific management almost a negligible force.[4] In other countries, the international scientific management movement passed through various stages: first, the "propagandizing" and translations of men such as Le Chatelier; second, adaptation by various countries to meet their own needs; and finally, adjustment through various committees, conferences, and international organizations.[5] Different countries had varying political and economic structures which made it difficult to apply Taylorism in its pure form. Consequently, managers often grasped the mechanics of time study, incentive schemes, and so on, without applying the philosophy. Europe, having a long history of organized labor of an often radical nature, also encountered more resistance from unions than America. Further, an "anti-American" sentiment led to a less than favorable reception before and during the war. The 1920s were marked, however, by a widespread rec-

---

[3] For further information on Filene, see Lyndall Urwick, *The Golden Book of Management*, London: Newman Neame, 1956, pp. 85–88; and Tom Mahoney, *The Great Merchants*, New York: Harper and Row, 1949, pp. 76–99.

[4] Urwick and Brech, *The Making of Scientific Management*, p. 111.

[5] Paul Devinat, *Scientific Management in Europe*, Geneva: International Labor Office, 1927.

ognition of the need for efficiency, and Taylorism was adapted to fit varying national goals. For example, the Germans stressed coordination between educational institutions and industry; the English emphasized industrial psychology and fatigue research; the Swedes were primarily interested in standardization and simplification; and the Russians charted their five-year plans on Gantt charts and studied American mass production techniques.

European interest in Gantt's charts was stimulated by the work of Wallace Clark, who popularized them and provided a basis for the European "productivity movement." Before Gantt, however, Poland's Karol Adamiecki had developed a "harmonogram" which was a graphical device for simultaneously charting several complicated operations and thus enabling their harmonization.[6] According to Mee, the harmonogram was similar to the idea of a PERT network. The harmonogram, developed in 1896, received some acceptance and use in Poland and Russia but Adamiecki's work was never translated into English. In brief, scientific management caught the fancy of Europe and translations flowed in that direction, but not vice versa. Taylor overshadowed Fayol, and Gantt was accepted before Adamiecki; the industrial climate in Europe was ready for the ideas of scientific management but it took other times to bring recognition to Europe's own sons.

Formalizing the Study of Management

Academic and editorial interest signaled a maturity of the scientific management movement in the texts, management handbooks, journals, professional associations, and in the college curricula beginning in the early 1900s. Despite Taylor's belief that one had to "live" management and learn through shop experience, the study of industrial management was becoming more formalized.

[6]John Mee, "History of Management," *Advanced Management—Office Executive,* Vol. 1, No. 10 (October, 1962), pp. 28–29; see also Edward R. Marsh, "The Harmonogram of Karol Adamiecki," *Academy of Management Journal,* Vol. 18, No. 2 (June, 1975), pp. 358–364.

Education for Industrial Management

Harlow S. Person brought academic recognition to the Taylor movement long before it became popular. In 1905, before the Harvard entry into the management field, Dartmouth College began the teaching of management *per se* under Person's guidance at the Amos Tuck School of Administration and Finance. Later, as dean, Dr. Person played host to the first scientific management conference in the United States.[7] Person had a broadening effect on the Taylor movement as president of the Taylor Society (successor to the Society to Promote the Science of Management). Person extended the group's membership and its range of interests and took a broad view of industrial education. He tried to dissipate the prevailing notion that scientific management was merely the use of a stopwatch and methods analysis; in his view, educators should emphasize the philosophy of scientific management and focus on the creative study of leadership in industry.

Person also gave early recognition to the need to bring the social scientist into the study of management. His thesis was that the manager and the worker were so closely entwined in everyday activities that they failed to see larger relationships; however, the social scientist would be able to take a larger, more objective view of industrial evolution in order to chart a future course of action for research and practice.[8] Person also made a distinction between "administration" and "management," lending a philosophical subtlety to the propagation of scientific management. He viewed administration as the moral, social, and political aspects of running an enterprise, while management dealt with the technical aspects. Hence management could be more "scientific" while science in administration would be more difficult to achieve.[9]

---

[7] *Scientific Management*, Addresses and discussions of the conference on Scientific Management held October 12–14, 1911, Hanover, N.H.: Amos Tuck School of Administration and Finance, Dartmouth College, 1912.

[8] H. S. Person, "The Manager, the Workman, and the Social Scientist," *Bulletin of the Taylor Society*, Vol. 3 (February, 1917), reprinted in Edward E. Hunt (ed.), *Scientific Management Since Taylor*, New York: McGraw-Hill Book Co., 1924, pp. 226–237.

[9] H. S. Person, "Scientific Management," *Bulletin of the Taylor Society*, Vol. 4 (October, 1919), pp. 8–14.

Through his own writings and those he edited, Person became a significant figure in refining scientific management thought.[10]

Louis D. Brandeis, who eventually was to serve as an associate justice on the Supreme Court, had brought the spotlight to bear on scientific management through the railroad rate hearings. In later work Brandeis continued to stress scientific management as a solution to American industrial problems. He was "anti-bigness" and felt that industry could be more efficient, more competitive, and more professional through scientific management.[11]

Clarence Bertrand Thompson (1882–1969) was "an educator, a missionary of the gospel" who taught at Harvard from 1908–1917 and was instrumental in inducing Taylor to give his famous "Harvard lectures." Thompson compiled the most extensive bibliography of scientific management for that period, became a consultant (getting his start from Taylor), and did much to further the scientific management movement in both academia and in industry.[12]

Also among those contributing to early management education was Leon Pratt Alford (1877–1942). He was trained as an electrical engineer, worked in industry, became editor-in-chief of the influential journals *American Machinist, Industrial Engineering, Management Engineering,* and *Manufacturing Industries,* and pioneered the concept of "management handbooks" as an editor and vice-president for the Ronald Press Company.[13] His role in management education has not been generally acknowledged by management historians; nevertheless, his influence in the journals, on various professional committees, and in his books, was

[10] See for example H. S. Person (ed.), *Scientific Management in American Industry,* New York: Harper and Row, 1928.

[11] An excellent biography is Alpheus Thomas Mason, *Brandeis: A Free Man's Life,* New York: The Viking Press, 1956. See chapters 20 and 21 for Brandeis and the hearings. Brandeis himself wrote *Scientific Management and the Railroads,* New York: Engineering Magazine, 1911; *Business: A Profession,* Boston: Small, Baynard and Co., 1914; and *The Curse of Bigness,* New York: Viking Press, 1934.

[12] Ronald G. Greenwood and Regina A. Greenwood, "C. Bertrand Thompson—Pioneer Management Bibliographer," *Academy of Management Proceedings* (August, 1976), pp. 3–6. See also: C. B. Thompson (ed.), *The Theory and Practice of Scientific Management,* Cambridge, Mass: Harvard University Press, 1917.

[13] An excellent biography, including a complete bibliography of Alford's work, may be found in William J. Jaffe, *L. P. Alford and the Evolution of Modern Industrial Management,* New York: New York University Press, 1957.

substantial. Among Alford's early writings was an attempt to provide a correct interpretation of "science" in management. Writing with Alexander Hamilton Church, he deplored the term *scientific management* in that it was interpreted to mean that there was "a science rather than an art of management."[14]

The weakness of the Taylor approach, in Alford and Church's view, was that it superseded the art of leadership by substituting an "elaborate mechanism" or system. This did not mean that the mechanism was useless but rather that it overlooked the dynamic possibilities of effective leadership. Alford thought that Taylor's so-called "principles" were too mechanical, and to remedy this he (and Church) proposed three broad principles: (1) the systematic use of experience; (2) the economic control of effort; and (3) the promotion of personal effectiveness. The first emphasized both personal experiences of executives plus scientific studies; the second was based on subprinciples of division of labor, coordination, "conservation" (least effort expended to a given end), and remuneration; and the third stressed personal rewards, developing contented workers, and promoting the workers' physical and mental health. From these three broad regulative principles, a truly scientific basis for the art of management could be discovered.

Alford's call for art plus science in management is a reflection of his admiration of Henry Laurence Gantt, about whom he prepared an excellent biography. In the style of Gantt, Alford pleaded for industrial engineers to become involved in leading the economy toward "service" to the community and toward better relations between employers and employees. Alford continued to stress this theme as a member of the prestigious American Engineering Council and contributed to the better-known works of this group such as the reports on *The Elimination of Waste in Industry*, *The Twelve Hour Shift*, and *Safety and Production*. Parallel to his efforts on the council, Alford turned to disseminating management knowledge through the device of "management handbooks." The pioneering concept of the handbook was to organize

14 A. H. Church and L. P. Alford, "The Principles of Management," *American Machinist*, Vol. 36, No. 22 (May 30, 1912), pp. 857–861. Reprinted in Harwood F. Merrill (ed.), *Classics in Management*, New York: American Management Association, 1960, pp. 197–214.

information on all facets of administering and operating business and industrial enterprises.[15] It was through the handbook and his other publications that L. P. Alford sought to develop both the art and science of management.[16]

Dexter S. Kimball (1865–1952) was another influential figure in education for industrial management. As professor of machine design and construction at Cornell's Sibley College of Engineering, he became enthralled by Taylor's ideas and became one of America's first management professors. His course on "Works Administration" began in 1904; in it he taught the application of scientific management to plant location, equipment policies, plant organization, coordination, control of production, and labor compensation.[17] Kimball expanded the concept of scientific management in production and called for the scientific study of the distribution side of enterprise.[18]

Another who followed this "works administration" approach was John Richards. Richards, whose works were never published, gave a series of lectures in 1895 and 1896 on "works administration" before engineering students at Leland Stanford Junior University (Palo Alto, California).[19]

Early management education was largely of this works administration–industrial engineering genre. The number of institutions offering such courses on a regular basis increased from none in 1900 to 10 in 1922 and to 35 in 1931.[20] The typical course outline for the period included such subjects as: designing the proper organizational structure, policies for plant and equipment, motion and time study, wage incentives and payment schemes, procurement, materials handling, materials control, and "industrial

---

[15] L. P. Alford (ed.), *Management's Handbook*, New York: Ronald Press Co., 1924; and later, *Cost and Production Handbook*, New York: Ronald Press Co., 1934.

[16] See also: L. P. Alford, *Laws of Management Applied to Manufacturing*, New York: Ronald Press Co., 1928, and *Principles of Industrial Management*, New York: Ronald Press Co., 1940.

[17] His lectures were published in text form in *Principles of Industrial Organization*, New York: McGraw-Hill Book Co., Inc., 1913.

[18] D. S. Kimball, "Another Side of Efficiency Engineering," in C. B. Thompson, pp. 734–740.

[19] Richard J. Whiting, "John Richards—California Pioneer of Management Thought," *California Management Review*, Vol. 6, No. 2 (Winter, 1963), pp. 35–38.

[20] C. W. Lytle, "Collegiate Courses for Management: A Comparative Study of the Business & Engineering Colleges" (1932), cited by Jaffe, p. 233 and p. 294.

relations."[21] While the approaches were largely shop oriented à la Taylor, the study of industrial management was brought to its apogee in the 1920s.

The Impact of Scientific Management on Other Disciplines

Beyond the industrial engineering flavor of management thought, education for general management responsibilities began to take on new dimensions. Stimulated by scientific management, other disciplines began to reflect the search for efficiency through science. William H. Leffingwell applied the principles of scientific management to office management.[22] The University of Chicago's Leonard D. White picked up where Morris Cooke had left off and made numerous contributions to public administration.[23] White was the first to teach public administration in the classroom and also pioneered in personnel management for governmental offices. In marketing, Arch W. Shaw, Ralph Starr Butler, Louis D. H. Weld, Paul T. Cherington, and Paul D. Converse were pioneering the scientific study of that field.[24]

[21]The following represents a sample of such early management texts: A. G. Anderson, *Industrial Engineering and Factory Management*, New York: Ronald Press Co., 1928; Norris A. Brisco, *Economics of Efficiency*, New York: Macmillan Co., 1914; Hugo Diemer, *Factory Organization and Administration*, New York: McGraw-Hill Book Co., 1910; John C. Duncan, *The Principles of Industrial Management*, New York: Appleton-Century-Crofts, 1911; H. P. Dutton, *Factory Management*, New York: Macmillan Co., 1924; E. B. Godwin, *Developing Executive Ability*, New York: Ronald Press Co., 1915; E. D. Jones, *The Administration of Industrial Enterprises*, New York: Longmans, Green and Co., 1916; R. H. Lansburgh, *Industrial Management*, New York: John Wiley and Sons, 1923; and E. H. Schell, *The Technique of Executive Control*, New York: McGraw-Hill Book Co., 1924.

[22]William Henry Leffingwell, *Scientific Office Management*, Chicago: A. W. Shaw Company, 1917.

[23]Leonard D. White, *Introduction to the Study of Public Administration*, New York: Macmillan Co., 1926; and L. D. White, *The City Manager*, Chicago: University of Chicago Press, 1927.

[24]For the extent of the influence of scientific management on these pioneers, see Joseph C. Seibert, "Marketing's Role in Scientific Management," in Robert L. Clewett (ed.), *Marketing's Role in Scientific Management*, Chicago: American Marketing Association, 1957, pp. 1–3; Robert Bartels, *The Development of Marketing Thought*, Homewood, Ill.: Richard D. Irwin, 1962; 2nd ed. published as *The History of Marketing Thought*, Columbus, Ohio: Grid, Inc., 1976; and Paul D. Converse, *The Beginnings of Marketing Thought in the United States*, Austin: Bureau of Business Research, University of Texas, 1959.

It was from combining engineering economy ideas and accounting techniques that management was to be first exposed to
"contingencies" in financial planning and control. A vexing problem for management has always been the relationship between
the volume of production, fixed costs, variable costs, sales, and
profits. An engineer, Henry Hess, developed a "crossover chart"
in 1903 which showed these variables and their relationships.[25]
The position on the graph where total costs equaled total revenues
was the "crossover" point, that is, the point where losses turned
to profits. Walter Rautenstrauch, a professor at Columbia University, coined the term "break-even point" in 1922 which described
this same phenomenon.[26] John H. Williams, an accountant, conceived the idea of a "flexible budget" in 1922, showing how management could plan and control at various levels of output.[27]
Taken all together, these tools provided means for management to
forecast, control, and account for unforeseen developments.

James O. McKinsey (1889–1937) also sought to expand upon
traditional notions of accounting and pioneered in the development of budgets as planning and controlling aids. F. W. Taylor
had deplored the traditional post-mortem uses of accounting and
McKinsey furthered this notion by viewing accounting information as an aid to management rather than as an end in itself. For
McKinsey, the budget was not a set of figures but a way of placing responsibility and measuring performance.[28] As a one-time
professor at the University of Chicago and later as a senior partner
of McKinsey and Co., McKinsey was also influential in the early
days of the American Management Association. The A.M.A. was
founded in 1923 as sort of an adult extension university for practicing managers. Its objective was to broaden the study of man-

[25] Henry Hess, "Manufacturing: Capital, Costs, Profits, and Dividends," *Engineering Magazine*, Vol. 26 (December, 1903), pp. 367–379.

[26] Walter Rautenstrauch, "The Budget as a Means of Industrial Control," *Chemical Metallurgical Engineering*, Vol. 27 (1922), pp. 411–416.

[27] John Howell Williams, *The Flexible Budget*, New York: McGraw-Hill Book Co., 1934.

[28] James O. McKinsey, *Budgeting*, New York: Ronald Press Co., 1922; *Organization*, New York: Ronald Press Co., 1922; *Budgetary Control*, New York: Ronald Press Co., 1922; and *Managerial Accounting*, Chicago: University of Chicago Press, 1924. See also: William B. Wolf, "James Oscar McKinsey: Pioneer in Modern Manage-ment," *Academy of Management Proceedings* (August, 1976), pp. 7–11.

agement to encompass not only production and personnel but to include sales, financial, and other facets of managerial responsibilities. In brief, education for management responsibilities was beginning to shift from that of production shop management toward a broader view encompassing allied areas.

Taylorism in Industrial Practice

Many industrialists played a large role in putting Taylor's theories to the test in their own factories. Henry S. Dennison, president of the Dennison Manufacturing Company, pioneered in employee selection, created an early "Personnel Office," and made his plant a testing ground for scientific management. Henry P. Kendall, manager of the Plimpton Press of Norwood, Massachusetts, was an early promoter of scientific management in the printing industry. He thought that plants could become efficient by being "systematized" but that a greater long-run effect could be achieved only if the philosophy of scientific management was fully accepted by all parties.[29] James Mapes Dodge pioneered the link-belt conveyor which became the basis for belt assembly line operations and the Link-Belt Company (Philadelphia) was one of the major installations of the Taylor system.[30] Wilfred Lewis, president of the Tabor Manufacturing Company (Philadelphia), a machine-tool producer, was an authority on gearing and a friend of metric reform. Taylor's system, installed at Tabor, increased output 250 percent.[31] Horace King Hathaway was general manager of the Tabor Company and assisted Taylor in the installation. Hathaway advocated careful planning before installation, including an extensive program of educating the workers and supervisors as to the principles and purposes of the Taylor system. George Babcock, with the assistance of Carl Barth, pioneered scientific management in the automobile industry at the Franklin Motor Car Company

[29]H. P. Kendall, "Unsystematized, Systematized, and Scientific Management," in C. B. Thompson, pp. 103–131.

[30]See George P. Torrence, *James Mapes Dodge*, New York: Newcomen Society of North America, 1950; and James M. Dodge, "A History of the Introduction of a System of Shop Management," in Thompson, pp. 226–231.

[31]Wilfred Lewis, "An Object Lesson in Efficiency," Thompson, pp. 232–241; see also H. K. Hathaway, "Wilfred Lewis," *Bulletin of the Taylor Society*, Vol. 15 (February, 1930), pp. 45–46.

from 1908 to 1912. He also initiated an employee counseling program there long before Mayo and Roethlisberger did so at Western Electric.[32]

Early Organization Theory

During this era, the study of organization was largely production shop oriented and focused on designing a formal structure of authority-activity relationships. The early factory system, based upon the widespread division of labor, demanded the coordination of efforts, and the grouping of activities into departments satisfied that need. Military, governmental, and church hierarchical models permeated early industrial organizational thought. Daniel McCallum prepared America's first organizational chart and Joseph Slater Lewis pioneered in the same task for British industry.[33] Emerson continued in the military tradition but Taylor had sought modification through his functional foremen. Taylor's functional foreman concept did not become widely accepted but there was widespread recognition among others that new organizational forms were necessary.

In 1909 Russell Robb gave a series of lectures on organization at the newly formed Harvard Business School in which he attempted a compromise between the old military style and the new conditions of industry.[34] His thesis was that the objectives of business differed from that of the military and therefore the organizational emphasis had to differ. Much could be learned from the military framework of fixing responsibility and authority, of clearly defining duties and channels of communication, and of providing for order and discipline. However, the military stressed control and discipline, those being essential to its objectives, to an

---

[32] George D. Babcock, *The Taylor System in Franklin Management*, New York: Engineering Magazine Company, 1917.

[33] Joseph Slater Lewis, *The Commercial Organization of Factories*, London: Spon Books, 1896.

[34] Russell Robb, *Lectures on Organization*, privately printed, 1910. Chapter 1 is reprinted in Harwood E. Merrill, *Classics in Management*, pp. 161–175. Mr. Robb was an engineer with Stone & Webster, Inc. of Boston, managers of public service corporations. Further insights into his life and writings may be found in Edmund R. Gray and Hyler J. Bracey, "Russell Robb: Management Pioneer," *S.A.M. Advanced Management Journal*, Vol. 35, No. 2 (April, 1970), pp. 71–76.

extent not necessary in industry. The industrial organization, built upon an extensive division of labor, needed to provide for *coordination* of effort to a greater extent than the military. Success in industry was not based upon obedience but economy of effort; therefore the industrial organization had to be different. More stress had to be placed on worker and manager selection and training, processes had to be arranged for economy, and the manager must be aware that a "great factor in organization is 'system,' the mechanism of the whole."[35] An industrial organization was more than a machine based on order and discipline and must be infused with *esprit de corps* by leadership. Structure, discipline, and definitions of authority and responsibility were not enough; the industrial organization had to take into account "system . . . records and statistics . . . *esprit de corps,* cooperation, and team play."[36]

Webster Robinson, professor at the University of California, sought universal "fundamentals" of industrial organizations which were:

1. *"Policies"—ranging from general to specific and guiding all effort.*

2. *"Function"—the specialization of labor.*

3. *"The Right Man: The Right Place"—proper selection and assignment of duties.*

4. *"Direction"—purpose and objectives defined for all.*

5. *"Supervision"—which followed through to insure compliance with "direction."*

6. *"Control."*

7. *"Delegation and coordination of authority and responsibility."*

8. *"Incentives."*[37]

While Robb had emphasized the organic whole of the organization, Robinson was more concerned with the operative aspects of organization or what might be more closely akin to "principles" of organization.

[35] Robb, *Lectures,* p. 173.

[36] Ibid., p. 175.

[37] Webster Robinson, *Fundamentals of Business Organization,* New York: McGraw-Hill Book Co., 1925.

Scientific Management at DuPont and General Motors

No story is more fascinating to business historians than the growth of giant enterprise. Mingled into the development of two giants, DuPont and General Motors, we find the ideas of scientific management. One of Frederick Taylor's strongest suits was cost accounting and control techniques for manufacturing, and he had installed such a system at the Steel Motor Company, which later found its way to the DuPont Powder Company (see chapter 6).

In 1902, Coleman, Pierre, and Alfred I. DuPont bought control of the DuPont Powder Company from their cousins for $12 million in 30-year notes—no cash—and were subsequently to mold this company into an industrial giant. The DuPonts, and especially Pierre as president, sought to broaden Taylor's cost concepts to include a measure of overall performance rather than just manufacturing efficiency. As early as 1903, the DuPont Powder Company inaugurated "return on investment" as a measure of organizational performance, apparently the first use of this important managerial tool.[38] It is Pierre who is credited with bringing the necessary financial, operational, and managerial techniques to the DuPont Company which made it into an effective organization. Pierre learned from Taylor and Carnegie (who had learned McCallum's methods while working on the Pennsy).[39] One of Pierre DuPont's key people was Hamilton McFarland Barksdale, the firm's general manager, who stressed the human factor and was using psychological tests for personnel selection in 1910. He also pioneered in separating the line and staff functions, in developing uniform objectives and policies for the company, in the concept of decentralization of authority, and in the development of managerial talent.[40]

[38] H. Thomas Johnson, "Management Accounting in an Early Integrated Industry: E. I. DuPont de nemours Powder Company, 1903–1912," *Business History Review*, Vol. 49, No. 2 (Summer, 1975), p. 189.

[39] Alfred D. Chandler, Jr., and Stephen Salsbury, *Pierre S. Dupont and the Making of the Modern Corporation*, New York: Harper and Row, 1971, p. xxi.

[40] Ernest Dale, *The Great Organizers*, New York: McGraw-Hill Book Co., 1960. See also: Ernest Dale and Charles Meloy, "Hamilton McFarland Barksdale and the DuPont Contributions to Scientific Management," *Business History Review*, Vol. 36 (Summer, 1962), pp. 127–152.

Another key figure was Barksdale's cousin, Donaldson Brown. Brown's contribution was to refine the return on investment concept into a device for measuring and comparing the performance of various departments (rather than just measuring overall return on investment for the firm). Brown developed the formula $R = T \times P$ where R represented the rate of return on capital invested in each department, T stood for the rate of turnover of invested capital, and P for the percentage of profit on sales.[41] Brown also developed the famous "DuPont Chart System," which endures yet today, and used this ROI formula to portray the relative performances of various departments, to forecast, and to control.

The organizational legacy of DuPont carried over to the emerging General Motors Corporation. William C. Durant conceived the idea of creating General Motors out of an amalgam of motor car and parts producers. The union was unwieldy and General Motors was plucked from the brink of financial disaster by an infusion of DuPont money in 1920. Durant resigned and Pierre came out of semiretirement to become president of General Motors. Pierre made at least two key personnel decisions: one was to bring Donaldson Brown to General Motors; the other was to hand-pick a successor to himself as president, Alfred P. Sloan, Jr. (1923). Sloan created the concept of decentralized administration and operations with centralized control and review. By decentralizing operations and centrally coordinating control, the separate parts of General Motors could work toward a common end. Establishment of this multidivisional structure enabled organizational units to grow larger without the encumbrances of organizing by function.[42]

The concept of decentralization into product divisions made use of Brown's ROI formula. Each division or unit, given a certain amount of resource investment, could then have its performance measured and controlled by judging the rate of return on in-

---

[41] Donaldson Brown, *Some Reminiscences of an Industrialist*, privately printed, n.d., pp. 26–28.

[42] The General Motors story is a classic and is examined, to name only a few, by: Alfred D. Chandler, Jr. (ed.), *Giant Enterprise*, New York: Harcourt, Brace Jovanovich, 1964; Peter Drucker, *The Concept of the Corporation*, New York: John Day Co., 1946; and Alfred P. Sloan, Jr., *My Years with General Motors*, New York: Doubleday & Co., 1963.

vestment. The result was a correlation between efforts expended and results obtained which enabled central management to judge and compare the effectiveness of each product division.

From Taylor, Pierre DuPont learned the necessity of a rational basis for organizational and managerial control. He used these techniques to build DuPont, he applied them to General Motors, and, through Sloan, enabled the overtaking of the Ford Motor Company. Pierre DuPont, Barksdale, Brown, and Sloan were the major men in the making of the concept as well as the reality of the modern corporation.

Management:
Synthesis and Functions

In 1914, two years before the appearance of Henri Fayol's description of the elements or functions of management, Alexander Hamilton Church (1866–1936) put forth a functional approach to the study of management.[43] Church began his career in England, became a consultant in cost accounting systems, and moved to America at the turn of the century. Tutored by Joseph Slater Lewis, one of England's management pioneers, Church sought a broader approach to the study of management than he saw existing in Taylor's approach.[44] To Church, every industrial undertaking consisted of two elements: (1) the "determinative" element, which fixed the manufacturing and distribution policies of the firm; and (2) the "administrative" element which took the policy as determined and gave it practical expression through buying, manufacturing, and selling. In making these two elements operational, the manager used two fundamental "instruments": (1) *analysis*, consisting of cost accounting, time and motion study, routing, machine layout, and planning; and (2) *synthesis*, combining workers, functions, machines, and all activities effectively to achieve some useful result.

In Church's view, Taylor's ideas were analytical and formed a restricted view of the task of management. Management should be

[43] A. H. Church, *The Science and Practice of Management*, New York: Engineering Magazine, 1914.

[44] Joseph A. Litterer, "Alexander Hamilton Church and the Development of Modern Management," *Business History Review*, Vol. 35 (Summer 1961), p. 214.

concerned with total efficiency, not just with the efficiency of the production unit, of stores, or of any other single unit in isolation. This regard for the whole led Church to derive five "organic functions" of management:

1. *Design, which* originates.

2. *Equipment, which provides physical* conditions.

3. *Control, which specifies duties, and which* orders.

4. *Comparison, which measures, records, and* compares.

5. *Operation, which* makes.[45]

"Organic" was a physiological analogy meaning that these functions were essential, independent, and yet closely coordinated. Performance of the whole could be adversely affected if any of the parts were malfunctioning, just as in the human body. The manager needed knowledge of these functions just as the doctor needed knowledge of anatomy and physiology. Concerning the functions themselves, design was essentially planning; control was basically coordination, initiating orders, and supervising to insure compliance; and comparison was setting standards and measuring performance. The organic functions of Church do not have the logical appeal of Fayol's nor do they appear as comprehensive due to Church's predilection toward manufacturing concerns. In a later book, Church stated that "it is not, of course, possible to teach executive ability".[46] The executive aspirant needed certain physical and moral traits and when he learned from his predecessors and had the experience, he would become effective. Again, Church lacked the foresight of Fayol but his notion of examining the organization as a whole and his "organic functions" earn him his place in management history.

An Early Philosophy of Management

Scientific management had a fundamental philosophy in what Taylor had called the "mental revolution," the fusing of labor and management's interests into a mutually rewarding whole. How-

[45] Church, *The Science and Practice of Management,* pp. 37–38.

[46] A. H. Church, *The Making of an Executive,* New York: Appleton-Century-Crofts, 1923, p. 2.

ever, it was an Englishman, Oliver Sheldon (1894–1951), who was the first to lay claim to developing explicitly a "philosophy of management."[47] Sheldon began and ended his business career with Rowntree & Company, Ltd., an English chocolate-manufacturing company headed by B. S. Rowntree. Sheldon had undoubtedly read H. L. Gantt and his notion that business had a larger responsibility of "service" to society. Sheldon stated his own rationale for a philosophy:

> . . . *we should devise a philosophy of management, a code of principles, scientifically determined and generally accepted, to act as a guide, by reason of its foundation upon ultimate things, for the daily practice of the profession.*[48]

Adoption of isolated principles was not adequate to Sheldon's thesis; he sought a body of managers who would develop common motives, common ends, a common creed, and a common fund of knowledge. The basic premise of his philosophy, like that of Gantt, was that of "service" to the community:

> *Industry exists to provide the commodities and services which are necessary for the good life of the community, in whatever volume they are required. These commodities and services must be furnished at the lowest prices compatible with an adequate standard of quality, and distributed in such a way as directly or indirectly to promote the highest ends of the community.*[49]

This combination of the efficiency values of scientific management with the ethics of service to the community was the responsibility of each manager. Each manager must adopt three principles: (1) "that the policies, conditions, and methods of industry shall conduce to communal well-being"; (2) that "management shall endeavor to interpret the highest moral sanction of the community as a whole" in applying social justice to industrial practice; and (3) that "management . . . take the initiative . . . in raising the general ethical standard and conception of social justice."[50]

In applying these principles, management must maintain industry upon an *economic* basis and consider both human *and* tech-

[47]Oliver Sheldon, *The Philosophy of Management,* London: Sir Isaac Pitman & Sons Ltd., 1923.

[48]Ibid., p. 283.

[49]Ibid., p. 284.

[50]Loc. cit.

nical efficiency. This duality of efficiency was based upon: (1) scientific methods of work analysis; and (2) development of human potentialities to the greatest extent possible. In Sheldon's philosophy, the economic basis of service, the dual emphasis on human and technical efficiency, and the responsibility of management to provide social justice would all lead to a "science of industrial management" of benefit to all parties. Management, through the application of science in work and cognizant of its responsibility for justice, served by being both technically and humanly efficient.

Summary

Scientific management was a significant force in industry, in academia, and in other countries. In bringing the movement to its maturity, a number of individuals played relatively minor, though important, roles. Harlow Person began teaching management as a separate subject, Louis Brandeis called for a widening of the use of scientific management in professionalizing business, and individuals such as C. B. Thompson, Dexter Kimball, and L. P. Alford were bringing education for industrial management into the classroom as well as into industry. In Europe, the reaction was mixed; scientific management achieved international acclaim and recognition but took on varied forms in practice. Taylorism overshadowed the work of Fayol, for awhile, and became the *zeitgeist* of this era. The movement had its adherents as well as its dissenters. It was along all of these dimensions that scientific management reached its apogee of influence in college curricula, in industry, and in the international management movement.

9

The Human Factor:
Preparing the Way

Scientific management was sired and nurtured in an era which stressed science as a way of life and living. It is not surprising, therefore, that the credo of scientific investigation would spread to many areas and shift them from traditional, intuitive, pseudoscientific bases to more empirical, rational ones. Progress needs a spark; this chapter will examine how scientific management provided the ethic for industrial psychology and led to the emergence of personnel management as a discipline. Eras in management thought typically blend into one another and find their roots in earlier theory. Hence we will also find concurrent developments in sociology which anticipated and formed the intellectual basis for a subsequent era in evolving management thought.

Psychology and the Individual

Before the advent of scientific management, psychology was largely introspective, i.e., based on the premise that people could learn what they needed to know about others by studying themselves. Pseudosciences such as astrology, physiognomy, phrenology, and graphology were abundant as managers sought to select personnel on the basis of the movement and position of the stars, on their physical characteristics, on the basis of bumps on the skull, and on handwriting analysis.[1] Even in such reputable

[1] Cyril Curtis Ling, *The Management of Personnel Relations: History and Origins,* Homewood, Ill.: Richard D. Irwin, 1965, pp. 232–233.

consulting firms as that of Harrington Emerson, Katherine H. M. Blackford, a physician, emphasized the study of physiognomy and graphology as aids to selection. She advocated the study of facial and hair coloring, the shape of noses, facial expressions, and head proportions such as "convex and concave faces," and other "psychophysical" variables in selecting employees. She found nine such psychophysical variables and also concluded that handwriting analysis, like the person's voice, was an expression of a person's character and should be taken into account.[2]

Toward Scientific Psychology

Elsewhere, psychology was escaping its introspective, pseudoscience beginnings. When Wilhelm Wundt opened his Leipzig laboratory in 1879, the scientific method first appeared in psychology. Wundt did not entirely abandon introspection but began to examine behavior through controlled experiments. As the father of experimental psychology, he opened the way for applied and eventually industrial psychology. Wundt was searching for "psychological man," just as Taylor sought "economic man," through studying the individual for universal mainsprings of human conduct. Observation of human behavior, combined with the emergence of the psychoanalytical theories of Freud, soon led to a widespread search for instincts to explain behavior and thought. People were not rational, as Adam Smith had postulated, but controlled by instincts and, by understanding these instincts, the secrets of the hitherto unexplored mind could be opened for examination. Thorstein Veblen laid great stress on the instinct for workmanship; William James thought there were 28 separate instincts; and Ordway Tead discovered 10.[3]

The disparities and disagreements among the lists of instincts soon proved that this approach was futile, and instinct theory was dismissed as an oversimplified view of behavior. How-

[2] Katherine H. M. Blackford, *The Job, The Man, The Boss*, New York: Doubleday and Co., 1915, chapter 7, p. 176 and p. 184.

[3] Ordway Tead, *Instincts in Industry: A Study of Working Class Psychology*, Boston: Houghton Mifflin Co., 1918. Tead's list consisted of the parental, sex, workmanship, possession, self-assertion, submissiveness, herd, pugnacity, play, and curiosity instincts.

ever, the human variabilities which were noted in the attempts to develop instinct theory led to the recognition of individual differences. The study of human behavior had to study the individual and it was here that the psychologists found their alliance with scientific management.

The Birth of Industrial Psychology

Scientific management gave industrial psychology its ethic, its scope, and its direction for research. The earliest objective of industrial psychology was

> the maximum efficiency *of the individual in industry and his optimum* adjustment . . . *in the belief that, in the final analysis, the maximum efficiency of that individual in the industrial situation can only be achieved by insuring his most satisfactory adjustment in that situation.*[4]

While the engineer studied mechanical efficiency, the industrial psychologist studied human efficiency with the same goal in mind of improved overall greater productivity. Acceptance by industry of the heretofore ivory-tower psychologist was facilitated by the psychologist's interest in efficiency.

Hugo Munsterberg (1863–1916) was the father of industrial psychology. Born in Danzig and educated in Wundt's Leipzig laboratory, he was soon enticed to America by William James, the great Harvard psychologist.[5] In 1892, Munsterberg established his psychological laboratory at Harvard, which was to become the foundation stone in the industrial psychology movement. His interests were far-ranging, including the application of psychological principles to crime detection, to education, to morality, and to philosophy. In 1912 he published *Psychologie und Wirtschaftleben*, which was translated as *Psychology and Industrial Efficiency* in 1913.[6] In the spring of that year, he visited with Pres-

---

[4] Morris S. Viteles, *Industrial Psychology*, New York: W. W. Norton and Co., 1932, p. 4.

[5] A sympathetic but interesting account of Herr Doktor Munsterberg may be found in Margaret Munsterberg, *Hugo Munsterberg: His Life and Work*, New York: Appleton-Century-Crofts, 1922.

[6] Hugo Munsterberg, *Psychology and Industrial Efficiency*, Boston: Houghton Mifflin Co., 1913.

ident Wilson, Secretary of Commerce Redfield, and Secretary of Labor W. B. Wilson in Washington to win them to the idea of creating a government bureau dedicated to scientific research in the application of psychology to the problems of industry. National interest in scientific management was high and Munsterberg sought to put science in the study of human behavior at the same level of national concern. According to Munsterberg:

> While today the greatest care is devoted to the problems of material and equipment, all questions of the mind . . . like fatigue, monotony, interest, learning . . . joy in work . . . reward . . . and many similar mental states are dealt with by laymen without any scientific understanding. [7]

Even though the government bureau never materialized, Munsterberg's research efforts sought to answer certain perplexing industrial questions:

> We ask how we can find the men whose mental qualities make them best fitted for the work which they have to do; secondly, under what psychological conditions we can secure the greatest and most satisfactory output from every man; and finally how we can produce most completely the influences on human minds which are desired in the interests of business. In other words, we ask how to find the best possible work, and how to secure the best possible effects. [8]

Munsterberg's *Psychology and Industrial Efficiency* was directly related to Taylor's proposals and contained three broad parts: (1) "The Best Possible Man"; (2) "The Best Possible Work"; and (3) "The Best Possible Effect." Part one was a study of the demands jobs made on people and the necessity of identifying those people whose mental qualities made them best fitted for the work they had to do. Part two sought to determine "psychological conditions" under which the greatest and most satisfactory output could be obtained from every person. Part three examined the necessity of producing the influences on human needs which were desirable for the interests of the business. For each of these objectives, Munsterberg outlined definite proposals for the use of tests in worker selection, for the application of research on learning in

[7] Margaret Munsterberg, p. 250.
[8] Hugo Munsterberg, pp. 23–24.

training industrial personnel, and for the study of psychological techniques which increased the worker's motives and reduced fatigue. In character with experimental psychology, Munsterberg illustrated his proposals with his own evidence gathered from the study of trolley motormen, telephone operators, and ship's officers.

Taylor and others, such as Harlow Person, had envisioned contributions from psychologists for research into the human factor. Munsterberg fitted into this scheme and the ethic of scientific management was readily apparent in (1) the focus on the individual, (2) the emphasis on efficiency, and (3) the social benefits to be derived from application of the scientific method. As Taylor had called for a mental revolution and the recognition of the mutuality of interests between employees and employers, Munsterberg noted:

> *We must not forget that the increase of industrial efficiency by future psychological adaptation and by improvement of the psychophysical conditions is not only in the interest of the employers, but still more of the employees; their working time can be reduced, their wages increased, their level of life raised.* [9]

Concern for the human factor was increasing and it was within the ethics and objectives of scientific management that it began. After Munsterberg, other industrial psychology texts appeared and followed a fairly definite pattern: first, developing a "psychological point of view of industry" by pointing out the need to study human behavior; second, establishing the roots and justification of the industrial psychology movement in scientific management; and finally, examining such recurring subjects as fatigue, vocational guidance, improving efficiency through testing and placement, and overcoming "industrial unrest" through understanding the human factor. [10]

---

[9] Hugo Munsterberg, pp. 308–309.

[10] Typical works would include: Frank Watts, *An Introduction to the Psychological Problems of Industry*, London: Allen and Unwin, 1921; Charles S. Myers, *Mind and Work: The Psychological Factors in Industry and Commerce*, New York: G. P. Putnam's Sons, 1921; and Charles S. Myers, *Industrial Psychology*, New York: People's Institute, 1925. Charles Samuel Myers, inspired by Munsterberg, pioneered industrial psychology in England.

Personnel Management: A Dual Heritage

The field of personnel management has a dual heritage and a beginning during this period of our study. The dual heritage comes from: (1) The notion of personnel work as "welfare" or "industrial betterment"; and (2) scientific management.

Personnel as "Welfare Work"

Paternalism, whether by the state, the church, or business, is as old as civilization. The feudal system was based upon paternalistic ideals and many of the early factory owners, such as Robert Owen, sought to provide various benefits such as recreation, dancing lessons, meals, housing, education, sanitation, etc. The New England "Waltham Plan," discussed in chapter 5, had paternalistic overtones as management looked after the education, housing, and morals of its employees. The first recorded attempt to establish an office for "welfare work" appears to be at the National Cash Register Company in 1897. The company's founder and president, John H. Patterson, appointed Lena H. Tracy as the firm's first "welfare director."[11] Joseph Bancroft and Sons had a "welfare secretary" in 1899, the H. J. Heinz Company employed a social secretary in 1902, the Colorado Fuel and Iron Company had one in 1901, and the International Harvester Company followed in 1903. The goal of the social secretary was to improve the life of workers, both off and on the job, hence the terms "welfare" and "industrial betterment." The social secretary listened to and handled grievances, ran the "sick room" of the workshop, provided for recreation and education, arranged transfers for dissatisfied workers, administered the dining facilities, prepared nutritious menus, and looked after the moral behavior of unmarried female factory employees.[12] In brief, one branch of thought regarding

[11] See Lena Harvey Tracy, *How My Heart Sang: The Story of Pioneer Industrial Welfare Work*, New York: R. R. Smith Publisher, 1950.

[12] For other companies and other duties of the "social secretary," see William H. Tolman, *Social Engineering*, New York: McGraw Publishing Company, 1909, pp. 48–59. See also: Stuart D. Brandes, *American Welfare Capitalism: 1880–1940*, Chicago, Ill.: University of Chicago Press, 1976; and Daniel Nelson, *Managers and Workers: Origins of the New Factory System in the United States, 1880–1920*, Madison, Wis.: University of Wisconsin Press, 1975, especially chap. 6.

personnel relations was founded in the idea of concern for worker welfare which would better industrial conditions and, hopefully, lead to greater productivity.

Scientific Management and Personnel

The second branch of the dual heritage of personnel management began with scientific management and was furthered by industrial psychology. In the early days of the factory, the personnel or "employment" function was the responsibility of the line manager, typically the foreman. The B. F. Goodrich Company developed the first "employment" department in 1900, although it performed a very limited number of functions. Taylor had described the duties of the "shop disciplinarian," one of the functional foremen, as keeping performance records, handling discipline problems, administering wage payments, and serving as a "peacemaker." While this early idea was sketchy, Plimpton Press, one of Taylor's model installations, had a full-fledged personnel department in 1910.

A clash between the welfare version of personnel work and scientific management was inevitable. It came at the Joseph Bancroft textile firm (Wilmington, Delaware). Bancroft's first "welfare secretary" was Elizabeth Briscoe, who was appointed in 1902. Her job was to perform the social secretary functions much as they were described previously. In 1903, Bancroft ran into some severe productivity problems and Henry L. Gantt was employed as a consultant. Gantt's recommendations soon ran counter to the welfare orientation when he tried to improve personnel selection, to transfer or dismiss inefficient employees, and to insist upon regular attendance. Miss Briscoe insisted that all workers, even inefficient ones, should be retained. Gantt argued that poor personnel relations and assignments were a contributing factor to the productivity problem he had been hired to solve. The younger, junior managers backed Gantt; the older, senior managers backed Briscoe; and Gantt lost this first battle between scientific management and the welfare movement.[13] The battle lines were drawn

[13] The full account of this clash may be found in Daniel Nelson and Stuart Campbell, "Taylorism versus Welfare Work in American Industry: H. L. Gantt and the Bancrofts," *Business History Review*, Vol. 46, No. 1 (Spring, 1972), pp. 1–16.

and the early 1900s were to find both interpretations of personnel work in various stages of development. Modern personnel management was to be a wedding of welfare work and scientific management, a marriage which occurred when both partners were very young.

Further Advancements in Personnel Management

Growing concern for improved personnel practices touched off a vocational guidance and personnel testing and placement movement. The first national organization to deal with personnel matters was the National Association of Corporation Schools, founded in 1913. It considered its work "human relations," meaning employee relations. In 1918, the National Association of Employment Managers was formed to focus on employment practices. In 1922, these two groups merged to form the National Personnel Association, which indicated national recognition of the need to study and improve employment practices and relations.

Walter Dill Scott (1869–1955) received his Ph.D. under Wundt at Leipzig in 1900. In America, Scott turned his efforts to psychological research into advertising, to the selection and placement of salesmen, and eventually to helping devise a system for classifying and testing officer candidates for the Army. In his early work Scott focused on the psychology of persuasion and on proper personnel selection to enhance industrial efficiency.[14] From this work, Scott turned to a broader view of personnel and pioneered in formalizing the emerging "personnel management" function.[15]

The early developmental period of vocational guidance efforts had few well-developed tools and techniques for personnel administration. World War I led to greater refinement, and the postwar period found great strides in the management of personnel. Henry Ford, faced with a tight labor market and a worker turnover

---

[14]Edmund C. Lynch, "Walter Dill Scott: Pioneer Industrial Psychologist," *Business History Review*, Vol. 42, No. 2 (Summer, 1968), p. 150; see also: W. D. Scott, *Influencing Men in Business*, New York: Ronald Press Co., 1911; and W. D. Scott, *Increasing Human Efficiency*, New York: Macmillan Co., 1911.

[15]W. D. Scott and R. C. Clothier, *Personnel Management: Principles, Practices, and Point of View*, Chicago: A. W. Shaw Co., 1923. (Revised in 1931, 1941, 1949, and 1954).

rate of 10 percent, formed an early personnel department in 1914 called the "Sociological Department."[16] The $5 minimum wage, announced the same year, was "neither charity nor wages, but profit sharing and efficiency engineering."[17] Ford feared that the easy money of $5 per day would lead the workers astray, so he employed 100 investigators—"advisers"—who visited the workers' homes to insure that their homes were neat and clean, that they did not drink too much, that their sex life was without tarnish, and that they used their leisure time profitably. The sociological department was a far cry from modern concepts of personnel management, but its formation symbolized the notion that concern for the human element was the very best investment a business firm could make.

The war experiences with the refinement of psychological tests, plus a tight labor market, and growing labor unrest in the postwar period as evidenced by the Wobblies (I.W.W.) and the Bolsheviks in Russia spurred many firms to emulate the personnel departments of Ford and other companies. The early personnel and employment management texts followed the theme that concern for people would lead to greater prosperity for all. Farseeing industrialists such as James Hartness of Jones and Lamson Machine Company pointed out that management approaches were too mechanistic and relied too heavily on the efficiency engineers. Greater increases in efficiency must come through psychology in the work place as well as from engineering and economics.[18] In England, Benjamin Seebohm Rowntree (1871–1954) brought to his York Cocoa Works an interest in human welfare which stopped slightly short of paternalism. Rowntree employed a sociologist in a "psychological department" who supervised company education, health, canteens, housing, and recreation.[19] Mary Follett, (who will be discussed later) chose Rowntree's firm as a prime example of how a business should develop a social philosophy. Rowntree also influenced the lives and ideas of two other significant con-

[16] Loren Baritz, *The Servants of Power*, New York: John Wiley and Sons, 1960, p. 33.

[17] Henry Ford, quoted by Baritz, loc. cit.

[18] James Hartness, *The Human Factor in Works Management*, New York: McGraw-Hill Book Co., 1912.

[19] Lyndall Urwick and E. F. L. Brech, *The Making of Scientific Management; Thirteen Pioneers*, vol. 1, London: Sir Isaac Pitman and Sons, 1951, pp. 58–70.

tributors to management thought, Oliver Sheldon and Lyndall Urwick.

Interest in the human side of enterprise and in the potentialities of personnel administration would lead to significant changes in assumptions about people in organizations. For instance, Ordway Tead partially recovered from his "instinct" explanation of work behavior to coauthor an early personnel text with Henry C. Metcalf.[20] They concluded that instincts and inborn tendencies still had a great deal to do with human conduct but that advances in personnel research were opening new vistas enabling more scientific selection, placement, and training. Executives should adopt a "personnel point of view," which assumed that there was a cause-and-effect relationship in behavior which could be studied for purposes of guiding human conduct.[21] Proper work habits could be formed, emotions controlled, and creative leadership could lead to reduced conflict and improved morale.

The typical personnel management text of this era examined such subjects as job analysis, writing job descriptions and specifications, psychological tests, interviewing and selecting employees, merit rating, promotion policies, analyzing labor turnover, training, and dealing with problems such as tardiness and absences. The training of foremen was also included but relatively little attention was paid to developing higher management. "Industrial democracy" and employee representation were often mentioned but in the 1920s the stress was largely on company unions, partially due to some residue of Taylorism and partially to the fact that the twenties was a paternalistic, "union-busting" decade.

The 1920s witnessed a decline in psychological testing and an upswing in company paternalism and welfare schemes designed to woo worker loyalty. People became the firm's most important asset, not out of sentimentality nor moral uplift, but based on the view that concern for employee welfare would increase worker efficiency. Personnel departments proliferated and worker welfare

[20] Ordway Tead and Henry C. Metcalf, *Personnel Administration: Its Principles and Practice*, New York: McGraw-Hill Book Co., 1920.

[21] Ordway Tead, *Human Nature and Management: The Applications of Psychology to Executive Leadership*, New York: McGraw-Hill Book Co., 1929, p. 9.

schemes were designed with the hope that workers would reciprocate by expressing their appreciation through higher productivity. Psychological testing had proved inadequate to the task of selection since research had failed to show any correlation between tests and job success.[22] An early employment manager noted that tests were unscientific, administered by amateurs, used as a substitute for judgment, and were little better than fortune-telling for predicting human success.[23] Quacks abounded, throwing reputable psychologists into disrepute, as firms sought quick and simple solutions to human problems. After 1925 the testing fad declined and managers had less faith in measuring traits that would predict greater efficiency. Eventually this breach would be filled by the ethic of human relations as the road to greater productivity.

Foundations of Social Man: Theory and Research

Scientific management did not neglect the human factor, as it is frequently alleged, but focused on the individual. There were reasons for this, as we shall see later, but changing cultural conditions and new theories were emerging in the scientific management era to lay the foundations for a new emphasis in evolving management thought.

Sociology and Industry

The human relations movement, to be discussed in chapter 13, found its roots in earlier sociological theory. Max Weber, Émile Durkheim, and Vilfredo Pareto formed an intellectual triad of sociological theorists of the nineteenth century. Max Weber, who will be discussed in more detail later, established sociology as a field of inquiry and was concerned with the relationship between eco-

---

[22]For example, Henry C. Link suggested that more effort should be devoted to testing *tests* rather than men. H. C. Link, *Employment Psychology*, New York: Macmillan Co., 1921.

[23]Mary Barnett Gilson, *What's Past is Prologue*, New York: Harper & Row, 1940, p. 64.

nomics and society. Émile Durkheim's first book, his doctoral dissertation on *The Division of Labor*, was published in 1893.[24] He divided societies into two primary types, *mechanical*, or those dominated by a collective consciousness; and *organic*, or those characterized by specialization and division of labor and societal interdependence. Mechanical societies were bound together by friendliness, neighborliness, and kinship; however, such solidarity did not exist in organic societies and led to anomie or a state of confusion, insecurity, and "normlessness." According to Durkheim, restoration of social solidarity in organic societies must come through the law and a new "collective consciousness" which created values and norms and imposed them on the individual. In organic societies people must cooperate, "love" one another, and be willing to sacrifice self to the group in order to promote solidarity. In Durkheim there arises the antithesis of Adam Smith's self-interest as the basis for exchange. Instead, Durkheim would substitute the group as the source of values and norms and as the new collective consciousness. It was in Durkheim's anomie that Elton Mayo found a new prescription for industrial solidarity.

Vilfredo Pareto (1848–1923) was the father of the notion of "social systems."[25] By social system Pareto meant the state which society takes both at a specified moment and in the successive transformations which it undergoes within a period of time. Pareto was a "macro" sociologist and concerned with larger societal systems but his ideas were later adopted by Elton Mayo and the human relationists in their own analytical framework. Pareto's theories were introduced to Mayo and the Hawthorne researchers by Lawrence J. Henderson, a physiologist in the research group.[26]

William G. Scott further traced the comparison between Pareto and the Mayo group and found that Pareto's ideas of the so-

[24] E. Durkheim, *De la Division du travail Social*, Paris: F. Alcan, 1893: translated by George Simpson, New York: Free Press, 1947.

[25] Vilfredo Pareto, *The Mind and Society*, translated by Andrew Bongiorno and Arthur Livingston, New York: Harcourt Brace Jovanovich, 1935.

[26] John B. Knox, "Sociological Theory and Industrial Sociology," *Social Forces*, March, 1955, cited by W. G. Scott, *Organization Theory: A Behavioral Analysis for Management*, Homewood, Ill.: R. D. Irwin, Inc., 1967, p. 38. Henderson's study of Pareto may be found in L. J. Henderson, *Pareto's General Sociology*, Cambridge, Mass.: Harvard University Press, 1935.

cial system, of logical and nonlogical behavior, of equilibrium, of the functions of language, and of the circulation of the elite were all adopted by the Hawthorne researchers.[27] For example, Pareto's social system viewed society as a cluster of interdependent but variable units. The human relationists were concerned with the interdependence of the social and physical aspects of the work environment and viewed the system as something which must be considered as a whole because each part bore some interdependent relationship to every other part.

Aside from the pioneering work of Pareto and Durkheim, a major school of sociological theory called "social behaviorism" was forming during the scientific management era. This school introduced the idea of the "social person" as the object of study and established social psychology as a fundamental branch of sociology.[28] Charles Horton Cooley contributed the "looking glass self" or the idea that the social self arises reflectively in terms of one's reactions to the opinions of others. Through group experiences the person forms his first notions of both self and social unity. George Herbert Mead fathered social psychology by suggesting that one learns his own self through a process of taking the role of others in interaction situations. Society enters every person through the process of interaction and the self is constantly being reshaped through these encounters.

In psychology, the notion of *Gestalt* was coming into prominence due to the work of the Austrian Christian von Ehrenfels (1890) and the German Max Wertheimer (1912). Prior to the Gestalt idea, Martindale characterized psychological theories as "mechanistic" in that they tended to emphasize fundamental units of study, e.g. an element, a particle, or an individual. Gestalt psychology, on the other hand, represented an "organismic" approach which emphasized not the parts or units but the patterns, wholes, configurations, etc., which made the whole appear to be more than the sum of its parts.[29] From these beginnings, Gestalt

[27] W. G. Scott, Figure 1–3, pp. 40–41.

[28] Don Martindale, *The Nature and Types of Sociological Theory*, Boston: Houghton Mifflin Co., 1960, pp. 285–435.

[29] Ibid., pp. 451–453.

theory would pervade the ideas of social systems, group dynamics, and other behavioral research right up to the modern-day notion of general systems theory.

Some Early Empirical Investigatons

The group and social facets of human behavior were gaining recognition in sociological theory and in the Gestalt idea of configurations and systems. Empirical investigations into the human facet of industrial life were sparse but becoming more frequent. Whiting has uncovered the work of Paul Goehre, a German theological student, who took a job in a factory to investigate working conditions in 1891. Goehre observed that the workers took more pride in producing a complete unit of work rather than an unidentifiable fragment, that higher productivity occurred when supervisors instilled a feeling of group interdependence and teamwork, and that there were informal group pressures for adherence to norms. Lower morale and lower efficiency were the result when people were isolated and felt a lack of "community of labour [sic]." According to Whiting, Goehre formed a "missing link" between Robert Owen and the more modern human relationists.[30]

In the post-Taylor era, two other individuals were developing some unique ideas on motivation. Henri DeMan anticipated by more than three decades Frederick Herzberg's methods of probing. worker motivation. DeMan asked both wage earners and salaried workers in various parts of Germany to make a statement "concerning their own feelings about their daily work."[31] DeMan concluded that there was a natural instinct in people to find "joy in work." In this drive, positive motives were instincts for "activity," "self-assertion," to be "constructive," and a longing for "mastery" (power). The negative factors which inhibited this natural impulse for joy in work were found: (1) in the job itself in factors such as detailed work, monotony, reduction of worker initiative, fatigue,

---

[30]Richard J. Whiting, "Historical Search in Human Relations," *Academy of Management Journal,* Vol. 7, No. 1 (March, 1964), pp. 45–53. Goehre's work was translated in English as *Three Months in a Workshop,* London: Swan Sonnenschein & Company, 1895.

[31]Henri DeMan, *Joy In Work,* translation by Eden Paul, New York: Holt, Rinehart and Winston, 1929, p. 9.

and poor working conditions; and (2) in "social hindrances" such as the dependent position of the worker, unjust wage systems, speed-ups, insecurity of livelihood, and lack of social solidarity. DeMan's sample (78 subjects) was limited but his findings bear a remarkable similarity to Herzberg's later "motivation-hygiene" theory in many respects. DeMan felt that work itself was a motivator and that management's job was to remove the "hindrances" which prevented the worker from finding joy in work.

Whiting Williams quit his white-collar job as personnel director of the Hydraulic Pressed Steel Company to become a blue-collar "industrial hobo" to study working conditions first-hand. Williams worked in coal mines, ship building, iron mines, oil refineries, and a multitude of other industries to gauge the temper of the times. By living and working with his research sample, Williams was able to form some very definite impressions about labor-management relations: (1) that workers restricted output ("stringing out the job") because they perceived scarce job opportunities and employers tended to hire and lay off indiscriminately; (2) that unions arose out of worker concern for security and the unions would not have made much progress if employers had evidenced concern for this worker need; (3) that long factory hours (12-hour shifts in steel) made both workers and foremen grouchy and tired, causing interpersonal conflict; and (4) that the workers listened to radical agitators because employers failed to speak "of the plans and purposes, the aims and ideals—the character of the company."[32]

In later writings, Williams argued that pay was relative in the worker's view; i.e., it was not the absolute amount of pay but the amount in relation to what others were receiving that counted. Hence incentive plans were less than effective as motivators. The "mainspring" of workers was the ". . . wish to enjoy the feeling of our [the worker's] worth as persons among other persons."[33] "Togetherness" in thinking, feeling, and working in groups was important to the workers. It was from their peers that the workers drew their social sustenance, security, and concept of self-worth.

[32] Whiting Williams, *What's on the Worker's Mind*, New York: Charles Scribner's Sons, 1920, pp. 283–290.

[33] Whiting Williams, *Mainsprings of Men*, New York: Charles Scribner's Sons, 1925, p. 147.

Workers chose to "get along" with their coworkers because they could always find another job but could not always move from the community. From the employer, and especially the foreman, they expected recognition and treatment conducive to preserving self-worth. It was not the paternalistic clubs, cafeterias, and recreation activities that won worker loyalty, but successful relations with the foreman as a representative of management. Williams recommended an Eleventh Commandment, "Thou Shalt Not Take Thy Neighbor For Granted" and urged management to change from appeals to fear to appeals to "hope and surety of reward."[34] Latent in Williams' study of the worker was Cooley's "looking glass self" and the group as the primary social unit. Williams' experiences had taught him that the worker was not the rational "economic man" as assumed by many. Workers acted on the basis of emotion, sought to maintain social status, and considered the nature of their job more important than any pecuniary considerations.

The view and analysis of people as social beings did not begin at Western Electric. From Durkheim's identification of anomie, through Pareto's analysis of the social system, through the social behaviorists such as Mead and Cooley, through the Gestaltists, and to the empirical evidence of Whiting Williams and others, economic man was on the wane and social man began to wax.

Summary

Industrial psychology was a spin-off of scientific management, and academic and industrial interest was stimulated in vocational guidance, personnel testing for selection, and individual motivation. A secondary theme of the period was a growing interest in worker behavior, and social scientists began to add new dimensions to understanding behavior in industry. Times were changing and the social facet of people, including their interactions, their needs for security, and their drives for social solidar-

---

[34]Williams, *What's on the Worker's Mind*, pp. 312–313. Williams also studied the worker in foreign settings. His study of England may be found in *Full Up and Fed Up*, New York: Charles Scribner's Sons, 1921; and his experiences in France, Germany, Italy, and Spain are reported in *Horny Hands and Hampered Elbows*, New York: Charles Scribner's Sons, 1922.

ity, began to appear. In theory and practice, Durkheim, Pareto, Whiting Williams, and others were laying the intellectual foundations for a new era in evolving management thought.

10

The Emergence of Administrative Theory

History rarely measures the full contribution of a man during his own lifetime. Epitaphs are often prematurely written and other times bring added appreciation to men such as the two presented in this chapter. Both of our subjects lived during the latter nineteenth and the early twentieth centuries; both wrote during the scientific management era in America; both were Europeans; and both made lasting contributions to the evolution of management thought. One was a practicing manager and one an academician; one was trained in the physical sciences, the other in the social sciences; and neither was accorded the full measure of his contribution until some decades after his death. Henri Fayol, the French manager-engineer, fathered the first theory of administration through his study of the management process. Max Weber, the German economist-sociologist, sired a theory of organizations through his conception of bureaucracy as the ideal of technical efficiency. Both sought to generalize theory and practice; yet it was the task of others to bring full appreciation to the impact of their thinking on modern management.

Henri Fayol: The Man and His Career

Henri Fayol (1841–1925) was born of a family of the French *bourgeoisie* and in 1860 graduated from the National School of Mines at St. Etienne.[1] Trained as a mining engineer, Fayol joined the Commentary-Fourchambault Company in 1860 and spent his entire career with that coal-mining and iron foundry combine. From 1860 until 1866, he worked as an engineer; but his administrative talents were recognized and he was made manager of the Commentary pits at age 25. Six years later, he was promoted to manager of a group of coal mines and also published numerous works on geology and mine safety. In 1888, the company was in dire financial straits and headed for bankruptcy when Henri Fayol was named the managing director. As the coal pits of Commentary neared exhaustion, the pits and iron works at Décazeville were procured in 1892 and the new combine became known as "Comambault." Faced with the overall problems of the new combine, Fayol was able to bring the company from near bankruptcy to an unassailable financial position by the time of his retirement at the age of 77. Today, this company continues as a part of Le Creusot-Loire, the largest mining and metallurgical group in central France.

During his lifetime, Fayol made significant technical contributions to geology and metallurgy as well as to the field of management. He was awarded the Delasse Prize in 1893 for his technical accomplishments, the Gold Medal of the Society for the Encouragement of Industry, and was a member of the Legion of Honour. From his own experiences, Fayol began to formulate his ideas of administrative theory as early as 1900 when he read a paper on administration before the International Mining and Metallurgical Congress. In this particular paper, he indicated the importance of the administrative function but did not present the "elements" of management for which he later became famous. In 1908, he prepared a paper for the Jubilee of the Society of Mineral Industry in which he put forth his 14 "general principles" of administration. His first mention of the "elements" of administration came in 1916 with the publication of his *Administration indus-*

[1] The original source of personal data on Fayol is the *Dictionnaire de l'organization et de Science du Travail*, published by the Comité National de l'organization française, and translated by J. A. Coubrough in Henri Fayol, *Industrial and General Administration*, Geneva: International Management Institute, 1930, pp. 4–5. Further insights in a more readily accessible form may be found in Lyndall Urwick and E. F. L. Brech, *The Making of Scientific Management* (vol. I), London: Sir Isaac Pitman and Sons, 1951, pp. 39–47, and L. Urwick's "Foreword" to Henri Fayol, *General and Industrial Management*, (translation by Constance Storrs), London: Sir Isaac Pitman and Sons, 1949, pp. v–xxix.

trielle et générale.[2] The first English translation was by Coubrough and appeared in 1930 under the auspices of the International Management Institute at Geneva.[3] One of Fayol's other papers, "The Administrative Theory of the State," was translated in 1923 and published in America in 1937 as a part of a collection entitled *Papers on the Science of Administration*.[4] However, America was not thoroughly exposed to Fayol's theory until 1949 when Pitman's of London published a translation by Constance Storrs.[5]

Ignorance of Fayol's work was not limited to the United States; even in France his work was largely overshadowed by that of Taylor, due to the efforts of Henry Le Chatelier and Charles de Freminville. Le Chatelier had translated and popularized Taylor in France and the contributions of scientific management to the French war effort were substantial. From Fayol's retirement (1918) to his death in 1925, he founded and presided over the meetings of the Center of Administrative Studies, a group formed to promote the advancement of *"Fayolisme."* Shortly before his death, this group merged with the Le Chatelier-de Freminville or *"Taylorisme"* group to form the Comité National de l'Organisation Française.

This merger was significant in that it brought the two main French schools of management together. Early interpretations of Fayol had placed his work in competition or contrast with Taylor's. Fayol insisted that this was not so and that the two were complementary in the sense that both sought to improve management through different avenues of analysis. In comparing the lives of these two men, one can see the reasons for their different perspectives.

These two fountainheads of management thought were quite dissimilar in many respects; and, though both were born of relatively well-to-do parents and both were educated as engineers, their similarities soon vanish. Fayol was born and educated to the managerial elite in a French culture which stressed position based on tradition. Social classes were more distinct and the French

[2] Published as a monograph by the Societé de l'Industrie Minérale in 1916 and in book form by Dunod Frères (Paris) in 1925.

[3] The title was translated by Coubrough as *Industrial and General Administration*.

[4] Edited by Luther Gulick and Lyndall Urwick; pp. 99–114.

[5] The title was translated by Storrs as *General and Industrial Management*.

manager achieved success through genetics and long and faithful service. Taylor started at the bottom and worked his way up in the open culture of America and the functioning Protestant ethic. Fayol faced no hostile organized labor, never encountered the resistance of installing his system into a plant, and never appeared before any investigating committees. Taylor started as a worker and worked his way up while Fayol started as a junior executive and from the beginning identified with the management group. Taylor began by implementing his methods in the shop and then generalized from them while Fayol built his system of general management from the executive viewpoint and then applied them to lower organizational elements. Taylor died relatively young amidst much turmoil and controversy. Fayol lived a long life, did not publish his major work until he was 75, and avoided the boiling waters of controversy. Taylor's star shone brightly while Fayol's was eclipsed, awaiting other times and other men who could write his proper epitaph.

Management or Administration?

Fayol intended to write a four-part treatise on administration which would have included: Part I, the necessity for and possibility of teaching management; Part II, the principles and elements of management; Part III, his personal observations and experiences; and Part IV, the lessons of the war. Parts III and IV never appeared but the beginnings were enough to establish Fayol's stress on the importance of management in all undertakings, "large or small, industrial, commercial, political, religious, or any other."[6] This "universality" of management marked a major contribution since it proposed to overcome parochial views and set the study of management apart as a study in itself.[7] Fayol began by identifying six groups of activities found in

[6]Henri Fayol (the Storrs translation), p. xxi. Except where specifically noted, the Storrs translation will be used since it is more readily available.

[7]Cf. Taylor's introduction to *Principles:* "Third . . . to show that the fundamental principles of scientific management are applicable to all kinds of human activities, from our simplest individual acts to the work of our great corporations . . ." (p. 7). Fayol certainly knew of Taylor's work via Le Chatelier who translated it in the *Revue de Metallurgie* (1911). Thus Taylor perceived a universality of the methods and philosophy of scientific management but not the universality of the activity of management as Fayol developed it.

all industrial undertakings: (1) "technical," such as production and manufacture; (2) "commercial," or buying, selling and exchange; (3) "financial," or the search for and optimum use of capital; (4) "security," or the protection of property and persons; (5) "accounting," or stocktaking, balance sheets, costs, and statistics; and (6) "managerial," or "planning, organization, command, co-ordination, and control."[8] Of the six activities, Fayol devoted his attention only to managerial activities since the others were commonly understood.

At this point, it is necessary to develop an analysis of the variations which appear between Fayol's original French, Coubrough's 1930 translation, and Storrs' 1949 rendition. Lyndall Urwick criticized the Storrs translation for substituting the word "management" for "administration" but acceded to this change since it was "accurate and convenient" in modern terminology.[9] However, a comparison of these three editions will indicate how the course of management thought might have been changed by the translation of only *one* word.

In the original French, Fayol developed his *"fonction administrative"*:

> J'ai donc adopté la définition suivante:
>
> Administrer, c'est prévoir, organiser, commander, coordonner et contrôler;
>
> Prévoir, c'est-à-dire scruter l'avenir et dresser le programme d'action;
>
> Organiser, c'est-à-dire constituer le double organisme, matériel et social, de l'entreprise;
>
> Commander, c'est-à-dire faire fonctionner le personnel;
>
> Coordonner, c'est-à-dire felier, unir, harmoniser tous les actes et tous les efforts;
>
> Controler, c'est-à-dire veiller à ce que tout se passe conformément aux règles établies et aux ordres donnés.[10]

Coubrough rendered this as:

> I have, therefore, adopted the following definition: To administrate *is to plan, organize, command, coordinate and control.*

[8]Fayol (Storrs), pp. 3–6.

[9]"Foreword," ibid., pp. xii–xiii.

[10]Fayol, p. 11.

To plan means to study the future and arrange the plan of operations.

To organize means to build up the material and human organization of the business, organizing both men and materials.

To command means to make the staff do their work.

To co-ordinate means to unite and correlate all activities.

To control means to see that everything is done in accordance with the rules which have been laid down and the instructions which have been given. [11]

In the Storrs' version:

Therefore I have adopted the following definition: To manage *is to forecast and plan, to organize, to command, to co-ordinate and to control. To foresee and provide means examining the future and drawing up the plan of action. To organize means building up the dual structure, material and human, of the undertaking. To command means maintaining activity among the personnel. To co-ordinate means binding together, unifying and harmonizing all activity and effort. To control means seeing that everything occurs in conformity with established rule and expressed command.* [12]

The major distinction between the translations of Fayol's *"administrer"* is in Coubrough's "to administrate" and Storrs's "to manage." How did Fayol distinguish between management and administration? In the original French:

La fonction administrative se distingue nettement des cinq autres fonctions essentielles.

Il importe de ne pas la confondre avec le gouvernement.

Gouverner, c'est conduire l'entreprise vers son but en cherchant à tirer le meilleur parti possible de toutes les ressources dont elle dispose; c'est assurer la marche des six fonctions essentielles.

L'administration n'est que l'une des six fonctions dont le gouvernement doit assurer la marche. Mais elle tient dans le rôle des grandes chefs une si grande place qu'il peut parfois sembler que ce rôle est exclusivement administratif. [13]

[11] Fayol (Coubrough), p. 9. Italics added.

[12] Fayol (Storrs), pp. 5–6. Italics added.

[13] Fayol, pp. 11–12. Italics added.

According to Coubrough:

> *It is important not to confuse* administration *with* management. To manage *an undertaking is to conduct it towards its objective by trying to make the best possible use of all the resources at its disposal; it is, in fact, to ensure the smooth working of the six essential functions. Administration is only one of these functions, but the managers of big concerns spend so much of their time on it that their jobs sometimes seem to consist solely of administration.* [14]

And, the Storrs translation:

> *The* managerial *function is quite distinct from the other five essential functions. It should not be confused with* government. To govern *is to conduct the undertaking towards its objective by seeking to derive optimum advantage from all available resources and to assure the smooth working of the six essential functions. Management is merely one of the six functions whose smooth working government has to ensure, but it has such a large place in the part played by higher managers that sometimes this part seems exclusively managerial.* [15]

Thus Fayol made a definite distinction between *administrer* and *gouverner* which Coubrough interprets as "to administer" and "to manage" and which Storrs renders as "to manage" and "to govern." To a Frenchman, *gouverner* is a general function of steering or guiding a totality toward a goal; for example, the captain of a ship, the head of a state, or the chief of an enterprise. Depending on the context of the writer, *gouverner* may become steering a ship, governing a state, or *managing* an enterprise. On the other hand, *administrer* also means to manage but is less comprehensive and applies to executing smaller matters. Briefly stated, Coubrough's translation is the better of the two and Storrs's rendering of *gouverner* as "to govern" was not appropriate in the business context of Fayol's writing. [16]

The point in this comparative analysis is to clear up some

---

[14] Fayol (Coubrough), p. 9. Italics added.

[15] Fayol (Storrs), p. 6. Italics added.

[16] The author is indebted to Dr. Joseph Allaire, Chairman, Department of Modern Languages, Florida State University, for his assistance in comparing, translating and making the above distinctions.

semantic problems. For many, management is "getting things done through people" and this view has persisted because of the Storrs translation:

> *The managerial function finds its only outlet through the members of the organization (body corporate). Whilst the other functions bring into play material and machines the managerial function operates only on the personnel.* [17]

Coubrough's version reads:

> *The administrative function is only concerned with the human part of an undertaking; while the other functions control material and machines, the administrative function only affects the personnel.* [18]

If one accepts Fayol's original intent to distinguish between *administrer* and *gouverner*, then the Storrs translation which confined the definition of management to working with and through people was an erroneous one (Figure 10-1). Fayol's intent was to establish management as an overall function of conducting an undertaking "towards its objective by trying to make the best possible use of all the resources at its disposal . . . to ensure the smooth working of the six essential functions. Administration is only one of these functions . . ."[19] Alas, this was not the case; and the Storrs translation became the standard translation of Fayol.[20]

Managerial Skills and Abilities

Fayol did not develop a discussion of this general "management" function separate from his "administrative elements." In presenting the abilities needed by a manager, he did stress the idea that each manager would need "special knowledge" which was peculiar to any function, such as technical, financial, and so on. In general, every manager needed these qualities and abilities:

---

[17] Fayol (Storrs), p. 19.

[18] Fayol (Coubrough), p. 19.

[19] Fayol (Coubrough), p. 9.

[20] This author prefers the Coubrough translation but will confine himself in the following pages to using the Storrs terminology in order to preserve historical continuity and to keep the material within the commonly accepted frame of reference of the reader.

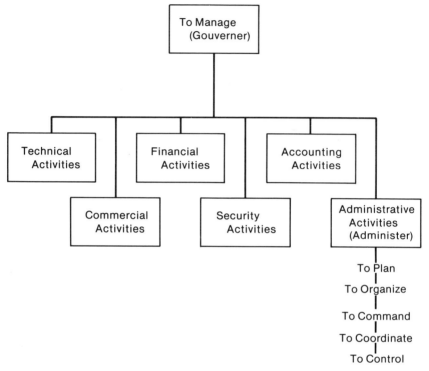

Fig. 10-1.   Fayol's "management" function.

1. *Physical qualities: health, vigour, address.*

2. *Mental qualities: ability to understand and learn, judgement, mental vigour and adaptability.*

3. *Moral qualities: energy, firmness, willingness to accept responsibility, initiative, loyalty, tact, dignity.*

4. *General education: general acquaintance with matters not belonging exclusively to the function performed.*

5. *Special knowledge: that peculiar to the function, be it technical, commercial, financial, managerial, etc. . . .*

6. *Experience: knowledge arising from the work proper. It is the recollection of lessons which one has oneself derived from things.*[21]

[21] Fayol (Storrs), p. 7.

Fayol then graphed the relative importance of requisite abilities for personnel, depending on their location in the management hierarchy. At the worker level, technical ability was most important; but as one moved up the scalar chain, the relative importance of managerial ability increased while the need for technical ability decreased. The higher the level of authority, the more dominant became the need for managerial ability. Ability in commercial, financial, security, and accounting matters also diminished in importance farther up the scalar chain. In terms of differences in the size of the enterprise, the manager of a small firm must have relatively more technical ability, while in larger concerns, the upper levels needed managerial rather than technical ability.

The distinction between the relative importance of abilities was crucial to Fayol's development of the notion of *teaching* management. Regarding the proliferation of large firms and other organizations, he noted that future leadership must receive managerial training rather than clinging to the past precepts of education for technical, commercial, etc. abilities. Schools did not teach management and it was assumed by industrial leaders that practice and experience were the only pathways to a managerial position. The reason for the absence of management teaching was the "absence of theory." Each manager followed his own methods, principles, and personal theories, but no one had ever tried to fit the acceptable precepts and experiences into a general framework of administrative theory. Management knowledge came through osmosis and generalized concepts were lacking. Fayol had built his case for theory: (1) the fact that management was a separate activity applicable to all types of undertakings; (2) that managerial ability was sorely needed as one moved up the hierarchy; and (3) the premise that management could be taught.

The Principles of Management

The notion of "principles" of management is often misunderstood and subject to controversy. Fayol's conception of a principle was not as rigidly based as one might conceive of a rule or law in the physical sciences. He used the term "principles" very reluctantly:

> *For preference I shall adopt the term principles whilst dissociating it from any suggestion of rigidity, for there is nothing rigid or absolute in management affairs, it is all a question of proportion. Seldom do we have to apply the same principle twice in identical conditions; allowance must be made for different and changing circumstances . . .*
>
> *Therefore principles are flexible and capable of adaptation to every need; it is a matter of knowing how to make use of them, which is a difficult art requiring intelligence, experience, decision and proportion. Compounded of tact and experience, proportion is one of the foremost attributes of the manager. There is no limit to the number of principles of management, every rule or managerial procedure which strengthens the body corporate or facilitates its functioning has a place among the principles so long, at least, as experience confirms its worthiness. A change in the state of affairs can be responsible for change of rules which had been engendered by that state.*[22]

Fayol's principles were derived from those that he used "most frequently" in his own experience. They were not immutable but served as "lighthouses" to show the way to theory. Fayol's famous 14 principles were:

1. *Division of work.*

2. *Authority.*

3. *Discipline.*

4. *Unity of command.*

5. *Unity of direction.*

6. *Subordination of individual interests to the general interest.*

7. *Remuneration.*

8. *Centralization.*

9. *Scalar chain (line of authority).*

10. *Order.*

11. *Equity.*

12. *Stability of tenure of personnel.*

[22]Ibid., p. 19.

13. *Initiative.*

14. Esprit de corps.[23]

Division of work was the classic idea of specialization of labor and the advantages which accrued in reducing waste, increasing output, and easing the task of job training. Like Taylor, Fayol thought that division of labor was not limited to technical work but could apply also to a "specialization of functions and separation of powers,"[24] i.e., to managerial effort also.

Authority was defined as "the right to give orders and the power to exact obedience."[25] Fayol distinguished between the *formal* authority held by the manager by the virtue of his office or rank and *personal* authority which was "compounded of intelligence, experience, moral worth, ability to lead, past services, etc."[26] A good manager would *complement* his official authority with personal authority. Further, authority and responsibility were corollaries in the sense that wherever authority was exercised, responsibility arose. Fayol stated the classic case for authority being commensurate with responsibility and this principle has appeared throughout management literature to become as inseparable as Mary and her little lamb.

Discipline was in essence based on obedience and respect between the firm and its employees. It was essential to success and based on respect rather than fear. Poor discipline was inevitably the result of poor leadership and good discipline came from good leaders, clear agreements between management and labor regarding rules, and the judicious use of sanctions (penalties).

Unity of command, Fayol's fourth principle, brought him into opposition to Taylor's functional foremen. The principle that "For any action whatsoever an employee should receive orders from one superior only" was fundamental to Fayol's concept of an organization. Just as no man can serve two masters, dual command was a threat to authority, discipline, and stability.

Unity of direction meant "one head and one plan for a group

---

[23]Ibid., pp. 19–20. Note: Coubrough translated number five as "unity of management" and number nine as "the hierarchy."

[24]Ibid., p. 20.

[25]Ibid., p. 21.

[26]Ibid., p. 21.

of activities having the same objective."[27] Unity of direction came from a sound organization structure and was essential to "unity of action, coordination of strength, and focusing of effort."[28]

The principle of *subordination of individual interests to the general interest* was a plea to abolish "ignorance, ambition, selfishness, laziness, weakness and all human passions" which caused conflict when the individual or a group tried to prevail over the organization. The *remuneration of personnel* principle was Fayol's version of economic man. After discussing day wages, piece rates, bonuses, and profit sharing, he concluded that the mode of payment was dependent upon many factors and that the objective was to "make the personnel more valuable . . . and also to inspire keenness."[29] His analysis certainly fell short of suggesting a clear concept of a remunerative principle or of any clear notion of motivation. The principle of *centralization* was more lucid and showed some brillant insights into organization:

> *Centralization is not a system of management good or bad of itself, capable of being adopted or discarded at the whim of managers or of circumstances; it is always present to a greater or less extent. The question of centralization or decentralization, is a simple question of proportion, it is a matter of finding the optimum degree for the particular concern. In small firms, where the manager's orders go directly to subordinates there is absolute centralization; in large concerns, where a long scalar chain is interposed between manager and lower grades, orders and counter-information too, have to go through a series of intermediaries. Each employee, intentionally or unintentionally, puts something of himself into the transmission and execution of orders and of information received too. He does not operate merely as a cog in a machine. What appropriate share of initiative may be left to intermediaries depends on the personal character of the manager, on his moral worth, on the reliability of his subordinates, and also on the condition of the business. The degree of centralization must*

---

[27] Ibid., p. 25. Coubrough rendered this as "unity of management" which was "one manager and one plan for all operations which have the same object in view" (p. 23).

[28] Ibid., p. 25.

[29] Ibid., p. 32.

vary according to different cases. The objective to pursue is the optimum utilization of all faculties of the personnel.[30]

The continuum of possibilities for centralization and decentralization, the possible communication distortions in the scalar chain, and the variables affecting the degree of decentralization were pillars for evolving theory. Fayol's notion of the centralization–decentralization continuum was explicit: "everything which goes to increase the importance of the subordinate's role is decentralization, everything which goes to reduce it is centralization."[31]

The *scalar chain* was "the chain of superiors ranging from the ultimate authority to the lowest ranks."[32] It showed the routing of the line of authority and the channels for the transmission of communications. To counter possible communication delays caused by the unity of command principle, Fayol developed his "gang plank" which allowed communications to cross lines of authority but only when it was agreed to by all parties and superiors were kept informed at all times.[33] Thus Foreman *F*, desiring to communicate with Foreman *P*, could do so directly without reporting upward (*F* through *E* to *A*) and having that message in turn transmitted downward to *P*. The gang plank (see Figure 10–2) permitted swift, sure lateral communications without overloading circuits and preserved the unity of command principle.

Order, the tenth principle, insured a place for everything and everything in its place. It applied to materials, shop cleanliness, and to personnel. For people, it was each to his task and that task set neatly into a structure of activities. *Equity* resulted from kindliness and justice and provided a principle for employee relations. The twelfth principle, *stability of tenure of personnel*, sought to provide for orderly personnel planning and provisions to replace the human resource. *Initiative* as a principle exhorted individuals to display zeal and energy in all efforts. Finally, *esprit de corps* stressed building harmony and unity within the firm. "Dividing

[30] Ibid., p. 37.
[31] Ibid., p. 34.
[32] Ibid., p. 34.
[33] Ibid., p. 34. Coubrough translated Fayol's *passarelle* as a "bridge" (p. 28).

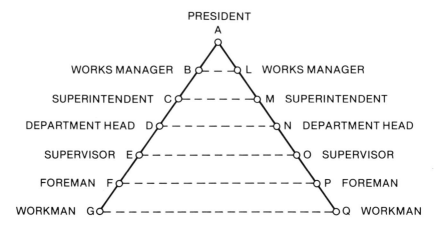

Fig. 10-2.   Fayol's gangplank.

enemy forces to weaken them is clever, but dividing one's own team is a grave sin against the business."[34]

Fayol's 14 principles represented building blocks for his discussion of the elements of management. They were intended as guides to theory and practice and were not exhaustive in scope nor to be interpreted as rigid in application. The early factory system reflected many of these principles in practice but it was Fayol's contribution to codify them into a conceptual schema. So much of our present management literature has been built upon Fayol's ideas and terminology that we cannot see the uniqueness of his insights. For his time and in the context of the paucity of management literature, his ideas were fresh, illuminating, and milestones on the path of the evolving discipline of management.

The Elements of Management: Planning

Henri Fayol did not use the term "process" to describe the manager's functions but chose instead "elements of management." The first element and one he stressed a great deal was *prévoyance* or *planning*. To Fayol, "managing means looking ahead" and foresight was an essential element of management.[35] Any plan of ac-

[34] Ibid., p. 40.

[35] Ibid., p. 43.

tion rested upon: (1) the firm's resources, i.e., the buildings, tools, materials, personnel, sales outlets, public relations, etc.; (2) the nature of present work in process; and (3) future trends in all activities of the firm whose occurrence could not be predetermined. In developing the plan of action, Fayol put forth an early concept of participation:

> *The study of resources, future possibilities, and means to be used for attaining the objective call for contributions from all departmental heads within the framework of their mandate, each one brings to this study the contribution of his experience together with recognition of the responsibility which will fall upon him in executing the plan.*[36]

Such participation insured that no resource was neglected and it promoted managerial interest in the plan. More attention would be given to planning by lower-echelon managers since they had to execute what they themselves had planned. A good plan of action had the characteristics of *unity* (one overall plan followed by specific plans for each activity); *continuity* (both short range and long range); *flexibility* (to bend to unexpected events); and *precision* (eliminating as much guesswork as possible). Based on these characteristics, Fayol advised a series of separate plans which would all together comprise one entire plan for the firm. Daily, weekly, monthly, annual, five-year, and ten-year forecasts (or plans) were prepared and redrafted as time passed or as conditions changed.

Fayol's stress on long-range planning was a unique contribution to management thought and his ideas are as important today as they were for his own time. He also displayed some unique insights into national planning for the French nation. The French government planned and budgeted on an annual basis with little or no regard for long-term development; the result was hand-to-mouth operations and a lack of exercise of fiscal responsibility by the chiefs of state. Fayol attributed the blame to "instability of tenure" for the prime minister and evidently this failing has been a continuing one for the French government. This first element of management, a combined function of planning and forecasting, was to be universal in applicability and a fundamental building block for all organizations.

[36] Ibid., p. 48.

Organizing

Organizing, the second element, included provisions for the structuring of activities and relationships as well as the procurement, evaluation, and training of personnel. As this element evolved, later writers split Fayol's organizing element into two elements, organizing and staffing (or human resource administration). For Fayol, to organize a business meant "to provide it with everything useful to its functioning: raw materials, tools, capital, personnel" and it was the duty of management to "see that the human and material organization is consistent with the objective, resources, and requirements of the concern."[37] The organization structure must be so arranged that it provided unity of direction toward the objective of the firm. The proper structure defined duties clearly, encouraged initiative and responsibility, harmonized activities and coordinated efforts, and insured control without an "excess of regulation, red tape, and paper control."[38]

In organization theory, the organizational "pyramid" is a product of functional growth. Functional growth is horizontal in that more people are added to functions as the organizational workload expands; scalar growth is vertical and caused by the need to add layers of supervision to direct and coordinate lower echelons. Each addition of workers in functional growth brings fresh foremen and in turn these added supervisors require the addition of higher levels of management, resulting in continued scalar growth. Fayol built his functional and scalar growth processes on the basis of 15 workers to a foreman and a ratio of 4 superiors to every other superior. For example, 15 workers required 1 manager, 60 workers required 4 superiors, and in turn these 4 required 1 common manager. The organization grew in simple geometrical progression whose first term was 15 (workers) and a common ratio of 4; by following this progression, Fayol envisioned a method of keeping the number of levels in an organization to a minimum. An organization of 251,658,240 people, for example, would require only 13 levels of management. Fayol advocated a relatively narrow span of management throughout the organization. Whatever his level of authority, one manager was to

[37] Ibid., p. 53.
[38] Ibid., p. 54.

have direct command over a small number of subordinates, "less than six, normally" according to Fayol, and only the first line supervisor would have more. At the foreman's level, Fayol judged him to be capable of handling 20 or 30 men, provided "the work is simple."[39]

On the subject of staff, Fayol visualized a group of men who had the "strength, knowledge, and time" to assist a manager by acting as a "sort of extension of the manager's personality."[40] The staff was to take orders only from the general manager and Fayol compared it to the military concept of the general staff. The functions of the staff were to aid in carrying out the manager's personal duties such as correspondence, interviews, conferences, etc., to aid in liaison and control, to gather information and assist in formulating future plans and to "search for improvements." The latter function of the staff was unique to Fayol; he postulated that operating management had neither the time nor the energy to devote to long-term research because they were too absorbed in current and weighty problems of running the business. The staff, freed of daily cares, could search for better work methods, perceive changes in business conditions, and concern itself with long-range matters.

Fayol's staff concept brought him into direct opposition to Taylor's functional foremen. Fayol agreed with Taylor's goal, i.e., the necessity for specialized assistance, but disagreed with the means. Functional foremen negated the unity-of-command principle and to Fayol this was treading on dangerous ground. Order must be maintained and this was possible only if one man was clearly responsible to one other person: "So . . . let us treasure the old type of organization in which unity of command is honored. It can, after all, be easily reconciled . . . with the assistance [i.e., staff] given to superintendents and foremen."[41]

Organization charts were a *sine qua non* of every enterprise. The preparation of a formal organization chart enabled one to visualize the organization as a whole, specified lines of suthority, provided channels of communication, prevented the overlapping

[39] Ibid., p. 98.
[40] Ibid., p. 63.
[41] Ibid., p. 70.

or encroachment of departments, avoided dual command situations, and clearly assigned duties and responsibilities. The chart itself was a managerial instrument for analyzing relationships between departments, for specifying individuals and their tasks, and for making modifications in the organization. Fayol did not completely develop his ideas or methods of departmentalizing operations since this was to be reserved for Part III of his work, which was never finished. Turning from the organizational framework, Fayol developed the rudiments of a personnel or staffing function which consisted of selection, evaluation, and training. Selection was examined only briefly and was viewed as a function of finding the qualities and knowledge in people to fill all levels of the organization. The consequence of poor selection was "commensurate with the rank of the employee"; Fayol advised that the length of time spent on selection should be increased as the level of position being filled rose. Evaluation of both managers and workers was based on similar essential characteristics but varied according to the level within the organization:

1. *"Health and physical fitness" were essential to all personnel.*

2. *"Intelligence and mental vigour" became more important further up the hierarchical chain. Mental vigour, as Fayol used the term, was the ability to "deal simultaneously with many varied manifold subjects" and was essential for higher managers.*

3. *"Moral qualities," such as initiative, acceptance of responsibility, loyalty, and discipline were important at all levels.*

4. *"General education," i.e., knowledge apart from job knowledge, was necessary if one wished to rise in the organization.*

5. *"Management knowledge" or that concerned with the elements of planning, organizing, command, coordination, and control became increasingly important as one moved up the organizational ladder.*

6. *"Knowledge of other functions" was necessary as one's responsibility expanded to include other spheres of activity.*[42]

Fayol confined himself to describing qualities and did not examine problems of evaluating performance, nor did he recom-

[42]Ibid., pp. 76–77.

mend methods and procedures for its conduct. Like Taylor's, his view of the personnel function was limited; this is not in criticism, however, since personnel practices of the day were very rudimentary in all cases. Training was dealt with at length primarily because Fayol had an axe to grind. He advocated a diminution of technical training and an increased teaching of managerial knowledge. Contemporary education was based on the premise that the value of engineers and industrial leaders bore "a direct relationship to the number of years devoted to the subject of mathematics."[43] Fayol deplored the emphasis on mathematics: "Long personal experience has taught me that the use of *higher* mathematics counts for nothing in managing businesses . . ."[44] Basic mathematics helped train the mind but further study should be devoted to management rather than more mathematics. Fayol sought balance and advised young engineers to study people, "their behavior, character, abilities, work, and even their personal interests."[45] For Fayol, *everyone* should study management for it was necessary in the home as well as in industrial and non-industrial undertakings.

Command

Command, Fayol's third element, had as the manager's object "to get the optimum return from all employees of his unit in the interest of the whole concern."[46] Command was an art which rested upon certain personal qualities and knowledge of general principles of management. The manager who exercised command should:

1. *Have a thorough knowledge of his personnel.*

2. *Eliminate the incompetent.*

3. *Be well versed in the agreements binding the business and its employees.*

4. *Set a good example.*

[43] Ibid., pp, 83–84.

[44] Ibid., p. 84. Later he referred to "higher" mathematics as special studies such as calculus.

[45] Ibid., p. 91.

[46] Ibid., p. 97.

5. *Conduct periodic audits of the organization and use summarized charts to further this.*

6. *Bring together his chief assistants by means of conferences, at which unity of direction and focusing of effort are provided for.*

7. *Not become engrossed in detail.*

8. *Aim at making unity, energy, initiative and loyalty prevail among the personnel.*[47]

Most of these aspects of command are self-explanatory and, together with the 14 principles, form a fairly coherent picture of Fayol's concept of leadership. He deemed conferences a very useful device for insuring unity of direction and stressed that the chief must be constantly aware of all business activities. The *caveat* to avoid being engrossed in detail was not antithetical to keeping informed. The manager should be aware of everything but not neglect large problems while lavishing attention on small ones. Through use of staff, by proper definition of the organization, and through the use of oral and written reports, the manager could maintain direction and control of the main business issues. To achieve initiative, the manager should allow subordinates "the maximum share of activity consistent with their position and capability, even at the cost of some mistakes . . ."[48] This was mostly delegation and not full-blown participation in management since a sound organization could be used to circumscribe activities to prevent too much initiative at the wrong times and in the wrong places. However, Fayol did recognize the importance of such delegated participation as a useful device for developing young managers.[49]

Coordination

Coordination, viewed by Fayol as a separate element of management, meant "to harmonize all the activities of a concern so as to facilitate its working, and its success."[50] Later writers have

---

[47] Ibid., pp. 97–98.
[48] Ibid., p. 103.
[49] Ibid., p. 103.
[50] Ibid., p. 103.

stressed the role of coordination in all elements rather than treating it as a separate one. To Fayol, coordination was a balancing act of keeping expenses equivalent to revenues, of maintaining equipment to meet production goals, and of insuring that sales and production were consonant. Organization and planning facilitated coordination by specifying duties, establishing schedules, and focusing responsibilities on the objective. Command instilled initiative and the conferences between the manager and his subordinates provided a clearing house for airing problems, progress, and plans. The conference was a quick, simple way of keeping informed and of insuring organizational cohesion. Liaison officers, typically staff personnel, should be used to enhance coordination in the interim between conferences and in the care of establishments located far from the main office. The liaison position supplemented coordination but did not replace the direct responsibility of the chief.

Control

Control consisted of "verifying whether everything occurs in conformity with the plan adopted, the instructions issued, and the principles established."[51] The objective of control was to identify errors in order to correct them and to prevent recurrence. Control was to be applied to people, objects, and activities. Effective control was based on prompt action, followed by sanctions if necessary. Control was impartial and Fayol advised separation of the inspector from those being inspected to insure independence of the control element. Control permeated all elements of the undertaking, including personnel, execution of plans, quality of work, financial activities, security, and information. Control also had an integrative effect on the other four elements because it stimulated better planning, simplified and strengthened the organization, increased the efficiency of command, and facilitated coordination. In effect, control completed a cycle of managerial activities which then could be improved as the cycle (or the process) of management continued.

[51] Ibid., p. 107.

A Final Note

Henri Fayol had the orientation of the top manager. He was not as philosophical as Taylor, nor did he stress mechanics to the same extent. Of the five elements he developed for his theory of administration, planning and organizing received the majority of his attention. The stress on these two was not necessarily an imbalance but illustrated the primacy that Fayol gave to these elements with respect to the performance of the others. Planning and organizing set the stage by making forecasts, developing a plan of action, establishing an organization, and selecting personnel. In Fayol's terms: "The organization, having been formed, must be set going, and this is the mission of command."[52] Command actuated the plans and the organization; coordination kept the parts of the organization in harmony; control checked up on plans and instructions with respect to actual performance; and the cycle was renewed as new plans were made in light of past operations.

It is easy to underestimate the work of Fayol. His ideas and terminology are so commonplace to present management literature that they are taken for granted. Yet his notion of an administrative theory applicable to all types of organized undertaking was an important milestone in the history of management. Though Taylor did suggest the applicability of a science of management to a multitude of activities, Fayol receives the credit for "universality" because he was much more explicit and far reaching. Taylor had more confidence in "principles" than Fayol, who saw them as flexible guides for action and not as immutable laws.

The "universality" of management principles was also tempered by Fayol. The manager who operated solely on the principles and who was armed only with knowledge of the elements would not be effective. In essence, the manager needed to know more than how to plan, organize, command, coordinate, and control. He had to have some knowledge of the business activities (technical, commercial, etc.) which he was managing, even if he were the chief executive. The elements did not operate in a vacuum but were applied to *something* which for Fayol were the essential activities and resources of the firm.

---

[52] Ibid., p. 97.

Bureaucracy: Max Weber

The life and work of Max Weber (1864–1920) run chronologically parallel to that of Henri Fayol and Frederick Taylor. Born to a life of affluence in Germany in a family of considerable social and political connections, Weber was an intellectual of the first degree with far-ranging interests in sociology, religion, economics, and political science.[53] As a professor, editor, consultant to government, and author, he established himself as one of the leading scholars of his period. *The Protestant Ethic and the Spirit of Capitalism* was one of his major works but his interests also led him to consider the relationships between economic organizations and society. Weber was a theorist who introduced a significant number of new interpretations and emphases which were unique to the economic-historical discussions of the time. His contributions greatly facilitated understanding of the relationships and the continuity between nineteenth-century family-firm capitalism, which he called "patrimonial," and the emerging era of the large-scale organization of industry and big governmental units in Europe of Weber's day.

Bureaucracy as the Ideal

For Weber, bureaucracy was management by the "office" (German *büro*) or position rather than by the person or "patrimonial." Weber perceived the need to establish a rational basis for the administration of large-scale undertakings and the result of his work was the conception of *bureaucracy* as an ideal organizational arrangement. "Ideal" to Weber did not mean desirable, but the "pure form" of organization.[54] Combinations or alloys of various organizational arrangements would appear in practice but Weber wanted to characterize an ideal type for the purpose of theoretical analysis. The bureaucratic ideal would serve as a normative model

---

[53] Biographical information on Max Weber is based on Hans Gerth and C. Wright Mills, *From Max Weber*, New York: Oxford University Press, 1946; Reinhard Bendix, *Max Weber: An Intellectual Portrait*, Garden City, N.Y.: Doubleday & Co., 1960; and Marianne Weber, *Max Weber: A Biography* (trans. and ed. by Harry Zohn), New York: John Wiley and Sons, 1975 (a reprint of a 1926 edition).

[54] S. M. Miller (ed.), *Max Weber*, New York: Thomas Y. Crowell Co., 1963, p. 10.

to ease the transition from small-scale entrepreneurial ("patrimonial") administration to large-scale professional administration. Weber's conceptualization of bureaucracy merits substantial consideration for naming him the "father of organization theory."

Though other writings of Weber were translated earlier (i.e., Frank Knight's translation of Weber's *Economic History* in 1927 and Talcott Parsons' rendition of *The Protestant Ethic* in 1930), his work on bureaucracy was not rendered into English until 1947. However, Chester Barnard, who will be discussed later, was influenced by Talcott Parsons and read Weber in the German.[55] Weber's writings thus formed a partial foundation for Barnard's own analysis of the formal organization. Weber was the intellectual progenitor of the formal analysis of organizational structures. He was concerned with designing a blueprint structure of authority-activity relationships which would facilitate the attainment of the objective of an organization.

Kinds of Authority

Weber postulated three *pure* types of legitimate (i.e., socially acceptable) authority: (1) rational-legal authority which rested on "legality" or the "right of those elevated to authority . . . to issue commands"; (2) a "traditional" type which rested on a belief "in the sanctity of immemorial traditions and the legitimacy of the status of those exercising authority under them"; and (3) "charismatic" authority which was based "on devotion to the specific and exceptional sanctity, heroism, or exemplary character of an individual person . . ."[56] In the case of rational-legal authority, the obedience of subordinates was owed to the legally established hierarchy such as a business, a state office, military unit, or any other organization. It was obedience to the authority of an established *position* or rank. In traditional authority, obedience was due to the *person* who occupied the traditionally sanctioned position of

---

[55]The author is indebted to Professor William B. Wolf for his indication of the influence of Parsons on Barnard. Letter to author, December 16, 1970.

[56]A. M. Henderson and Talcott Parsons (ed. and trans.), *Max Weber: The Theory of Social and Economic Organization*, New York: Free Press, 1947, p. 328. In reality, Weber would recognize that authority may be legitimated on a combination of these so-called "pure" types.

authority. In charismatic authority (i.e., charisma from the early Christian concept of "the gift of grace"), the leader was obeyed by virtue of the follower's personal trust and belief in his powers or revelations.

Some form of authority is the cornerstone of any organization. Without authority of some type, no organization can be guided toward an objective; authority brings order to chaos. Of the three pure types of authority, Weber said that rational-legal must provide the basis for a bureaucracy, since it: (1) provided a basis for *continuity* of administration; (2) was "rational," i.e., the member occupying the administrative office was chosen on the basis of *competence* to perform his duties; (3) the leader was provided a legal means for exercising authority; and (4) all authority was clearly defined and carefully delimited to the functions necessary to accomplish the organization's task.[57] In contrast, tradition as legitimate authority would be less efficient since the leaders were not chosen on the basis of competence and since the administrative unit would act to preserve traditions of the past. Likewise, charisma as authority was too emotional and irrational in the sense that it avoided rules and routine and depended upon mystique and divine revelations.

The Administrative System

Weber's concept of the best administrative system is strikingly analogous to that of Taylor. For both men, management or administration meant the exercise of control on the basis of knowledge. Both sought technical competence in leaders who would lead by virtue of fact and not whim, by ability and not favoritism. The essential elements of Weber's ideal bureaucracy were:

1. *A division of labor in which authority and responsibility were clearly defined for each member and were legitimatized as official duties.*

2. *The offices or positions would be organized in a hierarchy of authority resulting in a chain of command or the scalar principle.*

3. *All organizational members were to be selected on the basis of*

[57] Ibid., pp. 330–331.

technical qualifications through formal examinations or by virtue of training or education.

4. *Officials were appointed, not elected. (With the exception in some cases of the chief of the whole unit, for example, an elected public official.)*

5. *Administrative officials worked for fixed salaries and were "career" officials.*

6. *The administrative official was not an owner of the unit being administered.*

7. *The administrator would be subject to strict rules, discipline, and controls regarding his conduct of his official duties. These rules and controls would be impersonal and uniformly applied in all cases.* [58]

For Weber, bureaucracy embodied the ideal administrative system and was not rule-encumbered inefficiency as the term has come to connote in modern parlance:

Experience tends universally to show that the purely bureaucratic type of administrative organization—that is, the monocratic variety of bureaucracy—is, from a purely technical point of view, capable of attaining the highest degree of efficiency and is in this sense formally the most rational known means of carrying out imperative control over human beings. It is superior to any other form in precision, in stability, in the stringency of its discipline, and in its reliability. It thus makes possible a particularly high degree of calculability of results for the heads of the organization and for those acting in relation to it. It is finally superior both in intensive efficiency and in the scope of its operations and is formally capable of application to all kinds of administrative tasks. [59]

Weber perceived a spreading of the growth of large-scale organizations in the church, state, the military, in political parties, in economic enterprises, and in all types of organizations. The growth of these large undertakings required a rationalization in administration. In Weber's view, capitalism had played a major role in the development of bureaucracy. Capitalism created an urgent need for stable, strict, intensive, and calculable administra-

---

[58] Adapted from ibid., pp. 329–333.
[59] Ibid., p. 337.

tion. It was this need which gave bureaucracy a crucial role in society as the central element in any kind of large-scale organization.

From a historical perspective, Weber's writings reflected what he saw as a breakup of tradition-based society. The process of industralization in Germany had been rapid but largely constrained by the strong political regime of the Junkers. Germany stood at the crossroads between the old family-based business system and the rapid rise of large-scale enterprise. Weber's response to the breakup of tradition was to rationalize organizations to provide efficiency for a new capitalistic state. In essence, Weber was the Adam Smith of Germany.[60] Whereas Adam Smith had struck a blow to destroy the mercantile policies of England which were retarding the development of capitalism, Weber's attack on tradition and the use of political control in the economy, which were to be replaced by administration by knowledge and technical competence, was a similar thrust to advance capitalism. Bureaucracy was conceived as a blueprint for efficiency which would emphasize rules rather than men and competence rather than favoritism.

Weber's work on bureaucracy remained largely unrecognized in America until the 1940s and 1950s. Like Fayol, he had to wait until cultural conditions created the need to think in terms of administrative theory. As organizations grew in size and complexity, men began to search for a theory of organizations. In their search they discovered Max Weber and his bureaucratic ideal.

Summary

The emergence of administrative theory took place in two forms; one, Fayol's contribution of the principles and elements of management; and two, Weber's search for a blueprint of idealized structural arrangements for the purpose of insuring technical efficiency. From different backgrounds and perspectives, both Fayol and Weber attempted to present administrative schemes for coping with large-scale organizations. Henri Fayol stressed education for management rather than technical training, the importance of planning and organizing, and the ongoing phases of command, coordination, and control. He distinguished between "manage-

[60]S. M. Miller, p. 6.

ment" as an integrating force and "administration," which worked solely through people. Max Weber took an administrative viewpoint in his bureaucratic ideal. He sought to avoid leadership and organization by tradition and charisma, to establish a ratio-nal-legal basis for authority, and to present orderly arrangements for the selection of personnel and the execution of activities. Both Weber and Fayol had history's misfortune of having to wait until others could give them their proper credit in the evolution of management thought.

11

Scientific Management and Organized Labor

There was never any doubt about Taylor's stand on organized labor. His insistence on science rather than bargaining in determining wages and working conditions and his preference for dealing with the individual worker rather than the union intermediary was to bring a surfeit of criticism. Our purpose here is to examine the critics, the opposing philosophies of organized labor and scientific management, and the changing tides in labor-management relations during this era.

The Stance of Organized Labor

Preceding the publicity given scientific management by the railroad hearings, organized labor had paid scant attention to Taylor and his followers. The existing philosophy of the American Federation of Labor, as represented by Samuel Gompers, was to bargain for more wages and to achieve gains for labor through "power" and not productivity.[1] As public interest was aroused by the possibilities of increasing national productivity through scientific management, labor leaders were stirred from their former positions. The strike at the Watertown Arsenal and the subsequent House investigation were results of organized labor's increased interest in and hardened attitudes toward the new vogue of efficiency engineering. Conceptually, the evolution of relations

[1] Jean Trepp McKelvey, *AFL Attitudes Toward Production: 1900–1932*, Ithaca, N.Y.: Cornell Studies in Industrial and Labor Relations, vol. II, 1952, pp. 6–11.

between organized labor and scientific management may be classified into rather discrete time periods: (1) a period of vitriolic hostility from 1911 to 1915; (2) an informal truce during the war production years 1916–1918; and (3) a new era of revisionism in management and cooperation on the part of labor lasting up to the Great Depression.

The Hoxie Report

The early position of organized labor vis-à-vis scientific management found its critical articulation in an investigation by the U.S. Commission on Industrial Relations. The chief investigator was Robert Franklin Hoxie, professor of political economy at the University of Chicago, and his assistants were Robert G. Valentine, an investigator and consultant in labor problems who was to represent management's viewpoint, and John P. Frey, editor of the *International Molder's Journal*, representing labor.[2] The purpose of the study was to investigate all systems of shop management, including Taylor's, Gantt's, and Emerson's, and the final report was the most comprehensive statement of the relations between scientific management and labor for that era.[3] The investigators examined 35 shops employing scientific management during the period January to April 1915. In addition, they consulted 150 industrial leaders, labor officials, and authorities on scientific management, including Taylor, Gantt, and Emerson.

An early inkling of controversy occurred when Hoxie insisted on making no distinction between the theory and the practice of scientific management. To Hoxie, scientific management was what was practiced, regardless of the ideas and theories it advocated; to Taylor, scientific management "ceased to exist" if its principles and philosophy were violated in practice. Hoxie's distinction did not impress Taylor and this undoubtedly led to his

[2] Though calling himself a consultant to management on labor relations, Valentine had only brief experience in industry and that in banking. He taught English at the Massachusetts Institute of Technology and was at one time assistant commissioner of Indian affairs. L. Urwick and E. F. L. Brech, *The Golden Book of Management*, London: Newman Neame Ltd., 1956, p. 163.

[3] Robert F. Hoxie, *Scientific Management and Labor*, New York: Appleton-Century-Crofts, 1915.

unfavorable reception of the report and the inclusion of a separate statement on his position in the appendix.[4]

The core of the Hoxie report was the analysis of the practice of scientific management in 1915. Contrary to the view that acceptance of the movement was widespread, Hoxie found a marked degree of diversity among the various shops studied. In the shops which were supposed to represent scientific management in practice, *not one* had a complete and faithful installation of either the Taylor, Gantt, or Emerson systems. Further, the systems which did appear did not conform precisely to the ideas and principles of the scientific management advocates since each management had modified the system to fit the idiosyncrasies of its own firm as it perceived them. This diversity led to an analysis of various features of the theory and how they became modified in practice. First, Hoxie found that practice violated the precepts of careful study and analysis prior to installation of any efficiency system. The lack of individuals trained in time study methods, coupled with employer pressure for quick payouts, resulted in hasty and incomplete job study. Standardization of tools, methods, and work conditions were lacking in most shops studied. The fault fell equally on management and on the efficiency engineer. Management's prevailing attitude was to opt for quick returns with small regard for the long-range outcome and with little concern for or knowledge of the impact of the system on the workers. On the other side, the efficiency experts who offered their services worked for the short run and did not have "the ability or the willingness to install scientific management in accordance with the Taylor formula and ideals."[5] Hoxie did not specifically fault Taylor or his close followers, but indicated that there were others who were picking and choosing from his system and discarding and violating the spirit and principles of what Taylor advocated.

Second, the concept of functional foremen found few adherents in practice. Some firms made the attempt but soon returned to the military, line type of organization. Hoxie found that in practice the Taylor ideal of substituting obedience to knowledge

[4] Ibid., Appendix II, pp. 140–149. Mr. Gantt, in Appendix III (pp. 150–151), and Mr. Emerson, in Appendix IV (pp. 152–168), also filed their positions regarding Taylor's claims. The three do not present a unified theory of the movement but do agree on the fundamental aims of scientific management.

[5] Ibid., p. 29.

and fact for obedience to personal authority had not come about. The old-time foremen continued to retain and use arbitrary authority to the detriment of fair dealing with the worker as Taylor had envisioned. In a third area of inquiry, Hoxie found that little or no progress was being made with respect to the scientific selection of workers. "Labor heads," an early designation for the employment or personnel manager, were poorly trained and of "doubtful experience and capacity."[6] The work of the labor heads was further complicated by the ubiquitous presence of line-staff conflict. Line foremen and superintendents clung tenaciously to their traditional prerogatives and worked overtly and covertly to nullify the advice and assistance of the personnel managers. With due respect to scientific management, Hoxie noted that these problems also existed in other establishments and was not confined to those firms being studied. Personnel selection, and indeed the entire personnel function, was in a rather embryonic state in all shops, not just those attempting the scientific management system. Although initial selection was no better in scientific management shops, the overall general class of workers did appear to be higher through some ill-defined process of weeding out. Hoxie did not examine the reasons; but one is led to conclude that the incentive schemes, standards of work, or some form of the first-class-man concept was evolving in scientifically managed shops.

Instruction and training of workers was another area where practice fell far short of theory. There were few attempts to execute the Taylor precept of "setting each man to the highest task for which his physical and intellectual capacity fits him." Learning proceeded by trial and error, specially trained instructors were scarce, and instruction more often than not focused on attaining the standard rather than on learning the job. Despite these faults, Hoxie concluded that training practices in scientific management shops were generally better than those that could be found elsewhere in industry.

A fifth area, and one of greater criticism, was in the use of time study and task setting. It was here that Hoxie found the greatest diversity in practice and the most deviations from scientific inquiry. Standards and incentive rates were often estab-

[6] Ibid., p. 32.

lished after only a cursory inquiry and led to a variety of inaccuracies and injustices. In theory, time study is supposed to yield a quantitative measure of performance by deriving standard times taken to perform a task. In practice, qualitative factors caused by the time study engineer's judgment and experience tended to make the results less and less scientific. To the elementary times recorded from observation, allowances must be added to cover fatigue, unnecessary delays, "human necessities" (personal time), and possible errors in the work of the observer. Rather than substituting "exact knowledge for prejudiced opinion in the setting of the task" as Taylor had advocated, Hoxie found some seventeen variables which could be affected by the judgment and subjectivity of the person doing the study. In general, the time study personnel were poorly trained, inexperienced, and often set rates based upon management's desires and not upon true scientific inquiry and observation.

Once more, the criticisms were not lodged against the concept of time study and Taylorism per se, but against the use of stop watches by untrained, inexperienced observers. Hoxie found the typical time study engineers to be technicians with little knowledge of the subject of fatigue who displayed little understanding of the psychology and temperament of workers. They were "prevailingly of the narrow-minded mechanical type, poorly paid, and occupying the lowest positions in the managerial organization."[7] Some employers recognized the limitations of time study and were attempting to improve; to others, time study became "religion" and was leading to overstrain, exhaustion, and underpayment of the workman. On this question of time study, Hoxie was the most pessimistic. He saw no future for time study, even under the most enlightened management.[8]

Incentive schemes also came under close scrutiny. Hoxie found no pure adoptions of either the Taylor, the Gantt, or the

[7] Ibid., pp. 5–6.

[8] Professor Hoxie's doubts about time study are reinforced by modern prolabor writers. For example, see William Gomberg, *A Trade Union Analysis of Time Study*, New York: Prentice-Hall, 1948. Mr. Gomberg was director of the Management Engineering Department of the International Ladies' Garment Workers Union. His position is that physiological, mechanical, psychological and sociological variables make time study "unscientific" and therefore the results of time study should be used for further bargaining and not as *the* standard.

Emerson plans. The Taylor differential piece-rate plan was infrequently encountered and most plans were modifications of the Gantt and Emerson plans. Taylor had maintained that once rates were established they must never be cut "without an absolute change in the direction governing the work and the time demanded for doing it." In practice however, employers often interpreted very liberally the phrase "absolute change"; slight changes were made in tools, jigs, or materials in order to justify restudy of the job and rate cuts. Hoxie did not give evidence of the prevalence of this practice but noted that some managers were unscrupulous and eager to take advantage of the worker.[9] It must be added, however, that this may occur under any system and was not the fault of scientific management. While Taylor maintained that scientific management would protect the worker against overspeeding and exhaustion, Hoxie found no evidence in practice that it in fact did so. Of course, this would be expected since the Taylor precepts which would protect the worker, i.e., standardization of tools, methods, and conditions, substitution of knowledge for guess-work, careful studies of fatigue, proper instruction, admonitions against rate-cutting, rest periods, etc., were all being evaded in practice. Without these safeguards, the spirit of scientific management was putty in the hands of the unscrupulous.

Philosophies in Conflict

On a broader plane, Hoxie tried to reconcile the opposing views of unions and Taylor regarding industrial democracy. Taylor maintained that scientific management was the essence of industrial democracy. Taylor's argument hinged upon harmony and the mutuality of interest between labor and management. Individuals were stimulated and rewarded on the basis of effort, discipline fell under scientifically derived laws and not under autocratic, driving management, and protests were to be handled by reliance upon scientific inquiry and mutual resolution. On the other hand, organized labor declared that scientific management was essentially autocratic by forcing the employee to conform to the employer's concept of fairness and by limiting the democratic safeguards of

[9]Hoxie, p. 86.

the workers. Scientific management, according to the union view, monopolized knowledge and power in the hands of management by denying the worker a voice in setting work standards and in determining wage rates and conditions of employment. It introduced a "spirit of mutual suspicion" among workers and destroyed the "solidarity and cooperative spirit of the group" by emphasizing the individual worker. It destroyed unions, the protection that unions gave workers, and in turn obviated the collective bargaining process.

The result, in Hoxie's view, was an inevitable, fundamental conflict between organized labor and scientific management. Hoxie maintained that Taylor's philosophy was a "Utopian ideal" which would not be practical until management knew more of worker psychology, was able to stabilize and regularize employment to a greater extent, and would recognize the need to build "group solidarity" (i.e., through organized labor). Channels must be opened for grievances, presumably through union representation, and management must accept worker (and union) participation in decision making. In Hoxie's words, "with rare exceptions, then, democracy under Scientific Management cannot and does not exist apart from unionism and collective bargaining."[10] The rare exceptions were the "very few" managers who were truly democratic in spirit and practice; but Hoxie characterized most managers as benevolent despots or solid autocrats. Hoxie concluded that scientific management was not promoting industrial democracy: "In practice, Scientific Management must, therefore, be declared autocratic; in tendency, a reversion to industrial autocracy, which forces the worker to depend on the employer's conception of fairness, and limits the democratic safeguards of the workers."[11]

In fairness to Taylor, Hoxie attempted to pinpoint the causes of the shortcomings of scientific management in practice. In part these were caused by the infancy and immaturity of the movement since all new social and industrial ideas fall short of the ideal in their younger days. On this point Hoxie was optimistic that many of these shortcomings would disappear in time. More spec-

[10]Ibid., p. 109.
[11]Ibid., p. 112.

ifically, Hoxie blamed management for seeking shortcuts to efficiency, he faulted Taylor for trying to generalize his machine shop experience to all types and sizes of industries, and indicted efficiency experts who were guilty of selling patent medicine panaceas to employers in dire financial straits and eager to improve performance. "So the Scientific Management shingles have gone up all over the country, the fakirs have gone into the shops, and in the name of Scientific Management have reaped temporary gains to the detriment of . . . the employer and the worker."[12]

Criticisms of the Hoxie Report

Those who criticize are also open to criticism. What can be said of the research methodology of the Hoxie team? Professor Hoxie and his associates made numerous attempts to be fair to Taylor by noting that practice fell far short of theory. However, the predilections of Hoxie, Frey, and Valentine toward labor yielded a research bias which is inescapable. There is also evidence that the methodology of the research group was less than meticulous. Mary Barnett Gilson, who was employment manager at Clothcraft Company of Cleveland, one of the shops included in the study, wrote that Hoxie was "brilliant" but "prejudiced."[13] When Hoxie and Frey visited Clothcraft, they held a short interview with the president, Richard Feiss, and some of his managers, took some notes, but never visited the factory area itself. They promised to return to see the working conditions but never did. Gilson also wrote that Frey was especially antagonistic during the interview because Clothcraft had no union. If this encounter at Clothcraft was characteristic of the researchers' conduct at the other 34 shops in the study, one must conclude that the Hoxie group was less than thorough. The investigation lasted only four months (January to April 1915) and could have been conducted only in a superficial manner. It is unfortunate that those who had the best opportunity to do a thorough empirical investigation of scientific management in its early days approached this chance with closed minds and hasty feet.

[12] Ibid., p. 117.

[13] Mary B. Gilson, *What's Past is Prologue*, New York: Harper & Row, 1940, p. 93.

Hoxie took the position that industrial democracy could come only through the process of collective bargaining. He saw no other avenue, included no possibility for an educated, enlightened management, and seemed dedicated to the proposition that labor and management interests were inalterably opposed for all times and in all places. He brought no true bill against union leadership nor its membership for soldiering or resistance. On this count, his examination was less than equitable.

In later work, Professor Hoxie began to equivocate on whether the philosophies of scientific management and trade unionism were reconcilable or inalterably opposed. He maintained: "We surely cannot afford to give up the vast possibilities of increased productiveness which Scientific Management holds out"; further, "Scientific Management holds out possibilities of substantial benefits to labor."[14] The paradox he was unable to resolve was based on an essential philosophical incompatibility between labor and scientific management. In organized labor's case, it "can function successfully only through the maintenance of a fixed industrial situation and conditions." On the other hand, "Scientific Management can function successfully only on the basis of constant and indefinite change of industrial conditions."[15] In the final analysis, the proper application of scientific management "would spell the doom of effective unionism as it exists today."[16]

Was Taylor a Utopian idealist? Was the fault with Taylor or with those who grasped at the straws of expediency and forgot the philosophy? From the Hoxie study, one is led to conclude that American management failed in the pressures of the moment to thoroughly understand and apply the Taylor system. Many are called to be mechanics, but there are few who can execute a grand design. Both labor and management were guilty of checkmating Taylor's call for a mental revolution. To Hoxie's credit one must indicate that he stimulated an interest in bringing practice closer to the high ideals of scientific management.

[14]Robert F. Hoxie, *Trade Unionism in the United States,* New York: Appleton-Century-Crofts, 1924, p. 324. Published posthumously since Professor Hoxie took his own life in June 1916.

[15]Ibid., p. 341.

[16]Ibid., p. 348.

Changing Times in Labor–Management Relations

The ideas of scientific management inspired both faithful adherents and determined antagonists. From within and without the movement, new ideas to meet new demands were coming to the fore. The Hoxie report provided a seedbed for others who were beginning to explore new vistas for scientific management, pointing out the positive features, and yet also beginning to nurture the seeds of dissent to be reflected later in a revisionist movement.

Defenders and Revisionists

H. H. Farquhar was pro-Taylor, yet had some interesting insights into the unexplored opportunities of the scientific management movement.[17] For Farquhar, the positive aspects of scientific management were both technical and human: on the technical side, it resulted in greater productivity at no greater worker exertion, led to more efficient utilization of equipment and materials, improved regularity of production, and enhanced the power and stimulus of scientific knowledge gained through investigation. On the human side, scientific management improved industry by better worker selection and training, higher wages, reduction of worker turnover, greater worker security, and by allowing a wider scope for individual initiative.

After putting forth the positive contributions, Farquhar examined "neglected opportunities." He indicated that these were not so much criticisms as guides for future work in management. First, he questioned whether or not "we have given sufficient weight to the question of personality in management . . ." and had forgotten that management was an art which required human direction and control. Second, he asked whether or not enough stress had been given to the fact that scientific management re-

---

[17] H. H. Farquhar, "Positive Contributions of Scientific Management," in E. E. Hunt (ed.), *Scientific Management Since Taylor*, New York: McGraw-Hill Book Co., 1924, pp. 37–59. Originally published in the *Bulletin of the Taylor Society*, Vol. 9, No. 1, (February, 1924). Professor Farquhar at the time was assistant professor of industrial management at the Harvard Graduate School of Business Administration.

quired better leadership than any other management system. Instead of developing leaders, management had focused on "carefully outlined procedures" and substituted them for the lack of leadership abilities. Finally, he wondered whether or not scientific management, by focusing on the individual as an individual, had "obscured the possibility of making that individual and his fellows more productive and more contented through recognizing the psychological benefits to be gained through group dealings." Farquhar felt that it was unfortunate that Taylor stressed soldiering and the profit motive of the individual worker "almost to the exclusion of other instincts and motives in life and which at heart, he [Taylor] knew every workman is interested."[18] Taylor was an engineer, not a psychologist, and, though he knew from his own experience the values of being a "regular fellow" in the group, he did not write extensively on the problems of people in groups. Farquhar, though a defender of scientific management, was one of the first to question the omission of the social and group facet of people in industrial research.[19]

H. B. Drury (of the Ohio State University) was primarily a defender of scientific management and only secondarily a revisionist. He noted that total productivity improved 100 percent at Midvale, 50–75 percent at Bethlehem and on the Santa Fe, 250 percent at the Tabor Manufacturing Company, 200 percent at Link-Belt, and that substantial savings accrued at the Watertown Arsenal, in the cotton industry (Gantt), and in the construction industry (Gilbreths).[20] Under the guidance of scientific management pioneers, substantial improvements were achieved without labor strife or widespread worker displacement.

In answering the critics, Drury pointed out that organized labor was fighting scientific management because unions would have difficulties in recruiting membership if science replaced bar-

[18] Ibid., pp. 48–49.

[19] Professor F. J. Roethlisberger indicates that the Hawthorne research team was not influenced in its research by Professor Farquhar's writing. Letter to author, January 28, 1969.

[20] Horace B. Drury, *Scientific Management: A History and Criticism*, New York: Columbia University Press, 1915, pp. 163–168. Drury noted that there were 60 installations of the Taylor system and 200 of the Emerson system by 1912 (pp. 144–146).

gaining over terms and conditions of employment. Point by point, Drury examined and answered the allegations of the Hoxie report. First, scientific management did not have as its goal the placement of all industrial jobs on piecework. Taylor, in testimony before the Industrial Relations Commission, had said that only 17 percent of the nation's industrial workers held jobs appropriate for the use of piece-rate incentives.[21] Therefore, the unions had little to fear that piece rates and incentive schemes based on time study would be applied to all jobs. Second, job monotony and routinization of work had actually made the worker more productive and better paid. If workers were to be judged automatons in a factory, then the blame must be placed on the process of industrialization and not on scientific management. Third, there was no evidence that scientific management per se led to overwork and exploitation of employees. Greater output came from better methods and not greater worker exertion. Neither the Congressional investigating committee nor the Hoxie group found evidence of overwork or injury to worker health in factories where Taylor's procedures were strictly followed.[22] Fourth, there was no evidence that scientific management led to greater industrial strife. Drury noted that most opposition came from labor leaders and not from the workers. At Watertown Arsenal, for example, the workers were told to resist by the labor leaders. At the Frankford Arsenal, "several hundred" workers petitioned to continue the installation of the Taylor system even though instructed to the contrary by their leadership.

Finally, Drury felt that scientific management was more aware of the human element in management than any previous management method:

[Scientific Management] is based upon the principle that cheerful workmen are more profitable than sullen ones, that to fit the work

[21] Ibid., p. 166. It is interesting to note that a modern researcher says 27 percent of the 11½ million U.S. workers in manufacturing were paid on some incentive basis in 1959. L. Earl Lewis, "Extent of Incentive Pay in Manufacturing," *Monthly Labor Review*, Vol. 83, No. 5, May 1960. Lewis found variations among industries but the percentages of workers on incentives were fairly constant over time.

[22] Drury, p. 190. Based upon his own studies and upon his own experiences as a worker, Stanley Mathewson concluded that a vast majority of managers of the times were not autocrats. Further, he maintained that the charge that scientific management exploited the worker was the "myth" of "popular magazine writers." S. B. Mathewson, *Restriction of Output Among Unorganized Workers*, New York: Viking Press, 1931, p. 151.

*to the man is better than to try to fit the man to the work, that
the individual is a more satisfactory unit of study and administration than the mass.*

In conclusion, Drury was much less critical than Hoxie and
therefore must be classified primarily as a defender of scientific
management. As a revisionist, he did not accept the movement as
a final answer to industrial problems. He saw scientific management as a stage in industrial evolution, not entirely original and
not yet complete. Progress and study would yield more "science"
in management to replace the autocracy of driving and whimsical
practices. His prognosis was that scientific management would
not dominate American industry but that it would become transformed and differentiated as industry turned more and more toward scientific investigation. His forecast was particularly perceptive; management did turn toward more investigation, especially
in the social facet of the workplace, and subsequently in applying
more rigorous quantitative tools.

The Hoxie report, coming on the heels of the Congressional
investigation, represented a turning point in the evolution of
management thought. The war years had brought an uneasy truce
but after the war a new breed was rising in counterpoint to the
Taylor movement to bring a series of changes in management philosophy, especially with regard to labor relations. In varying degrees, a number of people were instrumental in reformulating the
"official" viewpoint of scientific management toward labor.
Robert G. Valentine, a member of the Hoxie team, was one early
revisionist who attempted a *rapprochement* between unions and
scientific management as represented by the Taylor Society.
Viewed with suspicion by the Taylorites but praised by union
leadership, he argued that the labor-management relationship was
properly one of "consent." Consent was based on worker participation, and especially union participation, in reaching all decisions affecting labor.[24] Ordway Tead, a former partner in Valentine's consulting firm, urged the formation of company unions in

---

[23] Drury, p. 202.

[24] R. G. Valentine, "The Progressive Relation Between Efficiency and Consent," *Bulletin of the Society to Promote the Science of Management*, Vol. 2, No. 1 (January,
1916), pp. 28–29.

order to get worker participation.[25] The American Federation of Labor was opposed to this viewpoint although company unions did achieve some large measure of acceptability during the 1920s. Although Tead and Valentine pushed for worker and union participation in management, the major intellectual break over Taylor's union position was by Morris L. Cooke. Cooke became friendly with labor leaders, especially the patriarch Gompers, and was the most influential in opening up a new era for labor-management relations. Cooke proposed to "humanize" management by advocating collective bargaining over rates, standards, and all matters affecting worker welfare. This break by one of Taylor's disciples was hailed by labor leaders but condemned by such stalwarts as Harrington Emerson.[26]

Additional strength to labor's position came with the publication of *Waste in Industry*. Originally proposed by then Secretary of Commerce Herbert Hoover and appearing a decade after the appearance of Taylor's *Principles*, this report undertook an appraisal of the progress of industrial management in reducing the national waste that Taylor had decried in his original work. In its essence, the report left a very gloomy view of American management by stating that ". . . over 50 percent of the responsibility for these wastes can be placed at the door of management and less than 25 percent at the door of labor, while the amount chargeable to outside contacts is least of all."[27] The chief causes of low productivity were faulty material control, faulty production control, lack of cost control, lack of research, ineffective workmanship, and faulty sales policies. The report was more of an indictment of American management's failure to use known methods and procedures and not a criticism of scientific management itself. In view of Professor Hoxie's findings about the uneven acceptance of scientific management methods and almost a complete rejection of the requisite mental revolution, the *Waste in Industry* report is not surprising in its conclusions.

[25] Ordway Tead, *Instincts in Industry: A Study of Working Class Psychology*, Boston: Houghton Mifflin Co., 1918, pp. 56–58 and pp. 218–220.

[26] Milton J. Nadworny, *Scientific Management and the Unions: 1900–1932*, Cambridge, Mass., Harvard University Press, 1955, pp. 116–117.

[27] *Waste in Industry*, Federated American Engineering Societies, New York: McGraw-Hill Book Co., 1921, p. 9.

Labor leaders welcomed the conclusions that the responsibility for waste lay primarily with management and not with labor. Further, the report suggested that others (labor, owners, the buying public, and trade associations) could contribute to waste elimination by "cooperating" with management. This became a signal to Samuel Gompers to push for union participation in helping management eliminate waste.[28] The practical implications of this marked change in union attitudes toward waste elimination and improvement of industrial practices were to lead to an era of labor-management cooperation, a phenomenon so far largely confined to the 1920s. The wheel was to come full circle in the relations between organized labor and management.

The Union-Management Cooperation Era

It would be easy, almost too easy, to attribute the change in labor leadership attitudes to the influence of men such as Morris Cooke. The *rapprochement* of labor and scientific management also was based in the economic conditions of the twenties. While younger men in the Taylor Society did change the pure alloy of Taylor's attitudes concerning unions, the unions themselves were facing unusual environmental pressures. A short, steep depression in the early 1920s weakened unions; further, companies were becoming increasingly paternalistic, management was waging intense drives for the open shop, and government and the courts were becoming increasingly hostile to unionism. Americans saw radicals and Bolsheviks in every picket line and reacted against any concerted effort to change the status quo. Accordingly, union membership suffered, declining from around 5 million in 1920 to 3½ million in 1921.[29] In this relatively hostile environment, labor leadership adopted the protective coloration characterized by a decade of union-management cooperation.

Numerous examples and industries can be cited to illustrate the shifting sands of labor-management relations. The clothing unions, under the capable leadership of Sidney Hillman, were among the first segments of organized labor to agree to co-

[28] Jean T. McKelvey, p. 70.

[29] Nadworny, p. 122.

operation and to implementation of scientific management techniques. The Rochester Plan, composed of nineteen manufacturers representing the Clothiers' Exchange of Rochester and the Amalgamated Clothing Workers of America, was an attempt to guarantee certain rights to both labor and management under a collective agreement. Management had the right of an open shop and the right to install efficiency techniques; in turn, labor's rights were to bargain collectively, to elect bargaining representatives, and to participate through "price committees" in the fixing of piece rates.[30] This early attempt was successful and modern clothing unions are the most favorable advocates of piece rates set through collective bargaining.

The railroads also developed extensive plans for cooperation, first on the Baltimore and Ohio and then later the Chesapeake and Ohio, the Chicago and North Western, the Canadian National Railway, and others. In each instance the union implicitly accepted the principles of scientific management and participated through joint union-management shop committees in improving work routing and scheduling, hiring practices, and job analysis.[31] As in the garment industry, scientific management had gained greater acceptance than previously possible under resistant leadership. When William Green succeeded Gompers as AFL president in 1925, he increased the emphasis on cooperation. The AFL hired its own management consultant and in a 1930 statement of "Labor's Principles of Scientific Management" urged complete acceptance of scientific management. Using "management research" departments within the union, labor leadership emphasized that the worker actually *needed* the management engineer.[32] This "new unionism" completed a cycle in organized labor-scientific management relations. Except for worker participation through unions and recognition of the union's right to bargain, Frederick Taylor's *Principles* were now accepted as valid by the labor world.

---

[30]Meyer Jacobstein, "Can Industrial Democracy Be Efficient? The Rochester Plan," *Bulletin of the Taylor Society*, Vol. 5, No. 4 (August, 1920), reprinted in E. E. Hunt, pp. 212–221.

[31]Otto S. Beyer, "Experiences with Cooperation between Labor and Management in the Railway Industry," *Wertheim Lectures on Industrial Relations* (1928), Cambridge, Mass., 1929.

[32]Nadworny, p. 138–139.

The AFL abandoned the idea of union-management co-operation in 1932. The new political regime promised better days for labor, and union efforts turned from cooperating with management to influencing legislation in order to insure its survival and strength. The crash in 1929 and the deepening deterioration of economic conditions doomed most cooperative schemes to failure. Thus ended an era in scientific management. The era began with the adamant Taylor who wanted to substitute scientific knowledge for bargaining, and the movement was redirected by the revisionists who wanted worker and union participation. Spurred by adverse economic conditions, the labor movement itself began its move toward almost complete acceptance of Taylorism. The 1920s are remembered for Babe Ruth, bathtub gin, short skirts, the Charleston, and Al Capone: it was during this decade that unions found a haven in scientific management.

Summary

The publicity which brought scientific management into the national spotlight also aroused the ire of organized labor. Organized labor and the proponents of scientific management found themselves bound up in a fundamental conflict of philosophies. On the one hand, labor felt that scientific management meant autocracy in the workplace and placed the worker at a disadvantage vis-à-vis management. Taylor recognized the abuses in practice which violated the spirit of the mental revolution. However, he felt that the worker, and everyone else, would benefit the most from scientifically determined pay and standards, from individualized treatment of the worker, and from a spirit which tried to create more rather than fighting over the division of the surplus. In the end, both positions were being reshaped. Labor, influenced by the economic and political environment, came to accept a modified version of Taylorism. The scientific management movement, influenced by the revisionists, also changed in response to new demands for industrial cooperation.

12

Scientific Management
in Retrospect

The death of Taylor was the demise of a man and not that of an idea. Bedeviled and discouraged in his latter days, Taylor must have felt that he had failed in his life's work. From its orthodox conception, scientific management was evolving inexorably as new individuals and ideas came forth in an ever changing cultural environment. Interacting to form a giant web of currents and eddies of change, very substantial economic, social and political forces shaped the emergence, course, and progress of the scientific management movement. In examining the cultural environment of scientific management, economic, social, and political forces are separated for expository purposes, although in reality they were interacting and mutually reinforcing. Within this framework, the whys and wherefores of Frederick W. Taylor and his intellectual heirs will form a more coherent picture.

The Economic Environment:
From the Farm to the Factory

In 1800, 90 percent of America drew its sustenance from agriculture; by 1900, the proportion was 33 percent, and by 1929, 20 percent. The transformation from an agrarian to an industrial nation placed America at the world's helm in output of products and services, in wages, and in the standard of living of its citizens. The typical citizen who awakened on the morning of January 1, 1900, saw little change between the old and the new centuries. Yet the change was there and America had in reality moved into a new era. The accumulation of resources, though moving at varying speeds in various industries, was culminating in a new phase. New industries, in their embryonic stage in the latter part of the nineteenth century, were growing to influence and eventually dominate the course of American life. Spindletop (near Beaumont, Texas) ushered in a new era for petroleum; chemical discoveries were proliferating and the DuPont firm opened up synthetic fibers with an "artificial silk" later called rayon; at Kittyhawk in 1903, the airplane industry was launched; and in steel, meat packing, electricity, rubber, tobacco, agricultural implements, and retailing, corporate giants began to take shape. These large-scale industrial forms presaged profound changes for Mr. and Mrs. Citizen-Consumer.

Energy developments of the period also merit mention. Coal was the primary source of energy for the steam-driven wheels of industry. While coal continued to dominate, new discoveries of petroleum deposits were soon to reshape the energy base. Electrical energy also entered the scene. While not "invented" in the usual sense, the principles of electricity were applied to generate a new power source for factory gears and home lights and appliances. Edison's central power plant in New York City was built in 1882. By 1920 one-third of the nation's industrial power came from electricity. Half of the urban homes had electricity. In the rural areas 98 percent of the homes still relied on kerosene lamps and candles, but not for long.

Urban and suburban transportation made marked advances during this period. Intra- and interurban trolley cars were at first horse-drawn, and the tracks were laid in the streets. After 1890 and the appearance of the electric trolley, the horses were retired, street sweepers' jobs were less onerous, and pedestrians could walk with greater assurance. By 1920 there were 50,000 miles of urban and interurban streetcar tracks. Retail markets were extended, and suburban living was facilitated by these improvements in transportation.

The automobile was one technological advancement which brought about substantial economic and social change during this period. Exhibited at the Paris Exposition in 1896 by the German Nicholas Otto, the gas-buggy was soon to become more than an amusement. Basic industries such as petroleum, steel, rubber, and glass were given added impetus by the automobile. Spin-off industries in tourist inns and restaurants, garages, and highway construction were created. The automobile gave people a new mobility, a new freedom of movement which led to a decentralization of the cities into suburban living and posed a new threat to older, established forms of transportation. The new economics of the automobile industry was based on a minute division of labor and on the interchangeability of parts. Henry Ford and his associates took these old ideas and transformed them into a logic of mass production on an assembly line basis which could be called the Second Industrial Revolution. Mass production yielded cost savings which in turn were passed on to the consumer via lower prices. In 1910, the "Model T" cost the consumer $950; by 1924 the purchase price was $290 and Ford was selling over 1¼ million cars. Using lowered product prices to expand the market and the greater market to achieve greater production savings, Ford divided work into small elements and personified Adam Smith's idea that the market was the only force limiting the division of labor. Ford's startling announcement of a $5 a day minimum wage in 1914 (when the average wage in the auto industry was $2.40 a day) operated on two premises: (1) that the best workers could be attracted and retained; and (2) that the worker needed the wherewithal to buy industry's output. In large part an economic man concept, it brought success to Ford and lent credence to Taylor. Although Ford lost his domination of the automobile industry as consumer preferences changed, his introduction of the logic of mass production had a lasting impact on American thought.

American labor prospered, too. Immigration to America remained open until an isolationist fever in the 1920s closed the door to some nationalities. The Negroes were in America before the Civil War, the Chinese had been brought in to build the western railroads, and Irish, Germans, and Swedes populated the coal fields, steel mills, auto factories, and the farms of America. After 1880, another flow of Slovaks, Poles, and Italians added to the swelling force. The increased supply of workers did not result in lower wages for the American worker. Real wages (i.e., the purchasing power of the worker's income) *doubled* between 1865 and 1890. From 1890 to 1921, the annual compound increase in real wages was 1.6 percent per year, enabling another doubling. In addition to gaining in terms of real wages, the hours of labor were starting to decrease: in 1890 the average industrial work week was 60 hours; in 1910, 55 hours, and in 1920, 50 hours.[1]

Administratively, the new economics of mass production demanded an even sharper focus on the development of management. Large accumulations of resources were requisite to meet the demands of mass markets and mass distribution. As the industrial giants grew, the men who had built the empires were passing from the helm and being replaced by a new breed of salaried manager. The personalized, informal structures of the family business yielded to the logic of size in industrial administration. No longer could owner-entrepreneurs depend upon their own personal supervision. Technology demanded specialized knowledge and staff personnel were added to handle engineering, production, purchasing, legal affairs, and other functional activities. Motives changed from the risk of loss or possibility of gain in one's equity as an entrepreneur to those germane to a salaried manager. This separation of ownership and management required the development of an enlarged fund of managerial talent trained or wise in the administration of industrial affairs.

Support for this growing need for professional managers was also found in economic theory. Alfred Marshall (1842–1924), of the "neoclassical school" of economic thought, indicated the differential advantage that management could provide:

> *A manufacturer of exceptional ability and energy will apply better methods, and perhaps better machinery than his rivals: he will organize better the manufacturing and the marketing sides of his business; and he will bring them into better relation to one another. By these means he will extend his business; and therefore he will be able to take greater advantage from the specialization both of labour and of plant. Thus he will obtain increasing return and also increasing profit . . .*[2]

Marshall wrote of the "earnings of management" in his theory of

---

[1] Ross M. Robertson, *History of the American Economy*, 3rd ed., New York: Harcourt, Brace, Jovanovich, 1973, pp. 379–380.

[2] Alfred Marshall, *Principles of Economics* (8th ed.), New York: MacMillan Co., 1949, p. 614. First published in 1890.

distribution and of marginal analysis, and thereby laid the basis for managerial economics.

The Rationalization of Resource Utilization

Chandler has noted that phase I (the resource accumulation phase) was complete in American industry by the beginning of World War I. Industrial growth in the latter part of the nineteenth century had created the giant enterprise, and in the first two decades of the twentieth century it was the task of the salaried manager to design and implement the appropriate administrative structures. The large corporation demanded a formal structure of relationships between the firm's activities and personnel and required also a formalization of administrative procedures. Culmination of the resource accumulation phase meant that the typical corporation of the early twentieth century was faced with basically two problems: (1) the need to reduce unit costs by improving productive techniques and processes; and (2) the need to facilitate planning, coordination, and appraisal of performance.[3]

This set the stage for phase II, the rationalization of resource utilization. The work of Taylor and other scientific management writers was focused on meeting the industrial needs of the economic environment with respect to rationalizing resource utilization. The rational, scientific approach to problem solving was the foundation of scientific management. Time and motion study set standards, intended to reduce fatigue, and sought to eliminate wasted motions; it was a logical approach to work design rather than whimsical or rule-of-thumb methods. The "first-class man" and the scientific selection of personnel were attempts to provide a better match between people's abilities and job requirements. The Taylor piece-rate incentive sought to boost production and lower per unit labor costs even while paying higher wages. The functional foremen were to bring specialized, expert advice and leadership; the separation of planning and doing was a concept designed to improve the planning of work; and the exception

[3] A. D. Chandler, Jr., *Strategy and Structure*, Cambridge, Mass.: MIT Press, 1962, pp. 386–390.

principle sought to focus managerial attention on critical performance problems. Even Taylor's philosophy of a "mental revolution" was an attempt to reduce friction and to rationally bring together the interests of labor and management into a mutually rewarding whole.

Those who followed in Taylor's wake also followed this rationalization-of-resource-utilization theme. The Gilbreths sought motion economy and waste reduction and their "systems" books were detailed how-to-do-it procedures manuals. Gantt's work provided visual aids for scheduling, routing, dispatching, and control of work. Carl Barth, Morris Cooke, and the others who followed the gospel of efficiency all focused on basically this same problem of productive efficiency. Harrington Emerson, among others, wrote of efficiency through organization, a matter of some consequence to industrialists of that period. Stated succinctly, the economic milieu of the era created and accounted for the appeal of Taylor and scientific management.

Economically, scientific management was a product of its environment in the sense that it grew out of the pressing needs of industry for efficiency. Resources were accumulated, phase I completed, and rationalization of resource utilization (phase II) became important. Many have criticized the scientific management era as characteristic of a "machine civilization" or a mechanistic view of man in industry. According to Daniel Bell, for example, the enterprise was rigidly structured to obey three "logics": (1) the "logic of size," based on large-scale production in a central work place: (2) the "logic of measured time" or the scientific determination of work standards: and (3) the "logic of hierarchy," resulting in a transfer of control of work and the work pace from the worker to the management.[4] In Bell's opinion, Taylorism resulted in a "social physics" which reduced the social facet of man to solely physical laws and determinants. Human movement was detached from the human and made abstract through motion study. Science in enterprise made workers passive and dependent, and removed all thought from their jobs. Bell represents one school of modern criticism whose thesis is that scientific management built a one-dimensional machine model of people and organizations.

[4] Daniel Bell, *Work and Its Discontents: The Cult of Efficiency in America*, Boston: Beacon Press, 1956, pp. 3–10.

Whatever the merits of such criticism, it simply does not portray the whole story. Placed in the cultural imperatives of his era, Taylor was meeting a legitimate need of industry. The "logics" which Bell uses in criticism were the logics that created scientific management. Taylor was not a social scientist and never claimed to be; his forte was efficiency, which was the watchword of the day. As cultural conditions changed, views on Taylorism were revised accordingly and management thought assumed new forms. The social scientist of today may find fault with Taylor but the historian must see the man from the perspective of his times.

Increasing Industrial Efficiency

The post-Taylor period witnessed great gains in industrial efficiency. Although the 1921 *Waste in Industry* report castigated American management, the period 1919–1929 was one of increasing productivity. One historian attributes the increase to (1) the methods of mass production, (2) Taylorism, and (3) better and cheaper sources of power.[5] In manufacturing, the number of man hours input per unit fell from an index number of 74 in 1919 to 42 in 1929 (1899=100) for a gain in efficiency of 43 percent. While output per person was rising rapidly, unemployment remained low, wages were rising, and the purchasing power of the dollar was relatively stable.[6] The prosperous 1920s held forth the promise of economic abundance for all. A great outpouring of products from the industrial machine and gains in real income gave the consumer more than ever before. The 1920s canonized the salesman and Madison Avenue. The ambitious young person avoided prosaic occupations, took sample case in hand, and sold Everyman the wares of abundance. "The business of America is business," said the taciturn Calvin Coolidge to capsulize the era. Retailing giants such as Woolworth's, the A and P, and Sears, Roebuck invaded every hamlet so that Mr. and Mrs. Everyman could dress, eat, and partake of America's goods in a manner never before possible in history.

[5] George Soule, *Prosperity Decade: From War to Depression*, New York: Holt, Rinehart and Winston, 1947, pp. 127–128. Professor Soule did not rank nor assign any weights to the influence of these three factors.

[6] Solomon Fabricant, *Labor Savings in American Industry: 1899–1939*, New York: National Bureau for Economic Research, pp. 43–46 and p. 50.

Economically, America came of age in this period. Large-scale administrative structures were required to cope with the economics of mass production and mass distribution. Rationalization of resource usage was required and scientific management became the conventional wisdom to fill that void. It was an age of concern for economic efficiency. With a tremendously productive industrial system, rising real wages, low-level unemployment, and mass marketing and distribution, America had never known such abundance. Many were buying stocks and land in sunny climes such as Florida and California to prepare for early retirement with their affluence. In October of 1929, there were only a few who thought that anything could go wrong; and after all, these were the pessimists who had not grasped the American dream.

The Social Environment: From Horatio Alger to Babbitt

Between the Civil War and 1900, Horatio Alger, Jr., wrote more than 100 books for boys with such piquant titles as *Bound to Rise, Luck and Pluck, Sink or Swim,* and *Tom, the Bootblack.* At least 20 million copies were sold and "Horatio Alger" became a synonym for a success story.[7] The typical plot was the tale of a young but poor hero, beset by the unscrupulous on all sides, who worked his way to wealth by the virtues of diligence, honesty, perseverance, and thrift. Quite often he was befriended by a benevolent benefactor who recognized his latent talent for capital accumulation and aided him in his climb to the pinnacle of the financial world. The hero of Alger's books was a personification of McClelland's "high achiever" and of Riesman's "inner-directed" man who had his own gyroscope to keep him on the path to success.[8] He exhibited the virtues of self-control, hard work, and fru-

[7]The life of Horatio Alger, Jr., (1832–1899) formed an interesting paradox to the type of novels he wrote. He wrote success stories of rags to riches yet he himself was neither born poor nor did he die rich. About 15 of the 20 million copies of his books were sold after his death. Frederick Lewis Allen, "Horatio Alger, Jr.," The *Saturday Review of Literature,* Vol. 18, No. 21 (September 17, 1938), pp. 3–17.

[8]McClelland, in *The Achieving Society,* found that *n* achievement increased regularly from 1800 to 1890, peaked, and declined thereafter. See also David Riesman, *The Lonely Crowd,* Garden City, N.Y.: Doubleday and Co., 1950, pp. 28–32.

gality of the Protestant ethic and of Ben Franklin's Poor Richard.[9] The hero learned in ·the school of hard knocks and no formal schooling could prepare him for success in business. Charles M. Schwab, a protégé of Andrew Carnegie, stated the case:

> If the college man thinks that his education gives him a higher social status, he is riding for a fall. Some college men . . . have pride in their mental attainments that is almost arrogance. Employers find it difficult to control, guide, and train such men. Their spirit of superiority bars the path of progress.[10]

Elbert Hubbard sketched the traits of the man who was desired by industry in his "A Message to Garcia." In this story, Rowan was asked to carry a message from the president of the United States to the insurgent Cuban General Garcia during the Spanish-American War.[11] Without questioning and whining, Rowan took the initiative and, operating on a minimum of guidance, got the message through. This display of the virtues of a self-starting, self-directed, highly motivated man exemplified the business ideal. The ideal was that of individual effort and initiative with a minimum of guidance from without.

Early scientific management theory was consonant with the social values of reward for individual effort and the classical virtues of "rational man" directed by his own self-interest. Utilitarian economics, then in vogue, held that individuals rationally calculated what was to their own advantage based on the seeking of pleasure and the avoidance of pain. Workers, like every other human being, were motivated by their own self-interest. In the classical period of economics, this self-interest was largely the monetary reward that came from work, giving rise to the idea of "economic man." Before Taylor, management by incentives had failed largely because management had not cleared the obstacles for gain from the workers' paths and had indulged in rate cutting when earnings became too high. Taylor's conception of a management which facilitated worker effort by study and proper job de-

---

[9] An interesting anthology of success stories based on these virtues is Moses Rischin, *The American Gospel of Success*, New York: Quadrangle Books, 1965. Rischin discusses such individuals as Cotton Mather, Benjamin Franklin, Clarence B. Randall, and Billy Graham.

[10] Charles M. Schwab, "The College Man in Business," in Altha G. Saunders (ed.), *The Literature of Business*, rev. ed., New York: Harper & Row, 1923, p. 5.

[11] Elbert Hubbard, "A Message to Garcia," ibid., pp. 190–194.

sign was supposed to open the door and free the workers' basic drive for economic rewards. Rate cutting was not in management's self-interest because it only served to force workers to return to their former habits of soldiering. The mental revolution between labor and management was the recognition of mutual self-interest. From management's vantage, a rational system of work, proper incentives, no cutting of rates, and leadership by knowledge and not by "drive" would lead to lower costs and higher profits. From the workers' viewpoint, they would recognize that standards had been properly established by scientific study and that by following instructions and procedures they would be able to rationally calculate that they could best serve their own self-interest by following Taylor's system.

The ideals of scientific management were compatible with the prevailing views of people's needs, and aspirations. As Hugh Aitken has so capably pointed out, scientific management was a manifestation of the rationalist's philosophies of the eighteenth century and earlier. All phenomena, including human activity, were subject to rational laws, and scientific management was an attempt to apply these laws to people at work.[12] The notion of rational, economically motivated people and the spirit of scientific inquiry leading to the reduction of all activity to physical laws were both commonly held concepts deeply rooted in the culture.

The "Collision Effect"

Cultural change, that third eternal inevitability like death and taxes, is always difficult to pinpoint historically. But times were changing and the milieu of scientific management slowly assumed new dimensions that affected the course of management thought. Two disparate yet strangely congenial forces were forming to mark a new era in American cultural thought: (1) the closing of the frontier and (2) the rise of progressivism. America of the early twentieth century was in the turmoil of urbanization and industrialization. The noted historian, Frederick Jackson Turner, identified four forces which were tending to reshape American economic, social, and political ideals: (1) the exhaustion of the supply

---

[12] Hugh G. J. Aitken, *Taylorism at Watertown Arsenal*, Cambridge, Mass.: Harvard University Press, 1960, pp. 15–16.

of free land and the closing of the West; (2) the concentration of wealth and power in the hands of a few fundamental industries; (3) the political expansion by America into territories beyond her own borders; and (4) the rise of populism.[13] The West in America typified the ideals of individualism, economic equality, freedom to rise on one's own initiative, and democracy. Whenever social conditions became too oppressive or capital pressed upon labor or political restraints became too great, the West provided an avenue of escape. When the "safety valve" of the West closed, new institutional arrangements were necessary to attain the American ideal of democracy which had long been provided for by the West.

William G. Scott has built on Turner's thesis and has called the culmination of these cultural forces the "period of collision" (Figure 12-1). The "collision effect" was characterized by conflict and resulted from forces which had drawn people into an inescapable proximity and dependency upon one another. Left unmitigated, the collision effect would have led eventually to social and psychological degeneration. However, Scott's thesis was that the decline of the "individualistic ethic" of the period of expansion was slowly being replaced by a "social ethic" which substituted human collaboration for human competition "with a prayer that a social philosophy would lead to industrial harmony."[14] Basic to this search were Taylor's notions of "harmony, not discord," "cooperation, not individualism," and the "mental revolution" on the part of both labor and management.

There were elements of both the individualistic and the social ethics in Taylor's philosophy. In Scott's analysis, the social ethic began with the group as a source of value while the individualistic ethic started with the person as the primary value. Taylor's "cooperation, not individualism" would suggest that he accepted the social ethic. However, people are neither purely individualistic since they normally desire social intercourse, nor are they purely group-oriented because of their own ego needs. Taylor's philosophy bridged the gap between the two ethics by stressing the mutuality of interests and collaboration at work (the social

[13] Frederick Jackson Turner, *The Frontier in American History*, New York: Holt, Rinehart and Winston, 1921, pp. 244–247.

[14] W. G. Scott, *The Social Ethic in Management Literature*, Atlanta: Georgia State College of Business Administration, 1959, p. 9.

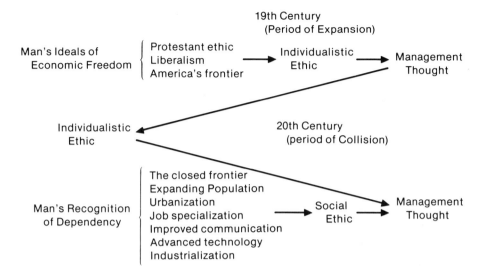

Fig. 12-1. **Management thought in a changing culture. (Adapted from William G. Scott,** *Organization Theory: A Behaviorial Analysis for Management,* **Homewood, Ill.: Richard D. Irwin, Inc.; by permission. This diagram appeared originally in William G. Scott,** *The Social Ethic in Management Literature.* **Bulletin No. 4, Bureau of Business and Economic Research, Georgia State' College, Atlanta, Georgia, 1959, p. 10.)**

ethic) coupled with individually based economic incentives and the selection and development of each person to the highest extent possible (the individualistic ethic). Taylor was clearly in touch with the problems of the industrialized society of the period. Though not known nor regarded as a social philosopher, he clearly perceived the industrial dilemma and proposed one means of alleviating the detrimental effects of the disharmonies of urbanization and industrialization.

Taylorism and the Progressives

The Populist-Progressive movement was a parallel development which attempted to provide a broader base for democracy in order to mitigate the perils of the collision effect. It is a strange quirk of history that Taylor would never have been considered by modern critics "progressive," yet his work and philosophy eventually became imbedded in Progressive thought. Progressivism had its roots in the Populist movement of the seventies and eighties. Whereas Populism was overwhelmingly rural and provincial, Progressivism was urban, middle class, and nationwide.[15] Both were reform movements and progressivism picked up where the populism of William Jennings Bryan left off. For both movements, the central problem was to "restore" equality of opportunity by removing the interventions of government which benefited large-scale capital and by replacing those interventions with ones which favored men of little or no capital.[16] Populism waned because it was based on support from a declining segment of the population, the rural areas. Progressivism, both a social and a political force, succeeded because it was concerned with labor, small businessmen, and the urban population. The Progressives sought to enfranchise women, elect United States senators by direct popular vote, aid lower-income groups, establish a minimum wage, enact workmen's compensation laws, encourage trade unions, and enact a federal income tax.

There was probably little in the Progressive platform which would have appealed to F. W. Taylor but reform movements have a facility for making a union of odd couples. Scientific management caught the Progressive eye at the Eastern rate hearings. Brandeis, a leading Progressive, helped coin the catchy title ("scientific management") which made efficiency synonymous with morality and social order. The public could be "saved" from a rate increase if efficiency was introduced and labor and management denied unwarranted gains. Everyone could benefit from lower costs and higher wages if industrial leaders would accept Taylor's precepts. It was here that the Progressives' romance with scientific management began.[17] The reformers did not wish to root out capitalism but sought orderly change in the structure of industry vis-à-vis the public. Some reformers, like the Socialist Eugene Debs, wanted to replace the whole system. More moderate men, like

[15] Richard Hofstadter, *The Age of Reform*, New York: Vintage Books, 1955, p. 131. Hofstadter traced the reform movement in America from populism, through progressivism, to the "New Deal."

[16] Eric F. Goldman, *Rendezvous with Destiny*, New York: Vintage Books, 1952, p. 59. This is another excellent history of the Progressive reform movement.

[17] Samuel Haber, *Efficiency and Uplift: Scientific Management in the Progressive Era 1890–1920*, Chicago: University of Chicago Press, 1964, pp. 54–56.

Louis Brandeis, Herbert Croly, and Walter Lippman, thought that efficiency through science and leadership by professional experts would bring social order and harmony. Each envisioned a professionalization of business leadership which would remove the manager from the "cesspool of commercialism" and turn him into an "industrial statesman."[18] The appeal of scientific management to these men was that it offered leadership by expertise and knowledge and would hence rise above class prejudice and rule by drive and whim. The high wages and low costs promised by efficiency systems would check the greed of the employer and the laziness of the employee. Finally, scientific management showed that the interests of the employer and the employee were identical and the wastes of class conflict therefore unnecessary.[19]

The major snag between the Progressives and scientific management resided in Taylor's view of unions. To Progressives, unions were instruments of social and economic reform and men like Robert G. Valentine envisioned trade unions eventually being replaced by enlightened consumer unions in their evolution toward true industrial democracy.[20] The transition period was to be marked by a *rapprochement* between scientific management and organized labor based on "efficiency and consent." The revisionist movement was therefore a means whereby the Progressives could reconcile Taylorism with their own goals. Once the union view was resolved, the Progressives felt that scientific management had much to offer as a social force. The Progressives sought "industrial betterment" or "industrial welfare" which was an uneven mixture of philanthropy, humanitarianism, and business acumen.[21] Industrialists such as John H. Patterson of National Cash Register set the pattern for the industrial welfare movement.[22] Welfare schemes had the objectives of preventing labor problems and im-

---

[18] Walter Lippman, *Drift and Mastery*, New York: Mitchell Kennerly, Publisher, 1914, pp. 10–11. See also Louis Brandeis, *Business—A Profession*, Boston: Small, Baynard & Co., 1914.

[19] Haber, pp. 58–58 and 89–90.

[20] R. G. Valentine, "Scientific Management and Organized Labor," *Bulletin of the Society to Promote the Science of Management*, Vol. 1, No. 1 (January, 1915), pp. 3–9.

[21] Haber, p. 18.

[22] Samuel Crowther, *John H. Patterson: Pioneer in Industrial Welfare*, Garden City, N.Y.: Doubleday and Co., 1923.

proving performance by providing hospital clinics, lunchrooms, bath houses, profit sharing, recreational facilities, and a host of other devices to woo worker loyalty. To this group, human happiness was a business asset and it was the wise, profit-minded employer who nurtured worker loyalty to the firm through various employee welfare schemes. The efficiency engineers, especially Taylor, complemented the work of the betterment or welfare proponents by linking efficiency and morality.[23] For Taylor, hard work led to morality and well-being; for the industrial betterment advocates, morality and well-being yielded hard work. This reciprocal work-welfare equation was the core of the romance between the Progressives and scientific management. Societal uplift through efficiency was in vogue.

In retrospect, social forces were generating and sanctioning an efficiency craze during the Taylor era. A proliferation of popular and technical literature appeared on efficiency in the home, in education, in conservation of natural resources, in the church, and in industry. The noted psychologist H. H. Goddard thought that the efficiency of group endeavors was not a function so much of intelligence but of the proper assignment of workers to a grade of work which met their mental capacity.[24] This psychological notion of the "first-class man" reflected the grip of Taylor's ideas on the academic community. American educational institutions, seeking reform and a broader base for their efforts, seized upon Taylorism and discovered the efficiency expert.[25] Conservationists, spurred by Presidents T. R. Roosevelt and William Howard Taft, also found comfort in the gospel of efficiency.[26] Feminists saw a saving grace in efficiency which would release the woman from the drudgery of housework and free her to assume her equal role in society. The Reverend Billy Sunday recommended functional fore-

---

[23] Haber, p. 20.

[24] Henry Herbert Goddard, *Human Efficiency and Levels of Intelligence*, Princeton, N.J.: Princeton University Press, 1920.

[25] See Raymond E. Callahan, *Education and the Cult of Efficiency*, Chicago: University of Chicago Press, 1962; and J. M. Rice, *Scientific Management and Education*, New York: Hinds, Noble, and Eldredge, 1914.

[26] Samuel P. Hays, *Conservation and the Gospel of Efficiency*, Cambridge, Mass.: Harvard University Press, 1959.

manship for the church so that each department could obtain expert advice and lasting results.[27]

This cultural fetish for efficiency was soon to wane. By the 1920s, a marked shift had occurred from the individualistic ideal of Horatio Alger. The gospel of production efficiency was dying as factories poured forth an abundance. Prosperity reigned and a new gospel of consumption emerged with a heavy stress on sales and selling all Americans on the importance of being "middle class." Individuals such as Whiting Williams, Elton Mayo, and Mary Parker Follett were beginning to play down the emphasis on the individual and stress the importance of the group in industry. The burgeoning discipline of personnel management emphasized industrial welfare, better selection, improving morale, and worker happiness as both a social and business asset. Fictional critics of society were deploring America's preoccupation with business, and the vulgar, crass fellow Babbitt symbolized conforming mediocrity. There was security in conformity and people were becoming more conscious of social relations and less aspiring in maximizing individual return. The frontier was closed and new social values were replacing the Western ideal of rugged individualism. The seeds were sown for "social man."

The Political Environment: From one Roosevelt to Another

The task of government and political institutions throughout time has always revolved around balancing two basic themes: (1) the need to establish equity and order to protect one man from another, and (2) the need to limit governmental power to protect man from the state. Political theorists like Machiavelli and Hobbes saw a central role for the state over man; Rousseau and Locke sought a system of balances through which man could check the excesses of governmental power. Constitutional or representative government, the philosophy of Locke and Rousseau made man-

---

[27] Haber, p. 63. See also: Ernest J. Dennen, *The Sunday School Under Scientific Management*, Milwaukee: The Young Churchman Co., 1914; and Eugene M. Camp, *Christ's Economy: Scientific Management of Men and Things in Relation to God and His Cause*, New York: The Seabury Society, 1916.

ifest in America, makes consent of the governed the proper source of all legislative authority. Pluralism is characteristic of a constitutional society and it "seeks to diffuse power into many organizations and groupings and thus to prevent the development of imbalance of power and to assure the freedom of the individual from the tyranny of the one, the few, or the many."[28] The ballot box is the medium for making pluralism a reality. America of the late nineteenth century was seeking to perfect democracy, and dissatisfied groups and individuals were responding to the collision effect with an outpouring of legislation to change the relations between individual and state and between business and government. Founded on the premises of limited government, private property, freedom of economic opportunity, stress on individual initiative, and a government which should keep its hands off business, America was finding imbalances and imperfections between the ideals and practice of economic democracy. Instead of *laissez-faire* capitalism perpetuating itself as Adam Smith envisioned, business men were taking collective action to ration and monopolize the market, organized labor took on economic and political objectives, and special interest groups fought to expand their opportunity at the expense of other groups. People were feeling powerless as individuals, and collective action became more prevalent.[29]

The change in public attitude, that is, as espoused by the Progressives, was that government should look out for interests of all the people, not just a privileged few. Farm groups, especially the Grange movement, sought to protect themselves against the unholy alliance of the government bureaucrats who gave railroad franchises and the business men who bribed to get franchises and cheated to keep them. Workers organized through the Knights of Labor and later the American Federation of Labor in order to offset what they perceived to be an imbalance in bargaining power. Other groups sought subsidies, tariffs, and special legislation to enhance their own advantage. In 1900, there was no Department of Commerce, no Department of Labor, no Federal Reserve Sys-

---

[28] Richard Eells and Clarence Walton, *Conceptual Foundations of Business,* Homewood, Ill.: Richard D. Irwin, 1961, p. 363.

[29] Samuel P. Hays, *The Response to Industrialism: 1885–1914,* Chicago: University of Chicago Press, 1957, p. 190.

tem, and no Federal Trade Commission. The United States Senate was composed of members elected by the various state legislatures and was a citadel of privilege. Women did not have the right to vote and immigrants were crowding into the cities. "Boss" rule prevailed in many cities and the muckrakers were only beginning their scathing attacks on governmental corruption and business malpractices. Upton Sinclair had not yet penned *The Jungle*, which aimed for the nation's heart, but hit its stomach and led to enactment of the Pure Food and Drug Act.

Business and the Progressives

The "Big Change" came in 1901 after the assassination of President McKinley and the succession of Theodore Roosevelt.[30] At first, the new president gave business men and the financial interests no cause for alarm. His well-phrased first message to Congress did well to balance his own Progressive inclinations with a probusiness stance. Mr. Dooley, Peter Finley Dunne's fictional Irishman, aptly summarized President Roosevelt's position:

> "Th' trusts," says he, "are heejus monsthers built up be th' inlightened intherprise in th' men that have done so much to advance progress in our beloved counthry" he says. "On wan hand I wud stamp thim undher fut; on th' other hand not so fast."[31]

The honeymoon was brief. In 1902, President Roosevelt brought suit to dissolve the Northern Securities Company by invoking the Sherman Act. This direct blow at Northern Securities, a holding company set up by J. P. Morgan and Edward H. Harriman to control three major railroads, opened a new era in government-business relations. Known as a prime proponent of conservation of natural resources as well as a "trust-buster," the first Roosevelt placed government in a new role as a regulator of business activity. Antitrust suits were filed against the Beef Trust (1905), the Standard Oil Company of New Jersey (1906), and the American Tobacco Company (1907); and new legislation regulated the railroads (Elkins Act in 1903 and Hepburn Act in 1906), and the telephone, telegraph and wireless industries (Mann-Elkins Act in 1910). Other state and federal legislative enactments sought to

---

[30] Frederick Lewis Allen, *The Big Change*, New York: Harper & Row, 1952.

[31] Cited by Allen, ibid., p. 85.

limit hours of work and regulate female and child labor. The Clayton Act and the Federal Trade Commission Act (1914) strengthened the Sherman Act and made more explicit other discriminatory business practices. The Federal Reserve Act (1913) created a more elastic currency and weakened the hold of big New York City banks over cash and reserves.

To illustrate further the decline of *laissez faire,* taxpayers lost their earlier reprieve with the passage of the Underwood-Simmons Tariff Act of 1913. The act provided for a 1 percent tax on personal incomes over $3,000 and a surtax was added progressively on incomes up to $20,000; the maximum rate was 7 percent on incomes in excess of $500,000 and taxpayers reported their income on Form 1040. The Supreme Court let this act stand; only the rates have changed.

In retrospect, the political environment of the early scientific management era sought to bring a new balance between the power of business vis-à-vis the public. Though Taylor did not concern himself with the political environment to any large extent, his own battles with entrenched, resistant business leadership, for example Bethlehem Steel, indicate that he sought to replace management by privilege with management by science based on expertise. The mental revolution was to deemphasize the division of the surplus and stress production for lower prices and higher wages. The romance of Taylor and the Progressives had political as well as social ramifications. Postwar America witnessed the decline of the progressivism of Roosevelt and Woodrow Wilson and welcomed the "return to normalcy" of Warren Harding. America withdrew from the world arena of politics and turned inward to enjoy a decade of prosperity. Congress and the Supreme Court relaxed controls over business, the influence of organized labor declined, sales were predominant over production, company unions and industrial welfare schemes abounded, and revised Taylorism led to union-management cooperation.

Politically, the 1920s were a nonactivist period. There was a brief restoration of the philosophy of *laissez-faire* and its belief in the self-regulating nature of an economy. Judge Gary held his famous dinners to get agreement on the price of steel, and banks and lending institutions gave free rein to finance whatever speculative impulse, be it land or stocks, the public might have. Blissfully ignoring the Florida land bust in 1926 and a downturn in economic activity in 1927, Mr. and Mrs. America enjoyed their bath-tub gin, rumble seats, jazz, and short skirts. The great collapse of 1929 signaled the end of an era. After that, America turned in desperation to the New Deal of Franklin Delano Roosevelt in the hope that government could do something, anything, to pull America from its cultural morass.

Summary of Part II

Figure 12-2 depicts the emergence, growth, and evolution of the scientific management era in a visual summary form. Scientific management was not an invention, it was a synthesis, a stage in evolving management thought. Charles Babbage could lay a valid claim for the paternity of a rational, systematic approach to management, but it was Frederick W. Taylor who gave systematic management a voice.

Taylor was the man of the hour, the *deus ex machina* who became the focal point for an idea. Scientific management was more than methods and time study; it was a much deeper philosophy of administering human and physical resources in a technologically advanced world where people had gained greater control over their environment than ever before. The Industrial Revolution had provided the impetus; Taylor provided the synthesis. As people gained greater power over the physical world, they sought to direct and guide the products of that greater prosperity to more rational ends. Taylor had an idea, a great idea, on how that might be done—by a mental revolution for all parties, founded on science and not whim, and leading to harmony and cooperation. Perhaps he was idealistic, even Utopian, but it would be wrong to criticize him for holding forth the promise of coupling industrial harmony, individual betterment, and greater productivity.

Those who followed Taylor represented divergences from his orthodoxy. Some were major figures, leaving larger footprints in the sands of time, while others left merely tracings. But each in his own way provided for industrial education, for academic awareness of management, and for improved productivity and service to society by industry. Two of Taylor's contemporaries, Fayol and Weber, were to achieve acclaim only in more modern times; but

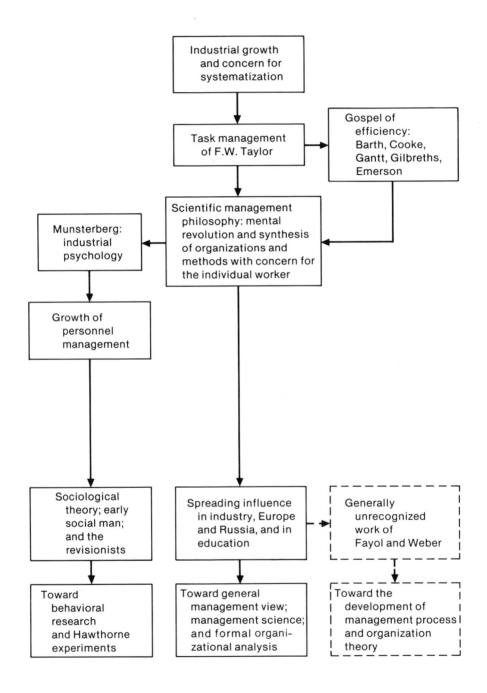

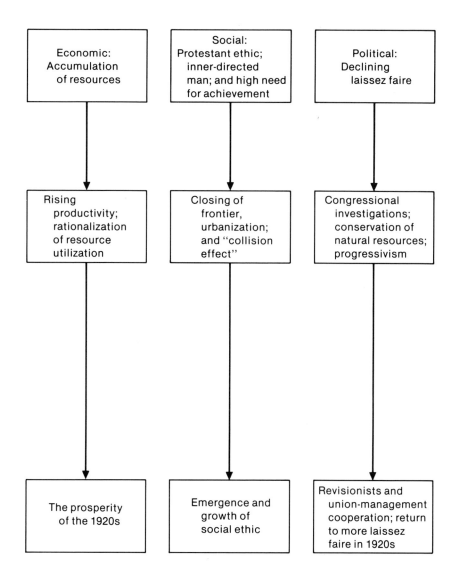

Fig. 12-2.   Synopsis of the scientific management era and its cultural environment.

all of those examined during this era reflected the imprint of Taylor's search for administrative rationality in a world of large enterprise.

The historical question of whether the person makes the times or vice versa cannot be begged. Certainly it is a mutually reciprocating force, an action-reaction throughout history. Taylor and his followers were the products of an era which economically sought a rationalization of resource utilization, which socially sanctioned individual reward and effort, and which politically encouraged uplift through efficiency. In return, the individuals affected the times by giving voice to a movement toward material prosperity, toward industrial harmony to retard the collision effect, and toward making America into the world's economic and political leader. Scientific management was the child of its culture and in turn made its culture an adult of industrial, social, and political vigor.

 # THE SOCIAL MAN ERA

Eras in management thought never begin and end neatly in any particular year. Instead there is a blending of movements and the themes are played in a shifting of major and minor keys. The notion of a "social man era" reflects more of the philosophy which was emerging than any settled criterion for managerial action. "Social man" was born late in the scientific management era but did not achieve any large degree of recognition until the 1930s. In part III, we will examine first the Hawthorne research and the emerging Mayoist philosophy which ushered in the human relations movement. Next, the work of Mary Parker Follett and Chester Barnard will be examined to illustrate some unique notions of authority and organizational integration. Then evolving management thought will be viewed in separate, parallel branches: one, the growth of widespread interest and research into industrial behavior; and two, the writings of a number of scholars who were slowly developing a top-management viewpoint of organizations. We will conclude part III by examining the critics of the human relationists and by discussing the economic, social, and political environment of social man.

13

Serendipity at Western Electric

At times, many managers and professional students of the subject have held that there was a clear-cut cause and effect relationship between the quality of the physical work environment and the well-being and productivity of the worker. Surrounded by the proper ventilation, temperature, lighting and other physical working conditions, the worker would have the optimum environment for working on scientifically measured tasks while motivated by some wage incentive scheme. Other impediments to efficiency, such as fatigue and monotony, were believed in large measure to be due to improper job design, poor materials flow, working under stressful conditions, or other factors which posed environmental obstacles to workers' efforts. Fatigue, believed to be caused by the buildup of lactic acid toxins in the blood, could be reduced by removing wasted motions and by the introduction of scientifically determined rest periods. Some researchers even suggested that acid sodium phosphate pills taken daily were the panacea to all the ills of industrial fatigue. Illumination of the workplace was also believed important since it affected the quality, quantity, and safety of work. In 1924, the National Research Council of the National Academy of Sciences decided to determine the precise relationship between illumination and individual efficiency by initiating research at the Hawthorne plant of Western Electric, the equipment-producing and supply arm of the American Telephone and Telegraph Company. The Hawthorne works employed 25,000 people at the time and the factory was located near Cicero on Chicago's dreary industrial west side.

In customary experimental style, the research began with the designation of two groups of female workers, each performing the same tasks and located in two rooms equally illuminated.[1] One group, the "control," was to have no changes made in its illumination or work environment. The other, consisting of six operatives, was the treatment group in which, by varying levels of illumination, the effects of lighting on efficiency could be scientifically determined. The task in each group consisted of assembling telephone relays, a highly repetitive job. Carefully designed, the research took into account room temperature and humidity as well as the level of illumination. The researchers observed the groups and kept accurate records of production. As the research proceeded, the results became more and more enigmatic. Regardless of the level of illumination (even when in one instance it was reduced to almost the level of moonlight),[2] production in both the control and the experimental groups rose. Puzzled, the researchers abandoned illumination as the significant variable and began manipulating methods of wage payments, rest periods, length of work day and work week as other possible causes of increased productivity. During one period, moving from a group incentive plan to an individual piece-rate resulted in a large increase in output. The introduction of five-minute rest pauses at 10:00 A.M. and 2:00 P.M. also led to increases in productivity. Shortening the work day, reducing the work week, and providing refreshments at the rest pauses all yielded increases in output.

Exasperated by their results, the researchers decided to abolish all "privileges" and to return to the conditions under which there were no rest pauses, no refreshments, and no shortened day or week, i.e., the original conditions of work with the sole exception that the individual piece rate was retained. Expecting the workers' spirits to be crushed, the researchers were amazed to find that "the daily and weekly output rose to a point higher than

[1] Descriptions of this early research may be found in Elton Mayo, *The Human Problems of an Industrial Civilization*, New York: MacMillan Co., 1933, pp. 55–69; and in Fritz J. Roethlisberger and William J. Dickson, *Management and the Worker*, Cambridge, Mass.: Harvard University Press, 1939, pp. 15–86. See also: Charles D. Wrege, "Solving Mayo's Mystery: The First Complete Account of the Origin of the Hawthorne Studies—The Forgotten Contributions of C. E. Snow and H. Hibarger," *Academy of Management Proceedings* (1976), pp. 12–16.

[2] At one point, the level of illumination was 0.06 of a footcandle. F. J. Roethlisberger and W. J. Dickson, p. 17.

at any other time . . ."[3] Reinstatement of rest pauses and re-freshments led to yet another boost in output to an all-time high. In brief, during the whole period of experimentation, individual output had risen from an average of 2,400 relays per week to 3,000 per week per worker.

These initial experiments of the National Research Council lasted from 1924 to 1927 and the results were so inconclusive that nearly everyone was prepared to abandon the whole project as useless. Output had increased but no one knew why. The illumination hypothesis was rejected; fatigue did not appear to be a factor, nor did there appear to be any consistent relationship between incentive schemes, hours of sleep, humidity or any of the other variables and worker output. George Pennock, Western Electric's superintendent of inspection, surmised that the key point was the interest shown in the workers by the experimenters.[4] But this was not considered totally conclusive and the management of Western Electric, at the urging of Pennock, decided to explore further the complexities of human reactions to the workplace. At that point, no one could have anticipated the scope and significance of what was to follow.

The Ivy League Comes to Hawthorne

During the winter of 1927–1928, Elton Mayo addressed a group of personnel managers at the Harvard Club in New York City. In attendance was George Pennock, who told Mayo of the test room experiments and invited Mayo to come into the study as a consultant. George Elton Mayo (1880–1949) was an Australian who had received his M.A. degree in logic and philosophy from the University of Adelaide in 1899. Mayo had taught logic and philosophy

---

[3] Ibid., p. 65. Among those who were puzzled was the renowned scientist, Dr. Vannevar Bush. Bush, then professor of electrical power transmission at the Massachusetts Institute of Technology, took part in the original experiments and recalled that none of the researchers could explain the variations in output. Loren Baritz, citing correspondence with Dr. Bush, in *The Servants of Power*, New York: John Wiley and Sons, 1960, p. 80.

[4] George Pennock, "Industrial Research at Hawthorne," *The Personnel Journal*, Vol. 8 (1930), p. 296. This was the first known appearance of the Hawthorne research in the management literature.

at Queensland University and later studied medicine in Edinburgh, Scotland.[5] While in Scotland, he became a research associate in the study of psychopathology; this experience was to serve
as a basis for his later development as an industrial researcher.
Under a grant from the Laura Spelman Rockefeller fund, Mayo
emigrated to America and joined the faculty of the Wharton
School of Finance and Commerce of the University of Pennsylvania. In early research Mayo found that the problems of workers
could not be explained by any one factor but had to be dealt with
in what he called "the psychology of the total situation."[6] This
was a Gestalt concept and formed the basis for Mayo's view of the
organization as a social system. In his research, Mayo followed the
conventional wisdom of the times and sought a relationship between working conditions and human performance in a textile
mill near Philadelphia. By introducing rest pauses, Mayo was able
to reduce turnover from 250 percent to 5 percent and improve efficiency. The work pauses, in Mayo's terms, reduced the "pessimistic reveries" of the workers, hence improving morale and
productivity. Joining the Harvard faculty in 1926 as associate professor of industrial research, Mayo was about to embark on an intellectual journey that would reshape the course of management
thought.

The Harvard Research Group

Intrigued by the initial results of the National Research Council
experiments, which were then still incomplete, Mayo perceptively
noted that "a remarkable change of mental attitude in the group"
was the key factor in explaining the Hawthorne mystery.[7] In his
opinion, the test room workers became a social unit, enjoyed the

[5] Personal data on Mayo are from Lyndall Urwick (ed.), *The Golden Book of Management*, London: Newman Neame, 1956, pp. 220–224.

[6] Elton Mayo, "The Basis of Industrial Psychology," *Bulletin of the Taylor Society*,
December 1924; reprinted in Donald Delmar and Rodger Collons (eds.), *Classics in
Scientific Management*, University, Alabama: University of Alabama Press, 1976,
pp. 264–277. See also Elton Mayo, "The Irrational Factor in Human Behavior: The
Night Mind in Industry," in the *Annals of the American Academy of Political and So-
cial Science*, Philadelphia, Pa., Vol. CX (November, 1923), pp. 117–130.

[7] Elton Mayo, *Human Problems*, pp. 71–72.

increased attention of the experimenters, and developed a sense of participation in the project.

> *The most significant change that the Western Electric Company introduced into its "test room" bore only a casual relation to the experimental changes. What the Company actually did for the group was to reconstruct entirely its whole industrial situation.*[8]

With this recognition of the social milieu of industrial life, Mayo had opened the door to research into social man. Social man was the creation of group efforts in which Mayo became the focal point for collaborative research between company officials and the Harvard research group. Along with Mayo, Fritz Jules Roethlisberger (1898–1974) became a cornerstone in these efforts and a leading exponent of the nascent philosophy of human relations. Roethlisberger received his A.B. degree from Columbia University in 1921 and his B.S. from the Massachusetts Institute of Technology in 1922. From 1922 to 1924 he was engaged in industrial practice as a chemical engineer and then he returned to Harvard to take his M.A. in 1925. He stayed on at Harvard to join the Industrial Research Department and soon became involved in the Hawthorne research.[9]

In addition to the primary intellectual inspiration of Mayo and Roethlisberger, others also made significant contributions to the research group. For the company, G. A. Pennock, William J. Dickson (chief of the Employee Relations Research Department), and Harold A. Wright (chief of personnel research and training) were the prime movers. From academia, the roll call was to become a *Who's Who* in management research: W. Lloyd Warner, the anthropologist who designed the experiments to reveal the impact of the group upon the individual; T. North Whitehead, who did detailed statistical studies of the relay assembly room;[10] and L. J. Henderson, the physiologist who introduced the Har-

[8] Ibid., p. 73.

[9] F. J. Roethlisberger, *The Elusive Phenomena* (ed. by George F. F. Lombard), Cambridge, Mass.: Harvard University Press, 1977. A special tribute to Roethlisberger appears in George F. F. Lombard (ed.), *The Contributions of F. J. Roethlisberger to Management Theory and Practice*, Cambridge, Mass.: Harvard University Graduate School of Business, 1976.

[10] T. N. Whitehead's work may be found in *Leadership in a Free Society*, Cambridge, Mass.: Harvard University Press, 1936; and *The Industrial Worker* (2 volumes), Cambridge, Mass.: Harvard University Press, 1938.

vard group to the work of Vilfredo Pareto.[11] Others were to follow but here was the beginning of a fateful voyage in management history.

Rejecting Traditional Hypotheses

The mythical three princes of Serendip did not find what they sought on their voyage but found things far more important than the original object of their search. Likewise, the Harvard group picked up the loose threads of the National Research Council experiments and found far more valuable insights into industrial behavior than the original intent of the illumination studies. Mayo and his associates entered the Western Electric experiments in period 10 of a 13-period project and immediately began to try to make sense of the previously incoherent results. The absence of a positive relationship between environmental changes, such as rest pauses, etc., and worker output led the Harvard group to examine the traditional hypotheses of management in an effort to find a new scope and role for management and the worker.

Five hypotheses of management were proposed to explain the failings of the original illumination research: (1) that improved material conditions and methods of work were present in the test room, leading to greater output; (2) that rest pauses and shorter days had provided relief from fatigue; (3) that rest pauses had provided relief from the monotony of work; (4) that the individual wage payment incentive had stimulated increased output; and (5) that the changes in supervisory techniques, i.e., improved interpersonal relations, had improved attitudes and output.[12] One by one, each hypothesis was tested. The first explanation was rejected since some working conditions, e.g., the level of illumination, had been purposely deteriorated and yet production had increased. Second, rest pauses and length of workday did not explain the results since output still increased after all of these "privileges" were taken away. The third hypothesis, relief from

[11]Lawrence J. Henderson, *Pareto's General Sociology: A Physiologist's Interpretation*, Cambridge, Mass.: Harvard University Press, 1935. Henderson's work on Pareto provided a bond of interest between him and Chester I. Barnard and also influenced the work of another social systems analyst, George C. Homans.

[12]Roethlisberger and Dickson, pp. 86–89.

monotony, was less conclusive since monotony was deemed a state of mind and could not be assessed on the basis of output data alone. The researchers knew that worker attitudes had improved, probably due to their being singled out as a special group receiving increased attention, but were loath to attribute the large rise in output to this factor alone.

The hypothesis of incentive payments struck at the core of traditional management theories of motivation and merited a deeper examination. Two new groups were formed, a second relay test assembly group and the mica splitting test room. Five experienced relay assemblers were selected to form a new group for study. Prior to the experiment, they were on a group incentive plan and for the first nine weeks of the experiment they were placed on an individual incentive plan. Initially total output went up, leveled off (for all but one worker whose output decreased), and then remained constant at the new higher level (112.6 percent over the base period of 100 percent). After returning to the original group incentive plan for a period of seven weeks, the second relay assembly group's performance dropped to 96.2 percent of the initial base of 100 percent before the experiment. The mica splitters had always been on an individual incentive system and the only change in the experiment was to place a selected group in a special observation room while retaining the same incentive plan. Rest pauses and the length of the workday were varied, as they had been in the earlier experiments, and changes in output noted. The mica-splitting experiment lasted 14 months and average hourly output rose 15 percent.

In explaining the results of these two groups, the researchers rejected wage incentives as a cause of increased output. Although total output increased 12.6 percent in the second relay assembly group, the researchers concluded that this was due to a desire on the part of the new group to equal the record of increase of the first relay assembly test group in the original experiments. Since the mica splitters had retained the same incentive scheme throughout the experiment, and since average hourly output had increased, the increase had to be due, in the researchers' opinion, to factors other than the payment scheme.[13] The conclusions they reached, which can be viewed as tenuous, were that it was not

---

[13] Roethlisberger and Dickson, p. 158–60.

wages but improved morale, supervision, and interpersonal relations that led to greater output in both groups. This conclusion formed the fifth hypothesis and the bulk of Roethlisberger and Dickson's book was devoted to examining the influence of improved interpersonal relations on industrial behavior.

The Interviewing Program

The "new man" of industry was to be socially motivated and controlled. Improvements in efficiency and morale were postulated to be due to improved social or human conditions rather than material or environmental conditions. This did not mean that all previous thought was completely erroneous but that management must be concerned with both the technical *and* the social facets of work. While the Harvard group's methodology may be suspect, their findings opened a new direction for management thought.

In the early experiments, the researchers removed the workers from the factory floor, placed them in special test rooms, and assumed many of the supervisory functions. This shift in control from the former line supervisor to the experimenters created a new social situation for the worker. As Mayo noted, the experimenters created a "freer and more pleasant working environment" under an experimenter-turned-supervisor "who is not regarded as the 'boss'."[14] The change in the quality of supervision was not a difference in its closeness but in the special attention given the workers with regard to their sentiments and motives. This special attention of experimenter for the subject conjures up the charge of the "Hawthorne effect" or the notion that the observers biased the experiment by their personal involvement. The experimenter (observer), who became the *de facto* supervisor, altered the previous managerial practices. Workers were advised and consulted about changes, their views were listened to sympathetically, and their physical and mental health became matters of great concern to the experimenters. As the research progressed, it became less of a controlled experiment and more inclined toward creating "a social situation" in which workers felt free to air their problems and one in which they established new interpersonal bonds with their coworkers and superiors.

[14] Elton Mayo, *Human Problems*, p. 78.

It would be fallacious to reject the Western Electric research findings on the basis that the observer biased the experiment. On the contrary, the significance of the Hawthorne work was that it opened new vistas in which the supervisor was called upon, and could be trained, to play a different role, one far removed from personal, idiosyncratic traits and one which enabled him to take a personal interest in the subordinate and to play the role as the experimenter played it. What was this new role and how did it evolve? A turning point in the experiments was the initiation and conduct of the interviewing program which was initially a plan for improving supervision. Since the test room studies had demonstrated a close relationship between employee morale and supervision, the Harvard group set out to reeducate the supervisors by teaching them to play the role as the observer-supervisor had played it.

The basic premise of the interviewing program was that the new supervisory role was one of openness, of concern, and of willingness to listen. The observers had noted that the female workers were "apprehensive of authority" but once the experimenter became more concerned with their needs, they lost their shyness and fear and talked more freely to company officials and to the observers. The workers developed a greater zest for work and formed new personal bonds of friendship both on the job and in after-hours activities. Their improved morale seemed to be closely associated with the style of supervision and with greater productivity. This link between supervision, morale, and productivity became the foundation stone of the human relations movement.

The interviewing program was quite lengthy and will be summarized for its unique features, rather than catalogued. The initial concept of the interviews was to have workers respond to directed questions about management's programs and policies, how well they were treated by their boss, working conditions, etc.; however, this patterned interview led to more serendipity at Hawthorne. The interviewers found to their surprise that the workers wanted to talk about things other than those included in the patterned format. What the workers thought was important were *not* those things deemed significant by the company or the investigators! Realizing this, the procedure was changed to a nondirective technique in which the interviewers allowed the workers to express their minds. The interviewers' job was to keep the workers talking and the average length of interview went from thirty minutes to one and one-half hours. After this change, workers expressed the opinion in follow-up interviews that working conditions had improved (although they had not changed) and that wages were better (even though the wage scale was the same). In short, the opportunity to "let off steam" made the workers *feel* better about their situation even though it had not changed.

The "complaints" gathered in the interviews were thoroughly investigated and found generally to be irrelevant to the facts.[15] This separation of fact and sentiment led the researchers to conclude that there were two levels of complaints, the *manifest* or material content versus the *latent* or psychological form of the complaint. For example, one interviewee was preoccupied with the noise, temperature, and fumes in his department. Further examination revealed that his latent concern was the fact that his brother had recently died of pneumonia and the worker feared that his own health might be impaired. In another case, complaints about a low piece rate were traced not to verification of this fact but to a worker's concern for medical bills arising from his wife's illness. In essence, "Certain complaints were no longer treated as facts in themselves but as *symptoms* or indicators of personal or social situations which needed to be explored."[16] From the researchers' viewpoint, worker preoccupation with personal concerns inhibited their performance, a conclusion which Mayo had called "pessimistic reveries" in his early research. The outcome of the interviewing program was supervisory training in the need to listen and understand the personal problems of workers. The supervisors were trained to be interviewers, to listen rather than to talk, and "to exclude from their personal contacts with employees any moral admonition, advice, or emotion."[17] Supervisory use of this nondirective interviewing technique enabled the supervisor to handle more intelligently workers' personal problems, to locate those factors affecting worker performance, and to re-

[15] Roethlisberger and Dickson, p. 255 passim.
[16] Ibid., p. 269. Italics added.
[17] Ibid., p. 323.

move events or factors in the workers' social or physical environment which were affecting their performance. The new supervisor was to be more people oriented, more concerned, less aloof, and skilled in handling social and personal situations. The product of this human relations style of leadership was to be better morale, fewer "pessimistic reveries," and improved output.

Group Behavior: The Bank Wiring Room

The final phase of the research program at Western Electric ran essentially chronologically parallel to the interviewing program and concerned the study of informal group behavior in the bank wiring room. The discovery of the informal organization and its machinations should not be solely attributed to the Harvard group. Frederick W. Taylor was keenly aware of systematic soldiering and group pressures; Whiting Williams had recounted his own experiences of informal relationships and attitudes toward work; and Stanley Mathewson had made an extensive study of pressures leading to restriction of output.[18] Despite these early recognitions of group pressures, the Harvard group was apparently surprised that "attention had been called to the fact that social groups in shop departments were capable of exercising very strong control over the work behavior of individual members."[19] Restriction of output was a new discovery to the researchers since they "had hitherto been unaware of its implications for management practice and employee satisfactions."[20] Knowledge builds on knowledge; and the failure of the researchers to glean from prior writings on informal group behavior is a fault, although it should not detract from the significance of their own research.

    The group chosen for study was isolated in an observation room and was composed of male operatives who assembled switches for central office switchboard equipment. The "bank wiring" task involved three groups of workmen whose work was highly interrelated: (1) the wiremen who wired the terminals;

[18] Stanley B. Mathewson, *Restriction of Output Among Unorganized Workers*, New York: Viking Press, 1931.

[19] Roethlisberger and Dickson, p. 379.

[20] Ibid., p. 380.

(2) the soldermen who solidified the connections; and (3) the inspectors who judged the quality of their work. In total, nine wiremen, three soldermen, and two inspectors were the objects of study. Wage payments were based on a group incentive plan which rewarded each worker on the basis of the total output of the group and would necessarily stress the need for collaborative effort. One of the first things noted by the researchers was that the workers had a clear-cut notion of what comprised a "fair day's work" and that this was *lower* than management's standard of output. If output exceeded that informal standard, the workers expected a cut in the wage rate or an increase in the "bogey" (i.e., management's standard) upon which the incentive was based. The worker therefore faced two dangers: one, high output which led to rate cuts or increased bogeys; or two, low output which resulted in arousing the ire of the supervisor. Group sentiment prevailed upon each worker not to exceed the informal output agreement and hence become a "rate buster" not to injure his fellow workers by parasitically falling below the standard and becoming a "rate chiseler." To enforce the group norm, the members engaged in some interesting intragroup disciplinary devices such as sarcasm, ridicule, and "binging." "Binging" involved a rather firm blow upon the upper arm of the object of disfavor and was used to enforce all violations of group norms. Avoiding bruises became a motivator and workers engaged in numerous subterranean devices to maintain informal group membership. For example, on high output days, a worker would hide the surplus and report only what conformed to the norm; later he would slow down, and take the previous surplus units from his cache and turn them in. Three facts neatly summarize the Harvard researchers' discoveries: (1) that restriction of output was deliberate and set by the group regardless of management's notion of expected output; (2) that workers smoothed out production reports to avoid the appearance of working too fast or too slowly; and (3) that the group developed its own devices to bring recalcitrant members into line.

A second facet of the bank wiring room research was the assessment of interpersonal relations for the purpose of studying social structure or group "configuration." In this phase the Harvard group could lay claim to far more originality than was possible in its study of restriction of output. Analysis of social relations in the bank wiring room revealed two cliques or informal groups within the formal structure. The formal structure consisted of three work groups of three wiremen each, one solderman serving each group, and inspection duties split between the two inspectors. The circles (Figure 13-1) indicated the presence of the two cliques A and B and the members of those sets. Wireman W_2 was shown with dotted lines to indicate that he was not a member of Clique A. Clique A was called the "front group" and worked toward the front of the observation room and Clique B was the "back group" because of its physical location. In analyzing these cliques, the researchers attempted to isolate the factors determining clique membership. Physical location (front and back) was one factor but did not govern; neither was occupation a determining factor since Clique A contained wiremen, solderers, and an inspector. Members of the same clique engaged in intragroup activities such as "games" (betting, binging, etc.), by trading jobs, and by helping one another even though company policy forbade all of these activities. Each clique excluded members from the other clique in these particular activities, and Clique A considered itself "superior" to Clique B.

Wiremen W_2 and W_5, solderer S_2, and inspector I_2 were "isolates" who did not participate in clique activities and were ex-

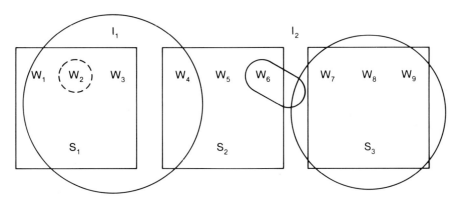

Fig. 13-1. Internal organization of the bank wiring room. (Adapted from Roethlisberger and Dickson, op. cit., p. 509. Copyright 1939 by the President and Fellows of Harvard College; by permission.)

cluded for various reasons: S_2 had a speech impediment and did not contribute to social interaction; W_2 was self-reliant and a non-conformist; W_5 was ostracized from the group because he "squealed" to the foreman about group activities which violated company policy. The inspector "isolate" (I_2) was excluded bacause he took his inspection duties very seriously whereas I_1 often pointed out errors without formally charging them against the worker and acted more like one of the boys than did I_2. In the final analysis, certain sentiments seemed to govern clique membership:

(1) *You should not turn out too much work. If you do, you are a "rate buster."*

(2) *You should not turn out too little work. If you do, you are a "chiseler."*

(3) *You should not tell a supervisor anything that will react to the detriment of an associate. If you do, you are a "squealer."*

(4) *You should not attempt to maintain social distance or act officious. If you are an inspector, for example, you should not act like one.*[21]

What was to explain the variations in output between the relay assembly test room and the bank wiring room? In the former case the female workers had increased their productivity but in the latter, restriction was the rule. Both groups were observed but the role of the observer was different. In the relay assembly experiment, the observer took the workers into his confidence, asked for suggestions, and encouraged participation in decisions affecting their welfare. In the bank wiring room, however, the observers merely watched impassively while the workers perpetuated the same informal schemes practiced in the past. The eventual explanation of the differences in output would add ammunition to the Harvard group's arsenal of arguments for new managerial skills. In explaining the cliques, new vistas for social systems would be opened.

The researchers found that the cliques performed two functions for the workers: (1) it protected them from internal indiscretions of members, such as rate busting or chiseling; and (2) it

[21] Ibid., p. 522.

protected them from the outside interference of management officials who would attempt to raise standards, cut rates, or stop their "games." The group was an instrument for controlling the activities and sentiments of the workers. Analogous to the findings of the interview program that in studying group behavior one had to separate fact from sentiment, the Harvard group began an exploration of the "facts" as the workers perceived them versus actual company practices as the researchers saw them. In regard to restriction of output, the researchers concluded that the fear of depression and layoff was not the sole reason for soldiering since workers restricted output in both good *and* bad times. Restriction was not a depression phenomenon and actually worked to the worker's detriment since restriction increased unit cost and might therefore actually induce management to make changes in rates, standards, or technology to offset the higher costs. Since the management of Western Electric had a long record of fair dealing with the workers, the researchers deemed the turning inward of the groups for protection to be "non-logical" and a worker misconception of reality.

Failing to find that mismanagement or general economic conditions caused the informal groups to form, the Harvard researchers sought an explanation by viewing the bank wiring room as part of a larger social organization. Relations with extradepartmental personnel, such as "efficiency men" and other "technologists," were viewed as disturbing since their actions could impinge on worker welfare. The technologist tended to follow a "logic of efficiency" which the workers perceived as an interference and a constraint on their activities. Further, supervisors (as a class) represented authority and the power to discipline to insure that the workers conformed to management rules. Apprehensive of such authority, the workers resisted supervisory attempts to force work behavior into an efficiency mold. Again, the researchers concluded that this was nonlogical behavior on the workers' part but stressed that management must recognize this and take into account "sentiments" along with the logic of efficiency. This position resulted in the admonition to management to view every organization as a "social system." The logic of efficiency in the technical system failed because it omitted the sentiments and nonlogical components of the social system.

The Organization as a Social System

The development of the social-system viewpoint must be classified as a major contribution of the Hawthorne research. The technical aspect of needs for efficiency and economic return should be viewed as being interrelated with concern for the human aspect of every organization. The employees have physical needs to be satisfied; but, more importantly, they have social needs. These needs arise from early social conditioning and persist through organizational life in relations with fellow workers and others in organizations. Events and objects in the physical work environment "cannot be treated as things in themselves. Instead they have to be interpreted as carriers of social value."[22] For example, a physical desk has no social significance; but if people who have desks are the ones who supervise others, then the desk becomes a status symbol and a carrier of social value. Other items, such as type of clothing worn, age, sex, seniority, and so on can also take on social significance. The researchers concluded that since people are not motivated by facts and logic, sentiments about things of social value become very powerful considerations in dealing with personnel.

The existence of the formal organization with its rules, orders, and payment plans, coupled simultaneously with an informal organization with its bases of sentiments and human interactions, posed problems for management. The informal organization should not be viewed as "bad" but as a necessary, interdependent aspect of the formal organization. Viewing the organization as a social system enabled management to attack the conflict between the "logic of efficiency" demanded by the formal organization and the "logic of sentiments" of the informal organization.[23] The manager should strive for an equilibrium between the technical organization and the human one by securing the economic goals while "maintaining the equilibrium of the social organization so that individuals through contributing services to

---

[22] Ibid., p. 557.

[23] Ibid., pp. 556–564. "Logic of sentiments" was a contradiction since Roethlisberger and Dickson concluded that sentiments were nonlogical.

this common purpose obtain personal satisfactions that make them willing to cooperate."[24]

In short, the outcome of the Hawthorne research was a call for a new mix of managerial skills. These skills were ones which were crucial to handling human situations: first, diagnostic skills in understanding human behavior and second, interpersonal skills in counseling, motivating, leading, and communicating with workers. Technical skills alone were not enough to cope with the behavior discovered at the Hawthorne Works.

A New View of Industrial Behavior

The new view of industrial behavior à la Mayo and Roethlisberger was in reality a new social philosophy for an industrial civilization. Mayo's education reveals the basis for this new emerging interpretation of people in industry. For a short time, Mayo had studied medicine and, though he never received a medical degree, he developed an interest in "psychopathology," the scientific study of mental disorders. Two individuals were in the vanguard of analyzing psychopathological thought, Pierre Janet of the French school, and Sigmund Freud, the originator of psychoanalysis. Mayo claimed more affinity to Janet, including writing a scholarly work on his theories.[25] Janet was of the opinion that the primary mental disorder was "obsession" or preoccupation with certain ideas to such an extent that the individual could not cope with them even though he knew such ideas to be irrational or untrue. The Freudians called this "compulsion" and Mayo thought the work of Janet and that of Freud were complementary.[26] The essence of Mayo's obsession-compulsion interpretation was that individuals were incapacitated by their obsessions to such a degree that they were inflexible in their responses to life, including their personal, social, and industrial behavior. Ob-

---

[24] Ibid., p. 569. The authors acknowledged their indebtedness to Chester Barnard (who will be discussed later) for this distinction.

[25] Elton Mayo, *Some Notes on the Psychology of Pierre Janet,* Cambridge, Mass.: Harvard University Press, 1948.

[26] Elton Mayo, *Human Problems,* pp. 107–110.

sessions, by reducing one's ability to adapt, had dysfunctional consequences for the worker and the supervisor. Although Mayo never once concluded that any large number of the workers at Hawthorne were severe cases, he did think that the interviewing program had demonstrated that minimal levels of obsession (or preoccupation) existed in the sense that "conditions of work tended in some way to prevent rather than facilitate a satisfactory personal adaptation."[27]

In Mayo's view, workers had been unable to find satisfactory outlets for expressing personal problems and dissatisfactions in their work life. This blockage had led to "pessimistic reveries" and preoccupations with personal problems at a latent level which emerged on the manifest level as apprehension of authority, restriction of output, and a variety of other forms of behavior which reduced morale and output. To Mayo, industrial life caused a sense of personal futility which led to social maladjustment and eventually to obsessive, irrational behavior:

> *Human collaboration in work, in primitive and developed societies, has always depended for its perpetuation upon the evolution of a non-logical social code which regulates the relations between persons and their attitudes to one another. Insistence upon a merely economic logic of production . . . interferes with the development of such a code and consequently gives rise in the group to a sense of human defeat. This human defeat results in the formation of a social code at a lower level and in opposition to the economic logic. One of its symptoms is "restriction."*[28]

It was from this psychopathological analysis of industrial life that Mayo and Roethlisberger formed the philosophical rationale for the human relations movement.[29] The goal was effective human collaboration; the means was the restoration of a social code to facilitate adjustment to industrial life.

---

[27] Ibid., p. 114.

[28] Ibid., pp. 120–121.

[29] Professor Roethlisberger also adopted this obsession-compulsion approach of Janet and Mayo. See F. J. Roethlisberger, "The Nature of the Obsessive Thinking," *Man-In-Organization: Essays of F. J. Roethlisberger,* Cambridge, Mass.: Belknap Press of Harvard University Press, 1968, pp. 1–19. This paper was originally written in June 1928 but was not published until 1968.

Anomie and Social Disorganization

To develop his thesis for human collaboration, Mayo borrowed Émile Durkheim's anomie as the basic premise for a new view of industrial man. In traditional societies people knew their place and their future and there was social solidarity. The domestic system, built around the family and kinship, gave people an identity in work as well as in their social life. The factory system and the process of industrialization destroyed this solidarity through widespread division of labor, increased social and physical mobility and the growth of large-scale organizations in which the manner of dealing with interpersonal relations shifted from a personal, friendship base to one of an impersonal nature. The result was a normless, rootless mode of life in which individual identities were lost along with the social bonds that provided continuity and purpose to human existence. This anomie led to social disorganization in personal lives and in communities and effected a general overall sense of personal futility of defeat and disillusionment.[30] Social invention to cope with industrial changes had not kept pace with technical inventions. It was this "social lag" that caused the widespread sense of futility and the resultant social disorganization. Rapid economic growth, such as America had experienced both before and after the turn of the century, had disturbed "communal integrity."

Mayo argued that the advance of technically oriented society placed undue emphasis upon engineering and yielded a technological interpretation of the meaning of work in the sense that achievement criteria were based on the economic logic of efficiency. Social needs of individuals were pushed into the background, thereby reducing the individual's "capacity for collaboration in work."[31] Managerial emphasis on the logic of efficiency stifled the individual's desire for group approval, for social satisfactions, and for social purpose gained through communal life. Drawing from Pareto's notion of an "elite," Mayo postulated that the administrative elite was technically oriented and that "in the important domain of human understanding and control,

[30]Mayo, *Human Problems*, pp. 128–131.
[31]Ibid., p. 166.

we are ignorant of the facts and their nature."[32] The "new administrator" must be one who effectively restored opportunities for human collaboration in work and in life by recognizing people's need for social solidarity. This would be accomplished by training in the human and social aspects of industrial organization, by developing "listening" and counseling skills, and by recognizing and understanding the nonlogical side of the social code. The human problem, as Mayo perceived it, was that administrators thought that the answers to industrial problems resided in technical efficiency, when in fact, the problem was a social and human one.

The Rabble Hypothesis

Elton Mayo was concerned with the human, social, and political problems of an industrial civilization, and a preponderance of his productive writing era was marked by substantial conflict in a world characterized by depression, war, and social upheaval. In the foreword to *The Social Problems of an Industrial Civilization*, he wrote:

> . . . the atomic bomb arrives at this moment to call our attention both to our achievement and our failure. We have learned how to destroy scores of thousands of human beings in a moment of time: we do not know how systematically to set about the task of inducing various groups and nations to collaborate in the tasks of civilization.
>
> It is not the atomic bomb that will destroy civilization. But civilized society can destroy itself . . . if it fails to understand intelligently and to control the aids and deterrents to cooperation.[33]

In his *Social Problems*, and later in *The Political Problems of an Industrial Civilization*,[34] Mayo was concerned with the failure of social and political institutions to provide means for effective human collaboration in the huge aggregations of people and materials which characterized a mass-producing society. Overemphasis on

---

[32]Ibid., p. 177.

[33]Boston: Division of Research, Graduate School of Business Administration, Harvard University, 1945, p. xvi.

[34]Boston: Division of Research, Graduate School of Business Administration, Harvard University, 1947.

technical progress and material life to the neglect of human and social life would be the downfall of civilization. Mayo traced the roots of this problem to faulty economic and political theory and laid the blame at the feet of David Ricardo and his "rabble hypothesis." In Mayo's view, the offender was *laissez-faire* economics and Ricardo's interpretation of society, which held that:

1.   *Natural society consists of a horde of unorganized individuals.*

2.   *Every individual acts in a manner calculated to secure his self-preservation and self-interest.*

3.   *Every individual thinks logically, to the best of his ability, in the service of this aim.*[35]

Since people were brutal, and unthinking except in the service of their own interest, the necessary corollary to cope with this "rabble" was the absolute state. This centralization of power was characteristic of Hobbes and Machiavelli; for Mayo, the era of Hitler and Mussolini was a continuation of this rabble hypothesis. Mayo attempted to refute the rabble hypothesis by: (1) postulating that it was collaboration with others, not competition among a disorganized horde, that was important; (2) stating that all individuals acted to protect their *group* status and not their self-interest; and (3) repeating the Hawthorne findings that thinking was guided more by sentiment than by logic. The Hawthorne research was used by Mayo to support all of these positions in the sense that the research found group collaboration and group sentiments to override the logic of efficiency.

In all fairness to David Ricardo, it must be noted that his "rabble hypothesis" was much less explicit than Mayo's interpretation. Ricardo, like Malthus, was one who earned for economics the title of "the dismal science" and he wrote in a gloomy world in which perhaps society did appear to be a horde to one from the educated class. Likewise, it was inappropriate to classify Ricardo's views of society with the *laissez-faire* of Adam Smith. Where Ricardo saw chaos, Smith saw order; in place of tragedy, Smith saw progress.[36] In linking the rabble hypothesis to *laissez-faire*, Mayo

[35]Elton Mayo, *Social Problems*, p. 40.

[36]Robert L. Heilbroner, *The Worldly Philosophers*, 3rd ed., New York: Simon and Schuster, 1967, especially pp. 86–95.

served his own purpose and not that of valid criticism. In linking it to Ricardo, he gave the gloomy prophet less than he deserved.

Aside from improper attributions, Mayo's idea was that the world must rethink its concepts of authority by abandoning the notion of unitary authority from a central head, be it the state, the church, or the industrial leader. Drawing heavily from Chester Barnard, Mayo concluded that authority should be based on social skills in securing *cooperation* rather than technical skill or expertise. By building from small groups to larger ones, and by basing leadership on securing cooperation, social solidarity could be restored and democracy preserved. It was through the group that the horde could be avoided.

Developing the New Leadership

Elton Mayo had set the stage for "social man" by seeking a new leadership buttressed by social and human skills which would overcome anomie, the rabble hypothesis, and social disorganization. In its very essence, Mayoism espoused the same goal as Taylorism, that of collaboration and cooperation in industry. The means to this goal differed but the end which both anticipated was the recognition of a mutually beneficial relationship between the worker and management. It is not a question of who was right, Taylor or Mayo, but more significantly, whose ideas most logically followed the cultural premises of the times.

In chapter 12, Taylor's views were seen to be logically consistent with his economic, social, and political environment. Begging the question on Mayo at this point and reserving that analysis for chapter 18, let us examine the implementation of this philosophy of social man. The "new" leader was to be one who acted as an investigator of social sentiments for the furtherance of collaborative efforts to achieve organizational goals. Since people spent so much time in a group, and since many of their satisfactions were the product of cooperative effort, management must focus its efforts on the maintenance of group integrity and solidarity. The group became the universal solvent and now it was management's task to find the universal container.

A marked shift for the leader of social man was in the basic assumption about why people work. Money or economic motivation was deemed of secondary importance in stimulating higher productivity. Instead:

> *Whether or not a person is going to give his services whole-heartedly to a group depends, in good part, on the way he feels about his job, his fellow workers, and supervisors . . .*[37]

Money formed only a small part of satisfaction and the worker reported that he wanted

> *. . . social recognition . . . tangible evidence of our social importance . . . the feeling of security that comes not so much from the amount of money we have in the bank as from being an accepted member of the group.*[38]

The Hawthorne evidence seemed to support this view that workers did not respond rationally to calculate the pleasure to be derived from meeting the bogey and earning the bonus reward but instead conformed to group pressures to restrict output. If workers did not respond to an economic calculus, managers found their job more complex. They had first to insure the economic function of the business by meeting production goals and keeping costs down. Second, they had to fulfill a *social* function to satisfy individual and group needs. For the human relationists, satisfaction of the social function led to fulfillment of the economic function. The manager satisfied needs and the worker reciprocated by increasing output. In a catchphrase—"satisfied workers are productive workers."

The foreman as the primary point of contact between the worker and management played a particularly crucial, and often conflicting role.[39] The problem for industrial leadership revolved around the premise that it was a rare supervisor who possessed both technical-economic skills and human relations skills. The ability to meet the logic of efficiency was different from the ability to meet the nonlogic of worker sentiments. Supervisors tended to confuse fact with sentiment and, as the Harvard research group had found in the interviewing program, assumed that what the workers told them was the way things really were. Communi-

[37] F. J. Roethlisberger, *Management and Morale*, Cambridge, Mass.: Harvard University Press, 1942, p. 15.

[38] Ibid., pp. 24–25.

[39] See Roethlisberger's often reprinted "The Foreman: Master and Victim of Double Talk," in *Man-in-Organization*, pp. 35–58.

cations and listening skills hence became an important part of the supervisors' tool kit.[40] The answer to preparing leaders for the new human relations role was training at all levels to teach skills in human understanding of logical and nonlogical behavior, understanding of the sentiments of the worker through listening and communications skills, and developing the ability to maintain an equilibrium between the economic needs of the formal organization and the social needs of the informal organization. Equilibrium became the keynote of organizational effectiveness. Through the social structure, workers obtained the recognition, security, and satisfactions which made them willing to cooperate and contribute their services toward the attainment of the organization's objectives. Disequilibrium occurred when technical change was introduced too fast and/or when management was out of touch with worker sentiments. This was the new leadership, one which could distinguish fact from sentiment and one which balanced economic logic and the nonlogic of sentiment.

Organized Labor and the Mayoists

Conspicuous by its absence in the writing of Mayo and others of the early human relations movement is the subject of organized labor. During the course of the 20,000 interviews at Hawthorne, no employee mentioned the subject of unions. The Hawthorne Works had successfully resisted organizing efforts and only in 1937 did a company union form.[41] It is true that most of the 1920s and part of the 1930s were periods of low union influence in industry. However, it is strange that the human relationists with their emphasis on group solidarity omitted unions from their view of industrial society. Loren Baritz, among others, has suggested that the Mayoists were antiunion and promanagement. "Cooperation" meant worker cooperation on management's terms. While this conclusion may not be perfectly accurate, the Mayoists were less than explicit on the role of unions. Apparently,

---

[40]The literature of the human relationists on communications is quite exhaustive. To sample the main ideas, see: F. J. Roethlisberger, "Barriers to Communication between Men," in *Man-in-Organization*, pp. 154–159; and F. J. Roethlisberger, "The Administrator's Skill: Communication," in ibid., pp. 160–175.

[41]Loren Baritz, p. 113.

the Mayoists thought that management could obviate the necessity for union representation by substituting human relations-oriented supervisors who would fill the workers' needs for security, recognition, and the expression of grievances.

Organized labor, apparently unaware of the Mayoists' views, did not lash out initially at the Mayoists as they had at Taylor. Scientific management was a threat to union leadership, explicitly striking at the core of unionism; Mayoism was more subtle, posed no explicit threat, and passed over the head of union leaders rather than hitting them in the gut as Taylor had. After initial apathy, the publication *Ammunition* of the United Auto Workers in 1949 lashed out petulantly at Mayoism:

> *The prophet is Elton Mayo, a Harvard University professor who has been prying into the psychiatric bowels of factory workers since around about 1925 and who is the Old Man of the movement. The Bible is his book, the Human Problems of an Industrial Civilization. The Holy Place is the Hawthorne Plant of the Western Electric Company (the wholly owned subsidiary of one of the nation's largest monopolies, the AT and T). At Hawthorne, Ma Bell, when she wasn't organizing company unions, allowed Professor Mayo to carry on experiments with a group of women workers for some nine years . . .*
>
> *For these nine years about every kind of experiment a very bright Harvard professor could think of was tried on the women. Everything you do to white mice was done to them, except their spines and skulls were not split so the fluid could be analyzed . . .*
>
> *What did make them produce and produce and produce with ever-increasing speed was the expression of interest in their personal problems by the supervisor; interviews by psychiatrically trained social workers and (later on) the way they were paired off with friendly or unfriendly co-workers.*
>
> *Now obviously this is the greatest discovery since J. P. Morgan learned that you can increase profits by organizing a monopoly, suppressing competition, raising prices and reducing production.* [42]

Labeling the Hawthorne researchers as "cow sociologists" (contented workers give more "milk"), this union view contained

---

[42] From "Deep Therapy on the Assembly Line," quoted by Loren Baritz, pp. 114–115.

much of the same illogical venom that characterized the hearings on the Taylor system.

A Final Note

Further criticisms by organized labor and academia will be examined in chapter 17. At this point, it is necessary only to draw some parallels between Taylor and Mayo as representatives of two major approaches to solving industrial problems. To this author, it is amazing to note the high degree of similarity of goals between the two men. Both perceived industrial conflict between the worker and management and put much of the onus on management; both sought a harmony or mutuality of interests between labor and management, Taylor through a mental revolution and Mayo through human collaboration. In this sense their goals are strikingly similar though their means to these ends differed. Both sought higher productivity and agreed that the worker must have the attention and aid of management in order to achieve that goal. Whereas Taylor would place on management the responsibility to reduce obstacles to higher performance through study, planning, and organizing, Mayo would increase the social skills of the supervisor. With this striking similarity in goals, the means to these ends bear the brunt of the dissimilarities. Taylor focused on the individual worker, Mayo on the worker as a group member; Taylor was not concerned so much with interpersonal relations, the Mayoists were; Taylor thought that the physical work environment was a major impediment to higher productivity, the Mayoists thought it was the social environment; and Taylor thought that, given the opportunity, people would seek to optimize their economic return, while the Mayoists downgraded the lure of money and stressed group membership. The training, backgrounds, and cultural perspectives of these two men do much to explain their dissimilarities. Taylor the engineer operated in an environment which demanded efficiency. Mayo was trained in logic and philosophy and was intrigued by psychopathology. Mayo lived in an era of different cultural imperatives. But more must be said of that matter later.

Summary

Embarking upon a voyage to explain the mysterious discrepancy between traditional assumptions about work behavior and observed behavior, the Hawthorne researchers disclosed new facets of industrial man. Output was not related to physical conditions of work but to how people were treated and how they felt about their work, their supervisors, and their coworkers. Economic motives became suspect and social motives paramount. The Mayoists concluded that individuals were more responsive to their peer group than to management controls, that people obtained their basic sense of identity through relationships with others, and that it was through social relations that meaning could be restored to industrial life. The new leaders for the new industrial man needed social, not technical skills. They should maintain an equilibrium between the logic of efficiency and the nonlogic of worker sentiments. By separating fact from sentiment and by developing listening and human skills, the human relations-oriented supervisor could overcome the dysfunctions of anomie and restore group solidarity, and thereby achieve a dualization of satisfying both human social needs and organizational economic needs.

14

The Search for Organizational Integration

The Western Electric research provided the impetus for the study of social behavior and social systems. Outside the Harvard circle, two individuals made significant contributions to the development of new ideas regarding the nature of authority, the necessity for coordination of effort, the resolution of conflict, and the design of organizations which would provide maximum opportunities for cooperative effort. One was a political philosopher turned business sage who never met a payroll in her life; the other, a utility executive whose hobby was classical piano and the work of Johann Sebastian Bach. Together, they were integrators who provided insightful links between the eras of scientific management and social man.

Mary Parker Follett: The Political Philosopher

Born in Boston in 1868 and educated at the Thayer Academy and the Annexe at Harvard (later renamed Radcliffe College), Mary Parker Follett brought a wide variety of interests and knowledge to bear upon management thought before her death in 1933.[1] Trained in philosophy and political science, Mary Follett became

[1] Biographical information on Miss Follett may be found in Henry C. Metcalf and Lyndall Urwick (ed.), *Dynamic Administration: The Collected Papers of Mary Parker Follett,* New York: Harper and Row, 1940, pp. 9–29; and in L. Urwick, *The Golden Book of Management,* London: Newman Neame, 1956, pp. 132–137.

interested in vocational guidance, adult education, and in the emerging discipline of social psychology. Chronologically, Follett belonged to the scientific management era; philosophically and intellectually, she was a member of the social man era. She had a foot in each world and served as a link between the two eras by generalizing from Taylor's concepts and by anticipating many of the conclusions of the Hawthorne researchers.[2]

In order to understand Mary Follett, one must examine her philosophical predilections. She was an ardent admirer of Johann Fichte (1762–1814),[3] the German philosopher who espoused a nationalism in which the freedom of the individual had to be subordinated to the group. Fichte did not think that individuals had free will but that they were bound up in an interpersonal network to which all people were committed. Thus an individual's ego belonged to a wider world of egos, making the ego a social one, until all together swelled up into one "Great Ego" which was part of a common life among all people.[4] Fichte's philosophy was made manifest in Follett's *The New State,* in which she challenged the prevailing political assumptions of her era.[5] Follett's thesis was that "we find the true man only through group organization. The potentialities of the individual remain potentialities until they are released by group life. Man discovers his true nature, gains his true freedom only through the group."[6]

The "group principle" was to be the "new psychology" and was designed to renounce the old ideas that individuals thought,

---

[2] Robert J. Daiute, *Scientific Management and Human Relations,* New York: Holt Rinehart and Winston, 1964, p. 30. Other useful sources on her philosophy are: Joel M. Rosenfeld and Matthew J. Smith, "Mary Parker Follett: The Transition to Modern Management Thought," *Advanced Management Journal,* Vol. 31, No. 4 (October, 1966), pp. 33–37; and Eliot M. Fox, "Mary Parker Follett: The Enduring Contribution," *Public Administration Review,* Vol. 28 (November–December, 1968), pp. 520–529.

[3] Urwick, *Golden Book,* p. 133.

[4] Henry D. Aiken, *The Age of Ideology,* New York: New American Library, 1956, pp. 54–60. Fichte was a disciple of Immanuel Kant and in his early years followed Kantian notions of rationalism and the absolutely inalienable rights of the individual. In his later years, Fichte broke with Kant, turned to nationalism and statism, and became part of the "romantic" revolt against reason.

[5] Mary Parker Follett, *The New State: Group Organization the Solution of Popular Government,* London: Longmans, Green and Co., 1918.

[6] Ibid., p. 6.

felt, and acted independently. Groups of people lived in association, not as a separate ego, and individuals were created by reciprocal social intercourse. This view demonstrated her acceptance of Gestalt psychology and reflected Charles Horton Cooley's idea of the enlargement of the social self through association and the social "looking glass." Using phrases such as "togetherness," "group thinking," and "the collective will," Miss Follett sought a new society which would be based upon a group principle and not upon individualism. The underlying rationale was not to destroy the individual but was based upon her premise that only through the group could the individual find his "true self." Following the group principle, she concluded that a person's "true self is the group-self" and that "man can have no rights apart from society or independent of society or against society."[7] In negating the notion that the purpose of government is to protect individual rights, she proposed a new concept of democracy:

> Democracy then is a great spiritual force evolving itself from men, utilizing each, completing his incompleteness by weaving together all in the many-membered community life which is the true theophany.[8]

For Follett, democracy was the development of a social consciousness, not individualism, and she felt that "the theory of government based on individual rights no longer has a place in modern political theory."[9] The new and true democracy was to build from small neighborhood groups, to community groups, to state groups, to a national group, and eventually to an international group "will." Without really coming to grips in this book with the problems of groups in conflict, she had faith that people could create a new "social consciousness" and live together peaceably in the "World State."[10] She demonstrated little confidence in ballot-box democracy, believing that this idea reflected crowd psychology and "right" being defined by the sheer weight of numbers.

In *Creative Experience,* Follett followed the same theme: that through conference, discussion, and cooperation, people could

[7] Ibid., p. 137.

[8] Ibid., p. 161. "Theophany" is "the visible manifestation of God or a god."

[9] Ibid., p. 172.

[10] Ibid., pp. 359–360. Cf. Fichte's "Great Ego."

evoke each other's latent ideas and make manifest their unity in the pursuit of common goals. Relying heavily upon Gestalt psychology, which held that every psychological situation has a specific character apart from the "absolute" nature of the component parts, i.e., the "whole" is a configuration greater than the sum of the parts, she felt that through group experiences individuals could reach a greater release of their own creative powers.[11] The goal of group effort was an *integrative unity* which transcended the parts. In essence, she began to answer the questions of group conflict which she failed to examine in *The New State*. She hypothesized that any conflict of interests could be resolved in any one of four ways: "(1) voluntary submission of one side; (2) struggle and the victory of one side over the other; (3) compromise; or (4) integration." Both one and two were clearly unacceptable because they involved the use of force or power to *dominate*. Compromise was likewise futile because it postponed the issue and because the "truth does not lie 'between' the two sides."[12] *Integration* involved finding a solution which satisfied both sides without compromise and domination. In a later lecture she gave her best examples of this concept of integration:

Let us take some very simple illustration. In the Harvard Library one day, in one of the smaller rooms, someone wanted the window open, I wanted it shut. We opened the window in the next room, where no one was sitting. This was not a compromise because there was no curtailing of desire; we both got what we really wanted. For I did not want a closed room, I simply did not want the north wind to blow directly on me; likewise the other occupant did not want that particular window open, he merely wanted more air in the room . . . Let us take another illustration. A Dairymen's Co-operative League almost went to pieces last year on the question of precedence in unloading cans at a creamery platform. The men who came down the hill (the creamery was on a down grade) thought they should have precedence; the men who came up the hill thought they should unload first. The thinking of both sides in the controversy was thus confined within the walls of these two possibilities, and this prevented their even try-

---

[11] Mary Parker Follett, *Creative Experience*, London: Longmans, Green and Company, 1924, chapter 5.

[12] Ibid., p. 156.

ing to find a way of settling the dispute which would avoid these alternatives. The solution was obviously to change the position of the platform so that both up-hillers and down-hillers could unload at the same time. But this solution was not found until they had asked the advice of a more or less professional integrator. When, however, it was pointed out to them, they were quite ready to accept it. Integration involves invention, and the clever thing is to recognize this, and not to let one's thinking stay within the boundaries of two alternatives which are mutually exclusive. [13]

The search for integrative unity, for commonality of will, and for human cooperation earned Mary Follett an international reputation as a political philosopher. *Creative Experience* was widely read by businessmen of the day and Miss Follett was drawn even more closely to the problems of industrial administration. In 1924–1925, she was asked to give a series of lectures in New York to a group of business executives under the auspices of the Bureau of Personnel Administration. It was from these lectures and subsequent work that she made the transition from a political to a business philosopher.

The Business Philosopher

If one views management as a universal phenomenon, the processes which underlie political administration would necessarily apply to business as well. The same problems of achieving unity of effort, of defining authority and responsibility, of achieving coordination and control, and of developing effective leadership exist. It was toward the goal of drawing this parallel that Mary Parker Follett turned her attention. First, from *Creative Experience* she developed further the ideas of "constructive conflict" and the integrative unity of business. Since domination and compromise led to further strife and futility, integration was paramount in all business activities. In dealing with labor, she deplored the notion of collective bargaining because it rested on the relative balance of power and inevitably ended in compromise. Bargaining meant that there were two sides to fight over and both parties tended to lose sight of that which they had in common. In taking sides, e.g.,

[13] H. C. Metcalf and L. Urwick, pp. 32–33. Copyright 1940, Harper and Row; by permission.

prolabor or promanagement, positions solidified and the parties failed to see the business as a "functional whole" for which they had joint responsibilities. This collective responsibility began at the departmental level where workers were to be given group responsibilities:

> When you have made your employees feel that they are in some sense partners in the business, they do not improve the quality of their work, save waste in time and material, because of the Golden Rule, but because their interests are the same as yours [the manager's].[14]

In Miss Follett's view, this was not a reciprocal back-scratching arrangement, but a true feeling on the part of both labor and management that they served a common purpose. She suggested that in the past an artificial line was drawn between those who managed and those who were managed. In reality, there was no line and all members of the organization who accepted responsibility for work at any level were contributing to the whole. Beyond the view of the firm as a unity, all should recognize the relation of the firm to its environment of creditors, stockholders, customers, competitors, suppliers, and the community. This larger view of the firm and its environment would enable an integrative unity of society and the economy. Integration then became an associative principle applicable to all levels of life.

Integration as a principle of conduct would be less than fully effective unless people rethought their concepts of authority and power. It was in this second area that Follett sought to develop "power with" instead of "power over" and "co-action" to replace consent and coercion. When there was an "order giver" and an "order taker," integration was difficult to achieve. The role of "boss" and "subordinate" created barriers to recognizing the commonality of interests. To overcome this, Follett proposed to "depersonalize" orders and to shift obedience to the "law of the situation":

> One person *should not give orders to another* person, *but both should agree to take their orders from the situation. If orders are simply part of the situation, the question of someone giving and someone receiving does not come up.*[15]

[14]Ibid., p. 82.

[15]Ibid., p. 59.

The rationale for the law of the situation was based on scientific management in the sense that Taylor's functional management sought obedience to facts determined by study and not based on the will of one person. In a paper for the Taylor Society, Follett put it this way:

> If, then, authority is derived from function, it has little to do with hierarchy of position as such. . . . We find authority with the head of a department, with an expert . . . the dispatch clerk has more authority in dispatching work than the President . . . authority should go with knowledge and experience . . .[16]

By shifting authority to knowledge, personal confrontations could be avoided as each person felt the dictates of the situation and thereby acted with less friction in achieving an integrative unity. Miss Follett admired this facet of scientific management, which divorced the person from the situation because it was good psychology in dealing with subordinates. For her, the essence of good human relations was creating the feeling of working *with* someone rather than working *under* someone. In practice this became "power-with" versus "power-over" in her terms. Management should not exercise power over the worker, nor should the worker through unions exercise power over management. Jointly exercised power was "co-active," not coercive. The analogy she used was that "you have rights *over* a slave, you have rights *with* a servant."[17] Displaying a number of insights into the psychology of power, she rejected both the authoritarian's striving for power and Gandhi's "non-cooperation" as being insidious uses of power. Gandhi's concept of power through humility and non-violence was still the desire for "power-over." It was conflict, a search for bending the will of the British to his own movement. Integration and constructive conflict could not be found in any effort to dominate.

In all forms of life, from interpersonal relations to the handling of international disputes, "power-over" had to be reduced and obedience had to be shifted to the law of the situation. The basis for such integration was what she called "circular response." By this she meant a process based on the opportunity for each

---

[16]"The Illusion of Final Authority," *Bulletin of the Taylor Society*, Vol. 2, No. 5 (December, 1926), p. 243.

[17]Metcalf and Urwick, p. 101. Italics added.

party to influence the other and through open interaction, over a period of time, "power-with" could be obtained. For labor and management it would come through open disclosure of costs, prices, and market situations. In international affairs, diplomacy became disclosure, not withholding, and facts, not triumphs. Demands for power were demands to share in control, especially for the labor movement; yet the demands focused on getting power without accepting responsibility. Employee representation plans were designed to share power by wresting it from management. Management, in retaliation, strove to retain all power and this led to inevitable industrial conflict. For Mary Follett, this struggle for power overlooked the mutual interests of both parties. She thought that "final authority" was an illusion based on a false premise of power; authority accrued in the situation, not the person or his position. Likewise, "final responsibility" was an illusion. Responsibility was inherent in the job or function performed and was "cumulative" in the sense that it was the sum of all individual and group responsibilities in a system of cross-relationships. At the individual level, a person was responsible *for* work, not *to* someone. At the departmental level, the responsibility for work was jointly shared by all those who contributed, with the manager merely *interweaving* the various individual and group responsibilities. The chief of the organization also had cumulative responsibility for interweaving interdepartmental work.

In this second area of analysis, Miss Follett had put forth some iconoclastic notions of authority and responsibility. Traditional notions of the military or other organizations that authority was "power-over" and that responsibility accrued at the source of final authority were rejected. Authority resided in the situation, not the person or position. Logically then, responsibility was inherent in the function performed and accumulated in interweaving functions. This was heady material for thought from this modest spinster to the corporate manager.

Two facets of her philosophy have been explored: (1) the reduction of conflict through an integration of interests; and (2) the necessary corollary of obeying the law of the situation. A third facet of her philosophy concerned building the underlying psychological processes necessary to achieving goals through coordinating and controlling effort. Follett's view of control reflected her

Gestalt psychology of dealing with wholes and the total situation to achieve unity. Control was impossible to achieve unless there was unity and cooperation among all elements, material and people, in a given situation. Any situation was out of control when interests were not reconciled. The basis for control resided in self-regulating, self-directing individuals and groups who recognized common interests and controlled their tasks to meet the objective. The manager did not control single elements, but complex inter-relationships; not persons, but situations; and the outcome was a productive configuration of a total situation. How was this configuration achieved? Mary Follett called for a new philosophy of control which (1) was "fact-control rather than man-control," and (2) "correlated control" rather than "super-imposed control."[18] Each situation generated its own control because it was the facts of the situation and the interweaving of the many groups in the situation that determined appropriate behavior. Most situations were too complex for central control from the top to function effectively; therefore controls were to be gathered or "correlated" at many points in the organizational structure. This interweaving and correlation was to be based upon coordination which Follett saw as:

1. *Co-ordination as the reciprocal relating of all the factors in a situation.*

2. *Co-ordination by direct contact of all the responsible people concerned.*

3. *Co-ordination in the early stages.*

4. *Co-ordination as a continuing process.*

These were considered the "four fundamental principles of organization" and involved the conclusion that the organization *was* control since the purpose of organizing and coordination was to insure controlled performance. Coordination achieved unity and unity was control. For an illustration, Miss Follett took the age-old conflict between the purchasing agent who desired to reduce the cost of purchased materials and the production manager who

---

[18] Mary Parker Follett, "The Process of Control," in L. Gulick and L. Urwick (ed.), *Papers on the Science of Administration*, New York: Institute of Public Administration, Columbia University, 1937, p. 161.

[19] Ibid., p. 161. Also in Metcalf and Urwick, p. 297.

maintained that he needed better material with which to work. If they followed the principle of early and continuous coordination, each could see the reciprocal problems and would turn their search toward finding or developing a material which met both of their requirements. Neither sacrificed his goals and unity was achieved for their particular departments, for the firm, and for the consumer or the community. This synthesis of interests was self-regulation through coordination to achieve integration. The final facet of Miss Follett's business philosophy concerned the type of leadership it would take to make her system work. Leadership would no longer be based on power but on the reciprocal influence of leader on follower and follower on leader in the context of the situation. The primary leadership task was defining the *purpose* of the organization; the leader should

> . . . *make his co-workers see that it is not* his *purpose which is to be achieved, but a common purpose, born of the desires and the activities of the group. The best leader does not ask people to serve him, but the common end. The best leader has not followers, but men and women working with him.*[20]

Company purposes were to be integrated with individual and group purposes and this called for the highest caliber of executive leadership. The leader did not depend upon commands and obedience but upon skills in coordinating, defining purposes, and in evoking responses to the law of the situation. Recognizing that mere exhortation would not achieve this new definition of leadership, Miss Follett called for executive development aimed at: (1) developing more science in making both physical and human decisions; and (2) developing a motive of service to the community. The combination of science and service would lead to a "profession" of management which enlisted knowledge for the service of others. To those who aspired to be managers, she advised:

> *Men must prepare themselves as seriously for this profession as for any other. They must realize that they, as all professional men, are assuming grave responsibilities, that they are to take a creative part in one of the large functions of society, a part which, I believe, only trained and disciplined men can in the future hope to take with success.*[21]

[20]Metcalf and Urwick, p. 262.

[21]Ibid., p. 131. Copyright 1940, Harper and Row; by permission.

The notion of service was not to be substituted for the motive of profit but integrated into a larger professional motive:

> We work for profit, for service, for our own development, for the love of creating something. At any one moment, indeed, most of us are not working directly or immediately for any of these things, but to put through the job in hand in the best possible manner. . . . To come back to the professions: can we not learn a lesson from them on this very point? The professions have not given up the money motive. I do not care how often you see it stated that they have . . . Professional men are eager enough for large incomes; but they have other motives as well, and they are often willing to sacrifice a good slice of income for the sake of these other things. We all want the richness of life in the terms of our deepest desire. We can purify and elevate our desires, we can add to them, but there is no individual or social progress in curtailment of desires.[22]

A Final Note

Are the elements of Mary Parker Follett's business philosophy the idyllic notions of a political philosopher? The naturalistic simplicity of people living and working together without the use of coercion and without the need to sacrifice themselves through compromise is certainly worthy of merit. Integration, moving to a broader plane for a solution, would call for much more creativity and imagination than one commonly witnesses in daily industrial, academic, political, and social life. Nevertheless, the goal is a worthy one and should be considered to be akin to Taylor's "mental revolution" and Mayo's call for human collaboration. Depersonalization of authority and obedience to the law of the situation would certainly sound the death knell for tyranny and autocracy. However, perceiving and defining the law of the situation would be most difficult in a world of one-upmanship. Organizational control based on a perceived unity of purposes would make the world of the manager much more palatable. However, reward systems in practice often run counter to measuring one's contribution to total effort. A knowledgeable business leadership,

---

[22] Ibid., p. 145. Copyright 1940, Harper and Row; by permission.

dedicated to improving practices through science and service, is a recurrent plea throughout the evolution of management thought. Perhaps the ideals of Mary Follett can be attained, perhaps not. If not, it would be because too few heeded the pleas of this feminine philosopher.

The Erudite Executive: Chester I. Barnard

Chester Irving Barnard was a sociologist of organizations without portfolio. Born in Malden, Massachusetts, in 1886, he personified the Horatio Alger ideal of the farm boy who made good.[23] On a scholarship to Harvard, he supplemented his income by tuning pianos and running a small dance band. He studied economics at Harvard, completed the requirements in three years (1906–1909), but failed to receive a degree because he lacked a laboratory science. Since he had already passed the course with distinction, he was "too busy" and thought it pointless to take the laboratory section. Even without a bachelor's degree, he did well enough to earn seven honorary doctorates for his life-long labor in understanding the nature and purpose of organizations. Barnard joined the statistical department of the American Telephone and Telegraph system in 1909 and in 1927 became the president of New Jersey Bell. His unbounded enthusiasm for organizational work carried him into voluntary work in many other organizations: for example, he helped David Lilienthal establish the policies of the Atomic Energy Commission, he served the New Jersey Emergency Relief Administration, the New Jersey Reformatory, the United Service Organization (president for three years), the Rockefeller Foundation (president for four years), and was president of the Bach Society of New Jersey. Barnard was a self-made scholar who applied the theories of Vilfredo Pareto (whom he read in the French edition), Kurt Lewin, Max Weber (whom he read in the German edition), and the philosophy of Alfred North Whitehead in the first in-depth analysis of organizations as cooperative sys-

[23] Biographical data and an excellent discussion of Barnard's ideas are found in William B. Wolf, *The Basic Barnard: An Introduction to Chester I. Barnard and His Theories of Organization and Management*, Ithaca, New York: New York State School of Industrial and Labor Relations, 1974.

tems. By the time of his death in 1961, this Harvard "drop-out" had earned a place in history as a management scholar.

The Nature of Cooperative Systems

Barnard's best known work, *The Functions of the Executive*,[24] was an expansion of eight lectures given at the Lowell Institute in Boston in November and December of 1937. His explicit purpose for the lectures was to develop a theory of organizations and to stimulate others to examine the nature of cooperative systems administered by executives. To Barnard, the search for universals in organizations had been obstructed by too much emphasis on the nature of the state and the church and their concomitant stress on the origin and nature of authority. He complained that most research focused on social unrest and reform and included "practically no reference to formal organization as the concrete social process by which social action is largely accomplished."[25] Social failures throughout history were due to the failure to provide for human cooperation in formal organizations. Barnard said that the "formal organization is that kind of cooperation among men that is conscious, deliberate, and purposeful."[26]

By examining the formal organization, it was possible to provide for cooperation and accomplish basically three goals: (1) to insure the survival of an organization by the "maintenance of an *equilibrium* of complex character in a continuously fluctuating environment of physical, biological, and social materials, elements, and forces" within an organization; (2) to examine the external forces to which such adjustments must be made; and (3) to analyze the functions of executives at all levels in managing and controlling formal organizations.[27] Barnard's notion of including both internal equilibrium and external adjustment was an original view and brought criticism from those who adhered to the traditional view of intraorganizational analysis. Barnard rejected this traditional view of an organization having boundaries and comprising

---

[24] Chester I. Barnard, *The Functions of the Executive*, Cambridge, Mass.: Harvard University Press, 1938.

[25] Ibid., p. 3.

[26] Ibid., p. 4.

[27] Ibid., p. 6. Italics added.

a definite number of members; he included in his concept of organizations investors, suppliers, customers and others whose actions contributed to the firm even though they might not be considered "members" of the firm itself.[28]

Barnard's construction of a cooperative system began with the individual as a discrete, separate being; however, he noted that humans do not function except in conjunction with other humans in an interacting social relationship. As individuals, people can *choose* whether or not they will enter into a specific cooperative system. They make this choice based on their purposes, desires, or impulses of the moment, or by considering whatever alternatives are available. These are "motives," and the organization, through the executive function, modifies individual actions and motives through influence and control. However, this modification might not always attain the goals sought by the organization nor by the person. The disparity between personal motives and organizational motives led Barnard to his "effective"-"efficient" dichotomy. A formal system of cooperation required an objective or purpose; and, if cooperation was successful, the goal was attained and the system was *effective*. The matter of efficiency was different; cooperative efficiency was the result of individual efficiencies since cooperation was entered into only to satisfy "individual motives." *Efficiency* was the degree to which individual motives were satisfied and only the individual could determine whether or not this condition was being met.[29]

Cooperation within formal organizations afforded possibilities for expanding the powers of the group beyond those which the individual alone could accomplish, e.g., moving a stone, producing an automobile, building a bridge, etc. People cooperated in order to do what they could not do alone; and, when the purpose was attained, their efforts were effective. However, individuals also had personal motives, and the degree to which they continued to contribute to formal efforts was a function of the satisfactions or dissatisfactions they personally derived. If their motives were not satisfied, they withheld efforts or withdrew

---

[28]Barnard's rebuttal to his critics appeared in the *Harvard Business Review*, Spring, 1940, and is reprinted in C. I. Barnard, *Organization and Management*, Cambridge, Mass.: Harvard University Press, 1948, pp. 111–113.

[29]*The Functions of the Executive*, p. 44.

from the system, and from their point of view the system was inefficient. In the final analysis, "the only measure of the efficiency of a cooperative system is its capacity to survive"; by this Barnard meant its ability to continue to offer enough inducements to satisfy individual motives in the pursuit of group purposes.[30] Viewed in modern terms, the formal organization must renew its energy or acquire negative entropy by offering net satisfactions to contributing members. If it was inefficient, it could not be effective and therefore would not survive. For Barnard this was a universal principle of organization theory and one which was recognized by the Hawthorne researchers and by most organizational theorists thereafter. This attempt to bridge the requirements of the formal organization with the needs of the socio-human system was a landmark in management thought which persists to this day.

Formal Organizations: Theory and Structure

Barnard defined an organization as "a system of consciously coordinated activities or forces of two or more persons"[31] and used this to encompass all types of organizations, military, fraternal, religious, academic, business, or whatever.[32] Variations existed among organizations in terms of the physical or social environment, the number and kinds of persons involved, or in the bases upon which persons contributed to the organization. The organization consisted of human beings whose activities were coordinated and therefore became a system. The system was to be treated "as a whole because each part is related to every other part included in it in a significant way."[33] Levels of systems existed, ranging from departments or subsystems in the firm to a conglomeration of many systems forming "society" as a whole. Regardless of the level of the system being analyzed, all contained three universal elements: (1) willingness to cooperate; (2) common purpose; and (3) communication.

[30]Ibid., pp. 55–57.
[31]Ibid., p. 72.
[32]Ibid., p. 73.
[33]Ibid., p. 77.

An organization cannot, by definition, exist without persons. In Barnard's terms, *willingness to cooperate* was indispensable, the first universal element of all organizations, and "means self-abnegation, the surrender of control of personal conduct, the depersonalization of personal actions."[34] People must be willing to contribute to a system's objectives; but the intensity and timing of this willingness fluctuated, since it was based on the satisfactions or dissatisfactions experienced or anticipated by organizational members. The organization must provide adequate inducements, both physical and social, to offset the sacrifices individuals made by forgoing alternative systems and participating in the existing one. For the individual, willingness was the joint effect of "personal desires and reluctances" to participate; for the organization, it was the joint effect of "objective inducements offered and burdens imposed."[35] The net result was subjective and largely individual; hence the need for organizations to be efficient in Barnard's terminology. Securing willingness involved the "economy of incentives" and this consisted of two parts: (1) offering objective incentives; and (2) changing subjective attitudes through persuasion. Objective incentives were material ones (money), nonmaterial (prestige, power, etc.), and "associational" (social compatibility, participation in decision making, etc.). Barnard evaded the question of which of these devices was more effective (or more efficient), by stressing the subjectivity of individual motives. Persuasion, or changing attitudes, was a subjective incentive method which sought by precept, example, and suggestion to condition the motives of individuals. It was not coercion but inculcation of ideas designed to nurture cooperation. Appeals to loyalty, *esprit de corps*, belief in organizational purpose, and other abstractions would fit into this category.

Purpose, the second universal element, was a corollary to willingness to cooperate. Willingness could not be induced unless organizational members knew what efforts would be required of them and what satisfactions might accrue as a result of cooperating. The executive must inculcate members with the common purpose or objective of the organization. It was not necessarily what the purpose meant personally to the members, but

[34]Ibid., p. 84
[35]Ibid., pp. 85–86.

what they perceived as its meaning to the organization as a whole. Organizational motives and personal motives differed and individuals contributed not because their personal motives were the same as the organization's, but because they felt that their personal satisfactions would come from accomplishing the purpose of the organization.

The process by which these first two universal elements became dynamic was through *communication*. All activity was based upon communication, and Barnard developed some "principles": (1) that *"channels of communication should be definitely known"*; (2) that *"objective authority requires a definite formal channel of communication to every member of an organization"*, i.e., everyone must report to or be subordinate to someone; and (3) that *"the line of communication must be as direct or short as possible"* in order to speed communications and reduce distortions caused by transmission through many channels.[36] Barnard developed other principles but these will suffice to capture the essence of the stress he placed on communications, which he well might be expected to do, considering his industrial background.

Identification of these three universal elements in the formal organization led Barnard to seek universals in the "informal organization." He defined this informal organization as "the aggregate of the personal contacts and interactions and the associated groupings of people" which were not a part of nor governed by the formal organization.[37] Without structure, and often without conscious recognition of joint purpose, informal groupings arose out of job-related contacts and in turn established certain attitudes, customs, and norms. Informal organizations often created conditions leading to formal organizations and vice versa. Barnard found three functions served by the informal organization: (1) communication; (2) maintenance of cohesiveness in the formal organization by regulating willingness to serve; and (3) maintenance of feelings of personal integrity and self-respect. These functions appeared to be universal and made the informal organization an indispensable part of the formal organization. Informal activities served to make the organization more efficient and also facilitated effectiveness.

[36] Ibid., pp. 175–177.
[37] Ibid., p. 115.

The Acceptance Theory of Authority

One of Barnard's most unusual ideas was his theory of authority. He defined authority as "the character of a communication [order] in a formal organization by virtue of which it is accepted by a contributor to or 'member' of the organization as governing the action he contributes." According to this definition, authority had two aspects: (1) the personal, subjective *acceptance* of a communication as being authoritative; and (2) the objective, formal "character in the communication by virtue of which it is accepted."[38] In Barnard's theory, the source of authority did not reside in "persons of authority" or those who gave the orders but in the acceptance or nonacceptance of the authority by subordinates. If the subordinates disobeyed an order, they rejected the authority.

This notion was antithetical to all previous concepts of authority which had been based upon some hierarchy of rank or upon the power of organizational position. Whereas Follett would depersonalize authority and obey the law of the situation, Barnard retained the personal aspect but gave it a bottom-up interpretation. For Barnard, individuals must assent to authority and would do so if four conditions were met: (1) they could and did understand the communicated order; (2) they believed that the order was consistent with the purpose of the organization at the time of their decision; (3) they believed that the order was compatible with their personal interest as a whole; and (4) they were mentally and physically able to comply with the order.

To explain how an organization could function on such a unique concept of authority, Barnard developed a "zone of indifference" for each individual within which orders were accepted without questioning authority. The zone of indifference might be narrow or wide depending upon the degree to which the inducements outweighed the burdens and sacrifices for the individual. If a subordinate thought the order ran counter to his personal moral code, for instance, he had to weigh the advantages of staying employed against his own personal value system. Not all cases would be this clear-cut and Barnard admitted to many borderline possibilities; however, the individual must still balance the inducements versus the sacrifices to make the decision. In joining

---

[38] Ibid., p. 163.

organizations, the Army for example, certain "rules of the game" are preestablished and in those matters the zone of indifference would undoubtedly widen.

The objective aspect of authority was more closely akin to traditional ideas. It rested on the presumption that orders and communications were authoritative and had a "potentiality of assent" when they came from superior positions. In one case, the order might be accepted because authority was imputed to the superior regardless of his personal abilities; this was formal authority or the authority of position. In another, the order might be accepted because the subordinate had respect for and confidence in the individual because of his personal ability and not because of his rank or position; Barnard called this the "authority of leadership."

When the authority of leadership was combined with the authority of position, the zone of indifference became exceedingly broad. Nevertheless, Barnard stressed that "the determination of authority remains with the individual."[39] In retrospect, much more can be imputed to Barnard's acceptance theory than actually exists. In a free society, individuals always have the choice to go along with the costs and benefits of directives or not to do so. As long as labor is not conscripted, the acceptance theory is valid. What appears to be so striking in Barnard's theory is in reality another way of stating that all organizations depend upon leadership which can develop the capacity and willingness of members to cooperate.

The Functions of the Executive

In Barnard's analysis, executives operated as interconnecting centers in a communications system and sought to secure the coordination essential to cooperative effort. Communications was a central value in all of Barnard's writings and undoubtedly his views were influenced by his own industrial experience in the Bell System. To Barnard, executive work

> is not of the organization, but the specialized work of maintaining the organization in operation . . . The executive functions serve to maintain a system of cooperative effort. They are im-

[39]Ibid., pp. 173–174.

personal. The functions are not, as so frequently stated, to manage a group of persons.[40]

The executive function to Barnard was analogous to the brain and nervous system in relation to the rest of the body:

It exists to maintain the bodily system by directing those actions which are necessary more effectively to adjust to the environment, but it can hardly be said to manage the body, a large part of whose functions are independent of it and upon which it in turn depends.[41]

Barnard postulated three executive functions: (1) to provide a system of communication; (2) to promote the securing of essential personal efforts; and (3) to formulate and define purpose. In providing for communication, the executive must define organizational duties, clarify lines of authority and responsibility, and consider both formal and informal means of communication. Informal communications provided for organizational maintenance by allowing issues to be raised and discussed without forcing decisions and without overloading executive positions. The second executive function was to bring people into a cooperative relationship and to elicit their contributions to the organization. This was largely the task of recruiting and selecting those personnel who could best contribute and who would work together compatibly. It also included what Barnard called maintenance "methods": (1) the maintenance of morale; (2) the maintenance of a scheme of inducements; and (3) the maintenance of "schemes of deterrents" such as supervision, control, inspection, education, and training which would insure the viability of the cooperative system.

The third executive function, formulation of purpose and objectives, has already been examined in some depth. Slightly enlarging this function, Barnard included the functions of decision making and delegation. Delegation was a decision involving both the ends sought and the means to those ends. The results were decisions about the placement of various responsibilities and authority within the cooperative system so that individuals would know how they contributed to the ends sought. Decision making had two facets: (1) analysis, or the search for the "strategic factors"

[40] Ibid., pp. 215–216. Cf. Fayol's distinction between *gouverner* and *administrer*.
[41] Ibid., p. 217.

which would create the set or system of conditions necessary to accomplish the organization's purposes; and (2) synthesis, or the recognition of the interrelationships between elements or parts which together made up the whole system. As a capstone to the executive functions, Barnard postulated an "executive process" which was "the sensing of the organization as a whole and the total situation relevant to it."[42] This was the "art" of managing and was the *integration* of the whole with respect to internal equilibrium and adjustment to external conditions. Working from the micro level to the macro, Barnard viewed all aspects of society as one large cooperative system. Every organization must secure personal and other services from its environment and "can survive only as it secures by exchange, transformation, and creation, a surplus of utilities in its own economy."[43] The industrial organization, for example, must produce both physical utilities and social utilities in order to survive.

> *Thus in every organization there is a quadruple economy: (1) physical energies and materials contributed by members and derived by its work upon the environment and given to its members; (2) the individual economy; (3) the social utilities related to the social environment; and (4) a complex and comprehensive economy of the organization under which both material services and social services are contributed by members and material things are secured from the environment, and material is given to the environment and social satisfactions to the members. The only measure of this economy is the survival of the organization. If it grows it is clearly efficient, if it is contracting, it is doubtfully efficient, and it may in the end prove to have been during the period of contraction inefficient.*[44]

The moving creative force in this organization was moral leadership. Leaders must hold some moral code, demonstrate a high capacity for responsibility, and be able to create a moral faculty in others. Seeking a philosophical plane, Barnard concluded:

> *Executive responsibility, then, is that capacity of leaders by which, reflecting attitudes, ideals, hopes, derived largely from*

[42]Ibid., p. 235.

[43]Ibid., p. 245.

[44]Ibid., pp. 251–252. Copyright 1938 by the President and Fellows of Harvard College; by permission.

without themselves, they are compelled to bind the wills of men to the accomplishment of purposes beyond their immediate ends, beyond their times. Even when these purposes are lowly and the time is short, the transitory efforts of men become a part of that organization of living forces that transcends man unaided by man; but when these purposes are high and the wills of many men of many generations are bound together they live boundlessly.

For the morality that underlies enduring cooperation is multidimensional. It comes from and may expand to all the world, it is rooted deeply in the past, it faces toward the endless future. As it expands, it must become more complex, its conflicts must be more numerous and deeper, its call for abilities must be higher, its failures of ideal attainment must be perhaps more tragic; but the quality of leadership, the persistence of its influence, the durability of its related organizations, the power of the co-ordination it incites, all express the height of moral aspirations, the breadth of moral foundations.

So among those who cooperate the things that are seen are moved by the things unseen. Out of the void comes the spirit that shapes the ends of men.[45]

Chester Barnard was an erudite executive who drew upon his own experiences and upon sociological theory in order to build a theory of cooperative systems. His effective-efficient dichotomy was an attempt to synthesize the ever present conflict between organizational objectives and needs for economy of effort with the individual's personal objectives and needs for satisfaction. His theory of authority, his call for moral leadership, and his identification of universal elements in both the formal and the informal organization were all significant contributions to evolving management thought.

Summary

Mary Parker Follett and Chester Barnard were bridges between eras. Follett ushered in a group view of man and Gestalt psy-

---

[45] Ibid., pp. 283–284. Copyright 1938 by the President and Fellows of Harvard College; by permission. A plea for applying Barnard's moral code for executives may be found in George Strother, "The Moral Codes of Executives: A Watergate-inspired Look at Barnard's Theory of Executive Responsibility," *Academy of Management Review*, Vol. 1, No. 2 (April, 1976), pp. 13–22.

chology while living and working in the scientific management era. Barnard put forth an analysis of the formal organization, yet introduced the role of the informal organization in achieving an equilibrium. Both operated more on a philosophical plane and sought to create a spirit of cooperation and collaboration. Both were concerned with the individual, not per se, but as he achieved his being through cooperative group efforts. Both sought to reshape previous concepts of authority, both emphasized cooperation and unity, and both concluded that it was professional, moral leadership which would enhance the effectiveness of organizations and the well-being of people.

15

People and Organizations

This and the succeeding chapter will examine two branches of developing management thought from about 1930 to the early 1950s. This chapter will focus on the growth and refinement of the human relations movement as it passed through micro- and macro- phases. The micro- phase will reflect a significant amount of empirical research which led to substantial modifications in previously held views about people in organizations. The macro-phase will be characterized by a number of individuals who were building theoretical constructs of social systems analysis which were precursory steps for the later development of organization theory. The title of this chapter, "People and Organizations," indicates the human orientation of this branch of thought, with the structural aspects of organizations assuming a secondary subject of inquiry. Chapter 16, on the other hand, will examine a parallel branch of thought in which organizations and organizational structures assume a primary importance while the human element receives relatively less emphasis.

People at Work: The Micro View

Although social scientists had started to probe human behavior in industry in the first three decades of the twentieth century, it was not until the 1930s and 1940s that the greatest outpourings of behavioral research would appear. Whereas the engineer appeared to dominate the scientific management movement, the human relations movement was interdisciplinary, drawing from the contributions of sociologists, psychologists, and anthropologists. A

basic premise in their research into the social facet of human behavior was a Gestaltist notion that all organizational behavior involved some human "multiplier effect." Each individual, highly
variable and complex due to a unique genetic composition and
family, social, and work experiences, became even more variable
and complex when placed in interaction with other unique individuals. This multiplier effect meant that new means had to be devised to analyze, explain, predict, and control human behavior.

Developing Constructs
for Group Analysis

Two individuals, Jacob L. Moreno and Kurt Lewin, paved the way
in developing means for analyzing group behavior and their notions were frequently used in research during this era. Moreno
provided a new analytical tool, *sociometry*. Moreno stated its purpose as follows:

> *A process of classification, which is calculated to bring individ-
> uals together who are capable of harmonious interpersonal re-
> lationships and so create a social group which can function at the
> maximum efficiency and with a minimum of disruptive tendencies
> and processes.* [1]

Moreno felt that the psychological activities of groups were not
due to chance and that groups could be studied through the application of quantitative methods which probed the evolution and
patterning of attitudes and interactions. For purposes of analysis,
Moreno classified the basic attitudes which people showed toward one another as attraction, repulsion, and indifference.[2] In
Moreno's sociometry, the members of the group to be studied
were asked to indicate those with whom they would, and would
not, like to associate. The resulting chart, called a *sociogram*,
mapped the pairings and rankings of the individual's preferences
for other individuals. These mutual preferences were to be considered dynamic, not static, and changing as members of the group

---

[1] J. L. Moreno, *Who Shall Survive?: A New Approach to Human Interrelations*, Washington, D.C.: Nervous and Mental Disease Publishing Co., 1934, p. 11.

[2] Cf. Karen Horney's "moving toward people," "moving against people," and
"moving away from people." K. Horney, *Our Inner Conflicts*, New York: W. W.
Norton and Co., 1945.

changed and as problems facing the group changed. For example, in the New York Training School for Girls, where his basic sociometric research was conducted, Moreno found that different pairings appeared depending upon whether the expressed choice was for a roommate or a workmate. This task-versus-friendship preference formed a foundation for important distinctions in industrial research. In industry, sociometric research has sought to combine work groups such that they would be superior in quality and quantity of work as well as conducive to higher morale for the participants.[3]

Psychodrama and sociodrama were also the contributions of J. L. Moreno and together these ideas formed a basis for "role playing" techniques and for the analysis of interpersonal relations. Psychodrama, being both a method of diagnosis and of treatment of psychopathology, consisted of placing a person or patient "on stage" to act out his deepest psychic problems with the aid of other "actors" and a therapist.[4] The focal person (a patient or trainee) was mentally taken out of his immediate environment by means of a specially contrived situation and forced to play a role in which it was almost impossible to keep his private ego and personal needs and sentiments from emerging. Scarcely aware that he was expressing his own true self, something he might be loath to do if asked to do so explicitly, he displayed overtly in the role situation whatever his psychopathology might be. Since other actors were also in the situation, he exposed his manner of dealing with others in the role play. Once exposed, therapy could begin on whatever deviations in behavior were disclosed. Further, psychodrama was a *cathartic* experience, enabling the actor to release and relieve his innermost doubts, anxieties, and other disorders.

Sociodrama, an outgrowth of psychodrama, focused on the group as the method of analysis, whereas psychodrama focused on individual therapy. Sociodrama was based on the assumption that the contrived group was already organized by a set of previously held social and cultural roles. Catharsis and therapy were

---

[3] For example, see Raymond H. Van Zelst, "Sociometrically Selected Work Teams Increase Production," *Personnel*, Vol. 5 (1952), pp. 175–185. See also: J. L. Moreno (ed.), *The Sociometry Reader*, New York: Free Press, 1960.

[4] J. L. Moreno, *Psychodrama and Sociodrama*, Boston: Beacon Press, 1946, pp. 177–178.

oriented toward understanding social and cultural roles such as supervisor-worker, black-white, American-Oriental, etc. *Role reversal*, or taking the role of the opposite social or cultural group, for example, a white supervisor playing the role of a black worker, could be used to broaden role flexibility and create an understanding of opposite or alien members. In brief, it was group psychotherapy designed to reduce resentments, frustrations, and misunderstandings. Moreno's work would serve to supplement the counseling and interpersonal relations aspects of the human relations movement by providing methods for studying and changing a person's or group's behavior vis-à-vis other persons or groups. Psychology and psychoanalysis, both essentially concerned with the isolated individual, were inadequate for analyzing group behavior, which was the subject matter most frequently encountered in studying industrial behavior.

Another important construct for analyzing group behavior was that of "group dynamics." Credit for originating this concept is generally given to Kurt Lewin (1890–1947), a Jewish psychologist who fled Hitler's Germany in the early 1930s. Lewin studied at the University of Berlin under Max Wertheimer, one of the founders of the Gestalt movement. Lewin's own notions were subsumed under the heading of "field theory," which held that group behavior was an intricate set of symbolic interactions and forces which not only affected group structure but also modified individual behavior. A group was never at a "steady state" of equilibrium but was in a continuous process of mutual adaptation which Lewin called "quasi-stationary equilibrium." An analogy might be that of a river flowing within its banks; it appears relatively stationary but there is nevertheless gradual movement and change. In developing his field theory, Lewin borrowed the term "topology" from geometry and applied it to the study of groups. Topology is a branch of geometry which deals with problems of continuity rather than size or shape; topological space is a set of objects or points with a definite relation to one another.

Lewin saw behavior as a function of the person and his environment or "field" and sought to find some corollaries in psychological topology.[5] Using terms such as "life space," "space of

<hr>

[5] For more on Lewin's uses of topology, see: R. W. Leeper, *Lewin's Topological and Vector Psychology*, Eugene: University of Oregon Press, 1943.

free movement," and "field forces," i.e., tensions emanating from group pressures on the individual, Lewin and his associates embarked on a series of investigations into resistance to change and the effects of leadership on groups. For example, Lewin, Lippitt, and White examined the effects of "democratic," "authoritarian," and *"laissez-faire"* leadership on boys' groups and demonstrated that authoritarian leadership impaired initiative and bred hostility and aggressiveness while other styles were more effective in creating better morale and attitudes.[6] In research on changing family food habits during World War II, Lewin found that changes were more easily induced through group discussion than through individual methods. This was a new idea about the introduction of change, the idea that change would be facilitated when people thought *they* had discovered the need for change themselves rather than through being told to change.[7]

The emergence of group dynamics and the work of Kurt Lewin formed a significant milestone in evolving management thought. In 1945, Lewin founded the Research Center for Group Dynamics at the Massachusetts Institute of Technology; after his death, the center was moved to the University of Michigan in 1948. Besides fathering group dynamics, Lewin opened up and added to the study of subordinate participation in decision making and the use of the group to achieve changes in behavior. One of Lewin's disciples, Dr. Leland P. Bradford, established at Bethel, Maine (1947), the first "sensitivity training" or human relations laboratory, called the National Training Laboratory. The essence of this sensitivity training was to achieve changes in behavior through "gut level" interactions which led to increased interpersonal awareness.

Briefly, Moreno and Lewin brought a new focus to the group rather than the individual. Their work, reflecting Gestalt psychology, led to further studies of social change, social control, col-

---

[6]K. Lewin, R. Lippitt, and R. K. White, "Patterns of Aggressive Behavior in Experimentally Created 'Social Climates,' " *Journal of Social Psychology*, Vol. 10 (1939), pp. 271–299. For some application of group dynamics to industrial leadership situations, see: K. Lewin, *Resolving Social Conflicts*, New York: Harper and Row, 1948, pp. 125–141.

[7]For a summary of the applications of group dynamics work, see Dorwin Cartwright, "Achieving Change in People: Some Applications of Group Dynamics Theory," *Human Relations*, Vol. 4 (1951), pp. 381–392.

lective behavior, and in general the effects of the group on the individual. Research moved from the static state of the individual in isolation to the dynamic state of the individual in interaction with others.

The Growth of Human Relations Research and Training

The 1930s had witnessed the emergence of a more favorable political climate for organized labor in which explicit recognition of the role of the worker in industry was required. The passage of the National Labor Relations Act in 1935 (the Wagner Act) and the formation of the C.I.O. brought a new emphasis to collective bargaining. Morris Cooke found a better environment for his *rapprochement* between labor and management which would insure industrial peace and productivity through collective bargaining.[8] The theme became that of "industrial democracy," which was to mean in essence the application of human relations in the industrial setting in conjunction with organized labor.[9] Accordingly, a number of centers began to appear which would pave the way for the new "industrial human relations." In 1943, an interdisciplinary group at the University of Chicago formed the Committee on Human Relations in Industry. Drawing its members from business (Burleigh Gardner), sociology (William Foote Whyte), and anthropology (W. Lloyd Warner), this committee was to characterize the new style of interdisciplinary behavioral research.

Industrial relations centers also came into vogue. The first was the New York State School of Industrial and Labor Relations at Cornell (1945); others were to follow, such as the Yale Labor-Management Center and the Institute of Labor and Industrial Relations at the University of Illinois. In 1946, Rensis Likert, himself a psychologist and statistician, founded the Institute for Social Research at the University of Michigan.[10] In 1947, a group of aca-

[8] Morris L. Cooke and Philip Murray, *Organized Labor and Production,* New York: Harper and Row, 1940.

[9] Clinton S. Golden and Harold J. Ruttenberg, *The Dynamics of Industrial Democracy,* New York: Harper and Row, 1942.

[10] After the death of Kurt Lewin, The Institute for Social Research formed two divisions, the Survey Research Center and the Research Center for Group Dynamics.

demicians, labor leaders, and others interested in advancing the state of knowledge in personnel and industrial relations formed the Industrial Relations Research Association. It was in these centers and associations that a growing body of research literature on industrial behavior began.

Human relations training came into vogue during this period and was oriented toward overcoming communications barriers and enhancing interpersonal skills. The pathway to opening hidden talents in leaders resided in group-oriented techniques such as role playing, nondirective counseling, group discussion methods, and eventually the evolution of sensitivity training. Carl Rogers, a clinical psychologist at the University of Chicago, refined the nondirective counseling techniques of the Harvard group.[11] Michigan's Professor Norman Maier was one of the foremost advocates of "group-in-action" training techniques. For Maier, "group decision" was:

A way of controlling through leadership rather than force.

A way of group discipline through social pressure . . .

Permitting the group to jell on the idea it thinks will best solve a problem . . .

Pooled thinking.

Cooperative problem solving.

A way of giving each person a chance to participate in things that concern him in his work situation.

A method that requires skill and a respect for other people.[12]

In role playing and cases, technically oriented supervisors were asked to take on new role dimensions, to consult the group, and to discuss various decision alternatives in order to develop human relations skills. Case problems for training in human relations skills were growing in use in industrial and business school education. Many of these cases were adaptable to role-playing situations or otherwise lent themselves to sharpening the students' perceptiveness into human behavior or in developing interpersonal ability. Harvard, as might be expected because of the influence of Mayo and Roethlisberger, pioneered with its "Administrative Practices" course under the leadership of Edmund P.

[11] Carl P. Rogers, *Counseling and Psychotherapy*, Boston: Houghton Mifflin Co., 1942.

[12] Norman R. F. Maier, *Principles of Human Relations*, New York: John Wiley and Sons, 1952.

Learned.[13] Training to secure teamwork and to develop sensitive leaders led to a plethora of texts as managerial and employee education reached a new high in management history. The war had placed great emphasis on the need for trained managers; teamwork and group leadership notions were in vogue and academic institutions sought to fill an industrial void which called for both productive and satisfied workers. Founded upon the Mayoists' call for socially skilled supervisors, enhanced by the ideas and techniques of Moreno and Lewin, and carried out in research centers and associations, human relations training reached its apogee in the 1940s and early 1950s.

Changing Assumptions about People at Work

The Hawthorne experiments instigated a new thesis in evolving management thought. The Mayoists tilted with prior views about the nature of motivation, the role of the supervisor in eliciting human collaboration, and the importance of sentiments and informal activities at work. Investigations in the post-Hawthorne era furthered these challenges to previous ideas about the role of the manager. As an overview, these changing assumptions about people at work may be categorized as follows: (1) new ideas about motivation; (2) changing notions about the benefits to be derived from the division of labor; and (3) obtaining greater employee commitment to organizational goals through participation in decision making.

People and Motivation

One set of ideas about motivation is that human beings have certain needs which they try to satisfy. Need theory is one of our oldest notions about motivation, but research interest in the subject is fairly recent. In 1938, Henry Murray postulated 20 different

[13] The enduring casebook growing out of this course was John D. Glover and Ralph M. Hower, *The Administrator*, Homewood, Ill.: Richard D. Irwin, 1949, and revised in 1952, 1957, and 1963.

needs that people attempt to satisfy.[14] Abraham H. Maslow (1908–1970), an early "humanist psychologist," built upon Murray's work to give us one of our most widely recognized theories of motivation. Maslow proposed a theoretical hierarchy which identified at least five sets of these needs: "physiological," "safety," "love," "esteem," and "self-actualization" needs.[15] These basic needs were related to one another and were arranged in a hierarchy of "prepotency" (i.e., urgency of the drive). The most basic drives were physiological and, when these needs were satisfied, prepotency diminished and the next higher need emerged to dominate behavior. Once a need was gratified, it no longer motivated behavior. In Maslow's theory, people moved up the "ladder" of needs as each level was satisfied and they could move in a reverse direction if a lower-order need was threatened or removed. Since man was a perpetually wanting animal, all needs were really never fully gratified. The top rung of the hierarchy was self-actualization or "what a man *can* be, he *must* be."[16] This was self-fulfillment or the attainment of what a person had the potential of becoming.

The essence of Maslow's contribution was in the evolutionary, dynamic qualities of the nature of human needs. In a subsistence-level economy, physiological needs would appear to predominate. As the economy moved beyond that stage, other needs would become more important. The human relationists made the assumption that the American economy had in fact moved to a higher level of need priority. Fritz Roethlisberger stated the case for this position:

> *People at work are not so different from people in other aspects of life. They are not entirely creatures of logic. They have feelings. They like to feel important and to have their work recognized as important. Although they are interested in the size of*

[14] Henry H. Murray, *Explorations in Personality*, New York: Oxford University Press, 1938. In addition to inspiring Maslow, Murray also developed the Thematic Apperception Test (TAT) which provided the basis for the work of John Atkinson and David McClelland on the need for achievement.

[15] A. H. Maslow, "A Theory of Human Motivation," *Psychological Review*, Vol. 50 (1943), pp. 370–396. Maslow later expanded and refined these early notions in *Motivation and Personality*, New York: Harper & Row, 1954.

[16] "A Theory of Human Motivation," p. 380.

> *their pay envelopes, this is not a matter of their first concern. Sometimes they are more interested in having their pay reflect accurately the relative social importance to them of the different jobs they do. Sometimes even still more important to them than maintenance of socially accepted wage differentials is the way their superiors treat them . . . In short, employees, like most people, want to be treated as belonging to and being an integral part of some group.* [17]

Accordingly, the new focus of motivational efforts was to be on the social aspects of the workplace and on the group. Adhering to the Mayo thesis that industry must promote collaboration and social solidarity, individual incentive plans began to receive less prominence while group plans achieved more.

One such plan was the Scanlon plan, named after Joseph N. Scanlon, a steelworker, later union official, and eventually a professor at the Massachusetts Institute of Technology. [18] Scanlon's bailiwick was the La Pointe Steel Company, a marginal producer which was on the brink of bankruptcy in 1938. Scanlon, in consultation with steelworker officials, worked out a union-management productivity plan which provided that the workers would get a bonus for tangible savings in labor costs. The plan succeeded in saving La Pointe from bankruptcy and spread to other firms. The heart of the Scanlon plan was in a suggestion plan and production committees that sought methods and means to reduce labor costs. There were no individual awards for suggestions, and the first principle of the whole plan was group oriented. Cooperation and collaboration were stressed over competition and everyone benefited from the suggestions of any one individual. Rewards were plant- or company-wide, encouraging union-management cooperation to reduce costs and share benefits. The traditional suggestion system rewarded the individual, but under Scanlon's notion, the group was rewarded.

---

[17] F. J. Roethlisberger, from a speech entitled "The Human Equation in Employee Productivity," presented to the Personnel Group of the National Retail Dry Goods Association, 1950. Cited by Malcolm P. McNair, "Thinking Ahead: What Price Human Relations?", *Harvard Business Review*, Vol. 35, No. 2 (March–April, 1957), p. 17.

[18] Frederick G. Lesieur (ed.), *The Scanlon Plan: A Frontier in Labor-Management Cooperation*, published jointly by M.I.T. and John Wiley & Sons, 1958.

The Scanlon plan had great appeal to labor because it could save jobs in failing firms such as La Pointe and because it explicitly required union participation in the production committees which sought to solve pressing problems. According to Scanlon, such participation was not to create a "feeling" of belonging or a "sense" of participation, but management's explicit recognition of a definite role for the worker and union representatives in suggesting improvements. It was not profit sharing because it did not establish any fixed percentage of profits, nor was it based on profits which were made available to employees. The Scanlon plan was and is unique in these many respects: (1) a group reward for suggestions; (2) joint committees for discussion and proposing labor-saving techniques; and (3) the worker's sharing in reduced costs, not increased profits per se.

While the Scanlon plan typified the industrial human relations approach to motivation, economic man did not pass entirely from the industrial scene. James F. Lincoln pleaded for and gave experience-based confirmation of appeals to the individual in his *Incentive Management.*[19] Lincoln thought that people were giving up freedom for security, that they were relying on someone else (the government) to assume the responsibility for this security, and that pride in work, self-reliance and other time-tested virtues were declining. The proper answer to this decline, in Lincoln's view, was to return to the "intelligent selfishness" of individual ambition. People were not primarily motivated by money, nor by security, but by recognition for their skill. Lincoln's plan sought to develop employees to their highest ability and then to reward them with a "bonus" for their contributions to the success of the company. Over a period of 16 years (1935–1950), including the Depression, the "average total bonus for each factory worker in that time has exceeded $40,000."[20] This bonus was over and above the worker's other wages which were comparable to wage levels in the Cleveland area. At Lincoln Electric there was no history of work stoppages, labor turnover was almost nonexistent, individual productivity was five times as great as that for all manufacturing, dividends per share were constantly rising, product

[19]James F. Lincoln, *Incentive Management: A New Approach to Human Relationships in Industry and Business,* Cleveland, Ohio: Lincoln Electric Co., 1951.
[20]Ibid., p. 111.

prices were steadily declining, and worker bonuses continued high.[21] The individual incentive plan at Lincoln Electric is still in effect today and is as successful as ever.[22] Individual incentives à la Lincoln Electric were a minority case, however, and motivational research and advice during this era emphasized factors other than economic ones and stressed the group as the focal point for managerial stimulation.

Job Enlargement

A second facet of changing assumptions about people at work was a growing revolt against the division of labor. Walker and Guest found that assembly line workers rebelled against the anonymity of their work even though they declared themselves satisfied with their rate of pay and job security.[23] Having met these more basic needs, the workers sought to avoid the mechanical pacing of the conveyor belt, the repetitiveness of work, and the deskilling of their jobs. Feeling that they were mere cogs in the machine, discouraged about their inability to influence the quality of their work, and unable to fully engage in social interaction due to mechanical pacing of the line, workers were dissatisfied with industrial life. As a result of these pioneering efforts, job enlargement and job rotation assumed a new focus in studies of industrial behavior. Job enlargement served to relieve monotony, to enhance skill levels, and to increase the workers' feeling of commitment to the total product. In essence, this enlargement of job content was deemed a better motivating device than wages or security.[24] The economic benefits of the division of labor as espoused by Adam Smith and Charles Babbage began to become suspect as the hu-

[21] Ibid., Appendix, pp. 251–289.

[22] In 1976, for example, a total of $27,890,228 was distributed to 2,412 employees (an *average* of $11,563.11 per worker). This was the forty-third annual bonus and was in addition to regular pay, overtime pay, and fringe benefits. Correspondence with the company, December 3, 1976.

[23] Charles R. Walker and Robert H. Guest, "The Man on the Assembly Line," *Harvard Business Review*, Vol. 30, No. 3 (May–June, 1952), pp. 71–83.

[24] Ibid., p. 77. Cf. Whiting Williams, *Mainsprings of Men*, New York: Charles Scribner's Sons, 1925, pp. 58–60, who noted in 1925 that the "nature" of the job was more important than wages. Henri DeMan also noted the worker's search for "joy in work" through the nature of the task itself.

man relationists sought means to overcome industrial anomie through job enlargement.

Participation in Management

A third area of changing assumptions may be broadly viewed as a "power-equalization" thesis. This was an exhortation to play down the importance of the organizational hierarchy and to give a greater voice to subordinates through participation. Operating on the premise that worker participation would yield a greater commitment to organizational goals and would also further individual and group satisfactions, researchers sought to design work arrangements which would permit the involvement of subordinates in decision making. James C. Worthy, drawing upon his experiences in the Sears, Roebuck organization, argued for "flatter," less complex organizational structures, which maximized administrative decentralization and thereby led to improved subordinate attitudes, encouraged individual responsibility and initiative, and provided outlets for individual self-expression and creativity.[25]

William B. Given, Jr., and Charles P. McCormick were two industrialists who sought to apply the human relations philosophy to their organizations.[26] Using the catch-phrase "bottom up management," Given sought to develop and apply a philosophy of participation which essayed "to release the thinking and encourage the initiative of all those down from the bottom up . . ."[27] The notion involved widespread delegation of responsibility and authority, considerable managerial freedom in decision making, a free interchange of ideas at all levels, and the corollary acceptance of the fact that managers grow by having the freedom to fail. Recognizing that a "push from the top" was occasionally needed, Given tried to confine "top down" management to setting policy,

[25] James C. Worthy, "Organizational Structure and Employee Morale," *American Sociological Review*, Vol. 15 (April, 1950), pp. 169–179. A similar thesis by Worthy appeared in "Factors Influencing Employee Morale," *Harvard Business Review*, Vol. 28, No. 1 (January–February, 1950).

[26] Given was president of the American Brakeshoe Company and McCormick, president of McCormick and Company, producers and distributors of spices.

[27] W. B. Given, Jr., *Bottom Up Management*, New York: Harper and Row, 1949, pp. 3–4.

clarifying goals, and providing training programs for subordinates who needed them.

McCormick's plan of participation became a model for developing junior executive boards in three score or more companies by 1938.[28] The McCormick Multiple Management Plan used participation as a training and motivational method in the early Depression years with the selection of 17 promising younger men from various departments to form a junior board of directors. The board was given free access to financial and other company records, encouraged to elect its own officers and told that "every recommendation they made for the advancement of the business would have the serious consideration of the company."[29] The junior board met with the senior board once a month and at that time submitted its suggestions which were generally accepted and acted upon to a greater extent than McCormick himself had expected. In fact, McCormick attributed company success during the lean depression years to the efforts of the junior board. One example involved the redesign of the traditional bottle for extracts, which McCormick expected his older executives to wish to retain. The junior board conducted a market investigation, took housewives' ideas into account, and came up with a new design which had immediate acceptance by the senior board and in the marketplace.

The junior board evidenced other successes such as seeking out other capable young men and "sponsoring" them as protégés for further development. This early identification of management talent led to better appraisal methods, and the junior board members graduated to the senior board at an average rate of one man per year. Success with the junior board led to the creation of two others, the sales and factory boards, which operated essentially as the junior board for the sales and production departments. In brief, the entire system of boards involved a number of advantages: (1) it opened communication channels for the "Young Turks"; (2) it involved them in decision making; (3) it provided a

---

[28] Charles P. McCormick, *Multiple Management*, New York: Harper and Row, 1938, p. viii. McCormick's sequel, *The Power of People*, New York: Harper and Row, 1949, indicated further success and international acceptance in nearly 400 companies. The plan is still in use and is successful; see "Miniboards Give Spice Maker Zest," *Business Week*, May 10, 1969, pp. 174–176.

[29] McCormick, *Multiple Management*, p. 5.

means for identifying and developing executives; (4) it relieved senior board members of a great deal of detailed planning and research; and, last but not least, provided for interlocking arrangements between various departments to coordinate and follow through on company activities. The McCormick plan as participation in action his realized the ideals of Follett's integration and Barnard's effectiveness and efficiency.

Participation in decision making received greater and greater acclaim over this period of analysis. Participation was viewed as democracy in action, opening communication channels, diffusing authority, and motivating people to give a greater commitment of themselves to organizational goals.[30] Participative management was a challenge to hierarchical, unilateral authority and sought to bring group forces into play.

Another aspect of the psychology of participation came with early efforts to apply Lewinian concepts in overcoming resistance to change. The Harwood Manufacturing Company inspired some early research on using participation to overcome resistance to change.[31] Hypothesizing that resistance to changes in work standards and methods were the result of a combination of individual reactions to frustration and group-induced pressures, Coch and French manipulated three schemes for introducing change: no participation, participation through representatives chosen by the workers, and total participation. Total participation in change resulted in faster attainment of the new production rate, lower turnover, and reduced worker aggression. Interpreting these results, the researchers concluded that management must effectively communicate the need for change and must stimulate group participation in planning change. By involving the worker in change, resistance was lowered, new social structures could emerge, and the costs of change in terms of turnover and relearning skills could be minimized.

Coch and French's research in achieving organizational change was based on the theoretical work of Kurt Lewin. They used the notion of quasi-stationary equilibrium in their analysis,

---

[30]See Gordon W. Allport, "The Psychology of Participation," *The Psychology Review,* Vol. 53, No. 3 (May, 1945), pp. 119–127.

[31]Lester Coch and John R. P. French, Jr., "Overcoming Resistance to Change," *Human Relations,* Vol. 1 (1948), pp. 512–532.

and with other researchers turned to group dynamics theory in order to solve human relations problems. The *group* became the focal point for achieving change, and discussion of change and group reinforcement of attitudes was deemed much more effective than appealing to individual instincts. In brief, post-Hawthorne work was challenging prior assumptions by postulating: (1) that people were primarily motivated by social and group needs; (2) that overdivision of labor furthered anomie and could be allayed by job enlargement; and (3) that a greater commitment to organizational goals could be obtained and satisfactions enhanced by participation in decision making.

New Dimensions of Leadership

Early management thought held that the success or failure of the enterprise was due to the traits or characteristics of the manager-entrepreneur-leader. One either had the knack or he failed. Taylor identified the necessary qualities of foremen and, finding these qualities poorly distributed in the population, developed his functional foreman concept. Fayol wrote of the need for managerial knowledge, for technical skills, and for the proper moral, mental, and physical qualities of managers. He was much more optimistic than his predecessors that managerial skills could be taught. The Mayoists felt that the past had placed too much stress on the technical skills of the manager and that training should focus on the development of interpersonal skills. Chester Barnard wrote of leadership from a viewpoint of inducing others to follow and accept authority. Kurt Lewin and his associates appear to have been the first to view leadership as ranging along a continuum of possible "styles" from *"laissez-faire"* to *"democratic"* to *"authoritarian."* T. W. Adorno and his associates made a significant impact on leadership literature in 1950 with *The Authoritarian Personality.*[32] This behemoth volume, influenced by nazism and fascism, tried to relate personality structure with leadership, followership, morals, prejudices and politics. The F scale ("Fascist Scale"), developed as a part of the book, became an instrument for analyzing leadership styles as well as followers' preferences for leaders.

[32] T. W. Adorno, Else Frenkel-Brunswick, D. J. Levinson, and R. M. Sanford, *The Authoritarian Personality*, New York: Harper and Row, 1950.

Empirical research, however, was beginning to challenge these personal "trait" and unidimensional views of leadership. As early as 1945, the Institute for Social Research at the University of Michigan under the direction of Rensis Likert began a series of empirical studies in a variety of organizations in order to determine what kinds of organizational structures and what principles and methods of leadership resulted in the highest productivity, the least absenteeism, the lowest turnover, and the greatest job satisfaction. Over a period of years, this research led to the identification of two different leadership "orientations": (1) an *employee orientation* in which the supervisor stressed interpersonal relationships on the job; and (2) a *production orientation* in which the supervisor focused on getting out production and was more concerned with the technical aspects of the job.[33] The Michigan studies found that an "employee orientation," coupled with relatively "general" rather than "close" supervision, led to superior productivity, greater group cohesiveness, higher morale, less worker anxiety, and lower worker turnover.[34] The supervisor obtained higher productivity by building a team spirit, by showing concern for the worker, and by shifting from a close, production-oriented style to a looser, employee-centered, supportive style.

Chronologically parallel to the Michigan studies, the Ohio State University Bureau of Business Research began a series of investigations which would lead to the development of a "situational" approach to leadership. Professors Ralph M. Stogdill and Carroll L. Shartle formed the core of the research efforts but were aided by numerous others in analyzing leaders and their interaction with the group. Relying heavily on sociometric techniques, the researchers explored members' perceptions of the organization, status, measures of group performance, characteristics of groups, and effective leader behavior in various group sit-

[33] The bulk of this research and the findings may be found in Rensis Likert, *New Patterns of Management*, New York: McGraw-Hill Book Co., 1961.

[34] In addition to Likert's work, see: Nancy Morse, *Satisfactions in the White-Collar Job*, Ann Arbor, Mich.: Institute for Social Research, 1953; Robert Kahn and Daniel Katz, "Leadership Practices in Relation to Productivity and Morale," reprinted in Dorwin Cartwright and Alvin Zander, *Group Dynamics: Research & Theory*, Evanston, Ill.: Row, Peterson & Company, 1960, pp. 554–571; and S. F. Seashore, *Group Cohesiveness in the Industrial Work Group*, Ann Arbor: Survey Research Center, University of Michigan, 1954.

uations.[35] The Ohio State findings put forth a two-dimensional view of leadership: (1) an "initiating structure" dimension in which the leader acted to further the work objectives of the group; and (2) a "consideration" dimension in which the emphasis was on the needs of the followers and upon interpersonal relationships.

The analogies between the Ohio State and the Michigan studies of leadership are substantial: (1) both held a new view which was antithetical to a trait or a single-continuum approach; and (2) both identified two dimensions of leader behavior. One dimension was a production-oriented, initiating structure (task-oriented) axis; and another was an employee-oriented, consideration (interpersonal relations-oriented) axis. The two dimensions did not appear to be mutually exclusive; that is, a leader could combine a high initiating structure with high consideration. The advances in understanding leadership were in viewing every leadership situation as one of interaction between the leader and the group. Instead of a single style which led to the best results, there were more dimensions in every situation. Eventually this two-dimensional model of leader behavior would lead to a "grid" of possibilities, but more of that later.

In brief, the micro facet of people and organizations may be characterized as the generation and extension of significant research into industrial behavior. The emphasis was on people in the group, on social motivation, on redesigning organizational tasks to yield greater worker satisfaction, on participation in decision making, and on developing new dimensions of leadership.

People at Work: The Macro View

On the macro side, research was building into some essential notions of human behavior from a larger viewpoint. There were a

---

[35] The extent of this research is quite large; for only a sample, see: Ralph M. Stogdill and Carroll L. Shartle, *Methods in the Study of Administrative Leadership*, Columbus: Ohio State University, Bureau of Business Research Monograph No. 80, 1955: R. M. Stogdill, *Leadership and Structures of Personal Interaction*, Monograph No. 84, 1956; J. K. Hemphill, *Situational Factors in Leadership*, Ohio State University, Bureau of Educational Research Monograph No. 32, 1950; Ellis L. Scott, *Leadership and Perception of Organization*, Monograph No. 82, 1956; and Donald T. Campbell, *Leadership and Its Effects Upon the Group*, Monograph No. 83, 1956.

number of attempts to conceptualize and theorize about what was being discovered about people at work and the results were precursory steps to the later development of organization theory.

The Search for Fusion

One of the earliest and most perceptive studies of the interaction of the social system with the technical-work system was a study of restaurants by William Foote Whyte.[36] A key concept in his analysis was that of *status,* or the relative prestige of a job in a person's eyes or in the regard of others. The restaurant was characterized by many levels of job status, ranging from low-status bus-boys and dishwashers to relatively high-status cooks. Whyte found that the flow of work of taking customer orders, of food preparation, and of serving the food posed a number of human relations problems. Cooks, typically male, held a higher set of culturally derived status distinctions; on the other hand, waitresses, considered lower status, were typically in the position of *initiating* work for the cooks by placing customers' orders to be filled. Since those who initiated work for others were traditionally held to be in a higher status (e.g., supervisors initiate work for subordinates), it was inevitable that conflicts would occur when a lower-status person initiated work for a higher-status one. The conflict was mediated by placing orders on "spindles" and the use of higher counters such that the initiation of work was depersonalized. In this way the cook could remove and prepare the order under the pretext that it had not come from a lower-status person but from the spindle.[37]

Whyte developed other nuances of status on the job, such as differentiations among cooks who prepared different types of dishes, but his main argument focused on the use of social science knowledge to improve performance as well as human relations by (1) understanding the nature and functioning of the social system, and (2) developing teamwork through incentives which fostered

[36] W. F. Whyte, *Human Relations in the Restaurant Industry,* New York: McGraw-Hill Book Co., 1948.

[37] Ibid., p. 69–76. See also Elias H. Porter, "The Parable of the Spindle," *Harvard Business Review,* Vol. 40, No. 3 (May–June, 1962), pp. 58–66. The "spindle" was an ideal application of M. P. Follett's ideas; it depersonalized authority and required all to obey the "law of the situation."

collaboration rather than conflict. In brief, Whyte's work was a contribution to the analysis of the interaction of the work system with the social system in an effort to reduce interpersonal frictions which arose when these two systems met.

Another significant step in developing a macro view was an empirical investigation of a New England telephone company by E. Wight Bakke of Yale University.[38] Bakke sought to determine how the company and the union were bound together in an intricate social system. He found five major elements or "bonds of organization": (1) the functional specifications or the organization's definitions of jobs and departmental relations; (2) the status-system bond, which placed people in a vertical hierarchy of authority and deference with respect to direction; (3) a communication system, which accomplished the transmission of essential information; (4) the reward and penalty system, which provided incentives and controls in order to achieve organizational objectives; and (5) the organization charter bond, which included all those elements that contributed to giving the organization a "character" or a quality of entity. Through analysis of these bonds, Bakke sought to provide an understanding of the interaction between the formal system of relationships and the informal one. Bakke concluded that all five bonds could be analyzed to demonstrate that the formal and informal systems interacted to influence human behavior and that any initiation of change would affect both sides of the equation.

In later work, Bakke sought to classify the process by which the two systems, formal and informal, could be brought into conjunction. The elements of this "fusion process" were: (1) the "socializing process" by which the organization determined people's "position" in the organization and the "function" they performed; and (2) the "personalizing process," which was the individuals' determination of the "standing" they wanted to obtain in the organization and the "conduct" they expected of themselves. Fusion occurred when formal position and informal standing interacted to define the members' status and when formal function and infor-

---

[38] E. Wight Bakke, *Bonds of Organization: An Appraisal of Corporate Human Relations,* New York: Harper & Row, 1950.

mal conduct interacted to determine the members' role.[39]

Bakke was not giving answers to specific human relations problems but proposing a conceptual diagnostic tool for organizational analysis. In perspective, it was a building block for the later analysis of sociotechnical systems. The Tavistock Institute (London) was also responsible for a number of studies concerning the factory both as a social system and as a part of the broader social community. One extensive case study of the Glacier Metal Company was based on Lewin's field theory and sought to examine industrial changes as they moved through work groups into the larger community.[40] Such longitudinal research into the ongoing firm was rare, and the results indicated the general theme of studying organizations as interacting sociotechnical systems. While the Tavistock studies largely reaffirmed the theories of Barnard, they did provide empirical data for studying and coping with social adaptation to technological and organizational changes.

Technological change disrupts the social system, a factor that should be considered in any initiation of change by management. A classic instance was the introduction of new technology in the British coal industry following World War II.[41] The new technology required a breakup of small work groups which had high cohesiveness and the substitution of specialized, larger groups working in shifts. The logic of efficiency, i.e., the economic benefits of the new long wall method, resulted in severe emotional disturbances for the workers, low productivity, and an increasing sense of anomie. The object lesson in this case was that the imperatives of efficiency disrupted the social organization to such an extent that all of the hoped-for advantages of the new system could not come about. Technological changes cannot be effec-

---

[39] E. W. Bakke, *The Fusion Process*, New Haven, Conn.: Labor and Management Center, Yale University, 1953; and E. W. Bakke, *Organization and the Individual*, New Haven, Conn.: Labor and Management Center, Yale University, 1952, pp. 14–18.

[40] Elliott Jacques, *The Changing Culture of a Factory*, London: Tavistock Publications, 1951.

[41] E. L. Trist and K. W. Bamforth, "Some Social and Technical Consequences of the Longwall Method of Coal-Getting," *Human Relations*, Vol. 4 (1951), pp. 6–38.

tive unless there are corresponding provisions to redesign the system of social relationships.

New Tools for Macro Analysis

Herbert A. Simon (of Carnegie-Mellon) opened a new dimension in organizational analysis with his *Administrative Behavior*, which became an introduction to a later pioneering contribution in organization theory.[42] Simon was primarily concerned with decision making from the standpoint of the logic and psychology of human choice. He postulated that insights into the structure and function of an organization could best be gained by analyzing the manner in which the decisions and behavior of employees were influenced within and by the organization. All administrative activity was group activity; an organization took from the individual some of his decision-making autonomy and substituted for it an organizational decision-making process. To Simon, this was necessary since it was impossible for any single isolated individual to reach any high degree of objective rationality. Decision-making then became the result of the participation of many groups in the organization, rather than decisions residing in the scalar chain, and the effect was a "composite" decision.[43] This latter notion appears to be closely related to Mary Parker Follett's interweaving of individual and group decisions into a "cumulative" responsibility. Throughout his work, Simon reflected primarily the influence of Chester Barnard, especially on authority, inducements, and communications, and the ideas of Miss Follett to a lesser degree.

Simon's contribution came through his central theme that to study organization one must study the complex network of decisional processes, which were all directed toward influencing human behavior. By studying the distribution and allocation of decision-making functions, one could comprehend the influences on human behavior, the human choices with respect to organizational inducements, and the establishment of an effective and

[42] Herbert A. Simon, *Administrative Behavior*, New York: MacMillan Co., 1945. Revised in 1947 and 1957.

[43] Ibid., p. 221. Professor Simon says that the term was suggested to him by Chester Barnard. In retrospect, the notion sounds more like Follett than Barnard.

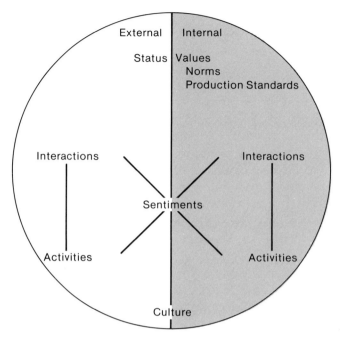

Fig. 15-1.   Homan's conceptual framework. (Adapted from Joseph A. Litterer [ed.], *Organizations: Structure and Behavior,* **New York: John Wiley and Sons, 1963, p. 144. Copyright © 1963, John Wiley and Sons, Inc.; by permission.**

meaningful equilibrium between the freedoms afforded the individual to make the decision on the job and the necessity for the organization to impose restrictions on the individual's freedom. Professor Simon's *Administrative Behavior* was an insightful link between Chester Barnard and later refinements in organization theory.

L. J. Henderson's work on Pareto formed the foundation for another step forward in the analysis of social systems by Harvard's George C. Homans. Homans attended Henderson's seminar on Pareto and coauthored a scholarly work on Pareto which formed the basis for the development of his own view of sociotechnical systems in *The Human Group*.[44] Homans divided the

---

[44] The results of Henderson's seminar may be found in George C. Homans and Charles P. Curtis, Jr., *An Introduction to Pareto: His Sociology,* New York: Alfred A. Knopf, 1934; the more modern work in George C. Homans, *The Human Group,* New York: Harcourt, Brace Jovanovich, 1950.

total social system of a group into an "internal system" and an "external system" (Figure 15-1). The external system was composed of forces or environmental factors, such as policies, job definitions, work flow, etc., outside the group. The internal system consisted of elements within the social life of the group which could influence the external system. Conversely, the external system impinged on the internal system, resulting in an interaction between the formal and informal organizations. Further, Homans categorized various dimensions of group behavior which interacted and could be found in both the internal and the external system: (1) *activities*, or what was formally required of members or behavior which informally emerged; (2) *interactions*, or any transaction between any two or more group members which could be either organizationally prescribed or informally originated; and (3) *sentiments*, an intangible, elusive concept which had to be inferred from observing behavior.[45]

Using the Hawthorne bank wiring room experiment for one example, Homans demonstrated how these three dimensions interacted in the two systems. Formal activities were the expectations and the work system devised by management for the wiring room; informal activities were restriction of output, "horseplay," games, and other nonsanctioned activities. Formal interactions were specified by job assignments and work flow among wiremen, soldermen, and inspectors; informal interactions and communications led to the formation of cliques A and B. Sentiments of management were essentially that the workers would act in their self-interest to earn wages; on the other hand, informal sentiments in the internal system tended more toward friendship and group acceptance. Homans proceeded to pair dimensions, such as the influence of interactions on sentiments, etc., to show the reciprocal influence of the external and the internal systems. While the Homans model was exceedingly broad and some of its dimensions elusive, it provided a building block for further developments in organization theory.

Talcott Parsons, the well-known Harvard economist-sociologist, also played his role in this emerging field of social systems analysis. Parsons received his doctorate from Heidelberg, wrote his dissertation on Max Weber, and introduced Chester Bar-

[45] Homans, *The Human Group*, pp. 34–40.

nard to Weber's bureaucracy. In an early work, Parsons drew together the ideas of Weber, Pareto, Alfred Marshall, and Durkheim and developed a "voluntaristic theory of social action."[46] His ideas influenced Barnard's search for a theory of "cooperative systems" and Parsons has provided further work in social systems analysis.[47] In brief, a number of individuals were paving the way for organization theory and a view of the organization as a sociotechnical system.

Summary

While Mayo and Roethlisberger had opened the door to human relations research in industry, it was the task of others to bring these notions to fruition. The "people and organizations" facet of evolving management thought was presented in two phases: (1) the micro level of inquiry into sociometry, group dynamics, participation in decision making, leadership, and the motivational appeals to group man; and (2) the macro search for analytical tools and conceptual models to explain the interactions of the formal and informal aspects of organizations.

The human relationists and their behavioral descendants were to bring about a substantial number of amendments to previously held concepts of management. Among them were: (1) an increasing emphasis on the social, group-belonging needs of people; (2) the desire to enlarge jobs to dispel the discouraging side effects of overspecialization of labor; (3) a marked decline in the emphasis on the hierarchy of authority and a call for "bottom up," participative management; (4) an increasing recognition of the informal side of the organization and the role of worker sentiments and informal activities; and finally, the development of means to study the interaction of the formal and the informal organizations.

The group was the process, social man the product. Management was exhorted to turn its attention to the social side of behavior, to get people involved, and to thereby couple worker satisfaction and higher productivity.

---

[46] Talcott Parsons, *The Structure of Social Action,* New York: McGraw-Hill Book Company, 1937.

[47] Talcott Parsons, *The Social System,* New York: Free Press, 1951.

16

Organizations and People

Chronologically parallel to the developments at Western Electric, the writings of Chester Barnard, and the empirical work in human relations, another stream of management thought focused on the structure and design of organizations. People were not entirely omitted from the equation but were placed in a relatively subordinate role to other problems of managerial concern. This chapter, covering the period from the advent of the Great Depression to 1951, will show an evolution through two phases: (1) interest in and concern for organizational structure, authority, coordination, span of control, and other issues relevant to organizational design; and (2) an increasing concern for a top administrative viewpoint which preceded renewed interest in the work of Henri Fayol.

Organizations: Structure and Design

The impact of the economic holocaust of 1929 on management thought has never been fully examined. While chapter 18 will attempt such an examination, the focus here will be on one set of theorems, the use of organizational design, to alleviate human want and misery. The Mayoist school put forth another set, that of group solidarity and human collaboration. The authors examined below felt that the efficient design and operation of organizations was another possible alternative for industry.

The Affable Irishman:
James D. Mooney

During the cold, dark days of the Depression, the exhortation *Onward Industry!* reflected the premise that through organizational efficiency, the lot of mankind could be improved. *Onward Industry!*, the joint efforts of a General Motors executive, James D. Mooney (1884–1957), and a historian-turned-executive, Alan C. Reiley (1869–1947), was an attempt "to expose the *principles of organization*, as they reveal themselves in various forms of human group movement, and to help industry to protect its own growth through a greater knowledge and use of these principles."[1] While joint authorship existed, it later became evident that the organizational aspect of the book was due to Mooney while Reiley assumed a lesser role and contributed primarily to the historical analysis of organizations. James Mooney was president of the General Motors Export Corporation and traveled over the world as a goodwill ambassador and negotiator for the General Motors Corporation. Described as "affable" and an "experienced diplomat," Mooney completed high school through correspondence, received a degree in mining engineering from Case Institute (1908), joined General Motors in 1920, and rose through the organization to head its Export Corporation.[2] Mooney was selected by President Roosevelt as his personal, secret emissary to Hitler when there were attempts to stop the war in 1939 and 1940 before America became involved. Failing in this, Mooney was given a special G.M. assignment to convert the company to defense production. He left G.M. in 1942 to head the U.S. Navy Bureau of Aeronautics and after the war became president and chairman of the board of Willys Overland Motors.

---

[1] James D. Mooney and Alan C. Reiley, *Onward Industry!: The Principles of Organization and their Significance to Modern Industry*, New York: Harper and Row, 1931, p. xiii. This book was revised by Mooney and Reiley in 1939 and retitled *The Principles of Organization*. Mooney revised the book again in 1947. References below will distinguish between *Onward Industry!* and the revised edition where appropriate.

[2] Personal insights into Mooney are from "Drawing the Rules from History," *Milestones of Management*, vol. I, by the editors of *Business Week*, pp. 10–11.

In *Onward Industry!*, Mooney and Reiley set out to develop principles of organizational efficiency which would meet industrial objectives of "profit through service" which they viewed as an obligation to contribute to "the alleviation of human want and misery."[3] Productive efficiency, though necessary, was not enough to insure the goal of industrial service. The entire organization, both production and distribution, must be efficient in terms of providing for organized group effort toward organizational aims and purposes. For Mooney and Reiley the efficient organization was based on formalism, which "means the efficient coordination of all relationships."[4] There is no evidence that either Mooney or Reiley had ever heard of Max Weber, the German who sought bureaucracy as the ideal, but the purposes and methods of these two sets of organizational theorists are more similar than dissimilar. Mooney and Reiley defined what they meant by organization: "Organization is the form of every human association for the attainment of a common purpose."[5] To clarify the role of management in organizations, they made this distinction:

> *Management is the vital spark which actuates, directs, and controls the plans and procedure of organization. With management enters the personal factor, without which no body could be a living being with any direction toward a given purpose. The relation of management to organization is analogous to the relation of the psychic complex to the physical body. Our bodies are simply the means and the instrument through which the psychic force moves toward the attainment of its aims and desires.*[6]

Using the body-mind analogy for organization and management, Mooney and Reiley formulated their principles of organization and put them in a framework of "principle," "process," and "effect." The first principle was that of coordination, which meant "the orderly arrangement of group effort, to provide unity of action in the pursuit of a common purpose."[7] Coordination was a

---

[3] Mooney and Reiley, *Onward Industry!*, p. xiii.

[4] Ibid., p. xv.

[5] Ibid., p. 10.

[6] Ibid., p. 13.

[7] J. D. Mooney, *The Principles of Organization* (rev. ed.), New York: Harper and Row, 1947, p. 5. The substance of Mooney's revision and the original *Onward Industry!* differ only slightly, the revision being more concise and definitive.

broad principle which contained all the principles of organization. Coordination found its own principle or foundation in *authority* or "the supreme coordinating power." This did not mean autocracy but the source of responsibility for direction. Authority was a "right" which inhered legitimately in the organization as opposed to power, which was an individual possession. In government, for example, authority represented *de jure* governments, while power represented *de facto* governments. Since coordination implied an aim or objective, every member of the organization must understand this common purpose, and Mooney and Reiley called this *doctrine* or the "definition of the objective."[8] This was similar to the religious concept of creed, but for industry it meant the attainment of "surplus through service" which was the objective of business. The greater the members' understanding of the organization's doctrine, the greater the degree of teamwork and the accomplishment of objectives.

The second principle was the *scalar* one, which meant that there was a hierarchy of degrees of authority and corresponding responsibility in every organization. Every organization, even of two people, had a scalar chain of superior to subordinate and thereby one found the scalar principle in operation. The scalar principle had its own principle in *leadership*, which "represents authority." Leadership was not always the "supreme authority" but was "the form that authority assumes when it enters into process."[9] The essence of this was that leaders were designated through the process of *delegation* which conferred authority on a subordinate by a superior. Delegation always meant the conferring of authority, whether it be authority over people or authority for task performance. Conversely, authority always carried with it responsibility for accomplishing what was authorized. The "effect" of this scalar principle was *functional definition*, which defined and assigned a task for each subordinate along the scalar chain.

The third principle, the *functional principle*, was not the same idea as functional definition but was the "distinction between different kinds of duties."[10] Every organization had functional differ-

[8]Ibid., p. 10.
[9]Ibid., p. 15.
[10]Ibid., p. 25.

entiation in the sense that people performed different kinds of duties such as production, sales, lathe operations, security, etc. To cite Mooney:

> *In every organized undertaking there must be some function that determines its objective, another that moves to its attainment, and a third that makes interpretative decisions in accordance with those rules of procedure that have been predetermined. These functions, which may be called the* determinative, *the* applicative, *and the* interpretative, *are related as principle, process, and effect. In secular government they are known as the* legislative, *the* executive, *and the* judicial *functions.* [11]

Every duty, function, or individual job involved either determination of what was to be done, the doing of that thing, or deciding on questions which arose in that performance.

Mooney also made a delineation of staff service as contrasted with authority or command. The task of staff service was to advise or counsel and it had three phases:

> *The* informative *phase refers to those things which authority should know in framing its decisions: the* advisory, *to the actual counsel based on such information; the* supervisory, *to both preceding phases as applied to all the details of execution. It is through this last phase that the informative and advisory phases become operative throughout an entire organization.* [12]

According to Mooney, there should never be any confusion about line and staff because line represented "the authority of *man;* . . . Staff, the authority of *ideas.*"[13] Line commanded, staff advised, and Mooney envisioned no potential conflict in line-staff relations as long as this was kept in mind.

Mechanically, Mooney and Reiley's principles resembled Weber's bureaucratic hierarchy, his rational-legal notion of authority, and his requirement for specifically defined duties and responsibilities. Mooney and Reiley made no reference to Weber and, since Weber's work had not been translated into English at this time, it must be assumed that they independently developed their format for efficiency through the proper organizational structure.

[11] Ibid., p. 26. Copyright 1947, Harper and Row; by permission.
[12] Ibid., p. 33. Copyright 1947, Harper and Row; by permission. Italics added.
[13] Ibid., p. 34.

Following their section on the principles of organization, Mooney and Reiley examined the history of organizations to demonstrate these principles in operation. Most probably the work of the historian Reiley, they examined Greece, Rome, and other ancient civilizations and rulers to show the scalar process and other principles. Though largely a description of governments and the military, the Catholic Church came in for some close scrutiny by the two Irish Catholics. The first principle, coordination, found its authority in God, by whom it was delegated to the pope as the supreme coordinating authority. The scalar principle operated from the pope, through the cardinals (who were often both line and staff), to the bishops and priests in the delegation of authority. Functional definition, though less clear, was based on a division between the secular and the regular clergy, who may or may not perform certain acts of consecration. In the development of staff, the church operated on a *compulsory staff service* concept. Under this rule, a superior must consult the elder monks even on minor matters. On matters of major importance, he must consult everyone for advice. This concept did not abridge his line authority but compelled him to consult everyone before rendering a decision. The superior could not refuse to listen. In industry, the compulsory staff principle would not protect the manager from errors in judgment but it would serve to allay errors of knowledge.

Briefly, Mooney and Reiley were concerned with the mechanisms of organization structure and design. The human element was not missing entirely but was relegated to a secondary role. For organization theory, Mooney and Reiley became a building block for a formalistic view of organizations.

Texts, Teachers, and Trends

A number of individuals continued the industrial engineering type of texts for management education and reflected more of a shop management view of organizations. Some were unique in their approach but for the most part they continued to stress production layout, scheduling, materials handling, organizing the shop, production control and other largely technique-oriented subjects. One unique approach was that of Henry Dennison (1877–1952), who had been a pioneer in the installation of the

Taylor system in his own firm. The title of Dennison's book, *Organization Engineering*, is misleading, for it advocated a design of organizational structure which was diametrically opposed to Mooney and Reiley's approach.[14] Dennison began with the idea that organization engineering was "making a success of group life" and built the organization structure up from groups of people who, under capable leadership, resolved their frictions and unified their motives in a single direction. Instead of designing the structure and tasks first, Dennison would find "like-minded" people, group them, and develop the total organization structure last. In this sense, Dennison actually anticipated by a decade or more the behavioralists who were advocating sociometrically selected work teams or other mutual-choice devices to group workers by compatibility.

Dennison also pioneered in a number of areas regarding employee welfare. He established, in 1916, America's first company-sponsored unemployment compensation fund which stabilized employment and provided worker security. He formed a "works committee" (1919) for employee representation and participation in management. Workers shared in company profits through a stock dividend plan, and Dennison has been hailed as an innovator because of his ideas on employee relations.[15]

Dennison's view of motivation was also unique:

Four general groups of tendencies which may actuate a member of any organization are: (1) regard for his own and his family's welfare and standing; (2) liking for the work itself; (3) regard for one or more members of the organization and for their good opinion, and pleasure in working with them; and (4) respect and regard for the main purposes of the organization . . . Only when impelled by the four combined can all of man's power be brought into steady and permanent play.[16]

Dennison would modify jobs so that more satisfaction would be obtained from them. He did not develop any notion of job en-

[14] Henry S. Dennison, *Organization Engineering*, New York: McGraw-Hill Book Co., 1931.

[15] W. Jack Duncan and C. Ray Gullett, "Henry Sturgis Dennison: The Manager and the Social Critic," *Journal of Business Research*, Vol. 2, No. 2 (April, 1974), pp. 133–143.

[16] Dennison, pp. 63–64.

largement but was on the fringe of later behavioral theory, which sought to make work satisfying. He recognized informal groups and their influence on restriction of output and proposed non-financial incentives which, when properly mixed with economic incentives, built loyalty. Principles of organization were not to be "sacred in and of themselves" and the final organization structure should be flexible to strengthen group performance, not to ossify it. Authority and responsibility should be clearly defined and a sound organization structure furthered organizational efficiency if it were flexible enough to meet changing group and organizational needs, i.e., if it promoted "success of group life." Dennison also recognized limits to and variations in the number of men to whom the executive could give his attention. The span of control, in his view, "seldom runs beyond six to twelve people."[17]

Other contributions during the 1930s were more production oriented. C. Canby Balderston and his associates defined management as "the art and science of organizing, preparing and directing human effort applied to control the forces and to utilize the materials of nature for the benefit of man."[18] They said that all managers, regardless of the type of enterprise, were concerned with four basic elements: men, money, machines, and material. They proceeded to analyze product design, physical facilities and equipment, power, heat, light, ventilation, inventory control, production control, and other shop-oriented subjects. Organization was treated within a formal framework in the Mooney and Reiley style; and personnel management, an emerging subject of consideration during the era, was one of the few subjects which appeared outside the shop management boundaries.

On the academic front, many were sensing a need for a synthesis in management education. Professors E. H. Anderson of the University of Alabama and G. T. Schwenning of the University of North Carolina perceived the fragmentary nature of management literature and made a contribution by attempting to "ap-

---

[17] Ibid., pp. 137–138.

[18] C. Canby Balderston, Victor S. Karabasz, and Robert P. Brecht, *Management of an Enterprise*, New York: Prentice-Hall, 1935, p. 5. Professors Balderston and Brecht of the Wharton School, University of Pennsylvania, later became influential in forming the Academy of Management and Professor Brecht served as president of the academy 1941–1947.

praise and synthesize" the work of others.[19] Though few new ideas were introduced, their synthesis and extensive bibliography provides a valuable research insight into this era. Anderson and Schwenning did note, however, the appearance of Coubrough's 1930 translation of Henri Fayol's work, although they did not give it more than a passing glance.

In 1936, Charles L. Jamison of the University of Michigan and William N. Mitchell of Chicago invited a group of management teachers to the University of Chicago's Quadrangle Club for the purpose of discussing the formation of a society to advance the philosophy of management.[20] Enough interest was evoked for Wharton's Balderston to invite the group to Philadelphia for another conference in 1937. R. C. Davis of Ohio State wrote the constitution in 1940–1941, officers were elected, and the Academy of Management began formal operations in 1941. The objectives of the academy were stated as follows:

> *The Academy is founded to foster the search for truth and the general advancement of learning through free discussion and research in the field of management. The interest of the Academy lies in the theory and practice of management, both administrative and operative. It is concerned also with the theory and practice of operative management as it relates to the work of planning, organizing, and controlling the execution of business projects. It is also concerned with activities having to do with the forming, directing, and coordinating of departments and groups which are characteristic of administrative management. It is not concerned primarily with specialized procedures for the control and execution of particular kinds of projects that are significant chiefly in narrow segments of a business field.*
>
> *The general objectives of the Academy shall be therefore to foster: (a) A philosophy of management that will make possible an accomplishment of the economic and social objectives of an industrial society with increasing economy and effectiveness. The public's interest must be paramount in any such philosophy, but adequate consideration must be given to the legitimate interests of*

[19] E. H. Anderson and G. T. Schwenning, *The Science of Production Organization*, New York: John Wiley and Sons, 1938.

[20] Preston P. LeBreton, "A Brief History of the Academy of Management," in the appendix of Paul M. Dauten, Jr. (ed.), *Current Issues and Emerging Concepts in Management*, Boston: Houghton Mifflin Co., 1962, pp. 329–332.

Capital and Labor. (b) Greater understanding by Executive leadership of the requirements for a sound application of the scientific method to the solution of managerial problems, based on such a philosophy. (c) Wider acquaintance and closer co-operation among such persons as are interested in the development of a philosophy and science of management.[21]

Academy membership was restricted to professors, although a few businessmen could be selected. The outbreak of World War II and consequent travel restrictions held academy activities dormant until 1947 when annual meetings were resumed. Jamison, as founder, presided from 1936 to 1940; Brecht was president from 1941–1947, and Davis became president in 1948. The academy reflected the increased awareness for the necessity of teaching management and for bringing together diverse ideas into a search for management theory.

Another trend appeared which indicated an increasing awareness of the relationship of industry to society as a whole. In 1928, Arthur G. Anderson of the University of Illinois had published *Industrial Engineering and Factory Management.*[22] This first edition was essentially of the works administration-industrial engineering approach which was typical of that era. In 1942, Merten J. Mandeville (University of Illinois), and John M. Anderson (of Minneapolis-Honeywell, Inc.), became coauthors with A. G. Anderson and introduced a larger view of the management function, which stressed the need for management to relate effectively to its public. In the authors' view, management must assume its social responsibility and promote both economic and social progress through productive and distributive efficiency as well as through emphasis on "the human side" of the company.[23] Discussing relations with customers, stockholders, the public at large, and employee relations, the authors took more of an environmental view of management than was apparent in any other management text since Gantt. Although a large portion of the remainder of the book

---

[21] Ibid., p. 330.

[22] A. G. Anderson, *Industrial Engineering and Factory Management,* New York: Ronald Press Co., 1928.

[23] Anderson, Mandeville, and Anderson, *Industrial Management,* (rev. ed.), New York: Ronald Press Co., 1942, p. 3. Professor Mandeville became president of the Academy of Management in 1959.

was devoted to traditional production subjects, it did reflect an increasing concern for a larger view of the management function.

Building Blocks for Administrative Theory

In 1937, Luther Gulick and Lyndall Urwick assembled a series of papers which reflected the divergences in management thought during the era under consideration.[24] This landmark in management literature contained essays by James D. Mooney, Henri Fayol, Henry Dennison, L. J. Henderson, T. N. Whitehead, Elton Mayo, Mary Parker Follett, John Lee, V. A. Graicunas, and the editors themselves. It included the first American rendition of Henri Fayol's work, including Urwick's comparison of Fayol with Mooney,[25] and an early account of the Hawthorne research.[26] Despite the inclusion of Follett and the Harvard experimenters, the whole of the collection was formalistic in terms of organization theory.

    Luther Gulick (1892–   ) was director of the Institute of Public Administration at Columbia University and served as a member of President Roosevelt's Committee on Administrative Management which attempted, without much success, to reform and reorganize the federal bureaucracy.[27] Amplifying Fayol's version of the process which appeared in the same collection, Gulick developed his famous POSDCORB, which was his view of the functions of the executive. The initials represented the following activities:

> *Planning, that is working out in broad outline the things that need to be done and the methods for doing them to accomplish the purpose set for the enterprise;*

[24]Luther Gulick and Lyndall Urwick (eds.), *Papers on the Science of Administration*, New York: Institute of Public Administration, Columbia University, 1937.

[25]Henri Fayol, "The Administrative Theory of the State," (trans. by Sarah Greer), ibid., pp. 99–114 and pp. 115–130.

[26]L. J. Henderson, T. N. Whitehead, and Elton Mayo, "The Effects of Social Environment," ibid., pp. 143–158.

[27]*Report of the President's Committee on Administrative Management*, Washington, D.C.: U.S. Government Printing Office, 1935. This report called for a restructuring of governmental agencies and offices to eliminate overlapping duties and to provide for more effective measures of executive responsibility.

Organizing, that is the establishment of the formal structure of authority through which work subdivisions are arranged, defined, and coordinated for the defined objective;

Staffing, that is the whole personnel function of bringing in and training the staff and maintaining favorable conditions of work;

Directing, that is the continuous task of making decisions and embodying them in specific and general orders and instructions and serving as the leader of the enterprise;

Co-ordination, that is the all important duty of interrelating the various parts of the work;

Reporting, that is keeping those to whom the executive is responsible informed as to what is going on, which thus includes keeping himself and his subordinates informed through records, research, and inspection;

Budgeting, with all that goes with budgeting in the form of fiscal planning, accounting, and control.[28]

Gulick visualized management as universal but his description of the functions was primarily applied to governmental administration. Gulick's contribution was not in his version of the process, even though this is most easily recalled, but in his theory of departmentation, which appears to be unique in the management literature for that time. Gulick began with the premise that the major purpose of organization was coordination. He then formulated a "principle of homogeneity" which required the grouping of similar activities under one head; otherwise friction and inefficiency would result. In grouping activities by this principle, Gulick noted four primary methods: (1) *purpose,* or function performed, such as "furnishing water, controlling crime or conducting education"; (2) the *process* being used, such as "engineering, medicine . . . stenography, statistics, accounting"; (3) *persons* or *things* dealt with or served, such as "immigrants, veterans, Indians . . ."; and (4) the *place* where the service is being rendered.[29]

In Gulick's scheme, these would be major groupings or primary levels of departmentation and any one could be chosen depending upon which best served the organization's objectives. For

---

[28] Luther Gulick, "Notes on the Theory of Organization," in Gulick and Urwick, p. 13. Italics added.

[29] Ibid., p. 15 and pp. 21–31.

example, if the primary level chosen was by place (i.e., geographical), the secondary level might be grouped by purpose, process, clientele, or even again by place. The same would be true for the third level and so on. Any decision about how to group activities must follow the principle of homogeneity, insure coordination, and maintain flexibility as the organization grew or as its objectives changed. While Mooney and Reiley stressed "functionalism" or the distinction between kinds of duties, Gulick demonstrated how these duties and activities could be grouped into homogeneous departments in order to assure coordination. It was on this point that Luther Gulick made his primary contribution to management and organization theory.

Lieutenant Colonel Lyndall Fownes Urwick (1891–   ), co-editor with Gulick of the *Papers on the Science of Administration*, has earned his place in management history. Educated at Oxford, he served in a distinguished manner in Her Majesty's Army and government in World Wars I and II, was organizing secretary of Rowntree and Company (1920–1928), was elected and served as director of the International Management Institute in Geneva (1928–1933), and was chairman of Urwick, Orr and Partners, Ltd., management consultants in London, until his retirement.[30] Influenced to a great degree by B. S. Rowntree and Oliver Sheldon of the Cocoa Works, Urwick has written on a wide range of subjects, such as his collaboration with E. F. L. Brech on biographical sketches of pioneers in scientific management, with Henry Metcalf on Mary Follett's papers, with Gulick, and on his own on various aspects of organizations.

Although his writings have spanned many decades, his work in the late 1920s and 1930s was heavily oriented along formalism in organization theory.[31] He identified eight principles applicable to all organizations: (1) the "principle of the objective," or that all organizations should be an expression of a purpose; (2) the "principle of correspondence," that authority and responsibility must be coequal; (3) the "principle of responsibility," that responsi-

---

[30] No author, L. *Urwick: A Bibliography*, London: Urwick, Orr and Partners, 1957.

[31] See L. Urwick, "Principles of Direction and Control," in John Lee (ed.), *A Dictionary of Industrial Administration*, London: Sir Isaac Pitman and Sons, 1928; L. Urwick, *Management of Tomorrow*, London: Nisbet and Co., 1933, in which he developed a "Pure theory of organization"; and L. Urwick, *Scientific Principles of Organization*, New York: American Management Association, 1938.

bility of higher authorities for work of subordinates is absolute; (4) the scalar principle; (5) the "principle of the span of control," concluding that no superior can supervise directly the work of more than five or six subordinates whose work interlocks; (6) the "principle of specialization," or limiting one's work to a single function; (7) a coordination principle; and (8) the "principle of definition," or a clear prescription of every duty.[32]

Urwick's discovery of Henri Fayol's elements led him to compare Fayol with Mooney and Reiley in a search for broader "principles of administration." He applied Mooney and Reiley's "principle, process, and effect" to Fayol's 14 principles and concluded that these independent developments in organization theory were remarkably correlated and that they suggested a possible avenue of integration for administrative theory.[33] In later work, Urwick expanded his search for a synthesis by deriving 29 major principles and a host of subprinciples by integrating his own ideas with those of Fayol, Mooney and Reiley, Taylor, Follett, and V. A. Graicunas.[34] He was optimistic that a general theory of administration could be attained, and his own work has represented a substantial step in that direction.

The Span of Control

While Gulick and Urwick were publicizing and synthesizing the work of Fayol and Mooney and Reiley, V. A. Graicunas was furnishing mathematical proof to support the concept of a narrow span of control. Graicunas, an American born of Lithuanian descent, was a noted international consultant in industrial administration. After a career in consulting, he served in the United States Army Air Corps during World War II. In Russia on a business trip in 1947, Graicunas was arrested by the Russian secret police and subsequently died somewhere in the "Gulag Archipelago."[35] Graicunas's ideas on the span of control were largely influenced

[32] L. Urwick, *Scientific Principles of Organization*.

[33] See L. Urwick, "The Function of Administration with Special Reference to the Work of Henri Fayol," in Gulick and Urwick, pp. 115–130.

[34] L. Urwick, *The Elements of Administration*, New York: Harper and Row, 1944.

[35] An interesting account of Graicunas's life, career, and demise may be found in Arthur G. Bedeian, "Vytautas Andrius Graicunas: A Biographical Note," *Academy of Management Journal*, Vol. 17, No. 2 (June, 1974).

by Lyndall Urwick, who, in turn, followed the theme of the British General Sir Ian Hamilton:

> . . . As to whether the groups [of subordinates] are three, four, five, or six, it is useful to bear in mind a by-law; the smaller the responsibility of the group member, the larger may be the number of the group—and vice versa . . . the nearer we approach the supreme head of the whole organization, the more we work towards groups of six. [36]

Graicunas observed that industrial managers were hampered by trying to supervise too many subordinates; this was due, in part, to their desire "to enhance their prestige and influence" by adding sections and departments to their responsibilities. Such ego bolstering could be deadly from the standpoint of delays, lack of coordination, and confusion from trying to control too many subordinates. Graicunas indicated two factors to support his argument for a narrow or limited span of control: (1) the psychological principle of "span of attention" which stated that the human brain could cope with only so many variables at any one time; and (2) his own development of "cross relationships" and "direct group relationships" in addition to "direct single relationships." On this second point, Graicunas described these relationships in this way:

> In almost every case the superior measures the burden of his responsibility by the number of direct single relationships between himself and those he supervises. But in addition there are direct group relationships and cross relationships. Thus, if Tom supervises two persons, Dick and Harry, he can speak to them as a pair . . . . Further what Dick thinks of Harry and what Harry thinks of Dick constitute two cross relationships which Tom must keep in mind in arranging any work over which they must collaborate in his absence . . . Thus, even in this extremely simple unit of organization, Tom must hold four to six relationships within his span of attention:
> Direct Single Relationships
>   Tom to Dick and Tom to Harry 2
> Direct Group Relationships
>   Tom to Dick with Harry and Tom to Harry with Dick 2

[36]Sir Ian Hamilton, *The Soul and Body of an Army,* London: Arnold Publishing House, 1921, p. 229.

Cross Relations
  Harry with Dick and Dick with Harry 2
   Total Relationships .... 6[37]

With the addition of these different sets of relationships, Graicunas postulated that when the number of direct single relationships increased arithmetically with the addition of one subordinate, the corresponding increase in the number of direct group and cross relationships caused the total number of relationships to increase in exponential proportion. Where n represented the number of persons supervised, Graicunas derived a formula to show this growth:

$$\text{Total relationships} = n\left(\frac{2^n}{2} + n - 1\right)$$

or, if there were three subordinates in direct single relationship, then:

$$\text{Total} = 3\left(\frac{2^3}{2} + 3 - 1\right), \text{ or } 3 \times 6 = 18$$

Further, to show the growth as subordinates were added:

n =	1	2	3	4	5	6	7	8	9	10	11	12
total =	1	6	18	44	100	222	490	1080	2376	5210	11374	24708

The significance of this geometric growth was that increasing n from 4 to 5 increased working capacity 20 percent, whereas the increase in the "possible" number of relationships increased 127 percent or from 44 to 100. Hence Graicunas argued that the span of control should be limited to a "maximum of five and most probably, only four."[38] Exceptions to this decision rule were permissible in the case of routine work at lower organizational elements where workers worked relatively independently of others, where they had little or no contact with others, and where supervisory responsibilities were less complex and therefore allowed a wider span of control. However, at upper levels, where responsibility was greater and often overlapped, the span should be less.

[37] V. A. Graicunas, "Relationship in Organization," in Gulick and Urwick, p. 184.
[38] Ibid., p. 185.

Graicunas noted also that "it is not possible to assign comparable weights to these different varieties of relationship," suggesting that he was aware that not all interaction possibilities were operative at all times. If some interactions were not required, for example, if Dick need not interact with Harry, or if the job was routine and interaction not crucial, then the number of relationships would be less and the span might be wider. Graicunas was using mathematics to prove a point. His formula represented "maximum possible" relationships, not what might actually be operative at one given point in time. His advice, highly influenced by military and governmental needs for control and coordination, reflected his formalistic concern for organizational efficiency and should not be generalized to other situations where other variables, such as subordinate motivation or development, might be of greater import.

Toward a
Top Management Viewpoint

A second facet of this era involved developments which were shifting management thought from a shop-management, production orientation to a larger view of the administrative function. The design of organization structures and the search for organizational principles were still subjects for discussion; however, organizations per se were beginning to take a back seat to the study of administration. Ralph C. Davis is an excellent example of this transition period in evolving management thought.

Ralph C. Davis:
Pater Familiae et Magister

Ralph Currier Davis (1894–   ) received his mechanical engineering degree in 1916 from Cornell where he studied under the pioneering Dexter Kimball.[39] After becoming a registered industrial engineer he went to work on the industrial engineering staff

[39] Biographical information is based on personal correspondence, Ralph C. Davis to author, May 18, 1969; and on John F. Mee, "*Pater Familiae et Magister*" (Father of Family and Teacher), *Academy of Management Journal*, Vol. 8, No. 1 (March, 1965), pp. 14–23.

of the Winchester Repeating Arms Company, where, as he puts it, "I quickly discovered that I knew practically nothing about management."[40] His experiences were soon enriched by observing Carl Barth, Dwight Merrick, and members of the staff of A. Hamilton Church's consulting firm, who were all on assignment at Winchester. In 1923, Davis was invited to the Ohio State University to establish a Department of Management in the College of Commerce and Administration. His first book was in the traditional shop-level, "operative management" orientation. Davis stated that the fundamental functions and principles of factory management were universal in their application and that a sound organization was essential:

> *In developing the organization, consideration should be given to (1) the fundamental functions to be performed and their relation to one another, (2) the proper division of responsibility, (3) the definite location of responsibility, (4) the proper functioning of the system, (5) the flexibility of the organization, (6) provision for future growth, (7) personal characteristics and abilities, (8) the creation of an ideal, and (9) the quality of the leadership.*[41]

Davis also questioned the wisdom of Taylor's functional foremen:

> *The employee in a functionalized organization must look to a number of executives for instructions. This may impair discipline by permitting him to play off one executive against another. Furthermore, it is difficult to draw sharp lines between many of the functions of management, and accordingly there is danger of conflict of authority between the various functions . . . Finally, the Taylor division of functions is adapted chiefly to shop conditions. It cannot be applied readily to the other units of the organization, as, for example, the purchasing department.*[42]

On personnel, Davis reflected the industrial psychology orientation of the period by stressing job analysis and scientific selection of workers: "Psychological methods have a scientific basis and seem to offer the only real hope for the development of scientific methods for the selection of applicants."[43]

[40]R. C. Davis to author, May 18, 1969.

[41]R. C. Davis, *The Principles of Factory Organization and Management*, New York: Harper and Row, 1928, p. 41.

[42]Ibid., pp. 47–48 and p. 50.

[43]Ibid., p. 338.

In 1927, Davis was asked by General Motors to set up a Department of Management in the General Motors Institute at Flint, Michigan. It was at General Motors from 1927 to 1930 that he was exposed to the philosophies and principles of Donaldson Brown and Alfred P. Sloan, Jr., and from that time on he began to formulate his "administrative" approach to management as opposed to his previous "operative" or shop-level approach. Davis's approach was further reshaped by his acquisition (in 1930 or 1931) of Coubrough's translation of Henri Fayol's *Industrial and General Administration*.[44] In 1934, this melding of ideas led Davis to develop his own "organic functions" of management as planning, organizing, and controlling.[45] R. C. Davis's life and work illustrate the ecology of evolving management thought over a span of more than four decades. His 1928 work was largely a shop-level, "operative"-oriented approach to management; in 1934, he developed his own organic functions of planning, organizing, and controlling; and in 1940, he developed the management process further but still devoted a large portion of this book to production shop subjects.[46] His notions of management theory and practice were clearly in transition when he published *The Fundamentals of Top Management* in 1951.[47] In this effort, he moved almost entirely to an "administrative management" viewpoint.

In *Fundamentals*, Davis defined management as "the function of executive leadership" and stressed the need for "professional" managers who had a sound philosophy of management with respect to leadership and the relations between business and the community. Since the business organization was largely an economic institution, its objectives were "any values that the busi-

[44] R. C. Davis to author, September 11, 1971.

[45] R. C. Davis, *The Principles of Business Organization and Operation*, Columbus, Ohio: H. L. Hedrick, 1935, pp. 12–13. John Mee has suggested that Davis's idea of "organic functions" reflected the influence of Alexander Hamilton Church. Church developed some "organic functions" of management in 1914 and Davis had encountered Church's ideas at the Winchester Repeating Arms Company. John Mee to author, August 26, 1969.

[46] Ralph C. Davis, *Industrial Organization and Management*, New York: Harper and Row, 1940. This book was a substantial revision of his 1928 text and its third edition appeared in 1957.

[47] Ralph C. Davis, *The Fundamentals of Top Management*, New York: Harper and Row, 1951.

ness organization is required or expected to acquire, create, preserve, or distribute."[48] Organizational objectives were constrained by community ideals or commonly held standards of business conduct. Executive leadership was a motivating force that stimulated and directed the members of the organization toward the satisfactory achievement of its objectives.

In developing the management process, Davis viewed his organic functions as universally applicable to all types of enterprises. Planning was the "specification of the factors, forces, effects and relationships that enter into and are required for the solution of a business problem" and provided "a basis for economical and effective action in the achievement of business objectives."[49] Planning was mental work of a creative nature which facilitated understanding and accomplishment of the organization's mission. Organizing included "any process that results in the antecedent provision of the necessary basic conditions for successful business accomplishment" and involved "bringing functions, physical factors, and personnel into proper relationships with one another . . ."[50] Organization rested on authority which was "the right to plan, organize, and control the organization's activities . . ."[51] This represented the traditional formal view of authority as the right to command and decide, which Davis found to be legitimatized ultimately in organized society. For example, society upholds the right of private property; individuals exercise this right through stock ownership in a company and delegate the management of their property to the board of directors who in turn delegate authority down through the scalar chain. With respect to the functional grouping of activities and his examination of other aspects of organizing, Davis reflected the formalism of Mooney and Reiley and other writers of this genre. He did not examine the in formal organization, made no mention of the Western Electric research, and in general made few references to the behavioral research being carried out during that era.

Control was defined "as the function of constraining and regulating activities that enter into the accomplishment of an objec-

[48] Ibid., p. 10.
[49] Ibid., p. 43.
[50] Ibid., p. 238.
[51] Ibid., p. 281.

tive."[52] Davis identified eight control functions: routine planning, scheduling, preparation, dispatching, direction, supervision, comparison, and corrective action. In this scheme, he did make a useful distinction by indicating the importance of *timing* in phases of control. For instance, routine planning, which provided information for the execution of plans, was a phase of control. On the other hand, creative planning involved advance planning of a general nature and was part of the organization's total planning function. The phases of control were: (1) *preliminary* control, which included routine planning, scheduling, preparation and dispatching; and (2) *concurrent* control, or direction, supervision, comparison, and corrective action. Preliminary control tried to design in advance constraints and regulations which would assure proper execution of the plan; on the other hand, concurrent control operated while performance was in progress. Corrective action completed the control cycle and began the preliminary phase again by identifying deviations and by replanning or taking other actions to prevent recurrence of deviations. While many of his predecessors had written of control, Davis presented a much more insightful and comprehensive view of this function.

In comparing Davis and Fayol, we note that each had his own uniqueness. Both stressed the universality of management, both recognized the necessity and importance of teaching management, and both held to a formalized view of management. Fayol's process added command and coordination to planning, organizing, and controlling. Davis did not include command but included it under a more descriptive label of "executive leadership" which permeated all other functions. Likewise, Davis treated coordination as operating throughout his organic functions and not separate, as regarded by Fayol. On the other hand, Fayol developed staffing as a subfunction of organizing while Davis paid relatively less attention to the personnel function.

Harry Hopf: Toward the Optimum

During this era another individual was to begin with the precepts of Frederick Taylor and conclude with a broader conception of the role of top management. Harry Arthur Hopf (1882–1949) was a

[52] Ibid., p. 663.

penniless emigrant to America who became a widely respected consultant, author, and executive.[53] Hopf began his career as a clerk in the office of a life insurance company and became acquainted with the ideas of Taylor, which were then in vogue. Hopf applied the principles of scientific management to office work and became more interested in efficiency and the scientific approach to work. He did studies of compensation methods for office workers and wondered why so little attention had been paid to the compensation of executives. In his studies of the problem, he was critical of the typical executive payment plans, such as profit sharing, stock options, and deferred payments. Hopf felt that these plans did not adequately tie payment to performance, which was a conclusion Taylor had reached about worker compensation some years before.

The conventional answer of Hopf's era was that executives did a "different" kind of work which was intangible and not subject to measurement. Not satisfied with that position, Hopf proposed principles and standards for measuring executive work in a manner which would link performance with pay.[54] Hopf felt all managers were judged (and should be rewarded) by the *results* they obtained. Some authors have suggested quite accurately that Hopf's work on measuring managerial performance antedated by some 20 years the concept of "management by objectives."[55] Indeed, Hopf had taken a giant step forward in measuring executive performance.

Hopf wrote of many ideas concerning the job of the manager: organizing work, the span of control, policies, coordination, and executive control, to name a few. None of these were as far-reaching, however, as his concept of "optimology." It was this idea that would take Hopf beyond Taylor's shop management in order to view the firm as a whole. Hopf defined the optimum as "that state of development of a business enterprise which tends to perpetuate an equilibrium between the factors of size, cost, and

---

[53] An outstanding treatment of Hopf is by Edmund R. Gray and Richard J. Vahl, "Harry Hopf: Management's Unheralded Giant," *The Southern Journal of Business*, Vol. 6, No. 2 (April, 1971), pp. 69–78.

[54] Harry Arthur Hopf, *Papers on Management* (2 vol.), Easton, Pa.: Hive Publishing Company, 1973, vol. I, pp. 267–286; vol. II, pp. 140–157, 169–174, and 231–245.

[55] Gray and Vahl, p. 74.

human capacity and thus to promote in the highest degree regular realization of the business objectives."[56] Hopf felt that business firms usually reversed the order of priority in fulfilling their societal role: the typical firm sought to maximize earnings and thereby serve society, while Hopf argued that the organization should serve society and thereby maximize earnings. He also felt that the goal of corporate growth was a *faux amis:* growth as a goal more often than not sacrificed one part to the whole, benefiting one party at the expense of another. Instead, the optimum would be a balancing of all factors and this could be done by a scientific approach based on measurement. Hopf's most significant contribution was that the scientific approach could be applied to the organization as a whole. In brief, Hopf's ideas had evolved from the application of scientific management to the office to a view of the total enterprise. Harry Hopf provided another step forward toward the top management viewpoint.

Analyzing Top Management

World War II mobilized vast productive capabilities and the postwar period found American enterprise trying to cope with the problems of managing operations on a larger scale than ever before. Top management faced greater responsibilities in determining common ends toward which efforts must be directed, in maintaining the coordination of functions, in relating growing and emerging activities brought about by new products, processes, and markets, and in harmonizing, measuring, and controlling the results of these efforts. It was toward these new responsibilities of top management that administrative analysts turned their attention. One pioneering work examined the top management of 31 "blue chip" companies for the purpose of compiling the state of the management art with respect to long-range planning and objectives, organization, staffing, and controlling. The authors found that only about half of their sample prepared detailed plans for periods up to a year in advance and that very few companies developed fully integrated systems of plans for the firm as a whole. Very few companies developed long-range objectives and the authors stated that "one of the greatest needs observed

[56] Hopf, vol. I, p. 91.

during the course of this study is for more adequate planning and clarification of future objectives, both near-term and long-range."[57] The authors traced this failing to inadequate organizational arrangements in which jurisdictions, responsibilities, and relationships were ill-defined, staff departments poorly conceived and coordinated, and in which committees, that bane of all organizational work, were poorly designed and used for the wrong tasks. In staffing, "many companies" left provisions for key management personnel development and succession "largely to providence."[58] Control practices brought little solace; only one-half of the companies studied used budgetary control as a means of planning and subsequently for measuring "over-all results of efforts."

It is difficult to evaluate the authors' findings since they failed to fully develop their own explanation of the discrepancy between apparently poor management practices on the one hand and success in the "blue chip" category on the other. The 31 companies sampled were studied for seven months and six months were taken for analysis. Perhaps such a short period of study explains the variance in that no long-range changes could be noted; or perhaps early war prosperity enabled successful performance regardless of managerial ability. Whatever the explanation, the Holden, Fish, and Smith report demonstrated increasing concern for a top management viewpoint with respect to objectives, planning, organization, staffing, and controlling.[59]

Executive leadership as a subject of analysis was appearing with increasing regularity during the 1940s. Professor Sune Carlson conducted an empirical study of executive communications and concluded that they occupied a major portion of the manager's time.[60] Stanford University's Robert A. Gordon presented a broader study of 155 larger corporations in which he focused on the direction and coordination of America's big business. Noting

[57] Paul E. Holden, Lounsbury S. Fish, and Hubert L. Smith, *Top Management Organization and Control,* Stanford, Calif.: Stanford University Press, 1941, p. 4.

[58] Ibid., pp. 6–8.

[59] In a more recent follow-up study of 15 leading corporations, many improvements in managerial practices were noted, especially with respect to long-range planning, executive development, and management information systems. See Paul E. Holden, Carlton A. Pederson, and Gayton E. Germane, *Top Management,* New York: McGraw-Hill Book Co., 1968.

[60] Sune Carlson, *Executive Behavior,* Stockholm, Sweden: Strombergs, 1951.

the separation of ownership and management of the large corporation and that many American industries were dominated by one or a few large firms, Gordon stressed the need for "professionalization" of management. The era of the entrepreneurial motive of profit from managing one's own investment had passed and the new era was one dominated by salaried managers hired by the board of directors. The result was a lessening of the profit motive in corporations, leading to inflexibility and bureaucracy in decision making.[61] Gordon saw dangers in this increased insulation of the decision makers from ownership, especially with respect to the establishment of a self-perpetuating oligarchy of an executive group which placed its own interests above the interests of stockholders and others whose welfare was involved. Gordon's answer to this corporate leadership dilemma was dynamic, professional executives who were responsive to the needs of the groups the organization served.

Jackson Martindell and Alvin Brown also sought the top management viewpoint characteristic of this era. Martindell formulated what was to become a continuing series of publications on appraising managerial competence in organizations.[62] Through his "management audit" approach, Martindell established criteria for the purposes of evaluating management practices. His criteria included: (1) the economic function of a company; (2) its organization structure; (3) the health of its earnings growth; (4) its practices with regard to fairness to stockholders; (5) its research and development practices; (6) its fiscal policies; (7) the value contributed by the board of directors; (8) the company's productive efficiency; (9) its sales organization; and (10) an evaluation of the executive abilities of the company. The method of evaluation consisted of allocating points for performance ratings in each of the 10 areas, summing these points for an overall evaluation, and then comparing the excellence of any particular company with the score obtained from companies in similar industries. While Martindell's techniques have been refined over the years, his approach was significant in that it sought to establish means for evaluating and

[61] Robert A. Gordon, *Business Leadership in the Large Corporation,* Washington, D.C.: The Brookings Institution, 1945.

[62] Jackson Martindell, *The Scientific Appraisal of Management,* New York: Harper and Row, 1950.

comparing overall company practices from a top management viewpoint.

Alvin Brown, an executive of the Johns-Mansville Corporation, was more organizationally oriented but also tried to weave in some administrative functions. Brown defined organization as a "means to more effective concerted endeavor" and thought that principles of organization were universally applicable to all types of human effort.[63] Brown identified 96 principles of organization, classifying them under headings such as purpose of organization, scope of organization, responsibility, delegation, authority, self-coordination, phases of administration, and so on. For instance, principle 9 was that "responsibility cannot be shared with another"; principle 25 read "authority includes all means necessary and proper for the performance of responsibility"; and the list continued to principle 96: "whereas organizational principle [i.e., theory] is a science, the practice of organization is an art." Brown was more concerned with organizational structure, viewing it as a means to more effective administration. Organization was the handmaiden of administration which consisted of the phases of *planning, doing,* and *seeing.* This administrative process was cyclical and overlapping in that planning was a mental process of anticipating and specifying activities, "doing" was the physical execution, and "seeing" was confirmation that planning and doing were consonant in contributing to organizational purposes. The organization structure was the body in which the planning, doing, and seeing phases came to life. Brown's ideas reflected the formalistic approach to organizations typical of others examined in this chapter. His search for a science of organizational principles, his classification of these principles, and his differentiation between organization and administration were a prelude to a search for management principles in succeeding eras.

Summary

Whereas the Mayoists sought greater productivity and satisfaction based on building social solidarity and collaboration, the individ-

[63] Alvin Brown, *Organization of Industry*, New York: Prentice-Hall, 1947, p. v. This book was an enlargement of his *Organization: A Formulation of Principle*, New York: Hibbert Printing Co., 1945. Alvin Brown was president of the Academy of Management in 1957.

uals examined in this chapter were more concerned with the proper structuring of activities and relationships in order to reach essentially the same ends. These "formalists" postulated that people worked better when they knew what was expected of them and that they would be more satisfied and productive under those conditions. Hence these "formalists" stressed organizational structure and design as a means to both employee satisfaction and organizational productivity. Their efforts were characterized by a search for *principles of organization* and eventually by the quest for broader *principles of administration.* Mooney and Reiley extricated rules of organization from history to increase organizational efficiency and thereby alleviate "human want and misery"; Henry Dennison built his structure from compatible work groups aimed toward flexible overall structures which would make work more satisfying; and Gulick, Urwick, Graicunas and others also tended toward formalizing relationships to reduce confusion and foster certainty and predictability. While this stress on organization structure and on management of production operations persisted for much of the period, Ralph C. Davis personified the shift in management thinking from the operative to the administrative viewpoint with his organic functions of management. Gulick and Urwick brought Henri Fayol to the fore and Urwick in turn attempted to synthesize administrative theory. Hopf applied the scientific approach to the study of the firm as a whole and others were displaying an increasing awareness of large-scale administrative problems in the 1940s. The stage was being set for a new focus on the functions of the manager.

17

Social Man and the Critics

The Hawthorne research did not inspire any investigating commission, congressional inquiry, nor any direct recriminations and strikes by organized labor. Mayo did not have his Hoxie, Senator Wilson or Redfield, nor any confrontations such as the Watertown Arsenal. Nevertheless, every thesis generates its own antithesis (as Hegel saw it) and the Mayoists have had their share of criticism.

Hawthorne Revisited

William H. Knowles reviewed the literature in 1958 and classified the criticisms of the human relations adherents under these categories: (1) their lack of scientific validity; (2) their overemphasis on the group; (3) their view of the nature of conflict; (4) their focus on group decision making; (5) their view of democracy; (6) their mysticism; (7) their evangelism; and (8) their methods of training for human relations skills.[1] Henry Landsberger performed for human relations the function that Horace B. Drury did for scientific management. Landsberger furnished an extensive list of critical reviews of *Management and the Worker* up to 1958 and put forth a defense of that work. Landsberger identified four separate areas of criticism: (1) the Mayoists' view of society as one characterized by anomie, social disorganization, and conflict; (2) their acceptance of management's views of the worker and management's "will-

[1] William H. Knowles, "Human Relations in Industry: Research and Concepts," *California Management Review*, Vol. 1, No. 1 (Fall, 1958); reprinted in S. G. Huneryager and I. L. Heckman (ed.), *Human Relations in Management* (2nd ed.), Cincinnati, Ohio: South-Western Publishing Co., 1967, pp. 31–58.

ingness to manipulate workers for management's ends"; (3) their failure to recognize other alternatives for accommodating industrial conflict, such as collective bargaining; and (4) their specific failure to take unions into account as a method of building social solidarity.[2] Since these reviews, more fuel has been added to the fire. The following analysis will build upon the work of Knowles and Landsberger by adding more recent criticisms and will combine the critical evaluations of "social man" into three broader conceptual categories: (1) the premises from which the Mayoists worked; (2) their methodology; and (3) their conclusions regarding the care and feeding of social man.

The Premises of Industrial Civilization

Mayo and Roethlisberger both began with a view of industrial society characterized by anomie. People, bound up in their obsessive-compulsive "pessimistic reveries," needed identification with others and constructive outlets for their latent fears and frustrations. Industrial civilization, though making giant strides in technological progress, had created a cultural lag by diminishing the importance of collaborative social skills. The Mayoists' response was to build from small group structures to a view of people in a larger social system. A number of critics have questioned these assumptions about the nature of industrial society and the Mayoists' view of social systems. Daniel Bell felt that the Harvard group lacked adequate basic hypotheses about the nature of the industrial system: "There is no view of the larger institutional framework of our economic systems within which these relationships arise and have their meaning."[3] Among the specific omissions, Bell cited changes in class structure with respect to an increase in white-collar and technical workers, a shift in technology which degraded the skilled worker and tended to replace the unskilled worker, and a leveling of jobs in which workers became largely semiskilled machine tenders. In short, the Mayoists viewed the firm as a closed social system and overlooked the im-

[2]Henry A. Landsberger, *Hawthorne Revisited*, Ithaca, N.Y.: Cornell Studies in Industrial and Labor Relations, Volume IX, Cornell University, 1958, pp. 29–30.

[3]Daniel Bell, "Exploring Factory Life," *Commentary*, January, 1947, p. 86.

pact of technological and economic changes which had a direct bearing upon the status of workers in the total industrial system.

Bell also charged that the Mayoists considered themselves "social engineers" who managed not people but a social system in an effort to "adjust" the worker so that the human equation fitted the industrial equation. Since pride in work and the satisfactions of craftmanship had been destroyed by the process of industrialization, the Mayoists felt that people must find their satisfactions in human association. Bell said that to think that contented workers were productive workers was to equate human behavior with "cow sociology," i.e., that contented cows give more milk.[4] Counseling at Hawthorne, for which Bell used the colorful phrase "ambulatory confessors," was to be the new method of controlling humans.[5] When employees exposed their innermost doubts and fears, they were more susceptible to managerial manipulation. The socially skilled supervisor could move from the use of authority to coerce humans to psychological persuasion for worker "manipulation as a means of exercising dominion."[6] Another facet of Bell's criticism was that the human relations style of supervision was to replace thinking about improving work itself. Social man, relieved of "pessimistic reveries" by the catharsis of counseling, would feel better and forget all of his other problems. Bell recalled a folktale to make this point:

> *A peasant complains to his priest that his little hut is horribly overcrowded. The priest advises him to move his cow into the house, the next week to take in his sheep, and the next week his horse. The peasant now complains even more bitterly about his lot. Then the priest advises him to let out the cow, the next week the sheep, and the next week the horse. At the end the peasant gratefully thanks the priest for lightening his burdensome life.*[7]

In short, Bell challenged what he perceived to be a basic premise of Mayoism—that the worker still was to be regarded as a

[4] Daniel Bell, *Work and Its Discontents: The Cult of Efficiency in America*, Boston: Beacon Press, 1956, p. 25.

[5] Ibid., p. 26. Professor Ghiselli also warned that employee counseling could be an "invasion of privacy." Individuals may reveal their innermost secrets to a psychiatrist, but not to their boss. Edwin E. Ghiselli, "Human Relations Revisited," *Public Personnel Review*, Vol. 21, No. 3 (July, 1960), pp. 193–198.

[6] Bell, *Work and Its Discontents*, p. 28.

[7] Ibid., p. 26.

means to an end of industrial productivity. The new means were social skills but the end was still manipulation of the worker. Instead of restoring pride in workmanship and allaying anomie, human relations substituted a catharsis for the worker rather than striking at the root of the problem, the nature of work itself. On this latter point, Bell's criticism has much merit.

Another attack on premises came from those who maintained that the Mayoists presented a naive view of societal conflict. According to these critics, the Mayoists assumed that a commonality of interests could be found between labor and management when in fact society was much more complex in terms of conflict between classes and interest groups. Some tensions and conflict were inevitable in every human situation and some may even be necessary. The goal should not be to eliminate conflict and tension but to provide healthy outlets for resolution.[8] The Mayoists' notion of a conflict-free state of equilibrium was a worthy goal but too idealistic for modern critics. The Mayoists, like the Taylorists, found faddists and perversions of their original intentions. The human relations cult which followed the original conception of man as a social being often concluded that the goal of their efforts was to keep everyone happy in a conflict-free state of equilibrium with resultant worker-management marital bliss. When bliss was attained, higher productivity was the corollary. As William Fox put it:

> *Among the guilty are the "human relationists" with an inadequate concept of human relations, who mistakenly preach participation, permissiveness, and democracy for all, and those employers who confuse popularity with managerial effectiveness and misinterpret the Golden Rule in dealing with their subordinates . . . Many mistakenly regard it [human relations] as an "end" toward which the organization shall endeavor rather than as what it should be—a "means" for achieving the organization's primary service objectives.*[9]

----

[8] Landsberger, pp. 30–35. See also Bernard Sarachek, "Elton Mayo's Social Psychology and Human Relations," *Academy of Management Journal*, Vol. 11, No. 2 (June, 1968), pp. 189–197.

[9] William M. Fox, "When Human Relations May Succeed and the Company Fail," *California Management Review*, Vol. 8, No. 3 (Spring, 1966), reprinted in Max S. Wortman and Fred Luthans (eds.), *Emerging Concepts in Management*, New York: Macmillan Co., 1969, p. 184.

According to Fox, the regard for human relations as an end rather than a means misled the manager to think that a conflict-free state and worker contentment would automatically lead to company success when in fact the company might fail. Human relations could not be substituted for well-defined goals, policies, high standards of performance, and other administrative functions which were necessary to organizational goal attainment.

In brief, the challenges to the basic premises of the Mayoists were: (1) that they displayed a lack of awareness of larger social and technological systems; (2) that they accepted a premise that the worker could be manipulated to fit into the industrial equation; (3) that they assumed that cooperation and collaboration were natural and desirable and thus overlooked more complex issues in societal conflict; and (4) that they confused means and ends in assuming that the goal of contentment and happiness would lead to harmonious equilibrium and organizational success.

The Research Methodology

The modern management researcher is much more sophisticated in statistics and research methodology than the group of men who entered the Western Electric plant in 1927. The bulk of human relations thought was based on relatively few studies, and these studies were full of intellectual pitfalls in the view of a more sophisticated audience.[10] References have already been made to the small samples upon which sweeping conclusions were reached and to the classic "Hawthorne effect" of biasing one's own results by observing and participating in the experiment. Industrial research is full of cracks and crevices and the researcher is pinioned between the need for the controlled experiments of a laboratory versus the empirical reality of ongoing activity. Seen in this light,

[10] Knowles, op. cit., pp. 45–46, said that the bulk of the literature on human relations had based its conclusions on primarily four sources: the original Hawthorne study, the Harwood Manufacturing Company, the Glacier Metal Company (English), and the University of Michigan Survey Research Center's comparative studies of the Prudential Life Insurance Company, the Detroit Edison Company, the Baltimore and Ohio Railroad, and the International Harvester Company. Knowles commented that the human relationists "got a lot of mileage" out of these studies; ibid., p. 46.

one can forgive the human relations researchers some of their peccadilloes but not all of them.

The issue of the Mayoists' conclusions regarding human motivation is particularly pressing. William Foote Whyte concluded that Elton Mayo destroyed the orthodox theory of the economic motivation of workers.[11] Alex Carey of the University of New South Wales has used data from Roethlisberger, Dickson, and T. N. Whitehead to challenge whether or not this was true.[12] For purposes of review without repeating too much of the discussion in chapter 13, the original experiments took a small group of female relay assemblers and subjected them to various changes in working conditions, including a new incentive scheme and a "new" supervisor (observer). Output increased but the Harvard researchers wanted to isolate the cause in order to test their five hypotheses regarding the puzzling results. They formed a second relay assembly group which was to be placed on a new incentive plan and a group of mica splitters who would have new supervision but who would retain their old individual incentive plan. In the second relay group, output rose 12.6 percent but the experiment was abandoned at the end of nine weeks because other workers who were not in the experiment wanted to go on the same individual incentive scheme as the experimental group. After the incentive plan was abandoned, output dropped 16 percent. However, the researchers rejected economic incentives as the explanation of these variations in output by saying: ". . . it is difficult to conclude whether the increase in output was an immediate response to the change in wage incentive or was merely representative of the top level of a more or less upward swing [in output]."[13]

The mica splitters were already on individual incentives. This scheme was retained but all the changes introduced in the original experiments, such as new supervision, separate rooms,

[11] W. F. Whyte, "Human Relations Theory—A Progress Report," *Harvard Business Review*, Vol. 34, No. 5 (September–October, 1956), pp. 125–132.

[12] Alex Carey, "The Hawthorne Studies: A Radical Criticism," *American Sociological Review*, Vol. 32, No. 3 (June, 1967), pp. 403–416. A similar criticism is by A. J. M. Sykes, "Economic Interest and the Hawthorne Researchers," *Human Relations*, Vol. 18 (1965).

[13] F. J. Roethlisberger and W. J. Dickson, *Management and the Worker*, Cambridge, Mass.: Harvard University Press, 1939, p. 133.

shortening of hours, and rest pauses, were made in the mica group. Thus the only variable held constant in the mica splitters experiment was the individual incentive scheme. Average hourly output rose 15.6 percent over a period of 14 months among the mica splitters.[14] Since the incentive scheme had not been changed, the researchers concluded that it was supervision and not wages that caused the increase. On this point, Carey demurred by noting that the researchers changed their methods of reporting increases in output. In both relay assembly group experiments, both "average hourly output" and "increase in total output" had been used to describe results. However, in the mica-splitting experiment, *only* "average hourly output" was used. If "total output" had been used in measuring mica-splitting results, the outcome would have been zero or less because output per hour went up 15.6 percent while the weekly hours worked decreased by 17 percent from 55½ to 46½.[15] In effect, Carey's point was that total output was constant (or less) and that the new supervision and other changes had no effect since the old individual scheme was retained. By changing their measurement base, the researchers had shown an increase in output due to the "new supervision" when in fact there had been no increase in total output.

To capsulize Carey's comparison of the three experiments: (1) in the original relay assembly experiments a piecework incentive was introduced and total hours decreased 4.7 percent from beginning to end and total output was up 30 percent; (2) in the second relay group total output rose 12.6 percent under the individual incentive but fell 16 percent when the incentive scheme was abandoned; and (3) among the mica splitters, incentives were held constant, hours were reduced, and there was no increase and perhaps even a decrease in total output. Hence Carey concluded that it was completely erroneous for the Harvard group to decide that wages were not a variable and that it was spurious research methodology to change the way of computing and reporting increases in output.[16]

Carey also chastised the researchers for their claims of

[14] Ibid., p. 148, Table XV.
[15] Carey, p. 408. Cf. Roethlisberger and Dickson, pp. 136–139.
[16] Carey, p. 410.

"friendly supervision." First, the group selected "cooperative" workers who were willing to participate in the experiments. Second, two workers from the original group began causing some problems and "were removed for a lack of cooperation, which would have otherwise necessitated greatly increased disciplinary measures."[17] After reviewing production records, Carey concluded that output did not increase until the two girls were dismissed and two "more cooperative" ones were added to the original group.[18] Was this "friendly supervision" or the old-time use of negative sanctions to increase output?

Carey, having available a number of years of hindsight and a more sophisticated understanding of research methodology, has aimed a number of damaging charges at the conduct of the Hawthorne experiments. He considered the whole study to be "worthless," not only because of the manipulation of data, the rejection of economic incentives as a possible explanation, and the use of dismissals to get added productivity, but also because of a number of other points: (1) that the samples in all cases were extremely small and that no further attempts were made to increase sample size; (2) that no attempts were made to correlate output records of girls not in the experiment with those who were; and (3) that statistically reliable results were not obtainable from a sample of five, thus making generalization very tenuous. Carey maintained that the Hawthorne experiments were really consistent with the old view of economic incentives and the use of a firm hand in discipline in order to get higher output.

Peter Drucker, though not using the statistical, research methodological approach of Carey, also criticized the human relationists for their lack of "any awareness of the economic dimension."[19] In concluding that people were motivated by social and psychological satisfactions, the Harvard group lost sight of the whole person. They neglected the nature of work itself, focused instead on interpersonal relations, and thereby failed to find

---

[17] T. N. Whitehead, *The Industrial Worker*, (vol. I), Cambridge, Mass.: Harvard University Press, 1938, p. 118. In *The Human Problems of an Industrial Civilization*, Mayo said they "dropped out" (p. 56); cf. Carey, p. 411.

[18] Carey, p. 415.

[19] Peter Drucker, *The Practice of Management*, New York: Harper and Row, 1954, p. 279.

that people derived satisfactions from more than their social relationships.

In defense of the Hawthorne experimenters, Shepard has indicated that Carey overstated his case, in some instances supported the researchers' findings which he had criticized, and was wrong in rejecting the results of the Western Electric studies. Shepard maintained that Roethlisberger and Dickson's intent was to place monetary incentives in their proper perspective, i.e., as "carriers of social value."[20] Perhaps so, but many followers of the human relationists did not see this subtlety and this led to a rejection of economic motivators. Many of Carey's other criticisms remain unchallenged and, though critics often overstate their case, he served to bring new questions to some old findings.

Conclusions Regarding Social Man

Does everyone desire to participate in decision making, in group "games," and want to feel the comfort of security through belonging? Robert N. McMurry has maintained that "democratic management runs counter to human nature."[21] Some people prefer regimentation and are unwilling or unable to make positive contributions. Further, McMurry regarded group decision making as an illusion in which the autocracy of the group may be substituted for the autocracy of an individual. Group decisions stimulate individuals' dependency on the group and lead to conformity through denials of their own perceptions of reality because of a desire to conform to group pressures. In the interests of group harmony, disagreement may be stifled, thus reducing organizational innovation and progress. William H. Whyte has also decried the exaltation of the group to the detriment of the individual. For Whyte, the ethic of social man had its roots in three forms: (1) "scientism"; (2) "togetherness"; and (3) "belongingness." Whyte's criticisms were aimed at these three points: first, that advocates of the social ethic sought a science of man such as that available in the physical sciences; second, that the Mayoists

---

[20]Jon M. Shepard, "On Alex Carey's Radical Criticism of the Hawthorne Studies," *Academy of Management Journal,* Vol. 14, No. 1 (March, 1971), pp. 23–32.

[21]Robert N. McMurry, "The Case for Benevolent Autocracy," *Harvard Business Review,* Vol. 36, No. 1 (January–February, 1958), p. 85.

sought to rebuild modern society along the same social bonds that were apparent in primitive societies; and finally, that the group was superior to the individual and all problems could be solved through collective efforts.[22] Consensus would replace creativity.

For Malcolm P. McNair, to speak of developing supervisory "human relations skills" often meant a "cold-blooded connotation of proficiency, technical expertness, calculated effect."[23] This danger of treating people with the same developed skills as one would develop for handling a machine reflected the idea of a cult of "people efficiency." McNair's indictment of the human relations approach was built around four themes: (1) that it ". . . encourages people to feel sorry for themselves, makes it easier to slough off responsibility, to find excuses for failure, to act like children"; (2) that it sapped individual responsibility by playing down the virtues of self-discipline, will power, and self-control; (3) that it emphasized keeping everyone happy, which resulted in conformity to group wishes and desires; and (4) that it developed a "one-sided" concept of the executive job. The executive needed more than "listening" and human relations skills to be effective in accomplishing organizational goals. In teaching human relations as a separate skill, McNair saw the dangers of compartmentalizing knowledge when in fact it should become an integral part of all managerial development, whether in marketing, management, or whatever. In essence, McNair concluded: "It is not that the human relations concept is wrong; it is simply that we have blown it up too big and have placed too much emphasis on teaching human relations as such at the collegiate and early graduate level . . . Let's treat people like people, but let's not make a big production of it."[24]

Many critics called for a better mix of managerial skills but one which would avoid the "evangelism" and the "mysticism" which so often characterized human relations training. Evangelism represented a thesis that only human relations could "save

---

[22] William H. Whyte, Jr., *The Organization Man*, Garden City, N.Y.: Doubleday & Co., 1956, p. 26, p. 40, passim.

[23] Malcolm P. McNair, "Thinking Ahead: What Price Human Relations?," *Harvard Business Review*, Vol. 35, No. 2 (March–April, 1957), pp. 15–23.

[24] Ibid., p. 23.

Western Civilization from impending doom."[25] The doom theme was an old one, having its roots in the revulsion of the Romantic philosophers at the perceived ravages of the Industrial Revolution. For social philosophers such as Durkheim, Mayo, and Toynbee, advancing technology and the specialization of labor destroyed social cohesiveness and yielded a loss of pride in work for mankind. Increased interpersonal competition and concern for material things destroyed primary groups, caused status anxiety, and created obsessive-compulsive reactions. The answer to "impending doom" was an evangelical zeal by the human relationists to play down material acquisitiveness, to rebuild primary groups, and to teach people to love other people once more. The world could be saved by belongingness and man could once more find himself by losing himself in some larger entity. This mystical overtone, reflecting the Gestalt psychology of the totality, attributed wisdom to groups which could not be found in individuals. It was not the logic of efficiency but the ill-logic of sentiments which would save people from the brink. The moral uplift of scientific management had been efficiency; for the human relationists, it was belongingness and solidarity.

The Mayoists were also placed under fire for a "promanagement antilabor bias." According to the critics, it was not man but management that the Mayoists sought to save. For example, Mary Barnett Gilson noted that:

> In all the more than six hundred pages describing the Western Electric experiments, costing hundreds of thousands of dollars and supported by some of the wealthiest groups of this country, no reference is made to organized labor except a short statement, unindexed, that it was so seldom mentioned by any workers that it was not considered sufficiently important to discuss . . .[26]

While it is true that the Mayoists made no reference to the role of organized labor, it would be unfair to conclude that this constituted an antilabor bias. It was labor, the worker, who was the cen-

---

[25]Knowles, p. 52.

[26]M. B. Gilson, "Review of Management and the Worker," *American Journal of Sociology*, July, 1940, p. 101. See also Harold L. Sheppard, "The Treatment of Unionism in 'Managerial Sociology'," *American Sociological Review*, April, 1949, pp. 310–313.

ter of their concern when they called for the application of human relations skills.

The Critics: A Final Note

The multitude of criticisms against the Mayoist-human relations axis have been conceptualized into attacks on their premises, their methodology, and their conclusions regarding the nature and nurture of social man. In defense of the movement, Landsberger indicated that the Mayoists were much less dogmatic than the critics maintained and that they realized any conclusions "would bear the stamp of human imperfection."[27] According to Landsberger, the critics' attacks should have been directed toward those individuals and groups who seized upon the infant theories of human relations and attempted to fashion out of them "cookbook" techniques for management's handling of people. If this defense sounds familiar, it should; the Hoxie report noted that managers in practice grasped the techniques but not the philosophy of scientific management. Likewise, human relations as *the* means to avoid impending social, political, and industrial doom led to evangelic, missionary exhortations about "getting along with people." The results were frequently insincere, often abortive, and derisive terms like calling the human relationists "the happiness boys" were the result.

In response to the promanagement-antilabor bias, Landsberger noted that the lag between the conduct of the interviews (1927–1932), and their publication (1939), explained the omission of unions. While *Management and the Worker* and the writings of Mayo omitted unions, Landsberger concluded that this did not automatically make them promanagement and antiunion. With respect to the omission of monetary incentives, Landsberger defended the researchers, as Shepard has, by stating that they did not omit them but instead held that wages were carriers of social value which should be viewed as only one aspect of a larger social phenomenon. In sum, Landsberger would conclude that the Hawthorne researchers were "not guilty," though they made their share of blunders, of most of the challenges of the critics. More serious challenges have been leveled since Landsberger's defense,

[27]Landsberger, p. 49.

especially the Carey analysis, and these pilgrimages to Hawthorne have served to bring a better perspective to the past.[28]

Summary

The critics have questioned a number of facets of the philosophy as well as the practice of the human relations-social man thesis. These were discussed in terms of attacks upon the premises, the methodology, and the conclusions regarding industrial man. The premises of Mayo and his associates were largely a product of the times, as we shall see in the next chapter. The methodology has only more recently been challenged and certainly leaves some doubt in terms of our modern insistence upon more rigorous research methods. However, the state of statistical knowledge at the time of the original experiments was rudimentary at best and we must recognize this state of the arts before issuing a wholesale indictment. In spite of all the limitations and shortsightedness, the Hawthorne experiments did signal a new direction in management thought. The experiments stimulated research, discussion, and a reexamination of managerial premises. In its time, the human relations movement witnessed all of the malpractices and misinterpretations to which any new idea usually falls prey. Today, the apogee of the movement has passed as the very research it stimulated is bringing fresh insights into human behavior.

---

[28] A more recent pilgrimage celebrated the 50th anniversary of the Hawthorne studies. See: Eugene L. Cass and Frederick G. Zimmer (eds.), *Man and Work in Society*, New York: Van Nostrand Reinhold Company, 1975.

18

Social Man in Retrospect

The ideas of individuals in the context of their times form an interesting topic for historical discussion. Within its cultural context, scientific management as the gospel of efficiency found its basis in the economic necessities of large-scale corporate organizations, in the social sanction of individual achievement and the moral uplift of efficiency, and in political concern for national productivity and the conservation of resources. What can be said of the era from the advent of the Hawthorne experiments to the early 1950s? It has been postulated that management thought forms a more coherent picture when viewed in its changing cultural milieu of economic, social and political forces. Management is both a process in and a product of its environment. The social man era was an age of individual hopes dashed on the reefs of economic misfortune, of social collisions and maladies, and of political shifts heralding a transformation in traditional relationships. Though treated independently below, these cultural facets interacted to form the cultural milieu of social man.

The Economic Environment: From Depression to Prosperity

The "great crash" of 1929 found the winter of its discontent in earlier days. The 1920s were prosperous, characterized by price stability, a doubling of industrial productivity, and a 55 percent rise in the real income of individuals.[1] Industrial efficiency and mass production technology were holding costs down and increasing the purchasing power of the dollar. On the human front, economic and political chauvinism led to restrictions on immigration, largely at the behest of organized labor. Quotas were established for various nationalities and sources of cheap labor began to evaporate. As an economic corollary to the emerging political withdrawal and isolationism, America turned to protection tariffs with the Fordney-McCumber Tariff of 1922. For a short time, this protection afforded American industry and agriculture a respite from the rigors of competition. In the long run, American productive capacity began to outrun its ability to consume and, with foreign markets relatively closed, pressures began to build which would lead to corporate mergers and to excessive speculation. Installment buying and easy credit, though intended to stimulate consumption to take up the productive slack, instead increased personal indebtedness to a dangerously high level.

The 1920s also saw a wave of business consolidations. Antitrust legislation and presidential activists had slowed the growth of trusts, pools, and holding companies but the postwar period saw a tripling in the rate of mining and manufacturing mergers. By 1925, the 16 principal holding companies in the electrical energy field held 53 percent of the nation's electrical productive capacity. Individuals like Samuel Insull were pyramiding company on company, borrowing and reborrowing on the resultant leverage.[2] Corporations with over $80 million in assets controlled 80 percent of the assets of stocks of corporations regularly traded on the New York Stock Exchange. In 1927, the 200 largest nonfinancial corporations controlled over 45 percent of the assets of all nonfinancial corporations.[3] According to Burns, the growth of giant enterprise led to a decline in the number of sellers, to a con-

---

[1] David N. Alloway, *Economic History of the United States*, New York: Monarch Press, 1966, p. 29.

[2] An interesting account of the use of holding companies and their rise and downfall is Forrest McDonald, *Insull*, Chicago: University of Chicago Press, 1962.

[3] Gardiner C. Means, "The Growth in the Relative Importance of the Large Corporation in American Economic Life," *American Economic Review*, Vol. 21 (1931), pp. 10–42.

centration of economic power in the hands of the few, and to a decline in competition.[4] This scramble for size to gain efficiencies of scale led to more consolidations, and big business was becoming Big Business. The public wanted a piece of this dynamic growth, money was cheap, margin requirements were low, and it was this orgy of speculation that led to Black Friday, October 24, 1929. On that day, the stock market fell 40 points and wiped out $30 billion worth of inflated stock values.

For more than a decade following, all of American life was to be substantially changed by that crash which preceded the Great Depression. In 1929, 48 million persons were employed and the unemployment rate was 3.2 percent. By 1933, 30 percent of the nation's workers were without jobs.[5] Businesses were failing, unemployment rampant, incomes dropping, homes lost, family savings wiped out, and worst of all, national morale was at an all-time low. Gone was the optimism of prosperity and promise; the old guideposts apparently had failed as "rags to riches" became the midnight pumpkin. Perhaps it was not the economic depression but the psychological one which left the lasting imprint on our forefathers.[6] Recovery from the economic morass was painfully slow, but from the social and psychological viewpoint, it was even slower. Feeling inept in adjusting to economic deprivation, people turned to the government for relief.

Attempts at Economic Recovery

The new political regime of Franklin Roosevelt promised freedom from fear, from want, and the other fears that bound America. President Hoover had tried the Reconstruction Finance Corporation in 1932 as a scheme to pump government funds into private business enterprise. President Roosevelt went much further with the "New Economics" of John Maynard Keynes. Keynesian economics was a challenge to the Protestant ethic dogma of thrift; Keynes held that savings which were withheld from consumption

---

[4] Arthur Robert Burns, *The Decline of Competition*, New York: McGraw-Hill Book Co., 1936.

[5] Lloyd G. Reynolds, *Labor Economics and Labor Relations*, 4th ed., Englewood Cliffs, N.J.: Prentice-Hall, 1964, p. 339.

[6] See Caroline Bird, *The Invisible Scar*, New York: David McKay Co., 1966.

could lead to dislocation and underutilization of economic resources. Therefore the federal government should intervene and
"prime" the pump to stimulate consumption and to provide for
economic recovery. This new capitalism was also designed to destroy the financial control of Wall Street, to link government assistance with industrial capitalism, to aid agriculture and small business in the Progressive tradition, and to increase benefits to the
workers who formed the chief electorate.

While Keynesians would hold that economic stimulation
through government spending contributed to recovery, the
Friedmanites have maintained that proper monetary action by the
Federal Reserve could have prevented contraction of the money
supply and allayed the Depression.[7] Robert Heilbroner concluded
that World War II was the factor that really pulled America from
its economic doldrums, not government pump-priming.[8] Economists may fuss and fume about proper remedial actions but in
reality "what might have been" is a matter for other historians.
The fact for management was that the government did become increasingly involved in economic life; though capitalism was preserved, with ownership and management remaining in the hands
of private individuals, control and policy guidelines became more
and more lodged in the hands of the dominant political party. The
new concept of the corporation tied it more closely than ever before to the public interest with concomitant calls for "economic
statesmanship" on the part of business leaders and for public regulation of corporate concentrations of power.

The Grass Roots and
Bottom Up Movement

Economically it was to be the age of the "little man," the farmer,
the worker, the small businessman, the unemployed, the hungry,
and all others who were the waifs of economic misfortune. Somehow it was Wall Street and Big Business who were considered the
primary contributors to the ills of the economy. Economic policy

[7]Milton Friedman and Anna J. Schwartz, *The Great Contraction: 1929–1933*, Princeton, N.J.: Princeton University Press, 1965.

[8]Robert Heilbroner, *The Making of Economic Society*, Englewood Cliffs, N.J.:
Prentice-Hall, 1962, p. 167.

was to be from the "grass-roots" up in aiding the little man to counterbalance the concentration of power in Big Business. People were concerned that there was an economic elite and sought to democratize industry, to reduce power differentials, and to restore the influence of those at the base of the pyramid. Berle and Means noted the separation of ownership and management and pointed out that control was passing from the hands of owners to the hands of a select body of top corporate managers whose decisions affected the entire economy.[9] Kenneth Boulding warned of the moral dilemma caused by the conflict between the industrial aristocracy of a hierarchy of authority with the democratic ideal of equality.[10] James Burnham foresaw that managers would become an elite ruling class in a "managerial society."[11]

For management scholars, the little man movement found its expression in "bottom up management," "multiple management," and participative leadership. The Mayoists saw the root of economic problems in social problems. For them, people's anomie was made manifest in pessimistic reveries, in obsessive-compulsive behavior, in the turning inward of groups to protect themselves from management, and in the expressed needs of the workers to find social satisfactions on the job. Once social solidarity was restored, primary groups rebuilt, communications channels opened, and social and psychological needs fulfilled, people could turn their efforts to being more productive. Follett would certainly support this thesis in her call for depersonalizing authority, for integration, and for enlightened leadership. Barnard indicated that an organization had to be efficient in terms of satisfying individual and group needs in order to be effective in meeting organizational goals. Cooperation was a reciprocal process for both management and the worker. From the "people and organizations" point of view, industrial problems were to be solved by democratizing the workplace and thereby improving human relationships within the organization.

[9] Adolf A. Berle, Jr., and Gardiner C. Means, *The Modern Corporation and Private Property*, New York: MacMillan Company, 1947.

[10] Kenneth E. Boulding, *The Organizational Revolution: A Study of the Ethics of Economic Organization*, New York: Harper and Row, 1953.

[11] James Burnham, *The Managerial Revolution*, New York: John Day Co., 1941.

Organization as the Answer

Whereas managerial concern for administrative structures to rationalize resource utilization dominated the first three decades of the twentieth century, industrial attention in the 1930s was primarily on survival. For Mooney and Reiley, Brown, Gulick, Urwick, and others of the organizational bent, the solution resided in the proper, orderly arrangement of formal relationships. People, preferring order and certainty, would function better within a well-structured system and management could better insure economic survival through the practice of sound organizational principles. In their cultural context, those who focused on people and those who focused on the organization were attempting to cope with the massive social and industrial dislocations presented by the Depression.

The Depression delayed the development of any growth which would have moved industry into phase III of Chandler's framework. Reduced sales and the general contraction in activity postponed any enlargement or elaboration of structures. However, the presence of excess productive capacity did stimulate interest in product diversification.[12] The advent of the war required industrial conversion to military production, and the postwar reconversion finally shifted the bulk of American industry into phase III. Mobilization for the war effort had created both technological and managerial advancements. Vast productive resources had been gathered, training within industry had created a deeper pool of managerial talent, consumer products had been rationed, worker earnings were high, and the postwar era found America with a pent-up demand for products and services. With demand outrunning productive ability, America did not experience the anticipated postwar business slumps. The war had created new products, new technologies, new markets and more highly skilled, broader-based labor force. Management thought was in transition in this era and the shift was from a production orientation to a top management viewpoint, which called for a changed executive role in balancing and coping with larger-scale enterprises and markets.

---

[12] Alfred Chandler, Jr., *Strategy and Structure*, Cambridge, Mass.: MIT Press, 1962, p. 44.

Managers were seeking a broader, more flexible conceptual framework, a process of action upon which they could build for a more dynamic interplay of inputs and outputs. The work of R. C. Davis was cited previously to show this transition in thought; Henri Fayol was awaiting rediscovery, and others were writing with more emphasis on top management.

The postwar period promised a new era of prosperity, expansion, and diversification. The regained prosperity and the further growth of industry was to create a new focus in evolving management thought.

The Social Environment: From Babbitt to the Organization Man

The economic temper of the times most certainly shaped the social values which came to dominate the period under analysis. Attitudes and aspirations are the founts of human strength, and the crushing economic burden for many was a violation of the previously held precepts of abundance and success for Everyman. The 1920s had brought Madison Avenue to Peoria and Dubuque, and American productive ability and salesmanship presaged more than a car in every garage and a chicken in every pot. What happened to social relationships and the assumptions which guided people's behavior in the troubled 1930s? Broadly viewed, two fairly distinct paths were reshaping social values: (1) a decline of the tenets of the Protestant ethic and the rise of a "social ethic"; and (2) a decline in the level of esteem given the businessman.

Shifting Social Values

The Lynds, in their famous study of the "typical" American city of the late 1920s, found a split in values between the "working class" man and the white-collar man. For the worker, economic motives appeared to be primary:

> This dominance of the dollar appears in the apparently growing tendency among younger working class men to swap a problematic future for immediate "big money." [13]

[13]Robert S. Lynd and Helen M. Lynd, *Middletown: A Study in Contemporary American Culture*, New York: Harcourt Brace Jovanovich, 1929, p. 81.

While the workers measured social status by financial status and tended to hold to the traditional virtues of individualism, including a declining interest in belonging to organized labor, the businessmen represented a different outlook. The Lynds noted a decline in individualism among businessmen and a rapidly increasing conformity and "need to belong." In their follow-up study, made during the Depression, the Lynds found that "the insecurity during the depression has brought with it greater insistence upon conformity and a sharpening of latent issues."[14] Workers were turning to unions for collective action and businessmen combined to maintain the "open shop"; these "latent issues" sharpened class distinctions and engendered social bitterness. The economic catastrophe had brought about a shift in social values for the worker as well as the manager.

After the crash, of what value were the time-tested Protestant ethic virtues of thrift and hard work? Apparently nearly everyone had been affected in some way, the loss of a job here, a savings account there, or a friend who had lost his shirt in the market. The new consciousness was that the disaster had struck the virtuous as well as the prodigals, the tycoon as well as the tyro, and the energetic as well as the feckless. People found their own fortunes intertwined with that of others in a pattern not subject to reason or justice. As time went on,

> . . . there was a continuing disposition among Americans young and old to look with a cynical eye upon the old Horatio Alger formula for success; to be dubious about taking chances for ambition's sake; to look with a favorable eye upon a safe if unadventurous job, social insurance plans, pension plans . . . They had learned from bitter experience to crave security.[15]

This craving for security, this turning inward of people to others who shared the same tribulations, marked that generation as well as their children, and even perhaps another generation or more. Perhaps people have a natural reaction to form groups when faced with threatening circumstances—when these circumstances assume a major cultural impact, such as a depression, then people become more and more group beings. The presence of oth-

---

[14] Robert S. Lynd and Helen M. Lynd, *Middletown in Transition: A Study in Cultural Conflicts,* New York: Harcourt Brace Jovanovich, 1937, p. 427.

[15] Frederick Lewis Allen, *The Big Change,* New York: Harper and Row, 1952, p. 132.

ers must offer some psychological sense of relief under threatening or frustrating conditions. Erich Fromm has also noted this desire of people to escape the loneliness of standing alone. In Fascist Germany, to escape this loneliness, people turned to an authoritarian regime which made their decisions for them and which gave them a sense of identity, however evil it might have been. According to Fromm, this "need to belong" also pervaded American industrial life and an individual more frequently than not would be willing to give up self to conform to the group. While the Reformation and the Industrial Revolution drove people from the security of medieval life, enabling them to find freedom in the spiritual, political, and economic spheres of life, industrialization created new threats to these new-found freedoms.[16] People felt alone in the individualism of capitalism and the Protestant ethic, and needed something larger than themselves, God, the Nation, the Company, the Union, or Something with which to identify and lose self.

The conditions of the troubled 1930s must have compounded this desire for group affiliation as a source of strength. McClelland found in his studies that the need for achievement had increased in America from 1800 to 1890 but had decreased regularly since that date. The trade-off between the need for affiliation and the need for achievement took a dramatic shift from 1925 to 1950. In 1925, the need for affiliation was primarily a familial concern; by 1950, affiliation had become an *alternative* concern for economic achievement.[17] By 1950 Americans were showing more concern for affiliative relationships and less concern for achievement.[18]

David Riesman and his associates have furnished additional evidence for this era by noting the shift from the "inner-directed" to the "other-directed" man. The inner-directed man represented the era of *laissez-faire* capitalism, the Protestant ethic, and emphasized self-direction and control. The "other-directed" man was characterized by high social mobility, emphasis on consumption

[16] Erich Fromm, *Escape from Freedom*, New York: Holt, Rinehart and Winston, 1941, pp. 7–10.

[17] David C. McClelland, *The Achieving Society*, New York: Van Nostrand Reinhold Co., 1961, p. 167.

[18] Ibid., p. 166; and McClelland's "Business Drive and National Achievement," *Harvard Business Review*, Vol. 40, No. 4 (July–August, 1962), p. 110.

rather than production, and on getting along and being accepted by others as the magic key to accomplishment.[19] Riesman would call the Taylor period "job minded" and the other-directed man of the Mayoist era, "people-minded."[20]

For Riesman, the shift from the "invisible hand to glad hand" actually began about 1900. Up until that time *laissez-faire* and the utilitarian philosophy of individualism had been the dominant force. After 1900, the closing of the frontier and restrictions on immigration began to bring less confidence in self-interest and a rise in confidence in "groupism."[21] The inner-directed man persisted for a period after 1900 but individuals began to feel more lonely in the crowd. People had to live where they were and were unable to move to a new frontier and to use the West as a safety valve. Most of the pressing problems of production began to disappear, and the problems of consumption became more apparent. Inner-directed individuals had to cope with a niggardly material environment; the new problems which arose following relative conquest of a hostile material environment were problems with people. Entrepreneurs could deal face-to-face with most of their employees—they knew them, their problems, their likes and dislikes. Growth made industry less personal, replacing the personal style of the entrepreneur with the bureaucratic style of the administrator. The personal touch of leadership was gone, only to be replaced with the directives from the technically trained specialists that an advanced industrial nation required. Social competence, the manipulation of people, began to assume a new importance, and technical skills were played down.

Individual loneliness in the organizational crowd led to the rise of "groupism" and social man. Progressive education began fitting the child to the group in the socialization process, and the parental socialization function was replaced by peer socialization. Small groups became the panacea for individual adjustment to the loneliness of industrialization. Getting along and being accepted was the magic key to accomplishment. People were judged by

[19] David Riesman, Nathan Glazer, and Reuel Denney, *The Lonely Crowd*, New Haven, Conn.: Yale University Press, 1950, pp. 19–40.

[20] Ibid., p. 151.

[21] Ibid., pp. 151–152; and David Riesman, *Individualism Reconsidered*, New York: Free Press, 1954, p. 31.

what others thought of them, not what they thought of themselves. The psychological gyroscope of inner-directed man began to waver and now needed the helping North Star of others.

The "Confusion of Souls"

Industrialization had not made people less religious but they found they could more easily segment their lives into religious and nonreligious duties. When God smiled on the division of labor, thrift, and success, people found a comfort in combining secular drives with spiritual grace. For one authority, the Depression caused a "confusion of souls" and a crisis for the Protestant ethic.[22] Self-help had failed and the notion of self-made man was rejected as the guarantee of economic order. Charity became a public rather than a private concern, and the power for the individual of the Protestant gospel of success fell into disfavor. Out of this confusion of souls and the debris of *laissez-faire*, the moral order needed to take on new dimensions. On the one hand there was the "mind cure" approach offered by Norman Vincent Peale in *The Power of Positive Thinking;* on the other hand, the "getting along" cure of Dale Carnegie. Peale advised seeking the "inner power" of Christianity to cope with stress and crises. This turning inward helped people escape their loneliness and malaise by drawing upon the greater power of God.

Carnegie established the personal-magnetism ethic in 1936 with his *How to Win Friends and Influence People.*[23] This book, replete with "how-tos" of human relations, advised that the path to success resided in: (1) making others feel important through a sincere appreciation of their efforts; (2) making a good first impression; (3) winning people to your way of thinking by letting others do the talking, being sympathetic and "never tell a man he is wrong"; and (4) changing people by praising of good traits and giving the offender the opportunity to save face. Although *Management and the Worker* had not been published at that time, the

[22] Donald Meyer, *The Positive Thinkers: A Study of the American Quest for Health, Wealth and Personal Power from Mary Baker Eddy to Norman Vincent Peale,* Garden City, N.Y.: Doubleday & Co., 1965, pp. 233–237.

[23] Dale Carnegie, *How to Win Friends and Influence People,* New York: Simon and Schuster, 1936. Dale Carnegie was founder and president of the Dale Carnegie Institute of Effective Speaking and Human Relations.

Carnegie formula bore a striking resemblance to the rules the Harvard researchers laid down for the counselors in the interviewing program. For Carnegie the way to success was through winning the cooperation of others.

These "positive thinkers" stressed two ways out of the "confusion of souls": (1) drawing on the inward power of faith; and (2) drawing personal strength by winning the cooperation of others through personal magnetism. The social ethic of the times played down achievement by individual striving because the Protestant ethic had run its course. This new ethic was "others"-oriented with moral uplift coming not from efficiency but from getting along with others. For the most part, social man was sired, born, and nurtured in these trying times. People sought belonging in the group, solace in association, and fulfillment in affiliation.

The Social Ethic

A second facet of this attempt to understand social man and his times must come through an analysis of the changing societal views toward the businessman and the manager. The businessman as represented in fiction may or may not be a barometer of his social esteem. Robert Kavesh has warned that the fictional businessman is generally portrayed in an unrealistic manner.[24] This is because of the writer's need to dramatize in contrasts and to gain sympathy for characters. While it would be impossible to hold the businessman to blame for the Depression era's hard times, it was evident that he became through fictional writings the *symbol* of society's ills. The 1920s had canonized the businessman as hero and symbol of prosperity and the good life; when times turned turbulent, was it not fair to heap the blame on the "bankster" who robbed people of their homes and savings? While such charges were not entirely just, the businessman as portrayed in fiction undoubtedly became a convenient focal point for public wrath.

William G. Scott has noted that the novels of the 1930s and

[24]Robert A. Kavesh, *Businessmen in Fiction*, Hanover, N.H.: Amos Tuck School of Business Administration, 1955, p. 11. An exception that he noted, however, was Cameron Hawley's *Executive Suite*.

1940s were of disillusionment with individualism. Individualism became futile and the novelists shifted the keynote to pleas for "humanitarianism and collectivism in the form of proletarian fiction."[25] The "hero" vanished to be replaced by a "they" who did things without reason and were beyond the control of mere mortals. "They" represented power, machines, and forces, not individual managers whom one could hold responsible. The corporation was a monster of oppression in which people and their lives were ground down piece by piece. Representative of this type of fiction were John Steinbeck's *Grapes of Wrath* and Nathaniel West's *A Cool Million*. For Steinbeck, it was not individuals but "they" who gave the migrants a hard time. For West, his hero of the Alger type found himself caught between the contending forces of "international bankers" and "world revolutionists" who slowly but surely destroyed his spirit of individualism and quest for free enterprise.

As the 1940s and 1950s unfolded, the manager completed the shift from the hero image by becoming more and more of an "organization man." In conformity there was security and the manager became a hero not because of "great or daring deeds, but because he tolerates grinding mediocrity and conformity."[26] In Marquand's *The Point of No Return*, Pawel's *From the Dark Tower*, and Sloan Wilson's *The Man in the Gray Flannel Suit*, the emphasis was on conformity and the futility of rebelling against the organization as a system. In Scott's thesis, these novelists portrayed the shift from the individualistic ethic to the "social ethic" in management literature. The reference point in the "social ethic" was the group and the collective nature of people, a need for collaboration and social solidarity. Not only did this occur in fiction, but also in the technical literature of Follett, the Mayoists, and others who were playing down the individual and reinforcing the group or collective nature of people.

The social ethic in fiction underscored conformity and depersonalization of the individual into a "they," and portrayed the corporation as a monster machine. In technical literature, the ideas

[25] William G. Scott, *The Social Ethic in Management Literature*, Atlanta: Bureau of Business and Economic Research, Georgia State College of Business Administration, 1959, p. 47.

[26] Ibid., p. 50.

of teamwork, participation, group decision making, small rather than large groups, committee management, the "interweaving of responsibilities," and democratic leadership were abundant. Scott's striking parallel between the fictional and technical writers of the social man era is food for thought. Taken together with the low esteem of the businessman as symbol of the corporate monster, it was understandable that the Mayoists and others sought to remodel organizations from the bottom up in order to meet people's needs. While the Mayoists and others would reform the organization through the group, the organizational engineers would reform the group through the organization. In their view, *Onward Industry!* was a rallying cry for coordinating and focusing group efforts, not to subdue individuals, but to release their potential. "Principles" were not only organizational rules, but also guides for human conduct toward a purpose. Mooney, Gulick, and others knew of people's need to belong and sought to provide that through organizational definition. To these writers, it was through structure and not catharsis that people could release their potential.

In another sense, some critics have held the businessman and industrialization responsible for the ills of modern civilization. Intellectuals have maintained an uneasy truce with industrial life by idealizing agriculture and denigrating business. Jeffersonian and Jacksonian democracy were examples of the praise of an agricultural, small-unit, family-owned, ideal base of society. To be big was to be bad, and to live in the "city" was a sign of the decline of man. Why have the intellectuals idealized agriculture and sullied business? Kavesh perceptively noted that "the growth of cities is the history of business: the big businessman is the symbol of the city, and the city became the symbol of degradation."[27] This idea of non-city living still prevails; the first sign of success is the ability to escape the city by moving to the suburbs. Here one can escape the hurly-burly of the city and "farm" a 100 × 200 lot in some semblance of an agrarian existence.

Baritz has suggested that Mayo was one of those who was committed to an "Agrarian Golden Age":

> [Mayo] . . . believed that there was a mystical but direct relationship between farming and truth . . . An industrial society,

[27] Kavesh, p. 6.

by definition, could not be virtuous, for as men lost sight of the soil they lost sight of nature; and in so doing, they lost sight of the meaning of life and fell victim to the glossy gadgetry of modern industrialism. For Mayo, then the problem of the modern factory was clear; how to make possible the re-creation of Agrarian Virtue, Agrarian Loyalty, and the Agrarian Sense of Community in the twentieth century's world of skyscrapers and subways, of smoke and steam? [28]

For Mayo, the answer was to rebuild social solidarity and collaboration through the small group. Once the communal integrity of agrarian life was reestablished, man could cope with the evils of the city, the deskilling of work, and the anomic depersonalization of factory routine. Perhaps the Australian Mayo was caught up in the American-Jeffersonian-Jacksonian democratic tradition. He was certainly influenced by Durkheim, who saw evils in industrial life much as Robert Owen had seen them in the early nineteenth century. While Durkheim admonished people to love one another unselfishly and Owen tried to build communal centers, Mayo accepted the parameters of industrialization and tried to rebuild people's interpersonal relations within that framework. The gloom of the Depression, World War II, and the threat of the atomic bomb would certainly cause Mayo to harken back to an Agrarian Golden Age in which people could find solace in small groups.

The Political Environment: From FDR to Eisenhower

While the economic cycle had gone from the bust to boom and the social environment reflected increasing needs for affiliation, the political cycle saw an increasing role for government in individual and business affairs. No other period in American history has seen a political administration begin in such dire times, endure for such a long period, and cope with as many adversities as the tenure of Franklin Delano Roosevelt. Roosevelt, scion of a patrician family, cousin of former President Theodore Roosevelt, and paralyzed from the waist down by polio, brought a charisma to the American people in the depths of their despair. In his accep-

[28] Loren Baritz, *The Servants of Power*, New York: John Wiley and Sons, 1960, p. 111.

tance speech for the Democratic nomination, he had said "I pledge you, I pledge myself, to a New Deal for the American people." This became the slogan of the policies of the Roosevelt administration, which promised to reshuffle the old cards of society.

The New Deal

FDR saw as his first task that of restoring confidence to a stricken nation. A landmark of the lengths to which he went were the "first hundred days" (March 9, to June 16, 1933) in which a special session of Congress passed a multitude of bills enabling emergency legislation and giving Roosevelt tremendous political and economic powers. Roosevelt's keynote phrase, "The only thing we have to fear is fear itself," hoped to instill in the American people feelings of confidence and hope. In those first hundred days, legislation created such agencies as the Agricultural Adjustment Administration (A.A.A.), Civilian Conservation Corps (C.C.C.), Securities Exchange Commission (S.E.C.), Tennessee Valley Authority (T.V.A.), the Home Owners Loan Corporation (H.O.L.C.), the Federal Relief Act, the Railway Reorganization Act, the Federal Deposit Insurance Corporation (FDIC), and the National Industrial Recovery Act (NIRA).[29] The day of alphabet soup government had been created.

While some viewed the New Deal as "creeping socialism" and prophesied the end of capitalism, others saw the reforms as a necessary adjustment of capitalism while the motor was running in order to save free enterprise. Private enterprise endured, but in the process a lot of socialism did creep in. The restacking of the social, political, and economic order was to bring an activist role for government. Hands-off as a policy was defunct and the role of government increased in an effort to shift the balance of power as people perceived it from the financiers of Wall Street to the farmers, organized labor, and the "little man." One of FDR's "braintrusters," Rexford Tugwell, wrote that the idyllic days of business doing what it willed were gone and that the new leadership of industry must recognize unions, democratize industry by encouraging participation, and keep in mind the "greatest good for the

[29]John Gunther, *Roosevelt in Retrospect*, New York: Harper & Row, 1950, pp. 278–280, and 283–287.

greatest number."[30] Tugwell felt that industry had failed to provide security for the working class and that government must fill this vacuum. The response to this craving for security was made manifest in a number of pioneering legislative acts: the Social Security Act of 1935 sought to provide for old-age assistance; the Fair Labor Standards Act of 1938 established a guaranteed minimum hourly wage for certain workers; and the Railroad Unemployment Insurance Act of 1938 was the first national unemployment protection. These and other acts marked the shift from Adam Smith's "invisible hand" to Riesman's "glad hand," from private to public charity, and from the Protestant ethic to the social ethic.

Augmenting the Position of Labor

The Roosevelt era was a bottom up view of society. The role of federal power achieved a new dimension in governmental-business relations that even the Progressives had not envisioned. The New Deal introduced a positive conception of public responsibility that emphasized federal responsibility for relief of want and employment, for individual security, for parity for farmers, for recognition of organized labor and for maintenance of industrial peace, and enlarged responsibilities for operation of the nation's credit system. It was a new age, a calling for a new balance of power which promised to restore society by: "new commitments, new interpretations of the American role."[31]

Of all the changes in the redress of power, none had more immediate significance for management thought than the new role for labor. The promanagement legal environment that prevailed in the 1920s and the reliance on union-management cooperation was abruptly altered in the 1930s. During this period, the New Deal addressed itself to remedying a perceived imbalance in labor-management relations and passed revolutionary legislation that greatly strengthened the position of organized labor. The first significant piece of labor legislation passed by the Congress was the Federal Anti-Injunction Act of 1932, more commonly

---

[30]Rexford Guy Tugwell, *The Industrial Discipline*, New York: Columbia University Press, 1933, p. 158.

[31]Dexter Perkins, *The New Age of Franklin Roosevelt: 1932–1945*, Chicago: University of Chicago Press, 1957, p. 3.

referred to as the Norris-LaGuardia Act. This act, for all practical purposes, completely divested federal courts of injunctive powers in cases growing out of a labor dispute. In 1933, Congress passed the National Industrial Recovery Act, the first in a series of New Deal enactments designed to lift the nation out of the depression of the 1930s. Section 7a of the NIRA, in similar but stronger language than that already existing in the Norris-LaGuardia Act, specifically guaranteed that "employees shall have the right to organize and bargain collectively through representatives of their own choosing . . . free from the interference, restraint, or coercion of employers. . . ." It further provided that "no employee and no one seeking employment shall be required as a condition of employment to join any company union or to refrain from joining, organizing or assisting a labor organization of his own choosing. . . ."

When the NIRA was declared unconstitutional by the Supreme Court in 1935 (*Schecter* v. *U.S.*), Congress quickly replaced it with a law that was even more pleasing to organized labor. The National Labor Relations Act, more commonly known as the Wagner Act, was far more definitive in what it expected of collective bargaining than was the NIRA. The Wagner Act guaranteed employees "the right to self-organization, to form, join, or assist labor organizations, to bargain collectively through representatives of their own choosing, and to engage in concerted activities for the purpose of collective bargaining." In addition, it placed specific restrictions on what management could do by specifying five "unfair" management practices. To implement these provisions, the act established a National Labor Relations Board which was granted the authority not only to issue cease-and-desist orders against employers violating the restrictions, but also to determine appropriate bargaining units and to conduct representation elections.

The NLRB was also instrumental in destroying employee representation plans such as the one described earlier in the Dennison Manufacturing Company. Organized labor bitterly opposed such plans, seeing them as "company unions" which prevented their organizing efforts. In 1938 the United States Supreme Court ruled that these plans were employer dominated and in violation of the National Labor Relations Act (*NLRB* v. *Pennsylvania*

Greyhound Lines). This ended one era in labor-management relations, while yet another began.[32]

The passage of the Wagner Act marked a critical turning point in labor-management relations and created a new style of industrial unionism to supplant craft unionism. John L. Lewis, president of the United Mine Workers, led the fight for industrial unionism within the American Federation of Labor. Rebuffed, Lewis formed the Committee for Industrial Organization (known after 1938 as the Congress of Industrial Organizations), whose purpose came to be that of bringing workers into unions regardless of occupation or skill level. The newly founded CIO enjoyed almost instant success and was able to claim almost 4 million members as early as 1937. By 1941, virtually all the giant corporations in the mass production industries had recognized the CIO-affiliated unions as bargaining agents for their employees. With the legal climate created by the New Deal legislation, union membership spurted from less than 3 million members in 1933 to more than 8 million by 1939.

In retrospect, labor gained substantial power during the 1930s through legislation. The New Deal labor policy was part of a power-equalization drive designed to restore the voice of the "little man" in the industrial hierarchy. This new role for the worker fitted into the calls for teamwork, cooperation, and democratization of the workplace through worker participation. During the war, all shoulders were turned to the wheels of industry and differences temporarily laid aside. Employment regulation, such as through the War Labor Board, prevailed and in general enhanced the power of labor. After the war, numerous strikes led to the public opinion that labor had too much power and resulted in the passage of the Labor-Management Relations Act (Taft-Hartley Act) in 1947. While this act did bring about some redress in the balance of power, no longer was the employer able to pursue unilateral actions with respect to labor policies. In general, the whole environment of management had changed, not just with respect to labor, but also in all relations with government.

[32] An excellent analysis is C. Ray Gullett and Edmund R. Gray, "The Impact of Employee Representation Plans Upon the Development of Management Worker Relations in the United States," *Marquette Business Review*, Vol. 20, No. 3 (Fall, 1976), pp. 85–101.

The political environment brought a new focus for management thought. The manager had a new set of variables with which to contend, new relationships to be managed, and a revised set of assumptions with respect to the balance of power. After World War II, the search for general administrative theory would emerge as a solution to the complexities of managing in the modern era.

Summary of Part III

Figure 18-1 depicts the cultural forces and the developments in the social man era. Scientific management was the dominant theme in the 1920s, but there were the seeds of dissent of the revisionists and the beginnings made by sociologists and social psychologists who were bringing into play the ideas of behavioralism in management before the advent of the Hawthorne experiments. Mary Follett, though chronologically belonging to the scientific management era, served as an intellectual bridge to the emerging group approach to management's problems. The Hawthorne experiments and the subsequent writings of Mayo, Roethlisberger, Dickson, and Whitehead brought the human relations movement to the forefront and led to the social man theme. The heirs of Taylor and scientific management found new dimensions in organizations and in the job of the manager in coping with the new *zeitgeist* of this era.

The Hawthorne experiments, beginning before but enduring through the early days of the Depression, brought about a shift in emphasis: (1) an increased concern for people rather than production; (2) exhortations to play down the rigidity of administrative structures in order to increase the fulfillment of people's needs; (3) less emphasis on wages and efficiency and more concern for interpersonal relations as motivators; and (4) more concern for the ill-logic of sentiments rather than the logic of efficiency. The human relations movement and the research which followed reflected several basic themes which were products of the cultural environment: (1) calls for social, human skills rather than technical skills; (2) emphasis on rebuilding people's sense of belonging through groups and social solidarity in order to overcome the "confusion of souls"; and (3) concern for equalizing power through unions, through participative leadership, and by fusing

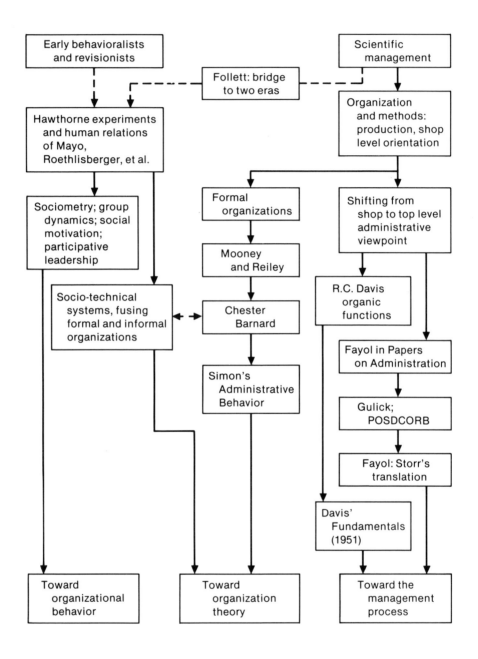

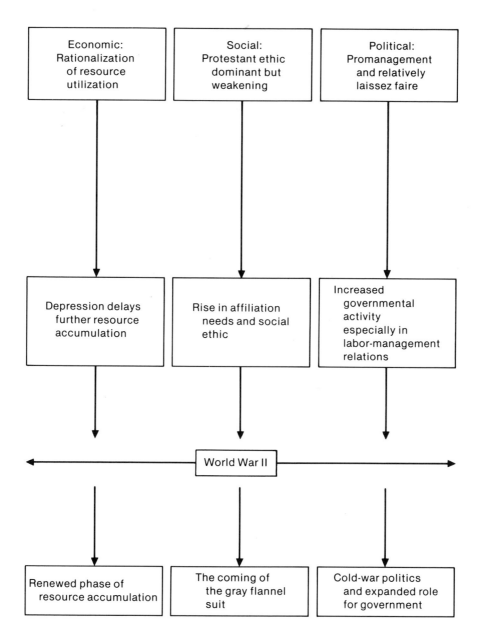

Fig. 18-1. Synopsis of the social man era and its cultural environment.

the formal organization with the social system of the factory.

The post-Hawthorne research assumed two separate yet congenial approaches: the "micro" researchers were establishing constructs for studying people in groups, were postulating a hierarchy of human needs, and were viewing leadership as a group-interactive-situational phenomenon. Along the "macro" branch, W. F. Whyte, George Homans, and E. W. Bakke were seeking to understand and to bring about an integration of the formal system with the informal system of sentiments, activities, and interactions. Each of these paths would lead to the "new humanism" and to the organization theory of the modern era.

Chronologically parallel to these developments in the human relations movement, the descendants of scientific management offered different types of solutions to the vexing problems of the Depression. Largely shop-management oriented at the beginning, as in the case of R. C. Davis, this branch of management thought also began to assume new dimensions. On the one hand, organizational constructs were offered as one way out of the cultural impasse. Mooney and Reiley urged *Onward Industry!* and Chester Barnard presented a sociological study of the formal organization and attempted to synthesize these "formalists" with the human relationists with his "efficiency-effectiveness" dichotomy. Alongside the organizational approach to management's problems, the elements of a top-level management viewpoint began to appear in the work of R. C. Davis, the translation of Fayol's process in the "Papers on Administration," and the efforts of Lyndall Urwick to synthesize principles of administration. A methods and analysis segment of scientific management was to receive increased recognition during World War II and would later emerge as operations research and management science in the modern era. Taken all together, the heirs of scientific management were establishing the foundations for the modern era of organization theory, the management process, and the search for quantification and systems in management.

In the cultural environment, management thought was shaped by the stressful times. Further economic growth was retarded by the Depression and the postwar boom was to create a need for a top-level administrative viewpoint. The Protestant ethic and the need for achievement, though not disappearing, declined in significance as people sought to find their identity and *raison d'être* through affiliation and getting along with others. People, not production, were the main concern of the administrator. Politically, an increased role for government and the growth, power, and legal protection afforded organized labor introduced new variables to be considered in managerial decision making. The world of management was much more complex than ever before with more advanced technology and communications, international markets, a broader-based, better-educated work force, and an increased awareness of the relationships between business and society. It was out of this age of confusion, trauma, and diversity that the modern era in management thought was about to begin.

IV THE MODERN ERA

Nestled between the knowns of yesterday and the unknowns of tomorrow, the present is the twilight of history. It is difficult to put more recent developments in perspective; some years from now we will be able to look upon this era with the aid of historical analysis, see the course of progress after it has evolved, and be better able to place our contemporaries in a clearer perspective. It is not possible to examine the full extent of modern management writings, for they are too diverse and too extensive for an in-depth analysis. Instead, we must be content to sketch the broad outlines of evolving management thought and try to perceive major trends, shifts, and influences in the modern era.

If one had to pick a general theme to depict the modern era, it would be one of a search for a Holy Grail, a quest to see which single "school" or combination of "schools" of management thought have that authentic piece of the True Cross of management knowledge. In examining this modern diversity, we will analyze first the search for a unified body of knowledge through the "principles and process" approach to management. Next, the focus will be upon the evolution of a modern view of organizational humanism, which will illustrate the search for harmony between the formal requirements of the organization and the informal dimensions of people in organizations. A search for order in management theory will be depicted as attempts to quantify variables in management decision making and efforts to bring order from chaos through general systems theory. These three objectives, unity, harmony, and order, characterize the quest of management scholars for a better understanding of the complex organizations and their societal interactions in the context of their environment. Finally, we will conclude by probing the lessons of history for evolving management thought. It is in this modern era that management thought experiences its adolescence of diversity and seeks the professional posture of maturity.

19

Principles and Process:
The Search for Unity

Management scholars have sought to reduce the theory and practice of management to an orderly body of knowledge for some time. The "principles and process" approach represents one view of how a general theory of management might be developed. The management "process," that is, *what* managers do in performing their job, provides a framework for theory. "Principles" allegedly describe *how* managers should manage and represent building blocks for the body of knowledge. In chapter 16 we saw an increasing concern for general management theory and postulated that this was necessitated by the further growth of organizations after World War II, by the proliferation of staff specialists, by the increased importance of new business functions beyond the realm of production and engineering, and by a greater awareness of relating management tasks to their more complex environment. If any one factor had to be chosen to explain the concern for a general theory, it had to be the increased number of variables to be taken into account in decision making. It was in this environment that management scholars turned from a shop-level management orientation to general management theory.

The first generation of the process approach to management thought consisted of the work of its intellectual progenitor, Henri Fayol; Ralph C. Davis and Luther Gulick were influenced by Fayol's elements and must be classified as "first generation" since their writings influenced more modern versions of the management process. It was in the writings of these men that the functions of the manager were established as a recurring, inter-dependent cycle of activity which led to the accomplishment of organizational goals. Though the elements included in the process differed among these authors, all saw management as universal, applicable to all types of organizations and at all levels within the management hierarchy. From these beginnings, new contributors whose names are more familiar to modern students began to re-shape the existing body of management knowledge. Less empha-sis was placed on production management and more began to be placed on general management theory.

With this brief link to the past, the modern era of the process approach will be developed as: (1) the proliferation of "principles and process" approaches in a second generation of writers; (2) the appearance of some serious challenges to the nature and content of management education; (3) the increasing awareness of the en-vironment and the responsibilities of managers; (4) the influx of ideas from the behavioral and quantitative sciences, leading to a theory "jungle"; (5) the influence of general systems theory; and (6) the rise of contingency and experiential approaches to management.

The Second Generation

Variations In the Management Process

The first effort of a second generation of authors was that of Wil-liam H. Newman of Columbia University. In 1950, Newman had copyrighted materials as *Principles of Administration* which was later published as *Administrative Action: The Technique of Organiza-tion and Management.*[1] Newman defined administration as "the guidance, leadership, and control of the efforts of a group of in-dividuals toward some common goal" and developed a logical process of administration as a separate intellectual activity. The el-ements in Newman's process were planning, organizing, assem-bling resources, directing, and controlling. For Newman, planning

---

[1] W. H. Newman, *Administrative Action: The Technique of Organization and Manage-ment*, Englewood Cliffs: N.J., Prentice-Hall, 1951. Newman was president of the Academy of Management in 1951.

was determining what is to be done in advance of doing it. It "provides the basis for organization, assembling resources, direction, and control."[2] Planning involved recognizing the need for action, investigation and analysis, proposing action, and a decision. The outcome of the planning process was the development of three broad groups of plans: (1) goals or objectives, which defined purposes of organizational effort and made integrated planning easier; (2) "single-use plans" which established a course of action to "fit a specific situation and are 'used up' when the goal is reached"; and (3) "standing plans," which endured over time and were changed only as the occasion warranted.

While Newman's version of the process was closely akin to Fayol's, it did have some unique features: (1) the distinction between the types of plans; (2) the "assembling resources" element; and (3) the treatment of coordination under directing rather than as a separate activity. Beyond this early contribution to the process approach, Newman has made significant contributions to business policy and to the importance of objectives in "shaping the character" of an organization. He felt that the basic objectives of the firm should define its place or niche in the industry, define the firm's social philosophy as a business "citizen," and serve to establish the general managerial philosophy of the company.[3]

George Terry was the first to call his book *Principles of Management*. Terry defined management as

> *the activity which plans, organizes, and controls the operations of the basic elements of men, materials, machines, methods, money, and markets, providing direction and co-ordination, and giving leadership to human efforts, so as to achieve the sought objectives of the enterprise.*[4]

Terry's version of the process included planning, organizing, directing, coordinating, controlling, and leading human efforts. "Leading human efforts" was a less definitive function but involved the utilization and development of an organization's per-

---

[2] Ibid., p. 28.

[3] William H. Newman, "Basic Objectives Which Shape the Character of a Company," *Journal of Business of the University of Chicago*, Vol. 26, No. 4 (October, 1953), pp. 211–223.

[4] George R. Terry, *Principles of Management*, Homewood, Ill.: Richard D. Irwin, 1953 (revised editions in 1956, 1960, 1964, 1968, and 1972). Terry was president of the Academy of Management in 1961.

sonnel and required the proper application of influence so that every member of the organization desired to work toward organizational goals. Leading human efforts, treated apart from directing, involved more consideration of developing executives and developing proper attitudes in order to achieve results. In later editions, Terry combined the directing and leading human efforts functions into an "actuating" function which sought to instill a desire on the part of subordinates to internalize the organization's objectives. Later editions also stopped treating coordinating as a separate function and recognized it as an integral part of all functions. Starting with six functions, Terry later reduced them to four; planning, organizing, actuating, and controlling. With respect to "principles," Terry defined a principle as "a fundamental statement providing a guide to action."[5] The principles, like Fayol's, were lighthouses to knowledge and not laws in the scientific sense. Among the principles that Terry offered were these:

[Principle of service:] The fundamental objective of every enterprise is service; it is eminently practical, stable, and sound.

[Principle of objective:] A clear and complete statement of the objective is essential, and it should be made known to all members of an enterprise affected by it so that management activities can be directed in a unified, orderly, gainful, and effective manner.

[Principle of Leadership:] Skillfully applied leadership contributes tremendously to smooth and successful group efforts.[6]

There were principles and subprinciples for planning, policies, decision-making, organizing, and other managerial tasks. In this first of many "principles and process" texts, Terry had established the theme for a search for a unified body of knowledge.

In 1954, the Department of the Air Force prepared and distributed for training and operational purposes Air Force Manual 25-1, *The Management Process.*[7] This manual established five functions of management: planning, organizing, coordinating, directing and controlling. Objectives, or "missions" in the military sense, were stressed a great deal as the foundation stone of all

---

[5] Ibid., p. 9.

[6] Ibid., p. 54, p. 56, and p. 229.

[7] *The Management Process,* Air Force Manual 25-1, Washington, D.C.: United States Government Printing Office, 1954.

managerial activity. This governmental interest in the process was significant for two reasons: (1) it signaled a further interest in the study of management as a separate activity; and (2) it was recognition of the universality of management beyond the previous emphasis on the study of management in the business concern.

Management by Objectives

Outside the notion of a Fayolian process approach to management, Peter Drucker made an enduring contribution to understanding the role of the manager in a business society. In contrast to the "functions" of the manager which were prevalent in the process texts, Drucker developed three broader managerial functions: (1) managing a business; (2) managing managers; and (3) managing workers and work. According to Drucker, in every decision the manager must put economic considerations first and management could justify its existence only through the economic results it produced:

> . . . *management has failed if it fails to produce economic results. It has failed if it does not supply goods and services desired by the consumer at a price the consumer is willing to pay. It has failed if it does not improve or at least maintain the wealth producing capacity of the economic resources entrusted to it.* [8]

Drucker recognized that there may be noneconomic consequences of managerial decisions, such as happiness and improved community welfare, but he felt that these were by-products of the emphasis on economic performance. In striving for economic results, the first function of "managing a business" was of an entrepreneurial character, innovative in the Schumpetrian sense of creating markets and products rather than being passive and adaptive. The second function of "managing managers" introduced the notion of "management by objectives." Without explicit recognition of the fact, Drucker followed Mary Follett's idea of depersonalizing authority and obeying the law of the situation:

> *A manager's job should be based on a task to be performed in*

---

[8] Peter F. Drucker, *The Practice of Management*, New York: Harper and Row, 1954, p. 8.

[9] Ibid., p. 137.

order to attain the company's objectives . . . the manager should
be directed and controlled by the objectives of performance rather
than by his boss. [9]

Management by objectives was to replace management by
drive, and control was to be self-control rather than control from
above. Knowing the objectives of his unit and those of the enterprise, the manager could direct his own activities:

The only principle that can do this is management by objectives
and self control . . . it substitutes for control from outside the
stricter, more exacting and more effective control from the inside.
It motivates the manager to action not because somebody tells him
to do something . . . but because the objective needs of his task
demand it. [10]

In the third managerial function of managing the worker, Drucker
advised treating humans as the most vital resource of the firm, engineering the work to fit the workers, giving the workers more
control over their job, and restoring challenge and "wholeness" to
the job.

". . . Getting Things Done Through Others"

While Drucker focused primarily on the practical aspects of management, others were continuing to further the use of the process
to find management theory. Harold Koontz and Cyril O'Donnell
of the University of California at Los Angeles defined management as "the function of getting things done through others."[11]
This definition reflected the Storrs rendition of Fayol's *administrer*

[10] Ibid., p. 136. Drucker disclaims inventing the term "management by objectives,"
crediting it instead to Alfred P. Sloan, Jr., of General Motors. See John J. Tarrant,
Drucker: The Man Who Invented Corporate Society, Boston, Mass.: Cahners Books,
Inc., 1976, p. 77. Drucker did, however, provide the major impetus to the MBO
concept as it moved into popular practice. Drucker's writings on management are
voluminous. For a sample, see Peter F. Drucker, *Management: Tasks, Responsi-*
bilities, and Practices, New York: Harper and Row, 1973.

[11] Harold Koontz and Cyril O'Donnell, *Principles of Management: An Analysis of Man-*
agerial Functions, New York: McGraw-Hill Book Co., 1955, p. v. and p. 3. Revised
editions appeared in 1959, 1964, 1968, 1972, and 1976. Koontz was president of the
Academy of Management in 1963.

as management, and the Koontz and O'Donnell definition became one of the more widely held views of the task of management. Koontz and O'Donnell furthered the Fayolian notion of the universality of management and sought in their book to provide a conceptual framework for the orderly presentation of the principles of management.

According to Koontz and O'Donnell, managers were known by the work they performed, and that was planning, organizing, staffing, directing, and controlling. These authors pointed out that some authorities maintained that these functions were exercised in the sequence given, but in practice managers actually used all five simultaneously. Koontz and O'Donnell stressed that each of these functions contributed to organizational coordination. However, coordination was not a separate function itself but was the result of effective utilization of the five basic managerial functions. In this first book, Koontz and O'Donnell offered a number of principles: in organizing, for example, "the principle of parity of authority and responsibility" and "the principle of unity of command"; in planning, "the principle of strategic factors"; and so on. The Koontz and O'Donnell principles and process approach has been an enduring, integral part of the search for a systematic body of management knowledge.

With the Koontz and O'Donnell offering and a revision by George Terry in 1956, the process appeared to be settling down to a four-function analysis of planning, organizing, directing, and controlling. Characteristic of this development was that of Dalton McFarland who interpreted management as a process by which resources were combined in achieving organizational goals. Management was performed by an executive who was "a person in an organization who possesses rank, status, and authority which permit him to plan, organize, control, and direct the work of others."[12] McFarland's effort reflected a greater concern for consideration of strategic and tactical factors in decision making, setting objectives, and in concern for the human resource as a utilizer of all other resources.

[12] Dalton E. McFarland, *Management Principles and Practices*, New York: Macmillan Company, 1958, p. 42 (revised editions in 1964, 1970 and 1974). Professor McFarland was president of the Academy of Management in 1965.

A Final Note

The period 1958–1960 marked a significant turning point for the evolution of the process school of management. Before examining the multitude of forces which would bring a number of changes to management theory, let us try to summarize and visualize the first and second generations of the search for theory through the process. In retrospect, the process approach was an attempt to identify management as a distinct intellectual activity which was universal in nature. The search was for a generally agreed upon body of knowledge which could be distilled into principles and hence would lead to a general philosophy or theory of management. The need for theory was evident: wider markets, advanced technology, widespread use of specialists, and larger, more intricate organizational forms demanded a more precise manner of handling human and physical resource problems. The underlying technical, human, and managerial problems of the early factory system still

Managerial Functions	Fayol (1961)	Davis (1934)	Gulick (1937)	Newman (1951)	Terry (1953)	AFM 25-1 (1954)	Koontz and O'Donnell (1955)	Terry (1956)	McFarland (1958)
Planning	✓	✓	✓	✓	✓	✓	✓	✓	✓
Organizing	✓	✓	✓	✓	✓	✓	✓	✓	✓
Coordination	✓		✓	✓	✓	✓			
Controlling	✓	✓		✓	✓	✓	✓	✓	✓
Command	✓								
Directing			✓	✓	✓	✓	✓		✓
Leading Human Efforts				✓					
Actuating								✓	
Staffing	✓		✓				✓		
Assembling Resources				✓					
Reporting			✓						
Budgeting			✓						

Fig. 19-1.　The first and second generations.

were present but the fund of managerial talent needed to be expanded to handle ever increasing masses of resources in ever increasing numbers of business, governmental, and other types of organizations. The search for unity through the process was the suggested answer to these problems.

As the process approach evolved, it began in classic simplicity with Fayol and Davis, became more diverse in the functions presented by Gulick, Newman, and Terry, and then began to settle down with more widespread agreement among AFM 25-1, Koontz and O'Donnell, and McFarland (Figure 19-1).

Of the managerial functions presented, planning, organizing, and controlling achieved the greatest agreement as to their applicability. A fourth function of the specified role of the manager in putting the bits and pieces together, starting the system, and keeping it together was a source of much disagreement in terminology. For some it was directing, for others supervising, leading, actuating, or whatever. Staffing, which Fayol had subsumed under organizing, was achieving some recognition as a separate function either explicitly for the human resource or more generally under the heading of "assembling resources." Coordination began and endured as a separate managerial function until 1954; afterwards, it became an integral part of the entire process. While scholars were settling down by 1958 to some degree of unanimity about the job of the manager, new developments in education, in other disciplines, and in the environment of management were beginning to impinge upon the process school and would lead to some changing notions about the manager's job.

Reshaping the Process Approach

The forces that were to reshape the first and second generations of the process came from a variety of sources. As an overview we will examine: (1) some challenges to both business and management education; (2) an increasing awareness of environmental forces on the role of the manager; and (3) the profusion of inputs from quantitative methods and the behavioral sciences which would lead to the management theory "jungle."

Challenges to Management Education

In 1959, two reports on business education appeared which would have a significant impact on the development of management thought. Unlike the study of education by Morris Cooke for the Carnegie Fund in 1910, these reports were taken more seriously by educators. The Ford Foundation commissioned and financed a study by Robert A. Gordon of the University of California (Berkeley) and James E. Howell of Stanford University.[13] Likewise, the Carnegie Corporation sponsored a study by Frank C. Pierson of Swarthmore College.[14] Although the authors of the two reports exchanged information, they reached their conclusions independently and both reports were sharp indictments of the state of business education in the United States. Both reports noted that schools of business administration were in a state of turmoil in trying to define just what should be taught and how it should be done. By adhering to outworn precepts of education, the business schools were not preparing competent, imaginative, flexible managers for an ever changing environment. Schools overemphasized "vocationalism," i.e., training for specific jobs, rather than preparing broadly educated individuals for maximum future growth in a business career.

While most schools claimed to be engaged in "professional education," the Gordon and Howell report questioned whether or not business was or could be a "profession." They suggested four criteria for defining a profession:

> First, the practice of a profession must rest on a systematic body of knowledge of substantial intellectual content and on the development of personal skill in the application of this knowledge to specific cases. Second, there must exist standards of professional conduct, which take precedence over the goal of personal gain. . . . A profession has its own association of members, among whose functions are the enforcement of standards, the ad-

[13] R. A. Gordon and J. E. Howell, *Higher Education for Business*, New York: Columbia University Press, 1959.

[14] F. C. Pierson, *The Education of American Businessmen: A Study of University-College Programs in Business Administration*, New York: McGraw-Hill Book Co., 1959.

ion of knowledge, and, in some degree,
e profession. Finally, there is some pre-
e profession through the enforcement of
minimum standard.......... ,   *ining and competence.*[15]

Applying these criteria, the authors found that business was developing a body of knowledge and moving toward meeting the first criterion. However, it had no clearly defined standards of conduct beyond those embodied in the law; it had no governing body or association; and there were no prescribed entry avenues for a business career. Failing on criteria two, three, and four, and partially satisfying the first criterion, business was not a profession. The authors concluded that business was beginning to resemble a profession and they were hopeful that further progress in defining standards and systematizing knowledge would move business toward the "professional" end of career spectrums.

The path to developing a profession resided in changing the content of the business school curriculum. More stress should be placed on a general education, especially in the humanities and the liberal arts; on an expansion of requirements in mathematics; and on extended study in the behavioral and social sciences. For management education, Gordon and Howell noted that there were at least four different aspects of the field of organization and administration: (1) managerial problem solving through the scientific method and quantitative analysis; (2) organization theory; (3) management principles; and (4) human relations.[16] Each played a part in the study of management and the authors recommended some integration of these ideas into a sequence of courses which would better prepare future leaders rather than leaving them with a fragmented picture of the tasks of management. Beyond the management area, the authors made numerous recommendations in other functional areas of business, in graduate education, and in teaching methodology. In total, both the Gordon and Howell and the Pierson reports were calling for a new shape in education for management and for business. Both reports led to scholarly introspection, debate, and a gradual reshaping of the area of study encompassed under the title of "management."

[15] Gordon and Howell, pp. 69–70.
[16] Ibid., pp. 179–182.

The Manager and Society

The Ford and Carnegie reports instigated a host of changes in management curricula and thought. It must not be presumed that managerial awareness of its environment began in 1959 but it does appear that these reports provided a new stimulus for some old ideas. While an extensive analysis is not possible at this point, certain areas will be examined to show the changing views of managers vis-à-vis their environment. The more significant changes came in quests for a profession of management, for a philosophy of management, for ethics, and for social responsibility in business. In practice, these four areas were interacting as scholars and practitioners sought a way out of diversity and a more solid foundation for systematizing managerial knowledge and behavior and for relating the business organization to its larger environmental context.

The notion of a profession or of being a "professional" has always connoted status beyond the ordinary. Business has been considered a base occupation by many cultures, the Greeks and Romans especially, and those associated with business would prefer to be recognized as a more integral part of society and regarded as an essential part of carrying out societal goals. If business or management could be regarded as a profession, then managers would feel that their role in society would be held in higher esteem. The 1960s witnessed an ever increasing body of literature on the pros and cons of management and business as a profession. Partially inspired by the Carnegie and Ford reports, partially a reaction to some highly questionable pricing practices in the electrical industry, and in part due to a deep concern for relating business to society, scholars sought to meet the missing criteria which would raise business to the level of a profession. Joseph Towle suggested that the Master of Business Administration degree be recognized as constituting the minimum prerequisite for entering the profession of management;[17] later, Professor Towle edited a volume of readings with the intent of integrating

[17] Joseph W. Towle, "The Challenge that Management is a Profession," in Paul Dauten (ed.), *Current Issues and Emerging Concepts of Management*, Boston: Houghton Mifflin Co., 1962, pp. 323–327. Towle was president of the Academy of Management in 1960.

ethics into the "emerging profession of management."[18] The term "professional" began to crop up more frequently in articles and books as scholars proposed to treat management as a profession. The aura was one of optimism and the theme presented was that through advancing knowledge, in professional associations for setting standards, and through ethical codes, management could truly become a profession.

A philosophy of management would be attractive to a management profession. Philosophy should serve to order knowledge, to provide values and premises, and to provide an epistemology or an answer to the question "how do we know?" R. C. Davis stated:

> *The problem of greatest importance in the field of management is and probably will continue to be the further development of the philosophy of management. A philosophy is a system of thought. It is based on some orderly, logical statement of objectives, principles, policies and general methods of approach to the solution of some set of problems.* [19]

For Davis, the premises of an American philosophy of management would be built upon private capitalism, the epistemology would be the spirit of scientific management, and orderly knowledge could be provided by sound business objectives and policies.[20] John Mee has stated that a management philosophy of the future "should provide managers and administrators with concepts, a scale of values, and a means to settle them without hindering the flow of economic and social progress."[21] Other scholars have taken various views of management philosophy, from pragmatic to metaphysical, and, though no clear-cut philosophy has

[18] Joseph W. Towle (ed.), *Ethics and Standards in American Business*, Boston: Houghton Mifflin Co., 1964, especially parts 4 and 5.

[19] Ralph C. Davis, "Research in Management During the '50's," in Arthur E. Warner (ed.), *Research Needs in Business During the '50's*, Bloomington, Ind.: Business Report #13, 1950, p. 32.

[20] Ralph Currier Davis, "Frederick W. Taylor and the American Philosophy of Management," *Advanced Management*, Vol. 24, No. 4 (December, 1959), pp. 4–7. Also see: Stewart Thompson, *Management Creeds and Philosophies*, New York: American Management Association, 1958.

[21] John F. Mee, *Management Thought in a Dynamic Society*, New York: New York University Press, 1963, p. 84. Mee was president of the Academy of Management in 1952.

emerged, the search continues for a deeper rationale and an orderly framework for management thought.[22]

Ethics, or agreements about codes of personal and interpersonal conduct, has been a subject of philosophers since time immemorial. Business transactions, so deeply imbedded in trust and confidence in one's fellows, have been an integral part of this search for guides to conduct beyond the question of legal boundaries. The antitrust prosecution of a number of electrical manufacturing companies in 1960 for price-fixing, coupled with the need for ethics in professionalism, touched off a number of inquiries into business ethics; the ferment has not abated to this day. The areas of inquiry were many: market collusion, conflict of interests, the morality of power, "reasonable" profits, advertising, and interpersonal relations, to name only a few. Father Baumhart revealed that more than 50 percent of the businessmen he interviewed believed that other businessmen would violate a code of ethics, if one existed, if they thought that they would go undetected.[23] While everyone would agree on the need for a code of ethics, the literature fails to reveal any clear-cut unanimity of opinion about what exactly would be the standards and the content of such a code. Would the code be applicable to an industry, a nation, a world? Would it be founded upon some Judeo-Christian or other religious base, or upon the "situation," or whatever? While the debate continues, this quest for ethics has revealed the challenges to management's desire to be a profession and to relate effectively to its environment.

"Social responsibility," or a broader concept of "business and society," represents another expectation regarding managerial performance. The philanthropy of business people is as ancient as business itself, as we saw in chapter 5. We also saw a legal precedent which clouded the situation and raised doubts about whether or not a corporation could give away a portion of its profits to nonbusiness-related endeavors. In the United States, a historic revision of the Federal Revenue Act in 1935 included the

---

[22] An excellent review of the literature and some questions which must be posed for management philosophy are discussed in William D. Litzinger and Thomas E. Shaefer, "Perspective: Management Philosophy Enigma," *Academy of Management Journal,* Vol. 9, No. 4 (December, 1966), pp. 337–343.

[23] Raymond C. Baumhart, "How Ethical are Businessmen?" *Harvard Business Review,* Vol. 39, No. 4 (July–August, 1961), p. 19.

famous "5 percent" clause, which permitted corporations to deduct up to that amount from net income for contributions to eleemosynary institutions. Despite this provision, deductions for corporate giving rarely reached 1 percent of taxable income. Another landmark case appeared in 1953, *A. P. Smith Manufacturing Company* v. *Barlow, et. al.* The company had donated $1500 to Princeton University for general educational purposes. Some stockholders sued, claiming that this action was outside the powers granted by the charter of incorporation. The New Jersey Supreme Court ruled for the company, reasoning that business support of higher education was in the best interest of a free-enterprise society. The case was not appealed, and the precedent for corporate involvement in social activities had been established.

To some extent post–World War II concern for social responsibility also grew out of the criticisms of business during the Depression and from those who felt that too much power was concentrated in the hands of too few business people. There was increasing concern that business firms had been unmindful of their relationship with their public constituency and their impact on the physical and social environment. For the advocates, business has a stake in societal development and must give as well as partake of the largesse. They argue that profits may be forgone to some extent but that the long-run benefits will outweigh the costs, i.e. "social responsibility is good business." The alternatives to accepting responsibility could be more government intervention or further criticisms of business. In part, acceptance of social responsibility takes some of the wind out of the sails of the critics.

The question of what to include in social responsibility is a broad one and extends into hiring the hard-core unemployed, to corporate giving to education, research, and other philanthropies, to the firm as a citizen of the community, to air and water pollution abatement, and a host of other questions.[24] Not everyone agrees with the idea of social responsibility; such individuals hold that the business organization is an economic institution. To take

[24]The literature of social responsibility and business and society is quite vast. For openers, see George Steiner, *Business and Society: Environment and Responsibility* (3rd ed.), New York: McGraw-Hill Book Company, 1975; Frederick D. Sturdivant, *Business and Society: A Managerial Approach,* Homewood, Ill.: R. D. Irwin, 1977; and Keith Davis and Robert L. Blomstrom, *Business and Its Environment* (3rd ed.), New York: McGraw-Hill Book Co., 1975.

on noneconomic, social goals would violate the interests of the stockholders, result in business imposing its views on others, and would be fundamentally subversive in a free enterprise economy.[25] The controversy will continue and our discussion here must be confined to a historical summary. The intent has been to show that these four factors, professionalism, philosophy, ethics, and social responsibility, were interacting to reshape the course of management thought. Together with the challenge to management education, a greater awareness of the environment of managers and their responsibilities would have a large impact on management thought in the 1960s.

The Generation Gap

The new wine that was testing the strength of the principles and process container came not only from the educational and societal

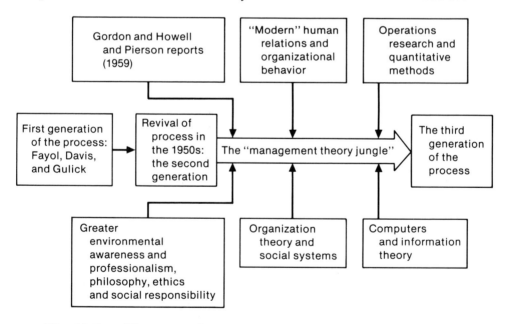

Fig. 19-2.   The generation gap.

[25]For examples of the critics, see: Milton Friedman, *Capitalism and Freedom*, Chicago: University of Chicago Press, 1962; and Theodore Leavitt, "The Dangers of Social Responsibility," *Harvard Business Review*, Vol. 36, No. 5 (September–October, 1958), pp. 41–50.

critics but also from an increasing accumulation of empirical research and new advances in other areas. From the social and behavioral scientists, new notions were arising about individual and group behavior and the human relationists were evolving toward different interpretations of people at work. The former production management-engineering approaches were availing themselves of more elaborate mathematical models and tools and attempting to quantify the management equation. General systems theory, still inchoate, was establishing some rudimentary notions about the nature of the universe and its parts. While each of these modern developments will be dealt with in greater depth in chapters 20 and 21, it is easy to visualize the forces that were reshaping the process approach (Figure 19-2).

While the Gordon and Howell report had noted the diversity of approaches to the study of management, it was Harold Koontz who delineated the differences and applied the catchy label of the "management theory jungle."[26] It was in this jungle that the gap between the second and the subsequent generations became painfully obvious. Koontz noted there were six main groups or "schools" of management thought:

1. The management process *school "perceives management as a process of getting things done through and with people operating in organized groups." Often called the traditional or universalist approach, this school was fathered by Henri Fayol and sought to identify and analyze the functions of the manager in order to bridge management theory and practice.*

2. The empirical *school identified management as the "study of experience" and used case analyses or Ernest Dale's "comparative approach"* (in The Great Organizers) *as vehicles for teaching and to draw generalizations about management. The basic premise of this school was that by examining the successes and failures of managers, understanding of effective management techniques would be furthered.*

3. The human behavior *school, variously called the human relations, leadership, or behavioral sciences approach, sought to*

[26] Harold Koontz, "The Management Theory Jungle," *Journal of the Academy of Management*, Vol. 4, No. 3 (December, 1961), pp. 174–188. See also: Harold Koontz, "Making Sense of Management Theory," *Harvard Business Review*, July–August 1962, pp. 24–30.

study management as interpersonal relations since management was getting things done through people. This school used psychology and social psychology to concentrate on the "people" part of management.

4. *The* social system *school saw management as a system of cultural interrelationships in which various groups interacted and cooperated. The sire of this approach was Chester Barnard and its adherents drew heavily upon sociological theory.*

5. *The* decision theory *school concentrated on analyzing and understanding who made decisions, how they were made, and the entire process of a selection of a course of action from among various alternatives. Economic theory, and especially the theory of consumer choice, represented the intellectual foundations of this approach to management.*

6. *The* mathematical *school viewed management as a "system of mathematical models and processes." This approach included the contributions of operations researchers, operations analysts, or management scientists who thought that management or decision making could be "expressed in terms of mathematical symbols and relationships."* [27]

Koontz conceded that each of these schools had something to offer to management theory but suggested that the student of management should *not confuse content with tools.* For instance, the field of human behavior should not be judged the equivalent of the field of management, nor should a focus on decision making or mathematics be considered as encompassing the entire area of analysis. Preferably, each of these areas would provide insights and methods to aid managers in performing their tasks, and hence were tools and not schools. The causes of confusion and the "jungle warfare" between the various approaches were many: (1) "the semantics jungle" of varying uses and meanings of such terms as *organization, leadership, management, decision making,* etc.; (2) problems in defining management as a body of knowledge since the term was used under such varying circumstances and in a variety of situations; (3) the *"a priori* assumption" or the tendency for some to cast aside the observations and analyses of the past since

[27] The preceding analysis was adapted from Koontz, "Management Theory Jungle," pp. 177–182.

they were *a priori* in nature; (4) the misunderstanding of principles through trying to disprove a whole framework of principles when one was violated in practice; and (5) the "inability or unwillingness of management theorists to understand each other" caused by professional "walls" of jargon between disciplines and personal and professional desires to protect their own idea or cult.[28] Koontz was hopeful that the jungle could be disentangled if these problems could be resolved.

The Quest for a Denouement

A direct result of the jungle article was a symposium of distinguished teachers and practitioners of management at the University of California, Los Angeles campus, in 1962. Koontz was the conference chairman and financial support came from the McKinsey Foundation and the Western Management Sciences Institute. The objective of the seminar was to convene a group of "eminent scholars with diverse research and analytical approaches to management, as well as perceptive and experienced practitioners of the managerial art from business, education and government.[29] Ernest Dale launched the conference by questioning the universality of management. Dale, deemed one of the "empirical school" by Koontz, put forth two arguments to refute the universal thesis: first he stated that the three best managed organizations (according to Jackson Martindell) were the Standard Oil Company of New Jersey, the Roman Catholic church, and the Communist party. Applying the doctrine of universality then meant that an executive "merry-go-round" of the chief executives of these three organizations was possible. Since this was obviously not true, the "universality and transferability of management" was therefore negated.[30] Finally, Dale held that the notion of a universal manager was contradicted by actual experience.

[28] The above is based on ibid., pp. 182–186.

[29] Harold Koontz (ed.), *Toward a Unified Theory of Management*, New York: McGraw-Hill Book Co., 1964, p. xi.

[30] Ibid., pp. 26–27. For a more comprehensive analysis of Dale's criticisms of the universalists, see E. Dale, *The Great Organizers*, New York: McGraw-Hill Book Co., 1960, pp. 5–11. A summary and analysis of more recent research may be found in John B. Miner, *Management Theory*, New York: Macmillan Co., 1971, chapters 6, 7, and 8.

Businessmen faced great frustration when assuming government posts and military men going into industry were chosen for their value in securing government contracts and not for any managerial ability they might have.

Dale's attack on the universalists was only the opening salvo. Roethlisberger was less critical, recognized the shortcoming of behavioral research, but felt that a general theory was possible if researchers turned some attention to explaining what previously had been found through experimentation. Harvard University's Robert Schlaifer, representing the decision theorists, stated that he was "convinced that decision theory is not and never will be a *part* of a theory of management.[31] Herbert Simon disagreed with the Koontz jungle from the onset. Simon maintained that there was no jungle, no semantic confusion, and was "exhilarated by the progress we have made . . . toward creating a viable science of management and an art based on that science."[32] According to Simon, management theory was far from being a jungle and was becoming a beneficiary of and a contributor toward systems theory. The study of complex systems required a variety of inputs, from empiricists, decision theorists, behavioralists, et al. and the future of management held forth the promise of a synthesis in management science.

From these diverse views, further discussion yielded few new insights. In reporting his observations of the discussion, Tannenbaum noted that semantics were a major problem and that people preferred to "play it safe" by using their own jargon and speaking only from familiar ground. Simon defended the use of jargon as marking the growth of a discipline which needed a new vocabulary to express new ideas. R. C. Davis challenged Dale's description of a "classicist"; others engaged in extensive attempts to define terms; and Wilfred Brown capsulized much of the conference sentiment when he said: "Frankly, gentlemen, I have not been able to follow much of what's been said in the discussions."[33]

As Koontz concluded, "Semantic confusion was evident

[31]Koontz, *Toward a Unified Theory*, p. 68.

[32]Ibid., p. 79.

[33]Ibid., p. 231. Mr. Brown was president of the Glacier Metal Co., Ltd., where a number of organizational systems studies were made.

throughout the discussions."[34] As a denouement, Koontz proposed an "eclectic approach" which would maintain management as a discipline of its own but one which would enable management to support itself by drawing upon relevant findings of many other disciplines. Koontz was still hopeful that the functions of planning, organizing, staffing, directing, and controlling would form the core of the management discipline and, when buttressed by eclecticism, that the process approach would lead to a general theory. The U.C.L.A. symposium was indicative of the incoherent state of management theory. Perhaps the seminar topic should have been subtitled "Is Anybody Listening?" Academicians could understand only those from their own specialty, practitioners could not understand academicians, and vice versa.

Koontz's perceptive analysis of the existing state of management theory in 1961 and the U.C.L.A. symposium encouraged a renewed interest in principles, universality, semantics, and other pressing problems in the search for a unified theory of management. In response to the jungle, some authors proposed new schemes although others were content to support the traditional, process approach while decrying the criticisms of the behavioralists. Waino W. Suojanen suggested that functional management theory (the process school) was appropriate to only certain types of organizations and that management must be viewed in biological terms as evolving toward more use of quantitative and behavioral sciences because of changing technology, the changing needs of people, and new types of research and development-oriented organizations.[35] From his retirement home in Australia, Lyndall Urwick joined the fray and questioned Suojanen's implication that the theories of the behavioral scientists were evolutionary and hence destined to supersede the functional theories of management.[36]

[34]Ibid., p. 238.

[35]Waino W. Suojanen, "Management Theory: Functional and Evolutionary," *Journal of the Academy of Management*, Vol. 6, No. 1 (March, 1963), pp. 7–17.

[36]Lyndall F. Urwick, "The Tactics of Jungle Warfare," *Journal of the Academy of Management*, Vol. 6, No. 4 (December, 1963), pp. 316–329. Urwick also attacked the behavioral scientists for contributing to much confusion in semantics and for rejection of past pioneering concepts. See Lyndall F. Urwick, "Have We Lost Our Way in the Jungle of Management Theory?" *Personnel*, Vol. 42, No. 3 (May–June, 1965), pp. 8–18.

Some individuals were optimistic that a general theory could be developed. Frederick thought that, by drawing upon the best of all schools of thought, a coherent body of management thought could be developed along the same lines as Lord Keynes' *General Theory of Employment, Interest and Money.*[37] One author developed a taxonomic matrix patterned after the periodic table which would aid in classifying management concepts in order to aid the development of a general theory.[38] Gordon suggested a multiple approach to the problem, including an "ecological" approach, which would fuse various schools into a larger process of administration.[39]

The pessimists were in a minority, or at least less vocal. In addition to Suojanen's notion that the evolution of the behavioral sciences would supersede the functional approach, George S. Odiorne posited that management situations were too complex for precise principles and propositions that would yield a sound theory.[40] Others indicated that researchers and authors interjected too many of their own value judgments and worked from diametrically opposed premises and that these facts of academic reality seriously hampered any hope for unification.[41]

To a great extent, the controversy only proved what Koontz had set out to do, that is, to show that there was a theory thicket. Often the proposed methods of disentanglement only led to more rain and the further growth of foliage. The jungle has not yet been

[37] William C. Frederick, "The Next Step in Management Science: A General Theory," *Journal of the Academy of Management*, Vol. 6, No. 3 (September, 1963), pp. 212–219.

[38] Authur C. Laufer, "A Taxonomy of Management Theory: A Preliminary Framework," *Academy of Management Journal*, Vol. 11, No. 4 (December, 1968), pp. 435–442.

[39] Paul J. Gordon, "Transcend the Current Debate on Administrative Theory," *Journal of the Academy of Management*, Vol. 6, No. 4 (December, 1963), pp. 290–303. Gordon was president of the Academy of Management in 1969. A later, similar scheme to reconcile and integrate human and organizational values may be found in Edwin B. Flippo, "Interactive Schemes in Management Theory," *Academy of Management Journal*, Vol. 11, No. 1 (March, 1968), pp. 91–98.

[40] George S. Odiorne, "The Management Theory Jungle and the Existential Manager," *Academy of Management Journal*, Vol. 9, No. 2 (June, 1966), pp. 109–116.

[41] See Orlando Behling, "Unification of Management Theory: A Pessimistic View," *Business Perspectives*, Vol. 3, No. 4 (Summer, 1967), pp. 4–9.

penetrated, the machetes are becoming somewhat duller, and the hope for unity is still the Holy Grail.

The Third Generation

Principles and process writers in the 1960s were the offspring of this era of diversity. If one were to choose a theme for their efforts, it would be that of a search for integration, an attempt to bring the various differing views about the behavioral sciences, social systems, and quantitative methods into the traditional management theory framework. One barometer of the confusion over defining just exactly what was the proper study of management was reflected in the number of "readings" books in the late 1950s and early 1960s. The suggested explanation is that these were attempts to provide vehicles for teaching management in the face of diversity in management knowledge. The readings were generally eclectic, allowing instructors or students to pick and choose if they preferred or to allow overall exposure to a number of ideas.

Principles-of-management texts also attempted to integrate the diversity which followed the identification of the "jungle." Within the process framework they sought to build more behavioral, mathematical, and decision theory ideas into the traditional approach. Most sought an "interdisciplinary" approach which would integrate such diverse areas as group dynamics, operations research, economic theory, electronic data processing, etc. It is impossible to explore in full the work of each of the authors of this period, but the intent has been to characterize the management process approach as being in a period of transition during the mid-1960s.[42] From the basic work of Fayol, the third generation sought to bring greater depth, a broader scope, and a better conceptual framework to management theory. Those who were char-

---

[42]Representative works would include: William M. Fox, *The Management Process: An Integrated Functional Approach,* Homewood, Ill.: Richard D. Irwin, 1963; Justin G. Longenecker, *Principles of Management and Organizational Behavior,* Columbus, Ohio: Charles E. Merrill Publishing Co., 1964; Edwin B. Flippo, *Management: A Behavioral Approach,* Boston: Allyn and Bacon, 1966 (revised in 1970); Max D. Richards and Paul S. Greenlaw, *Management Decision Making,* Homewood, Ill.: Richard D. Irwin, 1966; and Herbert G. Hicks, *The Management of Organizations,* New York: McGraw-Hill Book Co., 1967.

acterized as the third generation sought this framework in the process but it was supplemented by an interdisciplinary flavor.

The Fourth Generation

It would be presumptuous to conclude that a fourth generation supplanted the third. The "fourth generation" label is merely an expository device, a conceptual handle to reflect what many saw as an island of hope for unity in a stormy sea of diversity. One facet, general systems theory, was the product of interdisciplinary studies and of space-age technology; the other, comparative management, reflected the growing importance of the multinational corporation. Together, these elements were another stage in evolving management thought.

The Systems Approach

General systems theory, actually beginning in 1937 with the ideas of Ludwig von Bertalanffy, was finally achieving recognition in general management theory in the 1960s. The origin and development of general systems theory will be examined at length in chapter 21; it is sufficient to note here that the systems framework represented a newer quest for a general theory of management. In 1963, two separate publications marked the appearance of the systems approach to the manager's job. Seymour Tilles suggested that an organization was not merely a social system, nor an information-decision system, but an open-ended system of many interrelated parts.[43] Using the systems approach, the manager could define system objectives, establish criteria for evaluating systems performance, and better relate the firm to a variety of environmental systems. In essence, Tilles was using the systems framework to bring diverse subsystems into an integrated whole and also recognizing the influences of the external environment on managerial decision making.

Johnson, Kast, and Rosenzweig built upon the pioneering work of Bertalanffy and sought to integrate general systems theory

---

[43]Seymour Tilles, "The Manager's Job: A Systems Approach," *Harvard Business Review*, Vol. 41, No. 1 (January–February, 1963), pp. 73–81.

and the process approach to management.[44] These authors postulated that "managing by system" was a philosophical notion as well as a practical reality and that this blending of systems theory and management theory would lead to more effective management. Beyond these efforts, other authors sought to recast the principles and process approach into the general systems theory framework.[45] For these authors, the organization was an interacting complex of physical, human, and information resources which could be viewed conceptually and managed as an input-output system. The goal was to combine the familiar and traditional analysis of the management process with the newer systems concept of management. This spilling over of systems theory into the traditional process approach reflected an increasing concern for the increasingly complex environment of management and for the incorporation of behavioral, quantitative, information-theory, and systems-theory concepts into the traditional framework. The systems approach would decline eventually in importance, for reasons which we shall see shortly, but its remnants were not lost.

Comparative Management

Another facet of the search for theory was the attempt to analyze and integrate administrative concepts from cross-cultural, cross-institutional, and cross-disciplinary points of view. This movement, variously called "comparative management" or "comparative administration," was a reaction to the growth of multinational business organizations and to the need for management knowledge in such diverse fields as nursing, education, government, industry, librarianship, and other managerial settings. Various conferences were held in attempts to bring together scholars from many disciplines and professions in order to find out what administrative concepts might be held in common.

The main thrust of interest in comparative management came

[44]Richard A. Johnson, Fremont E. Kast, and James E. Rosenzweig, *The Theory and Management of Systems*, New York: McGraw-Hill Book Co., 1963 (revised in 1967).

[45]For example: Dan Voich, Jr., and Daniel A. Wren, *Principles of Management: Resources and Systems*, New York: Ronald Press Co., 1968; and Henry L. Sisk, *Principles of Management: A Systems Approach to the Management Process*, Cincinnati, Ohio: South-Western Publishing Co., 1969.

with publications and conferences in 1965. Richard Farmer and Barry Richman were among the first to develop a "model" which would identify the critical elements in the management process as they applied to individual firms in varying cultures.[46] The silver anniversary annual meeting of the Academy of Management in 1965 was devoted to the theme of "comparative administration" and Preston LeBreton, as president of the academy in 1966, started a task force to further explore how comparative management theory could be expanded and refined.[47] While the 1962 U.C.L.A. symposium seemed more concerned with intramanagement theory unity, the comparative management approach sought a broader base across cultures, across professions, and across disciplines. This approach was heavily influenced by general systems theory; as general systems theory waned, comparative management also lost some of its savor.

The Fifth Generation

In an age of social unrest, economic turbulence, and political turmoil, it would be expected that people would become less certain about standard prescriptions for life as well as for organizational and managerial roles. America in the 1970s experienced an age of uncertainty and in these times the newer theories of management reflected these doubts about any "one best way" to do things. The "fifth generation" label indicates yet another stage in management thought which was not wholly unique, but which was viewed by some as a path out of the management theory "jungle."

"It depends . . ."

General systems theory opened new frontiers of thought for the modern student of management. It was not that systems theory was new in the sense of being novel, but that it provided another insight into the job of the manager. Systems theory addressed the importance of studying the parts of a situation, their relationships,

[46]R. N. Farmer and B. M. Richman, *Comparative Management and Economic Progress,* Homewood, Ill.: Richard D. Irwin, 1965.

[47]Preston P. LeBreton (ed.), *Comparative Administrative Theory,* Seattle: University of Washington Press, 1968.

and the integration of the parts into a "whole." The systems approach also emphasized the notion of managing an "open system," one in which the environment affected and was in turn influenced by the actions of managers and organizations. From systems theory came the idea that the activity of management was made more difficult by environmental factors and by inter-relationships between the organization and its environment.

Traditional management theory, according to this emerging fifth generation, did not provide adequate guides to managerial decision making. There were no "universals," no "one best way," and no standard advice for practitioners of management. Instead, the fifth generation brought the phrase "it depends . . ." into the management literature. The idea was that management had to identify the variables in each situation, understand the relationships between these variables and their interactions, and recognize the complexities of cause and effect in every managerial situation. For example, an organization with a "job-lot" or batch-processing technology would be organized differently than a firm with a mass production technology. Or, a firm with a highly unstable environment would organize differently than a firm with a greater degree of certainty in its environment. Since organizations had different technologies and operated in different environments, and since research indicated that the more successful ones were those that adapted to their technology/environment, there was no one best way to manage or organize. Similarly, leadership research in the modern era had noted that there was no one best way to lead. Again, it depended upon the situation.

The challenge to this fifth generation was how to blend traditional general management theory with the variabilities that were being found in research on organizations and leadership.[48] The goal would be that of analyzing situations, recognizing relationships among the parts of each situation, and understanding what arrangement of the parts led to the best results. There would be no universal prescriptions, no single approach, but rather a *way* of approaching the job of the manager through under-

---

[48] Examples of a proliferating literature are: Fred Luthans, *Introduction to Management: A Contingency Approach*, New York: McGraw-Hill Publishing Co., 1976; Howard M. Carlisle, *Management: Concepts and Situations*, Chicago: Science Research Associates, 1976; and Gary Dessler, *Organization and Management: A Contingency Approach*, Englewood Cliffs, N.J.: Prentice-Hall Inc., 1976.

standing relationships in each situation. The search was to identify and specify *functional* relationships between situational elements and performance. Advice to managers then would be "if"
such and such a situation prevails, "then" do so and so. The prescription would be present, but it would not be the same pill for
every ailment.

The historian can bring a different perspective to understanding the contingency approach to management. Indeed it may
be argued that *all* management thought has a contingency flavor,
reflecting changing times and changing economic, social, and political environments. In chapter 3, we saw how the introduction of
steam power in the textile industry in the eighteenth century
changed organizational relationships. This new technology moved
firms from batch production to mass production and created more
formal organizational structures, just as modern contingency theory would advise. We saw how the ideas of Taylor and Mayo,
dominant figures in two different eras, fitted into their particular
cultural milieus. Fayol operated in a different environment, as did
Weber, and their ideas fitted the perceived situations of their time
and place. Fayol felt that management was a universal activity, but
was very explicit in saying that the *principles* of management must
be flexible and modified to fit varying circumstances. Later, Mary
Follett recognized the "law of the situation," but did not prescribe
how managers should identify the variables and their relationships in order to obey the situational imperatives.

In brief, what the moderns see as universal theories were not
intended to be that by authors such as Fayol, Weber, Taylor, et al.
Our historical figures were bound by their times, just as we are by
ours. Their slice of reality led to their theories, just as ours do. We
occupy but one moment in ever-flowing time; management
thought is a product of our perception of that moment in which
we work.

The future of contingency theory, or perhaps it should be labeled the contingency approach, is open to conjecture.[49] While it
was formed as a protest against the universalists, will future developments lead contingency theorists to prescribe "universal"

[49]For an excellent critical analysis, see Dennis J. Moberg and James L. Koch, "A
Critical Appraisal of Integrated Treatments of Contingency Findings," *Academy of
Management Journal*, Vol. 18, No. 1 (March, 1975), pp. 109–124.

prescriptions for similar situations? If so, that will be recognition that previous management writers were not universal for all time but for *their* time and their situation. If not, i.e., no uniform prescriptions can be found, then contingency "theory" will fall as a theory and every situation is up for grabs. If that occurs, then the implications for management education are so vast as to defy the imagination of any mortal. The most likely occurrence is that the contingency approach will evolve into another generation of thought which is more pragmatic. Research will enrich our understanding of managerial situations; some of this will be capable of being codified and communicated, and some of it will be the waste product of progress. The next generation will find theory and practice closer together as academicians move out into the real world to test their laboratory ideas.

Improving Education for Management

Participative management, previously taught in the classroom to be practiced elsewhere, had led to some rethinking of how students are to be prepared for their managerial positions. The criticism of education for management is not new, and generation after generation has sought to improve the delivery of its product, i.e., managerial knowledge. Taylor had his doubts about teaching management in colleges and universities (at least *his* system), but it was Fayol who argued that it not only could but must be taught in institutions of higher learning. (No wonder we professors prefer Fayol over Taylor.) Fayol essayed to codify knowledge so that management could be taught, but modern authors have found discrepancies between what managers do in practice and what "theory" says they do. Mintzberg observed managers in action and reported that their activities were sporadic, short-term copings rather than deliberative, analytical and logical as Fayol suggested.[50]

    Rather than engaging in the traditional functions (or Fayol's "elements") of the management process, Mintzberg classified the

---

[50]Henry Mintzberg, *The Nature of Managerial Work*, New York: Harper and Row, 1973; and Henry Mintzberg, "The Manager's Job: Folklore and Fact," *Harvard Business Review*, Vol. 53, No. 4 (July–August, 1975), pp. 49–61.

roles of the manager into: (1) interpersonal (figurehead, leader, and liaison); (2) informational (monitor, disseminator, and spokesman); and (3) decisional (entrepreneur, disturbance handler, resource allocator, and negotiator). Mintzberg was less clear on how these roles would be taught, but suggested that education for management should be through the simulation of situations and feedback to students to help them improve their skills. Of course Fayol learned management through real-world experience rather than its simulation, and it is doubtful that he and Mintzberg are as far apart as it seems on the surface. Fayol was an executive and it is unlikely that he arose, dressed, and took a carriage to the office so that he could plan and organize in the mornings and command, coordinate and control in the afternoons. It is more likely that Fayol encountered the same problems as the executives Mintzberg studied and Fayol realized the need to codify these experiences into a body of knowledge so it could be taught.

Nevertheless, the problem for modern management educators has been that of trying to make the students' transition from the classroom to the world of practicing less painful and more relevant. Teachers of management have long envied the scientists, lawyers, and physicians who would sharpen their skills in the laboratory, the moot court, and the clinic before graduating into the real world. Various vehicles for education have been tried: the case method (which began in the early 1900s), role playing (which started in the 1930s), computerized business "games" (which emerged in the 1950s), and a host of other traditional and nontraditional pedagogical devices. An amalgamation of many of these techniques reappeared in the 1970s as the "experiential approach" to education for management.[51] The common theme of these efforts was to create a situation in the classroom which *simulated* as much as possible real managerial situations and problems. In groups or alone, students became involved in accomplishing simulated tasks and learned by doing. The focus was on the process of interaction and interpersonal relationships rather

[51] Examples of this approach include Fremont E. Kast and James E. Rosenzweig, *Experiential Exercises and Cases in Management,* New York: McGraw-Hill Publishing Co., 1976; Hyler J. Bracey and Aubrey Sanford, *Basic Management: An Experience Based Approach,* Dallas, Texas: Business Publications, Inc., 1977.

than the content of knowledge itself, i.e., the applied skill as opposed to the textbook theory. Rather than just reading about planning, students were given a project which they planned; rather than reading about leadership, etc., students became involved in the activity. The approach did not eliminate the need for text theory, but supplemented it through these experiences.

The experiential approach, like the contingency approach, is a return to more pragmatism in management education. It is an endeavor to make education more relevant and to bridge theory and practice. In these approaches, the hope is that managers can be trained to analyze situations, sharpen their handling of them, and make the leap to the world of work without tripping over their college degree.

A Final Comment

The preceding analysis has focused on the evolution of the process approach to management theory without examining in depth the rich body of literature in the modern era. Of course the task of writing history is never done, for each day brings new ideas, new evidence, and new ways of examining the tasks of the manager. It is difficult for modern scholars, so steeped in their own daily activities and so influenced by the current press of today's ideas, to sit back and put them in perspective. The zoom lens of history often leaves the near present slightly out of focus.

The theme of this chapter has been that of a search for unity in management theory. Why search for unity? If unity in theory was achieved, would that lead to a stifling conformity in research, teaching, and practice? If one believes that unity is synonymous with conformity, then we all should be against unity. We recognize the need for constructive dissent, for innovative teaching and research that challenges the status quo, and for other new ideas which test the usefulness of conventional wisdoms. But unity need not mean conformity; the search for unity is the quest for agreement on terminology, for a common body of knowledge to be transmitted, for acceptance of various "tools" and "schools" for what each can contribute, and for attaining a perspective on what has been done and what needs to be done. Perhaps then unity should be viewed as a means, not the goal; a means whereby we can offer our students a more coherent view of the field, guide our research along more fruitful paths, offer users of our services more practical solutions to their problems, and reach out from a common baseline in our search for greater understanding of the job of the manager.

Summary

Post–World War II management found renewed interest in general management theory. The development of expanded markets, the technological advances which followed wartime research, and the continued growth of organizations required managers to operate on a sounder theoretical base. Management was to become more than providing for production operations, more than merely business management, and more than the straightforward performance of a limited number of activities. It was in this environment that scholars and practitioners sought to provide management principles and an intellectual framework for managing through the process approach. The early 1950s found a wide variation in terminology, especially with respect to directing or leading, and the second generation began to refine the Fayolian functions to fit modern organizations. Simplicity did not reign, however, as other areas spilled over into the process by contributing mathematical models, findings from the behavioral sciences, and the cybernetics of the computer age. The "jungle" was widely debated and the 1960s were characterized as an age of attempted integration of various new ideas into the traditional functions. The quest for unity continued through the systems approach and comparative management. The 1970s found a decline in the systems approach and yet another generation evolved. Less credence was placed in "one best way" and the contingency approach to management was the result. Pleas for relevance and recognition of the gap between theory and practice were met with the experiential approach to management.

Unity in theory has not come; perhaps it never will. Only the future and the hindsight it affords will bring this search into a better perspective. But the search continues, as it should, and if any lessons are to be learned from history, it is that we must learn to break down the walls of academic jealousy, to develop a better appreciation of our intellectual heritage, and to realize that we occupy only one point in time. Synthesis will come as we learn better to relate the technical and human problems of organizations.

20

Organizational Humanism: The Search for Harmony

Apace with the search for unity in management theory, modern behavioralists were gathering the harvest of the Western Electric and other researchers and sowing a new crop of ideas for managerial cultivation. The roots of concern for people in organizations may be traced historically to the "humanists" of the Renaissance who called for the overthrow of monolithic church authority, the participation and enlightenment of the citizenry, the breakup of rigid social structures, and the rediscovery of the human being as a unit of study. Throughout the preceding pages, we have seen varying views and assumptions about people vis-à-vis the organization. Robert Owen admonished the factory owners to pay as much attention to their "vital machines," their workers, as to their physical machines. Taylor, so often maligned by the modern behavioralists, was concerned with individual development and provided the roots for the empirical investigation of human behavior when he wrote: "There is another type of scientific investigation which should receive special attention, namely, the accurate study of the motives which influence men."[1] The industrial psychology of Hugo Munsterberg was the response to this call for better understanding of people at work. Others, such as Whiting Williams

[1] F. W. Taylor, *The Principles of Scientific Management*, New York: Harper and Row, 1911, p. 119.

and Henri DeMan, probed the human factor in industry. The roots of behavioralism were established before the Hawthorne studies; but that research, coming in such perilous days of industrial development, brought a new focus on people in organizations. This was "social man," and the Mayoists' call for the development of the manager's social skills.

The post-Hawthorne developments were presented as developing along two lines: (1) the micro analysis of human behavior in motivation, group dynamics, and leadership; and (2) the macro search for the fusion of the social and technical systems. This chapter will examine these micro and macro approaches as they evolved into modern views of people vis-à-vis the organization. Modern management makes more sense when viewed in the light of its foundations, and it will be seen that the modern behavioralists were engaged in a search for a harmony of people and organizations which began many years earlier. This search for harmony may be defined as the quest for a just adaptation of human needs and aspirations to the requirements and goals of the organization. Harmony means agreement between the parts of a design or composition which gives a pleasing unity of effect whether it be in music, art, or organizational life. This chapter will probe the modern quest to resolve the conflict between the logic of efficiency and the logic of sentiments, the search to meet human needs while fulfilling the objectives of organizations.

People and Organizations

The human relations movement was interdisciplinary in nature, bringing in the contributions of sociology, psychology, social psychology, anthropology, and political science as the primary disciplines to help to develop a body of knowledge about the behavior of individuals at work. The human relationists gathered many to their bosom to further the cause of industrial harmony. As the movement evolved, however, there came about: (1) a decline in the interpretation of people's needs as being primarily social; (2) mental health overtones of organizational humanism; and (3) an emphasis on job design and self-actualization through work.

Human Relations in Transition

In its early stages, the human relations movement bore the stamp of industrial sociology. Mayo and his associates were interested in rebuilding primary groups, in the factory as a social system, in status and role concepts, in the group as the source of human satisfaction, and in developing the social skills of the leader. The outcome of the Hawthorne studies was the establishment of various industrial relations centers, survey research centers, and other similarly titled organizations for carrying out behavioral research in industry. It was in these institutions that research was spawned which would eventually lead to the decline of social man.

The industrial sociologists attempted to overcome some of the criticisms levied against the Mayoists, and the early 1950s were to see the rise of "industrial human relations." Just as Robert Valentine and Morris Cooke tried to bring about a *rapprochement* between scientific management and organized labor, the post-Mayo revisionists quickly put unions into the human relations picture. Organized labor had made significant membership gains in the 1930s and 1940s, and the 1950s brought the merger of the A.F.L. and the C.I.O. The industrial sociologists devoted more and more space to organized labor and examined industry as an *institution* of groups of social classes, workers, foremen, managers, et al., who operated in a larger societal complex.[2]

A basic assumption which appeared to prevail in this approach to industrial human relations was that there was natural conflict between labor and management with respect to dividing the surplus created by an advanced technological society.[3] To the industrial human relationists, the answer to industrial conflict re-

[2]Examples of this may be found in George Friedman, *Industrial Society*, New York: Free Press, 1955; Wilbert E. Moore, *Industrial Relations and the Social Order*, New York: Macmillan Co., 1951; Eugene V. Schneider, *Industrial Sociology*, New York: McGraw-Hill Book Co., 1957; Delbert C. Miller and William H. Form, *Industrial Sociology*, New York: Harper and Row, 1951; and W. Lloyd Warner and James O. Low, *The Social System of the Modern Factory*, New Haven, Conn.: Yale University Press, 1947.

[3]See Arthur Kornhouser, Robert Dubin, and Arthur M. Ross (eds.), *Industrial Conflict*, New York: McGraw-Hill Book Co., 1954; and various selections in Conrad M. Arensberg, et al. (ed.), *Research in Industrial Human Relations*, New York: Harper and Row, 1957.

sided not in human relations training per se but in overcoming the conflicting interests and ideologies of management and the worker, usually meaning the organized worker. Industrial harmony would come through collective bargaining and from professional industrial relations specialists.[4]

In addition to bringing unions into the human relations fold, the human relations texts of the 1940s and early 1950s continued in the Mayoist tradition. They typically postulated that the "feelings" of people were more important than the "logics" of organization charts, rules, and directives.[5] Human relations was based on intangibles, not on hard scientific investigation, and there were no "final" answers, i.e., nothing positive nor fixed in solutions to human problems. In part, it was a rebellion against the absolutism of science and against the rigors of being responsible for one's actions. Malcolm McNair had criticized this lack of individual responsibility; an analogy might be that of the trend toward rehabilitating instead of punishing a criminal offender. In general, the texts of the early 1950s emphasized feelings, sentiments, and collaboration.[6] They were heuristic rather than specific or systematic, i.e., the texts encouraged others to investigate and discover for themselves rather than prescribing techniques.

The outpouring of behavioral research from various centers was to lead to the discoveries that: (1) the satisfied worker was not always the most productive worker; and (2) it was not necessarily the relationships between worker and manager nor the cohesiveness of the work group that led to higher productivity, but that it was the nature of work itself which was important. The beginning of the end of orthodox human relations appeared in the criticisms being levied in the 1950s of the abuses and corruption of the "happiness boys." For many, the term "human relations" represented "at best a rather pedestrian effort and at worst a cyn-

---

[4]See Ross Stagner, *The Psychology of Industrial Conflict*, New York: John Wiley and Sons, 1956; and William Foote Whyte's application of human relations to the bargaining problems of Inland Steel in *Pattern for Industrial Peace*, New York: Harper and Row, 1951.

[5]Schuyler D. Hoslett (ed.), *Human Factors in Management*, New York: Harper and Row, 1946, preface.

[6]For example: Burleigh B. Gardner and David G. Moore, *Human Relations in Industry*, Homewood, Ill.: Richard D. Irwin, 1955.

ical attempt to manipulate people."[7] The behavioral sciences were seen as one way in which more powerful analytical and conceptual tools could be put to use in handling the problems of human behavior.

The decline of social man was found in these dimensions: (1) the industrial research which discovered that man was more complex than orthodox human relations had assumed; (2) the criticisms of human relations as being too "happiness" oriented; and (3) the growing sophistication of the behavioral science disciplines themselves. Post–World War II America witnessed human relations in transition, and social man declined in importance to be replaced by a more rigorous way of examining human behavior in organizations.

The Changing Environment and the New Humanism

It is always difficult to pinpoint chronologically the decline of one set of ideas and the emergence of a new philosophy. However, there is evidence that the period from 1957 to 1960 can be specified as marking the emergence of a new philosophy concerning people in organizations. William G. Scott has called this emerging philosophy of the modern era "industrial humanism."

> [Industrial humanism] has both a philosophy and an assortment of practices with which it proposes to change the conventional structure of work relationships and the content of work itself . . . with the goal of the restoration of the individual's opportunity for self-realization at work.[8]

In its essence, industrial humanism sought to offset the authoritarian tendencies of organizations, to provide for democracy and self-determination at work, to integrate individual and organizational goals, and to restore man's dignity at work. A more comprehensive and more descriptive term might be *organizational humanism*; and this phrase will be used to describe the new

---

[7] William G. Scott, *Human Relations in Management: A Behavioral Science Approach*, Homewood, Ill.: Richard D. Irwin, 1962, p. 4.

[8] William G. Scott, *Organization Theory: A Behavioral Analysis for Management*, Homewood, Ill.: Richard D. Irwin, 1967, p. 43 and p. 258.

philosophy which was to replace the alleged softness and heuristic nature of the old human relations school.

What cultural phenomena are appropriate to mark this shift from social man to organizational humanism during the period 1957–1960? In the economic-technology sphere, two events serve as benchmarks: (1) the recession of 1957–58; and (2) the beginning of the space age. It has been noted that the human relations philosophy dominated until the recession of 1957–1958. During the recession, the human relations philosophy failed to meet the economic criteria of productivity and profitability. Afterward, the new emphasis was on "human resources" rather than "human relations." The human resources philosophy "viewed the productivity of employees as being an economic resource of a firm or nation. The employee himself . . . is viewed according to the concept of human dignity." This approach gave dual credence to economic efficiency while "recognizing and respecting the personal dignity of each human entity."[9]

The orbiting of Sputnik I thrust the world into the space age and America into a space race. In an effort to catch up, America began to fund large research and development programs. These programs generated the further development of computer-based information systems, the need for more quantitative bases for decisions, and the problems of managing engineers and scientists. The "professional" employee in research and development activities required new assumptions about motivation and leadership; the task of managing complex, interfacing projects demanded the rethinking of traditional line-and-staff organizational structures; and the requirements of a more highly technological, space-age economy required new modes of resource allocation and utilization.

Social values were in flux. Whereas the college students of the 1950s were accused of apathy, the new decade brought a new activism as institutions and their administrations began to be questioned more and more. Within business education itself, we

---

[9]Leon C. Megginson, *Personnel: A Behavioral Approach to Administration*, Homewood, Ill.: Richard D. Irwin, 1967, p. 87; see also Raymond E. Miles, "Human Relations or Human Resources?," *Harvard Business Review*, Vol. 43, No. 4 (July–August, 1965), pp. 148–163.

have already discussed the soul-searching of the Gordon-Howell-Pierson reports. Curricula were being reshaped and there was a revival of interest in management as a profession, in ethics, in philosophy, and in the social responsibility of business. In the political realm, the Eisenhower years were closing and the new decade promised the vitality and vibrancy of the youthful President John F. Kennedy. There was the promise of civil rights, of help to the disadvantaged, and of the opportunity to serve through the Peace Corps. In short, the late 1950s were presaging the close of an era and the 1960s were promising to bring in more of a bottom-up, power-equalizing humanism.

Self-Actualization Through Work

One of the criticisms of the human relationists was their emphasis on social relations to the neglect of a focus on the nature of work and the satisfactions in work for people. When viewed as a cultural value, work has a spotted history. As Purcell has pointed out, the Greeks used the word *ponos*, meaning sorrow or burden, for work; in medieval Europe, work was meaningful enough for men to derive their family names from their crafts and today we find names like Hunter, Weaver, Carpenter, Taylor, Miller, and so on. However, to derive names from jobs today, such as "Mike Machinist" or "Luella Keypuncher" would be folly.[10] The Protestant ethic saw work as an end in itself, not necessarily to be enjoyed but to serve as a sign of election and a means to achieving the grace of God. The critics of the Industrial Revolution and of the infant capitalism, such as Karl Marx, saw work as an imposition of the power of the exploiting capital class upon the working class. F. W. Taylor developed no explicit values for work but largely reflected the Protestant ethic that for each person there was a class of work at which he was best and, after assignment to that work, the worker would contribute the most to himself, to his employer, and to the community. Mayo and his associates played down work as a duty, as a means to fulfillment, and as a central theme of industrial life in order to substitute interpersonal re-

[10]Theodore V. Purcell, "Work Psychology and Business Values: A Triad Theory of Work Motivation," *Personnel Psychology*, Vol. 20, No. 3 (Autumn, 1967), pp. 235–236.

lations as a means of overcoming the anomie that industrial civilization had caused. Abraham Maslow established a hierarchy of human needs in the early 1940s and extended this theory in his *Motivation and Personality*. [11] Maslow saw a dynamic interplay of needs in which the summit was the need for "self-actualization." It was in this drive of self-fulfillment, for people being what they could be, that the modern behavioralists found blockages in previously held views of motivation, leadership, and organizations.

The modern era of organizational humanism has developed a new view of work, of people, and of how to achieve organizational harmony by designing organizations to allow people expression of what was assumed to be a natural urge to find satisfactions in work. In perspective, the themes developed by modern writers have mental health overtones as they seek to reduce organizational rigidity, as they strive to understand the personality needs of the healthy individual, and as they propose new managerial styles and philosophies to satisfy human needs while still fulfilling the formal goals of the organization.

Human Relations and Organizational Behavior

Nowhere was the evolution in human relations thought more evident than in the work of Arizona State's Professor Keith Davis, "Mr. Human Relations." In 1957 Davis defined human relations as "the integration of people into a work situation in a way that motivates them to work together productively, cooperatively, and with economic, psychological, and social satisfaction." [12] This view marked the beginning of a modern view of human relations which was more empirically rigorous in understanding organizational behavior and philosophically broader in understanding people's interactions in a more complex network of societal forces. Davis held that modern human relations really had two facets: one

---

[11] A. H. Maslow, *Motivation and Personality*, New York: Harper & Row, 1954. An extension of this thinking may be found in A. H. Maslow, *Eupsychian Management*, Homewood, Ill.: Richard D. Irwin, 1965; by *eupsychian*, Maslow means "moving toward psychological health" (p. xi).

[12] Keith Davis, *Human Relations in Business*, New York: McGraw-Hill Book Co., 1957, p. 4.

was concerned with understanding, describing, and identifying causes and effects of human behavior through empirical investigation; the other facet was the application of this knowledge into operational situations. The first could be termed "organizational behavior" and the second facet was "human relations." Both facets were complementary in that one investigated and explained while the other was a way of thinking about people at work and applying behavioral insights into operating situations.[13]

In other work, Davis developed techniques for the analysis of informal communications structures and has written extensively of the informal organization and of the social responsibility of business. The "modern" human relations of Keith Davis added economic and psychological facets to the social nature of people. He has brought unions into the equation, added broader consideration of societal forces, and based the new human relations era on a more rigorous empirical understanding.

Personality and Organization

Abraham Maslow paved the way for the "humanist psychologists" who argued for better employee mental health through improved organizational practices. Professor Chris Argyris enlarged upon this notion as a proponent of what had been variously called the "personality versus organization" hypothesis or the "immaturity-maturity" theory of human behavior. For Argyris there are some basic trends in the personality growth of healthy, mature individuals. From infancy to adulthood, there is a tendency for the "healthy" personality to develop along a continuum from immaturity to maturity by moving from being passive to being active; by moving from dependence to independence; by growing from a lack of awareness of self to awareness and control over self; and so on.[14] One could determine an individual's degree of self-actualization by plotting his position on the immaturity-maturity continuum.

---

[13] Davis' second edition was entitled *Human Relations at Work* (1962) and the latest edition (fifth) bore the title *Human Behavior at Work: Organizational Behavior* (1977).

[14] Chris Argyris, *Personality and Organization: The Conflict between the System and the Individual*, New York: Harper and Row, 1957, p. 50.

According to Argyris, the basic properties of the formal organization keep individuals immature and mediate against self-actualization. Criticizing Taylor and other organizational formalists, Argyris found four basic properties of the formal organization to be the seat of the problem: first, the specialization of labor limits individual initiative, chokes off self-expression, and requires individuals to use only a few of their abilities. "It inhibits self-actualization and provides expression for few, shallow, skin-surface abilities that do not provide the endless challenge desired by the healthy personality."[15] Second, the chain of command assumes that efficiency is a result of arranging the parts so that power and authority are lodged at the top and so that through a definite hierarchy of authority the top can control the bottom of the organization. The impact of this is to make the individuals dependent upon and passive toward the leader. Individuals have little control over their working environment, develop a short time perspective, and are made dependent by the incentive and control systems. Third, the unity-of-direction principle means that the path toward the goal is directed and controlled by the leader. Problems develop when these work goals do not involve the employees, when they are not allowed to aspire to use more of their abilities, and when they are not allowed to define their own goals in terms of their inner needs. Finally, the span-of-control concept tends to decrease the amount of self-control and the time perspective of the individuals at the bottom of the ladder. By limiting the number of subordinates under one manager, closer control may be exercised and this presupposes immaturity of these individuals.

Using these four organizational "principles," Argyris built his case for the incongruency between the needs of the healthy personality and the requirements of the formal organization. Faced with the demands of the organization, individuals may engage certain defense mechanisms to adapt or to react: (1) they may leave the organization; (2) they may climb the organizational ladder to achieve more autonomy; (3) they may daydream, become aggressive, use projection, regress, or use other defense mechanisms; (4) they may become apathetic or noninvolved; and (5) they may create and formalize informal groups to sanction

[15] Ibid., p. 59.

their own apathy, disinterest, restriction of output, aggression, and so on. Management, faced with the reactions of the workers, also reacts by using more autocratic, directive leadership, by tightening organizational controls, or by turning to "human relations." To Argyris, managers have adopted pseudo-human relations in many cases in order to "sugar-coat" the work situation rather than trying to remove the causes of employee discontent.

From Argyris' prolific writings, one can see his proposals for designing organizations to reduce the incongruency and to achieve harmony between the personality and the organization. Job enlargement, an increase in the number of tasks performed by the employee along the flow of work or a lengthening of the time cycle required to complete one unit, is one way to give individuals a greater opportunity to use more of their abilities and to give them a greater sense of power and control over their work. Participative, employee-centered leadership decreases feelings of apathy, dependence, and submissiveness, and helps individuals achieve self-actualization, while helping the organization meet its goals. In other areas, Argyris advises management to give employees a variety of experiences, to challenge them by giving them more responsibility, and to rely more on employee self-direction and self-control. Argyris requires a "reality-centered" leadership which has diagnostic skills, an awareness of self and others, and which keeps in mind at all times the worth of the individual and the worth of the organization. It is through awareness, understanding, and modification of organizational practices that the healthy individual can be nurtured in a healthy organization and that both can achieve their goals and needs. Harmony, then, for Argyris is not sweetness and light but the maturation of people in enlightened organizations.

Theories X and Y

Douglas McGregor (1906–1964) received his doctoral degree from Harvard University in 1935 and taught social psychology at Harvard from 1935 to 1937. He became an assistant professor of psychology at the Massachusetts Institute of Technology in 1937 and served that institution, except for six years as president of Antioch College (1948–1954), until his death. As president of Antioch College, McGregor found that the precepts of the human relations model were inadequate for coping with the rigors and realities of organizational life.

> *I believed, for example, that a leader could operate successfully as a kind of adviser to his organization. I thought I could avoid being a "boss." Unconsciously, I suspect, I hoped to duck the unpleasant necessity of making difficult decisions, of taking the responsibility for one course of action, among many uncertain alternatives, of making mistakes and taking the consequences. I thought that maybe I could operate so that everyone would like me—that "good human relations" would eliminate all discord and disagreement.*
>
> *I couldn't have been more wrong It took a couple of years, but I finally began to realize that a leader cannot avoid the exercise of authority any more than he can avoid responsibility for what happens to his organization.* [16]

In *The Human Side of Enterprise,* McGregor made a significant shift in his ideas from the human relations philosophy to the new humanism. He challenged the "classical principles of organization" as being inappropriate, since they were largely based on the church and the military; as being unrelated to the modern influences of the political, social and economic milieu; and as being based on erroneous assumptions about human behavior. [17] McGregor felt that managerial assumptions about human nature and human behavior were all-important in determining managers' styles of operating. Based upon their assumptions about human nature, managers could organize, lead, control, and motivate people in different ways. Managers who accepted one set of assumptions would tend to manage one way; those who held a different set would manage another way. The first set of assumptions McGregor examined was "Theory X," which was to represent the "traditional view of direction and control." Theory X assumptions were:

1. *The average human being has an inherent dislike of work and will avoid it if he can . . .*

[16] Douglas McGregor, "On Leadership," *Antioch Notes,* (May, 1954), pp. 2–3. Cited by Warren G. Bennis, "Revisionist Theory of Leadership," *Harvard Business Review,* Vol. 39, No. 1 (January–February, 1961), p. 34.

[17] Douglas McGregor, *The Human Side of Enterprise,* New York: McGraw-Hill Book Co., 1960, pp. 16–18.

2. *Because of this human characteristic of dislike of work, most people must be coerced, controlled, directed, threatened with punishment to get them to put forth adequate effort toward the achievement of organizational objectives . . .*

3. *The average human being prefers to be directed, wishes to avoid responsibility, has relatively little ambition, wants security above all.*[18]

McGregor thought that these X assumptions were the ones prevailing in modern industrial practice. He stated that he did not intend to make a "straw man" for demolition with his Theory X but his polarization of X as encompassing all traditional management certainly led to such an interpretation by others. He did not name individuals nor delve into past management thought very deeply; if he had, he would have found that Theory X was not quite as prevalent as he assumed. While he did note a shift from "hard" X (presumably scientific management) to "soft" X (human relations), McGregor maintained that no fundamental shift in assumptions or managerial philosophies had occurred.

Theory Y was put forth as a "modest beginning for new theory with respect to the management of human resources." The assumptions of Theory Y were:

1. The expenditure of physical and mental effort in work is as natural as play or rest. *The average human being does not inherently dislike work . . .*

2. External control and the threat of punishment are not the only means for bringing about effort toward organizational objectives. Man will exercise self-direction and self-control in the service of objectives to which he is committed.

3. Commitment to objectives is a function of the rewards associated with their achievement. *The most significant of such rewards, e.g., the satisfaction of ego and self-actualization needs, can be direct products of effort directed toward organizational objectives.*

[18]Ibid., pp. 33–34. Theories X and Y were first published in *Adventures in Thought and Action,* Proceedings of the Fifth Anniversary Convocation of the School of Industrial Management, Massachusetts Institute of Technology, Cambridge, Mass., April 9, 1957; reprinted in Warren G. Bennis, Edgar H. Schein, and Caroline McGregor (eds.), *Leadership and Motivation: Essays of Douglas McGregor,* Cambridge, Mass: MIT Press, 1966, pp. 3–20.

4. The average human being learns, under proper conditions, not only to accept but to seek responsibility. *Avoidance of responsibility, lack of ambition, and emphasis on security are generally consequences of experience, not inherent human characteristics.*

5. The capacity to exercise a relatively high degree of imagination, ingenuity, and creativity in the solution of organizational problems is widely, not narrowly, distributed in the population.

6. Under the conditions of modern industrial life, the intellectual potentialities of the average human being are only partially utilized.[19]

In the use of Mary Follett's terms, with a slight twist of Argyris, McGregor called Theory Y "the integration of individual and organizational goals" and held that it led to the "creation of conditions such that the members of the organization can achieve their own goals *best* by directing their efforts toward the success of the enterprise."[20] Under Theory Y, it was the essential task of management to unleash employees' potential so that they could achieve their goals by directing their efforts toward those of the organization. It was "management by objectives" in the traditional sense but the motivation came from the *commitment* of people to the objectives of the organization. Managers who accepted the Y image of human nature would not structure, control, or closely supervise the work environment. Instead, they would attempt to aid the maturation of subordinates by giving them wider latitude in their work, encouraging creativity, using less external control, encouraging self-control, and motivating through the satisfactions which came from the challenge of work itself. The use of the authority of external control by management would be replaced by getting people *committed* to organizational goals because they perceived that this was the best way to achieve their own goals. A perfect integration was not possible, but McGregor hoped that an adoption of Y assumptions by managers would improve existing industrial practice.

[19]McGregor, *The Human Side of Enterprise*, pp. 47–48. Copyright 1960, the McGraw-Hill Book Company; by permission.

[20]Ibid., p. 49.

McGregor served as a bridge from the old view of human relations to the new organizational humanism. It was McGregor's fundamental belief that harmony could be achieved, not by being "hard" or "soft," but by changing assumptions about people in order to see that people could be trusted, that they could exercise self-motivation and control, and that they had the capacity to integrate their own personal goals with those of the formal organization. To McGregor, how people were treated was largely a self-fulfilling prophecy; if managers assumed that people were lazy and treated them as if they were, then they *would* be lazy. On the other hand, if managers assumed that people desired challenging work and exploited this premise by increasing individual discretion, workers would in fact respond by seeking more and more responsibility.

The Motivation-Hygiene Theory

A high degree of consonance with Argyris and McGregor about why people work has been put forth by Frederick Herzberg and his associates. Based on extensive empirical investigation, Herzberg set forth a "motivation-hygiene" theory of motivation which has received both widespread support and many criticisms. The research was designed to discover the importance of attitudes toward work and the experiences, both good and bad, which workers reported. Herzberg asked his research samples to respond to this question: "Think of a time when you felt exceptionally good or exceptionally bad about your job, either your present job or any other job you have had . . . Tell me what happened."[21] Out of the responses to this question and a series of follow-up questions, Herzberg set out to discover the kinds of things which made people happy and satisfied on their jobs or unhappy and dissatisfied. In analyzing his data, he concluded that people responded in such a manner as to isolate two different kinds of needs which appeared to be independent. When people reported unhappiness and job dissatisfaction, they attributed this to their job environ-

[21] Frederick Herzberg, Bernard Mausner, and Barbara B. Snyderman, *The Motivation to Work*, New York; John Wiley and Sons, 1959, Appendix I, p. 141. The reader will recall from chapter 9 that Henri DeMan asked a similar question in 1929 in his search for "joy in work."

ment or the *job context*. When people reported happiness or satisfaction, they attributed this good feeling to work itself or to the *job
content*.

Herzberg called the factors which were identified in the job
context "hygiene" factors, "for they act in a manner analogous to
the principles of medical hygiene. Hygiene operates to remove
health hazards from the environment of man. It is not curative: it
is, rather, a preventive."[22] The hygiene factors included supervision, interpersonal relations, physical working conditions, salaries, company policies, and administrative practices, benefits,
and job security. When these factors deteriorated below what the
worker considered an acceptable level, job dissatisfaction was the
result. However, when the job context was considered optimal by
the worker, dissatisfaction was removed; this did not lead to *positive* attitudes, however, but to some sort of a neutral state of neither satisfaction nor dissatisfaction.

The factors that led to positive attitudes, satisfaction, and
motivation were called the "motivators" or those things in the
work itself which satisfied the individual's needs for self-
actualization. The motivators were such factors as achievement,
recognition for accomplishment, challenging work, increased job
responsibility, and opportunities for growth and development. All
of these factors were in the nature of the job itself and, if present,
led to higher motivation for the worker. In this sense, Herzberg
was saying that traditional assumptions of motivation about wage
incentives, improving interpersonal relations, and establishing
proper working conditions did not lead to higher motivation.
They removed dissatisfaction, acted to prevent problems; but once
these traditional "motivators" were optimal, they did not lead to
positive motivation. According to Herzberg, management should
recognize that hygiene was necessary but that once it had neu-
tralized dissatisfaction, it did not lead to positive results. Only the
"motivators" led people to superior performance.

In rebuttal to those who claimed success for wage incentive
plans such as the Scanlon and the Lincoln Electric schemes, Herzberg said that money in these cases was actually a direct reward
for recognition, achievement, and responsibility. It was not wage

[22] Ibid., p. 113. A more recent work is Frederick Herzberg, *The Managerial Choice: To
Be Efficient and To Be Human*, Homewood, Ill. Dow-Jones-Irwin, 1976.

increases in an across-the-board manner (which would be a hygiene factor), but added earnings which were merited as a reward for growth, achievement, and responsibility. For Herzberg, "hygiene is not enough" and the motivation to work must come from job enrichment ("vertical loading"), more challenging jobs and opportunities for growth, and supervisors who were aware of the need for recognition and achievement and gave employees chances for self-actualization.

Davis, Herzberg, McGregor, and Argyris form the pillars of this modern quest for organizational humanism. Harmony would not come from a mental revolution nor from social solidarity but from the use of the behavioral sciences to understand the nature and needs of people in organizations.

Fashions and Fads

The fashions of one age may appear to have been merely a passing fancy to a succeeding generation. Management knowledge is an evolving web of ideas which questions, yet builds upon, prior thought. The precepts of Argyris, McGregor, and Herzberg which advocated improved organizational practices to promote self-actualization have not escaped criticism. Those of the "contingency" viewpoint have questioned whether or not these precepts were "the one best way" (i.e., one must practice participative management, one must enrich jobs, or one must follow Theory Y). The challenges have been to the neatness and simplicity of following these precepts as the gospel of how to promote humanism in organizational life. For example, it has been suggested that organizations are not as tyrannical as Argyris supposed and that to assume that work is the sole life interest of workers, i.e., they must derive their life satisfactions from the job, is erroneous.[23] According to the critics, the self-actualizers neglect economic motivation, assume that all people want to be independent and creative, and err by concluding that the job should be the primary mode of need satisfaction for everyone. Opportunities for self-

[23] See Robert Dubin, "Person and Organization," in Robert Dubin (ed.), *Human Relations in Administration*, 3rd ed., Englewood Cliffs, N.J.: Prentice-Hall, 1968, pp. 90–93; and George Strauss, "Some Notes on Power Equalization," in Harold J. Leavitt (ed.), *The Social Science of Organizations*, Englewood Cliffs, N.J.: Prentice-Hall, 1963, pp. 41–48.

actualization should be offered where it is appropriate to the workers' abilities and aspirations. But where tasks are highly programmed and the organizational costs of self-actualization outweigh the gains, or when people do not desire to make work their central life interest, self-actualization would not be appropriate as a motivational device.

McGregor's ideas have also been tested in the crucible of organizational realities. Non-linear Systems, once a leading example of Theory Y in practice, returned to more traditional managerial practices as hard times hit the company and the industry.[24] Warren Bennis, a leading McGregorite, also encountered frustrations in applying these concepts in the world of work. One of the conclusions he formed was that "Bureaucracy is the inevitable—and therefore necessary—form for governing large and complex organizations."[25] The lesson for the modern has been that of adopting a situational posture—no one managerial style or precept can be appropriate in all situations and for all times.

This "beyond Theory Y" notion argued for a match (or "fit") between the nature of the task performed and the needs of the people doing that work.[26] Humans have varying need patterns and operate best when the task and the organizational design fit these needs. Those people who desire more structure, more formalism, and who perhaps do not desire to participate in decision making, could be effective and motivated under a Theory X manager. Those who desire more self-control, more responsibility, and more outlets for creativity would find their match in the Y set of assumptions. In brief, no one set of assumptions is going to cover all of the people all of the time.

Herzberg's formula for motivating has also been subjected to testing and criticism. Herzberg's methodology of asking people to report on satisfying and dissatisfying incidents has led to one set of criticisms. When asked to do so, people are not likely to attribute their satisfaction to job context factors—those events outside of

[24]"Where Being Nice to Workers Didn't Work," *Business Week* (January 20, 1973), pp. 98–100.

[25]Warren Bennis, "Who Sank the Yellow Submarine?," *Psychology Today* (November, 1972), p. 120.

[26]John J. Morse and Jay W. Lorsch, "Beyond Theory Y," *Harvard Business Review*, Vol. 48, No. 3 (May-June, 1970), pp. 61–68.

their own control. To the contrary, they will take the credit when things go well, attributing satisfaction to events they can control in the job content area. They will place the blame for dissatisfaction not on themselves, but on the job context—the work environment. The conclusion, then, is that Herzberg's way of asking his questions leads to the results he gets. The second general area of criticism involves Herzberg's conclusions.[27] If the dualfactor theory is correct, it should find that highly satisfied people are highly motivated and high producers. The evidence so far does not find a positive relationship between worker satisfaction and productivity. Satisfied workers are not always the best producers, nor are dissatisfied workers the worst producers. To illustrate, one worker may respond to the challenge of "plan-do-control" while yet another may prefer to be told what to do. Work is a means for some people, not an end. Finally, the position of organized labor with respect to job enrichment has not yet been fully articulated. One labor official has suggested that "to enrich the job, enrich the paycheck. The better the wage, the greater the job satisfaction. There is no better cure for the 'blue collar blues.' "[28] If this attitude prevails, yet another criticism will result, i.e., that job enrichment is opposed by organized labor.

From the debris of these notions, the emerging view has been that of less certainty and more variability in prescriptions for managerial practice. The conclusion should not be that Argyris, McGregor, and Herzberg were *wrong* (nor were Fayol, Taylor, Mayo, et al.) but that their ideas were bound by time and place. Organizational behavior, as the successor to human relations, has spawned a new lexicon for the manager. Organization Development (OD) represented a new label for a group of earlier developed techniques such as sensitivity training, change agents, role playing, MBO, etc., to meet the needs of changing attitudes and values of individuals and organizations. Behavior modification (an extension of classical learning theory) and transactional analysis (a neo-Freudian interpretation of interpersonal transactions)

---

[27] See Robert J. House and Lawrence A. Wigdor, "Herzberg's Dual-Factory Theory of Job Satisfaction and Motivation: A Review of the Evidence and a Criticism," *Personnel Psychology*, Vol. 20 (Winter, 1967), pp. 369–89.

[28] William W. Winpisinger, "Job Enrichment: A Union View," *Monthly Labor Review* (April, 1973), p. 54.

were also offered to improve organizational performance.[29] Path-goal theory represented an extended version of the contingency view of motivation to account for varying need structures. These fashions may become passing fancies; only the test of managerial practice will tell. Management thought is a product of its past as well as the harbinger of its future.

Leadership: Tasks and People

The concern for human interrelationships and the necessity for managerial social skills endured for some time after the Western Electric research. Early behavioral research, such as that of the group dynamicists, tended to place leadership styles on a continuum of possibilities ranging from authoritarian to democratic and finally to *laissez-faire.* This clustering of leader-behavior modes reflected the idea that the authoritarian would use formal authority, be production-oriented, and operate unilaterally in making decisions. The democratic or participative leader, on the other hand, would use formal authority sparingly, be employee-centered, and involve subordinates in the decision-making process.

Participative Leadership

Participative leadership, espoused by human relationists and organizational humanists, followed the theme of "power equalization." This was a movement to reduce the power and status differentials between the superior and the subordinate. The goal was to play down the organizational hierarchy of authority, to give the worker a greater voice in decisions, to encourage creativity, and to overcome apathy by getting people involved and committed to organizational goals.[30] The research which char-

[29] For some doubts about these techniques, see Edwin A. Locke, "The Myths of Behavior Modification in Organizations," *Academy of Management Review*, Vol. 2, No. 4 (October, 1977), pp. 543–553. For an excellent critique of different approaches to organizational behavior, see: L. L. Cummings, "Toward Organizational Behavior," *Academy of Management Review*, Vol. 3, No. 1 (January, 1978), pp. 90–98.

[30] Harold J. Leavitt, "Applied Organizational Change: A Summary and Evaluation of the Power Equalization Approaches," Seminar in the Social Science of Organizations, Pittsburgh, June, 1962; cited by George Strauss in Leavitt, *Social Science of Organizations*, p. 41.

acterized this drive to equalize power has already been discussed in some detail. The Ohio State studies described two dimensions of leader behavior as "initiating structure" and "consideration." The University of Michigan studies, under the direction of Rensis Likert, isolated two dimensions called the "employee orientation" and the "production orientation." Likert found that "supervisors with the best records of performance focus their primary attention on the human aspects of their subordinate's problems and on endeavoring to build effective work groups with high performance goals."[31]

Rensis Likert (1903–   ) has continued to be one of the foremost proponents of participative management. Trained as a psychologist, he developed the widely used "Likert Scale" for the measurement of attitudes and values in conducting organizational research. As long-time (1950–1970) director of the Survey Research Center at the University of Michigan, he has spent most of his life studying leadership in organizations. Likert thinks that of all the tasks of management, leading the human component is the central and most important one because all else depends upon how it is done. To express his ideas graphically, he developed a form in which the answers to various questions are scored in one of four columns, which range from "exploitive authoritative," System 1; "benevolent authoritative," System 2; "consultative," System 3; to "participative group," System 4.[32]

Likert's System 4 management involves three basic concepts: (1) the use by the manager of the principle of supportive relationships; (2) the use of group decision making and group methods of supervision; and (3) setting high-performance goals for the organization. The principle of supportive relationships means that the leader must insure that each member will view the experience as supportive and one which builds and maintains a sense of personal worth and importance. The second concept involves group decision making and an overlapping group form of structure with each work group linked to the rest of the organization by means of persons who are members of more than one group (called "link

[31]Rensis Likert, *New Patterns of Management*, New York: McGraw-Hill Book Co., 1961, p. 7.

[32]Rensis Likert, *The Human Organization: Its Management and Value*, New York: McGraw-Hill Book Co., 1967, p. 4, passim.

pins"). The third concept is high-performance goals. Superiors in System 4 organizations should have high-performance aspirations, as should every work group member. Employees are involved in setting the high-level goals which the satisfaction of their own needs requires.

Participative management, as espoused by Likert and others, gave employees a greater voice in setting goals, making decisions, and in obtaining more autonomy in their work. Managers became employee-centered, exercised a looser form of supervision, and tried to tap the creativity and commitment of subordinates. By practicing participation, by involving the workers in matters that concerned them, management was to be repaid by higher productivity and workers were supposed to exhibit higher morale and more cohesiveness, and to achieve greater satisfactions in their work.

Toward Adaptive Leadership

While Likert and others formed the primary support for participative management, empirical research often showed inconsistencies in the conclusion that this style was always best. Even Likert had found that high morale or high cohesiveness did not always lead to higher productivity nor did the production-centered supervisor always have a low-producing section. As Likert stated it:

> On the basis of a study I did in 1937, I believed that morale and productivity were positively related; that the higher the morale, the higher the production. Substantial research findings since then have shown that this relationship is much too simple.[33]

Often it was not a question of one or the other emphasis, i.e., employee-centered or production-centered, but under what circumstances did one work better than the other? Could "initiating structure" and "consideration" be combined or balanced in some way? These questions which arose out of the Ohio State and the University of Michigan work opened new vistas for leadership re-

---

[33] Rensis Likert, quoted in Warren G. Bennis, "Revisionist Theory of Leadership," *Harvard Business Review* (January-February, 1961), p. 31. The "revisionists," according to Bennis, attempted to reconcile classical management theory with modern behavioral sciences.

search and formed the basis for the development of the "manage-rial grid" by Blake and Mouton (Figure 20-1).[34]

The "grid approach" was an attempt to avoid the extreme "either/or" styles of leadership, such as either scientific man-agement or human relations, production-centered, or people-centered, and even Theory X or Theory Y, by showing the possibilities for various blends of leadership styles. This grid of al-ternatives reflected two dimensions, "concern for people" on the vertical axis, and "concern for production" on the horizontal axis. Each axis was expressed in terms of a nine-point scale, with the

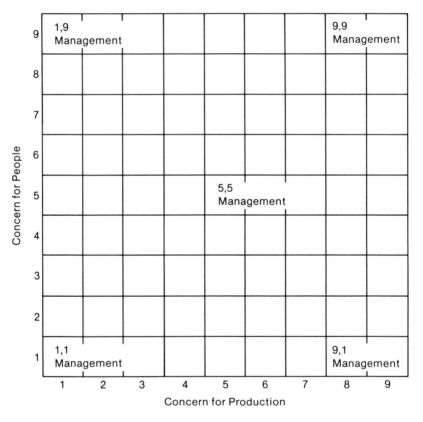

Fig. 20-1.   The "managerial grid."

[34]Robert R. Blake and Jane S. Mouton, *The Managerial Grid*, Houston, Tex.: Gulf Publishing Co., 1964.

number 1 representing minimum concern and number 9 standing for maximum concern. Although a number of different possibilities could be shown, Blake and Mouton emphasized those at the four corners and in the middle. Each of these five positions defined a definite, but different, set of assumptions regarding how managers oriented themselves for managing situations of production that involved people.

In the 9,1 style, heavy emphasis was placed on task and job requirements, with the manager occupying a position of authority and being responsible for planning, directing, and controlling the actions of subordinates so that production objectives of the enterprise could be reached. The 1,9 style emphasized satisfying the needs of people. The 1,1 showed little concern for either people or production. The 5,5 approach recognized the responsibility of the manager to plan, direct, and control, but the 5,5 manager led, motivated, and communicated, rather than commanded, to get the work done.

The 9,9 approach assumed that there was no necessary and inherent conflict between organizational purpose, production goals, and the needs of the people. With 9,9 as the "ideal," effective integration of people with production was possible by involving them and their ideas in determining the conditions and strategies of work. The general theme was to create work conditions where people understood the problem, had stakes in the outcome, and where their ideas made a real contribution to the results obtained. This 9,9 approach assumed that when individuals were aware of organizational purpose and of their real stakes in the outcome, there was no necessity for direction and control in an authority-obedience sense. Control and direction became self-control and self-direction. In short, Blake and Mouton presented a "grid" of possible leadership styles based on managerial assumptions about people and production. While the grid did not represent a new theory of leadership, it provided a diagnostic device for further leadership development.

The Contingency Model

Another approach which has achieved widespread recognition is the "leadership contingency model" of Fred Fiedler.[35] Fiedler has moved away from many of the normative statements about the best or "ideal" leadership style to suggest that a number of leader behavior styles may be effective or ineffective depending on important elements of the situation. Fiedler has devoted over 15 years to empirical testing of his model and many other researchers have contributed to its understanding and application.[36] To measure leadership style, Fiedler required a person (subject) to give a self-description and also a description of his least preferred coworker and his most preferred coworker. From this he derived "Assumed Similarity between opposites" (ASo) scores which indicated the differences or "distances" between the various descriptions. These ASo scores measured an attitude toward others which may best be described as emotional or psychological distance. A "high" ASo person tends to be concerned about his interpersonal relations, feels a need for the approval of his associates, and is less "distant" in describing himself and others. The "low" ASo person is relatively independent of others, is less concerned with feelings, and is willing to reject a person who cannot complete the assigned task. In essence, the high ASo is "consideration" oriented and the low ASo "task" oriented, in terms of the Ohio State studies.

In various studies Fiedler further identified three major factors in the leadership situation: (1) "leader-member relations," or the degree to which a group trusted or liked or were willing to follow the leader; (2) the "task structure," or the degree to which the task was ill- or well-defined; and (3) "position power," for the formal authority as distinct from the personal power of the leader. Fiedler then developed various models to show how these variables interacted and concluded that "the appropriateness of the leadership style for maximizing group performance is contingent upon the favorableness of the group task situation."[37] The most

---

[35] Fred E. Fiedler, *A Theory of Leadership Effectiveness*, New York: McGraw-Hill Book Co., 1967; and Fred E. Fiedler and Martin M. Chemers, *Leadership and Effective Management*, Glenview, Ill.: Scott, Foresman and Co., 1974.

[36] For example, see J. G. Hunt, "Breakthrough in Leadership Research," *Personnel Administration*, Vol. 30, No. 5 (September–October, 1967), pp. 38–44; and Walter Hill, "The Validation and Extension of Fiedler's Theory of Leadership Effectiveness," *Academy of Management Journal*, Vol. 12, No. 1 (March, 1969), pp. 33–47.

[37] Fiedler, *A Theory of Leadership Effectiveness*, p. 147.

favorable situation for a leader in which to influence a group is one in which the leader is well liked by the members (good leader-member relations), has a powerful position (high position power), and is directing a well-defined job (high task structure). The most unfavorable situation is one in which the leader is disliked, has little position power, and faces an unstructured task. As the model moves from a very favorable to a very unfavorable situation, Fiedler has concluded that (1) *task-oriented* (low ASo) leaders tend to perform best in group situations which are either very favorable or very unfavorable to the leader, and (2) *relationship-oriented* (high ASo) leaders tend to perform best in situations which are intermediate in favorableness (Figure 20-2).

Fiedler's model pioneered in the modern theme that there is no "one best way" to perform the leadership task. Other contingency approaches have been developed which reflect the complex interactions of individuals, aspirations, and situations.[38] The contingency approaches to leadership diverge from establishing participative leadership, System 4, the 9,9 style, or whatever, as the "one best way." Instead, the call is for flexibility in leading to fit the situation.

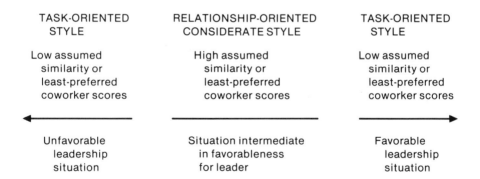

Fig. 20-2.   Appropriate leadership styles for various situations. (Adapted from Fiedler, op. cit., Figure 1-1, p. 14. Copyright © 1967, McGraw-Hill Book Company, Inc.; by permission.)

[38] For examples, see Robert J. House, "A Path-Goal Theory of Leadership Effectiveness," *Administrative Science Quarterly*, Vol. 16 (1971), pp. 321–338; and Jeffrey C. Barrow, "The Variables of Leadership: A Review and Conceptual Framework," *Academy of Management Review*, Vol. 2, No. 2 (April, 1977), pp. 231–251.

Organizations and People

Post–World War II management was faced with burgeoning masses of physical and human resources which were growing into ever more and more complex patterns and relationships. Management was faced with mass markets growing into an international scale and with mass assemblages of people of varying personal needs, educational backgrounds, and degrees of specialized knowledge. It was an emerging age of technological advancement which would bring the world beyond the atomic age and into the space age. Through electronic communications and the mass media, managers were becoming more aware of different markets, of different cultures, and of the political and economic race between East and West. Faced with more complexities, managers sought better means of analyzing alternatives in order to yield more efficacious results. One avenue of this search was for a new theory of organizations. These organizational theorists assumed a more macro stance and saw a larger view in which the search for harmony was implemented by the redesign of organizations to fit the diverse needs of people. The theorists were concerned with the processes of organizations as goal-seeking entities and how these organizations might assume a more pleasing form in light of what the behavioral sciences were revealing about the nature of individuals and groups.

This macro organizational quest for harmony was different from the organizational behavioralists only in the means to the end. In part III we saw that the Mayoists and the organizational formalists, such as Mooney, Gulick, and others, took opposite stances regarding the problems of their times. The Mayoists sought to rebuild organizations through primary groups and thereby to yield satisfied, productive workers; the formalists sought to redesign organizations to achieve efficient, coordinated effort and thereby to release people's potential to produce. In a similar manner, the modern organizational theorists sought to redesign organizations while the behavioralists sought to reshape our assumptions about the nature and nurturance of individuals. In reality, they both held the goal of organizational harmony.

The Roots of
Modern Organization Theory

Organizations are quite ancient and the views of management scholars have reflected a steadily evolving notion of how organizations might work both more efficiently and more effectively in terms of Chester Barnard's dichotomy. Organization theory itself is a product of its cultural environment and finds its roots in evolving ideas about the economic and the human problems facing organizations. Early organizations such as the church, the military, and the state were faced with the problems of getting predictable results. They did not face the rigors of market competition, and organizational structures were designed to keep humans within the boundaries of administrative desire. Early entrepreneurs, faced with both the rigors of competition and the vagaries of their labor force, adopted the precepts of prior organizations in their early structures. Earlier (in chapter 3), we saw how the advent of steam power technology led to longer production runs and an increasing need for formality in organization design. Hence, such ideas as a limited span of control, unity of command, a clearly defined hierarchy of authority, division of labor, and other such formal, blueprinted notions made sense to these early organizational writers.

It was not out of malice that they stressed the anatomy of the organizational structure but out of the economic and technological imperatives of bringing the multiplicity of human and physical resources together in a profitable concordance. Some scholars have labeled early organization theory as the "classical" approach because it was concerned with the anatomy of organizations and the assumed rational behavior of people.[39] Among the classicists we would find Weber, Fayol, Mooney and Reiley, Gulick, Urwick, Barnard, and others who stressed organizational goals, the division of labor, the scalar chain, and the formal aspects of the structure. Barnard, though primarily a classicist, was breaking with some of these chains with his efficiency-effectiveness dichotomy.

[39]William G. Scott, "Organization Theory: An Overview and an Appraisal," *Journal of the Academy of Management*, Vol. 4, No. 1 (April, 1961), pp. 9–11; and Joseph A. Litterer (ed.), *Organizations: Structure and Behavior*, New York: John Wiley and Sons, 1963, pp. 3–4.

A second stage in the development of organization theory came with the emergence of behavioralism, especially the Hawthorne studies. This period has been called the "neoclassical" school because it sought to overcome the "deficiencies" of the classicists by recognizing the people as part of the organization. Through emphasis on the informal organization, on the illogic of sentiments, and on the interactions of individuals and groups, the neoclassicists brought to the fore the recognition that many events may occur in organizations which could not have been anticipated by the planning and organizing genius of the classicist.

In the early 1960s, the power equalization thesis and the mental health overtones of the organizational humanists started to influence organization theory. It was in this era that scholars began to play down the formal blueprints of Weber, Mooney, and other classicists and began to relax the notion of a rigid organizational structure. While the Mayoists wrote of people and omitted structure, the modern organizational theorists sought to preserve both people and structure. It was in this modern era that organization theory was supposed to move beyond bureaucracy.

Is Bureaucracy Inevitable?

The 1960s held forth the great hope that organizations could be designed in such a manner that bureaucracy would not be a necessity. The theme was that of the humanists who called for a decline in the use of the hierarchy, less formality in design, and the use of the behavioral sciences and systems theory. The outcome would be a "new" theory of organizations to overcome the alleged deficiencies of the classicists and the neoclassicists.

March and Simon were the first to put forth a conceptual framework and a series of "propositions" about human behavior in order to present a "new" theory of organizations. March and Simon were critical of the "classical" advocates of organization theory and presented F. W. Taylor and Luther Gulick as prime proponents of this approach. March and Simon concluded that the Taylor branch of classical theory was "physiological" in that Taylor was more concerned with task specialization and definition, motion and time study, fatigue, and the engineer's approach to organizations. Gulick and his group (such as Mooney and

Reiley, Urwick and Fayol) were classified as "administrative management theorists" because they were concerned with broader notions of organization such as departmentalization, coordination, and other integrative schemes. March and Simon's indictment of these classicists was basically as follows: "First, in general there is a tendency to view the employee as an inert instrument performing the tasks assigned to him. Second, there is a tendency to view personnel as given rather than as a variable in the system."[40]

To March and Simon "traditional organization theory views the human organism as a simple machine."[41] In their view, the classicists failed on numerous counts by forming incomplete and inaccurate theories of motivation, by expressing little appreciation of intraorganizational conflict, and by omitting many significant elements of human behavior. The modifications which March and Simon sought to make in traditional organization theory were largely based on recent empirical discoveries in psychology and economics and upon the earlier theoretical derivations of Chester Barnard. Motivation was viewed as a "search process" among various "evoked alternatives" which would lead the organizational member to decide whether or not to participate in working toward the organization's goals. This decision to participate was based on the "inducements" offered by the organization which brought about "organizational equilibrium" in terms of earlier work by Barnard, and also by Simon in his *Administrative Behavior*. March and Simon also examined different kinds of conflict in organizations, rational and nonrational problem solving, centralization and decentralization, and the problems of innovating within the confines of organizations which were typically programmed and routinized.[41]

In essence, *Organizations* was a bold stroke against classical theory and a call for a new organizational design which recognized the limits of a decision maker's rationality, the need for understanding the human choosing process, and the need for a structure balanced with the needs and goals of organizational members. In depicting the classicists' views as a "machine-model" of organizations in which the human was merely a cog,

---

[40]James G. March and Herbert A. Simon (with the collaboration of Harold Guetzkow), *Organizations*, New York: John Wiley and Sons, 1958, p. 29.

[41]Ibid., p. 34.

March and Simon laid themselves open to questioning. It was naive on their part to capsulize Taylor's work as a machine model concerned only with the physiological organization of work. It is true that Taylor was an engineer and that he did not have much training in the behavioral sciences. It is also true that the behavioral sciences of Taylor's era were rather ill-conceived in comparison to modern standards and he, Gulick, and the other early writers should not be indicted for the poor state of the behavioral arts. In rebuttal, Lyndall Urwick has cited Simon's own work:

> We have a rapidly expanding body of empirical knowledge about how decisions are actually made in organizations, including in recent years successful attempts to simulate some kinds of middle management decision making quite accurately with digital computers.[42]

To this Urwick has added: "In the light of his enthusiasm for the computer, who is Professor Simon to criticize other writers for adopting a 'machine-model of human behavior?' "[43]

However, March and Simon had started a new direction in organization theory in which systems theory was to play a role. While organization theory did not divorce itself entirely from the classicists and the neoclassicists, the estrangement was enough to call for separate housekeeping. Organization theory became established as a separate area of study, and sociologists and political scientists joined management scholars in the study of complex organizations.[44] The notion of a duality of human and work systems in organizations had been established earlier in the work of W. F. Whyte, E. W. Bakke, George Homans, and Eliot Jacques of the Tavistock Institute. The phrase "sociotechnical systems" accurately describes this conceptual and analytical approach for the study of

[42] Herbert A. Simon, *The New Science of Management Decision*, New York: Harper and Row, 1960, p. 1.

[43] Lyndall F. Urwick, "Have We Lost Our Way in the Jungle of Management Theory?," *Personnel*, Vol. 42, No. 3 (May–June, 1965), p. 15–16.

[44] For merely a sample, see: Philip Selznick, *TVA and the Grass Roots*, Berkeley: University of California Press, 1949; Robert K. Merton (ed.), *Reader in Bureaucracy*, New York: Free Press, 1952; Peter M. Blau, *Bureaucracy in Modern Society*, New York: Random House, 1956; Amitai Etzioni, *Modern Organizations*, Englewood Cliffs, N.J.: Prentice-Hall, 1964; Theodore Caplow, *Principles of Organization*, New York: Harcourt Brace Jovanovich, 1964; Robert Presthus, *The Organizational Society*, New York: Alfred A. Knopf, 1962; and Victor A. Thompson, *Modern Organization*, New York: Alfred A. Knopf, 1964.

human work systems. Modern organization theory built upon these foundations as it sought through theorizing and empirical research to view the organization as a mutually interacting set of human, physical, and procedural variables in a complex system.

The "systems" approach to organization was a modification of the traditional views of structure, authority, division of labor, handling change and conflict, and other common organizational problems. It was a shift from the *form* or structure to the *process* and interaction of activities and people. The key notes were flexibility rather than formality, and process rather than form.[45] The use of the hierarchy of authority fell into greater disfavor, power was to be diffused, and managers were urged to use interpersonal influence rather than authority to get results. Social critics had a field day with the ineptitudes of bureaucrats and bureaucracy. Parkinson's Law and the Peter Principle became popular symbols of the disfavor with formality in organizational life.[46]

The systems approach to organizational design was an outgrowth of an aerospace age of missile systems as well as a rebellion against classical and neoclassical thought. An extension of the notion of sociotechnical systems, the emerging systems school emphasized an open environment of change and dynamics. As the systems approach to organizational design evolved, however, it became clear that many issues were too slippery and the notion too grand for any simple unravelings of how best to organize. It was noted by some that bureaucracy did indeed work well in some situations; perhaps bureaucracy was inevitable, depending . . .

The Contingency Approach

The contingency approach to organizational design was an out-

---

[45] For examples, see: Warren G. Bennis, *Changing Organizations*, New York: McGraw-Hill, 1966; Joseph A. Litterer, *The Analysis of Organizations*, New York: John Wiley and Sons, 1965; William G. Scott, *Organization Theory: A Behavioral Analysis for Management*, Homewood, Ill.: Richard D. Irwin, 1968; John A. Seiler, *Systems Analysis in Organizational Behavior*, Homewood, Ill.: Richard D. Irwin, 1967; and Rocco Carzo, Jr. and John N. Yanouzas, *Formal Organization: A Systems Approach*, Homewood, Ill.: Richard D. Irwin, 1967.

[46] C. Northcote Parkinson, *Parkinson's Law and Other Studies in Administration*, Boston: Houghton Mifflin Co., 1957; and Lawrence J. Peter and Raymond Hull, *The Peter Principle*, New York: William Morrow and Co., 1969.

growth of general systems theory and was also a reaction to any "one best way" of organizing and managing. We have already seen the influence of contingency thinking on the fifth generation of the principles and process approach to management, on organizational behavior, and on leadership theory. With respect to organization theory, two directions of thought have emerged, although they have a lot in common in terms of prescriptions with respect to organizational design. Each of these directions, i.e., technological and environmental, is based upon an open system view of an organization.

One set of studies regarding organizational design emerged from the research of the British scholar, Joan Woodward.[47] She classified organizations by the complexity of the *technology* they used in producing goods and found that technology influenced the organizational structure. Her classification, ranging from less complex (1) to more advanced (3) was: (1) unit and small-batch production systems which produced "to order" and "customized" products to meet consumers' needs; (2) large-batch and mass production which involved a fairly standardized or uniform product which had but few variations in its final appearance; and (3) long-run continuous process production which involved a standard product which was manufactured by moving through a predictable series of steps.

In her research, Woodward found that the more successful firms in each classification had similar structures. Organizations in classifications 1 and 3 (above) tended to place less emphasis on precise job descriptions for their personnel, delegated more authority, were more permissive in leading people, and had more loosely organized work groups. Successful organizations in classification 2 tended to use the line-staff type of organization, exercised closer supervision over personnel, used more elaborate control techniques, and relied more on formal, written communications. Woodward's findings demonstrated the influence of technology on organizational design. The "above average" firms in terms of success were those which adapted the organization to their technology. Firms in classifications 1 and 3 needed to be able to adjust readily to either changes in customers' needs or to sci-

[47] Joan Woodward, *Industrial Organization: Theory and Practice,* London: Oxford University Press, 1965.

entific advances in technology so the more successful firms exhibited more organizational flexibility. Firms in classification 2 did not need to respond so quickly; hence, the more successful firms could exhibit more formality. The answer to "it depends . . ." in organizational design, according to Woodward, would be technology.[48]

Another approach to organizational design was suggested by a number of researchers, notably Lawrence and Lorsch.[49] The emphasis of this group was that there was no one best way to organize, but that "it depends" upon *environmental* factors. Lawrence and Lorsch used the term "differentiation" to refer to the degree of segmentation in an organization's subunits with respect to how they related to the external environment. The greater the degree of differentiation, the greater the complexity of the organization. "Integration" was used to mean coordination or achieving unity of effort. Lawrence and Lorsch cited two approaches to integration: (1) the use of the formal management hierarchy of authority, plans, procedures, rules, and other more formal management practices; and (2) the use of crossfunctional teams and team leaders, more open communication, influence based on knowledge and expertise rather than formal authority, and other less formalized means of coordinating efforts. By "environment," these authors meant: (1) the market, corresponding to the sales or marketing subsystem of the firm; (2) the technical-economic, corresponding to the production subsystem of the firm; and (3) the scientific, corresponding to the research and development subsystem. Further, Lawrence and Lorsch identified three characteristics of these environments: (1) the rate of change in conditions; (2) the certainty of information available; and (3) the time span of feedback of results on decisions made or actions taken.

Lawrence and Lorsch found that differentiation was greater where (1) the rate of change was more rapid, (2) there was less certainty of information, and (3) the time span of feedback was longer. The greater differentiation brought about by these envi-

---

[48] For an example of support for Woodward's work, see William L. Zwerman, *New Perspectives on Organization Theory*, Westport, Conn: Greenwood Publishing, 1970.

[49] Paul R. Lawrence and Jay W. Lorsch, "Differentiation and Integration in Complex Organizations," *Administrative Science Quarterly*, Vol. 12 (June, 1967), pp. 1–47; and *Organization and Environment*, Homewood, Ill.: Richard D. Irwin, Inc., 1969.

ronmental conditions increased the need for integration. As discussed above, integration could be achieved in at least two ways —one relying more on formal means, and the other relying upon more flexible adjustments. Lawrence and Lorsch's study found that the more successful firms were those which adjusted to their relevant environments. The firms which faced a more stable, more certain environment, that is, had *less* differentiation, achieved integration through more formal means and were more centralized. Firms which faced more unstable, less certain environments, that is, had *more* differentiation, achieved integration through more flexible means and were more decentralized. In either case, success was due to organizational design consonant with the environment. The work of these authors and others led to a proliferation of research studies and books about the contingency approach to organizational design. There would be no "one best way" to organize, no standard prescriptions for the manager.

The jury is still out on contingency theory, however.[50] Viewed in historical perspective, contingency theory is a new label for what has been observed, but not codified, for some period of time. The church, the military, and the state long ago established formal mechanisms for handling situations requiring discipline, order, and unity of effort. Early economic enterprises were less formal until the advent of steam power technology. The job-lot shop was replaced by large-batch production of relatively standard products and the factory system became more formal in its organization and management. McCallum ran a railroad which required organizational formality; Taylor was essential to early twentieth-century large-batch production technology; and Fayol managed a large-batch producer in coal and iron. Weber advocated formality for large-scale organizations; Mooney's work reflected his experiences with General Motors; Gulick was influenced by governmental thinking; and Urwick liked being called "Colonel Urwick" although he had a vast range of other experiences. Each of these "formalists," or classicists if you prefer, wrote of the "one best way" from a perspective shaped by technology and environment. They were "right," at least for their times.

---

[50]For example, see P. M. Blau, C. M. Falbe, W. McKinley, and P. K. Tracy, "Technology and Organization in Manufacturing," *Administrative Science Quarterly*, Vol. 21 (March, 1976), pp. 20–40.

Historically, flexibility became the keynote as the work force became better educated with more skilled and more professional employees who needed less direction and structure. The pace of technological change accelerated after World War II and social and political turbulence called for less rigidity and more decentralized reactions. Hence the calls for job design which allowed more autonomy, for participation from a more capable work force, and for a humanism which stressed self-actualization. These proponents were "right" too, at least for their times.

An enduring theme throughout the preceding pages has been the interaction between management thinkers and their economic, social, and political environments. The notion of management responding to the imperatives of time and place is a given in an otherwise uncertain world. We must continue to observe, to learn, and to see our heritage as precursor to our posterity.

Summary

Organizational humanism emerged as a response to the alleged softness and deficiencies in empirical research in the traditional human relations mode of thinking. As a philosophy, organization humanism sought to bring a new focus on people and their varied needs, on work as a means of fulfillment, and on how organizations might be designed to accomplish the goals of people and of the organization. As an operational technique, this humanism challenged the assumptions we make about people and the motivational, leadership, and organizational styles most appropriate to the modern environment. Micro and macro facets of organizational humanism were examined to show the transition from human relations to organizational behavior and the influence of systems theory on organization theory. Contingency theory emerged to challenge any "one best way," including the precepts of organizational humanism. Despite doubts about how best to achieve it, the search for harmony between people and organizations continues. The goal of harmony is worthwhile but our means to that goal will evolve as we learn more about people and organizations. We must continue to seek a harmony in organizational life, a pleasing and productive arrangement of parts within the whole which would satisfy the requirements of people and the organization.

21

Management Science: The Search for Order

Numbers have always held a fascination for mankind; people have ascribed magical powers to some numbers, malignancy to others, and throughout history have used numbers to account for flocks of sheep as well as to reach for the stars. Having no intrinsic value in themselves, numbers have become symbols of the quest for knowledge because they lend a preciseness and orderliness to our environment. In observing nature, it was also noted that there was a natural rhythm of the seasons, of the solar system, and of life and death in all things. Our inquisitiveness led us to explore, to attempt to explain the inexplicable, and to search for a great force that bound the complexities observed in nature into some rational order of events. We sought to bring order from chaos by searching for interrelationships between observed events and activities. Although we are curious and seek variety in life, we also have a need for closure, a need to bring our observations into some unity of perception. We are basically orderly, rational beings who desire to control our environment insofar as that is possible.

For management, the search for order has been expressed throughout history in attempts to rationalize and systematize the workplace and to measure and control organization's operations. The modern era of management science has deep roots in prior management theory and this chapter will briefly trace those beginnings and developments in management's search for order.

The Quest for Quantification

In the search for order and predictability, the scientific method has denoted a rational approach to problem solving through the statement of hypotheses, the accumulation of data, the identification of alternatives, and the testing, verification, and selection of a path of action based upon facts. In his break with the mystics who held that reality was unknowable, Aristotle established the foundations for the scientific method. After Greece and Rome fell, reason submerged to the Age of Faith during the Middle Ages, only to reemerge in the Renaissance and the Age of Reason. It was during this time that the foundations for modern mathematics and science were to be established. René Descartes (1596–1650) thought the world operated mechanistically and prescribed the use of mathematics to describe its movements. Isaac Newton (1642–1727) developed calculus and stated laws of motion and gravitation, furthering Descartes' conception of the world as a giant machine. There were others who saw an orderly universe, and mathematics was to be the building block for bringing the parts together into one grand formula. The rediscovery of Aristotle during this time and the renewed interest in mathematics and in science led to the vast technological changes in mankind's environment known as the Industrial Revolution.

Charles Babbage, and to some extent Andrew Ure, applied a scientific approach to the solution of the problems of the burgeoning factory system. Industrialization demanded order and predictability and the engineers were a breed well equipped to cope with the scientific study and systematization of work. Scientific management and the work of Taylor, Barth, Gantt, the Gilbreths, Emerson, and others were the Age of Reason in twentieth-century management thought. In the 1930s, scientific management declined in emphasis as society had problems beyond the production of goods with which to cope. World War II and the renewed growth of large-scale enterprise, however, created a new environment for management. It was in the modern era that new ideas were being formed to add to the tradition of Aristotle, Descartes, Babbage, and scientific management.

Operations Research

World War I had given widespread recognition and acceptance to the notion of science in management. Governments and industrial organizations seized on the precepts of scientific management in order to cope with the mass assemblages of resources required to carry on the war. Likewise, World War II brought about a union of managers, government officials, and scientists in an effort to bring order and rationality to the global logistics of war. The British formed the first "operations research teams" of various specialists in an effort to bring their knowledge to bear upon the problems of radar systems, antiaircraft gunnery, antisubmarine warfare, the bombing of Germany, and civilian defense matters. One of the best known groups was under the direction of Professor P. M. S. Blackett, physicist, Nobel Prize winner, and co-developer of radar. Blackett's team, called "Blackett's circus," included "three physiologists, two mathematical physicists, one astrophysicist, one Army officer, one surveyor, one general physicist, and two mathematicians."[1] It was in groups such as this one that various specialists were brought together under one tent to solve the complex problems of the war and defense efforts.

In its conception, operations research was the application of scientific knowledge and methods to the study of complex problems with the stated purpose of deriving a quantitative basis for decisions which would accomplish the organization's objectives. While the British formed the first operations research groups, the Americans soon saw the potential of "operations analysis." James B. Conant, then chairman of the National Defense Research Committee, and Vannevar Bush, then chairman of the Committee on New Weapons and Equipment of the Joint Chiefs of Staff, saw the British groups in operation and were instrumental in forming similar staff groups for the United States Navy and the Eighth Bomber Command. The conclusion of the war did not bring the demise of operations research. The Army formed an Operations Research Office, the Navy established an Operations Evaluation

[1]Florence N. Trefethen, "A History of Operations Research," in Joseph F. McCloskey and Florence N. Trefethen (eds.), *Operations Research for Management*, Baltimore: Johns Hopkins Press, 1954, p. 6.

Group, and the newly formed Air Force established its Operations Analysis Division.[2]

Industrial organizations and private consulting firms also began to recognize that the methods of operations research were applicable to problems of a nonmilitary nature. Arthur D. Little, Inc., a private consulting firm, was one of the first to seek industrial uses. Other firms, some old and some new, began to apply the operations research concept and professional societies and professional journals began to form the first wave of an operations research boom. The Operations Research Society of America was founded in 1952 and began publishing its journal, *Operations Research*. In 1953, The Institute of Management Science (TIMS) stated its objectives as "to identify, extend, and unify scientific knowledge that contributes to the understanding of the practice of management" and began publishing the journal *Management Science*. It was merely a light staccato in the late forties and early fifties, but the environment of management was changing rapidly in its complexity after the war, and managers and academicians were seeking a more orderly basis for decision making. The war had resulted in an unprecedented accumulation of resources, and firms were faced with advancements in scientific knowledge which led to new products and markets, new technologies, and new developments in transportation and communication.

Historically, it is interesting to note the closing gap between the resource accumulation and the rationalization of resource utilization phases. It took America over a hundred years of resource accumulation (phase I) before scientific management appeared as phase II. Dormant during the Depression, phase III, the renewal of resource accumulation, began in postwar America. In less than a decade, attempts were being made to rerationalize resource utilization (phase IV) through the application of more science in managing.

The beginnings of operations research in industry came very naturally in the production management area. It was here that there were more structured kinds of problems and decisions for which decision rules could be rationally devised. There were

---

[2] Ibid., pp. 12–15. The reader will recall that Dr. Bush also participated in the original Hawthorne experiments under the aegis of the National Research Council.

problems of stocking the proper level of inventories, of scheduling production, of manufacturing in economical batches, of quality control, of capital acquisition, and a host of other physical resource problems. For industrial practice:

> O.R. (Operations Research) in the most general sense can be characterized as the application of scientific methods, techniques, and tools to problems involving the operation of the system so as to provide those in control of the operations with optimum solutions to the problems.[3]

As such, operations research has direct lineal roots in scientific management. Indeed, the similarities are striking. In his metal-cutting experiments, Frederick Taylor brought together a team of researchers which included a mathematician (Carl Barth), a metallurgist (Maunsel White), an engineer (Henry Gantt), and others to assist him in the solution of various problems. Further, Taylor, Gilbreth, and others spoke of the "one best way" as the objective of their scientific analysis. The modern management scientist has merely put the quest more euphemistically:

> The approach of optimality analysis is to take these alternatives into account and to ask which of these possible sets of decisions will come closest to meeting the businessman's objectives, i.e. which decisions will be best or optimal.[4]

The difference between the "one best way" and an "optimal" decision is a moot one. The old school and the new one have both sought through the scientific method to rationally evaluate alternatives in an effort to find the best possible decision. In Taylor's time, people had confidence that science could lead to societal perfectability; today, we are less confident in such a scheme and "optimal" sounds better to our ears than the "one best way."

Another striking similarity is that the moderns, like their predecessors, have sought to apply the scientific method in the analysis of human behavior. The Institute of Management Science has formed a functional interest group, the College on Management Psychology, and its purpose is "to investigate the processes of work and managing work by applying psychology, psychiatry,

[3] C. West Churchman, Russell L. Ackoff, and E. Leonard Arnoff, *Introduction to Operations Research*, New York: John Wiley and Sons, 1957, pp. 8–9.

[4] William J. Baumol, *Economic Theory and Operations Analysis*, Englewood Cliffs, N.J.: Prentice-Hall, 1961, p. 4.

and the behavioral sciences in order to enhance our understanding of management." Hugo Munsterberg could not have stated the case more clearly. Modern behavioralists frequently view management science as a continuation of a mechanistic view of man and feel that the behavioral and quantitative approaches are mutually exclusive. However, we should remember that it was not the wheel which was man's great invention, but the axle. We need to search for how these areas complement one another and how they might be brought together in some grand scheme.

Modern management science, inverted from scientific management, was not so much the search for a science *of* management as it was a striving for the use of science *in* management. It was here that the tools of mathematics and science were enlisted to help solve the age-old management problem of the optimum allocation of scarce resources toward a given goal.

Production Management in Transition

The Gordon and Howell report had been particularly critical of the state of business education with respect to mathematics. Sputnik launched the space age and new generations of computer technology were evolving to cope with the massive problem-solving and information requirements of the 1960s. The business student, being prepared for leadership in a computerized space age, had had few if any requirements for mathematics in the typical business school curriculum. The 1960s saw a reversal of this state of affairs and schools began to require more and more statistics and mathematics of their students. The burgeoning appearance of quantitative methods in curricula brought a proliferation of new management specialities and eventually an enrichment in the semantic problems of the management theory jungle.

For many, the language of the management scientist resembles the mumbo-jumbo of the witch doctor. There is the ritual of model building, the symbols to be manipulated during the ceremony, and the awe-inspiring incantation of magical phrases. To the uninitiated, the total ceremony inspires awe, fear, and reverence for the mathematical elite. Hence, there should be little wonder that the quantitative specialists had such an impact on traditional management theory. The 1950s saw a host of the new genre of production management textbooks which were heavily influenced by operations research techniques.[5] The outcome for management education was to move beyond the idea of factory/industrial/production management into an era which blended the old and the new into "production/operations management."

The new language of production/operations management was heavily oriented toward statistics and mathematics. At its base was the scientific method of problem solving; the body was composed of specific techniques for quantifying variables and relationships; and its apex was the notion of a model which represented the variables and their relationships for the purposes of prediction and control. Techniques such as statistics, linear programming, waiting line or queueing theory, game theory, decision trees, the transportation method, Monte Carlo methods, and simulation devices were part and parcel of the new language.[6] Statistics and probability theory aided in sampling for quality control purposes and other uses; linear programming and its special techniques facilitated the choice of a desirable course of action given certain constraints; and queueing theory facilitated balancing the costs and the services of a machine or other service facility. Competitive strategies could be best understood by drawing upon game theory;[7] capital acquisitions could be simulated through

[5] A suggestive but not comprehensive bibliography of the operations research approach to production management would include: C. West Churchman, Russell L. Ackoff, and E. Leonard Arnoff, *Introduction to Operations Research*, New York: John Wiley and Sons, 1957; Edward H. Bowman and Robert B. Fetter, *Analysis for Production Management*, Homewood, Ill.: Richard D. Irwin, 1957; Elwood S. Buffa, *Modern Production Management*, New York: John Wiley and Sons, 1961, 1965, 1969, 1974 and 1977; and Samuel B. Richmond, *Operations Research for Management Decisions*, New York: Ronald Press Co., 1968.

[6] In addition to references in the preceding footnote, the following would serve to explain more fully these techniques and their uses: Richard I. Levin and Rudolph P. Lamone, *Linear Programming for Management Decisions*, Homewood, Ill.: Richard D. Irwin, 1969; Daniel Teichroew, *An Introduction to Management Science: Deterministic Models*, New York: John Wiley & Sons, 1964; William T. Morris, *Management Science: A Bayesian Introduction*, Englewood Cliffs, N.J.: Prentice-Hall, 1968; and Harvey M. Wagner, *Principles of Management Science: With Applications to Executive Decisions*, Englewood Cliffs, N.J.: Prentice-Hall, 1970 and 1975.

[7] The mathematically inclined might wish to read John von Neumann and Oskar Morgenstern, *Theory of Games and Economic Behavior*, Princeton, N.J.: Princeton University Press, 1944; a lighter approach to game theory is John McDonald, *Strategy in Poker, Business, and War*, New York: W. W. Norton and Co., 1950.

computers and the use of probability theory; and quantitative models could be built and manipulated to test the impact of changes on one or more of the variables or the model as a whole.

Along with presenting the analytical techniques, serious attempts were being made to bring the operations research tools into a conceptual framework. The outcome of this was the "decision theorists," who sought to combine the economic concepts of utility and choice with the more modern quantitative tools. One early landmark attempt was by David Miller and Martin Starr, who stressed the executive's decision-making role in optimizing and suboptimizing corporate goals and placed less emphasis on the techniques.[8] By combining mathematics with computer technology, it became possible to simulate the entire operations and interactions of an enterprise, a city, an economy, and other systems.[9] In other developments, economic historians have sought to construct quantitative models of early and modern economies in order to better understand economic development.[10]

Statistical theory was substantially advanced in postwar America and probability theory became an important consideration in making managerial decisions. More esoteric ideas, such as those found in Bayesian statistics, added the subjective probability of events as a basis for the maximization of expected profit or utility in a decision. These more sophisticated decision-making tools were to reshape notions of educating managers through changes in business school curricula and would also bring about a new variety of specialists with whom the manager had to communicate. Henri Fayol, who had found the use of "higher mathematics" of no value in his experience, probably would have had his ideas of management education severely shaken in the business school of the 1960s.

Henry Gantt would also be surprised to find what the new quantitative methods had done with his ideas. The reader will recall that Gantt, under pressure to handle complex industrial-

---

[8]David W. Miller and Martin K. Starr, *Executive Decisions and Operations Research,* Englewood Cliffs, N.J.: Prentice-Hall, 1960. See also: David W. Miller and Martin K. Starr, *The Structure of Human Decisions,* Englewood Cliffs, N.J.: Prentice-Hall, 1967.

[9]Jay W. Forrester, *Industrial Dynamics,* Cambridge, Mass.: M.I.T. Press, 1961.

[10]For some exercises in "cliometrics," see *Purdue Faculty Papers in Economic History: 1956–1966,* Homewood, Ill.: Richard D. Irwin, 1967.

military interactions in World War I, had devised a graphic method of scheduling and controlling activities. In 1956–57, the DuPont Company developed a computerized arrow diagram or network method for planning and controlling which became known as the Critical Path Method (CPM). This method used only one time estimate and included only activities (arrows).[11] In 1957–58, in managing the development of the Polaris missile, the United States Navy encountered much the same problems in project scheduling and evaluation as it had in Gantt's day with shipbuilding. Together with the consulting help of Booz, Allen, and Hamilton, Inc., and the Lockheed Missile Systems Division (the prime contractor), the Navy devised the Program Evaluation and Review Technique (PERT). This technique used statistical probability theory to furnish three time estimates (pessimistic, most probable, and optimistic) and added "events" (circles) to the graphing of activities.

Taken together, these network techniques of PERT and CPM serve to plan a network of activities, their relationships, and their interaction along a path to a given completion date. They graph paths for the flow of activities, provide events as checkpoints, and focus managerial attention on a "critical path" or paths in an effort to keep the total project on course.[12] While these techniques are much more complex than this brief description implies, they are really little more than the Gantt chart concept enlarged and enriched by 40 or more years of advancing management and statistical knowledge.

Quantification: A Final Note

While the preceding pages have barely scratched the surface of what is a substantial and growing body of literature, the links with the past and the trends should be fairly obvious. Modern management science is a reemergence of the age-old quest for order, predictability, measurement, and control. In the development of management thought, the search for science in managing is an

---

[11] Russell D. Archibald and Richard L. Villoria, *Network-Based Management Systems (PERT/CPM)*, New York: John Wiley & Sons, 1967, pp. 12–15.

[12] For example, see Joseph Horowitz, *Critical Path Scheduling: Management Control Through CPM and PERT*, New York: Ronald Press Co., 1967.

old one and reflects the search for certainty of performance in operations. The search for order through quantification is an attempt to quantify variables in industrial and organizational problems, to enhance the measurement and control of performance, and to construct abstract models to represent the real world in order to manipulate and test these models for the purpose of aiding decision making.

Systems

A second part of this search for order in the modern era came with the development of systems theory or systems approaches to the study of management. We will see that the systems concept is really an old one and that modern developments have been an amalgam of many disciplines in an effort to sharpen managerial skills, to develop an operative theory of management, and to provide a better conceptual framework for organizational design and operation.

Early Notions of Systems

A dictionary definition of a system is "an assemblage of objects united by some form of regular interaction or interdependence; an organic or organized whole."[13] Throughout history people have observed such an orderliness in nature. They saw an ecological balance in plant and animal life, noted that the planets and stars operated predictably enough, and made gods of stars and used them to chart their own life forecasts; they saw that small streams flowed into larger and still larger ones to flow to the sea; and they saw a rhythm in the coming and going of seasons so that they could plant and harvest their crops. Primitive people built their life activities around rituals which were a part of this natural order; such ceremonies gave them the security of order and predictability. For example, the Egyptians depended upon the orderliness of nature in the rise and fall of the Nile in order to transport the materials for the construction of the pyramids.

---

[13]*Webster's New Collegiate Dictionary*, Springfield, Mass.: G. and C. Merriam Co., 1956, p. 863.

As people designed their organizations, they sought once more the orderliness in their operation that they observed in nature. Under the domestic system, entrepreneurs operated their various undertakings as a system built upon the receipt of orders for products, the "putting-out" of the work, and the return of the completed product. The early factory managers sought "systematic" management which would arrange the workplace, secure the proper flow of materials, and facilitate the performance of human effort in order to achieve some predictable result. Boulton and Watt designed a simplified inventory-production system by standardizing parts in such fashion that inventory level could be reduced to a minimum and customer reordering would be simplified. Taylor sought to systematize the selection of workers and the conditions of their jobs; Gilbreth wrote of "Field Systems" and "Concrete Systems" which were manuals for standardizing methods and procedures for work; and Gantt developed graphic aids to schedule, coordinate, and control the work of many agencies. Fayol separated management and administration and viewed management as the integration of all six functions of a business in directing it toward objectives. Mayo and his associates advised the manager to view the organization as a "social system" composed of many human parts; Lewin made "field theory" into a solid analytical tool; W. F. Whyte viewed the restaurant as a workflow social system; and Bakke and Homans wrote of the need to study the interactions of both formal and informal components. Follett spoke of integrative unity and Barnard wrote of formal and informal communications and the need to maintain an equilibrium both within the organization and with elements outside the organization.

If we examine all of these early notions of systems, we can see that they have in common a number of characteristics: (1) there was always a goal or purpose for the organization, some reason for its existence, whether it be tombs for the pharoahs, industrial products, governmental services, or social satisfactions; (2) there was some presumed inflow or input of materials, equipment, and human effort into the organization; (3) there was something being done in the organization to transform these inputs into some useful product or service to meet goals of the organization; and (4) there was some need to measure, to control, to acquire the necessary information about performance to see if plans were being carried out. Further, these early writers recognized the complex interactions which existed between the human and physical parts of the organization. There was a search to study the parts, to understand their interrelationships, and to so arrange the parts that they led to the desired outcome.

There is evidence that early management writers saw an interrelationship of parts and sought to bring these together into an organic whole or system. They sought to rationalize resource utilization, to understand human behavior, and to devise schemes whereby managers could bring the parts together. Some focused on organizational design, some on production processes, some on the factory as a social system, and others on the administrative activities performed by the manager in planning, organizing, and controlling work.

General Systems Theory

Although notions of systems existed, the major distinction between prior eras and the modern one was in the *way of thinking* or the *philosophy* of the systems approach. Here again we find deep roots in prior thought. It was in the early twentieth century that psychologists and sociologists began the "organismic" or Gestalt approach in theories of behavior. This was a break with the prior "mechanistic" or fundamental unit method of analysis. In 1926, a South African lawyer and general, Jan Christian Smuts, represented the coming *Zeitgeist* of following eras by noting a tendency toward "holism" (wholeness) in all form, matter, life, and personality. He spoke of "fields" before Kurt Lewin and put forth a synergistic view of the universe in noting that an organism consists of parts but is more than the sum of those parts.[14] Before Boulding, Smuts developed an idea of a "progressive grading" or levels of "holistic synthesis" (systems): (1) "mere physical mixtures," wherein the parts largely preserve their character; (2) chemical compounds, which form a new structure and the parts are not easily identifiable; (3) organisms, with central control of parts and organs; (4) "minds," with central control achieving a freedom and

---

[14] Jan Christian Smuts, *Holism and Evolution*, New York: Macmillan Co., 1926, pp. 1–2 and p. 101.

creativity; and (5) personality, the "most evolved" whole in the universe. Smuts' work represented a Gestalt view of the universe and must be considered as an attempt at what was to become the province of general systems theory.

Ludwig von Bertalanffy, a biologist, is credited with coining the phrase "general systems theory." Bertalanffy introduced the notion of "general systems theory" at a University of Chicago seminar in 1937 but did not publish his work until after the war.[15] He sought a unity of sciences which would go beyond merely relating physical phenomena at an atomistic level. He thought that it was possible to develop a systematic, theoretical framework for describing relationships in the real world and that different disciplines had similarities which could be developed into a "general systems model." Every science or discipline had a "model," i.e., a conceptual structure intended to reflect aspects of reality, but no *one* science had a monopoly on all knowledge since each science merely reflected a certain slice of reality. The goal, as Bertalanffy conceptualized it, was to search for parallelisms in disciplines and thereby be able to generalize a theoretical framework. Bertalanffy noted certain characteristics which were similar in all sciences: (1) the study of a whole, or organism; (2) that organisms tended to strive for a "steady state" or equilibrium; and (3) the "openness" of all systems in that the organism was affected by its environment and in turn affected its environment.[16]

Bertalanffy's efforts were the beginning piece in a jigsaw puzzle upon which others began to build. Norbert Wiener coined the word "cybernetics" from the Greek *kubernetes,* meaning steersman or helmsman.[17] The study of cybernetics showed that all systems could be designed to control themselves through a communications "loop" which "fed back" information allowing the organism to adjust to its environment. Of course, James Watt

[15] Ludwig von Bertalanffy, "General Systems Theory—A Critical Review," in Walter Buckley (ed.), *Modern Systems Research for the Behavioral Scientist,* Chicago: Aldine Publishing Co., 1968, p. 13. See also: Ludwig von Bertalanffy, *General Systems Theory: Foundations, Development, Applications,* New York: George Braziller, 1968; and Ludwig von Bertalanffy, *Organismic Psychology and Systems Theory,* Barre, Mass.: Clark University Press, 1968.

[16] Ludwig von Bertalanffy, "General Systems Theory: A New Approach to the Unity of Science," *Human Biology,* Vol. 23 (December, 1951), pp. 302–361. See also: Ludwig von Bertalanffy, *Problems of Life,* New York: John Wiley and Sons, 1952.

[17] Norbert Wiener, *Cybernetics,* Cambridge, Mass.: MIT Press, 1948.

had developed the first cybernetic control device, the "fly-ball governor," as a method of automatically regulating the speed of a steam engine. However, Wiener was seeking to study language and messages in a human sense in order to understand man-machine interactions and their broader implications for society. [18] Along a parallel path, Shannon and Weaver were developing some concepts of information theory as it pertained to the encoding, transmitting, and decoding of messages, to channel capacity, and to the mathematical study of communications. [19]

The economist Kenneth Boulding built directly upon Bertalanffy's ideas and tried to integrate Wiener's cybernetics with the information theory of Shannon and Weaver. Boulding suggested that general systems theory was one way of developing a means for specialists to find a common denominator, a language through which they could communicate. Boulding developed nine levels of systems for analysis and these are listed here in order of increasing complexity: (1) frameworks (static); (2) clockworks (simple dynamic systems); (3) thermostat (cybernetics); (4) cell (open, self-maintaining); (5) plant (genetic-societal); (6) animal; (7) man; (8) social organizations; and (9) transcendental. For Boulding, general systems theory "aims to provide a framework or structure on which to hang the flesh and blood of particular disciplines and particular subject matters in an orderly and coherent corpus of knowledge." [20]

The elements of general systems theory were flowing from a variety of sources and establishing a theoretical and philosophical framework for studying different levels of systems, for recognizing the openness of systems, for developing information feedback to maintain a relatively steady state, and for probing systems theory as a way of thinking. Along with this framework, industrial technology was advancing to make the dreams of systems theory come at least fairly close to reality. One advancement in particular, the computer, made a significant contribution because of its ability to

[18] Norbert Wiener, *The Human Use of Human Beings*, Boston: Houghton Mifflin Co., 1950.

[19] Claude E. Shannon and Warren Weaver, *The Mathematical Theory of Communication*, Urbana: University of Illinois Press, 1949.

[20] Kenneth E. Boulding, "General Systems Theory—The Skeleton of Science," *Management Science* (April, 1956), pp. 197–208; reprinted in Peter R. Schoderbeck (ed.), *Management Systems*, New York: John Wiley and Sons, 1967, pp. 7–15.

process masses of data, to simulate operations, to solve intricate problems, and to control production processes. Certain aspects of the development of the computer have already been discussed in the work of Charles Babbage, the Jacquard loom, and the punch card of Herman Hollerith. Hollerith had developed the punch card and sorter to aid the United States Census Bureau. He left the bureau and formed the Tabulating Machine Company (1903), and from that company the International Business Machines Corporation emerged in 1912. It was not until 1944 that Harvard's Howard Aiken developed for IBM the first automatic sequence controlled computer, an electromechanical, but not an electronic, model.

After more than a century from conception to reality, the computer evolved rapidly in technology and applications. The first generation of computers (ca. 1951) were space and energy consumers with vast arrays of vacuum tubes; the second generation (ca. 1959) replaced vacuum tubes with transistors, speeding up computational capability; and the third generation (ca. 1964) introduced miniaturized circuitry, improved software, and greater data-handling flexibility. The computer inaugurated the cybernetic-automated age: operating on the feedback of data, machines could be controlled, corrected, and guided by computer. Automated steel factories are in operation, and automated production processes are used in automobile assembly and a number of other operations.

It was the computer and all of its capabilities that arrived on the scene at the proper historical moment to aid the information theorists, the operations researchers, and the systems analysts in their work. Without the computer, management science would not have developed as rapidly as it did. With the computer, the complexities of mathematical models were simplified, simulation and game theory furthered, information systems enriched, and the automated control of factories made possible. The computer made possible a third Industrial Revolution based on cybernetics. The first had replaced human labor with machine labor, the second brought forth mass production through the assembly line, and the third replaced human control of production processes with machine control.

Systems Theory and Management Theory

Beginning with Bertalanffy as a hope in 1937 and evolving through the work of Wiener, Boulding, and others, general systems theory was not to make its major impact on management thought until the 1960s. It is true that more and more pieces of the puzzle were being inserted from organization theory, management process theory, information theory, decision theory, the behavioral sciences, and operations research. However, these specialized areas of study were evolving toward more and more of a "systems approach" until "systems" was to become the catchphrase of the 1960s.

While portions of the impact of general systems theory on the process approach to management were discussed in chapter 19, the focus here will be on various attempts to use the systems approach as an integrative framework for studying the job of the manager. The hope was that GST would provide a synthesis and a "systems point of view" which would enable the manager to have a conceptual framework for relating different specialities and parts of the company to one another. Further, the systems approach provided an open-ended view of the manager's job which facilitated an understanding of how a company related to its complex environment—to the other great systems of which it was a part. Johnson, Kast, and Rosenzweig put forth a comprehensive view of the systems approach as "a way of thinking about the job of managing . . . [which] provides a framework for visualizing internal and external environmental factors as an integrated whole."[21] Drawing heavily on Bertalanffy and Boulding, the authors felt the business organization typified a system in that it was an open system which was influenced by and in turn influenced its environment, strove to maintain a state of "dynamic equilibrium" of parts to whole, and was a dynamic interplay of both internal and external forces trying to satisfy goals of both the organization and of individual participants.

[21] Richard A. Johnson, Fremont E. Kast, and James E. Rosenzweig, *The Theory and Management of Systems*, New York: McGraw-Hill Book Co., 1963, p. 3 (rev. ed., 1967).

Others also sought to apply the systems approach in order to integrate management process theory by conceptualizing the organization as a complex input-output system in which the manager became a motivating and linking mechanism in applying the management process to a system of physical and human resources. The systems approach (1) facilitated understanding of the organization as a whole rather than as a chaotic arrangement of parts; (2) permitted the analysis of resource flows toward objectives; (3) described the manager's job in terms of the allocation and utilization of resources; and (4) revealed an awareness of the environmental forces which affected managerial decision making.[22]

General systems theory led to the "fourth generation" of the process approach to management theory (see Figure 21-1). This group took the view that the job of the manager could be accommodated within the realm of systems theory and that the systems view was a way of thinking about integrating management activities both internally and in relation to the organizational environment. As noted previously, systems theory formed one avenue of hope for unity in management theory.

A second stream of influence of general systems theory came through organization theory and systems approaches to organizational design. The Mayoists and other behavioralists conceived of organizations as social systems and as sociotechnical systems. The Tavistock Institute furnished early views on the analysis of organizations as open systems in which there was a dynamic interplay between the work system and the human system. The systems approach to organizations was an attempt to analyze the human, social, technical, and organizational "inputs" as aids to designing complex organizational systems. In numerous books, one could see attempts to blend information technology, quantitative methods, sociohuman factors, organizational technology, and management theory into the systems concept.[23]

The concept of project management or the "matrix organiza-

[22] Dan Voich, Jr., and Daniel A. Wren, *Principles of Management: Resources and Systems,* New York: Ronald Press Co., 1968.

[23] For examples, see William A. Shrode and Dan Voich, Jr., *Organization and Management: Basic Systems Concepts,* Homewood, Ill.: Richard D. Irwin, 1974; and Fremont R. Kast and James E. Rosenzweig, *Organization and Management: A Systems Approach,* New York: McGraw-Hill Book Co., 1970.

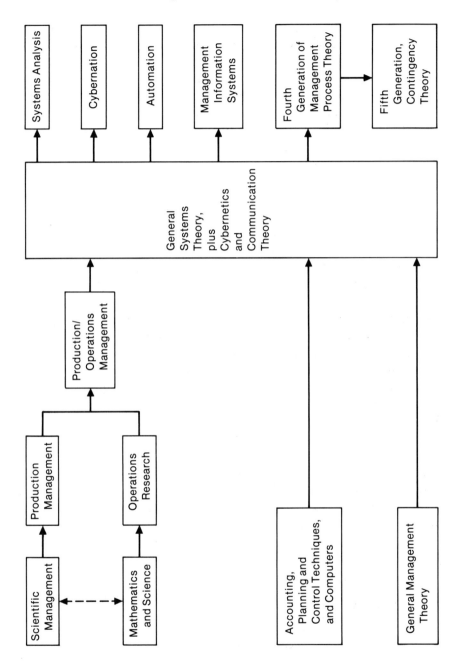

Fig. 21-1.   Influence of general systems theory.

tion" also became a part of organization theory. Emerging from the complexities of managing aerospace and other projects for the Department of Defense and the National Aeronautics and Space Administration, the project-management concept cut across functional lines to concentrate responsibility for accomplishment upon a project manager. The project-management concept also led to the development of planning-programming-budgeting systems (PPBS) which cut across functional lines to view activities as an integrated totality. PPBS had a short and glorious history during the Johnson administration when Robert McNamara was secretary of defense. Hailed as a major planning breakthrough, PPBS ran afoul of traditional bureaucratic minds and fell into disfavor.

Management science also felt the influence of systems theory and responded with a host of "systems analysis" techniques and models. Systems analysis may be characterized as providing problem-solving approaches, flow charting, simulation techniques, the use of computers, and the application of sophisticated operations research techniques.[24] To a large extent the systems analysts are making a specialty out of micro analysis of operations in contrast to more macro approaches in organization theory and in the systems approaches to the management process. Yet in another sense, the systems analysts have broadened management science, integrated into it a host of other analytical devices, and provided a link to the growth of information systems.

General systems theory also influenced the development of management information systems. Information has always been crucial to management decision making, and the Egyptian scribe who recorded his master's inventory with a stylus on a clay tablet was a forerunner of the modern information specialist. The need for management information existed prior to the Industrial Revolution, was made more crucial as organizations grew, and became a subject of major importance in a twentieth century of electronic computers, automated production, and cybernetic controls. With

---

[24]To merely scratch the surface, one might sample: Claude McMillan and Richard F. Gonzalez, *Systems Analysis: A Computer Approach to Decision Models*, Homewood, Ill., Richard D. Irwin, 1965 and 1968; Stanford L. Optner, *Systems Analysis for Business Management*, (2d ed.), Englewood Cliffs, N.J.: Prentice-Hall, 1968; Richard J. Hopeman, *Systems Analysis and Operations Management*, Columbus, Ohio: Charles E. Merrill Publishing Co., 1969; and Stanley Young, *Management: A Systems Analysis*, Glenview, Ill.: Scott, Foresman and Co., 1966.

an expanding view of the business environment and the doubling of our knowledge every five or so years, it is not surprising that information systems to cope with this expanding universe were necessary. Coupled with the computer and the development of cybernetics, a substantial body of literature has grown up around the theme of management information systems.[25] Wiener's concept of cybernetics has been expanded and refined in modern usage until the point has been reached where many activities are measured and controlled on a "real-time" basis, i.e., as the activity is actually occurring.

The area of management information systems is but one of many whose development has been affected by general systems theory. Information has become a more vital resource than ever before to the successful management of the modern, more complex organization which operates in an environment of manifold economic, social, and political constraints.

The Decline of a Grand Scheme

General systems theory did not pale from the want of attention, but from too much of it. In its robust youth, it was hailed by many as the grand scheme which would provide a means of synthesizing knowledge and integrating theory. Above we saw its impact on the fourth generation of general management theory, on organization theory, on management science, and on management information systems. What happened to this fair youth on its way to fame and fortune?

It was Aristotle, the Greek philosopher of many years ago, who said "The whole is more than the sum of its parts." General systems theory, that search for grand parallels among disciplines, sought to make this a reality in modern times. As scholars, and managers, seized this grand scheme, it proved elusive and abstract. Managers are action oriented, requiring ideas that can be translated into results; scholars are idea oriented, requiring phe-

---

[25] Typical of these developments are: John F. Dearden and F. Warren McFarlan, *Management Information Systems*, Homewood, Ill.: Richard D. Irwin, 1966; Stafford Beer, *Cybernetics and Management*, New York: John Wiley and Sons, 1959; and Dan Voich, Jr., Homer J. Mottice, and William A. Shrode, *Information Systems for Operations and Management*, Cincinnati, Ohio: South-Western Publishing Company, 1975.

nomena that can be isolated and studied for their relationships; and general systems theory proved inadequate for both groups. General systems theory provided abstractions while the practical world demanded concreteness; it offered the study of inter-relationships while the number of variables possible became in-finite; and it was based in the physical world of organisms, while the managerial world was one of contrived socioeconomic organi-zations. Critics of general systems theory found it too crude for fruitful research, too abstract for organizational realities, and too complex for meaningful decision prescriptions.[26] But all was not lost; from the debris would come contingency approaches, which were discussed earlier. The framework proved sound so that cy-bernation, automation, and management information systems could flourish (see Figure 21-1). The systems approach remains imbedded in the minds of those who practice and those who study management as a way of thinking about orderly problem solving. General systems theory was yet another step forward in the search for order.

Summary

This chapter has been characterized as the search for order through management science. The modern era demanded that managers refine their decision-making methods, that they enlarge their conceptual schema, and that they seek better ways of allo-cating and utilizing their physical and human resources. Oper-ations research was viewed as a modernized version of early sci-entific approaches to problem solving and of management's search to improve its ability to explain, predict, and control events. Gen-eral systems theory was viewed as a quest for universal hooks from which would hang general theories gleaned from specialized fields. In management science, the search was for order, for mea-surement, and for predictability.

[26] An excellent collection on general systems theory and its promises and breaches of promise can be found in the *Academy of Management Journal*, Vol. 15, No. 4 (De-cember, 1972). See especially Fremont E. Kast and James E. Rosenzweig, "General Systems Theory: Applications to Organization and Management," pp. 447–465; D. C. Phillips, "The Methodological Basis of Systems Theory," pp. 469–477; and Frederick Thayer, "General System(s) Theory: The Promise That Could Not Be Kept," pp. 481–493.

Advancements in computer technology and in the sophistication of quantitative methods have affected the education of prospective managers in profound ways. From specialized knowledge, the manager must grow into a generalist who can manage specialists and integrate people and activities in a rational, systematic, goal-directed fashion. In this discussion of the modern era, we saw the manifold ways of thinking about the manager's job: process theory offers a framework for the functions of the manager; organizational behavior offers understanding of the human facet; organization theory offers possibilities for designing authority and activity relationships; and management science offers quantitative techniques and ways of systematic problem solving. The challenge is great, and the evolution of management thought continues to enrich and to advance our understanding so that this challenge can be met.

22

The Past as Prologue

Lives of great men all remind us
  We can make our lives sublime,
And, departing, leave behind us
  Footprints on the sands of time;
—LONGFELLOW, *A Psalm of Life*

This has been a story about footprints, the individuals who left them, and the times in which these people lived. The past must not be buried but used as a foundation and guide for the footprints which will be made in the future. Within the practices of the past there are the lessons of history for tomorrow; there is a flow of events and ideas which link yesterday, today, and tomorrow in a continuous stream. We occupy but one point in this stream of time: we can see the distant past with a fairly high degree of clarity, but as we approach the present, our perspective becomes less clear. The future must be a projection, and a tenuous one at best. New ideas, subtle shifts in themes, and emerging environmental events all bring new directions to evolving management thought. The purpose of this concluding chapter is to present in summary form the past as a prologue to the future. Two broad areas will be examined: one, the evolving notions of the managerial functions; and two, the changing environment of management.

The Managerial Functions: Past and Future

The managerial functions form a convenient framework for a summary discussion of the past and the future. While the preceding pages have focused on the chronological evolution of contributors, ideas, and movements, there is a stream of changing ideas about what the manager does which can be used to link the past to the future.

Planning

Planning in early organizations depended in large part upon the seasons and upon natural events. Construction projects, planting and harvesting, and the hunt were seasonal activities. State planning and control of economic enterprises was often rigidly practiced by the Egyptians, Romans, Greeks, and other early civilizations. There was no separation of powers between the economic and political spheres, and this command philosophy prevailed for centuries prior to the cultural rebirth. The overthrow of mercantilism and the emergence of the *laissez-faire* economic philosophy severed the state from its role in economic planning. The market, through the consumer, was deemed the best method of allocating scarce resources toward human ends.

With this break in tradition, planning assumed a new importance for entrepreneurs. They had to be creative and innovative in meeting market needs. Shorn of the monopolies and franchises granted under mercantilism, entrepreneurs had to assume greater risks and take more cognizance of the future. The factory required large-scale capital investments, work flows had to be arranged to meet the new industrial technology, and human resources had to be recruited and trained to meet the demands of the factory system. At best, planning was intuitive and based upon the technological dictates of a particular industry. The standardization and interchangeability of parts facilitated planning but in turn complicated the problem of coordinating the efforts of others in bringing the pieces together. The widespread division of labor, though facilitating training of an essentially unskilled work force, furthered the problems of coordinating efforts.

As textile, steel, railroad, and other industries expanded, the planning problems became more acute. In scientific management, Taylor and his coworkers placed great stress on the planning function because of its crucial import to the existing industrial environment. Standards, to be set through motion and time study, were essential for scheduling and for incentive schemes. Taylor's separation of planning and doing and his concept of functional foremen were ideas designed to bring expert knowledge to bear upon production scheduling, work flows, and production control. Harrington Emerson spoke of "ideals," an early notion of the importance of objectives in organizations. H. L. Gantt developed visual aids to planning and controlling and added time as a vital ingredient in the planning process. Henri Fayol identified planning and forecasting as the first step in the process of managerial actions and wrote of the need for "unity of direction" in plans and in leadership.

An industrial engineering production orientation to management planning persisted in the early work of R. C. Davis. In later work he wrote of routing, dispatching, and scheduling as planning subfunctions and stressed objectives along with his organic functions. James Mooney also wrote of the concept of "doctrine" or commonly shared purposes in organizations. As management thought moved into the forties and fifties, shifts began to appear in the concept of planning. The human relationists spoke of the need for "participation" in planning and other managerial activities. Participation, whether of the "bottom up" style or of "multiple management," was to bring greater psychological as well as economic benefits.

The management process approach, emerging from the pioneering work of Fayol, based the planning concept on a broader plane than just production. Planning became almost synonymous with decision making and was intended to incorporate all business activities instead of just production. In the late 1950s and early 1960s, scholars were showing a greater concern for integrating the formal aspects of planning with the informal, human problems connected with budgeting, planning, and controlling. Long-range planning, though an age-old problem, assumed new dimensions with the growth of automated factories, the advent of the computer age, and the proliferation of international markets. From the quantitative specialists, new ideas were emerging for more precise and economical ways of allocating scarce resources through more sophisticated statistical and mathematical procedures. Model building and simulation came into vogue in this computerized cybernetic age. Management science, reflecting this historic concern for rational problem solving, enriched the planning activity with PERT/CPM, with operations research techniques, and with the application of more rigorous quantitative methods.

Thus the planning activity has evolved from a highly intuitive, command-oriented concept to one which is enriched by modern technology, by sophisticated aids, and by a broader understanding of people-machine interactions in a broader system. What, then, can be said of the future? Certainly there is no foreseeable diminution in the importance of the planning function to organized endeavors. The challenge will be to turn our accumulated knowledge of the planning function and the wealth and sophistication of our aids to planning to solve a variety of problems. We will be able to apply this knowledge and these tools to the more efficient utilization of physical resources and to the enhanced satisfaction of the human resource. We will be in a better position to handle the complex interfaces between organizations and between the public and the private sectors of our economy.[1] Model building and simulation of complex systems will be a necessity in planning for the large-scale investments required in automated factories and in social investments. A vast number of social problems, for example, urban development and ecological dilemmas, will lend themselves to systems analysis and design.[2] Also, we will be able to understand better how different organizations, facing different environments or technologies, can adopt a contingency approach to planning. It has been suggested that sometimes we need to formulate plans without having specific goals in advance.[3] Organizations facing a more stable environment and operating with a more formalized structure may well continue to plan from goals. However, organizations facing a more unstable, uncertain environment need to operate with a

---

[1] An example of how this might be done in electrical "power pools" may be found in Daniel A. Wren, "Interface and Inter-organizational Coordination," *Academy of Management Journal*, Vol. 10, No. 1 (March, 1967), pp. 69–81.

[2] A pioneering work in the simulation and systems approach to urban problems is Jay W. Forrester, *Urban Dynamics*, Cambridge, Mass.: MIT Press, 1969.

[3] Michael B. McCaskey, "A Contingency Approach to Planning: Planning With Goals and Planning Without Goals," *Academy of Management Journal*, Vol. 17, No. 2 (June, 1974), pp. 281–91.

more flexible structure and may need to plan toward certain "directions" rather than from specific goals.

The essence of the planning function itself will not change significantly in the future. But it will continue to evolve, as it has in the past, as we learn more and more about theories and methods of coping with the uncertainties of the future.

Organizing

Throughout history individuals have found their activities inextricably interwoven with organizational life. Since individuals were not held in a very high esteem in many early cultures, they were usually deemed subservient to the dictates of the monarch, the military leader, or the central source of church dogma. Authority was legitimatized on the divine right of kings or upon biblical delegation to the successors of Peter. Organizational structures were designed to keep human behavior within predictable bounds through discipline, a central decision maker, central doctrine, and a rigid hierarchy of authority. The early entrepreneurs could not depend upon doctrine, nor military discipline, nor divine right to legitimatize their authority; yet they adopted many of the precepts of organizational structures from the church, the state, and the military. The entrepreneurs divided labor and created problems of coordination; so they established departments under the leadership of kinsmen or salaried managers and acted themselves to both own and manage the organization. Finding their submanagers largely illiterate and often undependable, it is understandable that entrepreneurs tended to keep a tight rein on activities.

The railroads were really the first industry to pose organizational problems on a grand scale. Daniel McCallum and Henry Poor stuck basically to the centralized, rigid organizational structure. However, the human reaction in nineteenth-century America led to McCallum's resignation and to Poor's rethinking of the human versus the "system." As masses of resources continued to accumulate during America's dynamic industrial growth, the owner-manager began to give way to the salaried manager to a greater and greater extent. During the scientific management era, writers wrote extensively of structural and coordination problems and of the need to bring specialized advice and assistance to the work place. Taylor developed his scarcely used functional foreman concept; Emerson applied Prussian general staff ideas to industrial organizations; Fayol developed principles of organization; and Weber conceived bureaucracy as the epitome of technical efficiency. This era continued to stress the formal organization, although there was recognition of work restriction, morale, and other informal group phenomena.

The social man era really began to reshape substantially the thinking about organizations. On one hand, the Mayoists brought a new focus to informal groups, social needs, and interactions in a "social system." There were also the organizational formalists of the same era such as James Mooney, Luther Gulick, and Lyndall Urwick. For these formalists, the source of organizational authority resided in the right to hold private property, and this right was then exercised through the scalar chain. Follett followed more in the Mayoist tradition in playing down formal structure, in obeying the law of the situation, depersonalizing authority, and in "interweaving" responsibility. Chester Barnard, even though primarily a formalist, tried to synthesize the formal and informal organizations through his effectiveness-efficiency dichotomy. Like Follett, he radically revised the concept of authority in basing it on the subordinate's acceptance of a directive. Participation in organizations became a keynote in Given's "bottom up" management and in McCormick's "multiple management." Whyte, Bakke and Homans wrote of human-work systems and laid the basis for sociotechnical systems. Coexisting in the social man era, the formalists and the informalists both sought to improve the depressing environment: for one, it was through social skills and for the other, through sound principles of organization that the human problems of an industrial civilization could be overcome.

The modern era gave rise to the organizational humanists' view that people needed some structure in organized activity (which they say the neoclassicists neglected) but not so much that it would interfere with employee self-actualization (which they saw in the "man-machine model" of the classicist). The result was a decline in the worship of a hierarchy, the recognition of the human desire for power equalization in organizations, and the development of new organizational forms, such as the matrix or project organization, which emphasized flows of activities rather than structure. Research has shown the importance of technology and the environment as forces shaping organizational design, thus reflecting the growing use of contingency approaches.

Given this heritage, what may we expect of future organizational structures and strategies? To illustrate the dangers of prediction, one might refer to Leavitt and Whisler's forecast in 1958 that the computer and new information technology would: (1) result in a recentralization of authority in the hands of top management; (2) move certain classes of middle management downward in status and compensation while other middle managers would move upward into the top management group; and (3) lead to an organization structure which would resemble a football balanced on the top of a church bell.[4] Subsequent study has shown that there has been a trend toward more centralized decision making. However, predictions (2) and (3) have failed to develop.[5] The structure has not been reshaped so dramatically, nor have the jobs of middle managers changed so much. Middle managers, supposed to wither on the vine, have proliferated and assumed new roles in digesting for top management the masses of information generated by information technology.

With this in mind, one approaches prognostication with more caution and less fervor. The growth of knowledge-oriented industries, for example, the research-and-development-oriented firms, would seem to indicate that the project organization is here to stay. Employing highly educated specialists who tend to use as their reference group their profession rather than the company, this type of firm will have to seek fluid structures and other inducements for organizational participation. For other organizations, bureaucracy may be "inevitable." Managers will have to design organizations to give credence to human values while insuring that the organization can cope with changing markets, technology, and environmental factors.

[4] Harold J. Leavitt and Thomas L. Whisler, "Management in the 1980's," *Harvard Business Review*, Vol. 36, No. 6 (November–December, 1958), pp. 41–48.

[5] J. G. Hunt and P. F. Newell, "Management in the 1980's Revisited," *Personnel Journal*, Vol. 50, No. 1 (Jan., 1971). See also Thomas L. Whisler, *Information Technology and Organizational Change*, Belmont, Calif.: Wadsworth Publishing Co., 1970.

Automation may not cause the organizational problems that were once anticipated. Daniel Bell, former labor editor for *Fortune*, has estimated that if automation were introduced into all of the factories that could use it, only 8 percent of the labor force would be affected.[6] The growth of service-related industries, such as medical services, and of knowledge-related industries would certainly indicate a shift away from the industrial production firms of previous eras. For automated factories, the organizational problems will not be structural but one of making work meaningful.

Concern for maintaining relationships within a broader societal context, for example, in solving ecological problems, overcoming central city decay, and in providing jobs for hard-core unemployed, will also bring new dimensions to organization structures. One avenue will be that of liaison managers or offices who will act to interface the corporate organization with the Environmental Protection Agency or other governmental units, with a particular community, with other companies working on the same problem, or with concerned groups such as those representing various minorities. This interface manager or office would become an entry point for extraorganizational members and a contact point for purposes of planning, coordination, and for sensing and implementing necessary changes.

It has been suggested that future environmental events may require a substantial reassessment of the field of organization theory. Past approaches to organizations were based on the assumptions of growth, abundance of resources, and consensus among personnel. It may be that the future may bring antagonistic assumptions such as stability or decay, scarcity of resources, and greater conflict.[7] If so, then our conventional ways of designing organizations may need revision. Just what form this might take is unclear for the present. Whatever the form, the organizing function will continue to evolve to reflect the age-old need to provide structure without stifling initiative, to accomplish the goals of organizations and people, and to maintain organizational viability in a changing world.

[6]Daniel Bell, *Work and Its Discontents*, Boston: Beacon Press, 1956, p. 49.

[7]William G. Scott, "Organization Theory: A Reassessment," *Academy of Management Journal*, Vol. 17, No. 2 (June, 1974), pp. 242–54.

Leadership

In order to gain a perspective, leadership may be viewed as an all-encompassing function of guiding the human resource toward organizational objectives. This function has been subsumed under many labels throughout the years: entrepreneurship, supervising, leading, directing, commanding, actuating, and so on. As such, leadership has been closely allied with notions about the skills or traits leader-managers must have as well as how they go about motivating people. In early organizations, leadership was the function of the eldest, the strongest, or the most articulate, or often based upon some religious concept such as the divine right of kings. As such, leadership was often viewed as a function of custom and tradition or in many cases as one of the personal traits of the leader. Concepts of motivation were scarce at best: occupational and societal duties were expected to be fulfilled based upon tradition. Individuals were not expected to desire much beyond subsistence in this world. The command philosophy of leadership, as typified by Hobbes and Machiavelli, furthered the notion of centralized control to keep brute man in his place. The cultural rebirth was to shake mankind from these tradition- and command-based concepts and place a new emphasis on achievement in this world.

The early entrepreneurs acquired leadership positions through their power to command capital and their ability and zeal to transform this capital into productive enterprises. Within the factory system, the pressures for economies of scale soon forced entrepreneurs to hire salaried submanagers, and this was to lead to a number of problems in finding and developing talent and in motivating managerial performance. Adhering to the precepts of past organizations and to their own experiences, entrepreneurs thought that it was the personal idiosyncratic traits of the individual that led to leadership success or failure. The abilities and skills of the leader were not deemed transferable: managerial advice was based upon the industry or firm to be managed, and the early "text" of James Montgomery reflected this parochial view. Motivation in the early factory marked the first appearance of an "economic man" concept. Piece-work systems held forth the carrot, disciplinary fines provided the stick, and factory owners and religious officials combined to try to develop a factory "ethos."

Charles Dupin was the first to suggest that managerial skills could be taught, suggestive of the idea that management was more than a function of personal traits. Economic-man concepts continued in vogue and Babbage and Ure exhorted workers to accept the factory system as a means of improving their condition. Robert Owen urged a communal existence, had less confidence in the wage system, and fought to improve people's condition by improving their environment.

The scientific management era, following the growth of American industry and a continued rise in the employment of "professional," salaried, nonowning managers, viewed leadership as a function of knowledge. The best leader was the technical expert, and Taylor's functional foreman concept sought to provide specialized supervision for the worker. Gantt envisioned a leadership "elite" composed of industrial engineers. The factory ethos of that period was the "mental revolution," which was based on the premise that workers and managers would perceive that they had mutual interests in efficiency and productivity which would lead to high wages and low costs. In this age of Benthamite utilitarianism, the economic-man concept was in tune with a cultural environment of individual reward based on individual effort. But within the scientific management movement there were also motivational concepts beyond those of economic gain. Gantt recognized the importance of morale and teamwork; Taylor admonished leaders to know their workers and to build a personal rather than an impersonal system; and Lillian Gilbreth recognized the psychological factors bearing upon work.

Henri Fayol saw management as universal and teachable and identified the mix of skills needed as the manager moved up the scalar chain. Though his work was overshadowed by that of Taylor, Fayol's process and his notions of universality were to lead to the development of general administrative theory. By distinguishing between "management" as a total function of guiding the enterprise and "administration" as a cyclical subfunction of working through people, Fayol established a conceptual framework for the study of management.

The notion of social man found its roots in the early sociologists, such as Cooley and Mead, and in the work of Whiting Williams. There was a decline in the ethic of individual achievement motivation and a rise in the idea that people were primarily social creatures. This idea found its support in the work of the Mayoists and in the beginnings of human relations at the Hawthorne plant. This "new" view of people, though subjected to criticism, was that they were not motivated by money but by interpersonal relations and a need to belong. The cultural environment was perilous and the Mayoists sought to overcome industrial problems by building group solidarity and by developing social skills in managers. Thus the Taylor concept of leaders who led because they were technically the most competent was replaced by the notion that social skills were the most important to managers.

The Mayoists spawned a number of ideas and research about leadership and motivation. Participatory, democratic leadership came into vogue, interpersonal skills were to be developed, and sensitive, socially skilled leaders were deemed the best. At Ohio State and Michigan, leadership took on a "situational" aura which played down the traits of the leader and emphasized the interaction of leader and led in the situation.

The modern era brought another shift: motivation was to be found in challenge, responsibility, and in work itself in the idea of self-actualization. Leadership ideas also changed: the ideas of 9,9; System 4; and the "contingency" model of Fiedler brought new notions of leadership. The modern mix of skill required was that of adaptation—choosing the right style to fit task structure, position power, and leader-member relations. The ethos of the modern era was that of harmony, the bringing together of organizations and people in a Theory Y–self-actualizing notion of organizational productivity and human satisfaction.

There have been marked shifts in past notions of leadership and motivation. Our ideas have evolved as changing environmental conditions have reshaped our assumptions about people and as we have understood more about organizational behavior. What will the future bring? Certainly an advanced technological society will demand a variety of specialists who have higher educational and skill levels. Dealing with better-educated specialists will mean that managers will need to rely more and more on making work meaningful since these employees will be more inclined to identify with their "profession" than the company.

In the future we must see education for management as a "life-long" exercise which continues beyond the bachelor's level college degree into a series of seminars and experiences which managers will need to retool or to keep their knowledge and skills current. While business schools prefer to educate specialists, the future need will be for generalists who can bring a variety of specialists together in a productive fashion. A greater concern however, appears to lie in the caliber of managerial talent which will be available in the future. One author has noted some changes that indicate the supply of *effective* managers is declining. He feels that today's college students are deficient in the qualities of competitiveness, assertiveness, and a sense of responsibility—all attitudes required by effective managers. The predicted future shortage of managerial talent then would be caused in part by lacking this "will to manage," and in part by students choosing nonmanagerial careers.[8] Together, these factors threaten the supply of effective managers at the very time in the future when the demand will be the greatest.

The mix of managerial skills will most probably not change drastically. Managers will need some level of technical ability in order to communicate with and manage the work of specialists. Managerial skills in terms of the time-honored functions of planning, organizing, controlling, etc., will not change in their basic nature. One change which will most probably emerge will be a greater emphasis on *conceptual* skills for managers of the future. They will need to be able to see parts of the managerial situation, determine how these parts interact, and decide how to put all of these together in a total framework. This will be more than a conceptualization of the firm as a system and will include the relation of the firm to a broader context.

Education for this skill mix will undoubtedly be difficult. It will be at the polar extreme from the early idea of managing one type of industry. Education for management may shift from the business school setting, or the business school itself may evolve into a college of management arts and sciences. While this may

[8]John B. Miner, *The Human Constraint: The Coming Shortage of Managerial Talent,* Washington, D.C.: Bureau of National Affairs, 1974.

sound chauvinistic coming from a teacher of management, we will come to see business and industry as a subset of a larger institutional framework. The public sector (e.g., government, education, the military, and other nonprofit-oriented organizations) is continually growing in proportion to the private sector. This alone will demand a view of industrial organizations as a subset to the total concept of management.

Motivation will be a pressing problem of the future as it has always been. The advent of more leisure, the growth of automation, and the rise of service industries will move people further and further from physical work as it is presently conceived. Work, as we know it, will mean entirely different things to our children. There will not only be a physical removal of our direct ties to a physical product but also an intellectual separation. More mental functions will be turned over to machines and the human will be an observer rather than a participant. What will this mean to self-actualization? Certainly it will be difficult to obtain any pride or feeling of accomplishment while monitoring a machine. Our concern for the meaning of work in determining the quality of the lives we lead will continue.[9] But job enrichment will not be possible, if desired, for everyone. Self-actualization of the future may be found in the family, in how we spend our leisure time, or in other creative pursuits off the job. Whatever the skills and wherever they are applied, the leadership task will continue to be the crux of our age-old problem of balancing the needs and aspirations of people with the tasks required in goal-seeking organizations.

Human Resource Administration

The recruitment, selection, training, and administration of the human resource has a checkered history. Commonly called staffing or personnel management, this managerial function has grown into greater prominence over time. The early factory system posed all sorts of problems in inducing agrarian workers to go into the factory, in teaching them the skills of an industrial

[9]For a mixture of views on this subject, see James O'Toole (ed.), *Work and The Quality of Life: Resource Papers for Work in America*, Cambridge, Mass.: MIT Press, 1974.

civilization, in keeping their behavior within the parameters of sound, profitable practices, and in developing trustworthy salaried managers. The personnel function for many years was the responsibility of the line manager; it was not until around 1900 that "employment departments" and "labor chiefs" began to appear as a separate organizational function. Part of the dual heritage of personnel was "welfare" work, providing schemes such as meals, medical services, etc., in the hope of gaining satisfied workers.

The industrial psychology of Munsterberg, arising out of the ethics of scientific management, was the first attempt to develop a scientific basis for personnel management; this was the first break with pseudoscientific selection and the search for "psychophysical" variables. Taylor sought a "first-class man" but it was Munsterberg who sought through testing and empirical study to place the man in the right job. Vocational guidance was an early theme of industrial psychology, and personnel testing became the fad in the post–World War I era. People were being recognized more and more as a valuable asset of the firm, and the personnel function, through such offices as Henry Ford's "sociology department," achieved more recognition. In large part, the theme of early personnel departments was worker "adjustment" to the industrial situation. During the 1920s, companies took on various welfare schemes, partly to combat incipient unionism, partly to instill worker loyalty to the company, and partly because it was felt that concern for the human asset was sound business procedure.

The growth of unionism in the 1930s led to expansion of the personnel function into industrial relations-oriented activities. Industrial sociology, the product of the Mayoists, was amended as the "industrial human relations" of the 1940s. Industrial peace was viewed as a function of management's understanding and recognition of the role of unions in determining wages, hours, and conditions of employment.

For the management resource, early entrepreneurs looked for trustworthy, stable people who had the physical, social, or other personal attributes which would lead to success of the firm. This notion of managerial selection based on personal characteristics prevailed for an extended period. Under scientific management, Taylor had little confidence in any school (other than that of experience) for developing managers. Fayol made a major break with the personal trait-experience approach and thought that managerial skills could be taught in schools. However, there were few business schools and the general view still held that managers would best develop under the tutelage of an already proven manager. It was during the scientific management era that business schools began teaching management, and gradually these outputs would form a growing pool of talent for industry.

The human relations movement broadened education for management to include the development of social skills through the use of cases, incidents, and sensitivity training. The 1950s not only witnessed a renewed interest in general management theory but also the rapid growth of programs for industrial leaders commonly called "executive development" programs. Many industrialists returned to the classroom to renew their skills and reshape their attitudes to cope with the renewed growth of organizations.

The decline of the human relations philosophy in the late 1950s brought a new focus to the personnel function. The term "human resource administration" came more into vogue and scholars linked this philosophy to organizational humanism, to Rensis Likert's human asset accounting, and to the idea of productivity and efficiency through the satisfactions of work rather than through welfare-oriented, keep-people-happy schemes.

The future will bring into play many of the problems already commented upon with respect to future managerial skills and human motivation. A more affluent, leisure-oriented better-educated work force will make selection and placement more difficult and retention more tenuous. Unions will continue to play both an economic and a political role in influencing managerial decisions. After experiencing a stagnation in membership growth, i.e., as a percentage of the total work force, unions have expanded their efforts into heretofore unexplored areas such as teachers, governmental employees, and other white-collar workers. More organizations and managers of the future will find themselves engaged in the process of collective bargaining if these efforts succeed.

The bulk of future problems in human resource administration will lie in the area of social values and political imperatives. The modern era has witnessed a host of legislative enactments which dealt with employee health and safety, equal pay, equal employment opportunities, affirmative action plans, employee re-tirement income security, and other personnel issues. Businesses were asked to take on more social responsibilities and to move into slum areas to set up factories and training programs. The National Alliance of Businessmen moved vigorously to establish quotas for industries to hire the hard-core unemployed. In practice, experiences under these programs have reflected many of the problems encountered by the early entrepreneurs in the factory system. The hard-core unemployed have had little or no prior work experience, few usable skills, poor work habits (such as going on spending sprees after receiving a big check), and do not seem to be overly enthusiastic about the factory or office regimen. With a lowering of selection standards in order to bring the hard core into the factory, there will be more pressure for improved training, supervision, and motivation.

There will be more social pressures and legislative enactments which will affect the personnel function. Today's managers find their actions bound up more and more by "legalisms" in personnel administration; unfortunately, the future probably holds more of the same. Managers will find their human resource problems more closely aligned with both the social values and the political imperatives of the future.

Controlling

The managerial activity of controlling has existed since organized effort began. Controlling completes the managerial activity cycle by measuring and evaluating planned versus actual actions in order to take corrective action, if necessary. As such, controlling deeply reflects the premises of the controller. In preindustrial societies, controlling was based on unilateral command and rigid discipline in view of the low esteem with which people were held. The factory brought into play more variables to be controlled, yet the entrepreneur could not rely upon the power of dogma, military regimen, nor upon state fiat to achieve control. Standardization of parts helped somewhat but the widespread division of labor and the unskilled work force which was unaccustomed to working to close tolerances impeded development of any sophisticated, reliable control systems. Accounting as a means of providing information for decision making was in a relatively gross state, and cost accounting methods were undeveloped except for some early descriptive attempts by Charles Babbage.

Scientific management stressed controlling through empirical study to set accurate standards and made other advancements in measuring times and costs. As in the early factory, the emphasis was on the control of materials, schedules, and other facets of the production function. In this era, the first significant graphic aids to planning and controlling were developed by Gantt. The early factory owners and church officials had combined to urge a "factory ethos" upon the worker; under Taylor the "mental revolution" was to attempt to bring this same identity of managerial and worker goals. Though these attempts generally failed, they both sought an *internalization* of goals as both a motivating and as a control device. The premise that internal commitment to goals reduces the need for external control devices is thus an old one in management thought.

For the Mayoists, control was not an explicit function. Managers were to become aware of informal reactions to external control devices and how they affected the worker. The ill-logic of sentiments, once understood, would presumably lead managers to modify any stringent use of external controls, to open communications channels, to develop their interpersonal skills, and to recognize the importance of group influences on the task of the manager. Mary Follett would depersonalize control to obey the law of the situation, and Barnard would conclude that control was effective only to the extent that the group accepted managerial authority and standards. In general, the social man era was to lead to a softening of any rigorous notions of external control. Control was to become more of a democratic, internalized commitment to the inducements offered by management and the social skills the manager displayed.

R. C. Davis made a substantial contribution to the control function when he stressed the importance of timing. "Preliminary" control occurred through proper planning, preparation, and dispatching; "concurrent" control, on the other hand, operated while performance was in progress. Davis' notions of control added depth and practicality to the ideas of Fayol. The resurgence of interest in general management theory through the process approach broadened the concept of controlling beyond that of a production orientation. Controlling was viewed as completing a cyclical process of activities and as leading to replanning, resetting of objectives, and other kinds of corrective action.

The advent of the computer, the concept of cybernetics, and the growth of information systems combined to stress the role of feedback in managerial control. More sophisticated control devices were possible through computerized handling of masses of data such as PERT. Organizational humanism has been a modern attempt to reduce rigidity in organizational structures and to recognize the impact that controls have upon the human factor. The new "ethos" of the modern era has been self-actualization, again postulating that people should internalize the goals of the organization and see them as means to the satisfaction of their own needs and aspirations.

Our youthful contemporaries seem less inclined to accept at face value the dictates of their elders. As these individuals begin to assume the responsibilities of a corporate life, there will be strains and tugs at previously cherished notions of evaluating and measuring performance. "Doing your own thing" may be the desire, but history shows a clash between this ideal and the realities of controlled performance toward group goals. On the other hand, history also shows that statism and centralized controls lead to a rebellion against increased conformity and to a diminution of innovation and individual achievement aspirations. Organizations, like political systems, will find a continuation of this clash of the individual versus the system.

The very control devices which have the potential for increased efficiency carry within them their own self-destruct mechanisms. As centralized control is made more possible, it is also made less palatable to the individual. As activities become more centralized for efficiency's sake, they also become less flexible in meeting local needs and in allowing for individual discretion. In short, the institutionalization of the control function has been enhanced by modern technological developments; yet a proliferation of rules, forms, and procedures and other accoutrements of institutionalization may lead to dysfunctional consequences for both the human and the organization.

There will be future pressures for efficiency in resource utilization and modern control concepts can contribute to this goal. Yet there will be the strain between the individual and the system and the dangers of losing sight of the goal of controlling and the means of controlling. Cybernation will make possible a greater emphasis on external control devices; yet human values decree internalization of goals and self-control. Boguslaw has viewed the systems concept as a device to extend the mastery of mankind over nature; indeed, this is an old theme which has persisted throughout the evolution of management thought. Yet the systems concept poses its greatest threat "precisely in its potential as a means for extending the control of man over man."[10] Will the systems designer of today and tomorrow form the new leadership elite which Henry Gantt envisioned in the "New Machine"? Or will the systems designer formulate pleasing arrangements of parts and whole which will preserve those human values which have been our quest for such a long time? It is in resolving this paradox that management will find the challenges of the future.

The Cultural Environment

Management thought is the synthesis of many disciplines and the product of many forces. Throughout our study we have seen how the impact of technology, the changing of cultural values, and the ebb and flow of individuals and institutional arrangements have affected management thought. What we think about the allocation and utilization of resources in goal-directed organized effort is heavily influenced by our culture. Yet we are not slaves, not passive, not predetermined nor predestined to play our roles upon some great cultural stage. Our ideas in turn shape and change our environment in a historical action-reaction process of reciprocal interaction.

The Economic Environment

Management finds its roots in the economic problems of people. It is essentially an economic study in the broadest sense which is concerned with producing and distributing economic value in a

---

[10]Robert Boguslaw, *The New Utopians: A Study of Systems Design and Social Change,* Englewood Cliffs, N.J.: Prentice-Hall, 1965, p. 204.

directed manner. Management is not limited in its scope, however, to economic, i.e., business, institutions. Economic value must be created and sustained in all types of endeavors which seek to achieve some goal or goals with a certain amount of resource effort. Governments run on budgets financed by taxes which are not limitless. Churches operate on contributions which are not always forthcoming in abundance. Other organizations face this scarcity of resources and must engage in managerial activities to meet their manifold ends.

Management as an activity is also a resource. It carries the capability of producing value by guiding efforts more economically. There was a broad span of time before management became recognized as a legitimate factor in the process of creating value. Land and labor were first considered as the primary focus of economics; later capital was added as church strictures concerning usury loosened; but management has been viewed as a resource only recently. The nineteenth century brought some recognition of a managerial function, but it was not until the twentieth century that we began to isolate, identify, and study management as a separate function applicable to all types of organizations. It was here that we saw the problems of managing becoming so acute that they required a separate body of study.

Early societies had economic problems but sought their solutions either in past precepts or in a command philosophy of resource allocation. The market economy, as a part of the cultural rebirth, led to the generation of a new body of economic thought. A rapid advance in technology became the basis for a new economic order, the factory system. Here, coupled with steam power and changing cultural values, economics took on new dimensions. The factory system created both managerial and broader cultural problems. The managerial problems created the need to study management; the cultural problems created the first needs for managers to be responsible and aware of their environment.

Technology and science have evolved rapidly since the Industrial Revolution, and this advancement has continually placed greater pressures on management scholars and practitioners to cope with newer, more formidable problems. Advancements in power sources, communications, materials, transportation, and technology have removed the managerial activity from the domestic system to a world of international commerce. Chandler's cycle was used throughout this study to show how economic expansion led to changes in management thought. As resources are accumulated, managerial problems mount and forces arise which lead to a need to rationalize resource utilization. Administrative structures are formulated to meet industrial strategies and managers have had to cope with a dynamic economic environment in transportation, power, communications, and markets.

The early factory resulted in an accumulation of resources, and the first attempts at rationalization were made by Charles Babbage and Andrew Ure. The nineteenth century was depicted as the resource accumulation phase in American industry and scientific management was the response to this environmental pressure. Dormant during the Depression, the post–World War II world saw a renewal phase of resource accumulation. In a relatively rapid response, the reaction to this has been a search to rerationalize resource utilization through more science in managing.

In the future this cycle of accumulation, rationalization, renewal, and rerationalization may be slowed by the energy problems facing the United States and the world. We may indeed, as was suggested earlier, face the possibility of managing organizations under conditions of economic stagnation. Declining sources of petroleum and natural gas will seriously affect the costs of production and transportation as well as industrial employment. Danger signs have already been posted with respect to declining American productivity. In the past ten years, the rate of productivity and output per man hour in the United States has fallen behind all other major industrialized nations.[11] This has been caused by lowered levels of capital investment in the private sector and by a decline in the "work ethic," or the need for achievement. As productivity declines and as sources of energy cost more, managers will have to struggle to sustain organizational performance. There will be more emphasis on cost controls, on efficiency in production processes, and on improved motivation of employees.

[11]R. Joseph Monsen and Borge O. Saxberg, "When Workers Don't Work and Managers Don't Manage," *Bendrift Okonomen* (Norway) 8, 1976 (reprint 76-8 of the Graduate School of Business Administration, University of Washington, Seattle, Washington, 1976).

One author has suggested that scientific management will be "rediscovered" as a solution to future problems.[12]

As alternatives to fossil fuels are sought, the future will bring a race between technology and the question of whether or not we will freeze in the dark. Today, opinion seems divided: on the one hand, a "gloom and doom" camp predicts a return to a technology of natural energy sources which are not depletable; another group maintains that technology has met earlier challenges successfully and will do so again in the future. Only future events will determine the outcome; in any case, progress will not come without costs.

C. P. Snow has noted a resurgence of the "literary" intellectual, whom he calls the "natural Luddite," who scorns the material progress which science and technology have brought.[13] Toffler has suggested that we must avoid "Luddite paroxysms" yet keep technology responsible through such devices as a "technology ombudsman."[14] The challenge for the scientist and manager of the future will be to convince the intellectual Luddites, much as Babbage, Ure, and Dupin sought to do, that material advancement brings social betterment.

Organizational goals in the past have been largely economic ones. This did not preclude social goals, for example, early notions of social responsibility and service, but these were more frequently than not viewed as by-products of the economic goals. Future managers will find social values impinging more and more upon their economic decision-making framework. This social overlay of values may work to the detriment of economic return, and managers will find some degree of schizophrenia and social vertigo in the decision-making process. The task of future management thought is not an either/or proposition—either economic *or* social values—but one in the most enlightened sense of integration. In Taylor and Follett this notion of integration received vary-

[12] Peter F. Drucker, "The Coming Rediscovery of Scientific Management," *The Conference Board Record*, Vol. 13, No. 6 (June, 1976), pp. 23–27.

[13] C. P. Snow, *The Two Cultures: And a Second Look*, Cambridge, England: University Press, 1964.

[14] Alvin Toffler, *Future Shock*, New York: Random House, 1970, p. 381 and pp. 390–392.

ing interpretations. For Taylor, the "mental revolution" would bind all together in prosperity through efficiency; for Follett, it was the exercise of creativity in searching for a higher-level solution to lead to mutual resolution without compromise or conflict. While these ideals have been held high before, it is the task of the future to make them operative. Indeed, it will be a formidable challenge, one worthy of our best minds, to bring forth a mix of cultural values which would lead to both economic and social progress.

The Social Environment

While management finds its roots in the economic necessities of efficient and effective resource utilization, it also finds its actions affected by social values. Humans are the primary input of the management model and the outputs are used to satisfy human aspirations. Both internally and externally, managers are affected by prevailing social values. Finding its justification in being essential to organized efforts, the activity of management becomes inextricably interwoven with assumptions about people and about interpersonal relationships.

The individual has not been held as a primary value in many cultures. The tribe, the state, or other groups have often held that a person must be subservient to group or political needs. As evidence of this, slavery, the ownership of human beings, prevailed until relatively recently, historically speaking. Even the Greeks, who first flirted with democracy, thought that slavery was proper. It may or may not be historical coincidence, but the record shows that economic and social progress has been most rapid after enslavement ends. Early civilizations made little progress under slavery; and the feudal system, which was a more insidious enslavement device, kept society dormant. As people broke the bonds of feudalism, the monolithic authority of the church, and the dictates of the monarchy, they began to make economic and social progress.

An industrial society required a different set of assumptions about the nature of people; that they could have the freedom to choose their own government, that they could be self-directing, that they could pursue property and wealth as natural rights, and that they could devise means for the redress of grievances and injustices. It was in this context that individual liberty became a value, that the individual quest for wealth was morally sanctioned, and that creativity and innovation were encouraged. This individualism dominated the economic growth of the Industrial Revolution and fed the fires of industrialization. Even within America, it was the postslavery era that led to the greatest growth in resource accumulation and great social mobility for those fleeing Europe.

Interpersonal relations were bound up in traditional precepts for ages. Social customs and taboos were far more important than social progress, and it was the task of the tribe, the state, the church, or the feudal lord to preserve the social heritage. The cultural rebirth brought a redefinition of human relationships. The social solidarity of the community based on the agrarian life was sorely shaken by urbanization and industrialization. New neighbors, new customs, new environs, and new jobs were the social crises for industrial man. The family, formerly a prime social and economic unit, was to begin disintegration as parents and children went on their different paths to work in the new factory. Socialization, formerly a task of the family, became the province of the factory, the educational system, and of peers in work groups.

Robert Owen made an early attempt to restore communal integrity in the face of the perceived ravages of industrialization. Yet industrialization proceeded, and people guided by an inner gyroscope, furthered the specialization of labor, the factory system, and the expansion of markets. In rejecting the communal system of Owen, people accepted and furthered the notion of individualism. People were not entirely plastic in the early factory; they resisted technological advancement, factory regimen, and managerial discipline. Yet they accepted an innovative motivational premise in the concept of economic motivation. The carrot, supported by the stick and the moralistic overtones of the factory ethos, was held forth as the way of individual betterment.

Profits, long deemed a cardinal sin, became morally sanctioned by the Protestant ethic. Commerce and trade, deemed ignoble by many prior civilizations, became a stepping stone for the ambitious young person to cross the turbulent waters of social class. The ingredients of this social mix thus condoned trade, profits, and individual achievement. Holes were being torn in the social fabric but that was the way of progress. Stagnancy worships the untorn cloth. But even as these tears were appearing, there were a few who were beginning to put forth new philosophies which would help people in their newly found relations. Babbage sought an early identification of the mutuality of interests through profit sharing; Ure and Dupin established classes to prepare young men for more rewarding professions; and Henry Poor sought through leadership to overcome the conflict between the individual and the system.

Scientific management was a philosophy for coping with the social problems as well as the industrial problems of the age. Rooted in utilitarian economics, in the rationalism of nineteenth-century philosophy, and in the Protestant virtues of individualism, scientific management was a call for an integration of all interests in society. The mental revolution called for people to forget about dividing the spoils and to work toward creating more and more. The primary benefits were economic, but the social benefits were many: lowered prices, higher wages, individuals doing the work at which they were best, and everyone, manager, worker, and society ar large, benefitting from prosperity through efficiency.

Even during the apogee of scientific management thought, the credo of individualism, as personified in the Protestant and achievement ethics, was declining. The Depression and its aftermath was to bring a new focus in social values: affiliation needs became a trade-off for achievement needs; profits and efficiency delined as goals; self-help became government help; inner direction became other direction; and businessmen lost the esteem they had held previously. The Mayoists sought to rebuild social solidarity and to overcome a perceived cultural lag by exhortation to develop the social skills of the manager. Bottom-up management, in industry as well as in the Rooseveltian "little people" philosophy, became the goal. Getting along was valued before getting ahead. People were caught up in forces which they could not control and therefore someone else must help. The self-help doctrine was obsolete and the economic, social, and political climate was changing to offset the human dislocations of economic catastrophe.

In the modern era, social values appear to have shifted somewhat, but not much. Affiliation is still highly regarded but less so as self-actualization has moved to the forefront. Self-actualization is based on the social premise that people find their dignity and fulfillment in the challenge, rewards, and satisfactions which come from work itself. The trend is still away from authoritarianism, except today it is the antiestablishment movement. Calls for power equalization have led to programs for the poor, the black, and all others deemed disadvantaged. Profits are not too highly regarded and businessmen are asked to assume social goals and to diminish economic profitability if necessary. Hiring the hard-core unemployed, pollution control, and a host of other social issues have placed the manager in a potentially conflicting position of having to satisfy social demands while simultaneously keeping workers, customers, and creditors happy.

Peter Drucker has called these times "the age of discontinuity."[15] Drucker sees the discontinuities developing in new space age technologies, in the growth of the "knowledge industry," in the international development of economies, and in the political matrices of large organizations and ideological struggles. These discontinuities represent a break-up of previous bases and assumptions about economic arrangements for allocating resources, about social values, and about the nature and purpose of political institutions. It is in these stresses and strains on the cultural fabric that there will be continued pressures on leaders in all types of organizations.

The power equalization movement has not yet run its course, and the modern appearances of this phenomenon find its roots in a disenchantment with urbanization and industrialization. The businessman has been closely identified with the city, and the city is deemed degrading by many. Our inner cities are decaying today, yet it is the business sector that has the resource capability to rebuild them. Youth is disenchanted with business, and yet it is in the business sector that the resources and the know-how are accumulated which can provide jobs and housing, reduce or eliminate pollution, and solve other pressing cultural problems. Profits are suspect, yet it is profitability which is the key to research and

---

[15] Peter F. Drucker, *The Age of Discontinuity: Guidelines to Our Changing Society*, New York: Harper and Row, 1968.

development, to investments, and to long-run prosperity and growth of the total economy. Productivity and efficiency are no longer the cultural goals that they once were, yet it is productivity that enables higher wages, lower costs, and market proliferation and expansion.

Founded by stoics, America is begoming an epicurean society. Thrift is no longer a virtue, and neither is wealth. The biblical precepts of rights and wrongs are being threatened by "situation" ethics. It is in the future that the social fabric faces its most severe tests. It is in this uncertain future of shifting social values that management will have to summon forth its greatest energies of creativity and human understanding in the service of purposeful endeavors.

The Political Environment

The philosophical premises and the practical realities of the relation of the individual to the state are also deeply imbedded in the assumptions made about human nature. Early political philosophy was based on the premise that people in a state of nature were basically unreasoning brutes who could be civilized only by some central authority. Organizational structures reflected this premise and legitimization of authority tended to be based upon some time-hallowed or mystical source of power. The divine right of kings, based upon Adam's God-given power to rule his children, was such a source of authority. Tribal taboos, enshrined in ceremonial rites and ancestral worship, formed another such source of authority. Machiavelli and Hobbes were the spokesmen of lodging supreme power in the prince or the state.

John Locke broke with this command philosophy and established the framework for constitutional government. Coupled with the Protestant ethic, the market ethic, and the philosophical age of enlightenment, the liberty ethic provided a new source of power and a new legitimization of authority. Political thought with respect to economic thought followed the premise of self-governing individuals, guided only by their own self-interest in the pursuit of property, wealth, and happiness. This *laissez-faire* environment provided fertile soil for the Industrial Revolution, aided and abetted innovations in marketing and production, and gave a political sanction to the entrepreneur. But even as *laissez-faire* prevailed, there were early attempts through parliamentary investigations to check some of the abuses of power by individuals. Though generally unsuccessful, these efforts reflected a general scheme of societal checks and balances which constitutional government provided.

Early American political thought followed the *laissez-faire* precepts until the post–Civil War period. Increasing protests against an unholy alliance between government and business and against abuses by "robber barons" brought legislation to regulate business activities. First came legislation on the railroads, where the abuses were most severe, and then later antitrust legislation. Labor legislation lagged somewhat behind the development of other regulatory agencies, but that too was soon to pass. Laws regulating hours, working conditions, and child and female labor were slow to gain credence by the courts as the proper province of governmental activity.

The nineteenth century was still relatively *laissez-faire* but the twentieth century was to see an increasing role of government in business. The "new economics" placed government in a primary role through monetary and fiscal policy to stimulate economic recovery from the Depression. Labor legislation led to a spurt in union membership growth in the Rooseveltian "little man" philosophy. Post–World War II saw explicit recognition of the responsibility of the government to maintain high employment levels and sustained economic activity through the Employment Act of 1946. Some counterbalance to union power was achieved in the Taft-Hartley Act (1947) and in later labor legislation. Consumer advocates brought business to task for product safety, warranties, labeling, advertising, and a host of other consumer protection programs. Ralph Nader, a modern version of Upton Sinclair, tackled both the practices of business as well as those who regulated business (e.g., the Interstate Commerce Commission). Personnel practices became more circumscribed by legislation and administrative fiat. The Equal Pay Act (1963); Title VII of the Civil Rights Act (1964); The Age Discrimination in Employment Act (1967); The Occupational Safety and Health Act (1970); and the Employee Retirement Income Security Act (1974) impacted the job of the manager in a manner analogous to the alphabet-soup government

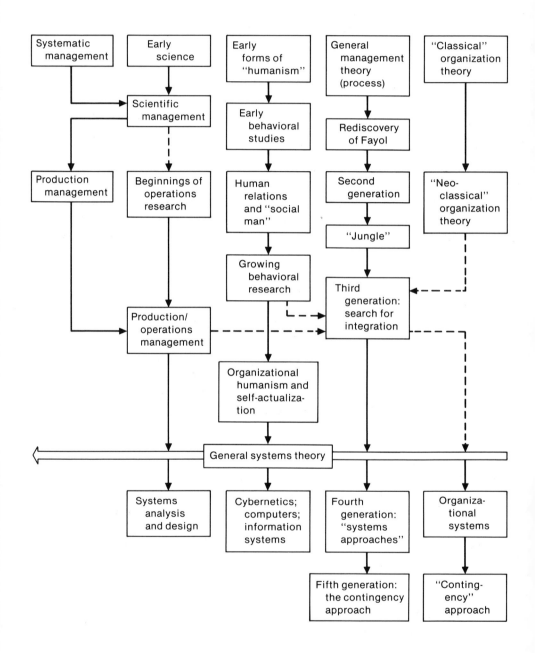

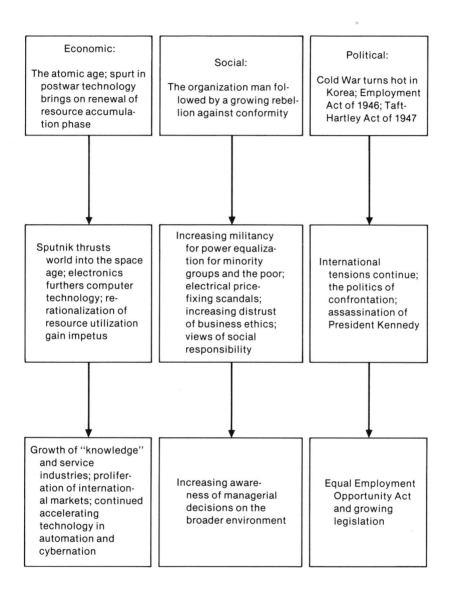

Fig. 22-1. Synopsis of the modern era and the cultural environment.

days of the 1930s. It has become fashionable to speak of "human rights" versus "property rights," forgetting Locke's admonition that without property rights, there are no human rights.

The political environment will continue to be exceedingly crucial in managerial decision making. Trade and tariff policy, foreign policy, defense spending, product regulation, wage-price guidelines, antitrust legislation, employment practices, pollution control, urban problems, and governmental emphasis on other social projects will continue to shape the objectives of the business sector for some time to come. Perhaps there will be increasing governmental regulation and control to bring continuity from discontinuity, order from chaos. Perhaps this centralization and regulation will lead to a stifling equalization of all to the point where creativity and achievement lose their value.[16] To restore innovation and progress, there may have to come a withering away of state controls of economic activity. If so, the twenty-first-century manager may find a new age of relatively *laissez-faire* political and economic philosophies.

Summary

This has been a long journey which is only just beginning. Throughout this trip, management has been viewed as an activity essential to all organized efforts. Management finds its basis in the economic allocation and utilization of human and physical resources in order to attain organizational objectives. However, management is more than an economic activity—it is a conceptual function which must mold resources into a proper mix within the economic, social, and political facets of its environment. Management thought is the mirror reflection of managerial activity. Management thought brings form to function and philosophy to practice.

Fairly definite trends, forces, and philosophies have emerged in this conceptual analysis of evolving management thought.

[16] Durant makes a significant point for modern man: "Hence the dream of communism lurks in every modern society as a racial memory of a simpler and more equal life; and where inequality or insecurity rises beyond sufferance, men welcome a return to a condition which they idealize by recalling its equality and forgetting its poverty." Will Durant, *The Story of Civilization, Part I; Our Oriental Heritage,* New York: Simon & Schuster, 1935, pp. 18–19.

Management is both a product of and a process in its environment. Internally, management thought has passed through phases of differing emphases on the human and on the organizational and methods facets of the problems encountered in guiding goal-directed systems. Externally, management thought has been affected by evolving technology, by shifting assumptions about the nature of man, and by the dynamics of economic, social and political values.

Figure 22-1 is a somewhat sketchy summary of the broad swath that has been cut through this study of management. The modern era has seen a proliferation of approaches to management thought and an increasing awareness of the environment of management. The search continues for unity in theory, harmony in organizations, and orderliness in problem solving and goal attainment. It is this search that makes the study of management most worthy of intellectual and practical exercise. Management is one of the most dynamic of all disciplines; as technology, institutions, and people change, our ideas of management evolve in order to cope with our oldest problem—the allocation and utilization of scarce resources to meet the manifold desires of human society. Today is not like yesterday, nor will tomorrow be like today; yet today is a synergism of all our yesterdays, and tomorrow will be the same. There are many lessons in history for management scholars, and the most important one is the study of the past as prologue.

Selected Bibliography

Part I:
Early Management Thought

BABBAGE, CHARLES, *On the Economy of Machinery and Manufactures*. London: Charles Knight, 1832.

BEARD, MIRIAM, *A History of Business*, Vols. I and II. Ann Arbor: University of Michigan Press, 1962 and 1963.

BURNS, TOM and SAUL, S. B., *Social Theory and Economic Change*. London: Tavistock Publications, 1967.

CHANDLER, ALFRED D., JR., *Henry Varnum Poor: Business Editor, Analyst, and Reformer*. Cambridge, Mass.: Harvard University Press, 1956.

CHANDLER, ALFRED D., JR., *Strategy and Structure*. Cambridge, Mass.: MIT Press, 1962.

CHANDLER, ALFRED D., JR., *The Visible Hand: The Managerial Revolution in American Business*. Cambridge, Mass.: Harvard University Press, 1977.

CHAPMAN, STANLEY D., *The Early Factory Masters*. New York: Augustus M. Kelley Publications, 1967.

CLARK, VICTOR, *History of Manufactures in the United States, 1607–1860*. New York: McGraw-Hill Book Co., 1916.

CLOUGH, SHEPARD B., *The Rise and Fall of Civilization: An Inquiry into the Relationship Between Economic Development and Civilization*. New York: McGraw-Hill Book Co., 1951.

COCHRAN, THOMAS C. and MILLER, WILLIAM, *The Age of Enterprise*. New York: Macmillan Co., 1944.

COOKE-TAYLOR, R. W., *Introduction to a History of the Factory Sys-

tem. London: Richard Bentley and Sons, 1886.

DEANE, PHYLLIS, *The First Industrial Revolution.* London: Cambridge University Press, 1965.

DUPIN, CHARLES, *Discours sur le Sort des Ouvriers.* Paris: Bachelier, Librairie, 1831.

DURANT, WILL, *The Story of Civilization, Part I: Our Oriental Heritage.* New York: Simon and Schuster, 1935.

DURANT, WILL, *The Story of Civilization, Part II: The Life of Greece.* New York: Simon and Schuster, 1939.

DURANT, WILL, *The Story of Civilization, Part III: Caesar and Christ.* New York: Simon and Schuster, 1944.

DURANT, WILL, *The Story of Civilization, Part IV: The Age of Faith.* New York: Simon and Schuster, 1950.

EELS, RICHARD and WALTON, CLARENCE, *Conceptual Foundations of Business.* Homewood, Ill.: Richard D. Irwin, 1961.

GAGER, CURTIS H., "Management Throughout History," in *Top Management Handbook,* H. B. Maynard (ed.). New York: McGraw-Hill Book Co., 1960.

GEORGE, CLAUDE S., JR., *The History of Management Thought.* Englewood Cliffs, N.J.: Prentice-Hall, 1968 and 1972.

GLADDEN, E. N., *A History of Public Administration* (2 vols.). London: Frank Cass and Company, 1972.

HAYEK, FRIEDRICH, *Capitalism and the Historians.* Chicago: University of Chicago Press, 1954.

HAYS, SAMUEL P., *The Response to Industrialism 1885–1914.* Chicago: University of Chicago Press, 1957.

HEILBRONER, ROBERT L., *The Worldly Philosophers: The Lives, Times, and Ideas of the Great Economic Thinkers.* New York: Simon and Schuster, 1953.

HEILBRONER, ROBERT L., *The Making of Economic Society.* Englewood Cliffs, N.J.: Prentice-Hall, 1962.

HOFSTADTER, RICHARD, *Social Darwinism in American Thought: 1860–1915.* Philadelphia: University of Pennsylvania Press, 1945.

HUGHES, JONATHAN, *The Vital Few.* Boston: Houghton Mifflin Co., 1966.

LARSON, HENRIETTA, *Guide to Business History.* Cambridge, Mass.: Harvard University Press, 1948.

LIVESAY, HAROLD C., *Andrew Carnegie and the Rise of Big Business.* Boston: Little, Brown, and Company, 1975.

McCLELLAND, DAVID, *The Achieving Society.* New York: Van Nostrand Reinhold Co., 1961.

OLIVER, JOHN W., *History of American Technology.* New York: Ronald Press Co., 1956.

OWEN, ROBERT, *The Life of Robert Owen.* London: Effingham Wilson, 1857.

PARSONS, TALCOTT, and SMELSER, NEIL J., *Economy and Society: A Study in the Integration of Economic and Social Theory.* New York: Free Press, 1956.

PIKE, ROYSTON, *Hard Times: Human Documents of the Industrial Revolution.* New York: Praeger Publishers, 1966.

POLLARD, SIDNEY, *The Genesis of Modern Management: A Study of the Industrial Revolution in Great Britain.* Cambridge, Mass.: Harvard University Press, 1965.

ROLL, ERICH, *An Early Experiment in Industrial Organization.* London: Longmans, Green and Co., Ltd., 1930.

SCHUMPETER, JOSEPH A., *The Theory of Economic Development.* Cambridge, Mass.: The Harvard University Press, 1936.

SMITH, ADAM, *An Inquiry into the Nature and Causes of the Wealth of Nations.* New York: Modern Library, 1937. Originally published in 1776.

SMITH, FREDERICK, *Workshop Management: A Manual for Masters and Men* (3rd. ed.). London: Wyman and Son, 1832.

SOMBART, WERNER, *Modern Capitalism.* London: T. Fisher Unwin, 1913.

TAWNEY, R. H., *Religion and the Rise of Capitalism.* London: John Murray, 1926.

TOYNBEE, ARNOLD, *The Industrial Revolution.* Boston: Beacon Press, 1956.

URE, ANDREW, *The Philosophy of Manufactures.* London: Charles Knight, 1835.

VEBLEN, THORSTEIN. *The Theory of the Leisure Class,* New York: Macmillan Co., 1899.

WEBER, MAX. *The Protestant Ethic and The Spirit of Capitalism,* New York: Charles Scribner's Sons, 1958. Originally published in 1905.

Part II: The Scientific Management Era

AITKEN, HUGH G. J., *Taylorism at Watertown Arsenal*. Cambridge, Mass.: Harvard University Press, 1960.

ALFORD, L. P., *Laws of Management Applied to Manufacturing*. New York: Ronald Press Co., 1928.

ALFORD, LEON P., *Henry Laurence Gantt, Leader in Industry*. New York: Harper and Row, 1934.

BARITZ, LOREN, *The Servants of Power*. New York: John Wiley and Sons, 1960.

BELL, DANIEL, *Work and Its Discontents: The Cult of Efficiency in America*. Boston: Beacon Press, 1956.

BENDIX, REINHARD, *Max Weber: An Intellectual Portrait*. Garden City, New York: Doubleday and Co., 1960.

BRANDEIS, LOUIS D., *Scientific Management and Railroads*. New York: Engineering Magazine Co., 1911.

CHANDLER, ALFRED D., JR., and SALSBURY, STEPHEN, *Pierre S. DuPont and the Making of the Modern Corporation*, New York: Harper and Row, 1971.

CHILD, JOHN, *British Management Thought*. London: George Allen and Unwin, Ltd., 1969.

CHURCH, ALEXANDER HAMILTON, *The Science and Practice of Management*. New York: Engineering Magazine Co., 1914.

CLARK, WALLACE, *The Gantt Chart*. New York: Ronald Press Co., 1922.

COOKE, M. L., *Our Cities Awake*. New York: Doubleday and Co., 1918.

CHURCH, ALEXANDER HAMILTON, *The Science and Practice of Management*, Vols. I and II. New York: Harper & Row, 1923.

DALE, ERNEST, *The Great Organizers*. New York: McGraw-Hill Book Co., 1960.

DEMAN, HENRI, *Joy In Work*. New York: Holt, Rinehart and Winston, 1929.

DRURY, HORACE B., *Scientific Management: A History and Criticism*. New York: Columbia University Press,1915.

EMERSON, HARRINGTON, *Efficiency as a Basis for Operation and Wages*. New York: Engineering Magazine Co., 1911.

EMERSON, HARRINGTON, *The Twelve Principles of Efficiency*. New York: Engineering Magazine Co., 1913.

FAYOL, HENRI, *Administration Industrielle et Générale*. Paris: 1916 and 1925; English trans. by Coubrough (Geneva: 1930); and trans. by Storrs, London: Sir Isaac Pitman and Sons, 1949.

FILIPETTI, GEORGE, *Industrial Management in Transition*. Homewood, Ill.: Richard D. Irwin, 1946.

GANTT, Henry L., *Work, Wages, and Profit*. New York: Engineering Magazine Co., 1910.

GANTT, HENRY L., *Industrial Leadership*. New Haven, Conn.: Yale University Press,1916.

GANTT, HENRY L., *Organizing for Work*. New York: Harcourt Brace Jovanovich, 1919.

GILBRETH, FRANK B. and LILLIAN M., *Applied Motion Study*. New York: Sturgis and Walton Co., 1917.

GILBRETH, LILLIAN M., *The Psychology of Management*. New York: Sturgis and Walton Co., 1914.

GILSON, MARY B., *What's Past is Prologue*. New York: Harper and Row, 1940.

HABER, SAMUEL, *Efficiency and Uplift*. Chicago: University of Chicago Press, 1964.

HEALD, MORRELL, *The Social Responsibilities of Business: 1900–1960*. Cleveland: Case Western University Press, 1970.

Hearings before Special Committee of the House of Representatives to Investigate the Taylor and other Systems of Shop Management, under Authority of House Resolution 90 (1912).

HOXIE, R. F., *Scientific Management and Labor*. New York: Appleton Century-Crofts, 1915.

KAKAR, SUDHIR, *Frederick Taylor: A Study in Personality and Innovation*. Cambridge, Mass.: MIT Press, 1970.

KIMBALL, D. S., *Principles of Industrial Organization*. New York: McGraw-Hill Book Co., 1913.

LING, CYRIL C., *The Management of Personnel Relations: History and Origins*. Homewood, Ill.: Richard D. Irwin, 1965.

MARTINDALE, DON, *The Nature and Types of Sociological Theory*. Boston: Houghton Mifflin Co., 1960.

MEE, JOHN F., "A History of Twentieth Century Management Thought." Ph.D. dissertation, Department of Business Organization, Ohio State University, 1959.

MEE, J. F., *Management Thought in a Dynamic Society*. New York: New York University Press, 1963.

MILLER, F. B. and COGHILL, M. A., *The Historical Sources of Personnel Work*. Bibliography Series No. 5. Ithaca, N.Y.: New York State School of Industrial and Labor Relations, Cornell University, September 1961.

MILTON, CHARLES R., *Ethics and Expediency in Personnel Management: A Critical History of Personnel Philosophy*. Columbia, S.C.: University of South Carolina Press, 1970.

MUNSTERBERG, HUGO, *Psychology and Industrial Efficiency*. Boston: Houghton Mifflin Co., 1913.

NADWORNY, MILTON J., *Scientific Management and the Unions: 1900–1932*. Cambridge, Mass.: Harvard University Press, 1955.

NELSON, DANIEL, *Managers and Workers: Origins of the New Factory System in the United States, 1880–1920*, Madison, Wisc.: University of Wisconsin Press, 1975.

POLLARD, HAROLD R., *Developments in Management Thought*. London: William Heineman, Ltd., 1974.

SHELDON, OLIVER, *The Philosophy of Management*. London: Sir Isaac Pitman and Sons, 1923.

STRAUSS, ANSELM (ed.), *The Social Psychology of George Herbert Mead*. Chicago: University of Chicago Press, Phoenix Books, 1956.

TAYLOR, FREDERICK W., *Shop Management*. New York: Harper & Row, 1903.

TAYLOR, FREDERICK W., *The Principles of Scientific Management*. New York: Harper & Row, 1911.

TEAD, ORDWAY, and METCALF, HENRY C., *Personnel Administration*. New York: McGraw-Hill Book Co., 1920.

THOMPSON, C. B. (ed.), *The Theory and Practice of Scientific Management*. Boston: Houghton Mifflin Co., 1917.

TILLETT, A., KEMPNER, T., and WILLS, G. (eds.), *Management Thinkers*. London: Penguin Books, 1970.

TROMBLEY, KENNETH E., *The Life and Times of a Happy Liberal: Morris Llewellyn Cooke*. New York: Harper and Row, 1954.

URWICK, LYNDALL (ed.), *The Golden Book of Management*, London: Newman Neame, 1956.

URWICK, LYNDALL and BRECH, E. F. L., *The Making of Scientific*

Management: Thirteen Pioneers, Vol. I. London: Sir Isaac Pitman and Sons, 1948.

URWICK, LYNDALL and BRECH, E. F. L., *The Making of Scientific Management,* Vol. III. London: Management Publications Trust, 1951.

WEBER, MAX, *The Theory of Social and Economic Organization* (trans. by T. Parsons). New York: Free Press, 1947.

WILLIAMS, WHITING, *What's on the Worker's Mind.* New York: Charles Scribner's Sons, 1920.

WILLIAMS, WHITING, *Mainsprings of Men.* New York: Charles Scribner's Sons, 1925.

YOST, EDNA, *Frank and Lillian Gilbreth: Partners for Life.* New Brunswick, N.J.: Rutgers University Press, 1949.

Part III: The Social Man Era

ALFORD, L. P., *Principles of Industrial Management for Engineers.* New York: Ronald Press Co., 1940.

ALLEN, FREDERICK L., *Only Yesterday.* New York: Harper and Row, 1931.

ANDERSON, A. G., *Industrial Engineering and Factory Management.* New York: Ronald Press Co., 1928.

ANDERSON, E. H., and SCHWENNING, G. T., *The Science of Production Organization.* New York: John Wiley and Sons, 1938.

BAKKE, E. W., *Bonds of Organization: An Appraisal of Corporate Human Relations.* New York: Harper and Row, 1950.

BARNARD, CHESTER I., *The Functions of the Executive.* Cambridge, Mass.: Harvard University Press, 1938.

BROWN, ALVIN, *Organization of Industry.* Englewood Cliffs, N.J.: Prentice-Hall, 1947.

BURNHAM, JAMES, *The Managerial Revolution.* New York: John Day Co., 1941.

BARNARD, CHESTER I., *The Functions of the Executive.* Cambridge, York: Simon & Schuster, 1936.

DAVIS, RALPH C., *The Principles of Factory Organization and Management.* New York: Harper and Row, 1928.

DAVIS, RALPH C., *The Principles of Business Organization and Operation.* Columbus, Ohio: H. L. Hedrick, 1935.

DAVIS, RALPH C., *The Fundamentals of Top Management.* New York: Harper and Row, 1951.

DENNISON, HENRY, *Organization Engineering.* New York: McGraw-Hill Book Co., 1931.

FOLLETT, MARY PARKER, *The New State: Group Organization the Solution of Popular Government.* London: Longmans, Green and Co., 1918.

FOLLETT, MARY PARKER, *Creative Experience.* London: Longmans, Green and Co., 1924.

GARDNER, BURLEIGH B., and MOORE, DAVID G., *Human Relations in Industry.* Chicago: Richard D. Irwin, 1945.

GIVEN, W., *Bottom-up Management.* New York: Harper and Row, 1949.

HOLDEN, P. E.; FISH, L. S.; and SMITH, H. L., *Top Management Organization and Control.* Stanford, Calif.: Stanford University Press, 1941.

HOMANS, GEORGE C., *The Human Group.* New York: Harcourt Brace Jovanovich, 1950.

JACQUES, ELLIOTT, *The Changing Culture of a Factory.* London: Tavistock Publications, 1951.

KAVESH, ROBERT A., *Businessmen in Fiction.* Hanover, N. H.: Amos Tuck School, 1955.

LANDSBERGER, HENRY A., *Hawthorne Revisited.* Ithaca, N. Y.: New York State School of Industrial and Labor Relations, 1958.

LEWIN, K., *Resolving Social Conflicts.* New York: Harper and Row, 1948.

LINCOLN, JAMES F., *Incentive Management: A New Approach to Human Relationships in Industry and Business.* Cleveland, Ohio: Lincoln Electric Co., 1951.

LYND, ROBERT S. and LYND, HELEN M., *Middletown: A Study in Contemporary American Culture.* New York: Harcourt Brace Jovanovich, 1929.

MAIER, NORMAN R. F., *Principles of Human Relations.* New York: John Wiley and Sons, 1952.

MASLOW, A. H., "A Theory of Human Motivation," *Psychological Review,* Vol. 50 (1943).

MAYO, ELTON, *The Human Problems of an Industrial Civilization.* New York: Macmillan Co., 1933.

MAYO, ELTON, *The Social Problems of an Industrial Civilization.* Boston: Division of Research, Graduate School of Business Administration, Harvard University, 1945.

MCCORMICK, CHARLES P., *Multiple Management.* New York: Harper and Row, 1938.

METCALF, HENRY C. and URWICK, LYNDALL, *Dynamic Administration— The Collected Papers of Mary Follett.* New York: Harper and Row, 1942.

MOONEY, J. D., and REILEY, A. C., *Onward Industry!* New York: Harper and Row, 1931.

MOONEY, J. D. and REILEY, A. C., *The Principles of Organization.* New York: Harper and Row, 1939.

MORENO, J. L., *Who Shall Survive?: A New Approach to Human Interrelations.* Washington, D.C.: Nervous and Mental Disease Publishing Co., 1934.

PERKINS, DEXTER, *The New Age of Franklin Roosevelt: 1932–1945.* Chicago: University of Chicago Press, 1957.

RIESMAN, DAVID (and others), *The Lonely Crowd: A Study of the Changing American Character.* New Haven, Conn.: Yale University Press, 1950.

ROETHLISBERGER, F. J., *Management and Morale.* Cambridge, Mass.: Harvard University Press, 1941.

ROETHLISBERGER, F. J., *Man-in-Organization.* Cambridge, Mass.: Belknap Press of Harvard University Press, 1968.

ROETHLISBERGER, F. J., *The Elusive Phenomena*, ed. by George F. F. Lombard, Cambridge, Mass.: Harvard University Press, 1977.

ROETHLISBERGER, F. J., and DICKSON, W. J., *Management and the Worker.* Cambridge, Mass.: Harvard University Press, 1939.

SCOTT, WILLIAM G., *The Social Ethic in Management Literature.* Atlanta: Georgia State College of Business Administration, 1959.

SIMON, HERBERT A., *Administrative Behavior. A Study of Decision-Making Processes in Administrative Organization.* New York: Macmillan Co., 1947.

STOGDILL, R. M., *Methods in the Study of Administrative Leadership.* Columbus: Ohio State University, Bureau of Business Research, 1955.

URWICK, L., *Scientific Principles of Organization.* New York: American Management Association, 1938.

URWICK, L., *The Elements of Administration*. New York: Harper and Row, 1944.

WHITEHEAD, T. N., *The Industrial Worker*. 2 vols. Cambridge, Mass.: Harvard University Press, 1938.

WHYTE, WILLIAM F., *Human Relations in the Restaurant Industry*. New York: McGraw-Hill Book Co., 1948.

WHYTE, WILLIAM H., JR. *The Organization Man*. Garden City, N.Y.: Doubleday & Co., 1956.

WOLF, WILLIAM B., *The Basic Barnard: An Introduction to Chester I. Barnard and His Theories of Organization and Management*, Ithaca, N. Y.: NYSSILR, 1974.

Part IV: The Modern Era

ALBERS, HENRY H., *Organized Executive Action*. New York: John Wiley and Sons, 1961.

ARGYRIS, CHRIS, *Personality and Organization*. New York: Harper and Row, 1957.

BEER, STAFFORD, *Cybernetics and Management*. New York: John Wiley and Sons, 1959.

BLAKE, ROBERT R., and MOUTON, JANE S., *The Managerial Grid*. Houston, Tex.: Gulf Publishing Co., 1964.

BOWMAN, EDWARD H., and FETTER, ROBERT B., *Analysis for Production Management*. Homewood, Ill.: Richard D. Irwin, 1957.

BROSS, IRWIN D., *Design for Decision*. New York: MacMillan Co., 1953.

BUFFA, ELWOOD S., *Modern Production Management*. New York: John Wiley and Sons, 1961, 1965, 1969, 1974, and 1977.

CHURCHMAN, C. WEST, ACKOFF, RUSSELL L., and ARNOFF, LEONARD E., *Introduction to Operations Research*. New York: John Wiley and Sons, 1957.

DAUTEN, PAUL M., JR., *Current Issues and Emerging Concepts in Management*. New York: Harper and Row, 1964.

DAVIS, KEITH, *Human Relations in Business*. New York: McGraw-Hill Book Co., 1957, 1962, 1967, 1972, and 1976.

DAVIS, KEITH and BLOMSTROM, ROBERT L., *Business and Its Environment*. New York: McGraw-Hill Book Co., 1966 and 1975.

DIEBOLD, JOHN and GEORGE TERBOUGH, *Automation—the Advent of the Automatic Factory.* New York: Van Nostrand Reinhold Co., 1952.

DRUCKER, PETER, *The Practice of Management.* New York: Harper and Row, 1954.

DRUCKER, PETER F., *Management: Tasks, Responsibilities, and Practices.* New York: Harper and Row, 1973.

FIEDLER, FRED E., and CHEMERS, MARTIN M., *Leadership and Effective Management.* Glenview, Ill.: Scott, Foresman, and Co., 1974.

FILLEY, ALAN C., and HOUSE, ROBERT J., *Managerial Process and Organizational Behavior.* Glenview, Ill.: Scott, Foresman and Co., 1969.

FLIPPO, EDWIN B., *Management: A Behavioral Approach.* Boston: Allyn and Bacon, 1966, 1970, and 1975.

FORRESTER, JAY W., *Industrial Dynamics.* Cambridge, Mass.: MIT Press, 1961.

FOX, WILLIAM M., *The Management Process: An Integrated Functional Approach.* Homewood, Ill.: Richard D. Irwin, 1963.

GALBRAITH, JOHN KENNETH, *The New Industrial State.* Boston: Houghton Mifflin Co., 1967.

GORDON, R. A., and HOWELL, J. E., *Higher Education for Business.* New York: Columbia University Press, 1959.

HAIRE, MASON (ed.), *Modern Organization Theory.* New York: John Wiley and Sons, 1959.

HAYNES, W. WARREN, and MASSIE, JOSEPH L., *Management Analysis, Concepts and Cases.* Englewood Cliffs, N.J.: Prentice-Hall, 1961.

HERZBERG, F., *Work and the Nature of Man.* Cleveland, Ohio: World Publishing Co., 1960.

HERZBERG, F., MAUSNER, B., and SNYDERMAN, B. B., *The Motivation to Work.* New York: John Wiley and Sons, 1959.

HICKS, HERBERT G., *The Management of Organizations.* New York: McGraw-Hill Book Co., 1967, 1972, and 1976.

JOHNSON, RICHARD A., KAST, FREMONT E., and ROSENZWEIG, JAMES E., *The Theory and Management of Systems.* New York: McGraw-Hill Book Co., 1963.

JUCIUS, MICHAEL J., and SCHLENDER, WILLIAM E. *Elements of Managerial Action.* Homewood, Ill.: Richard D. Irwin, 1960.

KOONTZ, H. and O'DONNELL, C., *Principles of Management*. New York: McGraw-Hill Book Co., 1955, 1959, 1964, 1968, 1972, and 1976.

KOONTZ, H. (ed.), *Toward a Unified Theory of Management*. New York: McGraw-Hill Book Co., 1964.

LAWRENCE, PAUL R., and LORSCH, JAY W., *Organization and Environment*. Homewood, Ill.: Richard D. Irwin, Inc., 1968.

LIKERT, RENSIS, *New Patterns of Management*. New York: McGraw-Hill Book Co., 1961.

LIKERT, RENSIS, *The Human Organization: Its Management and Value*. New York: McGraw-Hill Book Co., 1967.

LITTERER, JOSEPH A., *The Analysis of Organizations*. New York: John Wiley and Sons, 1965.

LUTHANS, FRED, *Introduction to Management: A Contingency Approach*. New York: McGraw-Hill Book Co., 1976.

MARCH, JAMES G., and SIMON, HERBERT A., *Organizations*. New York: John Wiley and Sons, 1958.

MASLOW, A. H., *Motivation and Personality*. New York: Harper and Row, 1954.

MCCLELLAND, DAVID C. and WINTER, DAVID G. *Motivating Economic Achievement*. New York: Free Press, 1969.

MCFARLAND, DALTON E., *Management Principles and Practices*. New York: MacMillan Co., 1958, 1964, 1970, and 1974.

MCGREGOR, DOUGLAS, *The Human Side of Enterprise*. New York: McGraw-Hill Book Co., 1960.

MCMILLAN, CLAUDE, and RICHARD F. GONZALEZ, *Systems Analysis —An Approach to Decision Models*. Homewood, Ill.: Richard D. Irwin, 1966.

MEGGINSON, LEON C., *Personnel: A Behavioral Approach to Administration*. Homewood, Ill.: Richard D. Irwin, 1967.

MILLER, DAVID, and STARR, MARTIN K., *Executive Decisions and Operations Research*. Englewood Cliffs, N.J.: Prentice-Hall, 1966.

MILLER, DAVID, and STARR, MARTIN K. *The Structure of Human Decisions*. Englewood Cliffs, N.J.: Prentice-Hall, 1967.

MINER, JOHN B., *The Human Constraint: The Coming Shortage of Managerial Talent*. Washington, D.C.: Bureau of National Affairs, 1974.

MINTZBERG, HENRY, *The Nature of Managerial Work*. New York: Harper and Row, 1973.

MORRIS, WILLIAM T., *Management Science in Action*. Homewood, Ill.: Richard D. Irwin, 1963.

NEWMAN, WILLIAM H., *Administrative Action: The Techniques of Organization and Management*. Englewood Cliffs, N.J.: Prentice-Hall, 1951 and 1960.

NEWMAN, WILLIAM H., and SUMMER, CHARLES E., JR., *The Process of Management*. Englewood Cliffs, N.J.: Prentice-Hall, 1961.

OPTNER, STANFORD L., *Systems Analysis for Business Management*. Englewood Cliffs, N.J.: Prentice-Hall, 1965.

PFIFFNER, J. M. and SHERWOOD, F. P., *Administrative Organization*. Englewood Cliffs, N.J.: Prentice-Hall, 1960.

PRESTHUS, ROBERT, *The Organizational Society*. New York: Alfred A. Knopf, 1962.

RICHARDS, MAX D., and GREENLAW, PAUL S., *Management Decision Making*. Homewood, Ill.: Richard D. Irwin, 1966, 1970, and 1975.

ROY, ROBERT H., *The Administrative Process*. Baltimore: Johns Hopkins Press, 1958.

SCOTT, WILLIAM G., *Organization Theory: A Behavioral Analysis for Management*. Homewood, Ill.: Richard D. Irwin, 1967.

SELZNICK, PHILIP, *Leadership in Administration*. Evanston, Ill.: Row, Peterson & Co., 1957.

SHARTLE, CARROLL, *Executive Performance and Leadership*. Englewood Cliffs, N.J.: Prentice-Hall, 1956.

SIMON, HERBERT A., *The New Science of Management Decision*. New York: Harper and Row, 1960.

SNOW, C. P., *The Two Cultures: And A Second Look*. Cambridge, England: University Press, 1964.

TERRY, GEORGE, *Principles of Management*. Homewood, Ill.: Richard D. Irwin, 1953, 1956, 1960, 1964, 1968, and 1972.

VON NEUMANN, JOHN and MORGENSTERN, OSKAR. *Theory of Games and Economic Behavior*. Princeton, N.J.: Princeton University Press, 1944.

WIENER, NORBERT, *Cybernetics*. Cambridge, Mass.: MIT Press, 1948.

WIENER, NORBERT, *The Human Use of Human Beings*. Boston:

Houghton Mifflin Co., 1950.

WOODWARD, JOAN, *Industrial Organization: Theory and Practice.* London: Oxford University Press, 1965.

WREN, DANIEL A., and VOICH, DAN, JR., *Principles of Management: Process and Behavior.* New York: The Ronald Press Company, 1968 and 1976.

Author and Name Index

Subject Index

Soviet Foreign Policy
1962–1973

ROBIN EDMONDS

Soviet Foreign Policy
1962–1973

THE PARADOX OF
SUPER POWER

LONDON

OXFORD UNIVERSITY PRESS

NEW YORK   TORONTO

1975

Oxford University Press, Ely House, London W.1

GLASGOW NEW YORK TORONTO MELBOURNE WELLINGTON
CAPE TOWN IBADAN NAIROBI DAR ES SALAAM LUSAKA ADDIS ABABA
DELHI BOMBAY CALCUTTA MADRAS KARACHI LAHORE DACCA
KUALA LUMPUR SINGAPORE HONG KONG TOKYO

ISBN 0 19 215810 4

*Printed in Great Britain by
Hazell Watson & Viney Ltd,
Aylesbury, Bucks*

To the memory of
C. H. K. E.

PREFACE

This book is indebted to a large number of people, both in Britain and abroad: to my colleagues in the Glasgow University Department of Politics and Institute of Soviet and Eastern European Studies, for the help and advice that they offered me during my time as visiting Research Fellow at the University—particularly Professor Alec Nove, Professor William Mackenzie, Professor Allen Potter, Dr. Vladimir Kusin, Dr. Christopher Mason, and Dr. Stephen White; to Lord Zuckerman, Sir Duncan Wilson, Mrs. Enid Balint, and Mr. Malcolm Mackintosh, all of whom read the whole manuscript and will, I hope, find in the book a reflection of their benevolent but unsparing criticisms; to Mr. Raymond Hyatt, for the maps; to Sir Edgar Williams, for reading the proofs; to Mrs. Jean Beverly, for typing the manuscript, with the help of Miss Carole Curtis, Miss Patricia Key, and Miss Charlotte Thompson; and to Sir Ronald and Lady Orr-Ewing, a corner of whose house provided the perfect setting for writing a book.

Long as it is, this list leaves unmentioned the many others whom I have consulted over the past year. Moreover, the book would never have been written if the Foreign and Commonwealth Office had not given me sabbatical leave and the University of Glasgow had not offered me both a Visiting Fellowship and a research grant that enabled me to exchange views on the spot with a wide range of those concerned with this field of international relations in the United States, France, and the Federal Republic of Germany. To all of them I am deeply grateful. Needless to say, the Office, the University, and all those who have helped over the past year are in no way responsible for the views expressed in the book, which are my own.

The dedication is to my Father, who taught me how to write.

Cardross
Port of Menteith
1974

CONTENTS

S.F.P.—I*

SELECTIVE CHRONOLOGY OF
INTERNATIONAL EVENTS

1956	February: October:	XXth CPSU Congress: Khrushchev denounces Stalin Second Arab-Israeli War (the Suez invasion); Hungarian revolt; Polish 'October revolution'
1957	October: November:	First *sputnik*; Sino-Soviet nuclear agreement Mao Tse-tung's speech in Moscow
1958		Year of the Chinese Great Leap Forward
1959	June: September: September– October:	Sino-Soviet nuclear agreement rescinded by Soviet Government Khrushchev's visit to USA Khrushchev's visit to China
1960	May: July:	U-2 incident; abortive summit meeting in Paris Recall of Soviet experts from China
1961	April: June:	Invasion of Cuba: the Bay of Pigs fiasco Meeting of Kennedy and Khrushchev in Vienna; beginning of second Berlin crisis
1962	October:	Cuban missile crisis; Sino-Indian war
1963	July: August:	CPSU Open Letter on Sino-Soviet dispute Partial Nuclear Test Ban Treaty signed in Moscow
1964	August: October:	Tonkin Gulf incident, followed by joint Congressional Resolution on Vietnam Fall of Khrushchev, replaced by collective Soviet leadership; explosion of first Chinese nuclear device
1965	February: September:	Kosygin visits Hanoi; US bombing of North Vietnam begins Soviet Economic Reform; beginning of Chinese Cultural Revolution
1966	January:	Kosygin mediates between India and Pakistan at Tashkent
1967	June: November:	Third Arab-Israeli war Security Council Resolution 242 on Arab-Israeli dispute
1968	January: July: August:	Dubček becomes First Secretary of Czechoslovak Communist Party Nuclear Non-Proliferation Treaty signed; end of Chinese Cultural Revolution Invasion of Czechoslovakia
1969	 March: July: September: October: November:	Year of Soviet-US numerical strategic nuclear parity Sino-Soviet border clash First withdrawal of US troops from Vietnam Meeting of Soviet and Chinese Prime Ministers in Peking Brandt elected Federal German Chancellor Soviet and US SALT delegations meet in Helsinki

	December:	Soviet-German talks begin in Moscow; Berlin talks proposed by Three Allied Powers; first moves towards multilateral European negotiations; CPSU Central Committee convened to discuss economic problems
1970	January	Soviet military intervention in Egypt
	March:	Ratification of Non-Proliferation Treaty by Great Britain, US, and USSR
	August:	Signature of Soviet-German Moscow Treaty; Egyptian-Israeli cease-fire
	September:	Allende elected President of Chile
1971	March-April:	XXIVth CPSU Congress adopts Programme of Peace
	July:	Announcement of US President's acceptance of invitation to visit China
	August:	The dollar declared inconvertible into gold
1971	September:	Quadripartite Agreement on Berlin signed
	October:	Nixon invited to Moscow
	December:	Indo-Pakistan war; Republic of China takes seat in UN
1972	February:	Nixon's visit to China
	May:	Nixon's visit to USSR; signature of first Soviet-US summit agreements; Quadripartite Berlin Agreement brought into force
	July:	Soviet troops withdrawn from Egypt, at Egyptian request
	August:	Last US combat troops withdrawn from Vietnam
	December:	Basic Treaty between the two Germanies signed
1973	January:	Britain, Denmark, and Ireland enter the European Economic Community; Vietnam cease-fire agreement signed in Paris
	April:	CPSU Central Committee approves Brezhnev foreign policy and changes in Politburo
	May:	Brezhnev visits Bonn
	June:	Brezhnev visits US; Agreement on Prevention of Nuclear War signed
	September:	*Coup d'état* in Chile; Geneva Conference on Security and Cooperation opens
	October:	Fourth Arab-Israeli War; Vienna talks on mutual reduction of forces and armaments in Europe open
	December:	World oil prices quadrupled
1974		Year of the Energy Crisis
	February:	Solzhenitsyn exiled
	May:	Indian explosion of a nuclear device
	June–July:	Third Soviet-American summit meeting
	July–August:	Cyprus crisis
	August:	Resignation of President Nixon, succeeded by Vice-President Ford
	October:	Kissinger's visit to Moscow; announcement of forthcoming working meeting between Brezhnev and Ford at Vladivostok

ABBREVIATIONS

ABM	Anti-ballistic missile
ASM	Air-to-surface missile
ASW	Anti-submarine warfare
CCP	Chinese Communist Party
CENTO	Central Treaty Organization
COMECON	Council for Mutual Economic Cooperation
CPSU	Communist Party of the Soviet Union
CSCE	European Conference on Security and Cooperation (the ordering of initials derives from the French translation)
DDR/GDR	East Germany (German Democratic Republic)
EEC	European Economic Community
FBS	Forward based system
FRG	West Germany (Federal Republic of Germany)
GATT	General Agreement on Trade and Tariffs
GNP	Gross National Product
ICBM	Intercontinental ballistic missile
IISS	International Institute for Strategic Studies
IMF	International Monetary Fund
IRBM	Intermediate range ballistic missile
MAD	Mutually assured destruction
MARV	Manoeuvrable re-entry vehicle
MBFR	Mutual and Balanced Force Reductions (the title finally agreed was Mutual Force Reductions and Associated Measures)
MFN	Most favoured nation
MIRV	Multiple independently targetable re-entry vehicle
MRBM	Medium range ballistic missile
MRV	Multiple re-entry vehicle
NATO	North Atlantic Treaty Organization
OECD	Organization for Economic Cooperation and Development

SALT	Strategic Arms Limitation Talks
SAM	Surface-to-air missile
SLBM	Submarine launched ballistic missile
SSBN	Ballistic missile submarine, nuclear
UNCTAD	United Nations Commission on Trade and Development

Note

Billion is used here as meaning a thousand million.

1

INTRODUCTION

In 1962 the Soviet Union and the United States suddenly found themselves on the brink of thermonuclear war. Had this war been fought, such historians as survived the holocaust would have recorded as its immediate cause each side's perception of the other's intentions regarding a Caribbean island whose revolutionary leader had recently professed himself a Marxist-Leninist.* The more perceptive among these historians, mindful of the belief of one of the two principal actors in the drama enacted during this seminal crisis, that the mysterious 'essence of ultimate decision remains impenetrable to the observer—often, indeed to the decider himself . . .',[1] would have added that the real reasons for the conflict lay much deeper, in the relationship between the two countries as it had developed since the end of the Second World War, during which they had been the senior partners in the Grand Alliance. The date on which the cold war was declared and Europe was split in two is debatable: perhaps 2 July 1947, when Molotov broke off negotiations in Paris, announcing that the Soviet Union would not take part in the Marshall Plan for the European Recovery Programme.[2] But there can be no question when the cold war came closest to becoming, literally, a hot war: 22 October 1962, the day on which the presence of Soviet ballistic missiles in Cuba was revealed to the world, and the six days that followed until Khrushchev announced his decision to withdraw them.

    * Lenin would hardly have recognized Fidel Castro as a disciple, although he might well have seen him, in traditional Russian terms, as a left-wing Social Revolutionary. Fidel Castro, who came to power as a radical, reforming *caudillo*, made his famous profession of Marxist–Leninist faith in a television broadcast three years later on 1 December 1961.

A decade later, although the Soviet Union and the United States each remained at the head of opposing alliances, the cold war was over. Again, there is no exact date for its conclusion, but as good as any is 22 June 1973, when the Soviet-American Agreement on the Prevention of Nuclear War[3] was signed in Washington, then being visited by the General-Secretary of the Communist Party of the Soviet Union (CPSU) for the first time since the brief armistice in the cold war marked by Khrushchev's visit in 1959. And again, this transformation of the Soviet-American relationship did not come out of the blue, but took several years to develop. That their relationship has undergone a radical change is beyond dispute. But the crucial question remains, what exactly is it that has changed and why? Is it Soviet as well as American foreign policy that has altered; or is it only American foreign policy, reacting to what Soviet observers of the international scene regard as a change in the 'correlation of forces'* in favour of the Soviet Union?

Defenders of the second view can point to the absence of any change in the doctrine of Soviet foreign policy as it has been formulated ever since 1956. (The one exception—the expansion of the concept of peaceful coexistence—will be examined in a later chapter.) The official History of Soviet Foreign Policy describes the policy's four basic tasks as:

1. To secure, together with the other socialist countries, favourable conditions for the building of socialism and communism;
2. To strengthen the unity and solidarity of the socialist countries, their friendship and brotherhood;
3. To support the national-liberation movement and to effect all-round cooperation with the young, developing countries.
4. Consistently to uphold the principle of peaceful coexistence of states with different social systems, to offer decisive resistance to the aggressive forces of imperialism, and to save mankind from a new world war.[4]

This formulation follows word for word the resolution on foreign policy approved by the XXIIIrd Congress of the CPSU in March 1966, which was repeated in turn by Leonid Brezhnev in his opening speech at the XXIVth Congress five years later.[5] To this formulation must be added two important riders. One is Lenin's statement that 'the deepest roots both of the international and of the external policy of our state are

* The Marxist concept of this correlation is of something inherently unstable, which it is the task of the statesman to turn to his country's advantage, with the aid of the forces of history—an important difference from the traditional Western concept of the balance of power, designed to preserve international stability.

determined by the economic interests ... of the ruling classes of our state':[6] the policy pursued by the Soviet Government abroad is a reflection and an extension of its policy at home. The other rider is the belief, also propounded in the Official History,[7] that the danger of war, including the danger of a Third World War, will continue as long as imperialism exists: peaceful coexistence is therefore a form of the Marxist class struggle. This belief was implicit in an article on strategic arms limitation published in *Pravda* on the eve of Brezhnev's visit to the United States in 1973, which reminded readers of his statement made six months earlier at the celebration of the fiftieth anniversary of the Soviet Union:

The ... class struggle of the two systems ... in the sphere of economics, politics and, it goes without saying, ideology, will be continued ... The world outlook and the aims of socialism are opposed and irreconcilable. But we shall ensure that this inevitable struggle is transferred to a channel which does not threaten wars, dangerous conflicts, and an uncontrolled arms race.[8]

True, there was a change in the conduct of foreign policy in 1964, when the present Soviet leadership took over from Khrushchev. But, at any rate at the outset, the way in which they described the difference between themselves and the man whom they had removed from power was primarily one of style or posture: their own approach they commended as that of prudent managers. As Brezhnev put it in a definition of Soviet foreign policy in a speech delivered to the Central Committee of the CPSU on 29 September 1965: 'we are striving to make our diplomacy active and thrusting, while at the same time showing flexibility and circumspection'.[9] Nevertheless, the doctrinal continuity of Soviet foreign policy from 1956 to 1973 has been remarkable.

The West, and particularly Western Europe, faces a bleak prospect if Soviet apologists are right in contending that for over seventeen years Soviet foreign policy has remained immutable, and that the only change is that the rest of the world, notably the United States, has had to adjust itself to an altered strategic power balance—at the moment, Soviet-American, but ultimately a triangular balance between China, the Soviet Union, and the United States. This view is not supported by the facts. The invasion of Czechoslovakia certainly demonstrated the paramount importance to the Soviet leadership of the first and second of the basic tasks of their foreign policy. But as for the third task (support of national-liberation movements), the Soviet Union gave North Vietnam enough help—and no more than that—both to keep it on its feet and to maintain Soviet influence in Indo-China against the Chinese; in Chile, the Soviet Union made no attempt to repeat its Cuban experience; Soviet commitment to this task is taken with a pinch of salt by Egyptians; and it is ridiculed by the Chinese Communist Party (CCP).[10] Above all, since 1972/3 the Leninist* principle of peaceful coexistence has been given an interpretation that goes far beyond anything ever suggested by Lenin (who described it to the VIIIth CPSU Congress as inconceivable over a long period of time). In short, although Soviet foreign policy may have remained unaltered on paper for nearly twenty years, in fact a gap has developed between its theory and its practice. For a Marxist, there can be no difference between theory and practice. In non-Marxist terms such a difference may be regarded as a conflict that cannot be tolerated indefinitely.

Is there another, tenable explanation of the contrast between the events of October 1962 and those of October 1973? The greatest achievement of the Soviet leadership since the fall of Khrushchev has been the Soviet Union's attainment of parity with the United States. Khrushchev's claim to this parity was proved hollow by the Cuban missile crisis. Under the flexible and circumspect management of his successors, however, the Soviet Union is today universally acknowledged to be a super-power, co-equal with its old adversary in the cold war, the United States. The relationship between the two super-powers is complex and ambivalent; and it has so far eluded attempts to define it in a single word or phrase. The word super-power is not part of the Soviet vocabulary; on the occasions when it is used, it appears in inverted commas; and Brezhnev brushed the term aside at his meeting with United States Senators in June 1973.[11] The reason for this modesty is partly the pejorative significance that the word has acquired in the political vocabulary of the Chinese, who disclaim any intention of aspiring to super-power status themselves. Instead, the Soviet Union is described as one of 'the two nuclear giants' or, in the History of Soviet Foreign Policy, as 'one of the greatest world powers, without whose participation not a single international problem can be solved':[12] a definition which foreshadowed Brezhnev's statement, during his television broadcast in the United States in June 1973, that the economic and military power of the two countries invested them with a special

---

* Although peaceful coexistence is the invariable phrase in contemporary Soviet usage, Lenin himself spoke rather of peaceful cohabitation (*mirnoe sozhitel'stvo*)—see, for example, *Collected Works*, English edition, vol. 40, p. 145; vol. 41, pp. 132–3; and vol. 45, pp. 327–44.

responsibility for the preservation of universal peace and the prevention of war.[13]

It is instructive to compare Brezhnev's statement with the plea for collaboration between the super-powers made nearly thirty years earlier by William Fox, who first coined the term 'super-power' and attempted its first definition (a great power, whose armed force is so mobile that it can be deployed in any strategic theatre, as opposed to a great power whose interests and influence are confined to a single regional theatre[14]). This definition, made before Hiroshima and Nagasaki, holds good today, when the central strategic fact underlying the world power structure is the nuclear armoury of the super-powers. It is this armoury, combined with the expanded Soviet conventional military forces, both at sea and in the air, that has at last entitled the Soviet Union to its global role. Yet in the process of achieving this goal, the Soviet Union, like the United States, has become in many ways the prisoner of its power, which it must control, and of its responsibility, which it must seek to define. Today both the Soviet Union and the United States possess what American theorists have defined as the capacity for mutually assured destruction (MAD). Although Soviet theorists have never officially accepted the MAD concept (that each super-power, even after an all-out first-strike attack on its strategic forces, would still be capable of inflicting an unacceptable degree of retaliatory damage on the other), both the Soviet Union and the United States now have at least one vital interest in common: not to destroy each other—an interest shared by most of the bystanders, who would be destroyed as well if the two super-powers were to come to thermonuclear blows.

At first sight, the determination simply not to destroy may appear a negative concept. But it implies a determination to survive; and the logic of strategic nuclear power is so inexorable, that sooner or later the relationship between two super-powers—however much they may pursue their rivalry in other, less dangerous fields—must become positive. If we examine the history of the past eleven years, we shall find that this is indeed what has come about between the Soviet Union and the United States, culminating in the twenty bilateral agreements signed between them during 1972–3: a paradox which, before the nuclear age, would have been inconceivable for Lenin, which in its first years Stalin could not understand, and which Khrushchev only partly perceived.

By a further paradox, at the end of the 1960s, just as the Soviet leadership finally scaled the peak of super-power status that they had expended so much national effort to reach, they found themselves confronted with a dilemma at home, which was both economic and political. The Soviet economy had reached a point in its development where it could not meet both the demands of the defence sector and the aspirations of the consumer except on one of two alternative conditions: either a root and branch reform of the Soviet system or a massive importation of Western technology, capital, and in the end, management techniques. In accordance with the doctrine of the class struggle, while the former alternative was inconceivable, the latter was acceptable, as the lesser of two ideological evils, provided Western imports did not infect the Soviet Union with the germ of alien political ideas—a proviso that necessitated a sharp tightening of ideological discipline in the Soviet Union in the 1970s. On the other hand, voices of dissent were raised in the Soviet Union, proclaiming the eternal truth that material progress and the liberty of the human spirit are indivisible. Among these voices the most authoritative urged the West not to give the Soviet Union economic help unless intellectual freedom were assured within its boundaries, at the very moment when promises of such help were forthcoming from the Soviet Union's traditional enemies—Germany and Japan—and from its principal adversary in the cold war—the United States, with which Brezhnev was now seeking a permanent relationship. These voices found a response in the West, both among those who believed that the Soviet Union should be helped only in return for political changes within that country, and among those who believed that such help would serve only to enable the Soviet Union to maintain and extend its military might.

This book is an attempt first, to reappraise Soviet foreign policy as it has been conducted in practice between October 1962 and October 1973, and in particular to study the evolution of the special relations now existing between the two super-powers; then, in the light of this evolution, to consider how these relations may develop further, over the next ten years; and in conclusion, to suggest how this development may affect Western Europe. It is hoped that this will throw some light on a third paradox: the gap between the theory and the practice of Soviet foreign policy, and the related question—what is the determining force that motivates the men who formulate and carry out this policy?

A professional diplomat writing history should bear in mind de Tocqueville's observation:

men of letters who have written history without taking part in public affairs . . . are always inclined to find general causes . . . politicians who have concerned themselves with producing events without thinking about them . . . living in the midst of disconnected daily facts, are prone to imagine that everything is attributable to particular incidents, and that the wires that they pull are the same as those that move the world. It is to be presumed that both are equally deceived.[15]

By allowing an equal weight in his scales both to particular incidents and to general causes, a wise historian may, with the advantage of hindsight, be able to penetrate Kennedy's 'mystery of ultimate decision', and to describe not only what really happened but why it happened in the way that it did. Can the tools of modern political science developed over the past quarter of a century help him in his task, particularly in assessing what de Tocqueville called general causes? In answering this question a distinction must be drawn between the study of the past, the present, and the future. In studying the past, provided that all the evidence is available (for example, governmental archives open to the public, private memoirs published), the historian may be able to learn something extra[16] by applying, among other methods of analysis, quantitative and scientific methods to the full range of the facts that he has assembled. Their value is doubtful when applied to the study of the immediate past, where all the evidence cannot yet be obtained, or of the present; and still more so if they are used in an attempt to construct a productive conceptual model of the future of international relations, since these are the product of a complex interplay of variables, which are not susceptible to treatment by the disturbance factor in a mathematical model. Indeed, as an eminent British scientist has observed in a criticism of abstract strategic analysis, these variables are 'of so qualitative a nature that no one could attribute numerical values to them.'[17]

Why is it that so much intellectual effort devoted since the Second World War to this form of analysis has helped us so little to understand the history of our times?[18] (For example, in the strategic field, games theory, though fascinating at first sight, becomes unmanageable when applied to a contest between more than two players; and in the political field, the astringent approach sought by structural functionalism ends by calling to mind Roy Campbell's: 'you use the snaffle and the rein all right, but where's the bloody horse?'). The reason is surely that history describes, and seeks to explain, the conduct of human beings, acting individually as well as in groups; and there is no instrument that can understand human beings better than the human mind.

Thucydides' approach to history was influenced by the medical theory of his day; he was a contemporary of Hippocrates. In my view, the scientific discipline which should most influence the modern historian, especially if he is studying the present and the recent past, is medicine. What the modern physician must do above all, if he is to make an accurate diagnosis and a successful prognosis, is to listen to the patient with a trained ear. The best service that the historian of our times can render is, so far as possible, to allow events to speak for themselves, in the hope that a comparison of what these events teach him with the lessons of the past may enable him to try to identify some of the parameters of the future. Such an approach to history is especially appropriate to a study of Soviet policy, because in the Soviet Union hard evidence is often lacking, and what is said and written, when studied in isolation from what actually happens, may be deceptive. Listening to the events of history is as difficult for the historian as listening to the patient is for the physician; the historian of a state inspired by a dialectical philosophy can best understand it if he observes closely what its rulers do; and if he observes a conflict between their thought and their actions, he must draw his own conclusions as best he can. This book will seek to observe events dispassionately, but as though from the Kremlin—a difficult task, because the Politburo of the CPSU, the supreme decision-making body in the Soviet Union and the hub of the lobbies that make up the Soviet élite, is not given to indiscretion. Moreover, its decisions on foreign policy are not based only on information and advice from the Soviet Ministry of Foreign Affairs. Other important bodies which submit to the Politburo views that are by definition closed to the outside observer, are the foreign departments of the Party's central apparatus and the foreign directorate of the KGB.[19] As if to emphasize the limitations of the Foreign Ministry, only one Soviet Foreign Minister—Vyacheslav Molotov—had been a member of the Politburo until April 1973, when Andrei Gromyko (who had succeeded Molotov as Foreign Minister in 1957)[20] became the first professional diplomat to enter it.

It has been well said that where the Soviet Union is concerned, there are no degrees of knowledge, only degrees of ignorance. Our knowledge of the years 1962–73 is indeed still fragmentary. But there are by now enough substantial fragments of evidence to make possible the work of reconstructing, as a coherent whole, the foreign policy of the Soviet Union during the period of its evolution from great power to super-power.

NOTES

1. J. F. Kennedy, in the foreword to Theodore C. Sorensen, *Decision-Making in the White House*, Columbia University Press, New York, 1963, p. xi.
2. In *Expansion and Coexistence*, Secker and Warburg, London, 1968, pp. 432 ff, Adam Ulam makes a good case for regarding this as the opening of the cold war. (The Soviet Government subsequently obliged Czechoslovakia, not yet a member of the Soviet bloc, to follow suit.) Soviet historians might prefer March 1947, when the Truman Doctrine was announced. Certainly the great divide must be set somewhere in 1947.
3. Text in *The Times*, 23 June 1973.
4. *Istoriya Vneshnei Politiki SSSR*, Moscow, 1971, edited by Ponomarev, Gromyko, and Khvostov, vol. 2, p. 486. The distinction between 'building socialism' and 'building communism' is that only the Soviet Union is regarded by Soviet theorists as having reached the latter stage of development (as was announced by Khrushchev in 1961).
5. L. I. Brezhnev, *Leninskim Kursom*, Moscow, 1972, vol. 3, p. 196. An even more recent, and identical, formulation is given by *Diplomatiya Sotsializma*, Moscow, 1973, p. 17.
6. V. I. Lenin, *Complete Collected Works*, Fifth Russian edition, vol. 36, p. 327, Moscow, 1962. This quotation comes from Lenin's report on Soviet foreign policy of 14 May 1918. (All other quotations from Lenin's *Collected Works* are taken from the English edition.)
7. Op. cit., vol. 2, p. 485.
8. *Pravda*, 5 June 1973.
9. Ibid., 30 September 1965.
10. Soviet treatment of Allende is discussed in chapter 12. For the Egyptian attitude towards the Soviet commitment to their country, see, for example, Sadat's speeches reported in *The Times* of 26 July 1973 and 19 April 1974, and his interview with *Al Ahram* reported by the Associated Press in the *International Herald Tribune*, 30/31 March 1974. For a recent statement of Chinese policy towards the Third World, and of Chinese criticism of Soviet policy towards the latter, see David Bonavia's article 'China Takes a New View of the World', *The Times*, 22 April 1974.
11. *Pravda*, 21 June 1973.
12. The first description is quoted from *Krasnaya Zvezda*, 9 July 1974. The second is from op.cit., vol. 2, p. 480.
13. *The Times*, 25 June 1973.
14. W. T. R. Fox, *The Super-Powers—their responsibility for peace*, Yale Institute of International Studies, 1944, pp. 20–1.
15. Alexis de Tocqueville, quoted on the fly-leaf of Graham Allison, *Essence of Decision: Explaining the Cuban Missile Crisis*, Little, Brown, Boston, 1971.
16. It is as well not to expect too much. Cf. Harold Guetzkow's remark (quoted by Nigel Forward in *The Field of Nations*, Macmillan, London, 1971) that 'if the use of quantitative methods and scientific analysis were to bring about an improvement of five per cent in the performance of nations in their relations with one another, he for one would be well pleased'.
17. Solly Zuckerman, *Scientists at War*, Harper and Row, New York, 1966, p. 25.
18. So far as Soviet studies are concerned, the title of a chapter in a book of American essays on Soviet foreign policy—'Ten Theories in Search of Reality'—is significantly disheartening: see *Process and Power in Soviet Foreign Policy*, edited by Vernon Aspaturian, Little, Brown, Boston, 1971,

ch. III, pp. 290 ff. But an interesting, if controversial, application of quantitative methodology to the past has recently been carried out by R. W. Fogel
and S. L. Engerman in their two-volume reappraisal of American slavery:
Time on the Cross, Little, Brown, Boston, 1974.

19. The KGB, or Committee for State Security, is the lineal descendant of the
Cheka, the 'Extraordinary Commission for combating counter-revolution,
speculation, sabotage and malfeasance in office', formed in 1917 on Lenin's
order. The KGB's activities abroad are not invariably directed against
Western interests: a notable exception to the rule was the important part
played by Fomin at the decisive moment of the Cuban missile crisis (Allison,
op.cit., p. 220).

20. Gromyko was Ambassador in Washington before the end of the Second
World War. The nearest Western parallel to his long experience of diplomacy
is that of David Bruce, although he has never held ministerial office.

PART ONE

Khrushchev's Foreign Policy: The Years of Adventure

2

THE THEORY

There is a long tradition in Soviet politics (of which Stalin himself took full advantage) of stealing the Whigs' clothes while they are bathing. In March 1954, seven months after he had announced the Soviet thermonuclear bomb, Georgyi Malenkov warned the Soviet people that a new world war fought with contemporary weapons would mean the destruction of world civilization.[1] It is clear that had Malenkov remained in power, he would have pursued a foreign policy designed to allow the Soviet consumer, at long last, a fair share of his country's economic resources. Khrushchev ousted Malenkov with a return to the long-standing priority of heavy industry, on which the modernization of the Soviet Armed Forces depended; and he at once increased the defence budget. Yet by 1964 he had become an advocate of minimum nuclear deterrence, at loggerheads with both the 'steel-eaters' and the military, having taken the first steps towards an accommodation with the United States.

In the process Khrushchev transformed Soviet foreign policy. During Stalin's last years, not only as dictator of the Soviet Union but also as the acknowledged[2] leader of the Sino-Soviet bloc, even though he referred to the principle of peaceful coexistence (for example, in the *Economic Problems of Socialism*, the year before his death), the image of the Soviet Union's relationship with the non-communist world which he projected was that of a besieged camp, with Europe as its citadel. Khrushchev staked out a new political claim for the Soviet Union (no longer seen as besieged by the West, but the latter's challenger throughout the world), while at the same time seeking an understanding with the United States, based on the premise that the Soviet Union was already its equal, with the prospect of superiority, economic and military in sight.

This new policy had to be based on an ideological reformulation, which was approved by the XXth Party Congress, held in February 1956. At this historic meeting, in parallel with his destruction of the Stalinist idol, Khrushchev introduced three major changes, two of which are reflected in the third and fourth basic tasks of Soviet foreign policy. First, he laid a fresh emphasis on the principle of peaceful co-existence between communist and non-communist countries. This was no longer seen as a temporary phenomenon. Although imperialism was perceived as being as aggressive as ever, the socialist commonwealth was now held to be strong enough to make war avoidable. This change, coupled with his second innovation—that a country's transition to socialism could be carried out by peaceful means—paved the way for Khrushchev's visit to the United States in 1959 (the 'spirit of Camp David') and the non-summit in Paris the following year. Thirdly, he propounded a new approach to the Third World. For Stalin, a country such as India was governed by bourgeois, who as such deserved no support from the communist states. Khrushchev, on the contrary, saw Soviet championship of countries that had recently won their independence from the colonial powers, or were seeking independence, as part of the Soviet Union's new global role. These countries, and the United Nations—where they were soon to form the majority—were perceived in a new light. The visits which Khrushchev and Bulganin made in 1955 to India, Burma, and Afghanistan marked the beginning both of the Soviet foreign aid programme and of the Soviet Union's special relationship with India, while the arms deal with Egypt in the same year was the first to be concluded as part of a new policy of military aid to non-communist countries. It has been estimated that by the time of Khrushchev's fall, about 3 billion dollars worth of arms had been supplied to thirteen such countries in the preceding decade, amounting to nearly half the total of all Soviet economic aid to underdeveloped countries in the same period.[3]

Although the doctrines of peaceful coexistence and of peaceful transition to socialism, against the background of the 'thaw' within the Soviet Union, made Khrushchev appear at first sight easier for the West to deal with than Stalin had been, his new policy towards the Third World brought his country to the brink of nuclear war. For Khrushchev's foreign policy to succeed, two projections into the future—one economic and the other technological—had to be fulfilled. According to the first, announced by Khrushchev at the XXIInd Party Congress in October 1961, not only would the Soviet Union enter the phase of communism by 1980; in twenty years it would overtake the per capita standard of living of any capitalist country, and specifically reach 80 per cent above the 1960 American standard of living.[4] (By the time Khrushchev died, Japan was already in sight of overhauling his country as the world's second greatest industrial power.) The second projection arose from the successful launching of the first *sputnik* in September 1957. Whether Khrushchev really believed that the initial Soviet success in rocket technology would enable him to deploy intercontinental ballistic missiles (ICBMs) swiftly enough to achieve strategic nuclear parity with the United States is a matter for speculation.

It has been argued[5] that the successive Soviet boasts made between 1957 and 1962 should be regarded as bluff: these ranged from Tass's statement in August 1957 that it was 'now possible to send missiles to any part of the world', through Khrushchev's own claim, made to the Supreme Soviet in January 1960, that the Soviet Union by then had enough nuclear weapons and rockets to wipe out any country or countries that attacked the Soviet Union or other socialist states, to Malinovsky's statement in January 1962, that approximate nuclear parity existed between the Soviet Union and the United States.[6] It is questionable whether the public debate on the 'missile gap'[7] that these boasts provoked in the United States really affected the pace of the six strategic nuclear Research and Development programmes already being carried out by the three US armed services in the fifties. The momentum of these immense, crash programmes was by that time so great that by 1962 the result would probably have been the same in any case: a large number of American ICBMs and *Polaris* submarines confronting a much inferior Soviet strategic nuclear force. Be that as it may, the possibility that the Soviet Union was indeed carrying out an effective crash programme of first generation ICBMs (in reality their design was one of extreme awkwardness) succeeded only in spurring on the Administration to greater efforts with their ICBMs and their *Polaris* submarines. In 1960 the first *Atlas* ballistic missile units became operational and the first *Titan* less than two years later, followed by the first *Minuteman* missiles towards the end of 1962; and the first *Polaris* missiles were deployed at sea in November 1960.[8] These American successes were such that in the autumn of 1962 Khrushchev resorted to a gambler's throw.

Khrushchev's changes in the doctrine of Soviet foreign policy, coupled with his claim for Soviet ballistic missile technology, contributed to the great schism in the communist world, which became public the year before his fall. Although both sides trace the origins of the Sino-Soviet dispute to 1957, the Chinese leaders seem unlikely ever to have forgiven the Russians for their ambivalent attitude to their cause from the 1920s onwards. Given the growing divergence in their economic and social policies, it is hard to see how the Soviet Union and China could have remained allies for long. Nevertheless, Khrushchev's impetuous nature, his conduct of the dispute by public abuse, and his attempt to have Chinese doctrines condemned by the majority of the international communist movement may well have loomed large in the minds of his colleagues when they finally decided to remove him from power.

Lenin's remark that 'abuse in politics often covers up the utter lack of ideological content, the helplessness, and the impotence of the abuser'[9] recalls the great schism between the Western and Eastern branches of Christianity, which offers the closest historical parallel with the Sino-Soviet dispute. Seen in retrospect, the Christian schism does indeed appear to have had remarkably little theological content. Yet the Sino-Soviet dispute has from the outset been a conflict of ideas, not simply of national interests stemming from a secular difference of cultural tradition. The ideological framework of the dispute may be summarized as follows.[10] Having—in Soviet eyes—accepted, at the XXth Congress, the CPSU's line on de-Stalinization, peaceful co-existence, and the peaceful transition to socialism, the Chinese afterwards opposed it. Basing themselves on the Maoist concept of contradictions within socialist society, the Chinese argued that revisionism, not dogmatism,[11] was the greater threat to the unity of the Sino-Soviet bloc, identifying the former first with Yugoslavia, and from 1963 onwards, with the Soviet Union itself. In their view therefore the CPSU had forfeited the position of head of the international communist movement. The CPSU responded by attacking the CCP as the exponent of dogmatism, and claimed that the class struggle had been virtually completed in the Soviet Union, where some relaxation was permissible. The Chinese alleged that bourgeois elements within the Soviet Union were increasing; and they regarded the picture of collectivist affluence painted by the XXIInd Congress as imitating the United States. For the Chinese, the commune experiment, together with the Great Leap Forward, showed them as pioneers, outstripping the Russians, on the path to pure communism; for the Russians, it discredited communism because it required a control over individual liberty even stricter than that which they themselves were in the process of discarding. The Russians maintained that the decisive event in world politics was the establishment of the world communist system, whose combined strength would expand communism by peaceful means. The Chinese replied that the imperialists would yield to force, if pressed, and that the tide was already running in favour of the communist movement.

Historically, the first duty of a Chinese Emperor was always the defence of the Empire. It was open to the Chinese Communists to choose to remain under the Soviet nuclear umbrella, which would have implied both an agreed policy over a wide range and a continuing trust in Soviet willingness to treat a threat to China as a threat to the Soviet Union. But their price for accepting this protection, and therefore opting out of the nuclear club themselves, was a more forward Soviet foreign policy than even the globalist Khrushchev could dare to contemplate. The fundamental differences between the Soviet and Chinese views of the nuclear issue were made plain by Mao Tse-tung in the speech which he delivered at the meeting of communist parties held in Moscow in November 1957 to celebrate the fortieth anniversary of the Russian Revolution. The full text has never been published, but it was on that occasion that Mao described the East wind as prevailing over the West, repeated his assessment of the United States as a paper tiger, and spoke of the millions of socialists who would survive a nuclear holocaust, which would leave imperialism razed to the ground.* At that moment Khrushchev was struggling to restore the unity of the world communist movement, in the wake of the Hungarian and Polish revolts of the preceding year. Perhaps therefore it was by way of compromise that he then granted Mao an agreement on new technology for national defence, which according to the Chinese version included the provision of a sample atomic bomb and the know-how for its manufacture.

The exact extent of defence cooperation between the two countries is uncertain.[12] In any event, according to the Chinese, 'the leadership of the CPSU put forward unreasonable demands designed to put China under Soviet control. These unreasonable demands were rightly and

---

* This historic speech, which must have chilled the blood of Mao's Soviet listeners, was summarized in the course of *Pravda*'s major survey of Chinese foreign policy on 26 August 1973 as a 'declaration that, for the sake of the achievement of a specific political goal, it is possible to sacrifice half mankind'. It is reconstructed, from published extracts, in ch. VIII of John Gittings's *Survey of the Sino-Soviet Dispute 1963–67*, Oxford University Press, 1968. Quotations for these years of the Sino–Soviet dispute are drawn from this comprehensive collection of polemical documents unless otherwise stated.

16

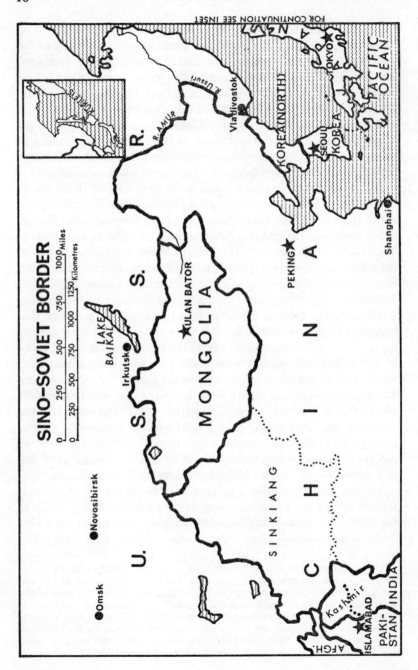

FOR CONTINUATION SEE INSET

firmly rejected by the Chinese Government.' This disagreement on defence policy came to a head in 1958, simultaneously with that on internal policy; the Chinese Great Leap Forward, openly denounced by Khrushchev, reached its peak in the autumn. Thus the Sino-Soviet bloc, whose titanic potential mesmerized the West, really lasted little more than eight years, from the Sino-Soviet Treaty of 1950 until 1958, the year in which the two major communist powers set out on their separate ways. As additional grievances in that year, the Chinese could also point to the inadequacy of Soviet support during the Matsu-Quemoy crisis, and to the solution of the Jordan-Lebanon crisis. They saw the latter as an example of collusion between the governments of the Soviet Union and the United States, since Khrushchev's proposal was for a summit meeting of the Powers, which was to include India, but exclude China. In January 1959, Khrushchev proposed an atom-free zone in the Far East and the whole Pacific Ocean, which Chou En-lai at first endorsed; but later he added the condition that this should apply to all countries bordering the Pacific. In June 1959 (coinciding with Khrushchev's visit to the United States) the Soviet Government revoked the 1957 atomic agreement and, according to the Chinese, refused to supply the sample. In August, the Chinese Defence Minister was dismissed. A year later Soviet specialists of all kinds working in China were recalled.

Within the world communist movement, the first break between the Soviet Union and China took place in June 1960 at the Romanian Communist Party Congress, where Khrushchev (fresh from the failure of the Paris summit meeting) clashed with the Chinese delegate. The watershed was reached at the meeting of eighty-one communist parties held in Moscow in December 1960, where in another confrontation Albania supported China up to the hilt, while the Indonesian, North Korean, and North Vietnamese delegates remained neutral, although inclined towards the Chinese. In October 1961, at the XXIInd Congress of the CPSU, to which Albania had not been invited, Khrushchev attacked Albania—and implicitly China—for opposing the line agreed at the XXth Congress. Chou En-lai protested, walked out, laid a wreath on the tomb of Stalin (whose body was removed a few days later from the Lenin Mausoleum), and then left Moscow. Only two thirds of the parties represented at the Congress endorsed the attack on Albania; all the Asians remained silent. In the following year, when by a remarkable (but genuine) coincidence the Sino-Indian border war broke out two days before the Cuban missile crisis began, the two communist governments for a few days lent each other moral support. But by 5 November

1962 the Chinese had begun to criticize the Soviet withdrawal of missiles from Cuba, and the Russians had reverted to their earlier attitude of neutrality towards the Sino-Indian dispute, urging the need for a negotiated settlement and continuing to provide military aid to India. Following the events in Moscow a year earlier, it was only a short step for the Sino-Soviet dispute to become both direct and overt, as it did in 1963, and for China to claim leadership of the world communist movement.

Seen from Moscow, the last straw came in March 1963, when—as if the ideological and defence aspects of the Sino-Soviet dispute were not enough—a third dimension was added to it by the publication of the Chinese territorial claims against the Soviet Union.[13] The Chinese Government then declared that the nineteenth-century treaties of Aigun, Peking, and Ili were 'unequal', in the sense that the Tsarist Government of those days, as part of its expansionist policy in Asia, had taken advantage of Chinese weakness (as did other European Powers). The treaties were described in a *People's Daily* editorial of 8 March as raising outstanding issues; these should be settled peacefully through negotiations; until the time for such negotiations was ripe, the Chinese Government was prepared to maintain the *status quo*. From subsequent statements by both sides, it appeared that the Chinese wished to renegotiate the entire Sino-Soviet frontier—some 4,000 miles—although they were willing to accept the existing treaties as a basis for negotiations, provided that the Russians accepted their 'inequality'. For their part, the Russians denied the concept of inequality —a Russian Tsar was no worse than a Chinese Emperor—and were prepared only to make certain sections of the frontier more precise (much of it has never been delimited).

Under the terms of the Aigun and Peking treaties, the Russian Empire incorporated within its boundaries all the territory north of the Amur river and east of the Ussuri river, which was previously under Chinese suzerainty and today constitutes the Soviet Maritime Province in the Far East. The Ili treaty ceded part of Chinese Sinkiang (then Turkestan) to Russia, where it now forms part of the Kazakhstan Soviet Republic in Central Asia. But the 1,540,000 square kilometres of Chinese territory annexed by the Tsarist Government were not all that was called in question by the Chinese Government a century later. The Sino-Soviet Treaty of 1950 (also perhaps unequal, but in a different sense) had confirmed the independence of Outer Mongolia. Four years later Mao Tse-tung re-opened this question with Khrushchev. That he had done so was revealed by Mao in July 1964, when he was reported by the Japanese press as having taken the opportunity of the visit of a Japanese Socialist Party delegation to back the Japanese claim for the return of the Kurile Islands, and even to criticize other Soviet post-war territorial acquisitions from Romania, Poland, and Finland.

No Soviet Government could fail to take seriously the claims of March 1963 (let alone the rest). The Soviet Union is the biggest land-owner in Asia; and east of the Urals it is inhabited by some 60 million people, most of whom are not Slavs. The Soviet press gave publicity to the Chinese territorial claims, including the question of the status of Mongolia. A year later *Pravda* published a mammoth report by Mikhail Suslov to a plenary meeting of the CPSU Central Committee on 'The Struggle of the Communist Party of the Soviet Union for the Unity of the International Communist Movement'. Dated 14 February 1964, its publication was delayed for nearly two months while the Romanian Communist Party attempted mediation (one of the first signs of Romania's independent foreign policy). The report was the bitterest and most comprehensive attack yet made by the Russians against the Chinese, whose deviation was described as *petit bourgeois*, nationalistic, and neo-Trotskyite, hard on the heels of a personal attack in the Chinese press on Khrushchev as the arch-revisionist. It was rumoured in Moscow that Suslov's report was not his own work; that whole passages were written by a member of Khrushchev's personal staff; and that Suslov agreed to accept authorship on condition that the report would not be published.[14] If true, this would explain why he was credited in October 1964, with organizing the removal of Khrushchev, who by that time had lost his colleagues' confidence in his conduct of Soviet policy both at home and abroad.

NOTES

1. *Pravda*, 13 March 1954. For an analysis of the differences between Malenkov and Khrushchev at that time, see J. M. Mackintosh, *Strategy and Tactics of Soviet Foreign Policy*, Oxford University Press, London, 1962, pp. 88 ff.
2. Marshal Tito alone dissenting, from 1948 onwards.
3. Thomas W. Wolfe, *Soviet Power and Europe, 1945–70*, Johns Hopkins Press, Baltimore, 1970, p. 130.
4. Quoted in *Problems of Communism*, vol. XI, no. 1 (Jan.–Feb. 1962), p. 40.
5. A. L. Horelick and M. Rush, *Strategic Power and Soviet Foreign Policy*, University of Chicago Press, 1966, pp. 36–120.
6. Ibid., pp. 42, 58, and 88 respectively. Khrushchev also allegedly remarked

that he had been obliged to hold down the megatonnage of one of the Soviet nuclear test explosions in the Arctic because it might have 'broken all the windows of Moscow': see Solly Zuckerman, op. cit., pp. 59–60.

7. In fact it was a 'space gap', rather than a 'missile gap', and even this was more apparent than real: see Herbert York, *Race to Oblivion*, Simon and Schuster, New York, 1970, pp. 109–12, and 144–6, and—for American R and D in the fifties—pp. 83 ff.

8. Ibid., p. 127 for Soviet ICBM design, and pp. 94–101 for the dates of deployment of American ICBMs.

9. This remark, taken from Lenin's article 'The Political Significance of Abuse' was quoted in a Chinese statement in the *People's Daily*, 13 September 1963: see William E. Griffith, *The Sino-Soviet Rift*, Allen and Unwin, London, 1964, p. 423.

10. See Zbigniew Brzezinski, *The Soviet Bloc*, Harvard University Press, Cambridge, Mass., 1967, pp. 399 ff.

11. In Western terms these may roughly be regarded as schools of Marxist thought representing liberal and conservative communism.

12. At the very least, the Soviet Government must have supplied the Chinese Government with the technology required to construct a plant for enriching uranium. See Gittings, op. cit., pp. 102–5, and Harry Gelber, 'Nuclear Weapons and Chinese Policy', *Adelphi Papers* no. 99, IISS, 1973, p. 13.

13. Gittings, op. cit., pp. 158–61 ff., contains a concise summary.

14. Michel Tatu, *Power in the Kremlin*, Collins, London, 1965, p. 367. Suslov's report, like the 'Open letter' of 1963 (see chapter 3), covered seven pages of *Pravda*.

3

THE ADVENTURES

During his years of secret ideological combat with the Chinese, Khrushchev stood in urgent need of a diplomatic victory over the West to prove his point. He tried in Europe, over Berlin; in Africa, over Egypt and the Congo; and finally on the Americans' own doorstep, in the Caribbean. The Berlin crisis lasted off and on for nearly four years from November 1958, when Khrushchev suddenly declared that the Soviet Government no longer recognized its obligations under the Potsdam Agreement, in particular those affecting Berlin. It had only one consequence of far-reaching importance: the erection of the Berlin Wall in August 1961. The Egyptian arms deal, together with the subsequent financing of the Aswan Dam, was a success. But in the Congo, after it became independent in 1960, the Soviet Union backed two successive losers—Lumumba and Gizenga. Khrushchev may have calculated that even though he lost in the Congo itself, this was compensated for by the influence that the Soviet Union began to win in Africa as a whole (hence the university in Moscow named after Lumumba). But the Congo affair led him into a quarrel with the United Nations Secretary-General, Hammarskjöld, whom Khrushchev accused of arbitrary and lawless behaviour. On 23 September 1960 Khrushchev addressed personally the special emergency General Assembly, calling on Hammarskjöld to resign and proposing instead his *troika* arrangement, whereby the office of Secretary-General was to be converted into a commission of three men, one representing the Western bloc, one the Soviet bloc, and one the neutrals. This proposal made little headway. Having declared in the following February that it would no longer recognize Hammarskjöld as an official of the United Nations, the Soviet Government was spared further embarrassment by his death in an air crash seven months later. Khrushchev's performance at the General Assembly was memorable for his shoe-banging during Harold Macmillan's speech: an incident which did not put the British Prime Minister off his stride but was no doubt chalked up by Khrushchev's opponents at home as *nekul'turnyi* behaviour, unbecoming to a Soviet statesman.*

The Cuban missile crisis

No Soviet Government has pursued the third of the four basic tasks of foreign policy listed in the first chapter to such extremes as did Khrushchev over Cuba. There is by now little doubt what happened during the fourteen days of this crisis, which lasted from 14 to 28 October 1962. Nor is there any lack of evidence about the American handling of the crisis or about American motives. But the precise nature of Soviet motives both before and during the crisis are a matter for speculation and are likely to remain so until much more Soviet and Cuban evidence is made public.

Of these fourteen days, three really matter. On 14 October, incontrovertible photographic proof of the presence of Soviet nuclear missiles in Cuba was submitted to the US President. On 22 October, after eight days of agonized debate with his closest advisers, Kennedy announced the presence of the missiles in an address to the American nation, and he imposed a naval quarantine (a word that he had personally substituted for the original 'blockade') of all offensive military equipment under shipment to Cuba. Kennedy described the quarantine as an initial step and declared that any nuclear missile launched from Cuba against any nation in the Western hemisphere would be regarded as an attack by the Soviet Union on the United States, requiring a full retaliatory response upon the Soviet Union. Finally, on 28 October, after an exchange of ten personal messages between Kennedy and Khrushchev (in two of which—those of 26 and 27 October—Khrushchev suggested the outlines of a compromise), Khrushchev announced publicly that a new order had been issued 'to dismantle the weapons, which you describe as offensive, and to crate and return them to the Soviet Union', and expressed his respect and trust for Kennedy's statement, in a message sent on the previous day, that 'no attack would

* According to a well-placed eye-witness, Khrushchev had both his shoes on at the time. *Nekul'turnyi*, literally 'uncultured', is the Soviet word for 'uncouth', 'boorish', 'ill-mannered'.

be made on Cuba and that no invasion would take place—not only on the part of the United States, but also on the part of the other countries of the Western hemisphere'.

That Khrushchev backed down in the face of American determination is not surprising. What is uncertain is why he decided to instal nuclear missiles in Cuba at all. At first the Soviet attitude towards the Cuban Revolution had been cautious. But from 17 April 1961 onwards —when the CIA-sponsored landing of Cuban exiles at the Bay of Pigs was repulsed—events moved swiftly. In June a Soviet-Cuban communiqué acknowledged Cuba's free choice of 'the road of socialist development'; in July Castro announced the formation of a new political party, whose creed was unmistakably proclaimed when five months later he declared 'I am a Marxist-Leninist, and I shall be a Marxist-Leninist until the last day of my life';[1] and thereafter the Soviet Government, whatever its earlier doubts about the orthodoxy of Cuban communism, had no choice but to admit Cuba to the socialist bloc, a decision which was made formally apparent at the May Day celebrations in Moscow. (One Albania was enough.) An exposed member of the socialist bloc, even though not a member of the Warsaw Pact, was bound to look to Moscow to ensure its physical survival. Moscow could not therefore afford to ignore any danger, however remote, to Cuba at a moment when the lunatic fringe in the United States was clamouring for a second attack on Cuba of a different kind from the Bay of Pigs fiasco. Yet it is a fact of history that Kennedy had no intention whatever of repeating the mistake of 1961; and Khrushchev himself in his 'Friday Letter' to Kennedy of 26 October 1962* recorded that he had regarded with respect the explanation for the Bay of Pigs affair which Kennedy had offered him at their meeting in Vienna shortly afterwards (namely, that the invasion had been a mistake). Yet the same letter stated emphatically that it was only the constant threat of armed aggression which hung over Cuba that prompted the despatch of Soviet nuclear missiles to the island. Did Khrushchev believe in this threat? We cannot altogether exclude the possibility that the Soviet

---

* The full text in translation of this famous letter, together with the other nine exchanged during the Cuban missile crisis, was at last published in November 1973, in the *State Department Bulletin*, vol. 69, no. 1795, pp. 643–5. The style leaves no possible doubt of its authorship. It differs in significant respects from previous attempts to reconstruct it, e.g. Allison, op. cit., pp. 221–3. Allison's book, although published before the full text of all the letters was available, remains the most complete exposition of the facts of the crisis as known from American sources; and unless otherwise stated, facts mentioned in the present section of this chapter are derived from it.

Government was misinformed.[2] Today, thanks to the hot line and to the expertise in Soviet-American relations built up over the past decade both in the Soviet Ministry of Foreign Affairs and the Soviet Institute for the USA (not to mention the Kremlin), such a misreading of American presidential intentions would scarcely be possible. In 1962 perhaps it was—just. But even if it was, it remains as obvious today as it must have been then that if the Soviet aim was only to deter an American attack on Cuba, it could have been achieved simply by stationing on the island 20,000 Soviet troops, equipped not with nuclear but with conventional weapons: a close symmetry with the Western presence in Berlin.[3]

The risks that Khrushchev ran were so high in 1962 that the only explanation which does justice to his undoubted intelligence, and also squares with Castro's own evidence, is that he decided that the risks were worth running because the prize was far greater than the security of Cuba, important though this had become to Soviet national interests. This prize was nothing less than to establish a strategic balance with the United States, which would make possible an accommodation between the Soviet Union and the United States across the board, leading not only to a settlement of the Berlin problem but also to the prevention of either West Germany or China from acquiring nuclear weapons—a diplomatic triumph of such brilliance that no one in the Soviet Union would ever have dared to challenge Khrushchev's personal leadership again.[4] The other possible explanations are: first, bad professional advice from the Soviet military; second, the possibility that Khrushchev's assessment of Kennedy's character, formed at the time of the Bay of Pigs and at their meeting in Vienna the previous year, was wrong; third, a false deduction by Khrushchev from the Suez crisis six years earlier that atomic blackmail always paid; and fourth, that by the time Kennedy issued his first, unmistakable warning, in early September, Khrushchev decided that it was too late to put the Cuban missile operation into reverse, and that he might as well be hung for a sheep as for a lamb.

For the first of these four explanations there is no evidence: if anything, it points the other way, in that Marshal K. S. Moskalenko, a Deputy Defence Minister, was relieved of his command of the Strategic Missile Forces in April 1962, about the time when contingency planning of the Cuban operation was presumably in its initial stage.[5] The reason for Moskalenko's removal is unknown, but it does not require much imagination to guess the likely reaction of the commander of this Soviet force when asked to commit part of it to a strategic theatre where, without almost inconceivable luck, it risked either destruction or capture by the American forces only ninety miles away. As for the second explanation, Khrushchev may well have hoped to frighten Kennedy, whom he perhaps regarded as a brash young man, and to establish a personal ascendancy over him at Vienna. Yet the detailed accounts of this difficult meeting given by three American eye-witnesses record only plain speaking, with no ground given on either side.[6] One records[7] that the President's greatest concern before his meeting with Khrushchev was that it might create another spirit of Camp David; and Kennedy's parting words to Khrushchev were not those of a broken man—'it's going to be a cold winter'[8] (he was referring to Khrushchev's ultimatum about West Berlin). What did happen,[9] was that Kennedy's private briefings of the press were 'so grim, while Khrushchev in public appeared so cheerful, that a legend soon arose that Vienna had been a traumatic, shattering experience, that Khrushchev had bullied and browbeaten the President, and that Kennedy was depressed and disheartened'. But this was a legend, and although Khrushchev may have helped to create it, it was not something in which he himself had any reason to believe. Finally, Khrushchev could hardly have convinced himself that it was his own atom-rattling, rather than the United States Government's sustained pressure, that obliged the British and French Governments to halt their Suez operation in November 1956, or that he lacked the authority to take voluntarily in September 1962 a decision that he was compelled to take six weeks later. This is surely a case of the simplest explanation being the best: Khrushchev was a man who played for the highest possible stakes; and on this occasion he miscalculated the odds.

For Khrushchev's Cuban plan to succeed, the United States had to be confronted, without warning, by the presence of a Soviet nuclear force in Cuba—already operational and manned by some 20,000 Soviet troops, in sites protected by surface-to-air missiles—consisting of twenty-four medium range and twelve intermediate range ballistic missile launchers, together with some forty Ilyushin-28 jet bombers capable of carrying nuclear weapons. The range of the former launchers was 1,000 and that of the latter 2,000 nautical miles. The exact number of IRBM launchers planned seems uncertain; none arrived, although their sites were constructed. Certainly, had the plan succeeded, it would have given the Soviet Union extra strategic deterrence on the cheap, by comparison with the cost of bringing Soviet intercontinental and

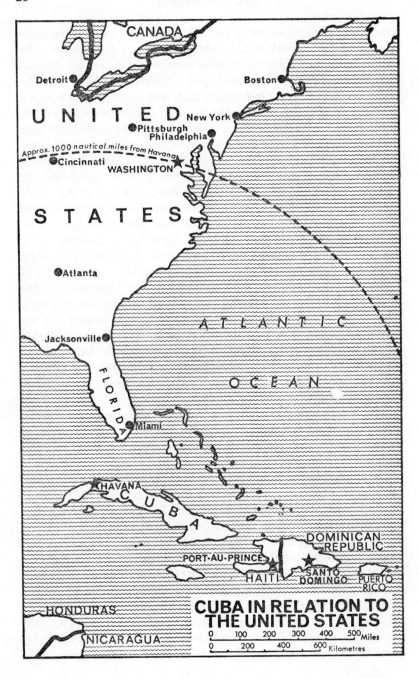

CUBA IN RELATION TO
THE UNITED STATES

submarine-launched ballistic missiles up to the American level; and the number of minutes' warning of oncoming missiles received by the Americans would have been greatly reduced. But even so, this would still not have given the Soviet Union anything resembling superiority. At the time of the crisis not only did the United States have about 144 missiles launched from *Polaris* submarines, as well as 294 ICBMs,[10] but the Caribbean was an area in which the United States possessed complete superiority in conventional weapons—at sea, in the air, and on land (during the crisis, a force of some 200,000 men was assembled in Florida). It can only be assumed that Khrushchev relied on everything going his way: that Cuba would be covered by ten-tenths cloud during the critical phase, that if the missiles were discovered, Kennedy (in the heat of a Congressional election) would dither, and that once he had decided on a course of action, it would be opposed by the United States' allies both in the Organization of American States and in NATO. Not one of these conditions was fulfilled—quite the reverse in each case. Granted what must have been known in Moscow about the performance of U-2 reconnaissance aircraft, from the one shot down over the Soviet Union in 1960, it is hard to see how the arrival of the missiles could have been expected to escape the notice of these aircraft, which overflew the island regularly, once American suspicions had been aroused. Moreover, the risks of the Soviet operation were increased still further by the number of mistakes made in its execution—for example, no attempt was made to camouflage the missile sites.[11]

Nor was there any lack of formal warning from the American side. On 4 September the White House issued a statement that 'the gravest issues would arise' if offensive ground-to-ground missiles were installed in Cuba'. On 12 September, four days after the first ship carrying Soviet missiles had docked in Cuba, *Pravda* published a governmental statement denying the need for the Soviet Union to 'set up in any other country—Cuba, for instance—the weapons it has for repelling aggression, for a retaliatory blow' and asserting that the power of Soviet nuclear weapons and missiles was such that there was no need to find sites for them beyond the boundaries of the Soviet Union. On the following day Kennedy himself repeated the warning of 4 September. Yet, according to all American sources, Khrushchev proceeded to give Kennedy the lie direct about the presence of the missiles in Cuba: speaking himself to the US Ambassador on 16 October—the day on which the photographic evidence of their presence was first submitted to the President—and via Gromyko to the President two days later. Whatever was said or left unsaid on these two occasions, as late as 25 October, *Izvestiya* observed that it was unnecessary to recall that both the Soviet Union and Cuba had recently emphasized that no offensive weapons and no long-range nuclear missiles were deployed on the island; and the next day two *Pravda* correspondents in Massachusetts described the allegation about the sudden appearance of Soviet nuclear long-range rockets in Cuba as a fantasy that did not inspire confidence among well-informed Americans.

From a crisis which, according to all the rules, should have ruined him, Khrushchev extricated himself with skill, by portraying himself as the world's peacemaker. In this he was helped by Kennedy, whose commitment not to invade Cuba cost him nothing, although it was sound as a means of saving Khrushchev's face. But it was paper-thin for the Chinese, who later accused the Soviet leadership of the double error of 'adventurism' and 'capitulationism' and enquired whether what had been done in the name of defending the Cuban Revolution was not in reality political gambling.[12] How do Soviet writers see their country's part in the crisis? Although there is nothing on the Soviet side of the Cuban equation remotely resembling Western analyses[13] in depth of the factors that made up its American side, what Soviet evidence there is should not be ignored. On one point all Soviet sources are unanimous: it was 'a damned nice thing'.[14] Making no precise mention of the missiles, which are referred to only as 'a series of new measures intended to strengthen Cuba's capacity for defence', the History of Soviet Foreign Policy describes the crisis as 'the most acute, in all the post-war years, which put mankind face to face with the threat of world-wide thermo-nuclear catastrophe'. There can be no quarrel with this verdict, which reflects the thought that (as the personal messages to Kennedy make clear) was in the forefront of Khrushchev's mind during the latter days of the crisis, which must have been as hard to manage in Moscow as it was in Washington. Western historians have tended to forget that during this crisis, Khrushchev had to contend not only with Kennedy's messages but also with Castro's. According to Khrushchev's subsequent report to the Supreme Soviet,[15] it was on the morning of 27 October that the Soviet Government became convinced, among other things, by telegrams from Havana 'displaying extreme alarm, which was well founded', that Cuba would be invaded within two or three days.*

The nearest approach to a Soviet explanation of why Khrushchev led with his chin consists of two articles published in 1971,[16] by Anatolyi

---

* This assessment was, as we know from American sources, correct.

Gromyko, son of the Soviet Foreign Minister, on the Caribbean crisis ('or, as they still sometimes call it in the West, especially in the USA, the "Cuban Missile Crisis" '). The articles draw mostly on American sources, but the first is notable for a lengthy account of the author's father's interview with Kennedy on 18 October, which in general counters the accusation that the Soviet Foreign Minister misled the President and in particular criticizes Robert Kennedy's account[17] of the interview as tendentious. The titles of the articles are themselves instructive: the first is 'The Instigation of the Caribbean Crisis by the Government of the USA' and the second is 'The Diplomatic Efforts of the USSR to Solve the Crisis'.

It is central to the argument of these articles that in 1962 it was the aim of the US Government's Cuban policy to prepare secretly a fresh attack against the island. The U-2 flights (which more than any other single factor wrecked Khrushchev's plan) are therefore portrayed as offensive, not defensive, in intention. But the accuracy of the deductions drawn in Washington from the critical U-2 flight of 14 October is in no way disputed: 'medium-range rockets' were indeed delivered to Cuba, for defensive purposes. American sources are quoted as proving that the presence of Soviet missiles in Cuba did not alter the strategic balance of power between the USSR and the USA, which the writer describes as based primarily on intercontinental strategic rockets. As Robert McNamara, then Defence Secretary, remarked during the crisis, 'it makes no great difference whether you are killed by a missile from the Soviet Union or from Cuba'. The conclusion is drawn that the Administration was governed more by political than by military considerations.

In his interview with the President on 18 October the Soviet Foreign Minister is said to have informed Kennedy unequivocally that since the governments of the USSR and Cuba feared a military attack on Cuba, the Soviet Union could not remain inactive, but that Soviet help to Cuba 'contributed only to its defensive capacity and to the strengthening of its economy'; Soviet specialists' training of Cubans in the handling of weapons intended for the defence of their country was a threat to no one. It is granted that the President read out to Gromyko, at the end of their talk, the text of his declaration of 4 September; but since Kennedy did not once raise directly the question of the presence in Cuba of Soviet missiles, he could not be given an answer. The tables are then turned, by accusing the President of deluding the Soviet side about his intentions, and this leads to the conclusion that it is enough to ask

why the diplomatic representatives of the USSR were obliged to inform
the United States Government in advance of these or other defensive
measures, taken for the protection of a friendly state, while the USA
never supplied the Soviet Union with information about the supply of
arms to its own allies. The contention that if only Kennedy had put a
straight question about the missiles to Gromyko, he would have got a
straight answer, is not as odd as it sounds: the interpretation of 'interesting silences'* forms an integral part of Soviet diplomatic style.

   The second theme that runs through both these articles is that if only
the President had sought an 'elucidation of the situation' through
diplomatic channels before embarking on a course as dangerous as a
naval blockade—let alone the attack on Cuba recommended by the
hawks among his advisers—the crisis would never have arisen. The only
credit given to Kennedy is that he stood his ground against right-wing
pressure. It is the Soviet Government that, according to the second
article, played the decisive part in ensuring that events were brought
under control. Khrushchev is nowhere mentioned by name, but his
letter of 26 October is credited with suggesting the compromise formula
which settled the crisis—correctly, although the recently published
text makes it clear that the letter did not propose the compromise in
precise terms, which were spelled out more clearly in Khrushchev's
'Saturday' letter of 27 October, this time linked with the suggested deal
over American bases in Turkey.† Robert Kennedy is also correctly
accused of omitting from his account the Soviet warning which accompanied this suggestion, namely that if the naval quarantine was
intended as the first step towards war, then the Soviet Union would
have no alternative but to accept the challenge.[18] This posture is twice
described in the article as one of firmness coupled with flexibility, a
phrase also used in the History of Soviet Foreign Policy. But the most
important message that these two articles were intended to convey was
this: in 1962 there would have been no crisis at all if at an early enough
stage the US Government had been willing to treat the Soviet Government as its equal and to settle the problem bilaterally at the highest
level. What they could not say was that in 1962 the Soviet Union was
still far from achieving parity with the United States.

   * Jane Austen, Emma, ch. XV, in which Mr. Elton says to Miss Woodhouse:
'Allow me to interpret this interesting silence. It confesses that you have long
understood me.'
   † The second letter, though it caused confusion and dismay in Washington,
did not, in my view, formally contradict the first, nor is there any marked
difference in tone between the two.

The temporary détente

Khrushchev survived this error of Himalayan proportions for two years. The remainder of his time in office was a period of relative *détente* between the Soviet Union and the West. Khrushchev allowed the Berlin crisis to fade away. In June 1963, in a major speech addressed to the American University, Kennedy called the cold war in question; the Soviet press published the text in full. Within a year following the crisis, the hot line was set up between Moscow and Washington, designed to eliminate the time factor in crisis management that had complicated the messages exchanged in October 1962; Great Britain, the Soviet Union, and the United States signed the partial Nuclear Test Ban Treaty in Moscow; at the United Nations it was agreed not to put into outer space 'any objects carrying nuclear weapons or any other kinds of weapons of mass destruction'. (This was to be embodied in treaty form in January 1967.) Other signs of the times were the dropping of the *troika* idea; the cessation of Soviet jamming of Western broadcasts; and the Soviet-American pledge to reduce the production of fissionable material for nuclear weapons. Why did Khrushchev not go further along the road towards a Nuclear Non-Proliferation Treaty, the conclusion of which would surely have been as much a national interest for the Soviet Union then as it was five years later? Perhaps he was held back by internal opposition to *détente*; or by Chinese criticism; or both.[19] The eruption of the territorial aspects of the Sino-Soviet dispute in March 1963 was bad enough, but the Nuclear Test Ban Treaty coincided with the final parting of the ways between the Soviet Union and China in July of that year. The three-power negotiations in Moscow before the signing of this document, rightly regarded at the time as a landmark in post-war history, opened simultaneously with an eleventh-hour attempt by the Russians and the Chinese to settle their differences through bilateral talks, also held in Moscow. The Soviet Central Committee's 'Open letter to Party organizations and all communists of the Soviet Union' published in *Pravda* on 14 July—the day before the Test Ban talks opened—provided the Soviet public with their first full account of their country's quarrel with China. Nearly 20,000 words in length, it included the vivid phrase: 'the nuclear bomb does not adhere to the class principle—it destroys everybody who falls within range of its devastating force'.[20] The Sino-Soviet talks were adjourned *sine die* on 20 July, just before the Test Ban Treaty was signed.

Meanwhile, having failed to attain parity with the United States on the cheap, Khrushchev fell back on the Malenkov concept of minimum nuclear deterrence. True, he had steadily increased the deployment, mostly in the western USSR, of a force of medium and intermediate range ballistic missile launchers targeted on Western Europe, which by 1964 levelled off at around 700. These served the purpose of a deterrent to Western European countries, but not the United States. Intercontinentally, the Soviet Union remained greatly inferior to the United States: in 1964, an estimated 200 Soviet ICBMs against 834 American, and 120 Soviet submarine-launched ballistic missiles against 416 American equivalents.[21] There is also abundant evidence[22] that by October 1964 Khrushchev intended to increase the production of consumer goods by cutting the defence budget, mainly at the expense of conventional ground forces; the Ground Forces Command was suspended as a separate entity shortly before his fall.[23]

The fall of Khrushchev

Things did not go well for Khrushchev at home after the Cuban crisis. True, in November 1962 he secured the Central Committee's approval of a reform of the Party apparatus, which was then divided into agricultural and industrial specialists. But in 1963 the harvest was poor and the rate of growth of Soviet national income was down. Khrushchev's de-Stalinization policy ran into the sand (but not before Alexander Solzhenitsyn's *A Day in the Life of Ivan Denisovich* was published, in November 1962). Perhaps the last straw for his colleagues was the knowledge that he was contemplating a sweeping reform of the agricultural system, which would have been submitted to the Central Committee in November 1964. Khrushchev's handling of the Party could have been sufficient reason in itself for his removal,[24] but the evidence points to a combination of factors. Certainly one of them was that Khrushchev was contemplating a fresh European initiative, this time directly with the new Federal German Chancellor (Erhard, who had succeeded Adenauer in October 1963), at a moment when the ink was scarcely dry on the signature of a new treaty of friendship concluded between the Soviet Union and the German Democratic Republic on 12 June 1964. The terms of this treaty cannot have satisfied Ulbricht —in particular, it explicitly left unaffected rights conferred on the Four Powers by their agreements on Germany, including the Potsdam Agreement—and it coincided with a series of signs that something was in the wind between Moscow and Bonn. These culminated in the visit of a party of three Soviet journalists to the Federal German Republic in July and August. This visit looked innocent enough. But the fact that the Volga Germans[25] were rehabilitated in August can hardly have been a coincidence; and it seems virtually certain that the senior member of the trio, Alexei Adzubei, Khrushchev's son-in-law (whom he had made editor of *Izvestiya*), was sent by Khrushchev to pave the way for a visit that he himself would pay to Bonn, probably in December. Had the visit taken place, it would have been historic: the first time, nearly twenty years after the German surrender, that the ruler of the Soviet Union had visited the Federal Republic. That Khrushchev should have entrusted his son-in-law with such an important mission was resented; it seems likely that he laid himself open to the suspicion that he was planning some deal with the West Germans over the heads of the East Germans (now no longer living in a slum, but on the way to performing their own economic miracle) and of the Poles; and two of his own colleagues, Brezhnev and Suslov, made speeches on the eve of Khrushchev's fall reassuring the East Germans, on the occasion of the fifteenth anniversary of the German Democratic Republic in early October.

As has been suggested earlier, the Soviet Politburo may well have felt that however intractable the Chinese might be, a change of Soviet leadership might increase the chances of at least a marginal improvement. Relations between the two communist parties had reached their nadir. Khrushchev was committed to holding a preparatory meeting in Moscow in December of the twenty-six members of the 1960 conference drafting committee; but it is unlikely that they would have given the CPSU unqualified support against the Chinese Communist Party. In their letter to the CPSU of 28 July 1964, the Chinese warned that 'the day of your so-called meeting will be the day you step into the grave'. By a superb coincidence, the Chinese exploded their first nuclear device on the day that Khrushchev fell—14 October.

NOTES

1. The profession of faith mentioned in the second sentence of this book; the full text of Castro's speech was carried in *Hoy* (Havana), 2 December 1961. For the evolution of the Soviet-Cuban relationship during this period, see Stephen Clissold, *Soviet Relations with Latin America 1918–68*, Oxford University Press, London, 1970, pp. 47–50.
2. For example, some publicity had been given to a large-scale amphibious

exercise which was to take place off the south-east coast of Puerto Rico, with the object of liberating a mythical republic from a dictator named Ortsac: see Allison, op. cit., p. 47. But Allison strains the imagination when he suggests that the importance of the Cuban issue in American domestic politics could have escaped the attention of any observer, Soviet or otherwise, in 1962.

3. See ibid., p. 49, for a fuller discussion of this proposition.
4. Khrushchev's complicated domestic position at this time is described in Tatu, op. cit., Pt. Three, 'The Cuban Fiasco'. For Castro's evidence—that the purpose of the Soviet missiles in Cuba was 'strengthening the socialist camp on the world scale' and 'we considered that we could not decline'—see *Le Monde*, 22 March 1963 (subsequently confirmed in a speech carried by *Pravda*). The idea that at this late hour China could have been prevented from joining the strategic nuclear club may seem far-fetched today, but it may not have been a pipe-dream for Khrushchev early in 1962: for an exposition of this view, see Ulam, op. cit., pp. 661 ff.
5. He was replaced as Commander-in-Chief of the Strategic Missile Forces by Biryuzov, a Ukrainian who may perhaps have been a political client of Khrushchev; see Tatu, op. cit., pp. 236–7.
6. P. Salinger, *With Kennedy*, Cape, London, 1967, ch. XI; A. M. Schlesinger, *A Thousand Days*, Deutsch, London, 1966, pp. 324–40; T. C. Sorensen, *Kennedy*, Hodder and Stoughton, London, 1965, pp. 543–600.
7. Salinger, op. cit., p. 176.
8. Ibid., p. 182.
9. Sorensen, op. cit., p. 550. There is nothing in the account given by A. A. Gromyko in *1036 dniei prezidenta Kennedi*, Moscow, 1968, to support this legend either.
10. *The Military Balance 1969–70*, IISS, London, p. 55. It is, however, conceivable that Soviet intelligence was less well informed about the relative strategic nuclear power of the two countries than was American intelligence, which had the benefit not only of U-2 but also of satellite reconnaissance—not to mention Penkovsky.
11. Op. cit., pp. 106 ff. In fairness to the Russians, the same book also points out some remarkable American mistakes, for example, the fact that no U-2 flight was directed over western Cuba between 5 September and 4 October: see p. 120.
12. Statement by Chinese Government spokesman, 1 September 1963, (*Peking Review*, 6 September 1963): text in Gittings, op. cit., pp. 181–3. The Soviet-US agreement over Cuba was not even registered officially at the UN, as was the original intention. For a discussion of the question whether there was also an unofficial US commitment to withdraw the fifteen obsolete Jupiter missiles from Turkey, see Allison, op. cit., pp. 229–30.
13. Allison, op. cit., pp. 200 ff., is the best recent example.
14. Wellington's much misquoted description of Waterloo: 'It was a damned nice thing—the nearest run thing you ever saw in your life'; Thomas Creevey, *The Creevey Papers*, p. 142, ed. John Gore, London, 1934.
15. *Pravda*, 13 December 1962. The relevant passage in the History of Soviet Foreign Policy is op. cit., vol. 2, pp. 364–5, to which the chapter concerned in *Mezhdunarodnye konflikty*, Moscow, 1972, eds. V. V. Zhurin and E. M. Primakov, adds little, summing up the outcome of the crisis as being that 'the USA was compelled to agree to renounce its plans of aggression against ... Cuba' after a 'fairly intensive exchange of messages between the two governments'—pp. 84 and 95. Gromyko told the Supreme Soviet flatly that

'the leaders of the USA brought the world one step, perhaps only half a step, from the abyss'—*Pravda*, 14 December 1962.

16. Anatolyi A. Gromyko 'Karibskii Krizis', *Voprosy Istorii*, nos. 7 and 8, Moscow, 1971.

17. Robert Kennedy, *Thirteen Days, a Memoir of the Cuban Crisis*, Macmillan, New York, 1969.

18. This accusation is borne out by the text of Khrushchev's 'Friday' letter. The 'Trollope ploy', whereby Kennedy replied to the 'Friday' letter rather than to the 'Saturday' letter, is described in Allison, op. cit., pp. 227 ff.

19. In Khrushchev's letter to Kennedy of 27 October 1962, which was broadcast over Moscow radio on that day, he said that agreement over Cuba would 'make it easier to reach agreement on banning nuclear weapons tests' and in his letter of the following day, which was also broadcast, he said that the Soviet Government would 'like to continue the exchange of views on the prohibition of atomic and thermonuclear weapons'. In Kennedy's letter of 28 October, which was released to the press, he suggested that the two governments 'should give priority to questions relating to the proliferation of nuclear weapons, on earth and in outer space, and to the effort for a nuclear test ban'. Macmillan (whose greatest achievement in foreign policy was perhaps the conclusion of the Nuclear Test Ban Agreement) also regarded a ban on tests as a measure that would enable the three governments 'to proceed rapidly to specific and fruitful discussions about the non-dissemination of nuclear power leading to an agreement on this subject': see the joint Anglo-American letter to Khrushchev of 15 April 1963, quoted in his *At the End of the Day*, Macmillan, London, 1973, p. 467. Ibid., p. 480 gives Macmillan's own view about this during the actual negotiations three months later.

20. *Pravda*, 14 July 1963: Griffith, op. cit., pp. 289–325, contains a translation of this document, which covered seven out of *Pravda*'s eight pages.

21. *The Military Balance 1969/70*, loc. cit.

22. In particular, *Pravda* of 2 October 1964, 'On the main directions for drawing up the plan for the development of the national economy in the next period'. In three columns describing Khrushchev's intervention there is only a single sentence on the needs of defence, which must be 'maintained at the appropriate level', whereas the need to make consumer goods top priority is repeatedly mentioned. Khrushchev's clear implication was that heavy industry was now strong enough to sustain both these objectives. This intervention is all the more striking in that it coincided with the publication of an article in the current issue of *Kommunist Vooruzhennykh Sil* which emphasized the continuing role of heavy industry as the economic foundation of the Soviet Union's progress: see the article reporting this in the *Guardian* of 2 October 1964 by Victor Zorza, whose articles in the *Guardian* of 18 and 25 September also described the controversy between Khrushchev and the Soviet military about the value of conventional weapons, particularly tanks.

23. T. W. Wolfe, op. cit. p. 464; Khrushchev's decision to subordinate the Ground Forces directly to the Defence Ministry was not revealed until 1968 (by Marshal Zakharov, Chief of the General Staff).

24. As was argued by P. B. Reddaway in his article on 'The Fall of Khrushchev' published in *Survey*, July 1965.

25. Deported from their homes by Stalin's order, for alleged collaboration with the German forces.

PART TWO

The Foreign Policy of
the Collective Leadership:
The Years of Consolidation

4

DEFENCE POLICY

The triumvirate which succeeded Khrushchev hastened to make it clear that the decisions of the XXth Congress, taken under his leadership, held good so far as doctrine was concerned: their validity was re-affirmed both in the CPSU Central Committee's communiqué announcing Khrushchev's resignation and in Brezhnev's speech delivered at the celebrations of the October Revolution. True, whereas the concept of peaceful coexistence between states with different social systems had, under Khrushchev, been described as the general line of the foreign policy of the Soviet state, in the formulation approved at the two party congresses presided over by his successors it was demoted to fourth place. But so long as American forces were fighting in Vietnam, the new leadership could scarcely have avoided this change of emphasis. Their indictment of Khrushchev was indirect: *Pravda* of 17 October 1964 described the Leninist Party as the enemy of subjectivism and drifting in communist construction; and as foreign to hare-brained scheming, immature conclusions, hasty and unrealistic decisions and actions, boasting, and idle talk. At a pinch, this could be construed as the indictment of an old man in a hurry at home, rather than in his foreign policy; and indeed radical changes on the home front were soon effected. The new leaders also lost no time in reassuring the military that the Party had the interests of the armed forces at heart;[1] and it is significant that the epithet 'hare-brained' recurred in the military newspaper *Krasnaya Zvezda* four months later, when Zakharov, reappointed Chief of Staff, wrote: 'with the appearance of nuclear weapons, cybernetics, electronics, and computer technology, a subjective approach to military problems, hare-brained schemes, and superficiality can cost very dear and cause irreparable harm'.[2]

The broad aims of Soviet foreign policy remained a global role for the Soviet Union and an accommodation with the United States. Both were to be pursued with prudence; there were to be no more games of bluff. At the same time, a further attempt would be made to restore order in the world communist movement. Finally—and this affected foreign policy as much as it did policy at home—the new leadership was collective. It is inconceivable that the great issues which the triumvirate has had to face have not given rise to sharp differences of opinion; but so far as we know, these have never attained the dimensions of a true struggle for power, and have been kept within reasonable bounds. None of Khrushchev's colleagues was dismissed with him. Brezhnev soon[3] emerged as *primus inter pares*, in his capacity as General-Secretary of the CPSU. But it is extremely unlikely that a single member of the Soviet élite will ever be allowed to assume all the offices held by Khrushchev.* The Soviet system of government is now so complex that these offices are too much for one man to hold efficiently, quite apart from the dangers ensuing from concentration of personal power. In short, in 1964 what the Soviet Union needed was a period of consolidation. This process was to be presided over by three serious men— Leonid Brezhnev, General-Secretary of the CPSU, Alexei Kosygin, Prime Minister, and Nikolai Podgorny, who succeeded Mikoyan as Head of State in December 1965. Their intentions were harder to interpret at first, since they were not well known to Western observers, who were to miss the outbursts that had often illuminated the policies of Khrushchev.

The Khrushchevian concept of minimum nuclear deterrence was set aside. It is a matter of debate whether the new leadership deliberately decided to achieve strategic parity with the United States; or whether

---

* The importance that the new leadership attached to the principle of collect-ive leadership, and their criticisms of Khrushchev's personal failings, emerge clearly from the leading article in *Pravda* of 17 October, which was intended as the keynote of the new regime. Khrushchev headed both Party and Govern-ment. Although in the Soviet system the former is, by definition, supreme, the latter's power resides in the fact that it is responsible for the day-to-day running of the Soviet economy, including the eight ministries relating to the military-industrial sector. In my view, Khrushchev also held the post of Supreme Commander-in-Chief: see the last paragraph of Grechko's article on Khrush-chev's seventieth birthday in *Izvestiya* of 17 April 1964. In any case, Khrushchev —like Brezhnev—was *ex officio* chairman of a body variously referred to as the War (or Defence) Committee and the Higher Military Council.[4]

they aimed at strategic superiority; or whether they embarked on the defence build-up over the next five years without any single clearly defined aim.* The factor common to all three of these is that the missile gap, which had grown even wider—to the advantage of the United States—since 1962, should be closed as quickly as possible. The underlying concept is summed up in a remark allegedly made after the Cuban missile crisis by a senior Soviet diplomat to an American interlocutor: 'you will never do that to us again!' At the same time the Soviet armed forces were now to be trained and equipped alike for general nuclear war, conventional operations, and operations in which nuclear weapons would be used on a limited scale. The management of defence industries, one of the victims of Khrushchev's policy of decentralization, was brought back to the centre. The subsequent investment in ICBMs and submarines carrying ballistic missiles was so enormous that by the end of the decade rough numerical parity had at last been achieved, enabling the Soviet Union to escape from its position of strategic hostage in Europe.

As between super-powers, what do the concepts of strategic nuclear parity, superiority, and inferiority mean?† This question can be evaded by taking refuge in the fact that today the governments of the Soviet Union, the United States, and China are all acting on the assumption that these concepts have a real meaning. Why otherwise would they be spending vast sums on their nuclear arsenals, and why are the first two of these governments currently engaged in negotiations the nub of which is to agree on a definition of what, in American terminology, is 'essential equivalence'?[5] But this is too simple. The argument that the concept of nuclear superiority and inferiority is, at any rate in a super-

---

* Each of these three views is examined in the final chapter of Wolfe, op. cit. Whichever is correct, it is also true that the Research and Development work on the weapons systems deployed by the end of the decade had already been begun under Khrushchev: the SS-9 ICBM did not spring out of the ground like the Theban warriors. In this sense it is arguable that Soviet defence policy developed continuously throughout the sixties. But there is a vast financial and economic difference between allowing resources to be committed to the Research and Development of a major weapons system and taking the final decision to produce and deploy it on a large scale.

† According to our definition, a super-power is a state possessing two military characteristics that differentiate it from medium or regional powers: the full range of the strategic nuclear armoury and the capacity to deploy its forces, whether armed conventionally or with nuclear weapons, in any strategic theatre of the world. Although the adjective 'strategic' is used throughout this book, the comforting distinction drawn by some between the effects of tactical and those of strategic nuclear weapons is dubious. For arguments to support scepticism about this distinction, see Zuckerman, op. cit., pp. 66–70.

power context, meaningless, is twofold. Would any sane man ever press the button unleashing a first-strike nuclear attack, knowing what the consequences[6] would be, for the population of just one of his country's major cities, of even a single megaton explosion forming part of a second-strike, retaliatory attack launched by the other super-power, still less the full consequences of an all-out second strike? Secondly, looking back over the period of nearly thirty years that has elapsed since the only atomic attack in history, how much weight have the Soviet and US governments given to each other's strategic nuclear power in the conduct of their bilateral relations? For example, it is maintained by some that in 1962, although the Soviet strategic arsenal was much smaller than that of the United States (intercontinentally,[7] not much more than a powerful *force de frappe*), it was already large enough to have inflicted an unacceptable number of American casualties; and that the nuclear capacities of the two sides in effect cancelled each other out in the Cuban crisis, which was in the end resolved by the superiority, not of American strategic power, but of American conventionally armed forces in the Caribbean. And even if this explanation of the outcome of the Cuban crisis contains only an element of truth, it is incontestable that all major wars since 1945 (Korea, Indo-China, the Middle East) have been fought with conventional weapons which for the most part are a technological extension of those used in the European theatre of operations during the Second World War.

The answer to the 'no sane man' question is to pose a counter-question: what is sanity in international relations? Both deterrence and security are largely states of mind; governments are controlled not by precise machines, but by fallible[8] men; and the governments of super-powers are no exception. Thus it may be scientifically demonstrable that the destructive capacity of modern megaton warheads must reach a point of 'overkill' where it no longer makes sense for one super-power to seek to increase its own destructive capacity, either quantitatively or qualitatively, regardless of whether the other super-power does so. Yet no computer will ever be devised whose calculations the leaders of any government will trust enough for it to determine for them exactly where this point lies. Therefore, so long as nuclear weapons exist, the government of a super-power must be haunted by the fear that the counsels of sanity may not prevail in the mind of its potential adversary, and that he will somehow or other contrive to steal a nuclear march, unless they can reach agreement to open their minds to each other, at least to the extent necessary to enable both of them to keep their fears within bounds.

With states, as with individuals, to be aware of the truth is safer than to act on fantasies conjured up by fear of the unknown; *omne ignotum pro magnifico.*

The answer to the historical argument[9] (that the super-powers' nuclear capacities have so far largely cancelled each other out) is that, although no one has used nuclear weapons in war since 1945, it remains equally true that all governments, and especially those of the Soviet Union and the United States, have been obliged to deal with each other, and to frame their foreign policies in the knowledge that, if the worst came to the worst, those weapons might be used—and 'might' is quite enough for international discomfort. The Cuban example is debatable— a study of the text of Khrushchev's messages to Kennedy leaves little doubt that, as the crisis developed, he became acutely aware of the danger that it would lead to a nuclear world war. A clearer example is provided by the course of Stalin's and Khrushchev's attempts to settle the question of Berlin in the Soviet interest. That they failed to do so is surely best explained by the assumption that each of them realized in his turn that, although Soviet forces possessed the local conventional superiority required to take West Berlin, they could not afford to press their aims beyond the point where there was the slightest risk of nuclear escalation;[10] and it is significant that Khrushchev never attempted to use Soviet local strength in and around Berlin as a bargaining counter during the Cuban crisis.* In my view, the concepts of nuclear inferiority, parity, and superiority, however questionable they may be as scientific-technological propositions, do have a profound significance, although their significance may be greater in political than in strategic terms. This distinction is sometimes tenuous but is always important, above all for the super-powers, for whom (as the US Secretary of State reminded the Senate Foreign Relations Committee in October 1974) 'the prospect of a decisive military advantage, even if theoretically possible, is politically intolerable'.

It was against this background that after the Cuban crisis Khrushchev settled for minimum nuclear deterrence. His scale of deterrence was minimal only by Soviet standards: that is to say, a defence posture of strategic nuclear inferiority which would still have assured the Soviet Union posthumous revenge in a second-strike, retaliatory attack that would have inflicted immense damage on the United States.

---

* The point about Berlin, though in reverse, struck the then British Prime Minister when compiling his impressions of the Cuban crisis on 4 November 1962: see Macmillan, op. cit., p. 218, 'What Are the Strategic Lessons?'.

His successors were content neither with this, admittedly high, status of inferiority, nor with the single, nuclear option on which Khrushchevian defence policy was based. Profiting by the Research and Development programmes already in the pipeline, they embarked on a defence effort, which, coupled with their space programme, required the allocation of a proportion of Soviet resources whose exact size has been the subject of much debate. In 1965 the Soviet military budget was actually cut by 4 per cent. Thereafter, it rose annually, reaching a figure of 17·9 billion roubles in 1969, while the figure for scientific research doubled in the same period. In a series of papers presented to the Joint Economic Committee of the United States Congress in September 1970, it was even argued that by the end of the Soviet Five-Year Plan in that year the Soviet armed forces might be getting as much as 40 per cent more hardware than the United States armed forces, which would have meant that Soviet defence and space expenditure had increased more than five-fold between 1958 and 1968.[11]

Any calculation of the proportion of the Soviet budget devoted to defence depends on how much defence expenditure is concealed in other sections of the budget: in particular, the cost of nuclear warheads, Research and Development on advanced weapons systems, and the military elements of the space programme. *Military Balance 1969/70* suggested that, on a conservative estimate, Soviet declared defence appropriations of 17,700 million roubles for 1969, if calculated on the basis of the real resources mobilized by the Soviet Union in equivalent American prices, were the equivalent of 42 billion dollars, and that the total defence expenditure was the equivalent of 53 billion dollars. (Based on a GNP over twice the size of that of the Soviet Union, United States defence estimates for 1969/70 were 78,475,000,000 dollars, of which an estimated 25–30 billions were attributable to the Vietnam war.) Brezhnev's allusions to defence expenditure, made at the XXIVth Party Congress and in a speech in June 1971, suggest that this is a delicate subject even within the Soviet Union. Of one thing there can be little doubt: the size of the resources committed to the defence sector in the second half of the 1960s was a major cause of the Soviet economic dilemma at the end of the decade.[12]

As well as the massive deployment of offensive strategic nuclear weapons, a start was made with the deployment of an anti-ballistic missile system round Moscow in 1966. But the Strategic Missile Forces —the élite of the Soviet armed forces, numbering some 350,000 men— were not the only recipients of funds designed for expansion. The substantial Soviet Mediterranean Squadron, which made its first appearance in 1963, is now an accepted feature of the strategic naval scene. The Indian Ocean was first visited in 1968 by a cruiser and a destroyer from the Soviet Pacific Fleet, which now detaches ships to provide a permanent naval presence there. The Soviet naval infantry arm (disbanded after the Second World War) was revived shortly before Khrushchev's fall; its strength was doubled between 1966 and 1969; and from 1967 onwards there was increasing emphasis on amphibious operations. The new Soviet Navy's role was no longer confined to defence of the Soviet Union's coasts, but became long range, as was to be demonstrated in 1970 by the *Okean* manoeuvres, in which over 250 Soviet ships took part, in every ocean (and some rivers) of the world. The new navy's main weakness was its lack of air support, although in 1973 this gap was partly filled by the first Soviet aircraft carrier. Finally, the size of the Soviet fishing fleet, the largest and most modern in the world, is also a factor to be reckoned with, given the electronic intelligence duties of its vessels. At the same time the Soviet Air Force was expanded and modernized, with the aim of establishing air superiority over the battlefield, and its capacity to intervene was also greatly increased. Already well demonstrated in the Middle East, this capacity is today an important factor in assessing the Soviet Union's ability to reinforce its divisions in the vital sector of Central Europe.

The collective leadership broadly continued Khrushchev's policy of re-equipping and modernizing the forces of the Soviet Union's allies in the Warsaw Pact, with the main emphasis on conventional warfare, although tactical nuclear missile launchers were also supplied (the nuclear warheads remaining in Soviet hands). The lion's share of new equipment went to the northern tier countries—Poland, Czechoslovakia, and East Germany—in whose territory most of the joint Warsaw Pact manoeuvres were held, these becoming much more frequent than under Khrushchev. Because of this policy, these three countries provided a large addition to Soviet military strength in Central Europe. The value of the Czechoslovak contribution became doubtful after 1968. But neither this setback, nor quarrels with the Romanians about burden-sharing and nuclear planning (both familiar concepts in the West), deterred the Russians from making full use of the Pact for both political and military purposes. The frequent meetings of the Pact's Political Consultative Committee (consisting of Communist Party First Secretaries, Heads of Governments, and Foreign and Defence Ministers of the member countries) became an important means of coordinating policy, for example, on the question of the European Conference; and in 1969 the command structure of the Pact was reformed. Whereas before the Eastern Europeans had little or no say, the new structure bore at least some resemblance to an integrated command, even though Soviet influence remained paramount.[13]

Finally, the Soviet Government introduced a major reform in 1967, when conscripted military service was cut to two years. This was followed in 1968 by compensating regulations which made participation in pre-conscription training obligatory. The 1967 law also established sixty as the compulsory retiring age for all senior officers below the rank of marshal. The second half of the 1960s was the period in which the Soviet officer corps was reformed and rejuvenated. (This process had been begun by Khrushchev, as part of his successive reductions of Soviet military manpower from the peak of 5·7 millions reached in 1955; in 1958–60, 250,000 officers were demobilized, and in 1960, 454 new generals were appointed.) What was most striking about this reform was the priority given to engineer officers, who by 1969 accounted for 80 per cent of the officer corps of the Strategic Missile Forces.[14] The influence of these military technocrats in Soviet society must be considerable, though this does not imply a conflict of interest between the military and the Party. In 1966, 93 per cent of all officers were members either of the Party or of the *Komsomol*. And Brezhnev's attendance at the final parade of the *Dvina* manoeuvres in 1970 (a year in which fifty-eight marshals, generals, and admirals were elected to the Supreme Soviet) marked the close relationship between the military and the Party—and particularly himself.

To sum up, the political consequence of this relationship, underpinned by the Soviet leadership's vast allocation of national resources to the armed forces, both nuclear and conventional, was that in the next decade Brezhnev was able to embark, with full military backing, on a Soviet-American dialogue of a different kind from that which had been attempted by Khrushchev.

NOTES

1. *Pravda*, 17 October and 8 November 1964. See also Brezhnev, *Leninskim Kursom*, vol. 3, p. 30.
2. *Krasnaya Zvezda*, 4 February 1965. It is evident from the context that Khrushchev—not Stalin, who is mentioned elsewhere in the article—is the target of this criticism.

3. At the latest, by March 1966, when Brezhnev resumed the old title of General-Secretary at the XXIIIrd CPSU Congress. But the first occasion on which he was specifically described by *Pravda* as leading a delegation abroad (to Poland) was on 5 April 1965.

4. About this little is known, but it is presumed to bear ultimate responsibility for strategic nuclear decisions. For a discussion of the present functioning of these three bodies, and also of the important role of the General-Secretary's personal secretariat, see Alain Jacob's article in *Le Monde*, 12 February 1974, *L'URSS, société socialiste développée*. Finally, Khrushchev was chairman of the Central Committee Bureau of the RSFSR, an office which was abolished in 1966.

5. This American term of art has been defined as rough equality in numbers of weapons and deliverable 'throw-weight' by Maxwell D. Taylor in an article in *Foreign Affairs*, April 1974, p. 580.

6. What these consequences would be for Birmingham are assessed by Zuckerman, op. cit., pp. 55-8.

7. Intercontinentally needs under-lining, because within the European continent Soviet medium and intermediate range nuclear weapons targeted on NATO countries could have wrought havoc, had the Cuban crisis ended in a nuclear exchange: see the final paragraph of 'The temporary *détente*' in the preceding chapter.

8. Fallible, but with brains, values, and judgements still perhaps 'superior to the mechanics and processes of electronic computers or guidance systems': Zuckerman, op. cit., p. 26.

9. This argument is deployed in Taylor, op. cit., for example.

10. For a criticism of this term, see Zuckerman, op. cit., pp. 63-4; also Tom Lehrer's marching song of the Third World War in his record *That was the year, that was* (in particular, the line 'describing contrapuntally the cities we have lost').

11. This argument was put forward by Michael Boretsky, whose conclusions were called in question by Alec Nove in *Survival* of January 1971, particularly those relating to comparative prices. For a discussion, see *The Military Balance 1973/4*, IISS, London, 1973, pp. 8-9.

12. For Brezhnev's allusions, see ch. 9. John Erickson, in *Soviet Military Power*, Royal United Services Institute for Defence Studies, 1971, p. 100, suggests that in macro-economic terms the Soviet leadership is prepared to see military expenditure 'move ahead at the rate of 4 per cent per annum within an annual growth rate of about 5 or 6 per cent'. The section of the present chapter that follows is indebted to Erickson's book.

13. The Budapest reforms of the Warsaw Pact introduced in 1969 are described in *Survival*, May/June 1974, 'The Warsaw Pact Today' by Malcolm Mackintosh, pp. 123-4, IISS, London, 1974.

14. By 1973 more than half the officer corps of the Soviet Navy also had engineering degrees, according to *Krasnaya Zvezda*; see *The Times*, 30 July 1973.

5

ASIA

The Vietnam War

It is the official Soviet view that the two principal causes of the worsening of Soviet-American relations in the second half of the 1960s were the Vietnam War and United States support of Israel. To these an objective historian must add the invasion of Czechoslovakia, although East-West relations did not take long to absorb this shock. But if the Americans had not become engaged in Vietnam on the vast scale which followed the Tonkin Gulf incident of August 1964, would the Soviet leaders have been ready for a full dialogue with them sooner than they were, that is to say, before they could conduct it as equal partners? It seems doubtful.[1]

The American involvement in Vietnam was a windfall for the Soviet Union, for a number of reasons: whereas Soviet support for North Vietnam was not expensive, the war took up a large slice of the United States defence budget (over 100 billion dollars in the years 1965–72); it increasingly antagonized world opinion against the United States Government; as Vietnam absorbed American attention more and more, the Administration found it increasingly difficult to give the problems of the rest of the world all the attention that they deserved; and finally it split American society and brought down President Johnson. Even so, the war in Indo-China must have given the Soviet leadership some anxious moments, for they could not tell for certain—any more than any other government—how far the war would develop; it complicated their quarrel with the Chinese still further; and the Soviet military may have envied their American opposite numbers their ability to test modern weapons systems in battle conditions (the Soviet armed forces, though highly professional, have barely heard a shot fired in anger since the Japanese Armistice, whereas the American armed forces saw active service almost continuously from 1941 until their final withdrawal from the war in Indo-China).

Following Khrushchev's agreement with Kennedy on the neutralization of Laos at their meeting in Vienna, the Soviet Government proposed in July 1964 that the Geneva Conference on Laos should be reconvened (a proposal to which the United States was known to be hostile), and gave warning that the Soviet Government might be compelled to withdraw from its position as co-Chairman of the Conference. Khrushchev may well have wished to disengage from Indo-China altogether. Certainly, the first Soviet reaction to the incident of August 1964 and to the Joint Congressional Resolution* which followed it was to support the American proposal, rejected by the North Vietnamese, to take the matter to the Security Council. The Chinese protested both against the incident and the proposal. One of the first decisions of the new Soviet leadership was to reverse Khrushchev's decision. In November the Soviet Government pledged its support for the North Vietnamese Government if North Vietnam was attacked by the Americans. No doubt they had several motives for this: conceivably, the hope that the United States Government might think again; certainly, the hope of winning back the support of the North Vietnamese and the North Koreans from the Chinese; and probably, the belief that failure to come out in support of Hanoi would be used against them by the Chinese, who had sent a senior delegation to the celebrations of the October Revolution in Moscow, while both sides had suspended polemics. Even so, when Kosygin visited Hanoi the following February (and also North Korea, calling twice at Peking, where he talked with the Chinese leaders), he not only supported the convening of a new Geneva Conference on Indo-China, but also, according to the Chinese, conveyed to the North Vietnamese an American warning to stop supporting the National Liberation Front (NLF) in South Vietnam and to put an end to attacks on cities there. In the event, while the Soviet Prime Minister was in Hanoi, American bombers raided North Vietnamese targets, in retaliation for an attack by South Vietnamese NLF forces on their base at Pleiku in South Vietnam. The United States Government declined to consider negotiations. In April 1965 the First Secretary of the Central Committee of the North Vietnamese Communist Party

* This Resolution approved Johnson's 'determination to take all necessary measures' in Vietnam.

visited Moscow at the head of a delegation; agreement was reached on the aid which the Soviet Union would give North Vietnam; and the NLF was allowed to establish a mission in Moscow. For the rest of the decade the Soviet role in Vietnam was no less important in the context of the Sino-Soviet dispute than in that of Soviet-American relations.

The Sino-Soviet dispute

The lull in polemics between the CPSU and the CCP did not last long. There was no meeting of minds between the new Soviet leadership and the Chinese delegation when they talked in Moscow in November 1964, and the year that followed exacerbated the dispute still further. The meeting of the drafting committee, which Khrushchev had intended to take place in December 1964, was held the following March. Only eighteen out of the twenty-six communist parties were represented, and the communiqué was equivocal, agreeing only that a new international conference should be held at a suitable time, after thorough preparation in which all fraternal parties should take part. But it did call for united action in support of the Vietnamese people. Coming just before the arrival of the Vietnamese delegation, this was a gain for the Russians, who from now on used the Vietnamese issue as a stick for beating the Chinese. Their accusations made at the time are repeated in the History of Soviet Foreign Policy: over several years the Chinese 'created obstacles to the transportation of arms and supplies across Chinese territory' and held up deliveries for a long time. How serious these obstacles were is hard to say; some could have been caused simply by the chaos of the Chinese Cultural Revolution, which in 1968 was such that in the border province of Kwangsi the Red Guards stormed the North Vietnamese consulate at Nanning and assaulted its staff, on 2 June.[2] But the Chinese were on weak ground in rebutting Soviet charges on this score, although they accused the new Soviet leadership as hotly as they had Khrushchev, not only of revisionism, but also of Soviet-American collaboration for the domination of the world, which in Chinese eyes made the Soviet call for united action over Vietnam fraudulent. (Not that the Chinese did not give the North Vietnamese military aid themselves—they did, although Soviet military aid, estimated at 1,660 million dollars in 1965–71, was nearly three times as great as the Chinese during the same period.)[3]

During the Indo-Pakistan war of August/September 1965, the Chinese accused the Russians of supporting the Indian reactionaries.

The success of the Tashkent meeting in January 1966, when the Indian and Pakistani leaders met the Soviet Prime Minister in the role of mediator, must have been galling to the Chinese, since it showed the Soviet Union as an Asian Great Power exercising its influence for peace. The Russians also scored over the Chinese in the affair of the Second Afro-Asian Conference, from which the Chinese sought to exclude them. It should have been held in Algiers in June 1965, but in the end it never took place. By that time the opening shots of the Cultural Revolution were being fired. This movement, literally translated 'a full-scale revolution to establish a working class culture', was to put the Chinese Government in baulk internationally in 1966. Not surprisingly, the Chinese sent no delegation to the XXIIIrd CPSU Congress in March of that year. But the eighty-odd parties who were represented included those of North Vietnam and North Korea. At the Congress Brezhnev spoke moderately about the CCP. In January 1967 Red Guards blockaded the Soviet Embassy in Peking; in February, the families of Soviet Staff were evacuated; and the Chinese withdrew their students from the Soviet Union after riots in the Red Square.

Whereas the Soviet Government gave full support to the North Vietnamese proposal of January 1967—that talks with the Americans could begin if the latter unconditionally stopped bombing and other acts of war against North Vietnam—the Chinese eventually condemned it as a Soviet-American conspiracy to compel the Vietnamese to give in, and accused the Russians of seeking to put the North Vietnamese and themselves at loggerheads. By now the Soviet leaders were 'the biggest group of renegades and scabs in history' for the Chinese, for whom Mao Tse-tung was Lenin's genuine successor. The Russians, as well as ridiculing the Cultural Revolution and the adulation of Mao, drew a distinction between the Maoist clique on the one hand and the CCP and the Chinese people on the other. Moreover they accused the Chinese of a tacit agreement with the Americans over Vietnam. This was partly based on Chinese statements that they would not intervene militarily in Vietnam unless themselves attacked by the United States, but may also have been connected with the Chinese formula for a North Vietnamese victory: a protracted people's war (such as they themselves had successfully fought for so many years), to be won primarily through self-reliant effort, rather than with the aid of sophisticated Soviet military equipment—a formula which, in Soviet eyes, could be interpreted as meaning that the Chinese would be content for the war to last indefinitely.

Thus there was too much at stake for a Sino-Soviet rapprochement to be possible: the leadership of the world communist movement and competition for influence throughout the Third World, to which the Chinese offered the Maoist slogan that the 'world city' must fall to the assault of the 'world village'. In Asia the only major communist parties to remain pro-Soviet, other than the Mongolian Party, were those of India and Ceylon. Elsewhere the Chinese had only modest success. Rival communist parties were set up in the 1960s in several countries with Chinese support; pro-Chinese groups appeared in Europe, where both ruling (Romania partially excepted) and non-ruling parties were broadly pro-Soviet; but in Latin America, where the existence of guerrilla movements and the Che Guevara mystique might have been expected to offer exploitable opportunities, such pro-Chinese groups as were formed remained minuscule. (Castro, who by the middle of the decade[4] had adopted a position somewhere between the Chinese and the Russians, was a complicating factor.) In the Middle East the Chinese continued to accuse the Russians of cooperation with the Americans. They officially recognized the Palestinian *fedayeen* (towards whom the Soviet attitude was ambivalent until 1974*), by signing an agreement with them in 1965, promising diplomatic, military, and economic support. And they worked hard further south: in Africa their most spectacular achievement was the offer, which was accepted by the governments of Tanzania and Zambia, of 400 million dollars for the construction of the Tanzania–Zambia railway—more than the Russians had given for the Aswan Dam.

Behind all this lay the Soviet Government's conclusion, reached towards the end of 1965, that it was to its advantage to sign a Nuclear Non-Proliferation Treaty, which the Chinese regarded just as they had the Test Ban Treaty: an obstacle deliberately set in the way of the nuclear capability that they were slowly developing. Given the state of Sino-Soviet relations in the 1960s, it would have been surprising if there had been no incidents along the 4,000 mile frontier. 60,000 Chinese Moslem inhabitants of Sinkiang are believed to have been given asylum by the Soviet Union in 1962, for example; and the climax was reached in March 1969, when a major engagement was fought on Damansky Island,[5] the first among a series of incidents between March and August of that year. More Soviet troops were moved eastwards (they had been stationed in Mongolia since 1967); a

* When the Soviet Government finally gave official recognition to the Palestine Liberation Organization: see *The Times*, 19 October 1974.

new Central Asian Military District was established, with responsibility for the Sinkiang border; and a missile specialist, General V. F. Tolubko, was appointed in August to command the Far East Military District. On 16 September Victor Louis, the Soviet journalist who had scooped the fall of Khrushchev, wrote an article in the *Evening News* about the danger of war, which included the following passage:

The Soviet Union is adhering to the doctrine that socialist countries have the right to interfere in each other's affairs in their own interests or those of others who are threatened. The fact that China is many times larger than Czechoslovakia and might offer active resistance is, according to Marxist theoreticians, no reason for not applying this doctrine.

In that month two Chinese nuclear tests took place in Sinkiang. Although the Chinese had not yet developed modern delivery systems for nuclear weapons, they were within sight of launching their first earth satellite (in April 1970). China was just reaching the most vulnerable point in the development of strategic nuclear power: the moment when its nuclear force was beginning to pose a threat but was not yet certain of being able to survive a first-strike attack. By the autumn there were rumours of a Soviet pre-emptive strike against China. They were no more than rumours; for if such an extreme course was ever considered in Moscow, by that time the strike would have had not merely to destroy the Chinese nuclear installations, both in Sinkiang and in eastern China, but also several thousand Chinese nuclear scientists as well. Undeterred, or perhaps even spurred on, by Soviet psychological warfare, the Chinese Government warned the population of the danger of a Soviet attack, and shelters were dug in the cities.

As had happened a decade earlier, this conflict coincided with ideological dissension. At the IXth CCP Congress, held in April 1969, the Chinese leadership formally elevated Maoism to a position of equality with Marxism-Leninism, denouncing the revisionism of the Soviet leadership, who became in Chinese terms 'social imperialists'. Yet in September the Soviet and Chinese Prime Ministers met in Peking, as Kosygin was on his way back from a visit to Hanoi. They agreed that, however acute their ideological rivalry, a working relationship between the two governments should be restored (both missions had been reduced to the level of Chargés d'Affaires, and the Chinese Embassy in Moscow had left its broken windows unrepaired as a reminder of the past). Ambassadors were exchanged in 1970, the year in which Chinese diplomacy[6] was released from the self-denying ordinance imposed by the Cultural Revolution. But talks on the frontier question, which have continued to this day, achieved no perceptible results. Even though the Soviet and Chinese governments were again on speaking terms, they remained as far apart as ever on questions of substance.

Conference of the world communist parties

In June 1969 the Soviet leadership did succeed in holding this long deferred conference. As it turned out, the delegates met with the invasion of Czechoslovakia as much in mind as the Sino-Soviet dispute (but for the invasion, the conference would have been held six months earlier). Seventy-five parties took part. Of the fourteen ruling parties, five boycotted the conference—China, Albania, North Korea, North Vietnam, and Yugoslavia—and Cuba sent only an observer. There were no representatives from Japan, Indonesia, or any East Asian or South-East Asian party. Exceptionally, *Pravda* published summaries of speeches even when critical of Soviet policies. These included a statement by Enrico Berlinguer, Secretary-General of the Italian Communist Party, sympathizing with the Czechoslovak experiment and condemning the invasion of 1968, and one by Nicolae Ceausescu describing China as the great socialist state and declaring that no force in the world could conquer a nation which was fully determined to defend courageously its freedom and national independence.[7] A group of parties submitted a draft declaration, which was chiefly the work of the Russians, the Hungarians, and the French. Over 400 amendments were submitted, of which a hundred found their way in one form or another into the compromise text, an anodyne document which some parties refused to sign (the Romanians did sign it). Even though the conference achieved little, the fact that it was held at all was a Soviet achievement.[8] Nevertheless, by the end of the decade, the Soviet leadership had proved no more successful than Khrushchev in restoring the unity of the world communist movement.

NOTES

1. Adam Ulam in *The Rivals*, Viking Press, New York, 1971, has argued that American diplomacy missed the opportunity for such a dialogue after the Cuban crisis had revealed the weakness of the Soviet position. But Khrushchev's personal position had also been weakened at home. Would he have had the authority to go further towards Kennedy than he did during his remaining two years of office?

S.F.P.—3

2. Op. cit., vol. 2, p. 422, gives the Soviet view. For the Nanning incident, see Stanley Karnow, *Mao and China*, Macmillan, London, 1973, p. 439.
3. *Strategic Survey 1972*, IISS, London, 1973, p. 50, which describes the estimated figures given as rough. For the Chinese view of the North Vietnam War in the sixties, see Karnow's analysis in op. cit., pp. 479 ff.
4. In 1966, Carlos Rafael Rodriguez, when asked by the author to which Communist Party Cuban Communists felt closest, replied without hesitation 'the North Korean'.
5. Chenpao Island for the Chinese, whose account of what they have claimed as a Soviet defeat was given in the *Observer* of 23 September 1973. For Sinkiang, see Karnow, op. cit., p. 135.
6. Chinese ambassadors who had been withdrawn from their posts returned, after years of absence; diplomatic relations were even restored with the capital of arch-revisionists, Belgrade; and Yugoslavia itself resumed relations with the arch-dogmatist Albania.
7. *Pravda*, 14 and 11 June 1969.
8. For details, see *Novosti*, Moscow, and the *World Marxist Review*, Prague, 1969.

6

THE THIRD WORLD

Policy towards the underdeveloped countries

Under Khrushchev, the stilted jargon of the third of the basic tasks of
Soviet foreign policy (to support national liberation movements and to
cooperate in every way with underdeveloped countries) expressed an
ambitious new approach towards former colonies comparable in scope
with Canning's calling in the New World to redress the balance of the
Old.

Khrushchev's new policy complicated relations between the CPSU
and the local communist parties, even in Cuba.[1] In the Middle East, the
communist parties of one country after another split under the strain of
Soviet support for the government that was suppressing them (a strain
that was aggravated by the Sino-Soviet dispute). True, this dichotomy
between Soviet national interests and those of a local communist party
was not a new phenomenon: one of the earliest examples was the sup-
pression of the Turkish Communist Party by Atatürk, who was cultiv-
ated by the Soviet Government soon after the Revolution. But it was
sharpened under Khrushchev. Moreover, his policy towards the Third
World met with some grievous disappointments, such as the fall of
Lumumba, Nkrumah, Kassem, Ben Bella, and Sukarno. Of these, by
far the worst blow to the international communist cause was the last.
Although Sukarno was not formally deposed as President until two and
a half years after the fall of Khrushchev, in the fighting that followed
the abortive *coup d'état* of September 1965 at least 100,000 members of
the Indonesian Communist Party were slaughtered, and an equal
number of the Party's sympathizers. Politically, this blow was as hard to
bear in Peking as it was in Moscow. But financially, it was the Soviet

Government that suffered. Not only was the new Indonesian regime left a handsome legacy of Soviet military hardware, including tanks and warships, but the Soviet Union was left with an unpaid Indonesian debt of over $1,000 million, 791 million of which was for military equipment; and in 1970 the debt rescheduling agreement finally reached between the Soviet and Indonesian governments provided for the period of repayment to be extended until the end of the century.[2]

In the early 1960s the approved model for a developing country was defined as an independent state of national democracy, which, based on a strong peasant-proletarian alliance with *petit bourgeois* support, could prepare the way for 'non-capitalist' development. Such a regime must be anti-imperialist, friendly towards the Soviet Union, and ready both to execute radical social and economic reforms and to give local communist parties full freedom of political action. But by 1964 Nasser, who did not treat Egyptian communists kindly, had been made a Hero of the Soviet Union. The role of local communist parties was now defined as that of friend and assistant of the national democrats: cold comfort for the parties concerned and grist to the Chinese mill. By the end of the decade, developing countries were broadly divided into three categories: those which had adopted the path of 'non-capitalist', or 'progressive social', development; those trying to strengthen their national independence and to create a modern economy with the broad participation of the national bourgeoisie; and those accepting a semi-colonial way of life and acting as the accomplices of imperialist exploiters. And in 1971 it was recognized by a Soviet theorist that in many, if not in most, of the developing Asian and African countries, no forces except the national democrats were capable of 'a nation-wide struggle for the attainment of the aims of the present stage of revolution'.[3] National democrats might well be army officers, as in Peru, whose military regime received Soviet support after the *coup* of October 1968. In short, the Khrushchevian belief that 'within the briefest period of time the overwhelming majority of former colonies would allegedly take, if not the socialist, then at least the non-capitalist, road of development' was acknowledged as an 'illusion'.[4]

Under the present Soviet leadership policy towards the Third World has become selective and pragmatic. The terms of Soviet aid are less generous than those of either the Chinese or the International Development Association: a Soviet loan, granted in inconvertible roubles, is usually repayable over 10–15 years, with interest at $2\frac{1}{2}$–3 per cent. Any comparison of the Soviet aid programme with that of the United States or of any major Western country is difficult, because Soviet aid figures are not published; according to the OECD's 1972 *Review of Development Cooperation*, three-quarters of the Soviet aid flow went to communist countries; and confusion frequently arises between amounts of Soviet aid offered and Soviet aid actually delivered. On a rough estimate, Soviet bloc and Chinese aid delivered to non-communist developing countries totalled about 600 million dollars in 1972, half of which came from the Soviet Union. But the rising flow of debt repayments from the developing countries to the latter probably reduced the net Soviet aid flow to the Third World from a high point of 300 million dollars, at the time of Khrushchev's fall, to less than 100 million dollars in 1972—a year in which one of the four major recipients of Soviet aid, economic and military, India, paid to the Soviet Union 35 million dollars more than the value of Soviet deliveries, even though India had been provided by the Soviet Union with a multi-million dollar turnkey project—the Bhilai steelworks, which was on a scale comparable to that of the Aswan High Dam in Egypt. It is significant that at the Second United Nations Conference on Trade and Development, held in Delhi in 1968, the representatives of the Soviet Union and its allies abstained from voting on the resolution committing developed countries to adopt one per cent of gross national product as the target for their annual transfer of resources to the developing countries.

American intervention in Vietnam made this country a special case for the Soviet Union, justifying almost any level of expenditure. Of all the aid programmes ever undertaken by the Soviet Government, the one that must have troubled the cost-effectiveness experts in the Kremlin most is the aid, direct and indirect, extended to Cuba. Whichever government originally suggested the installing of Soviet missiles in Cuba in 1962, it is certain that the negotiations for their removal were carried on over Castro's head; it is therefore not surprising that for the rest of the decade he remained a difficult ally for the Soviet Union. The difficulties were both economic and political. In the early years after the Cuban Revolution, its leaders looked to a combination of rapid industrialization and the establishment of giant state farms, run by officials responsible to highly centralized direction from Havana, as the key to economic progress, with unfortunate results,[5] which were accentuated by Che Guevara's belief that Cuba had already entered the final Marxist phase of pure communism. Under the terms of the original trade agreement negotiated by Mikoyan during his visit to Havana in February 1960, the Soviet Government had agreed to buy nearly 5 million tons of Cuban sugar over the next five years, and offered a credit of 100 million dollars in aid. At the end of 1963, in conditions bordering on economic chaos, Castro decided to abandon his original plan of economic autarky and to make agriculture the basis of Cuban economic development for the rest of the decade, sugar being given top priority. The Soviet Government was therefore obliged increasingly to underwrite the Cuban economy, mainly by taking annually rising quantities of Cuban sugar at prices higher than those on the world market. By 1973 it was estimated that in all, Cuba was costing the Soviet Union $1,500,000 a day and that repayment of the Cuban debt would last into the twenty-first century.

During the 1960s the basic political[6] difference between the Soviet Union and Cuba centred on the fact that Castro—who had come to power in Havana straight from his guerrilla base in the Sierra Maestra—continued to advocate the *via armada* (as opposed to the *via pacifica*) as the model for Latin American communist parties. At its XXIIIrd Congress the CPSU even found itself under Cuban fire for not doing more to help North Vietnam. For the Soviet Union, the Cuban alliance was an irritant in cultivating relationships with other Latin American countries. But Castro's qualified support of the invasion of Czechoslovakia (which, in a speech on 28 August 1968, he described as a bitter necessity)[7] marked the beginning of the closer alignment between the policies of the two countries that has followed in the present decade.

After what happened in October 1962, and with the Chinese as watchful rivals in Havana, Soviet historians would no doubt argue that no Soviet Government could have acted towards Cuba in any other way during the rest of the decade. Yet, if at some future conference Soviet and American historians were invited to re-write, with the advantage of hindsight, a fresh scenario for US-Cuban and Soviet-Cuban relations during the 1960s, it is hard to believe that they could not devise better policies than those actually pursued by their governments towards Cuba, and that they could not suggest ways in which both could have contributed to the development of a small island inhabited by a gifted people, with great natural resources.

The Middle East

If the Cuban aid programme was in financial terms the most costly legacy of Khrushchev's policy towards the Third World, in political and strategic terms by far the most important was the Soviet commitment to the Middle East, which in the 1970s was to replace South-East

Asia as the most explosive source of conflict in the world. Today this commitment has two aspects: one strategic and the other politico-economic. The former antedates Khrushchev, and for that matter the Russian Revolution itself. The traditional thrust of Tsarist diplomacy towards the Straits and southward from Central Asia was resumed by Stalin immediately after the Second World War (Stalin's request for a base in the Straits, the territorial claims made against Turkey, formally dropped only after Stalin's death in 1953, and the Azerbaijan episode of 1945–6). A glance at the map is enough to show that strategically the Middle East is for Russia—whether Tsarist or Soviet—what the Caribbean is for the United States: its backyard. After the failure of this forward policy towards Turkey and Iran in 1946, Stalin withdrew to his European fortress. Under Khrushchev, the strategic aspect of Soviet policy towards the Middle East received a fresh emphasis, beginning with the Egyptian arms deal. (Formally the arms then supplied to Egypt were Czechoslovak, but the deal must have received the approval of the Soviet Government, which by 1958 had assumed the main responsibility for equipping the Egyptian armed forces.) Soviet financing of the Aswan Dam and Soviet purchase of Egyptian cotton at premium prices in the mid-1950s added a new dimension to Soviet foreign policy: politico-economic rivalry in the Middle East with the Western countries whose exclusive preserve it had been ever since the break-up of the Ottoman Empire nearly forty years earlier. Among these countries Britain remained the predominant power in the Middle East until the collapse of the Anglo-French Suez expedition in 1956. The steady erosion of British power in the area left a vacuum which the United States found it hard to fill, because of its commitment to Israel, and which it would have been hard for the Soviet Union not to fill, even though it had been one of the State of Israel's original sponsors in 1948. As the Soviet Union gradually filled this vacuum, so too it assumed the role of the champion of the Arab cause against Israel, in the process acquiring a position in the Middle East which recalls that of Tsarist Russia in the Balkans.

The Middle East may indeed be described, in politico-strategic terms, as the Balkans of the late twentieth century. Thus, in pursuing its new policy in the Middle East, the Soviet Union has had to contend with the volatility of Arab politics, as well as with the problem of underpinning this policy with respectable ideological justification. In the northern tier, Soviet national interests—in particular mistrust of the CENTO[8] Alliance—obliged the Soviet Union to mend its fences with Turkey and

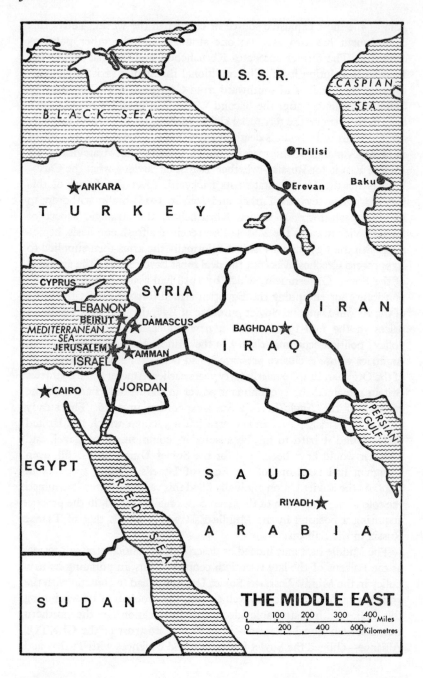

THE MIDDLE EAST

Iran. This rapprochement was cemented under the collective leadership by official visits paid by Kosygin to Teheran in 1968 and to Ankara in 1966. (The Soviet-Iranian agreement of January 1966, whereby Iran undertook to deliver natural gas to the Soviet Union for twelve years, in return for industrial projects in Iran carried out by the latter, also marked a turning point in Soviet oil policy.) Although all Arabs are anti-imperialist in the sense that they are anti-Israeli, the political spectrum of Arab regimes is extremely broad. The Soviet leadership began by attempting to define some of the Arab states as 'progressive social'—for example, the Ba'ath regimes in Iraq and Syria. But in the Middle East, as elsewhere, this attempt has ended with the acknowledgement of reality quoted in the previous section of this chapter; and the touchstone of Soviet policy in Arab eyes has become more and more the Soviet leadership's handling of the dispute between the Arab states and Israel.

The Arab-Israeli dispute

This dispute erupted again in June 1967. Soviet motives for stoking the fire that led to the Six Day War are obscure. On 21 April 1967, presumably under Arab pressure, the Soviet Government addressed a note of protest to Israel against the air raid which—as a reprisal—the Israeli Air Force had carried out on Damascus a fortnight earlier (previously the Soviet press had spoken only of border clashes). At the end of April Kosygin had talks in Moscow with a visiting Egyptian delegation, led by Anwar Sadat. According to a speech made by Nasser after his defeat, the delegation was told, presumably by the Soviet Prime Minister, that Israel was concentrating troops with the premeditated intent of attacking Syria. When Nasser closed the Straits of Tiran in May, the Soviet Government did not condone his action; but the Soviet press gave no hint of disapproval; on the contrary, *Pravda* of 26 May stated that the gulf waters could not be regarded as Israeli waters under any United Nations decision, three days after the Soviet Government had declared that aggressors in the Middle East would face not only the united strength of the Arab countries, but also a firm riposte from the Soviet Union. On this evidence, either the Soviet leadership completely mis-calculated the military situation on the ground, or 'no one calculated at all'; in any event, having urged restraint on both sides, Brezhnev, Kosygin, and the Defence Minister left Moscow, to spend the critical days from 31 May to 4 June inspecting the Soviet fleet at Murmansk and Archangel.[9]

Whatever the explanation for Soviet behaviour before the Six Day War, there is no doubt about the energy with which the Soviet Government reacted to it. The Soviet Prime Minister used the hot line to the US President more than once. After the cease-fire, a summit meeting of communist states was held in Europe. Soviet leaders visited their Middle Eastern friends; Soviet warships were sent to Alexandria and Port Said; the vast Egyptian losses of equipment were swiftly made good; and although the Algerian President publicly blamed the Russians* for the humiliating Arab defeat—which left Israeli forces occupying the Sinai peninsula, the west bank of Jordan, and the Golan heights in Syria— the Soviet position in the Arab world and the eastern Mediterranean was soon restored. In November 1967 the Soviet Union intervened militarily in the Yemeni civil war, from which Egyptian troops were at last pulling out, and in the following year an agreement on military and technical assistance was signed with the new South Yemen Government, which was established after the British withdrawal from Aden. In the Cyprus crisis of November 1967, the Soviet Government succeeded in maintaining an even-handed posture towards both the Turkish and the Cyprus governments, while blaming the West for allegedly pursuing policies in Cyprus which brought two NATO allies—Turkey and Greece—to the brink of war.

Meanwhile, in the aftermath of the Six Day War, Kosygin led the Soviet delegation to the United Nations. (While he was in the United States he met President Johnson at Glasboro, without result.) On the Arab-Israeli dispute the Security Council finally adopted a compromise resolution on 22 November, for which the British delegation was entitled to the credit. This resolution was an ingenious attempt to square the circle. The preamble to the resolution having emphasized, among other things 'the inadmissibility of the acquisition of territory by war and the need to work for a just and lasting peace, in which every state in the area can live in security.' the resolution itself consisted of three points. The first of these was:

the establishment of a just and lasting peace in the Middle East, which should include the application of both the following principles:

(i) Withdrawal of Israel armed forces from territories occupied in the recent conflict;

(ii) Termination of claims or states of belligerency, and respect for and acknowledgement of the sovereignty, territorial integrity and political

---

* The Russians themselves blamed both the superiority of Israeli equipment and Nasser's betrayal by the military bourgeoisie.

independence of every state in the area and their right to live in peace within secure and recognized boundaries free from acts or threats of force.

The resolution's second point affirmed the necessity for:

(a) guaranteeing freedom of navigation through international waterways in the area;

(b) achieving a just settlement of the refugee problem;

(c) guaranteeing the territorial inviolability and political independence of every state in the area, through measures including the establishment of demilitarized zones.

Thirdly, the Security Council requested the Secretary-General of the United Nations to designate a Special Representative to go to the Middle East, in order to help to achieve a peaceful and accepted settlement in accordance with the provisions and principles of the resolution.

This resolution, which the Security Council was to re-affirm in 1969 and in 1973, remains at the centre of the dispute. Whether it would have been passed unanimously if there were a definite article in the Russian language is an interesting speculation: the Soviet Union has supported its Arab clients in interpreting the word 'territories' in 1(i) of the resolution as meaning all 'the territories',[10] whereas it has been a cardinal point of the Israeli case that there are certain territories which they could never reasonably be expected to return to Arab hands, such as the Golan Heights, Sharm-el-Sheikh, and Jerusalem itself. U Thant's Special Representative, Gunnar Jarring, then Swedish Ambassador in Moscow, made repeated efforts over the years that followed to fulfil the mission entrusted to him. The main rocks that he hit were: on the Israeli side, their unwillingness not only to return all that they had conquered but also to negotiate other than directly with the Arab governments concerned; and on the Arab side, a matching reluctance to negotiate before a complete Israeli withdrawal—not to mention the special problem of Jerusalem and the future of the Arab refugees, their numbers swollen by the outcome of the 1967 war.[11]

The year 1969 opened with a Soviet initiative: on 2 January the Soviet Government suggested the outline of a settlement to the British, French, and United States governments. This led in the course of the year to discussions between the Representatives of the Four Powers in New York and to a Soviet-American bilateral dialogue, in which the two governments, as well as negotiating with each other, were also acting as lawyers for their respective clients in the Middle East. On the ground matters grew steadily worse. By April the United Nations

Secretary-General reported that open warfare was being waged: the War of Attrition, as it came to be called. Against a background of Arab guerrilla operations conducted in the territories occupied by Israel, in Israel itself, and in many other countries, the Egyptian Army used its superiority in artillery to conduct a shelling duel across the Suez Canal, while the Israeli Air Force, using the Phantom aircraft supplied by the United States, attacked targets nearer and nearer Cairo. These attacks were to lead the Soviet Union, early in 1970, to embark on a massive, direct intervention in Egypt. This will be described in later chapters; for present purposes, it must be recorded as marking a watershed in Soviet policy towards the Middle East and the Third World, and in the Soviet relationship with the United States.

NOTES

1. For example, the affair of Aníbal Escalante: see Stephen Clissold, op. cit., pp. 294 ff.
2. By 1970 the joint total of military and commercial Indonesian debt to the Soviet Union was still $750 million. The $400 million owed by Indonesia to Eastern European Governments was not rescheduled until 1971–2.
3. The evolution of Soviet aid policy is traced in ch. 6 of W. W. Kulski, *The Soviet Union in World Affairs 1964–1972*, Syracuse University Press, New York, 1973. For the threefold classification, see p. 161. The Soviet theorist is Ulyanovsky whose article in *International Affairs* is quoted in *The Conduct of Soviet Foreign Policy*, eds. Erik Hoffman and F. Fleron, Aldine and Atherton, Chicago, 1971, pp. 410 ff.
4. This 'illusion' is specifically attributed to the 'late fifties and in particular the early sixties' by V. Tiagunenko ,in *Nekotorye problemy natsional'no— osvoboditel'nykh revoliutsii v svete Leninizma*, 1970, quoted by Kulski, op. cit. pp. 188–9.
5. These were described soon afterwards by René Dumont, a left-wing writer sympathetic towards the Cuban Revolution, in his book *Cuba: socialisme et développement*, Editions du Seuil, Paris, 1964. In 1961/2, for example, only half the fruit and vegetables available in Cuba were collected by the Land Reform Agency, which was headed by a geographer, Professor Nuñez Jimenez; and in 1963 agricultural productivity on the state farms was less than half that in what remained of the private sector.
6. The Soviet-Cuban political balance sheet has been drawn up by Clissold, op. cit., pp. 42–59, although given the date of publication (1970), he had to end this chapter of his book with a question mark.
7. Ibid., pp. 304–6, which gives the full text. By the time of the Non-Aligned Conference held in Algiers in 1973, Castro had become an out-and-out defender of the Soviet Union against all comers: see *Pravda* of 9 September 1973, reporting his speech of the previous day.
8. The Central Treaty Organization, consisting of Turkey, Iran, Pakistan, and Great Britain. This succeeded the Baghdad Pact, from which Iraq withdrew after the *coup d'état* in 1958, in which both the King and the Prime Minister

were assassinated. Its headquarters was moved from Baghdad to Ankara in 1959.

9. Tatu, op. cit., 'Postscript', pp. 532 ff., gives the Soviet aspect of the chronology of the crisis. This particular incident is refered to on p. 536, from which the quotation is also taken.

10. Which is what the French text of the resolution said.

11. Of an estimated Palestinian Arab population of about three million, roughly half are now outside the 1948 frontiers of Palestine, and a further 600,000 are living in the West Bank area and the Gaza Strip under Israeli rule. 1,300,000 Palestinians are registered as refugees qualifying for United Nations assistance.

7

EUROPE

New ideas

Under Stalin, Europe was central to Soviet foreign policy. Under Khrushchev, in spite of his adventures in the Third World, it remained so. The heart of the matter was Germany. In 1958 the Soviet Government put forward a draft Treaty of Friendship and Cooperation of European States; and in 1960 the Warsaw Pact governments made, not for the first time, a proposal for a non-aggression pact between the NATO and the Warsaw Pact groups of states. Both these proposals would have involved recognition of the German Democratic Republic by the West, and hence the jettisoning of the Hallstein doctrine, which ostracized the GDR. In the 1960s new ideas were beginning to be discussed, both in Western and in Eastern Europe.

In Eastern Europe, the new look began in Romania, from which Soviet troops had been withdrawn in 1958, in the aftermath of the convulsions that had wracked Eastern Europe after the XXth Congress of the CPSU two years before. The Romanian attempt to mediate between the Russians and the Chinese in 1964 was part of a broad decision to pursue an independent foreign policy, based on what the Romanian leadership perceived as their country's national interests, while at the same time allowing no relaxation of party-imposed discipline at home. They began in the field of foreign trade, claiming the right to trade with whom they pleased, and rejected the Soviet proposal put forward in COMECON in 1962, for the division of labour between members of that organization in accordance with the directives of a central planning organ.[1] The new Romanian constitution of 1965 included a provision intended to prevent Romania from becoming involved in war except by its own decision. In May 1966 Ceausescu, who had become leader of the Romanian Communist Party the year before, delivered a speech[2] in which he publicly attacked the concept of military blocs and touched a raw Soviet nerve by referring to the lost provinces of Bessarabia and Northern Bukovina (acquired by the Soviet Union as a fruit of the Nazi-Soviet Pact of 1939). Romania was the first Eastern European country, other than the Soviet Union itself, to enter into diplomatic relations with the Federal Republic of Germany; and the Soviet Union had to acquiesce in Romania's maintaining relations with Israel after the 1967 war—and ultimately in her resumption of relations with China, where Ceausescu was to receive a lavish welcome in 1971.

'Polycentrism' (as it was described in the Italian Communist leader Togliatti's memorandum, published in *Pravda* after his death in September 1964) was matched in the West by de Gaulle's concept of Europe from the Atlantic to the Urals. According to Soviet theory, relations between communist countries are unique, because they involve not only their governments but also their whole peoples, led by their respective Communist parties.[3] The international obligations of the working class do not permit of any divergence of interest between one communist country and another. Nevertheless, the Soviet leadership decided to put up with the Romanians, and to foster a special Franco-Soviet relationship, because with it went the idea of Europe for the Europeans—not to mention the gap in the NATO order of battle left by the French forces, which de Gaulle withdrew from integrated international command before his visit to Moscow in 1966.

Most important of all, *Ostpolitik* was being re-thought in West Germany itself. On 26 January 1965, the *Frankfurter Allegemeine Zeitung* published a memorandum on this subject written by Willy Brandt the previous August. This memorandum took as its premise that it was a Western interest to support the independence of East European nations and their efforts to use their field of manoeuvre. Such a policy should concentrate on economic and cultural measures (linked with 'humanitarian regulations'), respecting each East European state as an equal partner, and taking into account its military and ideological links. Brandt foresaw, though he described the time as not yet ripe for it, a major increase in East-West trade, for which the Western countries would have to be prepared to grant substantial economic and financial support, and the development of joint projects on a European scale. The memorandum stopped short of recommending any change in the policy of refusing to recognize the Soviet Zone of Germany as an independent state, but contemplated greater economic and cultural contact between it and the Federal Republic, and expressed the hope that increased contact between the West and other Eastern European countries would affect the Soviet Zone as well. And towards the end, the memorandum recalled Brandt's remark in a speech made in New York in May 1964, that it was time to acknowledge the fact that Europe does not end at the Iron Curtain.

Six weeks before Brandt's article was published, the Polish Foreign Minister briefly remarked, at the United Nations General Assembly, that the time was ripe for convening a conference of all European states, to examine the problem of European security as a whole. (Rapacki expressly added that both the Soviet Union and the United States should take part.) On 20 January 1965 the political Consultative Committee of the Warsaw Pact countries endorsed the Polish initiative, proposing a conference of European states (with no mention of the United States or Canada) to discuss measures for collective security in Europe,[4] and followed this up at Bucharest, in July 1966, with a long 'Declaration on Strengthening Peace and Security in Europe'.[5] This foresaw an all-European declaration providing for pledges on the part of signatory states to be guided in their relations with one another by the interests of peace, to settle disputed questions only by peaceful means, to hold consultations and exchange information on questions of mutual interest, and to assist in the comprehensive development of economic, scientific-technical, and cultural ties with one another: a proposal repeated in the Karlovy Vary statement of European communist parties of 26 April 1967, according to which European security[6] depended on:

respecting the realities of post-war Europe . . . the inviolability of the existing frontiers in Europe, especially the Oder-Neisse frontier and the frontier between the two German states . . . the existence of two sovereign German states with equal rights . . . denying the Federal German Republic access to nuclear weapons in any form either European or Atlantic[7] . . . recognizing the Munich Pact as invalid from the very moment of its conclusion.

The Karlovy Vary statement was important not only because it made it clear that the idea of a European conference was already linked in the minds of its proposers with the German question, but also because it followed the announcement in the Bundestag, in December 1966, of the new *Ostpolitik* proposals of the Grand Coalition Government of Christian Democrats and Social Democrats, in which Brandt held the post of Foreign Minister. Although these proposals stopped well short of recognizing the German Democratic Republic, with whom a policy of 'regulated coexistence' was envisaged, they marked the beginning of the end of the Hallstein doctrine of 1955, whereby the Federal German Government had refused to recognize any government—with the single exception of the Soviet Union—which recognized the German Democratic Republic. Romania, which boycotted the Karlovy Vary conference, established diplomatic relations with the Federal Republic on this basis without delay. The East Germans and the Poles denounced the new policy as German revanchism in a new guise. After a period of apparent hesitation, the Soviet Union joined the Germans and the Poles. As though to emphasize the unity of the Eastern European bloc, in the course of 1967 all its members, except Romania, signed bilateral treaties of mutual assistance with the German Democratic Republic, and the Soviet Union began to bring its bilateral treaties with each member country up to date. But in the second half of 1967 and the first half of 1968 the Soviet Government did not feel inhibited from engaging in bilateral talks with the Federal German Government on the possibility of an agreement renouncing the use of force—with no result, although the talks proved to be the forerunner of the Soviet–German negotiations of 1970.

No direct response was made by the Western Alliance until the very end of 1969. But after the ministerial meeting held in Brussels in December 1967 the communiqué had annexed to it the Harmel Report on the future tasks of the Alliance.[8] The essence of this report was the concept that military security and a policy of *détente* were not contradictory, but complementary. The report spoke of 'realistic measures designed to further a *détente* in East-West relations', not as the final goal, but as 'part of a long-term process to promote better relations and to foster a European settlement'. Its final pragraph contained the first mention of balanced force reductions. Six months later—the French abstaining—NATO Ministers meeting at Reykjavik formally put forward a proposal for such reductions in Europe, and invited the Warsaw Pact countries to 'join in this search for progress towards peace'. But in August 1968 the dialogue was brusquely interrupted, when the forces of the Soviet Union, together with some units supplied by its Warsaw Pact allies (excluding Romania), invaded Czechoslovakia— some half million men in all.

Czechoslovakia

Ironically, it was Czechoslovakia, where Stalin's gigantic statue had been left standing in Prague long after Khrushchev had denounced him at the XXth CPSU Congress, that produced the most serious threat to Soviet authority in Eastern Europe since the Hungarian Revolution, and, in the process, retarded the Soviet grand design for Europe by one year. The origins of the Czechoslovak upheaval were complex: political (general dissatisfaction with fifteen years of rule by Antonin Novotny, who during most of this period combined the offices of President and First Secretary of the Czechoslovak Communist Party); regional (the Slovaks demanded the same rights as the Czechs); and economic. E. G. Liberman's thesis on profitability had been published in *Pravda* in September 1962; it was not followed up until three years later, when the Soviet leadership introduced a limited measure of economic reform, which was attacked by the Chinese as a big step towards the restoration of capitalism and 'a new *kulak* economy'. The success of the German economic reforms has already been mentioned; the Hungarian reform began in 1968; the Czechoslovak reform, approved in 1965, began on 1 January 1967, but was diluted by the conservatism of party officials. On all these grounds Brezhnev, who visited Prague in December 1967, cannot have been greatly surprised when Novotny was obliged to resign as First Secretary of the Czechoslovak Communist Party in January 1968 (three months later he was succeeded as President by General Svoboda). His successor as First Secretary, Alexander Dubcek, the Moscow-trained First Secretary of the Slovak Communist Party, may well have seemed reliable enough at first. From start to finish he was at pains to stress his commitment to the communist cause; and hence to keep Czechoslovakia in COMECON and in the Warsaw Pact. Indeed he reversed the Romanian experiment: his 'socialism with a human face' was loyal to Moscow abroad and became increasingly heterodox at home.

There is no evidence that when Dubcek, who combined diffidence with obstinacy in a remarkable way, took over in Prague in January 1968, he had any intention of liberalizing the Czechoslovak political system as he did during the next seven months, although he must have approved of Ota Sik's economic reforms. He was borne along by the wave of popular expectations, rather like Wladyslaw Gomulka in Poland twelve years earlier, but—unlike Gomulka—he did not drive it back again. Events moved so rapidly that on 2 May *Rude Pravo* was able to

EASTERN EUROPE

write of the springlike blossoming of a new public life and of the breath of fresh air brought by democratic freedoms. It might have been nearer the truth at that moment to describe Dubcek as unwilling to rule the country by force and unqualified to rule it by democratic means. He therefore fell between two stools. For example, having discontinued press censorship in March, at the end of May the Ministry of Interior announced that the formation of new political parties—in particular, this applied to the resuscitation of the Social Democratic Party—would be considered illegal. Yet the Ministry allowed a preparatory committee of the 'club of engaged non-party members' to operate, recognized the statute of the society for human rights, and permitted the Communist Party-sponsored youth organization to divide into a number of independent groups. Soviet influence in the Ministry of Interior and in the Czechoslovak Army was curbed. Worst of all perhaps in Soviet eyes was the Czechoslovak Party's decision, taken in May, to hold a Congress on 9 September, which was expected to consist of delegates holding reformist views.

Soviet concern at this trend of events was expressed to Dubcek and his colleagues at their first confrontation with representatives of five Warsaw Pact powers (Romania alone being absent) at Dresden on 23 March. This concern was heightened by the Czechoslovak Central Committee's approval, on 5 April, of the liberal Action Programme. On 27 June seventy prominent Czechoslovaks published a manifesto calling for even more radical reform, *The Two Thousand Words*, which led *Pravda* on 11 July to draw an ominous comparison between Czechoslovakia in 1968 and Hungary in 1956.[9] The Warsaw Letter of 15 July,[10] addressed to the Czechoslovaks by their five Warsaw Pact allies (they themselves had refused to attend the meeting), laid particular emphasis on the Czechoslovak Party's loss of control of the mass media. Of their allies' chief anxieties, the first was political: the fear that the Czechoslovak Communist Party would sooner or later lose control of the levers of power. ('Undermining the leading role of the Communist Party leads to the liquidation of socialist democracy and of the socialist system . . .') The second was military. ('The frontiers of the socialist world have moved to the centre of Europe, to the Elbe and the Sumav mountains.') The third was a bit of both: fear of West Germany, and the response among the ruling circles in Czechoslovakia which the Federal Republic's overtures were allegedly meeting. The Warsaw Letter was followed by a Soviet demand that the Czechoslovak Presidium should meet the Soviet Politburo, either in Moscow or in the

Ukraine. The Czechoslovaks agreed to the meeting, but succeeded in persuading the Soviet Politburo, all but two of whose members attended, to hold the meeting in Czechoslovakia.

Czechoslovakia was invaded on the night of 20/21 August, in spite of the apparent agreement reached between the Soviet and Czechoslovak party leaderships at Cierna[11] and between the leaders of all six parties at Bratislava,[12] at the end of July and the beginning of August respectively. The Czechoslovaks seem to have left the former meeting convinced that the Soviet troops who were conducting manoeuvres in Czechoslovakia would leave their country; that the Warsaw Letter was abrogated; and that Czechoslovak sovereignty was assured. Equally the Soviet leadership appear to have believed that the Czechoslovak leaders were now committed to regaining control over the mass media. The wording of the Bratislava Declaration was woolly. In any event, the political factor must have loomed larger in Soviet eyes after 10 August, when proposals for revising the statutes of the Czechoslovak Communist Party were published, condoning what in orthodox eyes was the crime of fractionalism: the right of the minority to state its views in public after a majority decision had been passed. Other visitors to Czechoslovakia during August included Presidents Tito and Ceausescu, Janos Kadar, and Ulbricht. The popular welcome given to the two presidents must have infuriated the Russians; Kadar, anxious for the future of his own economic reform, may well have advised Dubcek to slacken the pace; Ulbricht can only have reported in black. Throughout the summer the Soviet leaders were under pressure from Ulbricht and Gomulka, the second of whom feared the effect on his own regime (weakened by disorders that had taken place in Poland in March) if the Dubcek experiment succeeded. It was also widely believed that the Soviet leaders, particularly Piotr Shelest, then First Secretary of the Ukrainian Communist Party, were anxious lest the Czechoslovak liberal infection should cross the border into the Ukraine. Thus, the Russians were influenced by a domino theory in Eastern Europe similar to the one that obsessed American thinking on South-East Asia.

Was it the political or the military factor that in the end prevailed within the Soviet Politburo? Bismarck is reputed to have said that the master of Bohemia is the master of Europe. At the time of Dubcek's visit to Moscow in May, *Le Monde* published a report (later denied), according to which the Soviet Army was ready to answer appeals from faithful Czechoslovak communists for help in safeguarding socialism;[13] and Kovalev's article published in *Pravda* of 26 September alluded to the possibility that NATO troops might approach Soviet borders and that 'the commonwealth of European socialist countries might be dismembered'. (The same article included a warning shot against Yugoslavia, pointing out that non-aligned socialist states owed their national independence to the power of the socialist commonwealth and primarily to that of the Soviet Union.)

In my view, the political factor carried the greater weight. But the question remains why the members of the Soviet Politburo, beset by both political and military anxieties, took so long to make up their minds to take what the official History of Soviet Foreign Policy describes as an extraordinary but essential measure. (The role of the Central Committee seems to have been purely formal: it met on 20 August a few hours before the invasion began.) The delay in deciding on the invasion strongly suggests that there was a division of opinion within the Soviet leadership. No doubt all members of the Politburo must have hoped in the early months of the Dubcek regime that the combined pressure of five of Czechoslovakia's allies would eventually prevail without the need to resort to arms; and some of them may have gone on hoping against hope, as late as August. Those who believed in the *Westpolitik* of the Karlovy Vary meeting must have been prepared to go to considerable lengths to maintain the image of a Soviet Union dedicated to a peaceful Europe. On the other hand, with the Americans embroiled in a presidential electoral campaign as well as in Vietnam, and remembering the Western reaction to events in East Berlin in 1953 and Budapest in 1956, they can hardly have feared a Western response strong enough to outweigh the disadvantages of a Czechoslovakia ruled by reformists. As the summer went by, they could not have failed to note Western signals that any response would in no circumstances be military, but purely political. And politically, they had more reason to be concerned at the effect on the world communist movement, above all on China. It is also conceivable that the Soviet military, whose doctrine 'directs its primary attention towards the preparing of the nation and the armed forces for a world-wide thermonuclear war',[14] did not relish the prospect of the Soviet Army being employed in this uncongenial police role, more especially since the operation turned out to be based on the false premise that pro-Soviet members of the Presidium of the Czechoslovak Communist Party would at once come forward to take over from the leaders whom the invaders had imprisoned. It remains an interesting sidelight on the composition of the invasion force that it included units equipped with tactical nuclear weapons.[15]

The answer to the question why the Soviet leadership hesitated would throw a great deal of light not only on the whole Czechoslovak affair, but on the decision-making process in the Soviet Union and the relationship between the CPSU and the Soviet military. Once the decision to invade Czechoslovakia was taken, what it did demonstrate was both the paramount importance to the Soviet Union of maintaining its glacis in Eastern Europe and the frailty of the Eastern European communist regimes (Bulgaria being perhaps the only exception). As a military operation, the massive invasion of Czechoslovakia was effectively conducted. It is no reflection on the competence of the Soviet military planners to add that it could hardly have been otherwise, given that Warsaw Pact manoeuvres had been continuously in progress either in Czechoslovakia or on its borders since the beginning of June. But it was met with equally massive—though largely non-violent—opposition; Ludvik Svoboda refused to negotiate on the formation of a new government; and it became apparent that the invaders had no plan to cope with this contingency. Worse than that, they failed to gain control of either the mass media (which continued to operate, clandestinely) or the telecommunications network. The Soviet Union was therefore obliged to achieve its aims in Czechoslovakia according to a time-scale of months, instead of hours. This involved first releasing Dubcek, who had been abducted to the Soviet Union, together with other members of the Presidium, and then tolerating his remaining in office as First Secretary until the following April, when he was succeeded by Gustav Husak. But Dubcek had to accept, in October, a treaty sanctioning the stationing of Soviet troops on Czechoslovak territory (which not even Novotny had done), and he had to invalidate the XIVth Congress of the Czechoslovak Communist Party, which had met in a factory soon after the invasion. Slowly under Dubcek, and more effectively under Husak, Czechoslovak political life returned to normal. For his part, Dubcek refused to pronounce a self-criticism, and was stripped successively of his offices, including his short-lived mission to Turkey, and finally of his party membership.

Having done what was required of him (among other things, on 9 September 1969 the Czechoslovak Presidium rescinded its condemnation of the invasion a year before), Husak received the formal Soviet blessing during a visit to Moscow in October. That the Soviet leadership continued to feel uneasy about the intervention and the continuing presence of large Soviet forces in Czechoslovakia—eventually reduced to five divisions—is suggested by the fact that they sought to justify both by what has come to be known in the West as the Brezhnev doctrine. This was already implicit in the concluding paragraphs of the statement published in *Pravda* of 22 August, which declared flatly that counter-revolution could not be allowed 'to wrest Czechoslovakia from the family of socialist states', and described the defence of Czechoslovakia as an international socialist duty. It was also anticipated in the *Pravda* article of 26 September, which described socialism as indivisible and declared its defence to be the common cause of all communists. And although three years later—speaking at a banquet given in his honour by Tito in Belgrade on 22 September 1971—Brezhnev himself denied the existence of the 'so-called new doctrine of limited sovereignty',[16] he remains on the record as having told the Vth Polish Party Congress on 12 November 1968:

when internal and external forces, hostile to socialism, seek to reverse the development of any socialist country whatsoever in the direction of the restoration of the capitalist order, when a threat to the cause of socialism arises in that country, a threat to the security of the socialist commonwealth as a whole—this already becomes not only a problem of the people of the country concerned, but also a common problem and the concern of all socialist countries.[17]

The long term results of the Czechoslovak people's passive defiance of the Soviet Union, which threw a glaring light on the poverty of the Soviet concept of the socialist commonwealth, twenty years after the Prague *coup d'état*, will be considered later. The immediate effect of the Soviet intervention was a general outcry of horror. Not all the Soviet Union's non-communist friends joined in, however. (Cairo radio took the Soviet side in its broadcasts; so did the Iraqi Government; and Mrs. Gandhi, though expressing profound concern, blocked a parliamentary resolution condemning the invasion.) Perhaps the European non-ruling communist parties suffered most damage: only the Luxembourg and the Greek Cypriot communist parties supported the Soviet Union. Both the Romanians and the Yugoslavs publicly condemned the invasion of Czechoslovakia; the following February, when Tito met Ceausescu in Romania, their communiqué emphasized the importance of respect for the principles of the United Nations charter (an indirect attack on the Brezhnev doctrine). In March the Romanian Government adopted regulations making it impermissible for the troops of other Warsaw Pact countries to enter Romania (a country surrounded on all sides by Warsaw Pact countries, except for its common frontier with Yugoslavia) without Romanian consent, no doubt recalling the Warsaw

Pact manoeuvres of the previous June in Czechoslovakia. The Yugoslav leadership, for whom the years 1962–8 had been a period of rapprochement with the Soviet Union, took the Czechoslovak lesson to heart. The concept of total national defence was now adopted, whereby in the event of war units of the regular army would fight in depth alongside the newly created territorial defence force, transforming the whole country into a military 'hedgehog' and thus compelling the invader to fight all the way.[18] For the Chinese the invasion of Czechoslovakia (like the talks on the Arab-Israeli dispute) was an example of Soviet-American collusion. Much more important, seen from Peking, the Brezhnev doctrine offered a potential precedent for a Soviet attack on China.

East-West relations were frozen. In the communiqué[19] issued after their meeting in Brussels four months after the invasion, NATO foreign ministers continued to denounce both the invasion and the Brezhnev doctrine. Yet in May 1969 they announced their intention to explore possibilities for negotiation with the Soviet Union and the other countries of Eastern Europe.[20] The reason for this, at first sight remarkable, switch was neither Western cynicism nor Eastern cunning. Rather, both sides were led by a complex of reasons into a new era of multilateral diplomacy.[21]

NOTES

1. The Council of Mutual Economic Assistance was established in January 1949, as the Soviet response to the European Recovery Programme. The Soviet proposal of 1962 was abandoned and replaced by the concept of coordination of long-term planning. Some progress was achieved. In the following year *Intermetall*, which began as a programming centre for iron and steel planning, was set up in Budapest; the *Druzhba* pipeline began to bring Soviet oil to Eastern Europe; and in 1965 COMECON established an International Bank of Economic Cooperation and a joint Institute for Nuclear Research.
2. *New York Times*, 13 May 1966.
3. See, for example, *Istoriya Vneshnei Politiki SSSR*, vol. 2, pp. 61 ff.
4. Text in *Keesing's Contemporary Archives 1967/8*, p. 21981.
5. Text of communiqué in *Pravda*, 8 July 1966.
6. Compare *Istoriya Vneshnei Politiki SSSR*, vol. 2, p. 352.
7. The Soviet Government continued to be concerned at this prospect long after the American proposal for a NATO multilateral nuclear force (MLF), first launched in 1963, had been abandoned. Instead, in 1966 the NATO nuclear planning and consultative committee was established, which *Pravda* of 20 July 1965 described as 'perhaps even more dangerous than the MLF'. The NATO MLF nuclear planning proposals may have influenced the Soviet reversal of policy over the Non-Proliferation Treaty.

8. Text in *Keesing's Contemporary Archives 1967/8*, p. 22425. The original reason for the French abstention from the MBFR proposal was partly that French forces no longer formed part of the integrated NATO command and partly that the idea of negotiations conducted *de bloc à bloc* was contrary to French policy. As time went by the French Government also became increasingly opposed to any withdrawal of US forces from Europe in principle.

9. The name of the author, I. Aleksandrov, is a pseudonym used for articles cleared at the highest level of the CPSU. The text of *The 2,000 Words* was published in *East Europe*, August 1968, pp. 25–8. Aleksandrov described its authors as both counter-revolutionary and linked with reaction.

10. For the full text, see *Pravda*, 18 July 1968.

11. For the text of the Cierna communiqué, see *Washington Post*, 2 August 1968.

12. For the text of the Bratislava communiqué, see *Pravda*, 4 August 1968.

13. William Hayter, *Russia and the World: a Study of Soviet Foreign Policy*, Secker and Warburg, London, 1970, p. 37.

14. An excerpt from an article entitled 'The political side to Soviet military doctrine' and published in *Kommunist Vooruzhennykh Sil*, no. 22, November 1968: quoted by C. G. Jacobsen in *Soviet Strategy—Soviet Foreign Policy*, Glasgow University Press, 1972, pp. 191 ff.

15. Presumably, as Wolfe suggests (op. cit., p. 474), to serve notice on NATO that the Soviet Army meant business. But if so, on what possible sources of information did the planning staff base their supposition that any such notice was necessary? Perhaps the units formed part of the forces' establishment and it was simplest not to leave them behind.

16. *Keesing's Contemporary Archives 1971/2*, p. 24935.

17. *Pravda*, 13 November 1968.

18. The Soviet-Yugoslav rapprochement, coming after the stresses and strains imposed on Yugoslavia as an ideological pig in the middle during the early years of the Sino-Soviet dispute, was effected at the time of Tito's visit to Moscow in December 1962. For an account of 'hedgehog' defence, see *Survival*, March/April 1973, 'Yugoslav Total National Defence' by A. Ross Johnson, IISS, London, 1973, pp. 54 ff. A further rapprochement began with a visit by Gromyko to Belgrade in September 1969, although relations between the two countries have had their ups and downs since then.

19. *Keesing's Contemporary Archives 1969/70*, p. 23750. It stated that 'the use of force and the stationing in Czechoslovakia of Soviet forces not hitherto deployed there have aroused grave uncertainty about the situation and about the calculations and intentions of the USSR'; this uncertainty demanded 'great vigilance' on the part of the Allies.

20. Ibid., p. 23403.

21. As Nixon described it, in his report to the US Congress of 25 February 1971 on 'US foreign policy for the 1970s'.

PART THREE

The Brezhnev Foreign Policy:
The Years of Negotiation

8

THE TURNING POINT

By the middle of 1968 the momentum of nuclear logic carrying the Soviet Union and the United States towards each other had become so powerful that even the Czechoslovak tragedy could not arrest it for more than a brief interlude. The year 1969 was, both abroad and at home, a turning point for the Soviet Union.

On the eve of the invasion of Czechoslovakia—on 1 July 1968, five years after the signature of the Nuclear Test Ban Treaty—the three signatories of the earlier agreement, banning nuclear tests in the atmosphere, outer space, and under water, finally signed one of the most significant documents of international history since the Second World War: the Treaty on the Non-Proliferation of Nuclear Weapons. Under the terms of this treaty, each signatory possessing nuclear weapons undertook 'not to transfer to any recipient whatsoever nuclear weapons or other nuclear explosive devices or control over such weapons or explosive devices directly, or indirectly; and not in any way to assist, encourage, or induce any non-nuclear-weapon State to manufacture or otherwise acquire nuclear weapons or other nuclear explosive devices, or control over such weapons or explosive devices'. Each signatory not possessing nuclear weapons gave an undertaking complementary to that given by those possessing such weapons; and also undertook to accept certain safeguards designed to prevent diversion of nuclear energy from peaceful uses to nuclear weapons or other nuclear explosive devices. The treaty committed all parties to it 'to pursue negotiations in good faith on effective measures relating to cessation of the nuclear arms race at an early date and to nuclear disarmament, and on a treaty on general and complete disarmament, under strict and effective international control'. The treaty included a clause whereby it would not enter into force until forty-three signatories, including Great Britain, the Soviet Union, and the United States, had desposited their instruments of ratification (a point which was not reached until nearly two years later). A further clause laid down that five years after the treaty's entry into force the parties to the treaty would hold a conference in Geneva, in order to review its operation and to ensure that its purposes were being realized.[1]

Like its forerunner, this treaty was initially trilateral, in the sense that all three capitals—London, Moscow, and Washington—were designated for the depositing of instruments of ratification. But the second agreement was far more Soviet-American* than the first, because the protracted negotiations that led up to its signature were conducted in the forum of the Geneva Disarmament Conference, whose co-Chairmen were the Soviet Union and the United States, and because one of the conditions enabling other, non-nuclear, governments to accede to the non-proliferation treaty was in effect a joint guarantee offered them by the Soviet and the US governments. This guarantee took the form of Security Council Resolution No. 255, under the terms of which the Governments of Britain, the United States, and the USSR declared on 17 June 1968 that aggression with nuclear weapons, or the threat of such aggression, against a non-nuclear-weapon state 'would create a qualitatively new situation in which the nuclear-weapon states which are Permanent Members of the United Nations Security Council would have to act immediately through the Security Council to take the measures necessary to counter such aggression or to remove the threat of aggression. . . .' They also affirmed their intention, in such a contingency, to 'seek immediate Security Council action' to assist any non-nuclear-weapon signatory 'that is a victim of an act of aggression or an object of a threat of aggression in which nuclear weapons are used.'

Eighteen months before this second major nuclear treaty was signed, President Johnson had proposed that the governments of the United States and the Soviet Union should engage in what became known as

---

* The agreement was trilateral because France and China remained aloof, for the same reasons as in 1963. For the extent to which it was seen as bilateral in Washington as early as 1965, see William C. Foster (then Head of the State Department Disarmament Agency), 'New Directions in Arms Control and Disarmament', *Foreign Affairs*, 43, 1965, in which he suggested that a non-proliferation treaty would be worthwhile even if it meant some 'erosion of alliances resulting from the high degree of US-Soviet cooperation which will be required if a non-proliferation programme is to be successful'.

SALT—Strategic Arms Limitation Treaty—talks. There must have been divisions of opinion in Moscow about the wisdom of accepting this potentially far-reaching proposal, for it was not until June 1968 that the Soviet Foreign Minister formally did so, shortly before signing the Nuclear Non-Proliferation Treaty. One of the factors that no doubt weighed heavily in the Kremlin scales was the need to have rough numerical strategic parity at least in sight before accepting even the principle of such a negotiation. By 1969 the Soviet Union had at last achieved this goal. Although the United States remained well ahead in numbers of ballistic missile-launching submarines and strategic bombers, the Soviet Union had overtaken the United States in inter-continental ballistic missiles. The estimates of Soviet strengths for the end of the year were: 1,200 land-based ICBMs (including 270 massive SS-9s, with a yield of 20–25 megatons) against the United States' 1,054; 230 submarine-launched ballistic missiles against the United States' 656; and 150 strategic bombers against the United States' 540. The Soviet Union also had 67 anti-ballistic missile launchers round Moscow, while the United States had not so far deployed any.[2] On 20 January 1969—the day of Richard Nixon's inauguration as President of the United States—the Soviet Ministry of Foreign Affairs convened a special press conference in order to declare Soviet readiness to begin a serious exchange of views with the United States on the 'mutual limitation and subsequent reduction of strategic nuclear delivery vehicles, including defensive systems'. A week later Nixon referred in his first press conference to the doctrine of strategic sufficiency, thus in effect renouncing the American claim to strategic superiority over the Soviet Union; and he said that he was in favour of SALT.

By the time the delegations of the two super-powers finally began the SALT talks in Helsinki in November 1969, it was no longer simply a question of recognizing the fact that both sides now possessed a vast capacity of overkill. (In the course of his evidence given to the United States Senate Foreign Affairs Committee in 1969,[3] Melvin Laird, then Defence Secretary, estimated that 200 nuclear warheads of one megaton each would be enough to destroy 55 per cent of the American population and that it would take 1,200 equivalent American warheads to destroy 45 per cent of the more scattered Soviet population.) 'Lead-time' made it essential to plan as much as ten years ahead. Looking towards the end of the 1970s, both super-powers were aware that three technological developments in the strategic nuclear field threatened to make it just conceivable that a first-strike attack by one of the two powers might be successful—a perilously destabilizing factor—and to involve them in a further spiral of expenditure on strategic weapons. These developments were: first, new and more precise guidance systems, capable of increasing missile accuracy (down to a distance of 30 metres from the target), which is more important than yield in destroying land-based ICBMs; second, multiple re-entry warhead systems and—more important still— multiple, independently targetable re-entry vehicles (MIRV), each warhead being programmed for its specific target; and finally, anti-ballistic missile systems. On 14 March Nixon announced his decision to go ahead with the *Safeguard* anti-ballistic missile system, a decision which was confirmed in the Senate by a narrow vote in August. The SALT talks, which lasted until 23 December, were only preparatory. Nevertheless, they marked the opening of the first formally bilateral strategic negotiation between the two super-powers, each of whom had China's future potential in mind. As the Soviet Foreign Minister put it, in his report to the Supreme Soviet in July 1969, 'in questions of the maintenance of peace, the USSR and the USA can find a common language'.[4] Of a different order of importance, but none the less a sign of the times, was the Soviet-American agreement, in October, on a draft treaty banning the emplacement on the sea-bed of nuclear weapons, other weapons of mass destruction, or installations for the storing, testing, or using of such weapons.

By the end of this year the Soviet leadership must have had a further consideration in mind: in July the first American troops were withdrawn from Vietnam.* In November Nixon's broadcast about 'Vietnamization' made it clear that sooner or later, and if possible before the next presidential elections, he intended to pull out of Vietnam altogether. This was in line with the so-called Guam doctrine of stimulated self-help.[5] With the end of the United States' involvement in Indo-China at last in sight, and with no foreseeable conclusion to the Sino-Soviet dispute (which had erupted into armed conflict in March), it had become a major Soviet interest not only to engage the Americans in a direct dialogue but also to seek to bring about a European settlement. Here fate intervened: after the West German elections in October the Christian Democrats found themselves in opposition for the first time. Brandt became Federal Chancellor, depending for his majority in the Bundestag on his party's new alliance with the Free Democratic Party Liberals, whose leader, Walter Scheel, became Foreign Minister. On 28 October, in his inaugural speech, the Chancellor announced his

* Twelve days before the first American astronauts landed on the moon.

concept of two German states within one nation; a month later the Federal German Republic signed the Non-Proliferation Treaty; and on 8 December Soviet-German talks began in Moscow. In parallel, on 16 December the three Allied Powers renewed their proposal, first made to the Soviet Government in August, for talks on Berlin.

Meanwhile, the Warsaw Pact Political Consultative Committee had relaunched their proposal for an all-European conference at its meeting in Budapest in March, and seven months later in Prague they put forward two questions for the agenda: 'European security and the renunciation of the use of force or threats of force in relations between European states', and the expansion of 'trade, economic and scientific and technical ties'.[6] In May the Finnish Government had suggested Helsinki as the site of the conference, an offer which all the Warsaw Pact countries accepted. Finally, at Brussels in December 1969, NATO ministers made their first positive response to the prolonged barrage from Eastern Europe. It was guarded, mentioning careful advance preparation, prospects of concrete results, and the need for an assurance that such a meeting would not serve to ratify the existing division of Europe, and making it clear that progress in Soviet-German negotiations and in the Berlin negotiations would influence their future attitude to the proposal for a European Conference, 'in which, of course, the North American members of the alliance would participate'.[7]

These, then, were the beginnings—between the two super-powers, between the Soviet Union and West Germany, and between the two alliances—of the years of negotiation. Paradoxically, although the Soviet leadership entered this new era basking in American acknowledgement that their country had become a co-equal super-power, and confident that, at least for the time being, the Soviet presence in Eastern Europe had been made secure, they simultaneously faced a dilemma at home.

The change in the Soviet Union's international status was evident to any visitor to Moscow at the time. It was a city that had visibly arrived. In the year of Stalin's death, if the visitor could for a moment blot out from his mind both the dazzling cluster of monuments that form the Kremlin and the grotesque Stalinist skyscrapers, the greater part of Moscow looked like a provincial town, resembling a capital city far less than Leningrad, which still retained its elegance half a century after the transfer of the seat of government to Moscow. The boulevards were by Western standards almost empty of traffic; and what perhaps struck the visitor most of all was the queues of poorly-dressed Muscovites patiently waiting outside the shops. By contrast, the Moscow of 1970 was a bustling city. Still shabby and ill-lit at night—this, together with the large number of men walking about in uniform, recalled London towards the end of the Second World War—but none the less a great capital, it now accommodated the diplomatic missions of close on a hundred countries, compared with the handful represented in Moscow seventeen years earlier. (Most of the staff of these embassies lived in a diplomatic ghetto, their working hours spent in seeking Soviet attention and Soviet information, and their leisure in fulfilling the obligations of a social round whose formal character seemed to be accentuated, as through osmosis, by the hierarchical structure of the society by which they were surrounded.) An occasion which typified Moscow's trans-formation was the reopening of the magnificent Hall of St. George, the largest room in the Kremlin, its white walls decorated in gold with the names of Tsarist regiments and knights of the Order of St. George, the highest military distinction in Tsarist Russia. This gleaming chamber provided the setting for the first lavish evening reception offered by the Soviet leadership for several years, to which all ambassadors were invited, in honour of the visit paid to Moscow by Svoboda and Husak in October 1969.

By 1970 the Khrushchevian concept of the taxi had yielded to that of the private car; there were now a million on Soviet roads, with the factory built by Fiat[8] due to produce 660,000 private cars annually after its completion. The suburbs of the city now consisted of mile after mile of new blocks of flats, housing a population that had almost doubled in two decades. In the Arbat, the old quarter in the centre of the city, there were new buildings which would not look out of place in a Western capital. This new construction had already alarmed Soviet conservationists; still more dignified old buildings were threatened by future plans. Nevertheless, large sums were being spent on restoring old monuments, both secular and religious, in Moscow, as elsewhere in the Soviet Union. The city teemed with tourists, Soviet and foreign. True, there were still queues to be seen, but the woollen shawls, quilted jackets and felt boots of earlier years had almost disappeared. In short, the people of Moscow had 'never had it so good'. This was the centenary of Lenin's birth; and Moscow, even if no longer acknowledged by all Marxists as the Third Rome, had by universal consent become the centre of one of the world's two super-powers.

If this had been all that five years of power had given the Soviet leaders who succeeded Khrushchev, they would have had reason to congratulate themselves. The very fact that they felt able to enter into major negotiations proved the new confidence that they felt in themselves and in the immense military power that they had built up since October 1964. But this was not the whole story.

NOTES

1. Text in Command Paper 3683, HMSO, London, June 1968, reprinted 1969, which also contains the text of the security assurances given by the three nuclear powers which signed the treaty.
2. *Strategic Survey 1969*, IISS, London, 1969. One megaton = 1,000,000 tons of TNT, in terms of the yield of a nuclear explosion. For the fortuitous origin of the megaton, see York, op. cit., pp. 89–90.
3. *Keesing's Contemporary Archives, 1969/70*, p. 23291.
4. Quoted in *Istoriya Vneshnei Politiki SSSR*, vol. 2, p. 452.
5. This was more of an off-the-cuff statement than the exposition of a new doctrine, but none the less important for that. The difference between American global policy at the beginning and end of the decade can be seen by comparing the statement, in Kennedy's inaugural message, that the United States would help anyone, with Nixon's reformulation, that the United States would help anyone who would help themselves.
6. *Pravda*, 18 March and 1 November 1969.
7. *Keesing's Contemporary Archives 1969/70*, p. 23750.
8. This major contract was concluded by Fiat after Gromyko's visit to Italy in 1966, when he also became the first Soviet Foreign Minister to be received in audience by the Pope.

9

THE STATE OF THE UNION

The dilemma faced by the Soviet leadership, at the very moment when they should have been able to enjoy the fruit of their labours in the field of foreign relations, was both economic and political. It has been analysed in depth in *Kniga o sotsialisticheskoi democratii* by Roy Medvedev.[1] For him, as for Andrei Sakharov, the two sets of problems, in the economic and in the political field, are interdependent. Sakharov's book *Progress, Coexistence and Intellectual Freedom* includes this passage:

We are now catching up with the United States only in some of the old, traditional industries, which are no longer as important as they used to be for the United States (for example, coal and steel). In some of the newer fields, for example, automation, computers, petro-chemicals, and especially in industrial research and development, we are not only lagging behind, but are also growing more slowly. . . .[2]

Coming half a century after the October Revolution and seven years after Khrushchev's boast at the XXIInd Party Congress, this was a devastating indictment, even though what its author dared to write in 1968 was on the same lines as an article published in the Moscow *Journal of World Economics and International Relations* in January 1973, which listed the chemical industry, automobile construction, several branches of mechanical engineering, computer technology, gas processing, pulp and paper, and a range of branches of light industries among those sectors of modern industry in which Western development had reached a higher technical level. What had gone wrong with the Soviet economy? A great deal, as was reported to the CPSU Central Committee on 15 December 1969, and—in guarded terms—to the Soviet public by *Pravda*[3] a month later; so much so that the XXIVth Party Congress, which should have been held in 1970, and the publication of the new Five-Year Plan were both postponed.

In order to understand why it was that Soviet economic problems came to a head at the end of the 1960s, we must go back to Stalin's decision, forty years earlier, to abandon Lenin's moderate New Economic Policy and to launch the Soviet Union on its race to become a great industrial power, a ruthless transformation largely financed by the Soviet peasantry, whose land was forcibly collectivized in order to provide cheap food for the workers in the swiftly growing cities. This extraordinary feat, directed entirely from Moscow, from which every decision was handed down (*spuskat'*), lasted under Stalin's rule for a quarter of a century, through the purges, the Second World War, and the reconstruction of the country that followed, to be summed up afterwards by a distinguished Polish economist[4] as a *sui generis* war economy —surely one of the greatest understatements in history.

A year after the XXth CPSU Congress, Khrushchev attempted to put new life into the Soviet economy by decentralizing it. In consequence, all but two of the specifically industrial ministries were eliminated, and instead 105 regional economic councils were established (later reduced to 47). In September 1965 his successors abolished these councils and restored the ministries in Moscow, but with a difference— the Economic Reform.[5] The new Soviet leadership took a whole year to decide the terms of this reform, whose execution Kosygin described to the Central Committee as unthinkable without significant worker participation in management. In the event the scope of the reform was modest; its success was limited; and a most important measure—the formation of regional or all-union corporations, operating on the basis of autonomous profit-making—was not finally approved until April 1973.[6] By the end of the Five-Year Plan, not only had the notoriously inefficient and wasteful Soviet system of agriculture achieved a far smaller increase in production than had been hoped, because it had been starved of the capital investments and the quantity of machinery laid down in the plan (as Brezhnev reported to the Central Committee in July 1970), but many key Soviet industrial products had failed to achieve their planned targets, even though the industrial output plan as a whole was fulfilled.[7]

How was it that Soviet industry could produce hundreds of SS-9 intercontinental ballistic missiles and put the *lunakhod* vehicle on the moon, and yet find it difficult to cover the Soviet Union with a chain of modern hotels (as was done in the space of a few years in the impoverished Italian *Mezzogiorno*)? In its article reporting the Central Committee meeting of December 1969, *Pravda* admitted that the key problem was an increase in productivity; the quantitative approach to the Soviet economy was no longer good enough; new methods and new decisions were required. This was true. But there were many other things that *Pravda* did not, or could not, say. Among these, six may be singled out. The first is the growing technological gap between East and West, which Sakharov described in the passage quoted above, and which was to be publicly admitted later within the Soviet Union. The second is the managerial gap. The reasons for both these gaps are complex. They became evident at a time when the pace of change in industrial and in management techniques in the West was so great that it amounted to a second Industrial Revolution. One of the essentials of the technological revolution—the ability of an industrial society to diffuse new technology swiftly through all sectors of its economy—is discouraged by the very nature of the Soviet system, partly for reasons of security. As for management, to the sheer size of the Moscow bureaucracy must be added what has been described by a Soviet critic as the greatest single obstacle: the absence not only in the political system, but also in the economy, of an effective mechanism for renewing management.[8] Third, in a non-market economy, a qualitative as opposed to a quantitative approach depends on its planners' ability to identify success indicators that will encourage a prompt response to demand: this is something that Soviet planners have found hard, even though the economic reform of 1965 modified the cult of gross output—the essence of Stalinist economics.[9] Fourth, the Soviet economy no longer has at its disposal the reserves of labour which—through a concentration of effort on key sectors of the economy—helped it to win its greatest successes in the past. (In the construction industry: in September 1972, Kosygin revealed that the volume of investments immobilized in uncompleted projects had almost trebled in four years, to reach a total of 61·4 billion roubles.)[10] Fifth, the aspirations of the Soviet consumer are at last beginning to make themselves felt: for example, the meat shortage—the consequence of the deficiencies of Soviet livestock production—could in 1970 no longer be ignored. Finally, whatever the statistical doubts mentioned in an earlier chapter, it must be concluded that at least part—perhaps a major part—of the strain imposed on the entire Soviet economy by the end of the 1960s was caused by the overcommitment of resources to its defence sector.

At the same time there was a profound political malaise in the Soviet Union. Just when their country's military power had grown to a size which—for example—enabled them to carry out the military intervention in Egypt in 1970, the Soviet leaders seemed to see themselves as the embattled defenders of Marxist-Leninist orthodoxy in the Kremlin, assailed alike by any new idea put forward within the boundaries of the Soviet Union, by the schismatic Chinese, by the reformist Czechoslovaks, and by the New Left in the West. The Soviet Communist Party showed no sign whatsoever of sympathy with the perpetrators of the Parisian *chie-en-lit*[11] of 1968. Marcuse was described as an ideologist of *petit-bourgeois* rebels and an old fool. At first sight it may seem strange to find the General-Secretary of the CPSU devoting a whole paragraph of his report at the XXIVth Party Congress to an attack on a group of Marxist 'renegades' so disparate as Roger Garaudy, Ernst Fischer, the Italian 'Manifesto Group', and Teodoro Petkoff (formerly a member of the Venezuelan Communist Party), until one recalls that the heretic appears to the faithful to pose a greater threat than the infidel.[12] As if to break the monotony, the Soviet leadership decided to make a major event of Lenin's centenary year. Few of the thousands of words written and spoken about this extraordinary man in 1970 would have given him pleasure—certainly not *Pravda*'s misquotation of a passage from one of his works, which did not escape Chinese ridicule.

New ideas within the Soviet Union covered a wide spectrum. The connecting link was the convicton that scientific and industrial progress was inseparable from intellectual freedom. Sakharov emerged as the leader and co-founder of the first, unofficial, civil rights movement[13] in the Soviet Union. A group was formed of individuals resolved to see that the rights conferred on the citizen by the Soviet Constitution were observed to the letter. What these dissidents regarded as illegal acts began to be publicized in 1968 in the *Samizdat* news-sheet *Khronika Tekushchych Sobytii*—passed from hand to hand (like Akhmatova's lyric poems during the war)—and from 1970 in the *Ukrainian Herald*. Copies of these news-sheets regularly reached the West. This movement[14] arose in protest against constraints which have been interpreted by some observers as neo-Stalinism. If by neo-Stalinism is meant the arrest of liberalizing tendencies, coupled with the fact that, since his total eclipse under Khrushchev, Stalin has been partly rehabilitated in official statements (he is now depicted as a wise and benign leader in Soviet war films), there is no need to quarrel with this assessment. But there can be no question of a return to historical Stalinism, if for no other reason than that this involved the physical destruction of the CPSU, including most of the senior members of the Soviet officer corps.* Under the collective leadership, the literary freedom allowed under Khrushchev had been steadily eroded. True, Tvardovsky did what he could, so long as he was editor, to defend the literary journal *Novyi Mir* as a bastion of liberalism. Dimitri Shostakovich was allowed to compose as he wished: the performances of his tragic Fourteenth Symphony cannot have pleased the censors. And, after several years' delay, Moscow audiences were allowed to see Andrei Tarkovsky's politically ambivalent and intensely religious film *Andrei Rublev*. But what the regime found intolerable was the growing habit of publication in the West of works[15] banned in the Soviet Union. Thus, in February 1966 Andrei Sinyavsky and Yuli Daniel were sentenced to seven and five years' forced labour respectively for having published abroad, under pseudonyms, allegedly anti-Soviet writings; two years later Alexander Ginsberg and three others were convicted on charges based, *inter alia*, on their having compiled a White Book on the Sinyavsky-Daniel case; and in 1969 Solzhenitsyn, the heir to the great tradition of the Russian novel, all but one of whose major works have been published abroad, was expelled from the Writers' Union. In the same year Piotr Grigorenko, a dissident General who had espoused the cause of the Crimean Tartars (deported from their homes during the war by Stalin's order), was committed to a mental home—a way of dealing with political opposition which has since been repeated with other dissidents.[16]

The Soviet leadership could not accept the link between the solution of their country's economic problems and that of its political problems, in the sense advocated by men like Sakharov and Medvedev. To have done so would have led them down the path of pluralism, which the Czechoslovak reformers had followed and to which they themselves were adamantly opposed. But they were seized of the necessity to seek to meet the needs of the Soviet consumer and to close the economic gaps between East and West—technological and managerial. Their solution was a compromise: at home, an intensification of ideological discipline; abroad, an intimate economic cooperation with the Soviet Union's cold war adversary, the United States, and with its former enemies, Germany and Japan, which would, they hoped, make ultim-

* 'History never repeats itself—historians repeat themselves.' But if any analogy is to be drawn, the atmosphere of the reign of Tsar Alexander III (1881–94) offers a closer parallel than that of the Great Terror. For the important distinction between neo-Stalinists and moderate conservatives in the CPSU, see Medvedev, op. cit., pp. 55 ff.

ately possible the development of the vast resources of Siberia, such as the Tyumen' oil-field and the copper deposits of Udokan. A start in the direction of economic cooperation had already been made by one of the most forward-looking departments of the Soviet bureaucracy, the State Committee for Science and Technology, a new agency established under the collective leadership. It was this committee which was primarily interested in the conclusion of inter-governmental agreements for the exchange of scientific and technological know-how (a word now transliterated into cyrillics to form part of the Soviet vocabulary). The French Government led the way in 1965, followed by the Italian Government in 1966, and the British Government in 1970; by then Britain, France, and Italy all had considerable numbers of men helping to establish industrial plants in the Soviet Union, the biggest of which was the giant Fiat factory already mentioned. But at a time when Western firms were not yet allowed to open permanent offices for their representatives in Moscow, this was only a beginning.

The compromise solution was presented to the XXIVth Congress of the CPSU on 30 March 1971, by which time the Soviet leadership was also influenced by the events leading to the fall of Gomulka three months earlier (discussed in Chapter 10). The supreme aim of the Party's economic policy was described to this Congress as the raising of the Soviet standard of living, the planned increase in real income per head of the population being almost one third. For the first time priority for consumer goods was written into the Five-Year Plan, although this did not mean that concern for heavy industry was being slackened (the planned increase was 42–46 per cent). Kosygin made it clear that 80–85 per cent of the entire planned increase in material income during the period of the plan would have to be derived from increased productivity. And Brezhnev added two interesting footnotes: the first at the Congress, when he stated that 42 per cent of the defence industry's output was used for civilian purposes, and the second in the course of an electoral speech delivered in a Moscow constituency on 11 June, when he said that socialism was powerful enough to secure both reliable defence and the development of the economy, although the Soviet economy would have advanced much more quickly, had it not been for large defence expenditures.[17]

In the field of foreign policy, the basic tasks were reiterated in Brezhnev's report to the Congress, when he spoke of 'the great alliance of the three basic revolutionary forces of our day—socialism, the international workers' movement, and the peoples' national-liberation struggle'.[18] As is expected of a communist party leader on such an occasion, he described the general crisis of capitalism as deepening (accurately, in the event, since the dollar crisis finally erupted the following August). The conduct of affairs with the United States was, he said, complicated by the 'frequent zigzags of American foreign policy', which he attributed to internal political manoeuvres. Nevertheless, he left the door ajar. Soviet policy towards the United States was based on the premise that an improvement in relations between the two countries was possible: 'our line of principle in our relations with capitalist countries, including the USA, is consistently and fully to realize in practice the principles of peaceful coexistence. . . .'

About China Brezhnev pulled no punches. The CCP's ideological-political platform on the fundamental questions of international relations and the world communist movement was condemned as incompatible with Leninism. The talks about frontier questions were going slowly; if they were to be concluded successfully, a constructive attitude was required from both sides. The Chinese slanderous inventions about Soviet policy, instilled into the Chinese people from Peking, were rejected absolutely. Nevertheless, the CPSU and the Soviet Government were profoundly convinced that an improvement in relations between the Soviet Union and the Chinese People's Republic would correspond to the long-term interests of both countries; they were therefore ready to cooperate across the board not only in order to normalize relations, but also to restore good-neighbourliness and friendship; and they were certain that in the final reckoning this would be attained.

A last word had to be said about Czechoslovakia. The network of Soviet bilateral treaties with its Eastern European allies, taken together with the latter's treaties with each other, was described by Brezhnev as a comprehensive system of mutual commitments of a new, socialist type. Czechoslovakia had received international assistance in defending socialism against the forces of imperialism and counter-revolution in the exceptional circumstances of 1968, for reasons of 'class duty, loyalty to socialist internationalism, concern for the interests of our states and for the fate of socialism and peace in Europe'.

International communist attendance at the Congress must have satisfied the CPSU. Most Asian communist parties were represented; the North Vietnamese delegation repeated their 1966 practice of stopping in Peking on the way to Moscow, but they praised the CPSU, with only a passing reference to China. This time the Cuban delegate,

President Dorticòs, described his country's friendship with the Soviet Union as indestructible and he thanked the Soviet Government for its aid to Cuba.

The policy approved by the XXIVth Congress was presented by the leadership to the Soviet people and to the world as a Programme of Peace. True, the Soviet Government had, in August 1970, concluded its negotiations with the Federal German Government by signing the Moscow Treaty. But there was nothing essentially new in the programme; and it was not until 1972–3 that Soviet foreign policy underwent changes that proved to be as important as those of 1956. It is arguable that these changes would have taken place in any case. But they were, at the very least, greatly accelerated when, a few weeks after the Congress had ended, the Soviet leadership suddenly found themselves outflanked by the Metternichian diplomacy of Henry Kissinger.

The language of international relations is the poorer for its wealth of dead metaphors: bombshell, landmark, watershed. None of these is strong enough to describe the effect[19] of the announcement on 15 July 1971, that the United States President intended to accept an invitation from Mao Tse-tung to visit Peking the following year, with the object of restoring normal relations between the United States and China. This decision, secretly prepared by Kissinger during a 49-hour visit to Peking, which he reached from Pakistan, paved the way for the lifting of the ostracism imposed on the People's Republic of China by the United States for a quarter of a century, and for China's assumption of its seat in the UN Security Council. It was particularly dangerous for the Soviet Union, for which the worst of all possible worlds would be a nuclear China and a unified Western Europe—the Chinese make no secret of their wish to see Western Europe unite against the Soviet Union— backed by the United States, in alliance with Japan. The Soviet leadership lost little time in making the best of a bad job. In October of the same year, they invited Nixon to Moscow: the first visit ever paid to the Soviet Union by a US President.

NOTES

1. *Kniga o sotsialisticheskoi democratii*, Alexander Herzen Foundation, Amsterdam/Paris, 1972.
2. Circulated first in *Samizdat*; and the translation was published in London, in 1969, by Penguin Books; see p. 66.
3. *Pravda*, 13 January 1970. As late as July Brezhnev said that the Party Congress would be held during 1970.

4. Oscar Lange, who used this description in a lecture given in 1957 in Belgrade, quoted in Alec Nove, *The Soviet Economy*, George Allen and Unwin, London, 1968, p. 162. The closest quotation in Lange's collected works is in an article entitled *O niektorych zagadnieniach polskiej drogi do socjalizmu* (1957), reprinted in vol. 2 of his collected works, *Socjalizm*, Warsaw, 1973, p. 499.

5. The most important measures introduced in 1965 were some devolution of planning and decision-making to enterprise level and changes in the success criteria of enterprises, followed in 1967 by a revision of prices. Much has been written on this subject: see, for example, Medvedev, op. cit., pp. 287 ff., and Nove, op. cit., ch. 9.

6. *Pravda*, 3 April 1973. *Pravda* of 19 June foresaw the formation of transnational corporations.

7. Brezhnev, op. cit., vol. 3, p. 66. See ibid., pp. 62–9 for a strongly worded exposition of the shortcomings of Soviet agriculture. Cf. Nove, *The Soviet Economy*, p. 335. For an analysis of the 1965–70 Plan, see Nove, *The Soviet Five Year Plan*, Hong Kong Economic Papers, no. 6, 1971.

8. Medvedev, op. cit., p. 302.

9. The cult of the gross output, *kul't vala*, is a quotation from D. Kondrashev, *Tsenoobrazovanie v promyshlennosti*, Moscow, 1956, p. 32. The translation of *pokazatel'* as 'success indicator' is Nove's: see *The Soviet Economy*, passim.

10. Quoted by Alain Jacob in *Le Monde*, 15 February 1974: an example of the defect known by Soviet economists as *raspylenie sredstv*.

11. De Gaulle's own description of the students' revolt of May 1968.

12. For this attack, see Brezhnev, op. cit., p. 215. The description of Marcuse is in B. Bykhovskii's article *Filosofia mel'koburzhuaznogo buntarstva*, *Kommunist*, no. 8, 1969, pp. 114–24.

13. In November 1970. The text of the declaration of the programme of the *Committee for the Rights of Man* is given in Medvedev, op. cit., p. 91.

14. This movement has in effect performed the same gadfly function for Soviet society as the emigré intellectuals did for nineteenth-century Russia. For a description of how *Samizdat* (literally, 'self-publishing house') works, see Julius Taleshin's article in *Encounter*, February 1973.

15. An extreme case was *Can the Soviet Union Survive until 1984?* by Andrei Amal'ryk, Harper and Row, New York; Allen Lane, London, 1970.

16. Grigorenko was not released until 1974, despite the publicity given to his case in the West. A reply from a group of Soviet psychiatrists to Western criticism of this method of treatment was sent to the *Guardian*, which published their letter on 29 September 1973.

17. Brezhnev, op. cit., vol. 3, p. 390. All subsequent quotations from, and references to, this speech will be taken from this source.

18. Ibid., pp. 195–6.

19. The announcement came as an especially rude shock for the Japanese, who were not consulted in advance and took even longer than the Russians to absorb it; they had to adjust themselves not only to the US-Chinese rapprochement, but also to American economic demands. There had indeed been signs that the US and Chinese governments were moving towards a new relationship (such as the resumption of the US-Chinese talks at ambassadorial level in Warsaw, in December 1969, and the ping-pong diplomacy earlier in 1971), but the secret was well kept until 15 July 1971.

10

THE YEAR 1970

Europe

So far the evolution of Soviet foreign policy has been treated thematically, each chapter covering a span of several years. The next five chapters will seek to record, baldly, and with the minimum of comment, the conduct of Soviet foreign policy during the period 1970–3 (up to the end of October 1973), in roughly chronological order. This method may make the swift unfolding of events during these four years harder for the reader to follow, but it reproduces the kaleidoscopic effect that they presented to the leadership in the Kremlin as they occurred. My own assessment will be largely reserved for Part Four of this book.

In Europe, the critical date—from which everything that has followed in Europe stems—was 12 August 1970. Exactly thirty-one years to the day after the signature of the Soviet-Nazi Non-Aggression Pact,[1] the Soviet Union and the Federal Republic of Germany concluded the Treaty of Moscow. The preamble and the five articles that make up this brief document[2] formed the basis of what today amounts to a *de facto* European peace settlement. It was welcomed by most Europeans, Western as well as Eastern, although in the Federal Republic the Opposition remained unconvinced of the wisdom of the whole concept of Brandt's *Ostpolitik* and therefore opposed the treaty with all the means at their disposal. (The Bundestag did not ratify it until nearly two years later.)

At first reading, this treaty may appear to be no more than the mutual renunciation of force and the recognition of existing frontiers in Europe, including those between the two Germanies and the western frontiers of Poland. Indeed, on his return to Bonn after signing the treaty, the

Federal Chancellor claimed in a televised statement that with this treaty nothing had been lost which had not been gambled away long before. This remark, however, referred to the German loss of what are known as the Western Territories of Poland; a loss rendered virtually irrevocable by the fourth paragraph of Article 3 of the treaty, under whose terms the German signatories 'regard' the Oder-Neisse line as 'inviolable now and in the future'. But the wording of the treaty is subtle. At least in the Federal Government's view, the specific reference in the preamble to the Adenauer-Bulganin Agreement of 1956 and the implied reference in Article 4 to the Paris Agreements of 1954, coupled with the opening words of Article 3, provided sufficient legal backing to preserve the right of the ultimate reunification of Germany in the text of the treaty, in spite of the commitment to regard the frontier between the two German Republics as inviolable. And to make doubly sure, Scheel simultaneously wrote a letter to Gromyko, published five days later, stating that the treaty did not stand in contradiction to the political aim of the Federal German Republic; this remained a peaceful European settlement in which the German people would regain its unity through self-determination.

The Federal German side made it clear to the Soviet side that their ratification of the treaty was conditional on a satisfactory conclusion of the Four-Power talks on Berlin, which had opened in March, and that the question of Allied rights and responsibilities with regard to Germany as a whole and to Berlin was not affected by the treaty. This second statement—together with Gromyko's oral acknowledgement of it—was recorded in an exchange of notes between the Government of the Federal Republic and the British, French, and US governments. The treaty was also regarded by both sides as part of a package of other related agreements, the first of which was the Treaty of Warsaw,[3] signed between the Federal Republic and Poland in December. And both sides saw it as the prelude to a large expansion of trade; in the preceding February the two governments had already concluded an agreement whereby West Germany was to supply the Soviet Union with large-diameter pipe in return for future delivery, by pipeline, of large quantities of natural gas.

The Moscow Treaty was the cornerstone of Brandt's *Ostpolitik*. For the Russians it was a radical turning point not only in their relationship with the Federal German Republic, but also in the post-war history of Europe.[4] Two years after accusing the Czechoslovaks of yielding to the blandishments of German revanchists, why did the Soviet Union itself enter a close bilateral relationship with the Federal Republic—and this (suspected at the time and evident in April 1971, when Ulbricht was succeeded by Erich Honecker) in the teeth of the opposition of the redoubtable East German communist leader, one of the few survivors of the old guard who had known both Lenin and Stalin personally? It is significant that two meetings of the Warsaw Pact Political Consultative Committee were held, one in Moscow a week after the signature of the Moscow Treaty and the other in Berlin on 2 December, both of which set the seal of all the Eastern European governments' approval on the treaty. The turn of the decade may have seemed to the Soviet leadership to have constituted one of Hegel's unique moments in history: Brandt's electoral victory in 1969; his government's signature of the Nuclear Non-Proliferation Treaty;[5] and Soviet recognition of their country's urgent need of German capital and technology. A rapprochement with the West Germans may well have been considered a different matter in the Kremlin provided that it was made clear to the world that the way to it lay through Moscow, not through the capitals of the Soviet Union's Eastern European allies. And it was not at all untypical of Soviet diplomacy that the news of the rapprochement was broken to the Soviet public with little advance preparation, nearly eight months after talks had begun in Moscow with the Federal Chancellor's personal re-presentative, Egon Bahr, and three years after the beginning of the earlier round of talks between the two governments. Yet the fact remains that it was one of the most dramatic changes in post-war history, which cannot have been decided on by the Soviet leadership without much debate. Even now it is still too early to answer the Leninist question *kto kogo*?* The nearest historical parallel is the seventeenth-century Treaty of Westphalia; and it is to be hoped that the compromise enshrined in the Moscow Treaty of 1970 will be found by later historians to mark the beginning of the end of the twentieth-century European civil wars.

The Soviet Government succeeded in forming this new relationship with Bonn without disturbing the relationship with Paris that had developed steadily since de Gaulle's visit to Moscow in 1966. Indeed, in

* The question can roughly be translated as 'who is top dog?' Brezhnev's own answer, given in the course of a speech delivered to the Central Committee of the Azerbaijan Communist Party and the Azerbaijan Republic Supreme Soviet on 2 October 1970, was 'everyone won equally': Brezhnev, op. cit., vol. 3, p. 145. Apart from acquiescing in the legal niceties described, the main Soviet con-cession, which did not become effective until the conclusion of the Quadripartite Agreement on Berlin, related to the question of West Berlin.

October 1970, during a visit paid to the Soviet Union by his successor, Pompidou, the two governments signed a protocol whereby they agreed, should a critical situation arise, to 'enter into contact with each other without delay with the object of agreeing their positions'.[6] Britain, the Soviet Union's major trading partner in the late 1960s, was not included in the new set of bilateral relationships established by the Soviet Union both with its major opponents and with leading countries of the Third World, in spite of the comparatively successful visit paid to the United Kingdom by the Soviet Prime Minister in 1967. The fact that the negotiations following Kosygin's public—and unexpected—proposal of a new Anglo-Soviet friendship treaty during this visit subsequently petered out is hardly relevant. The coolness between Britain and the Soviet Union which lasted off and on from August 1968 until 1973 was due to a range of issues, some of which aroused strong feelings on both sides; one of these was the question of Soviet espionage, which finally erupted in September 1971.

In the summer of 1970 the proposal for a European Conference took what proved to be a decisive step forward, when the two alliances reached the point of exchanging memoranda on a possible agenda. In the communiqué issued after their meeting in Rome in May, the NATO Foreign Ministers suggested that (subject to progress in the talks already being conducted, especially on Germany and Berlin) the subjects to be explored should include: 'the principles which should govern relations between states, including the renunciation of force' and 'the development of international relations with a view to contributing to the freer movement of people, ideas, and information and to developing cooperation in the cultural, economic, technical, and scientific fields as well as in the field of human environment'. In a separate declaration (from which the French abstained, as at Reykjavik) NATO ministers laid down certain principles for their proposed negotiations on mutual balanced force reductions. The NATO proposals, which were communicated to the Warsaw Pact governments by the Italian Government, in its capacity as host at the Rome meeting, met with a rapid response. In a memorandum approved in Budapest on 21–22 June, the Warsaw Pact foreign ministers suggested three questions for the agenda of a very early meeting: 'the safeguarding of European security and renunciation of the use of force or the threat of the use of force in interstate relations in Europe; expansion on an equal basis of trade, economic, scientific, technical, and cultural ties, directed towards the development of political cooperation between the European states; and creation at the all-European conference of a body for questions of security and cooperation in Europe'. Although they continued to refer to the conference as all-European, they envisaged for the first time participation by the United States and Canada, as well as by both Germanies; and they also made another concession: the 'question of reducing foreign armed forces on the territory of European states ... could be discussed in a body whose creation is proposed at the all-European conference, or in another form acceptable to the interested states'.[7]

These quotations make the difference in the objectives of the two alliances evident. What the NATO countries had in mind was the Brezhnev doctrine and an opening up of Eastern Europe, including the Soviet Union, to Western ideas. The first objective was made still more explicit in the final communiqué of the Brussels ministerial meeting of December 1970, which listed three principles[8] which must in their view be respected as the basis for any genuine and lasting improvement in East-West relations in Europe. They were also well aware of the growing pressure in the US Congress, stemming from Senator Mansfield's resolution, first moved in 1966, for a reduction of the 300,000 American troops deployed in the European theatre.

The Warsaw Pact countries' original objectives in calling for a conference in the sixties are clear enough. They are listed in the History of Soviet Foreign Policy as: first, recognition of frontiers, including the Oder-Neisse line and the frontier between the two Germanies; second, recognition of the German Democratic Republic as a sovereign state; and third, denial of all nuclear armament whatever to the Federal Republic of Germany.[9] Each of these aims had either already been attained, or was on the point of being attained, by the time of the Budapest meeting. Why then did the Soviet Government in particular continue to press for the holding of a European conference, as it did again in Berlin the following December, after both the Moscow and the Warsaw Treaties had been signed, when it must have realized that once a conference was convened, it could not expect to avoid discussion of subjects which were sensitive for the Soviet Union? The least convincing explanation is that the idea of a conference had achieved such momentum through the years, thanks largely to Soviet effort, that the Soviet Government could no longer reverse it, especially as some of its allies wanted the conference to further their own national interests. Soviet diplomacy was fully capable of having made such an abrupt change of course, even later than 1970, if the Soviet leadership had judged this to be in the national interest. If so, we are left with two explanations, which do not exclude each other. Soviet diplomacy is not only flexible; it is also formal. However an agreement involving the Soviet Union may be arrived at, it must be recorded in black and white at the end of the day. The Soviet leadership may therefore have wanted some kind of overarching agreement, witnessed by the signatures of all Europe, as well as by Western Europe's trans-Atlantic allies, which would directly or indirectly constitute general approval of the *de facto* settlement of post-war Europe. They may also have been searching for some kind of all-European framework, jointly guaranteed by both the Soviet and the United States governments, within which they and their Eastern European allies would be able to contain the enlarged Western European Community, a factor that must have begun to loom large in the planning of Soviet foreign policy at the very latest after Edward Heath's agreement with Pompidou during his visit to Paris in May 1971. Some colour is lent to this interpretation of Soviet motives by the proposal made in the communiqué[10] issued on 19 April 1974 in Warsaw by the Warsaw Pact ministers, calling for the establishment of 'a permanent security council for Europe aimed at building new relations between all states'.

It has been argued by some that the main Soviet object in holding a conference in the 1970s was part of a wider plan to remove the United States forces from Europe, and to secure for the Soviet Union due recognition as the most powerful country in Europe; once the American forces were out of the way, the rest of Europe would, in effect be 'Finlandized'. It is questionable whether an immediate withdrawal of all US forces from Europe would be in the Soviet interest. In any case, the term 'Finlandization' does less than justice to the Finns, the one people of the former Russian Empire who have succeeded in remaining outside the borders of the Soviet Union ever since 1917.*

In the course of 1970 the Soviet Union also completed its network of bilateral treaties with its allies by signing new treaties of friendship with Czechoslovakia and Romania, in May and July respectively. Whereas the latter was worded to take account of Romanian susceptibilities, the former reflected the Brezhnev doctrine. Its preamble described the 'support, strengthening, and protection of the socialist achievements of

---

* The 1948 Soviet-Finnish Treaty (renewed for another twenty years in 1970 —see *Pravda* of 21 July 1970) is unique, as are Soviet-Finnish relations. It obliges Finland to defend its own territory in the event of an attack against the Soviet Union being directed across it: an echo of 1941.

the people' as 'the common international duty of socialist countries';
under Article V of the treaty the parties undertook to take the necessary
measures to this end; and in the words of the History of Soviet Foreign
Policy,[11] the treaty re-affirmed the principles of the Bratislava Declaration of 3 August 1968, regarding the collective defence of socialism in
any country of the socialist commonwealth. But at the very end of a year
which must otherwise have given the Soviet leadership much satisfaction, this commonwealth was shaken once again, in Poland, where the
government was overthrown—literally in the streets—for the second
time in fourteen years.

Unlike 1956, when the issues at stake were both political and economic,* this time they were chiefly economic—the mismanagement of
the economy by the Gomulka regime, culminating in increases in the
price of essential food items, tactlessly introduced just before Christ-
mas. The battles between strikers and police, reinforced by the army,
that followed in the Baltic cities were so severe (a total of 45 dead and
over 1,000 injured was officially admitted),[12] that Gomulka was obliged
to resign after over fourteen years as Party Secretary. Fortunately for
the Soviet Union, he was swiftly succeeded by Edward Gierek, who
rescinded his predecessor's economic measures, made concessions to
the workers, and—so it was rumoured—received Soviet economic aid
to help him meet his country's difficulties. Like Gomulka in 1956,
Gierek both admitted the errors committed by the previous Party
leadership and made it clear that there was no question of Poland seeking to break loose from the Soviet alliance. And unlike Dubcek, he not
only succeeded in restoring a measure of popular confidence but also
reassured the Soviet Union that the rule of the Party would be upheld in
Poland. Nevertheless, the Soviet leadership, however relieved they may
have felt at the outcome of the Polish crisis, must have asked themselves
how they would have reacted had it developed according to the Czechoslovak model. Poland lies athwart the lines of communication between
the Soviet Union and its forces in East Germany. Another invasion,
little more than two years after the invasion of Czechoslovakia, and only
a few days after the conclusion of the Treaty of Warsaw with the
Federal Republic of Germany, would have presented an appalling
prospect. The Polish crisis passed without any official Soviet comment;
but it left the Kremlin with food for thought; and as we have noted in
the preceding chapter, it may well have affected the decision of the

---

* 'Bread and freedom' was the demonstrators' slogan in Poznań in 1956.

XXIVth Party Congress to give priority to the needs of the consumer for the first time in the history of the Soviet Union.

Relations between the super-powers

Relations between the Soviet Union and the United States at the beginning of the decade could already be described as edging towards the 'middle ground of peaceful, if somewhat distant, coexistence ... lying somewhere between the intimacy we cannot have ... and the war there is no reason for us to fight'.[13] That this is how things seemed in the Kremlin is suggested by an article which appeared in the journal of the Soviet-USA Institute,[14] written by Lyudmila Gvishiani, an historian and daughter of the Soviet Prime Minister. The article consisted of an account of Bullitt's ill-fated mission to the Soviet Union in 1919, and quoted George Kennan's favourable verdict in his memoirs (that the peace proposals put to Bullitt by Lenin offered an opportunity that should not have been let slip by the Allied Powers). The chief interest of the article, however, lay in its opening and concluding paragraphs. The former described the principle of peaceful coexistence of states with different social systems as one of the basic principles of the Leninist foreign policy of the Soviet State, and went on to say that the 'realistic approach' of the Soviet Government and of Lenin personally appeared with the greatest clarity in the history of Soviet-American relations in March 1919. The article ended:

Lenin demonstrated the possibility of reaching agreement with capitalist countries, and first and foremost with the United States. To dogmatists the decisions of Vladimir Ilyich Lenin in the sphere of foreign policy might appear too bold, or, as G. V. Chicherin wrote, 'for all of us the sudden change from the early opinions of an underground revolutionary party to the political realism of a government in power was extremely difficult'.[15]

In the light of subsequent developments it is not fanciful to regard this as a prescription, inspired at a high level, for a new Soviet-American relationship, on a basis of equality, half a century after Lenin's death. But who were the dogmatists—the Chinese, or opponents within the CPSU Politburo of such a relationship, or both? This the author did not explain.

Meanwhile both sides continued their SALT talks—in Vienna from mid-April to mid-July and again in Helsinki from 2 November to 18 December, after which they were adjourned until the following March.

The Nuclear Non-Proliferation Treaty was brought into force in March 1970, when Great Britain, the Soviet Union, and the United States simultaneously deposited their ratifications. Over Indo-China, there could be no meeting of minds, particularly after the American–South Vietnamese 'incursion' into Cambodia in April-June (a similar operation was conducted in Laos in 1971). This followed the deposition *in absentia* of Prince Sihanouk, the Cambodian Head of State. It was the Chinese Government which acted as his host and sponsor in March, and in the following month joined with him in convening a summit conference of Indo-Chinese peoples. By comparison, Kosygin's denunciation of the incursion—although carried on television, the first such appearance by a Soviet Prime Minister within the Soviet Union— seemed a mild reaction; and the Soviet Union retained diplomatic relations with the new Cambodian Government for the next three and a half years.

In Latin America, both Chile and Cuba might have caused trouble between the two super-powers had the Soviet-US relationship still been as it was eight years before: Chile, when its electorate voted the Marxist leader of the Chilean Socialist Party, Salvador Allende, into power in September, and Cuba, when (following a visit by the Soviet Defence Minister to Havana) a Soviet submarine tender was anchored at Cienfuegos, accompanied by special barges for the storage of effluent from submarine reactors. As it was, the Soviet Government made no attempt to make Chile into a second Cuba, although it welcomed the new Chilean Government's nationalization measures and the swift reestablishment of Chilean diplomatic relations with Cuba; and the following May a modest Soviet-Chilean credit and technical assistance agreement was signed in Moscow,[16] which was visited by a Chilean trade delegation. The Soviet Government denied that it was building a base for ballistic-missile submarines in Cuba: an assurance that the US Government appeared disposed to accept.

By far the most difficult area was the Middle East, which in 1970 replaced South-East Asia as the principal source of conflict in the world, despite the fact that American involvement in Indo-China was to drag on for another three years. Here, while officially adversaries, the Soviet Union and the United States cooperated in practice, both in multilateral (together with the British and the French) and in bilateral talks, and notably by persuading Egypt and Israel to accept a cease-fire in August. In January, the Israeli Air Force's deep raids came within five miles of Cairo. Nasser could not be expected to survive a challenge on this scale. Following a hurried visit which he paid to the Soviet Union on 22 January, the Soviet Government took a major decision: to deploy in Egypt a force of about the same size as that despatched to Cuba in 1962 —150 MiG-21J aircraft and over 300 mobile and modern SAM-3 (surface to air) missiles.[17] This force, together with six Soviet-controlled airfields, was led by a Soviet air defence commander, General V. V. Okunev, from his headquarters in Cairo.

The Soviet Government took pains to assure the other governments concerned that the role of this force, which was sent to Egypt by air, was purely defensive and that the Soviet objective in the Arab-Israeli dispute remained a political settlement. Unlike 1962, on this occasion Moscow's assurances were accepted, as was the fact that the Soviet Defence Ministry could hardly forego side-benefits for Soviet national interests conferred by the operation that they had mounted: extra naval facilities at Mersa Matruh and an increased ability to keep watch on the US Sixth Fleet and allied navies in the Mediterranean from the air. The operation was successful, at a cost of the lives of four Soviet pilots shot down on 30 July. After mid-April Israeli deep raids virtually ceased; and the air defence of Cairo, the Nile valley, and the Delta was thus assured. The Israeli Air Force, which had hitherto enjoyed undisputed command of the air, now began to suffer losses, and by taking advantage of the cease-fire in August, the Russians were finally able to establish a complete air defence both of the Suez Canal itself and of a narrow stretch of Israeli-occupied Sinai immediately to the east of it.

Meanwhile, both advocates were exercising pressure on their clients, the United States Government by refusing, in March, to supply Israel with more Phantom aircraft, and the Soviet Government by applying pressure on Nasser in July, during another visit to the Soviet Union, to accept the American proposal for a cease-fire on the Canal and a military stand-still fifty kilometres either side of it. Unfortunately, the negotiations through Jarring, the UN mediator, that should have followed the cease-fire (which came into effect on 7 August), never got off the ground, because the Israeli Government withdrew from them in protest against the Soviet-Egyptian violations of the stand-still agreement. Had the Soviet Government resisted the temptation to move the SAMs forward to the Suez Canal in August, Jarring might have been able to make progress. As it was, an opportunity was missed, given the conciliatory statements made by both Golda Meir and Nasser before the cease-fire began. (Six months later, Soviet forces were withdrawn from the Canal, leaving the SAM-3 sites substantially in Egyptian hands.)

However, during the Jordanian civil war in the following month, both Nasser and the Soviet Government exercised a moderating influence, the former on the *fedayeen* and the latter on the Syrian Government, which was persuaded to withdraw the armoured force that had crossed the Jordanian frontier.[18] An anxious moment passed; this final exertion may well have hastened Nasser's death; but the cease-fire between Egypt and Israel, originally intended to last ninety days, held good. Nasser was succeeded as President of Egypt by Sadat, who in the course of the next three years was to set his country on a new course and, in the process, to bring the super-powers—for a few hours—closer to a nuclear confrontation than they had been at any time since the Cuban missile crisis of 1962.

NOTES

1. A Western European, especially from Britain, old enough to recall the events of 1938/9, might expect his Soviet contemporaries to prefer to forget this treaty, rather as he would prefer not to be reminded of the Munich Agreement: yet it appeared in posters displayed prominently in Moscow at this time, with a Nazi boot kicking through it.
2. Text in *Pravda* of 13 August 1970, translated in *Survival*, vol. XII, no. 10, October 1970.
3. Translated in *Survival*, vol. XIII, no. 2, February 1971.
4. The latter point was rammed home by Brezhnev again and again in his subsequent speeches: see, for example, the many references to the Moscow Treaty in Brezhnev, op. cit., vol. 3, indexed on p. 506.
5. Although the Federal Republic did not ratify this treaty for over four years after signing it: a measure of its importance.
6. *Istoriya Vneshnei Politiki SSSR*, vol. 2, p. 460. A similar protocol was signed during the Canadian Prime Minister's visit to Moscow in May 1971.
7. The texts of these two communiqués were reproduced in *Survival*, vol. XV, no. 8, August and no. 9, September 1970, respectively.
8. *Keesing's Contemporary Archives 1969/70*, p. 24348. These principles were 'sovereign equality, political independence and territorial integrity of each European state; non-interference and non-intervention in the internal affairs of any state, regardless of its political or social system; and the right of the people of each European state to shape their own destinies free of external constraint'.
9. Op. cit., vol. 2, p. 352.
10. See *The Times*, 20 April 1974.
11. Op. cit., vol. 2, p. 350.
12. In *Krajowa Agencja Informacyjna*, XII–XVI, no. 7/579, pp. 1, 3–13: Gierek's report to the Polish Central Committee, submitted early in February 1971.
13. George Kennan, in his article published in *Foreign Policy*, Summer 1972, p. 21, edited by Huntington and Manshel, National Affairs Inc., New York, 1972.

14. 'The Year 1919, the Mission of William Bullitt', *SShA*, Moscow, January 1970.
15. G. V. Chicherin, *Articles and Speeches*, Moscow, 1961, p. 227.
16. *Izvestiya*, 31 May 1971.
17. *Strategic Survey 1970*, IISS, London, pp. 46–9; the same source estimates the free market value of Soviet military equipment supplied to Egypt since the 1967 War as having increased during 1970 from 2,000 million to 4,500 million dollars.
18. Units of the US Sixth Fleet also moved eastwards towards the Syrian Coast. It is not clear whether this pressure on the Syrian Government was exerted by the super-powers acting in concert or in parallel.

11

THE YEAR 1971

The Middle East and the Mediterranean

On paper, the Soviet relationship with the new Egyptian President began well. In May, four months after the opening of the Aswan High Dam, the financing of which had first been undertaken by the Soviet Government in 1958, Podgorny signed a treaty of 'unbreakable' friendship between the Soviet Union and Egypt,[1] which provided for even closer cooperation between the two governments than did the Soviet-Indian Treaty concluded three months later. But its military clauses were carefully balanced. Article 7 laid down:

in the event of the development of situations creating, in the opinion of both sides, a danger to peace or violation of peace, they will contact each other without delay in order to concert their positions with a view to removing the threat that has arisen or to the reestablishing of peace;

while Article 8 stated that military cooperation, developed on the basis of 'appropriate agreements', would:

provide specifically for assistance in training the United Arab Republic military personnel, in mastering the armaments and equipment supplied to the UAR in order to strengthen its capacity, to eliminate the consequences of aggression as well as to increase its ability to stand up to aggression in general.

The phrase 'to eliminate the consequences of aggression' suggested the possible provision of more sophisticated offensive weapons by the Soviet Union than hitherto, while the phrases 'in the opinion of both sides' and 'appropriate agreements' seemed to safeguard the Soviet Union from being drawn into an adventure by Sadat, who had announced that 1971 was to be the Year of Decision.

Despite the treaty, it was a difficult year for the Russians in Egypt. Although Article 2 described Egypt as having 'set itself the aim of reconstructing society along socialist lines', it was in May that Sadat liquidated the pro-Soviet faction in Egypt, led by Ali Sabri. Worse still, soon afterwards the Sudan Government, which was being supplied with Soviet arms, executed the Sudanese Communist Party leader, Abdel Khalik Mahgoub. (The Chinese profited from the quarrel which arose between the Russians and the Sudanese by signing a 34 million dollar aid agreement with the latter in August.) Already perhaps sensing something of what was to follow in Egypt in 1972, the Soviet Government reinsured elsewhere. In the course of 1971 they supplied Syria with aircraft and surface-to-air missiles, accompanied by military advisers. The first Soviet arms deal with the Lebanon was announced in November, and in the following month the Soviet Prime Minister visited Morocco and Algeria—Morocco's armed forces being partly, and Algeria's wholly, supplied by the Soviet Union.

Although there were some anxious moments in the Arab-Israeli dispute, the cease-fire was maintained, amid a series of negotiations which were complicated by the fact that they were at times being simultaneously conducted by the Soviet and the US governments bilaterally; by the Russians with the Egyptians and by the Americans with the Israelis; and by Jarring with both the Egyptians and the Israelis. The idea which held the field at any rate in the earlier part of the year, was one which had first been floated by Moshe Dayan the previous October, namely that the Israelis should withdraw a certain distance from the Suez Canal, which would then be re-opened by the Egyptians. The negotiations foundered; in November Sadat said that he would go to war by the end of the month; once again both the super-powers were able to exercise restraint on their clients; but the Soviet Union was to pay the price for this in 1972.

Seen from Moscow, Cyprus is part of the Middle East. The island ended the year in a state of unrest, primarily because of the return of Grivas, the EOKA guerrilla leader, from Athens, where he had been living under surveillance since his recall from the island by the Greek Government nearly four years before. Despite the strength of the Greek Cypriot Communist Party, the immediate aim of Soviet policy in Cyprus was largely negative: to prevent the partition of the island between Greece and Turkey. While preserving its policy of friendship with the governments of both Turkey and Cyprus, it took the opportunity of the election of the new Moscow Patriarch to invite Archbishop Makarios to pay a state visit to the Soviet Union, which he did in June. As for the other former British colony in the Mediterranean, Malta (whose government had issued an ultimatum to the British Government), so far from the Soviet leadership emulating the Tsar Paul I,[2] it was the Chinese who granted the Maltese Government an interest-free loan of nearly £17 million, in April 1972. The Soviet Union was content to keep a watching brief on both these islands.

Europe

Notwithstanding the importance of the Soviet treaties with Egypt and India, by far the most significant agreement signed by the Soviet Government during the year 1971 was the Quadripartite Agreement on Berlin of 3 September. (The city was described as 'the relevant area' in the preamble and the first article of Part I of the agreement, in order to bridge the gap between the Soviet Government, mindful of its East German ally, and the other three governments.) The agreement,[3] which was expressly stated not to affect the Four Powers' quadripartite rights and responsibilities and their 'corresponding wartime and post-war agreements and decisions', was, like the Moscow Treaty, a compromise. It provided for unimpeded traffic between the western sectors of Berlin and the Federal Republic, for improved communications between these sectors and the rest of Berlin and the German Democratic Republic, and for the maintenance and development of the ties between the western sectors and the Federal Republic. Even though the western sectors of the city were not to be regarded as part of the Federal Republic, it was also agreed that the latter's government might perform consular services for permanent residents of the western sectors and might represent the interests of these sectors in international organizations and conferences; in return, the Soviet Union was authorized to establish a consulate-general in the western sector of Berlin.

In order to overcome the legal difficulty that the German Democratic Republic had not yet been formally recognized by the three Western signatories, or by the Federal German Government, the Quadripartite Agreement delegated the detailed arrangements for traffic and communications to be agreed by 'the competent German authorities'; and it was stated that these arrangements would be brought into force by a final quadripartite protocol when the latter had been concluded. These, broadly, were the legal niceties thanks to which the problem that had bedevilled East-West relations for twenty-three years was now in sight of solution. That the negotiations took eighteen months was, at least in part, the result of the opposition of the East Germans, whose object remained the complete *Abgrenzung** of the two Germanies.

The Berlin Agreement also opened the way for the first practical steps towards the holding of a European Conference. At their meeting held in Brussels in December, NATO ministers suggested four areas of discussion for an eventual meeting in Helsinki: 'questions of security, including principles governing relations between states and certain military aspects of security; freer movement of people, information and ideas, and cultural relations; cooperation in the fields of economics, applied science and technology, and pure science; and cooperation to improve the environment'.[4] And, following a remark about tasting the wine made by Brezhnev in a speech at Tbilisi in May (which perhaps helped to defeat the Mansfield amendment calling for US troop reductions), they also appointed Manlio Brosio, the former Secretary-General of NATO, to engage in exploratory talks about mutually balanced force reductions with the Soviet and other interested governments. To this offer there was no Eastern response; and there was no meeting in Helsinki for another year.

In 1971 Western and Eastern Europe each made what, at the time at any rate, seemed important advances towards closer unity. In the West, the enlargement of the European Economic Community was in sight. In the East, the COMECON Council approved in July its 'Complex Programme for the Development of Socialist Economic Intregration', with a time-scale of fifteen years for its execution. The lengthy text of the programme makes it clear at the outset that socialist economic integration is 'completely voluntary and does not involve the creation of supernational bodies; it does not affect questions of internal planning or of the financial and self-financing activity of organizations'. Given this restriction, which was essential for the Romanians (who had temporarily abstained from the previous year's decision to set up an Eastern European Investment Bank), integration meant the coordination by the member governments of their Five-Year Plans, through agreed decisions on product specialization, and implemented both by trade agreements for an equivalent period and by flows of capital, and in particular by the exchange of scientific and technological information between members. The basis of intra-COMECON trade remained the

* The concept of two German states, each with a completely different, irreconcilable, social system.

provision by the Soviet Union of long term supplies of raw materials in return for equipment manufactured by the Eastern European countries under specialization agreements.[5] But in deference to the smaller members of the organization, the programme included a schedule whereby the 1980 unit of COMECON accounting would become mutually convertible at unified exchange rates. The organization's principal task was defined as being gradually to bring closer and level up the economic development of member countries.[6] By Western European standards of the time the scope of this Eastern European economic programme was modest; and was, in the event, destined to be watered down still further.

Asia

The dramatic impact of the American decision to mend fences with China led the Soviet leadership to invite the US President to visit their country as well. But the Soviet response was not as clear-cut as this invitation may suggest. Some idea of the Kremlin's thinking may be derived from a comparison of the speech made by Brezhnev to the XVth Soviet Trades Union Congress, five months after the invitation was announced, with an article that appeared in *Kommunist* in January 1972. Having reaffirmed the need for a collective security system in Asia—a proposal that he had first launched in 1969—Brezhnev spoke with caution about the new Sino-American relationship: only time, perhaps the near future, would show how matters really stood, but the Soviet Union did not welcome the thought that the American and Chinese peoples held the future of our world in their hands.[7] According to the Chinese, Sino-Soviet relations should be based on principles of peaceful coexistence.[8] So be it, he said; and went on to recall Soviet proposals to the Chinese for non-aggression and the settlement of the frontier questions.[9] As for the United States, the key to success in the SALT negotiations was the recognition by both participants of the principle of identical security of both parties and their readiness to abide by this in practice—a Soviet formulation of the American concept of essential equivalence?

There was not yet, however, any public recognition of the responsibilities imposed on the two super-powers by their ability to blow up the globe. On the contrary, the *Kommunist* article repeated to its readers the conventional warning against the ideas, current in the bourgeois scientific world, of super-power, convergence, and bridge-building.

None the less, in February 1971 the Soviet Union joined with Great Britain and the United States in signing the Sea-bed Treaty; and on 30 September 1971 the United States and the Soviet Union signed two bilateral agreements, one to improve the hot line, which was converted to communication by satellite, and the other to reduce the risk of accidental nuclear war. Under the terms of the latter agreement, both sides agreed to do everything in their power to render harmless or destroy any nuclear weapon launched accidentally or without authority; each undertook to inform the other not only if its warning systems detected a possible missile attack, but also if warning or communication systems were themselves interfered with; and they committed themselves to give advance notice of any missile flights beyond their national territory.

On the ground in Asia, the Soviet leadership did all that they could to counter the Sino-American rapprochement. Whether they did indeed seek to influence some of their Chinese opposite numbers cannot be judged from Soviet sources; but two years later the Chinese Prime Minister publicly accused Mao Tse-tung's former right hand man, Lin Piao, of treason, plotting an armed *coup d'état* and fleeing 'surreptitiously . . . as a defector to the Soviet revisionists in betrayal of his party and country'.[10] (Lin Piao's death in an air crash in Mongolia in September 1971 was made officially public in August 1972.) Certainly, by the end of the year nearly a third of the two-year-old CCP Politburo had been dismissed by Mao. The number of Soviet divisions stationed along the Chinese frontier and in Mongolia was estimated to have risen to forty-four (from fifteen in 1968)—more than the number in Central Europe. Soviet support for India was given legally binding form by the Indo-Soviet Treaty concluded in August 1971,[11] on the eve of the Indo-Pakistan War, in which China and the United States both found themselves backing Pakistan—unsuccessfully, as it turned out.[12] There was a delicate moment in December when elements of the US Seventh Fleet were sent to the Bay of Bengal and elements of the Soviet squadron were sent northward from the Indian Ocean; but the war ended quickly with an overwhelming Indian victory. Soviet support for India was also diplomatic: two vetoes of cease-fire resolutions in the Security Council, where the representatives of the world's two great communist powers at once became engaged in a slanging match. As a Soviet commentator claimed, 'events in the Indian sub-continent led to the first joint defeat of the USA and China in the struggle with the national-liberation movement'.[13]

The Indo-Soviet Treaty looked like the first link in the Soviet system for containing Chinese power in Asia, which the Russians adopted just as the Americans were in the process of giving it up. (The number of US troops in Vietnam was halved in the course of 1971.) Its preamble affirmed both sides' belief in the principles of peaceful co-existence and of cooperation between states with different political and social systems. Could this have been designed to justify whatever agreements the Soviet Union intended to conclude with the United States in the following year? It was, however, balanced by Article 10, in which the parties declared that they 'shall not undertake any commitment, secret or open, towards one or more states imcompatible with the present treaty'. In essence, the treaty provided India with a Soviet umbrella against China for as long as India chose to stay out of the nuclear club: under the terms of Articles 8 and 9 respectively, each party solemnly declared that it would not enter into or participate in any military alliances directed against the other, and undertook to:

refrain from giving any assistance to any third party taking part in an armed conflict with the other party. In case any of the parties is attacked or threatened with attack, the High Contracting Parties will immediately start mutual consultations with a view to eliminating this threat and taking appropriate effective measures to ensure peace and security for their countries.

The message to China was clear enough.

NOTES

1. Full text in *Pravda*, 28 May 1971. In fact, Egypt was still called the United Arab Republic at that time, but it has seemed simpler to use the shorter form throughout.
2. In 1798 the Tsar Paul I accepted the Grand Mastership of the Order of the Knights of Malta.
3. *The Times*, 4 September 1971.
4. *Keesing's Contemporary Archives 1971/2*, p. 25015. The NATO communiqué was still cautious about the proposal for a meeting in Helsinki, expressing readiness 'to begin multilateral conversations intended to lead to a Conference on Security and Cooperation in Europe'.
5. As examples, Brezhnev mentioned at the XXIVth Party Congress the prospect that by 1975 the *Druzhba* pipeline would ship nearly fifty million tons of oil to Eastern Europe (as compared with 8·3 million tons in 1964), and that a gas pipeline would carry natural gas from Siberia to European Russia, thus facilitating the supply to Eastern European countries.
6. This analysis of the Complex Programme is indebted to Michael Kaser.
7. Brezhnev, op. cit., vol. 3, pp. 495 ff., contains the text of his speech. This

passage referred to Nixon's remarks, made on 21 and 27 February 1972, at the banquets given in his honour in Peking and Shanghai respectively: 'what we do here can change the world', and 'this is the week that changed the world'. For the 1969 proposal, see Brezhnev, op. cit., vol. 2, p. 413.

8. Not a flattering proposal, since in Leninist theory peaceful coexistence applies only to countries 'with different social systems'—i.e. between Marxist and non-Marxist countries.

9. At the end of the same year Brezhnev revealed that the proposal for a non-aggression pact with China, including nuclear weapons, had been put forward by the Soviet Union as early as January 1971.

10. *The Times*, 1 September 1973.

11. Full text in *Pravda*, 10 August 1971.

12. On the other hand, China supported the Government of Ceylon—as did the Soviet Union, among other countries—against the Maoist rebels there.

13. *Kommunist*, 'The Programme of Peace in Action', January 1972. But, in my view, Soviet policy in the sub-continent was aimed primarily against China. Soviet relations with Pakistan were restored in March 1972.

12

THE YEAR 1972

The year 1971 had been a transitional one for Soviet foreign policy. At the outset of 1972—the year in which Peking and Moscow were, each in turn, visited for the first time by the President of the United States— the concept in Washington of the structure of world power emerging in the late twentieth century seemed to resemble the nineteenth-century concert of the great powers, described as an even balance[1] between the United States, China, the Soviet Union, Japan, and Western Europe. In the event, things worked out differently. But the foundations of a new world power structure were laid during this memorable year.

China

Nixon visited China from 21 to 28 February 1972. Despite the American rear-guard action, fought only a few weeks beforehand in New York and many of the world's capitals, as a final attempt to retain Taiwan's seat in the United Nations, this visit came very close to achieving its stated objective, the normalization of relations between the United States and China. (Initially, diplomatic contact was maintained through their ambassadors in Paris, but liaison missions were exchanged in 1973.) The joint communiqué[2] consisted partly of points agreed by both sides and partly of statements of each side's position on the Taiwan question. The Chinese categorically described Taiwan as a province of China; its liberation was a Chinese internal affair; and they were opposed to concepts such as the two Chinas and an independent Taiwan. The Americans acknowledged that 'all Chinese on either side of the Taiwan Strait maintain that there is but one China and that Taiwan is a part of

China'; they affirmed as their ultimate objective the withdrawal of all US forces and military installations from Taiwan; meanwhile they would reduce them progressively, as tension in the area diminished. Both sides agreed to conduct their relations on the basis of the Five Principles;[3] neither would seek hegemony in Asia and the Pacific; each was opposed to efforts by any country or group of countries to establish such hegemony; major countries should not divide up the world into spheres of influence; and the Chinese declared that China would never be a super-power, and that it opposed hegemony and power politics of any kind.

The Soviet Union

This done, Nixon visited the Soviet Union from 22 to 30 May. Any doubt that by May 1972 the Soviet leadership had reached the conclusion that they must agree, at the highest level, the framework of a new Soviet-American understanding, was removed by the welcome that they gave the US President in Moscow, in spite of his decision (announced only a fortnight previously) to mine seven North Vietnamese ports and to attack supply routes from China to Vietnam.[4] Of the Soviet-American bilateral agreements concluded in 1972, by far the most important were the Treaty on the Limitation of Anti-Ballistic Missile Systems (ABMs), the interim agreement (lasting five years) on certain measures with respect to the limitation of strategic offensive arms, both signed during Nixon's visit, and the three-year grain agreement, signed in Washington on 8 July.[5]

The first of the SALT agreements is clear, the second less so. It will be recalled that one of the major destabilizing factors in the nuclear strategic equation by the end of the 1960s was the prospective deployment by both the super-powers of ABM systems. Under the terms of the treaty limiting such systems, each side was permitted to deploy them in two areas only: one centred on its capital and the other, at its own choice, containing some part of its ICBM force. Launchers so deployed must be capable of firing one missile with one warhead only; they must be static; and they must be land-based. These conditions, coupled with restrictions on the associated radar systems, meant that the Soviet Union could expand the existing ABM defences of Moscow to a total of 100 launchers, and also construct another site for the defence of some of its ICBMs.

The interim agreement was a holding operation, designed to set the ring for the second round of SALT talks, which were resumed in Geneva—their venue from then on—in November. Under its terms, each side was permitted a total of ICBM and SLBM launchers based on the number either operational or under construction on 1 July and 26 May respectively, although both sides were allowed to modernize and replace these launchers, subject to certain conditions. Quantitatively, this agreement sanctioned what had in the previous three years become a marked Soviet superiority: about 1,530 operational ICBMs (with another 90 under construction) as against 1,054 American ICBMs; and about 560 operational SLBMs (with another 245 under construction) as against 656 American SLBMs.[6] The Soviet Union had achieved an equally marked superiority in megatonnage, each of its 290 SS-9s having an estimated warhead yield of between 20 and 25 megatons, as opposed to the *Titan* 2's estimated yield of between 5 and 10 megatons. In order to assess the balance of the interim agreement, it is important to bear in mind not only that in strategic nuclear weapons systems accuracy matters more than megatonnage, but also that the agreement mentioned neither strategic bombers—an arm in which the US Air Force had retained its superiority—nor the so-called forward based systems (FBS)—US strike aircraft based on the territory of the United States' allies or on aircraft carriers stationed in the Mediterranean Sea and the Pacific Ocean—between two and three thousand in all— capable both of carrying out conventional attacks and of delivering nuclear warheads on Soviet targets.[7] Moreover, the ceilings on permitted numbers of American missile launchers were based on programmes laid down at the outset of the Kennedy Administration and had been accepted by successive US Administrations since 1967. Five years later, by which time both governments were probably spending about twenty-five billion dollars annually on strategic armament,[8] the US Government was already concentrating its efforts on quality rather than on quantity. In consequence, in 1973 US *Poseidon* submarines and *Minuteman-3* ballistic missiles were being deployed as quickly as possible, equipped with MIRVs, capable of doubling the number of Soviet targets at which, at any rate in theory, American missiles could strike by mid-1977.[9] MIRVs, which are unidentifiable by satellite, were not mentioned in the interim agreement, which was signed at a time when they had not yet been deployed by the Soviet Union.

The passage of the interim agreement through the US Senate was not an easy one. Ratifications were finally exchanged by the two governments in October, after the Senate had adopted an important amendment, submitted by Henry Jackson, urging the President to seek a further treaty with the Soviet Union—i.e. in SALT II—'which would not limit the United States to levels of intercontinental strategic forces inferior to the limits provided for the Soviet Union'.

The significance of the two strategic arms agreements of May 1972 is described by Soviet writers as difficult to overestimate.[10] Even though they did not mark a breakthrough towards the kind of disarmament to which both super-powers had been committed since their ratification of the Nuclear Non-Proliferation Treaty over two years previously, they did mark a potential beginning; and this must be assessed against the new kind of language used in the twelve points of the Joint Declaration on Basic Principles of Relations between the USA and the USSR, which formed part of the agreements signed in Moscow. In this declaration the two sides agreed that in the nuclear age there was no alternative to conducting their relations with each other on the basis of peaceful coexistence; they attached 'major importance to preventing the development of situations capable of causing a dangerous exacerbation of their relations'; they would therefore do their utmost to avoid military confrontations and to prevent the outbreak of nuclear war; they would always exercise restraint in their relations with each other and would be prepared to negotiate and settle differences by peaceful means; efforts to obtain unilateral advantage at the expense of the other, directly or indirectly, were inconsistent with these objectives; and the prerequisites for maintaining and strengthening peaceful relations between the USA and the USSR were 'the recognition of the security interests of the parties based on the principle of equality and the renunciation of the use or the threat of force. . . .'

These principles of parity were reaffirmed by Nixon in his speech at the Kremlin banquet given in his honour on 22 May, when he said that there was no longer such a thing as security in a preponderance of strength; the nuclear great powers had a solemn responsibility to exercise restraint themselves in any crisis, to take positive action to avert direct confrontation, and to exercise a moderating influence on other nations in conflict or crisis.[11] As if to play down the closeness of the special relations between the two super-powers implied by such language, he declared in his televised broadcast from the Kremlin on 28 May that it was not their aim to establish a condominium. And the joint communiqué ended by affirming that the Moscow agreements and understandings were not in any way directed against any other country.

Unlike the strategic agreements, the two commercial agreements, one covering the Soviet purchase of American grain and the other setting up a Joint Trade Commission, could be assessed in hard cash. Of these, the former came into immediate effect, whereas the Trade Commission, which held its first meeting in Moscow in July, could not exert its full impact on the Soviet-US economic relationship until Congress was willing to pass the legislation required to grant the Soviet Union most favoured nation treatment. Nevertheless, the Commission succeeded in settling the long outstanding Soviet Lend-lease debt to the United States; and the Trade Agreement contemplated that the volume of trade during its three-year period would be at least three times as much as over the 1969–71 period, to an aggregate of at least 1,500 million dollars; American business was on the point of making an assault on the Soviet market, which had previously been largely a West European and Japanese preserve.

The dimensions of the grain agreement were a measure of the Soviet crop failure. During the three-year period beginning on 1 August 1972 the Soviet Union was to buy at least 750 million dollars' worth of US grown food grains, at least 200 millions' worth of which was shipped in the first year. The US Government undertook to make available a line of credit not exceeding 500 million dollars for these purchases, repayable in three years from the date of delivery. The conclusion six days later of a five-year agreement with the Soviet Government by the Occidental Petroleum Company, for the joint development of Soviet oil and natural gas, seemed to open up a prospect of a longer term economic relationship between the two super-powers, with the Soviet Union an importer of American grain and the United States an importer of Soviet oil and natural gas.

One subject in the joint communiqué on which the two sides were able only to record their agreement to differ was Vietnam. Did the Soviet leadership use their influence in Hanoi on behalf of the US Government in the closing stages of the latter's painful negotiations with the North Vietnamese? The American bombing was halted while Podgorny visited North Vietnam in June; in August the last US combat unit was withdrawn from Vietnam; and by December (although it did not appear so at the time, when American bombing of the North was temporarily resumed) the end was at last in sight. In his televised address to the American people during his visit to the United States a year later, Brezhnev spoke of Soviet-US cooperation in halting the war in Vietnam.[12] Just how much ice Soviet representations cut with a government that had already held out so long,[13] and with the Chinese offering Hanoi free military equipment and materials for 1973, is questionable. In any case by January 1973, when Kissinger finally reached agreement with Le Duc Tho in Paris, the sigh of relief in the Kremlin must have been as deep as in every other country.

Japan

The political pattern that had been familiar for so many years in Asia was beginning to break up. The immediate[14] response of Kakuei Tanaka, the new Japanese Prime Minister, to the American announcement of 15 July 1971 had been to reinsure both with China and with the Soviet Union: in the words of the Japanese Foreign Minister, Japan must adapt to the multipolar age and pursue a foreign policy divorced from ideology. In September 1972 Tanaka visited Peking. The Japanese Government expressed its 'respect' for the Chinese position on Taiwan; the Chinese Government renounced its claims to war reparations; and the two governments re-established diplomatic relations. (In consequence Taiwan broke off diplomatic relations with Japan.) In October the Foreign Ministers of Japan and the Soviet Union began to discuss the negotiation of a peace treaty in Moscow.[15] Although the Japanese Government had earlier agreed to study positively the Soviet proposal for an Asian collective security system (during a visit paid to Tokyo in January by Gromyko), the only territorial concession that the Soviet Government felt able to offer Japan, no doubt with Chinese territorial claims in mind, was the return of two of the four Kurile Islands occupied by the Soviet Union in 1945—not enough for Japan, for whom half a loaf was unacceptable. This deadlock did not prevent a rapid expansion of trade. This had already increased in both directions from a mere 40 million dollars in 1958 to 822 millions in 1970; a new trade agreement concluded in 1971 had provided for an increase of nearly double over the next five years; and in June 1972 the two governments seemed to be nearing agreement in principle to engage in immense projects, the joint development of the Tyumen' oil field in Western Siberia and other areas, including Sakhalin, possibly with American participation, and natural gas resources at Yakutsk.

Japanese-Soviet participation in projects such as the Tyumen' development was viewed with suspicion by the Chinese Government, because this would in their view increase the potential Soviet military threat to China. By the end of the year, during which there had been another alleged clash on the Sino-Soviet border (this time between

Kazakhstan and Sinkiang, in which five Soviet border guards were believed to have been killed), China had built up, or was on the point of building up, a nuclear *force de frappe*[16] directed against the Soviet Union: 20–30 MRBMs probably deployed, mainly in north-eastern China, and an IRBM developed and possibly deployed with a range long enough to reach Moscow. No Siberian agreement was to be concluded between Japan and the Soviet Union for another two years.[17]

Europe

This was a year of fruition, both within Western Europe and between West and East. On 22 January the new members of the European Economic Community signed the Treaty of Accession in Brussels; on 18 October Great Britain ratified this treaty; on 19–20 October the heads of the Western European Governments, meeting in Paris, set themselves the goal of Western European unity by the end of the decade; and on 1 January 1973 the Treaty of Accession came into force.

It was against this background that on 17 May the Federal German Bundestag finally approved the ratification of the Moscow and Warsaw Treaties; on 26 May the treaty on traffic questions between the two Germanies was signed in East Berlin, thus opening the way for the foreign ministers of the Four Powers to sign the final Quadripartite Protocol of their 1971 Agreement on Berlin, which then came into force; and the West and East German governments went on—in December—to sign their Basic Treaty on relations between the two countries, which was signed in East Berlin.[18] Like the Moscow Treaty, from which this whole network of treaties stemmed, this agreement was a *de facto* compromise, which did not purport to settle the German problem *de jure*; indeed the rights and responsibilities of the Four Powers (who alone are legally entitled to bring about a *de jure* settlement) were expressly affirmed by both sides. Its most important practical consequences were threefold; preservation for the German Democratic Republic of its privileged position under the European Economic Community's Protocol on inter-German trade, whereby East German exports to West Germany are excluded from the EEC common tariff; the exchange of permanent missions—not described as embassies— between the two states; and application by both for membership of the United Nations (which they finally entered in September 1973).

Towards the end of the year the two conferences that had formed the subject of so many communiqués issued by the NATO Alliance and

the Warsaw Pact, at last entered the phase of practical preparation: the
Conference on Security and Cooperation in Europe (CSCE) at the level
of heads of mission in Helsinki, in November; and in the same month—
following Kissinger's discussions in Moscow two months earlier—
seven NATO countries invited five Warsaw Pact countries (the USSR,
Poland, Czechoslovakia, Hungary, and the German Democratic
Republic) to preparatory talks on Mutual Balanced Force Reductions
on 31 January 1973.[19] On 30 November, in a speech[20] delivered during
a visit to Hungary, Brezhnev declared his belief that it would be
possible to solve the problem of reducing armed forces and armaments
in Europe, and in his address to a joint session of the CPSU Central
Committee and the Supreme Soviet, on the occasion of the fiftieth
anniversary of the formation of the Soviet Union, he raised for the first
time the possibility that COMECON and the EEC might cooperate.

The Third World

Soviet multilateral diplomacy was impelled in 1972 both by the momentum which it had gathered during the two previous years and by the
Soviet understanding with the United States. In March, the Soviet
delegate to the Geneva Disarmament Conference presented a draft
treaty banning chemical weapons; in April, the convention banning the
production or possession of biological weapons was opened for signature
in London, Moscow, and Washington; and in May, the Seabed Treaty
banning the location of arms on the ocean floor was brought into force
by the ratifications of Britain, the Soviet Union, and the United States.
But in the Third World the Soviet leadership found their traditional
policy hard to reconcile with this new understanding. In the Middle
East,[21] Egypt became a test case. Having failed to make 1971 his Year
of Decision, Sadat paid two visits to Moscow in February and April
1972, doubtless in the hope of securing arms that would enable Egypt
to 'eliminate the consequences of aggression' as defined in Article 8 of
the Soviet-Egyptian Treaty of May 1971. The Soviet Defence Minister
visited Egypt in May. The Soviet-American agreements concluded in
that month induced a mood of despair in Egypt. On 18 July Sadat
demanded the withdrawal of all Soviet military advisers and experts,
estimated to number about 17,000. The Soviet Government took this
blow (the forerunner of Sadat's decision, nearly two years later, to adopt
a policy of 'positive neutrality' between the super-powers) on the chin.
Within a fortnight the withdrawal had substantially been completed;

only a few hundred Soviet advisers were thought to have remained; and the Soviet Union lost the use of Egyptian airfields, although their Mediterranean naval squadron retained some facilities on the northern Egyptian coast.

The Soviet response was to reinforce success further north. Soviet naval activity along the Syrian coast increased; the return of Soviet-trained military to Syria was accelerated; further arms were delivered; and a SAM-3 system was brought into operation. On 9 April the Soviet Prime Minister had visited Iraq to sign a fifteen-year Treaty of Friendship and Cooperation.[22] As in the Egyptian model, the friendship was unbreakable. The only military commitment was cautious, being to the effect that each side would assist the other in strengthening its defences and that they would coordinate their positions in the event of a threat to peace. The Iraqi armed forces had been largely dependent on Soviet arms since 1963 and wholly so since 1969. Soviet arms supplies were now increased; and a few SAM-3 sites were brought into operation by the end of the year. Equally important, the Soviet Union undertook to help to distribute oil from the Iraq Petroleum Company field at Kirkuk, which the Iraqi Government had at last nationalized on 1 June, and to bring the North Rumaila oil field into large-scale production (Soviet imports of oil from Iraq appeared for the first time in the statistics of Soviet foreign trade in 1972, published one year later). This tightening of Soviet-Iraqi relations suggested that the Soviet Government was seeking to make the Gulf, from which British troops had been withdrawn at the end of 1971, a new focus of its policy in the Middle East. Diplomatic relations had already been established with Kuwait, although not yet with the Union of Arab Emirates that had been formed after the British withdrawal. As long ago as November 1940, during Molotov's last round of negotiations with Hitler and Ribbentrop, the German side had described the natural tendency of the USSR as being to move in the direction of the Indian Ocean. But thirty-two years later there was an important difference in the political geography of this immensely rich area: although Britain had withdrawn its military presence, Iran was on the way to becoming a formidably armed country, using part of its vast oil revenues to buy sophisticated modern weapons. The Soviet Union's need to remain on good terms with Iran, therefore, acted as a restraining influence; and in October the Shah, while on a visit to Moscow, signed a fifteen-year treaty of economic cooperation and trade.

The Soviet dilemma in the Third World was presented to the

Kremlin personally by the leaders of the two Latin American Marxist governments, those of Cuba and Chile, both of whom visited Moscow in December 1972, in order to seek financial aid. The Soviet answer to their requests for aid was given in blunt terms: to Cuba, a great deal, to Chile, very little. Cuba had five months earlier become a full member of the COMECON, thus qualifying—like Vietnam—for aid within the socialist commonwealth. But by any standards the terms of the deal[23] secured by Castro were generous: deferment of the repayment of the Cuban debt (estimated at nearly three billion dollars, excluding military aid) until 1986, after which it would be repaid free of interest; Soviet credits to cover Cuban trade deficits in 1973–6, also to be repaid after 1986 without interest; and a 330 million dollar development loan, to be repaid at a low rate of interest after 1976. The Russians also agreed to buy Cuban sugar and nickel for the rest of the decade at prices well above the world prices then obtaining.

The joint communiqué[24] issued after Allende's visit to the Soviet Union could hardly have offered a greater contrast. It had much to say about the two governments' identity of views on the problems of the rest of the world and little about either Chile itself or Latin America— a recognized Moscow method of dealing politely with a distinguished visitor who has not been granted what he hoped for. Having made it clear early in his presidency that he would not accept a Soviet military presence in Chile, Allende did not seek military aid. But by the end of 1972 he was in desperate financial straits, with agricultural production lowered in the wake of the Chilean agrarian reform, and inflation already soaring at a rate of 160 per cent per annum. (The World Bank, the Export-Import Bank, and the Inter-American Development Bank had all suspended lines of credit to Chile, mainly because of the Chilean Government's decision to nationalize, without compensation, US copper interests in Chile.) Having received Soviet trade credits the previous June worth 260 million dollars and obtained Soviet agreement to import 130,000 tons of Chilean copper (despite the fact that the Soviet Union is a net exporter of copper itself), Allende was believed at the time[25] to have come to Moscow in search of 500 million dollars in hard currency loans. The paragraph in the joint communiqué relating to Soviet aid was not explicit, referring to Soviet agreement to extend aid to Chile for a number of stated purposes, but subject to the conclusion of 'corresponding agreements' reflecting the 'concrete measures for implementing this agreement'. All that Allende seems to have received by way of immediate help was 30 million dollars' worth of credit for

Soviet deliveries of food and of cotton for the textile industry, and agreement to reschedule the repayment of Chile's debt to the Soviet Union, amounting to 103 million dollars.

Once bitten, twice shy; after the Cuban experience, the Soviet leadership did not, as *Le Monde* gently put it, consider that the Chilean experiment should be defended by all available means. A Soviet apologist for his government's treatment of Allende—the CPSU Central Committee responded to the military *coup d'état* that overthrew his government with no more than a brief expression of sympathy— would no doubt recall the fact that, instead of heeding the economic advice given him by the Chilean Communist Party, Allende followed the ruinous path preferred by the extremists of his own, socialist, party. Yet if he had accepted communist advice and thus strengthened his claim to Soviet support (which even then would have had to be on a huge scale in order to keep Allende's regime afloat), would this claim have been met, given the Soviet experience in Cuba and the new Soviet understanding with the United States?[26] As it was, the award of the Lenin Peace prize, although a compliment to a septuagenarian socialist, cannot have been much consolation to Allende as a president who needed far more than that in order to stay in power, or, as it turned out, to stay alive (he committed suicide after being deposed by the Chilean armed forces on 11 September 1973).

So ended 1972, a year of great change for the international status of the Soviet Union, now formally acknowledged by the world's first super-power as its equal: a change that was to be reflected in the following spring by the first new formulation in the doctrine of Soviet foreign policy for nearly two decades.

NOTES

1. In an interview published in *Time* magazine of 2 January, Nixon said: 'I believe in a world in which the United States is powerful. I think it will be a safer world and a better world if we have a strong, healthy United States, Europe, Soviet Union, China, Japan, each balancing the other, not playing against the other, an even balance.' The President was echoing a remark made by Kissinger in 1968, in 'Central Issues of American Foreign Policy', Brookings Institution, Washington: 'in the years ahead the most profound challenge . . . will be . . . to develop some concept of order in a world which is bipolar militarily, but multipolar politically'.
2. *Keesing's Contemporary Archives 1971/2*, pp. 25150 ff.
3. Respect for the sovereignty and territorial integrity of all states; non-aggression against other states; non-interference in the internal affairs of other states; equality and mutual benefit; and peaceful coexistence.

4. The mines were laid and activated on 11 May.

5. *Keesing's Contemporary Archives 1971/2*, pp. 25309 ff. and p. 25291. Subsequent quotations from other documents signed in Moscow are derived from the same source.

6. *The Military Balance 1972/3*, IISS, London, 1972, Appendix I, pp. 83 ff., analyses the effect of the SALT agreement on the strategic balance.

7. *Strategic Survey 1972*, IISS, London, 1973, p. 15.

8. Ibid., p. 14.

9. Ibid., p. 16.

10. *Diplomatiya Sotsializma*, Moscow, 1973, p. 171.

11. Cf. Brezhnev's remark, quoted in ch. 1, made a year later in Washington.

12. *Pravda*, 25 June 1973.

13. The United States Air Force is estimated to have dropped three and a half times as many bombs on Vietnam as it did on all the United States' enemies in the Second World War. For rough estimates of the cost, in blood and in treasure, of the Vietnam War, see *Strategic Survey 1972*, IISS, London, 1973, pp. 48 ff.

14. For a Japanese assessment of the range of responses open to Japan in the longer term, see Kiichi Saeko, 'Japan's Security in a Multipolar World', *Adelphi Papers* no. 92, IISS, London, 1972.

15. The Soviet Union had refused to sign the Japanese Peace Treaty negotiated at San Francisco in September 1951, under Article 2 of which Japan renounced all claim to the Kuriles. The state of war between the Soviet Union and Japan was nevertheless brought to an end in October 1956, by the re-establishment of diplomatic relations between the two countries.

16. *The Military Balance 1972/3*, IISS, London, 1972, p. 44.

17. The 1972 agreement in principle led in the end to Japanese participation on a modest scale, a $450 million loan from Japan for the development of Siberia, not including Tyumen': see *The Times*, 23 April and *Pravda*, 27 June 1974.

18. An account of the three-cornered manoeuvres that preceded the momentous vote of 17 May is given in Kulski, op. cit., pp. 428 ff. The text of the Basic Treaty is in *Survival*, January/February 1973, vol. XV, 1, pp. 31–2.

19. At their meeting in Prague in January 1972, the Warsaw Pact ministers had declared that the interests of European security would be served by reaching an agreement on the reduction of armed forces and armaments in Europe, although it could not be 'an exclusive matter for the existing military and political groupings in Europe to consider and determine the way in which to solve that problem'.

20. *Keesing's Contemporary Archives 1971/2*, p. 25676.

21. In Africa south of the Sahara, on the other hand, Soviet policy, although troubled by fierce Chinese competition for influence, notably in Tanzania (whose armed forces were exclusively trained by the Chinese), could afford to be long term. In Southern Africa the principal source of the supply of arms for the major guerrilla movements remained the Soviet Union. The Soviet Government also made some well-judged offers to African governments: for example, field artillery to Nigeria, which made an important contribution to the ending of the civil war in 1970 (*New York Times*, 21 January 1970: 'Nigeria says Russian help was vital to war victory'); and cash ($7,500,000) to Somalia for the development of the Port of Berbera, which was to become a valuable port of call for the Soviet Navy's squadron in the Indian Ocean. And the Soviet Navy patrolled the coast of Guinea after that country had been attacked from Portuguese Guinea in 1971.

22. In turning to Iraq, the Russians did the same as the British had done twenty-

four years earlier, when the future of their Egyptian base began to look insecure.

23. Summarized in *The Economist*, 13 January 1973.
24. Text in *Pravda*, 10 December 1972.
25. For contemporary assessments of his mission, see *The Economist* of 9 December and *Le Monde* of 7 December 1972.
26. For a Soviet posthumous criticism of Allende's economic mistakes, see A. Sobolev's article in *The Working Class and the Contemporary World*, no. 2, Moscow, 1974. The CPSU's expression of sympathy was carried in *Pravda*, 14 September 1973.

13

1973—ANNUS MIRABILIS?

At the Moscow summit meeting in 1972 Brezhnev had accepted an invitation to visit Washington the following year. Before he paid this return visit, and before he visited Bonn—the first time that the General-Secretary of the Soviet Communist Party had ever set foot in the Federal Republic of Germany—the Central Committee held a meeting on 27 April 1973, which took two major decisions. The first of these was to set the seal of the Committee's formal approval on a foreign policy that had become more and more identified with Brezhnev personally. The second was to make the first important changes in the composition of the Party Politburo for eight and a half years. Two members of the Politburo were dropped: Voronov and Shelest, the latter having already been removed a year before from his powerful post as head of the Ukrainian Communist Party (perhaps because he was opposed to receiving Nixon, just as he had allegedly been the leader of the hawks over Czechoslovakia in 1968). The three newcomers were Andrei Gromyko, the Foreign Minister, Marshal Andrei Grechko, the Defence Minister, and Yuri Andropov, the head of the KGB. None of the holders of these three offices would normally qualify for membership of the Politburo; the last time that any of the incumbents had done so had been in the 1950s. Brezhnev was thus able to embark on his two delicate missions in the summer backed both by the maximum of departmental expertise concentrated inside the Politburo and by a fresh mandate of the Central Committee of the CPSU.

This mandate was expressed in a resolution, to which the Soviet press gave especial publicity, entitled 'On the international activity of the Central Committee of the CPSU regarding the realization of the decisions of the XXIVth Party Congress'. The resolution[1] began by describing the Party's international policy in conventional terms: active and thrusting, relying on Soviet strength, power, and authority. Although imperialist aggression against Vietnam had been brought to a halt, constant watchfulness was required against any intrigues of the aggressive, reactionary circles of imperialism; in particular, the legal rights of the Arab peoples in their struggle against imperialist aggression must be supported. So far, no change. But the nub of the resolution was its emphasis on the principle of peaceful coexistence 'as a general rule'* of relations between states with different social systems. From this rule stemmed the switch from cold war to *détente* and the need to 'ensure that the favourable changes achieved in the international sphere should acquire an irreversible character'. The value of summit meetings was affirmed; so was the role of foreign trade as a way to help peace as well as the interests of the Soviet people. The resolution ended with an attack on the CCP leadership's alleged opposition to the unity of the world communist movement and to international *détente*. The emphasis on peaceful coexistence as a general rule in this declaration, and the link between foreign and domestic policy, were both pointed up by Brezhnev during his visit to the Federal Republic the following month, when he declared, in the course of his televised address to the German people, published in full by *Pravda* on its front page on 22 May: 'our peace-loving foreign policy is the expression of the very essence of our society, the expression of its deep internal needs ... our aim is to ensure that the Soviet people live better tomorrow than they do today'.

Europe

Brezhnev visited Bonn from 18 to 22 May.[2] The chief fruit of the visit was economic: a ten-year agreement on the development of economic, industrial, and technological cooperation between the Soviet Union and the Federal Republic. (An agreement on cultural cooperation was also

---

* A literal translation of the three Russian words *v kachestve normy* will not suffice, because of the different significance of the word 'norm' in the two languages. Their inclusion in the resolution was an important doctrinal innovation, whose significance was made clear by their appearance among the officially approved slogans for the October Revolution celebrations six months later (see *Pravda*, 14 October 1973). On 26 October Brezhnev described the principles of peaceful coexistence as 'gradually becoming converted into the generally accepted role of international life' (*Pravda*, 27 October 1973) and on 15 August, in his speech at Alma Ata, he defined the aim of Soviet foreign policy as 'to render irreversible the phenomenon of *détente*' (*Pravda*, 16 August 1973).

signed.) Six months previously the two sides had signed a declaration of intent concerning the construction of an integrated steelworks using the direct reduction process on the Kursk ore-fields in central Russia, the largest Soviet-West German project so far (a further long-term agreement for the supply of Soviet natural gas to the Federal Republic had been signed in 1972). Its total cost was estimated at DM3,000 million, including orders from West German firms worth at least DM2,000 million, to be financed by long-term credits granted by a West German consortium, which were to be repaid by the supply to West Germany of the product of the plant. The joint statement issued on 21 May welcomed the current negotiations[3] on industrial projects, including the Kursk steelworks; agreed to promote cooperation in the development of advanced technology and the creation of new production facilities in the USSR; while, for its part, the Federal Government declared its interest in receiving large supplies of crude oil from the Soviet Union.

At the opening banquet on 18 May, the Federal Chancellor made it clear where he stood politically: 'the Federal Republic is a member of the Atlantic Alliance. It is embedded in the community of Western Europe, which has now grown beyond the Common Market.' As for Berlin, it was still not all plain sailing. Although both the Ten-Year Agreement and the Cultural Agreement contained clauses applying them to West Berlin 'in accordance with the Four Power Agreement of 3 September 1971', the joint statement referred to a detailed exchange of views on questions concerning that agreement, and the two sides agreed that strict observance and full application of the agreement were essential to lasting *détente* in Central Europe and to the improvement of relations 'between the states concerned', especially between the Federal Republic and the Soviet Union. Speaking in the Bundestag afterwards, the Federal Chancellor denied that there was any question of altering the Four Power Agreement on Berlin, or of giving it a special interpretation for the Federal Republic's bilateral relationship with the Soviet Union. It had become clear as the result of Brezhnev's visit that practical difficulties existed between the two governments regarding the application of the agreement, which must be, and indeed could be, solved, by using the facilities offered by the agreement. Brandt went on to say that the situation in Berlin was the touchstone of West German-Soviet bilateral relations, and that so far as economic relations were concerned, no negotiations on specific projects had been conducted or decisions taken. The difficulty to which Brandt referred concerned the precise nature of the consular representation of West Berlin to be under-taken by the Federal German authorities under the terms of the 1971 Agreement. This was not resolved until November, when a compromise was agreed in Moscow between the Federal German and Soviet Foreign Ministers.[4]

In June, after five months of preparatory talks in Vienna, the NATO and Warsaw Pact governments concerned agreed to begin negotiations on 30 October, again in Vienna, regarding 'mutual reduction of forces and armaments in Central Europe', with what amounted to an open agenda. Thus the adjective 'balanced' that had occurred in every NATO pronouncement on this question since the ministerial meeting at Reykja-vik in 1968, was dropped, although the communiqué[5] recorded agree-ment that specific arrangements would have to be carefully worked out in scope and timing in such a way that they would in all respects and at every point conform to the principle of undiminished security for each party. On the NATO side, the participants did not include France; and the Warsaw Pact side succeeded in securing agreement to the exclusion of Hungary, which would have only observer status, along with Romania Bulgaria, Norway, Denmark, Italy, Greece, and Turkey.

In the United States, Congressional pressure for a reduction in the number of US troops stationed in Europe, excluding the Sixth Fleet, mounted steadily. On 25 July Mike Mansfield proposed that the half million US ground forces overseas should be cut by half within three years, the axe to be applied most sharply to the 300,000 troops in Europe. In the event, he changed the 50 per cent to 40 per cent shortly before the Senate voted on his amendment, which was carried, by three votes, for the first time in a decade. Although the amendment was defeated in a subsequent vote,[6] and although the President could in any case delay cuts in Europe by beginning with a reduction of the 168,000 US troops stationed in the Far East and South-East Asia, substantial cuts seemed inevitable sooner or later in Europe, where, in the crucial central sector, the Soviet Union retained its massive margin of numeri-cal superiority in conventional forces. Leaving aside the number of formations, Soviet—as opposed to Warsaw Pact—forces in this sector had more tanks than all the NATO forces in the sector put together, and the total number of Soviet tactical aircraft was slightly larger than the NATO total, excluding France.[7]

When the thirty-five foreign ministers—from all Europe, except Albania, and from the United States and Canada—convened on 3 July in Helsinki to prepare for the Conference on Security and Cooperation in Europe, they adopted an agenda,[8] hammered out by their ambassadors over the previous six months, which bore a closer resemblance to what NATO ministers had suggested in the past than to what had been put forward by the ministers of the Warsaw Pact, although it was they who had launched the idea of a conference in 1965 and persisted in promoting it ever since. In particular, although the third section of the agenda, entitled 'cooperation in humanitarian and other fields', did not explicitly refer to the freer movement of ideas, it did contain several phrases which, if translated into action, would have that effect. The preparatory talks were notable both for Soviet resistance on this sensitive issue, and for a Romanian attempt to secure the inclusion of the phrase 'irrespective of membership of military and political groupings' in the list of principles which each participating country was committed to respect and apply in its relations with other participating states, by the terms of the first section of the agenda, entitled 'questions relating to security in Europe'. In the end, the words used were 'irrespective of their political, economic, and social systems'—less than the Romanians wanted and more than the Russians were at first prepared to concede. In his speech on 3 July,[9] Gromyko tried to claw this back, saying that cultural cooperation should observe fully 'the principles designed to govern relations between states', particularly those of sovereignty and non-intervention; and he pressed for a rapid conclusion of the conference before the end of the year. It was none the less agreed that the second stage of the conference should meet in Geneva on 18 September, and with such issues at stake, there was every indication that it would last for at least another year.

Thus, after years of bargaining, the Soviet Union and its allies got their European Conference and the United States and its allies got their negotiation on the reduction of forces in Central Europe, although both had to make concessions in order to secure their objectives. Meanwhile, Western Europe began 1973 with a bang—the signature of the Treaty of Accession by the three new members of the European Economic Community, Britain, Denmark, and Ireland—although by the end of the year the Community had been thrown into disarray. In Eastern Europe, COMECON's target of economic integration by 1985 had receded. This target, and the Complex Programme, remained a slogan, but in the course of 1973 the time-scale began to lengthen to twenty or twenty-five years. This was not simply the result of the four-fold increase in world oil prices at the end of the year, against whose effects Eastern Europe could not be immunized. The old idea of a crisis-proof

Eastern European monetary system was beginning to give way to a new concept of Eastern European cooperation, commercial and financial, with the Western economic community. The impulse for this change came from the needs of the Soviet economy, as much as from the desire of Eastern European governments for greater freedom to pursue their national interests. The old basis of the COMECON structure— broadly, an exchange of Soviet raw materials for Eastern European manufactured goods—weakened as the Soviet Union looked increasingly to the United States, Japan, and West Germany for help in the joint development of its natural resources, especially those located in Siberia. In consequence, Eastern European countries were, for their part, beginning increasingly to look westwards for sources of raw materials, for technical assistance in modernizing their industries, and for finance. Romania had become a member of the International Monetary Fund in 1972; Hungary joined Czechoslovakia, Romania, and Poland as a member of GATT; Eurodollar bank consortium loans to Eastern European countries rose sharply; the COMECON clearing bank itself raised loans in Western Europe; and there was even the prospect of joint ventures controlled by COMECON countries in Western countries. This loosening of COMECON made it increasingly important to establish some form of relationship between COMECON and the EEC. After Brezhnev had told the Luxembourg Foreign Minister (who happened to be visiting Moscow at the time) that COMECON wanted to begin working together with the Community on monetary, financial, and investment questions, on 27 August the COMECON Secretary-General formally proposed to the Chairman of the EEC Council of Ministers that both organizations should appoint delegations to discuss cooperation.[10]

The Washington Agreements

It has been suggested in the opening chapter that one of the agreements signed by Brezhnev during his visit to Washington may be regarded as terminating the cold war: the Agreement on the Prevention of Nuclear War of 22 June 1973. The contrast between the circumstances in which Brezhnev visited the United States, from 18 to 25 June 1973, and those of Khrushchev's visit fourteen years earlier could scarcely have been greater. True, in the intervening fourteen years the brave new communist world prophesied by Khrushchev had not materialized—the gap in living standards and gross national product between the two countries remained enormous. Militarily, however, the dialogue between the two leaders was now conducted between equals; and it was not just a dialogue, but—as in Moscow the year before—a negotiation expressed in written agreements. Moreover, by the time Brezhnev arrived in Washington, events there had reached a point where the visit of the most powerful leader in the communist world served to strengthen domestically the most powerful leader in the capitalist world, by diverting the attention of the American public for one week from the televised hearings of the Senate Watergate Committee, which suspended its activities while Brezhnev was in the United States as the government's official guest. This paradox was unknown to the rank and file of the Soviet public, who learned nothing about the Watergate scandal from Soviet sources until the second half of August, when Moscow radio broke the official silence by attributing it to the fears of Nixon's opponents that he might 'go too far in his steps towards the relaxation of international tension'.[11]

The key-note of the Washington agreements was the use of the word 'permanent'. The preamble of the communiqué issued on 25 June[12] recorded the decision of both sides to turn the development of friendship and cooperation between their peoples into a permanent factor for world-wide peace; and the United States President accepted Brezhnev's invitation to pay a second visit to the Soviet Union, in 1974. In spite of the constraints of Watergate, the 'broad network of constructive relationships' between the two super-powers—the aim of the new American diplomacy—was further strengthened.

Three nuclear agreements were signed, one relating to the peaceful use of atomic energy and the other two to the prevention of nuclear war and to the limitation of nuclear weapons. Under the terms of the first, for a duration of ten years, both sides agreed to expand and strengthen their cooperation in the fields of controlled nuclear fusion, fast breeder reactors, and research on the fundamental properties of matter, and to set up a joint committee to this end. The second agreement[13] was a Soviet initiative. It is of unlimited duration; its second article binds the Soviet Union and the United States to 'proceed from the premise that each party will refrain from the threat or use of force against the other party, against the allies of the other party and against other countries, in circumstances which may endanger international peace and security'. These last nine words provide a possible loophole, which Kissinger was at pains to close when, in an explanatory news conference held after the agreement's signature, he urged that the document should not be approached with the eye of a sharp lawyer; and he conceded that in the light of history, if either signatory wanted to go to war, it would, as before, find an excuse to do so.[14] This agreement also included an article (IV), which—although Kissinger said it did not make the United States an arbiter between the Soviet Union and China—defined the special relations between the super-powers in the strategic field in the following terms:

If at any time relations between the parties or between either party and other countries appear to involve the risk of a nuclear war between the USA and the USSR or between either party and other countries, the United States and the Soviet Union ... shall immediately enter into urgent consultations with each other. ...

The third agreement[15] committed the two governments to make serious efforts to work out the provisions of a permanent agreement on the limitation of strategic offensive arms, with the objective of signing it in 1974. They described the prospects for a permanent agreement in 1974 as favourable. The events of the following year have proved them wrong. Among the weaknesses of this agreement are the inadequacy of the national technical means of verification envisaged, and the contrast between the third and fifth articles, the former stating that limitations 'can apply' to the quantitative aspects of strategic weapons as well as to their qualitative improvement, and the latter envisaging their modernization and replacement, under conditions to be agreed between the parties. The present prospect is that by 1975 Soviet SS-18 rockets, the most powerful in the world, will be deployed, equipped with MIRVs, which have since been developed by the Soviet Union; meanwhile the United States has been reported to be developing a more sophisticated version of MIRV, known as MARV—manoeuvrable re-entry vehicle— the flight path of whose individual warheads can be influenced from the launching-point, instead of being pre-determined.[16] This technology is intended for use in the *Trident* submarine, whose rapid construction was approved by the US Senate in September 1973.[17] The first of these vessels should be ready by 1978, at a cost of 1,300 million dollars. Carrying 24 missiles, each armed with 10–14 independently targetable warheads with a range of 6,000 miles, it will be both faster and quieter— and therefore harder to hunt and destroy—than previous submarines, and will have a displacement larger than that of a modern British cruiser.

In the commercial field, American firms had governmental encouragement to work out concrete proposals on specific projects involving the participation of American companies, including the delivery of Siberian natural gas[18] to the United States. A sign of the times was the front page of *Pravda* on 24 June, which devoted a few lines to the CPSU General-Secretary's meeting with American Communist Party leaders, but the whole of the rest to his meeting with American businessmen, whose names and firms were spelled out in full. It was on this occasion that he spoke with candour both about the origins of the cold war— leaving it an open question which side had been responsible for it in the first place—and about deficiencies in the Soviet economy generally and in the handling of Soviet foreign trade in particular. In his televised address to the American people, which text took up the front page of *Pravda* of 25 June, Brezhnev reverted to the question of the cold war, describing it as 'a miserable substitute for real war', whose 'sombre influence is unfortunately preserved to some extent even to the present day'. He emphasized that both the Soviet Union and the United States respected the fact that each had its own allies and obligations to other governments. But the chief significance of what he and the President had discussed and agreed was the determination of both sides to make good relations between the USSR and the USA a permanent factor of international peace. He might well have added that this new relation-ship between the super-powers was symbolized by the plan for the meeting of their astronauts in space in July 1975.

Apart from the Watergate affair and related scandals, whose drama was resumed as soon as Brezhnev left America, two other shadows hung over the visit: the failure of the two governments to make any headway over the Middle East, their only point of agreement being that it caused both of them deep concern—with good reason, as events were soon to prove—and the question whether Congress would approve the granting of most-favoured-nation treatment to the Soviet Union. Two months later, a Soviet periodical[19] carried an abridged version of an article entitled 'USSR–USA and the Contemporary World', written by the chief editor of the Soviet journal *USA*, who had remained in the United States for some time after Brezhnev's visit, in order to sound the opi-nions of leading figures across the whole range of the American political spectrum. Basing himself on the premise that the changes both in Soviet-American relations and in the world as a whole were due to the decisive change in the Marxist correlation of world forces, which had obliged the leaders of the capitalist powers to carry out ' "an agonizing re-appraisal" of their foreign policy doctrines', the writer of this article went on to observe that the question that now interested many people both in the United States and in other countries was whether stability in US-Soviet relations was possible. So far as the Soviet side was concerned, the answer was clearly affirmative. As for the American side, it was not merely a matter of the good will of the present Administration or of external factors, but also of internal political problems in the United States which had necessitated new approaches and concepts both in the international and in the domestic field. The conclusions drawn were that the Administration's policy towards the Soviet Union had bipartisan support to a remarkable degree and that there were grounds for hoping that the world really was entering an era of *détente*.

What was significant in this article was the evident anxiety that this assessment should prove to be correct. By the autumn pressures were building up in the Western world with the object of making any concessions to the Soviet Union in the field of foreign policy dependent on Soviet willingness to modify internal policy—this in spite of the appeal of Kissinger, newly appointed Secretary of State,[20] for a fresh consensus behind US foreign policy and Brandt's statement that his government would have pursued the same *Ostpolitik* even if Stalin had still been head of the Soviet Government.[21] In the United States these pressures focused on the clause* in the Trade Reform Bill granting most-favoured-nation treatment to the Soviet Union, that is to say, the termination of the existing tariff discrimination against Soviet goods to which the Administration stood committed by the Moscow commercial agreement of 1972. Under the leadership of Jackson and Vanik, overwhelming support was secured in Congress for withholding not only MFN treatment but—more important—American credits and credit guarantees backed by the US Government, from countries denying free emigration or imposing more than nominal taxes on emigrants. This support was reflected in a non-binding resolution, passed in the Senate by an unopposed vote of eighty-five on 18 September, condemning Soviet treatment of political dissidents and calling on the President to use current negotiations to secure its end. As Jackson remarked, 'now, at the beginning of the road to *détente*, is the time to test the direction we are asked to travel'. Further evidence of Soviet awareness of the significance of the Jackson amendment was supplied by the description of Jackson as the darling of the military-industrial complex in *Pravda*,

* The object of this bill was to give the US Administration a mandate to negotiate further liberalization of world trade with other countries in the GATT framework. The clause relating to MFN treatment for the Soviet Union was tacked on to the bill by the Nixon Administration as an afterthought.

which accused him of interfering in the Soviet Union's internal affairs
for purely political motives.[22] Soviet anxieties were deepened by the
dramatic news of the President's dismissal of the Watergate Special
Prosecutor and the consequent resignation of the US Attorney-General
in October,* when the Fourth Arab-Israeli War had been raging for
nearly a week.

* *Novoe Vremya* gave the Soviet public this news at the end of October—by
Moscow standards, promptly—but it was not until this periodical appeared on
2 November 1973 that Soviet readers were informed for the first time of the
possibility that Nixon might be impeached by Congress, the word 'impeach-
ment' being transliterated into cyrillics. No comment was offered.

NOTES

1. Text in *Pravda*, 28 April 1973.
2. Once again, the Soviet leadership took pains to preserve their links with
   France: Brezhnev received Pompidou in January, before the French
   parliamentary elections, and he stopped in France for talks on his way back
   from Washington in June. He also visited the German Democratic Republic
   and Poland immediately before his visit to the Federal German Republic,
   and at a meeting of bloc party leaders, held in the Crimea at the end of July,
   he obtained their approval of his summit diplomacy: see *Pravda*, 1 April
   1973.
3. *Keesing's Contemporary Archives 1973*, pp. 25975 ff. The Kursk negotiations came to fruition two years later.
4. As a result of this compromise, the Federal German and Czechoslovak
   governments were able to sign a peace treaty on 28 November. Signature
   had previously been held up by this disagreement.
5. Text in *The Times*, 29 June 1973.
6. Ibid., 28 September 1973. The lobby for the cut in American forces abroad
   rests its case partly on political and partly on financial grounds. The latter
   can be summarized in a single statistic: the average cost of US military pay
   per man rose from 5,081 dollars in 1967/8 to 8,533 dollars in 1972/3. For
   leaked reports of an American plan for a 15 per cent cut in US troop levels in
   Europe, see *The Times*, 15 September 1973.
7. *The Military Balance 1973/4*, IISS, London, 1973, Appendices I and II,
   pp. 87 ff.
8. *The Times*, 2 and 3 July 1973.
9. Ibid., 4 July 1973.
10. Ibid., 28 August 1973: and for an assessment of the changes in COMECON,
    see *The Times*, 24 September 1973, 'Eastern Europe: Changing Priorities' by
    Kurt Weisskopf.
11. *The Times*, 21 August 1973, 'Mr Nixon Gets a Little Help from His Friends'
    by Victor Zorza. Soviet citizens able to listen to foreign broadcasts would of
    course have followed the affair throughout.
12. Text in *The Times*, 26 June 1973. The phrase was also used by Brezhnev in
    his televised address to the American people: see *Pravda*, 25 June 1973.
13. Text in *The Times*, 23 June 1973.

14. Ibid., 23 June 1973.
15. Ibid., 22 June 1973.
16. For MIRVs, see ibid., 18 August 1973, quoting James Schlesinger's press conference of the previous day. For MARVs, see *The Economist*, 26 January 1974, p. 56.
17. *The Times*, 28 September 1973.
18. Ibid., 22 June 1973, reported that an annual figure of 200 million dollars worth of natural gas, over twenty years, was being mentioned in Washington at the time, together with Export-Import Bank finance for a part of the cost of a 400 million dollar fertilizer plant.
19. Berezhkov in *Literaturnaya Gazeta*, no. 35, 29 August 1973. pp. 9 and 14.
20. Kissinger retained his post as Special Assistant to the President for National Security Affairs.
21. *The Times*, 10 October and 13 September 1973 respectively.
22. Ibid., 19 September, and *Pravda*, 7 October 1973.

14

1973: THE TEST

In October 1973, less than four months after the signature of the Washington Agreements, the new relationship between the super-powers was subjected to its first serious test, when war broke out between their clients in the Middle East, for the fourth time in a quarter of a century.

On the eve of this war, whose profound consequences are still being felt today—not only by the participants and the super-powers—how would the international scene have appeared to a well-informed observer in the Kremlin? Since anniversaries have a special attraction in Moscow, he might have begun his reflections by recalling that it was almost thirty years since what were then the world's Three Great Powers met at the Teheran Conference; just over twenty years since Stalin died; sixteen years since the first *sputnik*; eleven years since the first Soviet ballistic missiles were installed in Cuba; just over ten years since the Sino-Soviet dispute was publicly acknowledged in the Soviet Union and since the Soviet Government joined with the governments of its two former partners in the Grand Alliance in signing the partial Nuclear Test Ban Treaty; and not quite nine years since the resignation of Khrushchev and the explosion of the first Chinese nuclear device. What would have struck him most about the past decade was the increasing intimacy of his country's relations with the leader of the capitalist world, the United States, and the increasing acrimony of those with the leader of the great Marxist heresy, China. The Soviet Government was still theoretically* bound by the defence obligations of the

* *Pravda*, 16 October 1973, included, among Soviet proposals that the Chinese had rejected, 'confirmation of the validity of the Treaty of 1950'.

thirty-year Sino-Soviet Treaty of Alliance and Friendship signed in 1950. But by now dependable Chinese missiles could reach Moscow and other targets in European Russia.

It was no doubt with an eye to the Xth CCP Congress that, in a speech delivered on 15 August in Central Asia, at Alma Ata, Brezhnev repeated the offer that he had made to the Chinese Party leadership two years earlier at the XXIVth CPSU Congress (to normalize Sino-Soviet state relations and restore good-neighbourliness and friendship). Speaking on 24 September at Tashkent, again in Central Asia, he revealed that as recently as mid-June the Chinese Government had not even replied to a renewed Soviet offer of a non-aggression pact, although he simultaneously warned third parties against trying to make capital out of the Sino-Soviet dispute.[1] The Chinese response to the Soviet Union was not encouraging. At the end of August, the New China News Agency, after accusing the Soviet Union of having dismembered Romania and subjugated Bulgaria, concluded: 'The Romanov dynasty and the Khrushchev-Brezhnev dynasty are linked by a black line, that is, the aggressive and expansionist nature of Great Russian chauvinism and imperialism. The only difference is that the latter dons a cloak of "socialism"—"social imperialism" in the true sense of the term.'[2] The Chinese radio broadcast at length a speech made by the Chinese Prime Minister at the CCP Congress, in the course of which he went so far as to compare Brezhnev with Hitler and accused him of trying to get money from capitalist countries as a reward for opposing China.[3] On 28 July he said that both the contradictions between the two super-powers and their contention were ceaselessly intensifying, and that their temporary compromise and collusion would in no way change the nature of either of them.[4] Chinese opposition to the monopoly of world affairs by the super-powers was repeated by the Chinese Prime Minister at the banquet given in honour of Pompidou on 11 September, when he also reaffirmed Chinese support for the cause of Western European unity.[5]

The strength of the language used by the Chinese, who again spoke of the danger of a Soviet pre-emptive nuclear strike, may have been partly attributable to trouble on the Sino-Mongolian border (little more than 300 miles from the Chinese capital). In September a fresh element was injected into the Sino-Soviet dispute by a Mongolian press allegation that China had been violating this frontier.[6] (Of the forty-five Soviet divisions stationed in the Sino-Soviet border area, two are in the Mongolian Republic.)[7] But the two major attacks on Chinese policy that appeared in *Pravda* in August over the pen-name Aleksandrov provided enough explanation in themselves. The second[8] of these left nothing unsaid. The CCP, which represented the Soviet Union as its principal enemy, preached:

a reactionary pseudo-theory borrowed from bourgeois ideologists, according to which the march of historical development allegedly determines a 'conflict' of all small and medium states of the world with the two 'super-powers' . . . the absurd thesis of the 'two intermediate zones',[9] according to which the oppressed peoples of Asia, Africa and Latin America (the 'first zone') are allegedly not only 'linked by common interests' with certain basically capitalist countries of West and East (the 'second zone'), but they should and can unite with this 'zone' in a struggle against the 'super-powers'.

Thus China portrayed itself as the defender of the interests of small and medium countries and the leader of the Third World, to which it claimed to belong, instead of to the communist world. In spite of this, at the same time the Chinese leadership were forcing forward their country's conversion into a nuclear super-power, with the object of controlling the destinies of other countries. The chief proof of China's ideas of hegemony cited by Aleksandrov was Chinese policy in South-East Asia, where the Chinese aim was to establish a group of states under the aegis of Peking. China had aligned itself in an opportunistic alliance with the most aggressive circles of imperialism against the socialist countries, and had reoriented its foreign trade at the expense of its links with the communist world. China not only opposed the Soviet Union's European policy—the Moscow and Warsaw Treaties and the European Conference—but even pronounced panegyrics of NATO and the 'principles of Atlantism', and favoured the maintenance of the American military presence in Europe and a new Atlantic charter.[10] While opposing the Soviet suggestion of Asian collective security, China supported the US-Japanese security agreement and the US nuclear zone in the Far East; it had also tried to propagate the illusion in Tokyo that China had chosen Japan as its permanent partner for the joint decision of all Asian issues; it had encouraged Japanese territorial claims[11] against the Soviet Union; and had sought to dissuade Japan from pursuing a policy of peaceful coexistence with the socialist commonwealth.

China was further reproached for its refusal to sign the nuclear treaties;[12] for its refusal to consider the Soviet proposal for a treaty renouncing the use of force and its rejection of repeated proposals for the settlement of frontier questions; and for Chou En-lai's description of the Washington Agreement on the prevention of nuclear war as a mere scrap of paper. The absurd claims to broad areas of Soviet territory, false allegations about plans for a Soviet pre-emptive nuclear strike, and insinuations about an alleged 'threat from the North' were all spread by the Maoist leadership not only in order to work up a war fever and to justify the nuclear arms race, but also to divert popular attention from internal difficulties. Maoist ambitions of great power hegemony were described as being in contradiction with the needs of the Chinese people, whose interests did not coincide with the great power chauvinism of its leaders—a clear appeal to Chinese public opinion over the heads of the party leadership. For its part, the Soviet Union would continue its struggle against the theory and practice of Maoism, a trend hostile to Leninism, although it stood ready to restore its inter-state relations with China to normal.

Brezhnev's speeches and *Pravda*'s anathemas may have been aimed at a future Chinese leadership, rather than at the CCP Congress. So long as Mao Tse-tung remains in office, any normalization that goes beyond the courtesies required by the presence of ambassadors in the two capitals is hardly conceivable. What therefore is the best that our imaginary observer in the Kremlin could reasonably hope for? Anything resembling a renewal of the Sino-Soviet bloc would require a reconciliation between the two major communist parties that would resolve both the ideological and the state issues dividing the Soviet Union and China. By 1973 these divisions were so profound and so numerous that, from the Soviet viewpoint, the optimum goal had become simply an agreement to differ: perhaps something on the lines of the principles of the Belgrade Declaration of June 1955* (when Khrushchev made his Canossa journey, after seven years of Soviet-Yugoslav hostility), or at any rate a restoration of relations between the two governments to a state that would leave each party free to compete for world leadership— but not at the current level of mutual vituperation—and would enable both governments to devote less effort to preparing for a war that could benefit no one, and that would do incalculable harm.

Within the Soviet Union, our observer would have been aware that in spite of the Central Committee's April mandate for Brezhnev's

---

* The relevance of this declaration, which has served the Yugoslav leadership as the touchstone of their oscillating relationship with the Soviet Union ever since, is that it was an agreement of principles reached between the two governments, not the two parties: see Brzezinski, op. cit., pp. 177 ff., and Kulski, op. cit., pp. 339 ff.

foreign policy, of which the new concept of foreign trade formed an integral part, there were still autarkic voices prophesying woe among the planners trained in methods of the Stalinist era, who either could not or would not adapt themselves to the new model of compensation agreements, whereby credits from Western countries are devoted to producing commodities in the Soviet Union, part of which are used to repay the credits, over a long period of years. That these voices were audible in the Kremlin is suggested by the appearance of two articles in May 1973, defending the credit-barter compensation model. (In one of these[13] *Pravda* even felt obliged to cite Leninist principles to justify economic links with capitalist countries.) The natural allies of such critics of the new foreign policy would be those who feared its effects within the borders of the Soviet Union. Such fears would have been lessened by the tightening of the bonds of internal discipline and the steady weakening of the dissident movement in the Soviet Union.

The last edition—the twenty-seventh—of the *Samizdat* chronicle of current events had appeared in October 1972. At the end of August 1973—just before the second stage of the European Conference on Security and Cooperation was due to open in Geneva—two Soviet dissidents, Yakir and Krasin, pleaded guilty to offences under Article 70 of the Russian Federation's penal code, allegedly linked with the activities of organizations in the West. In the course of this trial, the names of Sakharov and Solzhenitsyn were implicated by the defendants. Both reacted forcefully. Solzhenitsyn said in a press interview in August that so long as permission to print his works in the Soviet Union was withheld, he would continue to have them printed by Western publishers; on 21 September he announced that he had begun underground circulation in the Soviet Union of two hitherto unpublished chapters of *The First Circle*;[14] and in the same month he decided to publish, in Paris, the most damaging attack on the Soviet system that he had ever written— *Gulag Archipelago*—for this reason:

with an uneasy heart I refrained for years from printing this book that was already completed; my duty towards those still alive outweighed my duty towards the dead. But now that the State Security has in any case seized this book nothing remains for me but to publish it at once.[15]

Adding what must have seemed to the Soviet leadership insult to injury, on 5 September Solzhenitsyn sent them a letter,[16] which was later published in the West. In this he put forward a programme of proposals aimed at preventing war with China, which he regarded as the chief danger facing the Soviet Union abroad, and at preserving the

Russian environment and the Russian nation: these proposals included repudiation of official support both of Marxism as a state ideology and of national liberation movements, termination of Soviet tutelage over Eastern Europe, permission for national republics to leave the Soviet Union, a Soviet agrarian reform on the Polish model, and concentration of Russian effort on domestic problems, especially development of the Siberian north-east. Five months later Solzhenitsyn was arrested by the KGB, and deported to the Federal Republic of Germany, on 12 February 1974.

For his part, Sakharov gave a long press conference on 21 August 1973 in his flat in Moscow, the full text of which was published in the West.[17] In the course of this he lamented the much stronger reprisals taken against Soviet political dissidents during the previous two years; he described the Soviet elite as having a 'sort of separate thinking' which prevented them from reacting differently from the way in which they did; and he declared:

a rapprochement while the West accepts our rules of the game . . . would be very dangerous . . . would not solve any of the world's problems, and would mean simply a capitulation to our real or exaggerated strength. It would mean an attempt to trade, to get gas and oil from the US, neglecting all other aspects of the problem . . . *détente* without any qualifications would mean the cultivation and encouragement of closed countries . . . no one should dream of having such a neighbour, especially if this neighbour is armed to the teeth.

The subsequent campaign in the Soviet press against these two world-famous figures caused a wave of indignation in the West. Ironically, this happened at a time when, following the outcry aroused by the Leningrad trials[18] of December 1970, an unprecedented number of Soviet Jews received permission to emigrate to Israel (70,000 in the period from 1971 to September 1973), and when the stiff emigration tax on Soviet Jews applying for exit visas was suspended, in deference to American pressure in April 1973. Moreover, in Marc Chagall's old age an exhibition was at last allowed of his works, which had lain for years in the cellars of Soviet museums; and just before the Geneva Conference opened, the Soviet authorities stopped jamming Western broadcasts in Russian. Nevertheless, when Soviet policy towards the dissidents was clearly intended either to silence them at home or to force them into exile, Sakharov had come uncomfortably close to the heart of the matter.

To sum up, in the autumn of 1973, although an observer in the

Kremlin would have been well satisfied with the Soviet-American agreements of the previous two years, he could not have ignored the shadows threatening the super-power relationship; and he would have been acutely conscious that the country that would gain most from a breakdown of this relationship would be China. In these circumstances it is hard to believe that on 6 October the Syrian and Egyptian combined attack on Israel, which achieved complete tactical surprise, can have been welcome to the Soviet leadership.

The Arab-Israeli War

The course of the war has been described in detail by other writers.[19] The war, which lasted from 6 to 25 October, was longer, more evenly balanced, more bitterly contested, and more costly in loss of life and of material than any of the three previous Middle Eastern wars. The Arab attack was launched on two fronts: the northern, on the Golan Heights, and the southern, in the Sinai Peninsula, both of which had been occupied by Israeli forces since the Six Day War of 1967. In the north, the Syrian forces were helped by Arab allies from as far afield as Morocco. Both attacks achieved initial success. But by 12 October the Israeli counter-attack on the northern front had reached a point twenty miles from Damascus, and on the southern front their counter-attacking force west of the Canal was about fifty miles from Cairo when the fighting stopped. Nevertheless, in strong contrast with previous Arab-Israeli wars, in this one neither side emerged as the victor; and because Israel had won the wars of 1948, 1956, and 1967 outright, this time it was the Arabs who acquired a new feeling of military confidence on the battlefields, whereas Israel's invincibility was called in question for the first time. This war also differed from earlier Middle Eastern wars in two other, highly significant ways: the use of economic warfare by the Arab oil-producing countries, and the involvement of the two super-powers, which culminated in the nearest approach to a nuclear confrontation between them since the Cuban missile crisis, exactly eleven years before.

In October 1973, for the first time, the Arabs used the power of their oil resources to apply political pressure to Israel's principal protector, the United States: an embargo on oil supplies to the United States, a cut-back in production and—above all—an increase in oil prices, which led to the world energy crisis of 1974 (a crisis which the war did not cause, though it hastened its onset).

The super-powers' intervention took two forms. As adversaries, the Soviet and United States governments each delivered vast supplies of arms by air to the combatants in the Middle East, to replace the losses incurred in battle. As partners, they conferred, both with each other and with their allies. At any rate so far as the public record is concerned, the first Soviet reaction to the Arab attacks was one of reserve. On 8 October the Soviet Union was warned by the United States that it could not disregard the principles of *détente* in any area of the world 'without imperilling its entire relationship with the United States.'[20] Brezhnev responded the following day with a message to the Algerian President suggesting that all possible aid should be sent to Egypt and Syria; and on 10 October the Soviet airlift of military supplies to the Middle East began. The American airlift to Israel was announced on 13 October; and on 19 October a bill was presented to Congress seeking 2·2 billion dollars military aid for Israel.

The day after the Israeli bridgehead had been established on the west bank of the Suez Canal, Kosygin arrived in Cairo, where he spent three days. On 20 October Kissinger visited Moscow, where agreement was reached between the two governments to sponsor jointly a resolution in the Security Council calling for an immediate cease-fire and for the implementation of the Council's Resolution 242 of November 1967. After Kissinger had flown from Moscow to Tel Aviv, both sides accepted the resolution, which brought the cease-fire into force on 22 October. The cease-fire soon broke down, with the prospect that the Egyptian Third Army, established in force on the east bank of the canal, would be cut off by the Israeli force that had by then reached Suez. After the super-powers had co-sponsored a second resolution in the Security Council, calling for a withdrawal to the positions of 22 October, the Egyptian Government pressed the Soviet and US governments to intervene militarily on the spot to ensure Israeli withdrawal. This was followed on 24 October by a personal message from Brezhnev to the US President, which was interpreted in Washington as a Soviet threat to intervene unilaterally in Egypt unless Israel observed the cease-fire of 22 October. For a few hours, in the early morning of 25 October, the American response took the form of a world-wide Defence Condition Three alert. Later on the same day, a third Security Council resoluton[21] was passed, which finally brought the war in Egypt to an end. It was agreed to send a United Nations Emergency Force to the Middle East, from which troops not only of the super-powers, but of all five permanent members of the Security Council, were excluded. On 28 October

146

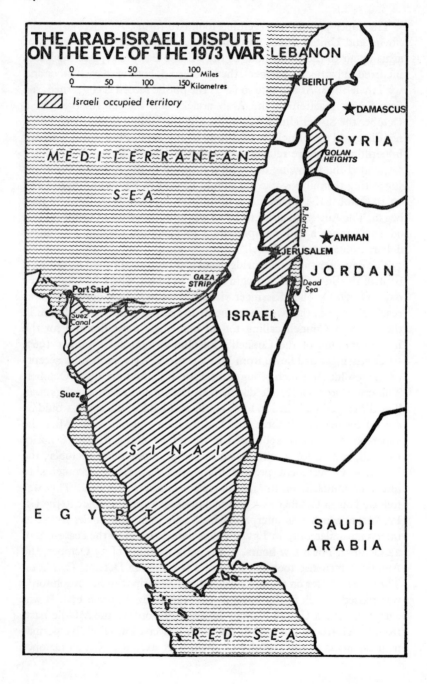

THE ARAB-ISRAELI DISPUTE
ON THE EVE OF THE 1973 WAR

the first meeting between Egyptian and Israeli officers for seventeen years took place, at Kilometre 101 on the Suez-Cairo road. Thus Soviet military intervention in Egypt was prevented; the encircled Egyptian Third Army was saved; and Sadat succeeded in making 1973 his year of decision.

To this brief account must be added a complicating factor: that the Middle Eastern crisis coincided with major developments in American domestic politics. On 10 October Spiro Agnew resigned as Vice-President under threat of indictment; two days later Gerald Ford was appointed Vice-President in his place; and on 12 October, by dismissing the Special Watergate Prosecutor, Nixon took a decisive step on the road that was to lead to his resignation nine months later as President of the United States.

Future historians will no doubt seek to provide the answers to four questions arising from the October war. First, in their attitudes towards the Middle East, where the temperature mounted steadily during the three and a half months that followed the signature of the Agreement on the Prevention of Nuclear War in Washington, to what extent did the Soviet and the US governments 'act in such a manner as to prevent the development of situations capable of causing a dangerous exacerbation of their relations, as to avoid military confrontations, and as to exclude the outbreak of nuclear war between them'? Second, once unmistakable signals that the Arab attack on Israel was imminent were received in Moscow (earlier, but perhaps not much earlier, than in Washington), did the Soviet Government act in the manner prescribed by the Treaty of June 1973, in relation both to the Arab governments concerned and to the US Government? Third, once the war had begun, how quickly did the Soviet and US governments 'enter into urgent conversations with each other'? (The meeting between the US Secretary of State and the Soviet leadership in Moscow did not take place until after two weeks of fighting and after both the Soviet and the US governments had started their air-lifts.) Fourth, what was the precise chain of events between the meeting in Moscow and the second cease-fire five days later; and in particular did the Soviet and United States governments misunderstand each other's intentions at any point during that critical period?

Without awaiting the full evidence required to answer these specific questions, some preliminary conclusions can be drawn with a fair measure of confidence. In general, although the strain to which the Middle Eastern War subjected the new relationship between the super-powers was severe, what matters is that their relationship survived it unimpaired. In particular, even in the early hours of 25 October what Soviet theorists call the *nekontroliruemyi element** in crisis management was contained. Each of the two governments achieved its immediate aim on that day. Moreover, the political outcome of the war was something completely new: the opening of negotiations between Arabs and Israelis at last—in December, in Geneva, under the co-Chairmanship of the Soviet and US governments. The contrast between the crisis of 14–28 October 1962 and that of 6–25 October 1973 speaks for itself.

* Literally translated, 'the uncontrollable element'—the factor of miscalculation—quoted from V. V. Zhurin and E. M. Primakov, *Mezhdunarodnye konflikty*, Moscow, 1972, p. 21, by Hannes Adomeit in *Adelphi Papers*, no. 101, p. 5, IISS, London, 1973.

NOTES

1. *The Times*, 25 September 1973.
2. Ibid., 27 August 1973.
3. Ibid., 1 September 1973.
4. Ibid., 30 July 1973.
5. *Glasgow Herald*, 12 September 1973.
6. *The Times*, 13 September 1973.
7. However, only about one-third of these Soviet divisions are 'first category' (between three-quarters and full strength and with complete equipment), whereas in Eastern Europe all thirty-one Soviet divisions are in this category: see *The Military Balance 1973/4*, IISS, London, 1973, p. 6.
8. *Pravda*, 26 August 1973. Both articles had been cleared at the highest CPSU level.
9. This concept, otherwise known as the 'changing geographical vortex of the revolution', had indeed been evolved by the Chinese in the early sixties, when they first began publicly to attack what they regarded as a Soviet-American attempt to establish a global hegemony: see Brzezinski, op. cit., pp. 403 ff.
10. A reference to Nixon's proposals for making 1973 the 'year of Europe', put forward on his behalf by Kissinger in a speech on 23 April 1973. By the end of the year the US and its allies were to have worked out 'a new Atlantic charter setting the goals for peace'. For the nine EEC governments' draft of such a declaration, agreed at Copenhagen in September, see *The Times*, 25 September 1973.
11. On 20 September the Japanese Diet voted unanimously, including the Communist Party, in favour of a demand for the return of the four southern Kurile islands.
12. The text in fact reads: 'the Nuclear Weapons Non-Proliferation Treaty of 1963'. The writer presumably had had both the Non-Proliferation and the Test Ban treaties in mind.
13. *The Times*, 12 June 1973, published an article by Nove summarizing it. In an article published by *The Times* on 11 July, 'Telling Omissions in Soviet Economic Performance', Nove pointed out that, for the first time ever in any

year in which Soviet foreign trade figures were published, those for 1972 (published in mid-1973) contained no word whatsoever about any grain, except rice.

14. A brief statement made it clear that Solzhenitsyn's purpose was to test how the Soviet authorities would in practice adhere to the international copyright convention, which the Soviet Government had at last signed in May: see *The Times* of 22 and 28 September 1973.

15. *Archipelag Gulag*, YMCA Press, Paris, 1973, on the fly-leaf.

16. This letter has since been published in paperback by Fontana, 1974.

17. See *The Times*, 22 August and 5 September 1973.

18. When several Soviet Jews were condemned to death for having tried to hijack an aircraft in order to fly to Israel.

19. For example, *Strategic Survey 1973*, IISS, London, 1974, examines the war in all its aspects. See also *Survival*, May/June 1974, 'Soviet Aims and the Middle East War', pp. 106 ff., by Galia Golan.

20. Kissinger's words at the *Pacem in Terris* conference, to which he added 'coexistence to us continues to have a very precise meaning: we will oppose the attempt of any country to achieve a position of predominance either globally or regionally'.

21. For texts of the three resolutions, nos. 338, 339, and 340, see *Survival*, January/February and May/June 1974.

PART FOUR

The Future of Soviet Foreign Policy

15

THE MOTIVATING FORCE

This reappraisal of Soviet foreign policy took as its starting point the Cuban missile crisis, or the Caribbean crisis as it is known in Moscow. Had this book been written in the immediate aftermath of that crisis, its author might reasonably have been expected to foresee both the limited *détente* that followed between the Soviet Union and the United States, based on a temporary coincidence of national interests, and at least the broad perspectives of the Sino-Soviet schism, although in public it had not yet led to a direct confrontation. Nevertheless, no study of Soviet foreign policy written eleven years before could have foreseen what would have happened by October 1973: on the one hand, Khrushchev long since obliged to resign from public life—he died, unforgiven and unhonoured by the Soviet state, seven years after his resignation—leaving his successors, at the zenith of Soviet military power, to grapple with the same domestic problems as he had himself, to seek an intimate, long term, political and economic relationship with the United States, and to extend their country's conflict with China to the military field; on the other hand, John Kennedy and his principal adviser during the Cuban crisis—his brother, Robert—both assassinated, the Camelot legend of the New Frontier cast on the scrap-heap of history, the United States brought to the brink of a constitutional crisis, the American people scarred by the self-inflicted wounds of a war in Indo-China that bore some resemblance to the Syracusan expedition of ancient Athens,*

---

* Although this analogy cannot be pressed too far—the Americans were not defeated in the field and American prisoners of war in Hanoi did not have to win their liberty by teaching their captors the choruses of Euripides—the points of resemblance are striking. The Syracusan expedition was undertaken outside the main strategic theatre; it was justified on the domino theory; its original purpose was to respond to a request for military aid from a weaker city (Segesta) against a stronger one (Syracuse); the ensuing war sucked a vast commitment of Athe-

and the hatchet buried between the United States and China after the rancour of quarter of a century. Nor could it have been foreseen in 1962 —the year of the Berlin crisis as well as of the Cuban crisis—that the focal point of the world conflict of interests, economic and strategic, would have shifted from Central Europe to the Middle East and that this conflict would have shaken the structure of the alliance between the United States and Western Europe.

Moreover, these examples must be viewed against the wider background of change over the past decade: the demographic explosion and the north–south economic gap (the poverty of many underdeveloped countries being still further increased by the new growth in the financial power of the oil-producing countries); the liquidation of the remainder of their empires by the Western European states; the accumulation of wealth in Japan and in Western Europe, the latter groping its way towards a closer unity within the European Economic Community; the collapse of the Bretton Woods international monetary system; the energy crisis; and the vertiginous pace and the complexity of scientific and technological innovation. In the strategic field, lead-time for modern weapons systems is now anything from ten to fifteen years. This means that so far as the systems which the super-powers will deploy in the 1980s are concerned, the initial decision to finance their Research and Development* was already taken by about 1970, and the decision to commit resources of men, money, and materials to their mass production and deployment must be taken not later than 1975. In the field of energy, the parameters of world demand for energy by 1985 can already be established with stark clarity, but precisely how this demand will in practice be met from then until the end of the century depends on a wide range of variables, political, strategic, financial, and technological, which is at the present moment anybody's guess. Nevertheless, a history of the past which is not written with at least half an eye on the future runs the risk of becoming no more than a literary or a statistical exercise. Therefore the attempt to see through the glass, however darkly, must be made.

There are those who argue that the recent change in Soviet foreign

---

nian manpower, materials, and money into a country of which the Athenians had little first-hand knowledge; it divided Athenian society (the mutilation of the Hermes and the trial of Alcibiades); and the Athenian withdrawal was followed by the establishment of a right-wing government in Athens.

* The process of Research and Development can best be defined as combining basic and applied research with the development of research into new products and processes, up to and including the prototype stage.

policy is only superficial, and that its underlying reality remains unchanged. Those who hold this view concede that the current decade has so far been a period of *détente*, but they compare it with the period of temporary *détente* that followed the Cuban missile crisis. They then divide into two opposed schools of thought. According to the first of these, Soviet foreign policy is devoid of principle, the lineal descendant of Russian foreign policy under the Empire, of which Curzon wrote, nearly a hundred years ago: 'so far from regarding the foreign policy of Russia as consistent, or remorseless, or profound, I believe it to be a hand-to-mouth policy, a policy of waiting upon events, of profiting by the blunders of others, and as often of committing the like herself.'[1] Even those who, like myself, find this view unacceptable, have to admit that some colour is lent to it by the fact that the most up-to-date Soviet book on Soviet foreign policy still stoutly defends the conclusion of the Soviet-German Non-Aggression Pact of 1939.* The second, more plausible, school of thought recalls Lenin's early definition of Soviet foreign policy in 1920, in which he ridiculed refusal 'to temporise and compromise with possible (even though transient, unstable, vacillating and conditional) allies' and defended the idea that 'at times we might have to go in zigzags, sometimes retracing our steps, sometimes abandoning the course already selected and trying out various others'.[2] For the adherents of this view, the whole history of Soviet foreign policy for the past half century reveals a grand design, which includes the zigzags recommended by Lenin in 1920; such a policy is the logical corollary of the doctrine of the correlation of forces; strategic nuclear parity with the United States is for the Soviet Union no more than a temporary halting place on its 'ascent of an unexplored and heretofore inaccessible mountain' (as Lenin described the path of Soviet foreign policy in the same passage); this ascent must sooner or later be resumed, with the ultimate aim of turning the correlation of forces, with the aid of the forces of history, to the advantage of the Soviet Union; in other words, to substitute a *pax sovietica* for the *pax americana* under which the peoples of the world lived, for the most part better than they had ever lived before, from 1945 until the beginning of the current decade; and meanwhile the Soviet leadership will, to allow time for modernizing their country's economy, rest content with a Soviet-American equilibrium. In short, the Soviet national game is chess.

An objective assessment of Soviet foreign policy suggests two replies.

* *Diplomatiya Sotsializma* (with a foreword by the Soviet Foreign Minister) in a paragraph explaining the flexibility of Soviet foreign policy: p. 38.

First, study of the past decade indicates that the parameters of the next decade (examined in the next chapter) will indeed continue to be different from those of the cold war, although the unstable equilibrium that has recently been established between the two super-powers could be upset. The second reply is related to the vexed question: what is the determining force that motivates the men who formulate and carry out Soviet foreign policy? To put it at its simplest, if the motivating force is Marxist-Leninist ideology pure and simple, the prospects of the existing equilibrium between the super-powers being maintained for long are more tenuous than they would otherwise be. If, on the other hand, the motivating force is Soviet national interest, the Soviet-American equilibrium may not only be maintained but rendered less insecure. This is a crude antithesis. We may not know much about the deliberations of the Soviet Politburo, but we do know enough to realize that it consists of politicians who share the motives of politicians the world over, such as the need to survive, physically and politically, which in turn involves a complex interplay of factors extending far beyond the sphere of foreign policy. Nevertheless, the manner in which they see their own motivation is of great importance; and this question has been given a new dimension by Sakharov's statement[3] commenting on Solzhenitsyn's letter to the Soviet leadership of 5 September 1973. The main thrust of this statement, after expressing his admiration for Solzhenitsyn as an author and as a man, was directed against overestimation of the role of ideology in present-day Soviet society and the Russian nationalistic and isolationist direction of Solzhenitsyn's thinking, which—for Sakharov—made his proposals Utopian and potentially dangerous.

For the official historians of Soviet foreign policy Marxism-Leninism and the interests of the Soviet state coincide. Soviet foreign policy is said to 'reflect the harmonious concurrence of the national interests of the Soviet state and the Soviet people with the international obligations of the working class which has come to power'.[4] Yet a conflict of interest between the two seems to have been recognized from the outset of the Russian Revolution. Although Lenin's initial reaction to foreign policy was that of an old Bolshevik—'What! are we going to have foreign relations?'[5]—he swiftly adapted himself to the realism of a government in power. This transition from the earlier opinions of an underground revolutionary party, observed by foreign diplomats serving in Moscow in the 1920s, was later described by Chicherin as having been difficult for other members of the Bolshevik Party.[6] Lenin was an exceptionally bold man, who had both the audacity and the wisdom not to keep to the rules; for him Marxism was the science which made possible the fearless prediction of the future and the daring needed to bring it about. What of his successors?

It is hard to conceive of a Soviet leader adopting a policy likely to damage the interests of the Soviet state while furthering those of the world communist movement. The history of the first half century of the Soviet Union's existence is rich in examples of the interests of fraternal parties being sacrificed to those of the CPSU. And the most notorious case of all—Stalin's conclusion of his pact with Hitler not only did grave damage to the world communist movement but almost led to the destruction of the Soviet Union. And yet Soviet historians and statesmen are guilty neither of dishonesty nor of cynicism when they claim, in effect, that what is good for their country is good for world communism. (A similar infallibility has been claimed at some time or other—often for long periods—by other European states, not to mention the United States during its messianic epoch.)

An analytic tool devised by two American writers[7] has shown that in selected public statements of Soviet leaders in the early 1960s, the impact of Marxist-Leninist ideology was weakest in their short-range formulations and their specific conclusions and perceptions, whereas it was at its strongest in their long-range thinking and their broad generalizations. This finding corresponds with everyday experience. In a private conversation a Soviet statesman or official appears to a non-Marxist observer to think and reason in the same manner as he does himself. But when time permits, or the occasion—such as a Party Congress—requires, the same statesman or official will speak in a different tongue. To take a concrete example, the Soviet Prime Minister may indeed have told his Japanese interlocutor in September 1968 that the invasion of Czechoslovakia in the previous month was unavoidable because the national survival of the Soviet Union was at stake[8]—an argument derived from pure *Realpolitik*—but publicly the invasion was justified by an appeal to the Marxist concept of proletarian internationalism. Without such a justification the Soviet leadership would have felt embarrassed, because their mandate to rule at home and to act abroad depends on the ultimate sanction[9] of Marxist-Leninist doctrine. In the last analysis—not always in the heat of a crisis,* but whenever

---

* Nevertheless, in his 'Friday' letter, written to Kennedy at the height of the Cuban missile crisis, Khrushchev found time to justify himself by the doctrine of peaceful coexistence.

action is being prepared or recollected in tranquillity—the general framework and guidelines of Soviet foreign policy must be seen to be justified by the doctrines of Marxism-Leninism: the ultimate sanction which gives those who formulate and carry out this policy the sense that they are moving forward with the forces of history and that their success is predicated on the truth of this ideology.

If this is how Soviet leaders think and how events in the Soviet Union are moulded, what happens when the Soviet Union reaches a point in history, as it did in 1956, when the inadmissible gap between Marxist-Leninist theory and Soviet practice becomes blatant? Sooner or later this gap must be closed—not by changing the practice, which will continue to be dictated, in Marxist terms, by Life Itself, but by changing the theory. Officially, theory never changes in the Soviet Union. In 1956, it was simply given a new formulation. But—as a Polish Marxist remarked to the author—all great communist leaders have been revisionists, from Lenin and Stalin onwards.[10] The adjective 'great' is an essential condition, because radical revision demands the courage to break the horizon—a quality that does not seem to be any more abundant in the Soviet Union than in other countries at the moment. Nevertheless, who could have foreseen Khrushchev's speech at the XXth Party Congress?

To sum up, the foreign policy of the Soviet Union, like that of any modern state, is conducted in the interests of the state, as perceived by its leaders. Their perception of Soviet state interests is at most only slightly distorted by the lens of Marxism-Leninism, whose doctrines provide the leaders with their ultimate sanction. And an eloquent contrast with the Curzonian thesis is afforded by comparing the principal characteristics claimed by Soviet apologists for their foreign policy—flexibility, firmness, and circumspection—with the source to which Tolstoy, writing not long before Curzon, ascribed traditional Russian self-confidence: 'a Russian ... neither knows anything nor wants to know anything, because he does not believe in the possibility of knowing anything'.[11] Half a century of Soviet rule may not have altered the fundamental scepticism of the Russian character; the Soviet claim to have evolved a new, Soviet type of man cannot be sustained; but the outward manifestation of the Russian character, observable in the conduct of Soviet foreign policy, has surely changed. A Soviet writer might trace this change back to the Marxist proposition[12] that one and the same idea in different, concrete, historical circumstances may be either reactionary or progressive.

NOTES

1. G. N. Curzon, *Russia in Central Asia*, Longmans Green, London, 1889, p. 315.
2. Lenin, *Left-Wing Communism—an infantile disorder*, Moscow, 1920: *Collected Works*, vol. 31, p. 70.
3. Full text in translation in *The Times*, 16 April 1974.
4. *Istoriya Vneshnei Politiki SSSR*, introductory chapter.
5. Leon Trotsky, *Moya Zhizn'*, Granit, Berlin, 1930, vol. 2, p. 64. Cf. Trotsky's own remark, when appointed Commissioner for Foreign Affairs, that he would issue some revolutionary proclamations to the peoples and then shut up shop.
6. See ch. 10, n. 15. For the views of foreign observers, see, for example, Arthur Hodgson's report to Austen Chamberlain of 6 May 1926, *Documents on British Foreign Policy*, Series IA, vol. I: 'the Soviet Government has been continually in conflict with the conceptions to which it owes its being—to cope with practical exigencies it has had to recede little by little from the ideas which inspired the Revolution . . . Moscow . . . has to deal with precisely the same problems as any of its neighbours—and is dealing with them in very much the same way.'
7. Jan F. Triska and David D. Finley, *Soviet Foreign Policy*, Macmillan, New York, 1968, pp. 118 ff.: the 'doctrinal stereotype quotient', representing the number of doctrinally stereotyped words or phrases in proportion to the total number of words in the statement being analysed.
8. Quoted by Hayter, op. cit., p. 63.
9. Compare Sakharov's description of 'ideological rituality' as a substitute for 'an oath of loyalty': *The Times*, 16 April 1974.
10. Julian Hochfeld, in conversation in 1959.
11. Leo Tolstoy, *War and Peace*, Bk. III, pt. I, section X.
12. See, for example, Andrei Zhdanov, *Essays on Literature, Philosophy, and Music*, p. 58, International Publishers, New York, 1950.

16

PARAMETERS AND VARIABLES

Soviet parameters[1]

The assumptions made in this chapter and the next will relate to the ten-year period 1973–83, a time span comparable with the years reviewed in this book. It is rather less than the period covered by the fifteen-year economic plan now being prepared in the Soviet Union, and far shorter than the twenty or thirty years of peaceful coexistence of which Brezhnev has been reported to be thinking.[2] But to look further ahead runs the speculator into a new era in which account must be taken of an entirely new factor in the world power structure, the possible emergence of China as a super-power. The span of ten years from 1973 onwards should include three congresses of the CPSU, one of which may be expected—in the course of nature—to produce a fresh Soviet leadership.

Since April 1973 personal responsibility for Soviet foreign policy has been attributed, both within the Soviet Union and abroad, to Brezhnev. However, with the world in the heat of the second industrial revolution and in the grip of the great bureaucratic age, the concept of the state as a rational actor is even less appropriate than half a century ago, when the image of states as individual characters or anthropomorphized animals —the Russian Bear, Uncle Sam, and John Bull—had already ceased to bear much relation to reality. As early as August 1914, when asked why the First World War had broken out, the German Chancellor Beth-mann-Hollweg replied: 'if only I knew!' In a crisis today the ruler of a modern state reaches a decision for which he will be held responsible before history not as a lonely figure, weighing up the pros and cons of the advice submitted to him by his personal staff, his specialist advisers, and his colleagues, but as the hub of a many-spoked governmental wheel and sometimes as the passenger, rather than the driver, of a bureaucratic machine carried forward by the momentum of its own procedures.[3] Nevertheless, the Soviet regime is nothing if not centralized. True, the growing complexity of Soviet society is reflected by the fact that, even though Brezhnev has long been *primus inter pares* in the Politburo, it still remains a collegiate body. A return to the Stalinist system of government, in the sense that every decision of importance was handed down by a single man, is inconceivable; and even a return to the Khrushchevian concentration of offices is improbable. But if we concede that the leading member of the Politburo, like any other national leader, is obliged to build up his majority round a consensus, the fact remains that during the ten years which we are now considering, he will wield immense power.

The first question is therefore this: if an alternative Soviet leadership were to accede to power tomorrow, either naturally or in the style of 1964, could it reverse the Brezhnev foreign policy? Given the intimate links between Soviet domestic and foreign policy, the answer is, theoretically, yes. But in my view such a leadership, however much it might commit itself publicly to a reappraisal of Soviet foreign policy, would sooner or later find itself constrained by the basic parameters of this policy.

The first parameter stems from nuclear logic. The statement that the nuclear bomb does not adhere to the class principle remains as valid today as when it was included in the CPSU Central Committee's Open Letter of 1963. By the end of 1973, the Soviet Union and the United States had already travelled some way towards a SALT II agreement; and eventually their negotiators are likely to reach the crossroads, where they must either put some trust in each other or abandon hope of preserving a civilized society. No Soviet leadership will opt out of the Great Game of strategic nuclear power; it will remain a vital national interest of the Soviet Union to preserve a strategic balance with the United States; but a way will have to be found of acknowledging the fact that strategic nuclear superiority for either super-power is a chimera.[4]

The second parameter is twofold: the East-West technological gap, which has been discussed in an earlier chapter, and the problem of the development of the natural resources of Siberia. Even if the gap could be closed in ten years, which seems improbable at the present pace of technological advance, the Siberian problem would remain for the rest of this century. Whatever Soviet ministers may say from time to time in public, no Soviet leadership can escape the fact that without Western help, the Soviet Union will not have the capital, the know-how, and the management techniques to solve it. Add to this the congenital weakness of Soviet agriculture and its climatic disadvantage—grain imports are likely to be needed in years of poor harvests—and it is clear that it will become increasingly difficult for the Soviet Union to avoid becoming an integral part of the world economic system. In Sakharov's words, 'not a single key problem can be solved on a national scale'.[5]

Because the Soviet leadership are well aware of this economic logic and of the greatly increased personal contacts between East and West that it is bound to involve, they are determined to do everything in their power to prevent these contacts from contaminating the ideological purity of the Soviet system. Hence, for example, Soviet opposition to concessions over the free exchange of ideas and information at the Geneva negotiations. As the Soviet Diplomatic Dictionary puts it, 'peaceful coexistence has nothing whatsoever to do with peace in the sphere of ideology ... those principles do not in any way exclude ideological struggle. Such a struggle goes on continually and is unavoidable. . . .'[6] One need only reflect on the impact that modern Western managerial techniques—let alone actual Western management —would have on the Soviet Union in the longer term, to wonder for how long the Soviet leadership will be able in effect to have its cake and eat it.

American parameters

The first of the three parameters described above (Mutually Assured Destruction) applies equally to the United States. As for the second, the United States could, in theory, revert to its previous policy of withholding from the Soviet Union both advanced technology and long term credit to finance the exploitation of Soviet natural resources. But is such a reversal now practical economics? However vast the resources that lie within its own boundaries, can the United States afford to play no part in the development of the largest known reserves of raw materials in the world?

Until the close of 1973 the obvious example was energy. The Soviet Union claims one third of the total sedimentary basins in the world; expert estimates of the ultimately recoverable oil, gas, and coal vary; not only are exact statistics lacking, but there are also problems of climate (permafrost) and distance (6,600 kilometres from the Tyumen' oilfield in Western Siberia to the Pacific port of Nakhodka). Until the world price of oil was quadrupled, it had seemed likely that by 1980 the United States, which consumes one third of the world's energy, would be as dependent on imported oil as Western Europe is today; that Saudi Arabia, whose estimated oil reserves are the greatest in the world, would become the world's 'swing' oil producer,[7] and that given the political uncertainties of the Middle East, a logical consequence for the United States would be large-scale investment in Siberian oil and natural gas. Today, it has become economic for the United States to develop alternative sources of energy (tar sands, shale, and coal), of which North American reserves are almost as large as those of the Soviet Union. Yet even Project Independence—the immense new American energy programme—is likely to leave room for a flow of oil and natural gas from the Soviet Union.*

In any case, the sudden increase in the cost of energy is only one aspect of the explosion in commodity prices which is central to the world inflationary crisis of today. Now that the Soviet Government has taken the plunge, by inviting Western firms to participate in major Siberian ventures in the energy field, it can only be a matter of time before Western investment is attracted to the rest of the Soviet Union's natural resources. It would be surprising if American capital were not in the van. This brings us back to American domestic politics, and in particular the Jackson Amendment, which in 1973 was linked with the conflict between President and Congress, with the Arab-Israeli dispute, and with the problem of Soviet Jewry—all three delicate issues in the United States. It is possible to construct scenarios in which Soviet resistance to concessions of the kind for which Jackson has pressed will continue for some years. No one knows how many[8] Soviet Jews wish to emigrate, nor at what pace Israel could absorb them, even assuming a crash programme. But given the strength of the logic, both strategic and economic, pulling any US Administration and any Soviet leadership down the path traced in 1972–3 by Kissinger and Brezhnev, a compro-

---

* Just how much will depend on a number of related but unpredictable factors: the success of the American programme (whose original target of complete oil self-sufficiency by 1980 is generally regarded as unattainable); the extent to which the Soviet Union decides to become a major oil and natural gas exporter; the extent to which Western oil and natural gas importers are prepared to become dependent on Soviet supplies; and the future reliability of Middle Eastern exporters, which is in turn connected with the outcome of the Arab-Israeli dispute.

mise solution of the problem of Soviet Jewry is by no means impossible, although it will take time.

Variables

This twilight world may be more easily explored by the political scientist than by the historian. There are at least four major factors that could, over the next ten years, upset the existing equilibrium between the super-powers.

The agreements concluded between the Soviet Union and the United States in 1972–3 established the ground rules of this equilibrium. However, whereas the rules of international behaviour by the super-powers have at last been established in South-East Asia, and have long been understood in Central Europe, they are less so in the rest of Europe, and above all in the Middle East—witness the US nuclear alert of October 1973. In Europe, Yugoslavia's non-aligned stance has allowed Tito to maintain close links with Moscow and Eastern Europe on the one hand, and with Washington and Western Europe on the other. But Yugoslavia's ability to combine the two has owed much to the unique position in the communist world that its leader has occupied since he out-faced Stalin a quarter of a century ago. Will his eventual successor have the strength and the stature to prevent outsiders from fishing in what could become troubled waters, as the Croatian troubles of 1971 showed?* What would be the Kremlin's reaction if the Italian Communist Party were, after a quarter of a century in opposition, at last to succeed in obtaining portfolios in central government? An attitude of caution, one would hope, as also towards the re-emergence of Marxism in Portuguese and Spanish political life. But can one be certain that counsels of caution would prevail if the Politburo were to find itself suddenly presented with a target of opportunity? Equally, given the importance of Israel in American domestic politics, how much effort will it cost any US Administration to recognize the Soviet claim (repeatedly put forward over the years, and reiterated by Brezhnev immediately after the Arab-Israeli War of October 1973)[9] that the Middle East and the eastern Mediterranean constitute an 'area in the immediate vicinity' of the frontiers of the Soviet Union, which is regarded in Moscow in much the same light as the Caribbean is in Washington?

* The trials of 'Cominformists' in Yugoslavia three years later pointed in the same direction.

Second, however high a degree of mutual trust may be established between the governments of the super-powers in whatever agreement flows from their SALT negotiations, this may not be enough to persuade either the scientific or the military community in both countries to resist technological temptation. The process of Research and Development of new nuclear weapons systems has an in-built momentum* that cannot be arrested at a stroke of the pen. The overall directive, on both sides, might well be to work towards the eventual deployment of such systems not against each other, but against China. But any technological break-through by one super-power must have a destabilizing effect on the other, particularly if the nuclear innovation is of a kind that cannot be verified by what are termed national technical means. The best contemporary example is the multiple independently targetable and the manoeuvrable re-entry vehicle; but what would be the effect, either in the Kremlin or in the White House, if one or other side were to succeed in deploying an effective system of anti-submarine warfare?

Third, if political and military constraints are once set aside, the economic obstacles in the way of developing and deploying a simple nuclear weapons system are less formidable than might be supposed. Indeed, a recent article[10] on this subject included the sobering statement that, given unlimited time, there is no country obviously incapable of a nuclear weapons programme. In 1968, a United Nations consultative group of experts estimated that an expenditure of 1,280 million dollars spread over ten years would allow an industrial country with a civil nuclear programme to develop and build a force of 100 plutonium weapons and 50 medium-range missiles, and to buy 30–50 aircraft as well. As the same article concluded, after allowing for inflation, in 1973 there were about sixteen countries capable of carrying that financial burden over the remaining years of the current decade, by diverting less than one per cent of GNP. These countries included India, Japan, and Italy, all of which have indigenous uranium and reactor capacity and which also have, or will have, reprocessing plants. Egypt would, according to the same estimate, need to divert 3·6 per cent and Israel about 4 per cent of GNP for this purpose.

* In the valedictory address which made famous the term military-industrial complex, Eisenhower added this warning: 'we must also be alert to the equal and opposite danger that public policy could itself become the captive of a scientific-technological elite'. The combined power of the two interest groups, in an advanced industrial society, is formidable.

If the super-powers succeed in persuading their clients in the Middle East to reach some kind of agreement, perhaps they will also be able to dissuade them from the folly of embarking on a nuclear programme. But could the accusation of folly be levelled at India or Japan if, in the second half of this decade, they decided that the growing strategic nuclear power of China obliged them no longer to rely on the nuclear umbrellas hitherto held over them by the Soviet Union and the United States respectively, especially if the 1975 review of disarmament required by the Non-Proliferation Treaty had borne no fruit? By exploding a nuclear device on 17 May 1974, India has become a member of the nuclear club. Japan's extreme vulnerability and the strength of public feeling against nuclear warfare in Japan are powerful constraints. Yet Japan will shortly become the second industrial state of the world, utterly dependent on long sea routes for its supply of raw materials. It will certainly wish to postpone the nuclear option, leaving it open, but no more, for as long as possible. But if it does finally decide to continue to rely either on the protection or the benevolence of others for the security of its life-line, it will prove to be the first great trading country in history to do so. Moreover, beyond such deliberate decisions of national policy, there is also the nightmarish possibility of a do-it-yourself nuclear, biological, or chemical device, in the hands of a guerrilla group, using it as an instrument of political blackmail, but this time with the survival of a whole capital city, not an airliner, or a team of athletes, at stake. It has been rightly said that the trouble with nuclear ploughshares is that they can be beaten into nuclear warheads.

Fourth, the most volatile variable of all is the pace of political change in Eastern Europe. We have noted the present Soviet leadership's dislike of anything new in Marxist thought; and we have taken as one of the Soviet parameters for the next ten years their determination to preserve Soviet society in its present form. Now that the Moscow Treaty and the agreements which followed it have removed the German bogey, in order to hold their Eastern European allies together, the Soviet leaders seem to be relying on a policy of *enrichissez-vous:* a pale image of the consumer society of the West, but a marked improvement, if measured against the standard of living which Eastern Europeans had experienced in the Stalinist period after the Second World War. Stalin needed Eastern Europe in the late 1940s as a defensive barrier, behind which he could glower or thunder at the West during the years of the Soviet Union's extreme weakness, with twenty million dead, European Russia ravaged by the most terrible campaign since the Mongol invasion in the thirteenth century, and the power of the Red Army rendered nugatory, in the eyes of Stalin and his advisers, by the American monopoly of the atomic bomb. Khrushchev, on the other hand, while not ignoring the military value of Eastern Europe, realized the political importance of its leaders as allies in his ideological struggle against the Chinese. Whichever of the two factors—political or military—weighed more in the present leadership's decision to invade Czechoslovakia in 1968, as the present decade advances, it will surely be the value of the Eastern European political frontier, beyond the administrative borders of the Soviet Union, that will be uppermost in the minds of Soviet policy-makers. The great political difference between the Soviet Union and its Eastern European allies (with the possible exception of Bulgaria) is that whereas in the USSR the Communist Party has deep roots, in Eastern Europe the Communist Parties consist of small oligarchies, brought to power, or the successors of men brought to power, by Soviet arms in 1944–5. The fragility of the socialist commonwealth has been proved repeatedly, most recently in Czechoslovakia in 1968: that a force of half a million men should have been required for the invasion of a country whose government had made no plan whatsoever for armed resistance speaks for itself.

What matters for the future is whether the pace of change in the Soviet Union will continue to be so slow as to exasperate one or more of the Eastern European peoples once again. Soviet society is not impervious to change; nor are Soviet political institutions; but they cannot be expected to evolve towards the Western model. The Warsaw Pact includes countries, notably Poland, Hungary, and Czechoslovakia, whose society remains rooted in the Western European tradition. Understandably, the Soviet fear is that if Pandora's box is once opened in Eastern Europe, the lid will sooner or later have to be lifted in the Soviet Union, which includes almost all the territories ruled by the Tsars. The Soviet constitution allows for any of the republics (some of which were independent countries[11] for over twenty years after the First World War) that compose the Union to secede; the official formula governing the principle of nationality within the Soviet Union is that it is 'nationalist in form, socialist in content'; but Lenin was not mistaken when he remarked in 1919, having concluded a treaty granting independence to Finland, 'scratch some communists and you will find Great Russian chauvinists'; and the last Soviet census, taken in 1970, gave the Russians a very narrow majority: 53·3 per cent.

Under the present Soviet leadership any radical change in the Soviet internal political system is inconceivable. The question therefore is, what will be the policy of their successors? A story was going the rounds in the summer of 1973 that Brezhnev had told a distinguished American visitor that he hoped to be succeeded by a man twenty years younger than himself. What would such a Soviet politician be like? A well educated man, perhaps a pious agnostic where Marxism was concerned, and a professional politician (the distinction sometimes drawn between conservative *apparatchiki* and liberal technocrats is not helpful). But above all he would be a man without any feeling of guilt. Not through any fault of their own, but simply because of their age, the triumvirs who ousted Khrushchev, like Khrushchev himself, owed their first steps on the ladder of success to the Great Terror. It is impossible to believe that this fact has not affected their attitudes profoundly: the importance of guilt in the Russian character is amply attested. John Rickman, who witnessed the Russian Revolution from a unique vantage point,[12] wrote in an essay that was published over thirty years later:

the Russian attitude towards guilt has always seemed strange alike to Western and Eastern peoples. In the religion of the old regime it was a central theme; in that of the new it is denied in relation to everything except the State. In the place of the old blasphemy . . . there is now the sin of not believing in the perfect suitability of the present rulers . . . for the needs of the Russian people. Discontent is taken as a sign of the unpardonable sin working in a diseased mind.

This prophetic passage is followed by the statement that, although violence may be necessary in politics, 'it generates feelings of guilt which may be unconscious. It is foolish and . . . in the long run politically imprudent to deny a factor so important in mental—or political—life.'[13] Khrushchev's revelations about Stalin at the XXth Party Congress may be regarded as a controlled attempt to free Soviet society from guilt and to release the energies of its people—including those of the millions of political prisoners who were then set free—for the task of working for a better life, by acknowledging, three years after Stalin's death, the extent of the trauma that the Soviet people had suffered from their leader's systematic use of violence on a titanic scale. It is the essence of the case pressed by men like Solzhenitsyn and the Medvedevs that this process, once begun, should have been allowed to run its full course. Perhaps the younger Soviet generation, unburdened by the nightmare of the purges, may feel able to allow some fresh air, and with it some new ideas, into the Soviet Union. If they do, it may help to lift the malaise that hangs over Eastern Europe and so contribute to the all-

European cooperation which has for so long been a primary aim of Soviet policy.

NOTES

1. In the Oxford English Dictionary's definition of this much misused term: 'a quantity which is constant (as distinct from the ordinary variables) in a particular case considered'.
2. Sadat, in his address to the Central Committee of the Arab Socialist Union on 16 July 1973, as reported by Cairo Home Service radio.
3. For an application of these three concepts to an historical process of decision-making, see Allison, op. cit.
4. Giles Bullard drew my attention to 'the Great Game', a phrase which his researches show to have been used for the first time in J. W. Kaye's *History of the War in Afghanistan*, in 1851, after which it became a shorthand for Anglo-Russian rivalry. The doctrine of Mutually Assured Destruction 'rests on two pillars: strength and vulnerability. Each side must be seen to have the strength to retaliate adequately for any attack. Each side must also permit the other to have the confidence that it too can retaliate intolerably. In other words, a sufficient retaliatory force must always remain invulnerable, and a sufficient hostage must always remain vulnerable. If A believes that B is trying either to reduce the invulnerability of A's retaliatory force or the vulnerability of B's hostage, A is driven either to strengthen his own forces or, *in extremis*, to attack before the tendency has gone too far.' This quotation comes from Ian Smart's 'Advanced Strategic Missiles', *Adelphi Papers* no. 93, IISS, London, 1969, p. 27.
5. Quoted from the statement translated in *The Times*, 16 April 1974. For a do-it-yourself line, see the remarks by the Soviet Minister of the Oil Industry, reported in *The Times*, 29 May 1974, but subsequently denied.
6. *Diplomaticheskii Slovar'*, vol. 2, Moscow, 1964, p. 176.
7. For the critical position of Saudi Arabia, see *The Changing Balance of Power in the Persian Gulf*, an international seminar report by Elizabeth Monroe, the American Universities Field Staff, New York, 1972, pp. 26–7.
8. The usual estimate—there are no statistics—is half a million.
9. In a speech delivered to the All-World Congress of Peace-Loving Forces in Moscow: *Pravda*, 27 October 1973.
10. *Strategic Survey 1972*, IISS, London, 1973, p. 74.
11. The Baltic States: in Lithuania, in May 1972, riots were reported to have taken place at and after the funeral of a young worker who committed suicide by burning himself—see *Strategic Survey 1972*, p. 84.
12. That of a doctor working in a Russian village during the years of the Revolution.
13. Geoffrey Gorer and John Rickman, *The People of Greater Russia*, The Cresset Press, London, 1949, pp. 88–9.

17

CONCLUSION

To return to the findings of this study of Soviet foreign policy since 1962, it is a paradox that, once rough numerical strategic parity with the United States had at last been achieved, Soviet rivalry with China grew more intense than it was with the United States at the height of the cold war (Soviet and American troops have not confronted each other directly for over half a century); that in spite of this rivalry, the Soviet Government entered into a network of agreements with the United States Government which made the stock Chinese accusation of super-power collusion still harder to rebut; that—except where Soviet national interests were involved—little more than lip service was paid by the Soviet Union to its doctrinal commitment to support national-liberation movements; that as Soviet military power, both strategic and conventional, became increasingly formidable, so the Soviet need for Western help in modernizing and developing the Soviet economy grew more apparent; that Western, and particularly American, willingness to provide this help evoked fierce controversy, in the Soviet Union as well as in Western countries; and finally, that so far the only Soviet attempt to explain this series of paradoxes to the Soviet people and to the world communist movement—to bridge the gap between the theory and the practice of Soviet foreign policy—has been to add three words to part of the fourth of its basic tasks. Yet, in reality, the adjectives now applied to the Soviet relationship with the United States—'permanent' and 'irreversible'—and to the two countries' joint responsibility for maintaining world peace—'special'—are a far cry from the Marxist class struggle.[1]

At the outset of this book it was observed that the nature of the new relations between the two super-powers was complex and ambivalent, and had therefore so far eluded attempts to define it in a single word or phrase. *Détente*, the shorthand currently used in the United States, is open to the objection that in the Soviet Union it is restricted (in my view, correctly) to its traditional meaning in diplomatic usage—the relaxation of tension: from the Soviet viewpoint this is a consequence of the policy of peaceful coexistence between communist and non-communist states as the 'generally accepted rule of international life', not the policy itself. Although the governments of both super-powers agree that their relations are special, this description contains a misleading echo of the Anglo-American special relationship of the post-war years. The most accurate, but an inelegant, definition is adversarial partnership, although this also echoes an earlier term—*frères ennemis*[2] —used in the different circumstances of 1961. Among the cluster of metaphors drawn from geometry and magnetism, the concept of bipolarity was useful in the past, because (as the inventor of the term super-power foresaw thirty years ago)[3] it need not necessarily imply the existence of polar opposites; but it has been obfuscated by adjectives—'loose' and 'tight'. Bipolarity has since been contrasted with multipolarity—the concept underlying Nixon's formulation of January 1972[4]—which has given rise to hexagonal and polygonal definitions. Multipolarity was in turn superseded by the passage in Kissinger's statement about the Year of Europe, delivered on 23 April 1973[5] on behalf of the United States President, in which he drew a distinction between the global interests and responsibilities of the USA and the regional interests of America's European allies: interests which were not necessarily in conflict, but in the new era not automatically identical. These words both recalled Fox's original definition of super-power and foreshadowed the conflict between American and European interests during the Middle Eastern crisis six months later. And it was at the height of this crisis—in his press conference of 25 October 1973—that Kissinger described the super-power relationship in two sentences that cannot be bettered:

the Soviet Union and we are in a unique relationship. We are at one and the same time adversaries and partners in the preservation of peace.

At the other end of the spectrum, there are those who maintain that the term super-power has become an archaism: in their view, in the late twentieth century, what determines the relative weight of a state in the counsels of the modern world is not the possession of a vast arsenal of strategic nuclear weapons capable of destroying the globe—no one today, they affirm, will ever commit national suicide—but the scientific, technological, and industrial capacity of the state, set in the context of its geographical position, the size of its population, and its natural resources. Since military power does not, as Kissinger has observed, automatically translate into influence, strategic nuclear power would indeed have little meaning if taken in isolation. (If, by a *reductio ad absurdum*, a government were to devote so much of its country's GNP to developing and maintaining a nuclear armoury that it was left with little or no resources to be used for the other weapons of modern diplomacy—trade, technical assistance, cultural cooperation—this twentieth-century Sparta would find itself in the unenviable position of having only a single international card to play.) On the other hand, if—as in the case of the super-powers—strategic nuclear power is combined with the full panoply of highly mobile conventional weapons and of conventional diplomacy, it means a great deal. As an American journalist wrote thirty years ago: 'even after you give the squirrel a certificate which says that he is quite as big as any elephant, he is still going to be smaller, and all the squirrels will know it and all the elephants will know it.'[6] These words remain valid today, except that the word 'both' should be substituted for the word 'all' before the word 'elephants'.

Rather than attempt to construct conceptual models of a world power structure that is changing before our eyes, it is wiser simply to accept two lessons of the past decade: that strategic nuclear capacity is indeed relevant to the exercise of super-power (or global power, as Kissinger has expressed it), and that the twin centres of such power, and of the decisions that flow from it, will remain Washington and Moscow, until such time as Peking becomes the third centre—a goal[7] which the Chinese leadership seem set to achieve even before their people reaches the 1,000 million mark. If so, what are the prospects for regional power? In particular what conclusions should be drawn in Western Europe, where most countries have, since 1949, been joined in a defence partnership with the Western super-power, and are together still facing not only the Soviet strategic nuclear armoury, but also the massed, and swiftly reinforceable, conventional forces of the Soviet Union and its allies in the centre of the European continent, and increasingly in the Mediterranean and on the south-eastern flank?

Subject to the reservation already made about the dangers of prophecy, an attempt will now be made to sketch briefly three possible paradigms, of which there could be many variants, for the development of super-power relations over the next ten years; beginning with what Wavell, when he was Commander-in-Chief in Cairo during the Second World War, used to call the Worst Possible Case. Whatever the disadvantages to other countries of the super-power equilibrium—the French President and his Foreign Minister suggested some in 1973[8]— it has one advantage of inestimable value: it sustains an international order within which the overwhelming majority of the world's inhabitants can live at peace. If this order were to collapse, under the strain of one or more of the dangers described in the previous chapter, the threat of large-scale conventional war, perhaps developing into nuclear war, would follow. And if, at the moment of this collapse, the Western European states—far from achieving their goal of unity—were still in a state of disarray, too weak to defend their wealth and their cultural and political heritage, Western Europe would then find itself no longer the partner of one super-power but the hostage of both.

Dismissing this vision of a helpless approach to Armageddon, let us next consider an intermediate paradigm. In this case, although the variables considered in the previous chapter may cause periods of extreme tension, the super-power equilibrium is maintained. Rather than see Western Europe united both as a political and as a defence entity, the Soviet Union encourages the United States to maintain a military presence in Europe. Nevertheless, this presence is gradually reduced between now and 1983, partly for financial reasons and partly because America's irritation with its European allies, voiced at the highest levels in the United States in 1973 and early in 1974, develops into disillusionment, so that interdependence—the watchword of the Atlantic Alliance—becomes a mockery in the later 1970s, until a point is finally reached where whatever American troops may still be stationed in the European theatre are either there on sufferance or have lost their credibility as a deterrent against the exercise of Soviet military power.[9] Here again the crucial question would be the state of Western Europe. If this were one of disarray, then each Western European country would have no alternative but to reach whatever accommodation it could with the most powerful state in Europe; and so far from being 'Finlandized', they might—depending on the circumstances obtaining at that time—find themselves so fragmented that their treatment by the Soviet Union would be less favourable than that received by the Finns during the past thirty years.

Lastly, the paradigm of the best that we can reasonably hope for: the equilibrium between the United States and the Soviet Union withstands all the stresses to which it may be subjected during the next ten years, in particular, those arising from the Middle East; both super-powers keep their present military partners and do not seek others; the Soviet Union finds a means of preserving the effectiveness of the Warsaw Pact, while allowing its members a greater measure of freedom to experiment with internal political reforms; the American military presence in Europe is reduced, but remains credible; a Western Euro-pean defence entity emerges, including a nuclear capability, despite all the formidable difficulties, both political and technological, which this would involve; Western Europe, without aspiring to the status of a super-power, is none the less able to exert widespread political influence and to avoid walking 'naked into the council chamber'—in Bevan's phrase.

None of these three paradigms has mentioned the world's fifth strategic nuclear power—the People's Republic of China. Sooner or later the Chinese nuclear force will rise from its present level, roughly equivalent to that of France,[10] to something resembling that of the United States and the Soviet Union. Once this transition has been effected, the scene of world politics will be transformed. The Soviet-American equilibrium could be destroyed and end in a chaotic scramble by each of the three super-powers to secure the alliance of one or the other, for both the United States and the Soviet Union would have important concessions to offer China, if they chose to do so. A world divided between three super-powers is indeed what Orwell foresaw in *Nineteen Eighty-Four*. Historically, the maintenance of a triangular balance of power has been fraught with danger for other, neighbouring, states.[11] Whatever happens, the moral remains identical: 'a choir of contradictory European voices is of no use to anyone'.[12]

It may be objected, first, that the disproportion between a nuclear deterrent force of the size and degree of sophistication which Western Europe (and specifically Britain and France) might be able to afford, on the one hand, and the nuclear armoury of the super-powers on the other, is so great that in practice the Western Europeans would become no better than the blackmailing nuclear guerrillas already mentioned; and secondly, that if this is the best projection that can be offered for the late twentieth century, some alternative machinery for keeping the world at peace must be found before the century draws to a close. To the first of these two objections the answer is that there is an important difference between the leader of a guerrilla group responsible to no one other than a distant headquarters with which, at the critical moment, he

may no longer be in contact, and the democratically elected head of a
European government, controlling a carefully safeguarded nuclear
deterrent; and that the international weight of a government known to
possess the nuclear ability to tear a limb from its adversary, even posthumously, must be greater than that of a non-nuclear power.

Nevertheless, if it is indeed unrealistic for Western Europe to aspire
to exert anything more than moral influence on the course of world
events in the rest of this century, should we turn our backs on history,
leave the super-powers to dispose of the world as they choose, and
cultivate our gardens—a policy of Little Europe? To this question the
reply must surely be: only if Little Europe could be sure of being able
to resist the Power of Menace.* True, the machinery of the United
Nations Organization is a useful, perhaps an indispensable, instrument
for helping to maintain world order, especially so long as the permanent
members of the UN Security Council are also the five strategic nuclear
powers. But it is rightly called an organization; it is no more than that.
A federal system of world government is inconceivable in this century.[13]
We are therefore thrown back on an ancient and admittedly imperfect,
because human, system of maintaining international order—what the
Peace of Utrecht described as a just balance of power, the best and most
solid foundation of mutual friendship and a lasting general concord. It
is a system that has had some distinguished advocates, across the
centuries. As Clausewitz pointed out, it is just the weak—the side that
must defend itself—which should always be armed in order not to be
taken by surprise;[14] and it was Richelieu who observed that of two unequal powers, allied by a treaty, it was the larger of the two which ran
the greater risk of being left in the lurch.[15]

In 1962 Acheson jolted British public opinion when he remarked
that Britain, having lost its empire, had not yet found a role. Today no
one doubts that Britain and its partners in Western Europe were wise to
give up their empires—the relic of another epoch, in which Western
Europe dominated the world. It has also become clear that even in the
new era of the super-powers the countries of Western Europe have a
role to play: a role which they cannot refuse, if they wish to survive.

* This striking phrase is Curzon's, used in *Russia in Central Asia*, ch. VIII.

NOTES

1. For Soviet definitions of the 'basic tasks' of foreign policy, the super-powers'
special responsibility, and the class struggle, see ch. 1.

2. Raymond Aron, *Paix et guerre entre les nations*, Calmann-Levy, Paris, 1962, pp. 527 ff.

3. See ch. 1, n. 14.

4. See ch. 12, n. 1.

5. *Keesing's Contemporary Archives 1973*, pp. 25933 ff.

6. Samuel Grafton in the *New York Post*, 23 November 1943.

7. For an assessment of Chinese nuclear policy, see 'Nuclear Weapons and Chinese policy', Harry Gelber, *Adelphi Papers* no. 99, IISS, London, 1973.

8. Michel Jobert (as reported in the *Scotsman* of 13 November 1973) said that the Nuclear Agreement of 22 June 1973 had set up a 'veritable condominium of the super-powers' and reduced the EEC to impotence. The super-powers' collusion was 'dangerous . . . because experience has shown that the direct dialogue between the US and the Soviet Union could lead not only to a *détente* but also to a generalized confrontation. . . .' The US and the Soviet Union had committed an error in 'brutally brushing aside' France and Europe while imposing a Middle Eastern settlement. 'Europe, treated like a non-person and humiliated in its very existence, because of its dependence on supplies of energy, is none the less the object of the second battle of the Middle Eastern War.'

9. For Nixon's remarks about Europe, made in Chicago on 15 March 1974, see *The Times*, 16 March 1974, which gives the full text. For a pessimistic view of American military credibility even in existing circumstances, see Taylor, *Foreign Affairs*, April 1974, p. 588, where he describes the US Seventh Army as a 'hostage force' in Central Europe.

10. For this comparison, see Gelber, op. cit., p. 8.

11. In *The End of the Post-War Era*, Weidenfeld and Nicolson, London, 1974, p. 81, Alastair Buchan points out that the price of the triangular power balance in Central Europe at the end of the eighteenth century was the Partition of Poland (a salutary lesson for Western Europe, should its leaders show the same inability to agree among themselves as did the members of the Polish Sejm two hundred years ago).

12. Brandt, addressing the European Parliament at Strasbourg on 13 November 1973: *Glasgow Herald*, 14 November 1973.

13. Indeed 'there has rarely been a less promising moment in modern history to advocate the disappearance of the nation state': Alastair Buchan, Reith Lectures, *Listener*, 20 December 1974, p. 844.

14. Carl von Clausewitz, *Vom Kriege*, translated by J. J. Graham, vol. 2, p. 155 (Bk. VI, ch. 5), Kegan, Paul, Trench, and Truebner, London, 1908.

15. Armand de Richelieu, *Testament politique*, part 2, Imprimerie Le Breton, 1764, p. 41: 'Bien que ce soit un dire commun, que quiconque a la force, a d'ordinaire raison, il est vrai toutefois que de deux Puissances inégales, jointes par un traité, la plus grande risque d'être plus abandonnée que l'autre.'

POSTSCRIPT: 1974

The account given in this book of the way in which the relationship between the Soviet Union and the United States evolved, from the Cuban missile crisis until the conclusion of the Fourth Arab-Israeli War, ended in the autumn of 1973. Up to October 1974—exactly twelve years after the Cuban crisis and twelve months after the cease-fire of October 1973—has anything happened to modify either this account of Soviet foreign policy or the attempt (in Part Four) to consider how the relationship between the two super-powers may develop further? The short answer is, nothing. Indeed, events have served rather to increase the lonely eminence of the super-powers.

None the less, much has happened in 1974. This has been, above all, the year of the world energy crisis and of the inflationary turmoil of the Western economic system. Politically, some of the outstanding international events of 1974 have been these: the replacement of the leaders of the United States and of the three principal countries of Western Europe; the quarrel between the United States and Western Europe, repaired at Ottawa and Brussels in June; the arcane struggle for power in China; the last stages of Nixon's struggle for survival as President of the United States; notwithstanding this, the feats of American diplomacy in the Middle East in the first half of the year; the ferment in Southern Africa, after the overthrow of the old regime in Portugal; the Indian explosion of a nuclear device in May; the United States Government's decision to give nuclear aid to the two principal antagonists in the Middle East a month later; the agreements between the super-powers reached at the third Soviet-American summit meeting in June/July, followed in October by the Soviet assurances[1] on freedom of emigration;

the Cyprus crisis; and the succession of Vice-President Ford as President of the United States.

This sequence must be considered against the Soviet domestic background: under Brezhnev's ascendancy, the authority of the collective leadership questioned less and less; approval of their foreign policy reaffirmed by the Central Committee immediately after Nixon's departure from Moscow; the import of Western technology and capital gathering speed; a reasonably good harvest in prospect; the first moves towards another meeting of at least the European branch of the world Communist Movement; and the voices of the dissident minority within the Soviet Union increasingly stifled—Sakharov cut off by the Russians from American television during an interview which he was giving while the United States President was the guest of the Soviet Government, and Solzhenitsyn living in exile, the first Soviet citizen to receive this punishment since Trotsky.

The change of American leadership on 9 August 1974 left the super-power relationship unchanged. The new US President kept Kissinger, the architect of American policy towards the Soviet Union in the present decade, as his Secretary of State; Ford's assurances regarding the continuity of this policy were publicly accepted in a speech delivered on 25 September[2] by Brezhnev, who said the same about Soviet policy towards the United States; and a month later it was announced that the two leaders would meet in Vladivostock on 23/24 November. Just after Nixon had left the Soviet Union and just before he resigned, the Cyprus crisis erupted. Although the consequences of this crisis on the south-eastern flank of the NATO alliance—in Greece* and in Turkey— affected the national interests both of the Soviet Union and of the United States, neither government became directly embroiled in the crisis.[3]

Chapter 14 offered some reflections on the world scene as it might have appeared to an observer in the Kremlin in the autumn of 1973. One year later, he might find two questions worth especially careful attention: first, the effect on the Soviet Union and on the super-power relationship of the world energy crisis and of world-wide inflation, and second, the value of the agreements reached between the Soviet Union and the United States in the summer of 1974.

The quadrupling of world oil prices at the close of 1973 brought to

---

* Constantine Karamanlis returned from exile to Greece, where democratic government was restored. Greek forces were withdrawn from NATO, on the French model.

an end the era of cheap energy: one of the basic premises on which the industrialized countries had predicated their unprecedented rate of development since the Second World War. These countries—unless (like the Soviet Union) they are self-sufficient in energy—now face a new dimension in the problem of balancing their external payments; and this has greatly accelerated their internal rates of inflation. This is bad enough. But for the Third World, excluding the oil-producing countries, the effect is far worse. From the Third World a Fourth World has now evolved, whose 'members are those who lack major resources or economic power ... are more dependent, more deprived, and more aware of it than any large segment of the world's population in history. That some of the desperate nations of the Fourth World now may have access to nuclear weapons only adds to the prospects for tragedy.'[4]

If he so chose, the Kremlin observer could shrug off this prospect as being the apocalyptic crisis of capitalism long foreseen by Marxist prophets: a crisis which must both justify and benefit the Soviet system. This was indeed the assessment that a member of the Politburo and the secretary of the Central Committee responsible for international relations both presented to a conference which had been convened in Moscow to discuss the teaching and the achievement of Lenin, on the fiftieth anniversary of his death.[5] But if the observer took a less super-ficial view, he would be bound to conclude that the world economic phenomena of 1974 were by no means an unmixed blessing for the Soviet Union. True, the Western countries were at sixes and sevens; and the Soviet Union's own reserves of foreign currency were swollen by the steep rise of world commodity prices, among which the fourfold increase in the price of oil was the most striking and the most significant element. But the observer would also be aware that the Soviet Union's Eastern European allies (themselves all importers of oil) were not im-mune from the consequences of Western inflation. And he could not turn a blind eye—although so far the Soviet Government seems to be doing just this—on the new problem of the Fourth World, which includes one of the Soviet Union's principal associates—India. Finally, even looking at the purely national interests of the Soviet economy, although he could take comfort in the fact that the Soviet Union can, in the last resort, be self-sufficient, he would also know well that the prospect of rapidly developing the Soviet economy still depended on the import of Western technology and capital, both of which had become much more expensive in 1974.

The agreements reached between the Soviet and US governments during Nixon's second presidential visit to the USSR, which lasted from 27 June to 3 July, were published on the front pages of *Pravda*:[6] among others, the ten-year agreement on economic, industrial, and technological cooperation, signed on 29 June; the Treaty of 3 July banning underground nuclear weapon tests having a yield exceeding 150 kilotons, with effect from 31 March 1976; the Protocol (also signed on 3 July to the 1972 Treaty on the Limitation of Anti-Ballistic Missile Systems, whereby the two governments bound themselves not to exercise their right, under the Treaty, to deploy an ABM system in the second of their two deployment areas; the agreement to open negotiations on environmental warfare; and—in the text of the joint communiqué of 3 July—the governments' conclusion that the 1972 Interim Agreement on Offensive Strategic Weapons should be followed by a new agreement between the Soviet Union and the United States on the limitation of strategic arms, covering the period until 1985 and dealing with both quantitative and qualitative limitations, which should be completed at the earliest possible date, before the expiry of the present agreement, their delegations being reconvened at Geneva 'in the immediate future on the basis of instructions growing out of the summit'.

In their communiqué the two governments also agreed to consider a joint initiative in the Conference of the Committee on Disarmament for the conclusion, as a first step, of an international convention regarding chemical warfare; they favoured an early date for the final stage of the CSCE conference, and they 'proceeded from the assumption that the results of the negotiations will permit the conference to be concluded at the highest level'; they considered it important that the Geneva peace conference should resume its work as soon as possible; and they agreed 'to remain in close touch with a view to coordinating the efforts of both countries towards a peaceful settlement in the Middle East', which should be based on UN Security Council Resolution 338, taking into account 'the legitimate interests of all peoples in the Middle East, including the Palestinian people, and the right to existence of all states in the area'.

In forming a judgement of these agreements, our observer would have been prepared by a good deal that had already appeared in the Soviet press both before and during the summit meeting. Thus, he would have been impressed by the paragraph of the joint communiqué[7] issued on 28 March, at the end of Kissinger's visit to Moscow, in which both sides expressed their determination 'to pursue . . . the established policy aimed at making the process of improving Soviet-American relations irreversible'—an adjective that was to be adopted by Nixon three months later. More recently, he would have noted Brezhnev's statement, in an electoral speech delivered in Moscow on 14 June: 'we wish Soviet-American relations to become really stable and independent of unfavourable combinations of events. We are in favour of both our countries and of the whole world receiving the benefit of their further development.'[8]

Unless he was a member of the Kremlin inner circle, he would not have been aware of the full extent of the American domestic controversy that surrounded the departure of the US President for Moscow, although he would have been warned by *Pravda* that the Chinese were seeking to support 'those who longed for the days of the cold war', and that recent invitations to visit Peking were 'no accident'.* And he would have observed Nixon's emphasis, in his speeches of 27 June and 2 July, on the value to relations between the two countries of the personal relationship established between their leaders ('able to meet together as friends'). He might also have compared Brezhnev's warning in his speech on 27 June—that if the two sides could not accomplish the task of assuring a stable peace between the Soviet Union and the United States, then all remaining achievements in the development of their mutual relations might lose their significance—with the remark made in his speech five days later, that although the nuclear agreements reached by the two sides, taken together, signified a substantial advance, this might perhaps have been even more comprehensive.† Nevertheless, he would have been impressed by the language used in the account of the reception given by the Central Committee to Brezhnev's report on the results of the summit meetings, described as 'a massive landmark in the history of the relations between the Soviet Union and the USA' and 'a massive contribution towards the improvement of Soviet-American relations', making possible a further relaxation of international tension.

A Soviet observer would not have known from his own press that the two governments had reached an (unwritten) understanding in principle that the inspection of peaceful nuclear explosions would involve the presence of observers—for the first time on Soviet territory. How much else he would have understood about what occurred between 27 June

---

* China was visited in the summer of 1974 by Heath and Jackson, among others.

† Speaking in Warsaw on 21 July, Brezhnev told the Sejm that he would have liked an agreement banning all underground nuclear weapons tests.

and 3 July 1974 would partly depend on whether he also received foreign reports of the summit meetings, in particular the transcript of the US Secretary of State's press conference on 3 July.[9] If he had read the latter, he would have known that these discussions about the nuclear arms race were the most extensive that had ever taken place, and with a frankness that would have been considered inconceivable two years previously ('indeed with an amount of detail that would have been considered violating intelligence codes in previous periods'); and he would have been struck by Kissinger's personal impression that both sides had to convince their military establishments of the benefits of restraint—'not a thought that comes naturally to military people on either side'. This last remark would have given any Soviet observer grounds for reflection. And another major anxiety left in his mind would have been the doubt whether the commitment simply to 'stay in close touch over the Middle East'* was enough to contain the continuing tensions between the Arab states and Israel, even though these were described in the communiqué of 1974—unlike that of 1973—as of 'paramount importance and urgency'.

In the West, fears were expressed before the summit meeting that it would become the occasion either of a 'quick fix' or of a deadlock on the paramount issue at stake between the super-powers—the future of the arms race. This requires a decision on the part of both governments whether or not to embark on a new generation of strategic nuclear weapon systems. In effect, they agreed in Moscow to defer the decision a little longer—in Kissinger's words: 'in the hope, not the assurance, that if such an agreement were reached next year, we should be talking of a ten-year agreement . . . to gain control of multiple warheads . . . by introducing some stability into the rate and nature of their deployment'. Therefore there was neither a quick fix nor was the third summit meeting merely a Field of the Cloth of Gold.

The excesses of optimism and of pessimism about this complex question have tended to be based both on an unwarranted assumption and on a misunderstanding of the nature of the strategic arsenals of the two super-powers. The assumption, which in the light of the history of the past twenty-five years is extraordinary, is that Soviet technology, following in the footsteps of its American counterpart, would not be capable of successfully testing multiple independently targetable re-entry vehicles and of equipping the gigantic new Soviet ICBMs with

* In the event, the Geneva Peace Conference is still in recess, at the time of writing.

MIRVs. The misunderstanding, which lies close to the root of the super-powers' nuclear dilemma, relates to the asymmetry of their strategic nuclear forces: at the risk of some oversimplification, it is broadly true to say that the USA has struck a balance between land, sea, and air, whereas the Soviet Union has until recently concentrated its principal strategic investment on land-based missile launchers.

Given this asymmetry, and given the inevitable Soviet determination to close the qualitative gap between the two systems obtaining in 1972 (the year in which the first strategic arms limitation agreements were concluded), it is hardly surprising that 1974 has not proved to be a year of nuclear restraint. It is indeed something that the two governments agreed on as much as they did in Moscow, including the underground test ban, which—for all its imperfections—may at least do something to inhibit the development of a new generation of warheads. Nevertheless, there is no ground whatever for complacency, especially since the explosion in the Rajastan desert on 18 May: thirty-nine governments have refused to sign the Nuclear Non-Proliferation Treaty.

If we have not reached an agreement well before 1977, then I believe you will see an explosion of technology and an explosion of numbers at the end of which we will be lucky if we have the present stability, in which it will be impossible to describe what strategic superiority means. And one of the questions which we have to ask ourselves as a country is: what in the name of God is strategic superiority? What is the significance of it, politically, militarily, operationally, at these levels of numbers? What do you do with it? ... We will be living in a world which will be extraordinarily complex, in which opportunities for nuclear warfare exist that were unimaginable fifteen years ago at the beginning of the nuclear age....

This was how the American Secretary of State felt the pressure of time in Moscow. Although there were no corresponding remarks on the Soviet side, in 1974 neither super-power could ignore the possible alternative to agreement:

> And yonder all before us lie
> Deserts of vast eternity.[10]

NOTES

1. *The Times*, 19 October 1974. But the Kissinger-Jackson exchange was not the end of the story, since the terms of the US Trade Bill (finally passed in December 1974) were regarded by the Soviet Government as inconsistent with the US undertakings of May 1972. A question mark therefore still remains over the development of Soviet-US trade in the immediate future.
2. *Pravda*, 26 September 1974.
3. The Cyprus crisis began with the overthrow of President Makarios by a right-wing *coup d'état* on 15 July. Cyprus was invaded on 19/20 July. Karamanlis was sworn in as Prime Minister of Greece on 24 July. Although the Soviet Government did not become embroiled in the crisis, it did not mince words about it: for an exposition of Brezhnev's view, see *Pravda* of 26 September 1974.
4. Walter Mondale, 'International Economic Society' in *Foreign Affairs*, vol. 53, no. 1, October 1974, p. 5.
5. *Pravda*, 19 January 1974, reported Suslov's and Ponomarev's addresses to this conference. The full text of Ponomarev's was given in *Kommunist*, no. 2, Moscow, 1974. Suslov spoke of the 'very sharp ideological struggle that is going on in the contemporary world' and Ponomarev of 'a definite qualitative shift in the development of the crisis of capitalism'.
6. *Pravda*, 30 June, 4 July, and 5 July 1974.
7. *The Times*, 29 March 1974, has the English text.
8. *Pravda*, 15 June 1974.
9. *Department of State Bulletin*, July 1974, vol. LXXI, no. 1831, pp. 205 ff. All subsequent quotations from Kissinger's press conference of 3 July 1974 are taken from this source.
10. Andrew Marvell (1621-78).

SELECT BIBLIOGRAPHY

Books

ALLISON, Graham, *Essence of Decision: Explaining the Cuban Missile Crisis*, Little, Brown, Boston, 1971.

AMAL'RYK, Andrei, *Can the Soviet Union Survive until 1984?* Harper & Row, New York; Allen Lane, London, 1970.

ARON, Raymond, *Paix et guerre entre les nations*, Calmann-Lévy, Paris, 1962.

ASPATURIAN, Vernon V., *Process and Power in Soviet Foreign Policy*, Little, Brown, Boston, 1971.

BREZHNEV, L. I., *Leninskim Kursom*, Moscow, 1972.

BRZEZINSKI, Zbigniew, *The Soviet Bloc*, Harvard University Press, Cambridge, Mass., 1967.

BUCHAN, Alastair, *The End of the Post-War Era*, Weidenfeld & Nicolson, London, 1974.

BUTTERFIELD, M. and WIGHT, M., *Diplomatic Investigations*, George Allen & Unwin, London, 1966.

CHICHERIN, G. V., *Articles and Speeches*, Moscow, 1961.

CLISSOLD, Stephen, *Soviet Relations with Latin America 1918–68*, Oxford University Press, London, 1970.

CURZON, G. N., *Russia in Central Asia*, Longmans, Green, London, 1889.
Diplomaticheskii Slovar', 2 vols, Moscow, 1964.
Diplomatiya Sotsializma, collective authorship, Moscow, 1973.

DUMONT, René, *Cuba: socialisme et développement*, Editions du Seuil, Paris, 1964.

ERICKSON, John, *Soviet Military Power*, Royal United Services Institute for Defence Studies, London, 1971.

FORWARD, Nigel, *The Field of Nations*, Macmillan, London, 1971.

FOX, W. T. R., *The Super-Powers—their Responsibility for Peace*, Yale Institute of International Studies, 1944.

GITTINGS, John, *Survey of the Sino-Soviet Dispute 1963–67*, Oxford University Press, London, 1968.

GORER, Geoffrey and RICKMAN, John, *The People of Greater Russia*, Cresset Press, London, 1949.

GRIFFITH, William E., *The Sino-Soviet Rift*, Allen & Unwin, London, 1964.

GROMYKO, Antolyi A., *1036 dniei prezidenta Kennedi*, Moscow, 1968.

HAYTER, William, *Russia and the World*, Secker and Warburg, London, 1970.

HOFFMAN, Erik and FLERON, F., *Conduct of Soviet Foreign Policy*, Aldine and Atherton, Chicago, 1971.

HORELICK, A. L. and RUSH, M., *Strategic Power and Soviet Foreign Policy*, University of Chicago Press, Chicago, 1966.

Istoriya Vneshnei Politiki SSSR, edited by Ponomarev, Gromyko, and Khvostov, two volumes, Moscow, 1971.

JACOBSEN, Carl, *Soviet Strategy—Soviet Foreign Policy*, Glasgow University Press, Glasgow, 1972.

KARNOW, Stanley, *Mao and China*, Viking Press, New York, 1972.

KENNEDY, Robert, *Thirteen Days, a Memoir of the Cuban Crisis*, Macmillan, New York, 1969.

KONDRASHEV, E., *Tsenoobrazovanie v promyshlennosti*, Moscow, 1956.

KULSKI, W. W., *The Soviet Union in World Affairs, 1964–1972*, Syracuse University Press, Syracuse, New York, 1973.

LANGE, Oscar, *Socjalizm*, Warsaw, 1973.

LENIN, V. I., *Collected Works*, Foreign Languages Publishing House, Moscow, 1960; Lawrence and Wishart, London, 1960.

MACKINTOSH, J. M., *Strategy and Tactics of Soviet Foreign Policy*, Oxford University Press, London, 1962.

MACMILLAN, Harold, *At the End of the Day*, Macmillan, London, 1973.

MEDVEDEV, Roy, *Kniga o sotsialisticheskoi democratii*, Alexander Herzen Foundation, Amsterdam/Paris, 1972.

MONROE, Elizabeth, *The Changing Balance of Power in the Persian Gulf*, an international seminar report, the American Universities Field Staff, New York, 1972.

NOVE, Alec, *The Soviet Economy*, George Allen & Unwin, London, 1968.

SAKHAROV, Andrei, *Progress, Coexistence, and Intellectual Freedom*, Penguin Books, London, 1969.

SALINGER, Pierre, *With Kennedy*, Cape, London, 1967.

SCHLESINGER, A. M., *A Thousand Days*, Deutsch, London, 1966.

SOLZHENITSYN, Alexander, *Archipelag Gulag*, YMCA Press, Paris, 1973; English translation, Collins, London, 1974.

SORENSEN, Theodore, *Decision-Making in the White House*, Columbia University Press, New York, 1969.

SORENSEN, Theodore, *Kennedy*, Hodder and Stoughton, London, 1965.

TATU, Michel, *Power in the Kremlin*, Collins, London, 1969.

TRISKA, J. F. and FINLEY, D. F., *Soviet Foreign Policy*, Macmillan, New York, 1968.

TROTSKY, Leon, *Moya zhizn'*, Granit, Berlin, 1930.

ULAM, Adam, *Expansion and Coexistence*, Secker and Warburg, London, 1968.

ULAM, Adam, *The Rivals*, Viking Press, New York, 1971.

YORK, Herbert, *Race to Oblivion*, Simon and Schuster, New York, 1970.

ZHDANOV, Andrei, *Essays on Literature, Philosophy, and Music*, International Publishers, New York, 1950.

ZHURIN, V. V. and PRIMAKOV, E. M., *Mezhdunarodnye konflikty*, Moscow 1972.

ZUCKERMAN, Solly, *Scientists at War*, Harper and Row, New York, 1966.

PERIODICALS

PUBLISHED IN BRITAIN

Adelphi Papers   *The Economist*   *Encounter*
Keesing's Contemporary Archives   *Military Balance*
Strategic Survey   *Survey*   *Survival*

PUBLISHED IN THE UNITED STATES

Foreign Affairs   *Foreign Policy*   *Problems of Communism*
State Department Bulletin   *Time Magazine*

PUBLISHED IN THE SOVIET UNION

Journal of World Economics and International Relations
Kommunist   *Kommunist Vooruzhennykh Sil*
Literaturnaya Gazeta   *Mezhdunarodnaya Zhizn'*
Novoe Vremya   *Novyi Mir*   *SShA*   *Voprosy Istorii*
The Working Class and the Contemporary World

PUBLISHED IN CZECHOSLOVAKIA

World Marxist Review

PUBLISHED IN CHINA

The People's Daily

NEWSPAPERS

Frankfurter Allgemeine Zeitung   *Guardian*   *Hoy*
International Herald Tribune   *Izvestiya*   *Krasnaya Zvezda*
Le Monde   *New York Times*   *Observer*   *Pravda*
Rude Pravo   *The Times*   *Washington Post*

INDEX